Henryk Grossman Works, Volume 1

Historical Materialism Book Series

The Historical Materialism Book Series is a major publishing initiative of the radical left. The capitalist crisis of the twenty-first century has been met by a resurgence of interest in critical Marxist theory. At the same time, the publishing institutions committed to Marxism have contracted markedly since the high point of the 1970s. The Historical Materialism Book Series is dedicated to addressing this situation by making available important works of Marxist theory. The aim of the series is to publish important theoretical contributions as the basis for vigorous intellectual debate and exchange on the left.

The peer-reviewed series publishes original monographs, translated texts, and reprints of classics across the bounds of academic disciplinary agendas and across the divisions of the left. The series is particularly concerned to encourage the internationalization of Marxist debate and aims to translate significant studies from beyond the English-speaking world.

For a full list of titles in the Historical Materialism Book Series available in paperback from Haymarket Books, visit:
https://www.haymarketbooks.org/series_collections/1-historical-materialism

Henryk Grossman Works

VOLUME 1

Essays and Letters on Economic Theory

Henryk Grossman

Edited and Introduced by
Rick Kuhn

Translated by
Dominika Balwin, Ian Birchall, Ben Fowkes, Joseph Fraccia, Julian Germann, Rick Kuhn, Geoffrey McCormack, David Meienreis, Einde O'Callaghan, Tom O'Lincoln, Nick Reynolds and Frank Wolff

Haymarket Books
Chicago, IL

First published in 2018 by Brill Academic Publishers, The Netherlands

Published in paperback in 2020 by
Haymarket Books
P.O. Box 180165
Chicago, IL 60618
773-583-7884
www.haymarketbooks.org

ISBN: 978-1-64259-044-9

Distributed to the trade in the US through Consortium Book Sales and Distribution (www.cbsd.com) and internationally through Ingram Publisher Services International (www.ingramcontent.com).

This book was published with the generous support of Lannan Foundation and Wallace Action Fund.

Cover design by Jamie Kerry and Ragina Johnson.

Printed in the United States.

10 9 8 7 6 5 4 3 2 1

Library of Congress Cataloging-in-Publication data is available.

Contents

Acknowledgements

Sandra Bloodworth, Tom Bramble, Günther Chaloupek, Liam Dee, Daniel Gaido, Andrew Gilbert, Ben Hillier, Peter Jones, John King, David Mayer, Fred Moseley and Thomas Weiss offered valuable comments on or advice for drafts of essays related to the introduction to this volume or issues encountered in editing Grossman's writings. I am grateful to Daniel Gaido, David Paenson, Geoff McCormack and the staff of the Archive of the Polish Academy of Sciences for access to materials. The translation of *Marx, Classical Political Economy and the Problem of Dynamics* benefitted from reference to previous translations by Pete Burgess and Paul Mattick Jr. The Australian National University provided funding and other support for the project of which this book forms a part. My partner Mary Gorman, especially, as well as close friends and Socialist Alternative comrades continue to provide emotional and intellectual support for my Grossmaniac endeavours.

Introduction

Rick Kuhn

On May Day 1905, Jacob Bros announced the formation of the Jewish Social Democratic Party to a rally of striking workers and other socialists in Kraków. Marching to join the rally organised by the Polish Social Democratic Party, the Jewish demonstrators' ranks had grown to over 2,000. Events were similar in Lviv, Przemyśl, and Tarnów. Henryk Grossman, a 24-year-old university student, was the principal author of the new organisation's manifesto, wrote an earlier pamphlet justifying the self-organisation of Jewish workers, and became the JSDP's founding secretary and principal theoretician.[1] He already had years of experience leading students and workers in associations and trade unions associated with the PPSD in Galicia, the Polish province of the Austro-Hungarian Empire.

From his first publications, as a leader of Jewish workers, through to his later academic works, Grossman was concerned to make the Marxist case for revolutionary working-class action. His investigations dealing primarily with economic theory and brought together here for the first time were always linked to this end.

Most of Grossman's works in this volume were first translated into English in the course of a broader project of making them more readily accessible. Three further volumes will contain his more politically focused writings, studies in economic history, and the first full translation of his *The Law of Accumulation and Breakdown of the Capitalist System*. His main contributions to the history of science have already been published together.[2] All of Grossman's letters, written after World War I, and reviews included in the project are in the current volume, even when their primary concerns are not economic theory.

The first substantive part of this Introduction outlines Grossman's life and the content of his writings. The second, 'Insights', focuses on his elucidation of Marx's method, the dialectic between use value and value, crisis theories, and revolutionary politics. These issues recurred in his economic works, highlighting aspects of Marx's theory that had been overlooked or misunderstood before

1 Grossman 1905; Komitet organizacyjny żydowskiej Partyi socyalno-demokraticyczney w Galicyi 1905. Grossman's name in most of his German publications was rendered as 'Henryk Grossmann'. The source for the present account of Grossman's life and work, unless otherwise referenced, is Kuhn 2007.

2 In Freudenthal and McLaughlin 2009.

Grossman. Many of them are still neglected or distorted, weakening efforts to analyse contemporary capitalism in order to overthrow it. The final part outlines the structure and the conventions employed in this volume of Grossman's works. It also indicates the content of subsequent volumes.

Grossman's Life and Work

University Student, Marxist Leader and Scholar: Kraków and Vienna

Born in Kraków to a prosperous Jewish family in 1881, Grossman became active in the PPSD while at school. The party's neglect of Jewish workers led to the formation of the JSDP, which immediately applied for but was refused membership of the federal General Austrian Social Democratic Party, alongside its German-Austrian, Czech, Polish, South-Slav, Italian and, most recently, Ukrainian organisations. An internationalist, Grossman was also involved in smuggling literature for Rosa Luxemburg's organisation, the Social Democracy of the Kingdom of Poland and Lithuania, into Russian-occupied Poland. Despite the hostility of the PPSD and the General Party, the JSDP grew rapidly, organised many Jewish workers into trade unions for the first time, mobilised them in struggles against their exploitation as workers and their oppression as (mainly Yiddish-speaking) Jews, undertook extensive educational and propaganda work, and within five months started publishing the weekly *Sotsialdemokrat*. The first item in this collection is an unsigned article on the fortieth anniversary of the publication of Marx's *Capital* from this newspaper, whose author may have been Grossman.[3] The JSDP led Jews in strikes and street protests alongside workers of other nationalities, particularly in the struggle for universal male suffrage. After completing his first degree, he moved from Kraków to Vienna in late 1908 to continue his studies, particularly under the economic historian Carl Grünberg, the most prominent socialist academic at a university in the Austro-Hungarian Empire, with whom he had already worked during the winter semester of 1906–07.

In his scholarly work before and during World War I, Grossman dealt with eighteenth-century economic policies and ideas in the Habsburg Empire. His main research project was a study of the Empire's trade policy for Galicia.[4] After army training in 1915 and service on the Eastern Front, Grossman held military administrative and research posts during the War. The extent of these

3 Anonymous 1907, see below pp. 42–43.
4 Grossmann 1914, also see Grossman 1912.

duties apparently left time for other investigations. One result was a substantial article on the relationship between the early theory of public policy (*Polizeiwissenschaft*, literally 'police science') and the origins of official statistics in Austria.[5]

A Communist Public Servant and Academic in Warsaw

Unable to take up the offer of a senior post in the Austrian Statistical Commission in Vienna after the War, as a result of the racist policies of the new, rump Austrian state, Grossman moved to Warsaw, where he joined the Communist Workers Party of Poland in 1920. He worked for over two years at the Polish Central Statistical Office, where he was in charge of the design of the new republic's first population census and published several articles related to his work, before being appointed to a full professorship in economic policy at the Free University of Poland. Because of his political activity, particularly in the illegal Communist Party's front organisations, Grossman was arrested five times and did prison stretches of up to eight months.

Before moving to Warsaw, Grossman had delivered a paper to the Polish Academy of Science in Kraków in June 1919. It was critical both of the reformist disproportionality theory of Mikhail Ivanovich Tugan-Baranovsky and Otto Bauer and, implicitly, the underconsumptionist approach of the revolutionary Luxemburg, who had recently been murdered in Berlin.[6] The paper was the first evidence of his work on Marxist crisis theory. Substantial manuscripts, written in Warsaw, elaborated on these ideas and a breakthrough he achieved by extending Otto Bauer's model of capitalist growth beyond just a few cycles. In Poland, apart from an abstract of the Kraków paper, he published statistical studies of the country's past and present. Then there were two essays in publications of Communist front organisations. One was a magazine article that provided a brief defence of Marx's economic theory against critics. The other introduced his own translations of Marx's critique of the German socialists' draft Gotha Program and focused on the early reception of Marx in Poland.[7] But Grossman's most substantial non-statistical publication while in Warsaw was a monograph, *Simonde de Sismondi and his Economic Theories: A New Interpretation of his Thought*.[8] It arose from a lecture to the Polish Society of Economists in December 1923, was published the following year in French by the Free University in Warsaw 'with the cooperation' of the Institute

5 Grossmann 1916.
6 Grossman 1922, see below pp. 44–49.
7 Grossman 1923b, see below pp. 50–54; Grossman 1923a.
8 Grossman 1924a, see below, pp. 55–119.

for Social Research in Frankfurt, and remains an important reference point in the literature on Sismondi's economic works.[9]

Following the publication of his *New Principles of Political Economy*, published in 1819, Jean Charles Léonard Simonde de Sismondi engaged in controversies with David Ricardo, as well as Jean-Baptiste Say and John Ramsay McCulloch,[10] proponents of the first phase of 'vulgar' political economy, who abandoned the insights of their classical predecessors, notably Adam Smith and Ricardo. Sismondi's work on the nature of capitalism[11] was not only a reference point for Karl Marx, but also in two major socialist controversies. The first was between the Narodniks (Populists), who invoked Sismondi, and Russian Marxists, pre-eminently Vladimir Ilyich Lenin, over the scope for the development of capitalism in Russia. In the second, among Marxists before World War I, over the nature of imperialism, Luxemburg drew critically on Sismondi.[12] The issue, in both cases, was the underconsumptionist argument that crises arose because, under capitalism, there is insufficient consistent demand to ensure the sale of all that has been produced.[13]

Unlike most of his predecessors, including Marxists but not Marx himself, Grossman's primary focus was not on Sismondi's underconsumptionism but on its deeper causes.[14] Grossman gave greater coherence to Sismondi's rather fragmented and unsystematic presentation,[15] in accord with the logic of his arguments, and stressed his originality. This was particularly true of Sismondi's method and grasp of the contradiction between commodities' use values – the concrete, practical and unquantifiable ways in which commodities with specific material, technical properties serve human purposes – and their exchange values – expressing their social aspects and arising, in Marx's more precise formulation, from the amount of socially necessary abstract labour embodied in them. Abstract labour is the common, quantifiable element of human labour – the expenditure of human energy, abstracting from its specific, concrete forms – that is the basis for determining the ratios at which commodities

9 International Institute of Social Research 1934, p. 14. For a more extensive account of the significance of Grossman's Sismondi monograph, see Kuhn 2016a.

10 Sismondi 1991d.

11 Sismondi 1837; Sismondi 1838; as well as Sismondi 1991d.

12 Lenin 1960, pp. 140–1, 142–5, 207–8, 247–8; Luxemburg 1951, pp. 218, 217, 328–31.

13 For a more detailed account of the main Marxist attitudes to Sismondi, see Kuhn 2016a. Of underconsumptionist arguments, Marx wrote: 'It is a pure tautology to say that crises are provoked by a lack of effective demand or effective consumption', Marx 1978b, pp. 486–7.

14 Grossman 1924a, see below p. 100.

15 Aftalion 1899, p. 41.

are exchanged for each other or money, under capitalism.[16] Like Grossman's 1919 lecture, his Sismondi monograph dealt not only with these issues but also the way disequilibrium could be intensified as producers increased output to compensate for falling prices.

According to Sismondi, the exchange value based system necessarily gives rise to disproportion between production and needs, and hence to crises, because production and consumption are separate.[17] Capitalists adjust production to their pursuit of profit, not demand. So demand does not tend to match supply, as mainstream classical political economists believed. The problem, Grossman insisted, is more profound than the concern about distribution and working-class poverty that previous commentators had identified in Sismondi's work.[18] Technological change also continuously disrupts the proportion between production and demand and gives rise to concentration of ownership, crises, pauperism, unemployment and unequal distribution of wealth.[19]

Grossman pointed out how the antecedents of a series of Marx's concepts were to be found in Sismondi's works: the fetishism of commodities;[20] socially necessary labour time, the foundation of commodities' values;[21] the commodity labour power (their capacity to work which workers sell for a wage), as distinct from the activity labour, which solved the conundrums of exploitation and the source of surplus value (newly created, additional value) under con-

---

16 Marx distinguished value, the amount of socially necessary labour time embodied in a commodity, from its 'manifestation' as exchange value, but observed that 'Once we know this, our manner of speaking [referring to value as exchange value] does no harm; it serves, rather, as an abbreviation', Marx 1976b, p. 152. On abstract labour, see Marx 1976b, pp. 142, 150, 188; Carchedi 1991, pp. 7–13.

17 Cf. '[T]he antithetical phases' of exchange involving money, that is the 'immanent contradiction' arising from the separation between the sale of one commodity and the purchase of another with the proceeds, that is intrinsic to the commodity form with its antitheses including that 'between use value and value', 'imply the possibility of crises, though no more than the possibility. For the development of this possibility into a reality a whole series of conditions is required, which do not yet even exist from the standpoint of the simple circulation of commodities', Marx 1976b, p. 209. Likewise, 'Hence, the quality of money as mediator, the separation of exchange into two acts, already contains the germ of crises, at least their possibility, which cannot be realised except where there exist the basic conditions of classically and fully developed circulation corresponding to its concept.' Marx 1986c, p. 133.

18 Grossman 1924a, see below pp. 69, 73, 75 et seq.

19 Grossman 1924a, see below pp. 93–94, 95; also Grossman 1922, see below pp. 44–49.

20 Korsch 1970, p. 64; Lukács 1971, pp. xlvi–xlvii, 11, 50, 164, 169; Grossman 1924a, see below pp. 79, 96. Marx's early discussion of alienation gave rise to the observations about commodity fetishism in *Capital*, see Marx 1975, pp. 290–1; Marx 1976b, pp. 163–77.

21 Grossman 1924a, see below pp. 86, 98, 102, 104; Marx 1976a, pp. 135–6; Marx 1987a, p. 300.

ditions of equal exchange;[22] capital, as 'permanent, self-multiplying value';[23] and crises, as a necessary feature of capitalism, arising from its contradictions between forces and relations of production, use and exchange value, production and consumption, capital and wage labour. His 'inkling ... that the bourgeois forms are only transitory ...'[24] was also distinctive. While Marx praised and built on Sismondi's theoretical insights, he was critical of the Swiss economist's policy proposals.

In conclusion, Grossman persuasively identified Sismondi as the 'first economist who ... scientifically demonstrated that an economic system based on abstract exchange value, as the sole purpose of production and regulator of it, necessarily leads to disruptions and to "insoluble questions"'.[25]

Sismondi was a recurrent figure in Grossman's research program. After leaving Poland in 1925, he joined the Institute for Social Research in Frankfurt am Main. In 1927 he was awarded his higher doctorate (*Habilitation*) for the major study of Austrian trade policy in Galicia, completed before the War in Vienna, under the supervision of Carl Grünberg (now the Institute's director), and a trial lecture on Sismondi and classical political economy.[26] Grossman's principal and best known work, on Marxist crisis theory, *The Law of Accumulation* published in 1929, drew attention to Sismondi's innovative stress on capitalism's transitoriness, a point on which he elaborated in his 1943 study of the emergence of evolutionist thinking in economics.[27]

Unlike the 1924 monograph, *The Law of Accumulation* included criticisms of Sismondi's unsatisfactory underconsumptionist explanation of crises. So too did two short reviews and his entry on Sismondi in the *Encyclopedia of the Social Sciences* in 1934.[28] The entry referred to Sismondi's hostility to democracy. Both it and his account of the development of Marxism, discussed in the next section, endorsed Lenin's critique of Sismondi's underconsumptionism, shared by Karl Kautsky and Luxemburg.[29] The arguments in the monograph were briefly recapitulated in the encyclopaedia entry, which offered a broader overview of his work. It referred to his studies of French and medieval Italian history as well as the way he and Madame de Staël 'paved the way' for

22 Marx 1988a, pp. 149, 157–8; Marx 1994, pp. 271, 418, 423; Marx 1976b, p. 277.
23 Marx 1988a, p. 12; also Marx 1991b, p. 341.
24 Marx 1989c, pp. 248, 274, 393.
25 Grossman 1924a, see below pp. 79–119.
26 Kuhn 2007, p. 119.
27 Grossmann 1992, p. 35; Grossman 1943a, see below pp. 573–576.
28 Grossmann 1934a see below p. 443; Grossmann 1934b, see below pp. 444–445; Grossman 1934, see below pp. 439–442.
29 Grossmann 1992, p. 35; Grossmann 1932f, see below p. 371–372.

the modern sociology of literature.[30] A later monograph on Marx's originality, issued in 1941, highlighted Sismondi's pioneering critique of the fundamental assumption of equilibrium in mainstream economics. Sismondi's appreciation of capitalism's transitoriness and developmental tendencies were considered in articles published in 1943, on the emergence of evolutionist thinking in economics, and in 1948, on William Playfair.[31]

Productivity and Prominence in Frankfurt

Political repression pushed Grossman into leaving Poland for a well-paid post at the Institute for Social Research, associated with the University of Frankfurt at which he also taught. The Institute was funded by an endowment secured by Felix Weil, the radical son of a very wealthy businessman, to conduct Marxist research. It was an excellent place to work. His period in Frankfurt, between 1925 and 1933, was Grossman's most productive, although his publications while there built on arguments developed in manuscripts written in Warsaw.

Grossman's first major study of Marxist economic theory was a restatement and recovery of fundamental features of Marx's approach and revolutionary politics, in 1928. In the course of demolishing a defective attempt in 1926 to construct an innovative synthesis of Marxist economics and strategy, Fritz Sternberg's *Imperialism*, he touched on the expositions of Marx's method and theory of economic crisis that were soon set out more extensively in *The Law of Accumulation* and his essay on the structure of *Capital*.[32] Sternberg made a living as a publicist in the extensive socialist space in Germany between the social-democratic and communist parties. A recent convert from left Zionism to Marxism, whose research had been supported by the Institute, he displayed a limited familiarity with Marx's works and accepted much of the revisionist critique of Marx's economic theory. Like many 'Marxists' today, Sternberg rejected the 'historical Marx', which amounted to the content of Marx's fundamental theories. The 'living Marx', Sternberg confidently asserted, would have acknowledged the mistakes he brought to light. As Grossman put it, this was 'beating up Marx with Marx himself'.[33]

Sternberg followed his PhD supervisor Frankfurt Professor Franz Oppenheimer and the quintessential revisionist Eduard Bernstein, by stating that Marx assumed intermediate social classes between the proletariat and bour-

30 Grossmann 1929a, p. 32; Grossmann 1934a, see below p. 443; Grossmann 1934b, see below pp. 444–445; Grossman 1934, see below pp. 439–442.

31 Grossman 1943a, see below pp. 556–599; Grossman 1948, see below pp. 600–623.

32 Sternberg 1971.

33 Grossmann 1928a, see below p. 122.

geoisie would disappear. In fact, Marx devoted considerable attention to them in discussions of ground rent in both the third volume of *Capital* and *Theories of Surplus Value*. Sternberg failed, Grossman also revealed, to understand the 'method of successive approximation' (*Annäherungsverfahren*)[34] that structured *Capital*, mistaking the production schemas in the second volume for Marx's final analysis.

While accepting the revisionists' conservative critique of Marx, Sternberg drew voluntarist conclusions. Revolution had to be made, even under unfavourable circumstances, because a new imperialist war would render a successful revolution forever impossible. Intellectuals and the revolutionary party could overcome this difficulty by 'hammering' 'correct consciousness' into the working class, irrespective of objective economic circumstances and the class struggle. Drawing on the critique of the revisionists' idealism by 'the great fighter' Luxemburg,[35] Grossman demonstrated that this had nothing to do with Marx's materialism. To Sternberg's voluntarism he counterposed Lenin's analysis of revolutionary situations.[36]

In asserting that Marx thought that the working class was consistently impoverished under capitalism, Sternberg again had recourse to Bernstein's arguments. He explained profits in terms of capitalist competition, in an argument that attributed Thomas Malthus's views to Marx. In contrast, Grossman provided a basic lesson in Marx's labour theory of value and recovered his neglected theory of wages.[37] Sternberg propounded an underconsumptionist theory, derived from Luxemburg and others, that economic crises were the consequence of the exhaustion of the possibility of sales to 'third persons' outside capitalist relations of production, which Marx had failed to discuss. This too derived from the mistaken idea that the reproduction schemas in *Capital*, Volume 2, embodied Marx's conception of concrete capitalist reality. Actually, capitalism's tendency to break down arises not from problems in *realising* surplus value, i.e. insufficient markets, but from the insufficient surplus value *produced*. Foreign trade, by transferring surplus value from less to more developed countries – the process now called 'unequal exchange' – and the export of capital, are only significant as factors that temporarily off-set this tendency.[38] Here Grossman was referring to the effects of the rising organic composition of capital (the ratio between living labour and means of production in the production

34 Grossmann 1928a, see below p. 129.
35 Grossmann 1928a, see below p. 141.
36 Grossmann 1928a, see below pp. 138–144.
37 Grossmann 1928a, see below pp. 144–166.
38 Grossmann 1928a, see below pp. 166–169, 174–176.

process) on the rate of profit, which his work in Warsaw had already identified as the core of Marx's explanation of capitalism's breakdown tendency.

'A New Theory of Imperialism' was republished in a German collection of Grossman's essays in 1971. The other essays in that collection are also in the present volume: 'The Change in the Original Plan for Marx's *Capital* and its Causes', 'The Value-Price Transformation in Marx and the Problem of Crisis', 'Gold Production in the Reproduction Schema of Marx and Rosa Luxemburg', and 'The Evolutionist Revolt Against Classical Economics'.[39]

In a devastating polemic, Grossman reviewed *Principal Theories of Economics*, by the conservative and later fascist academic Othmar Spann, exposing some of the multitude of errors in its section on socialist economics. The book was only worth attention because it served as a pre-exam, cramming aid for students and had gone through many editions after its original publication in 1910.[40] There was also a very short review in 1928 of a republished but dated empirical text by Maurice Bourguin. These two reviews, like 'A New Theory of Imperialism', appeared in Grünberg's journal, which had become the organ of the Institute.[41]

The Law of Accumulation was published in 1929. It spelt out the relationship not only between Marx's theory of the law of the tendency for the rate of profit to fall and its countertendencies, and crises, but also capitalism's tendency to break down. In dealing with these matters, the book explained and employed in its own structure Marx's method in *Capital*.

An article on Marx's method in *Capital* was a companion piece to the *The Law of Accumulation*. Elaborating on points in the book and earlier publications by Grossman, 'The Change in the Original Plan for Marx's *Capital* and its Causes' explained how and why Marx changed the structure of his work.[42] After initially conceiving it as dealing sequentially with different aspects of capitalism, Marx modified his plan. In accord with the method of successive approximation, *Capital* abstracted from the less important features of capitalism, which clutter our perception of it, and dealt first with the most fundamental. Subsequently the features that had been initially discarded were introduced in stages to build up a more complicated model, incrementally closer to the reality we perceive. Grossman argued that Marx's decision to change his plan was associated with the formulation of his reproduction schemas, even-

39 Grossmann 1971b. For the most recent comprehensive bibliography of Grossman's works and their republication see Scheele 2017a.

40 Grossman 1928b, see below pp. 177–181.

41 Grossman 1928c, see below p. 182.

42 Grossman 1929b, see below pp. 183–209.

tually published in the second volume of *Capital*. By at first abstracting from different empirical forms taken by surplus value – commercial profit, interest and ground rent – and focusing on it in aggregate, Marx was able to clearly specify and explain the tendency for the rate of profit to fall and capitalism's tendency to break down, as fundamental corollaries of his labour theory of value and the long-term rise in the organic composition of capital.

Luxemburg had tried to demonstrate that Marx's presentation of the conditions necessary for growth in the reproduction schemas was 'incomplete' because they should have demonstrated that expanded reproduction required the existence of non-capitalist areas and was impossible under pure capitalism. For her, this, rather than the tendency for the rate of profit to fall, explained why capitalism tended to break down. But the reproduction schemas were complete, Grossman explained, and non-capitalist areas, including foreign trade, are not necessary for the survival of capitalism. There was no gap, as Luxemburg asserted, in Marx's analysis. The case made in his essay still shines a spotlight of clarity into the convoluted debate over the structure of *Capital* that has continued to the present.[43]

While *The Law of Accumulation* was very widely reviewed, there was a condemnatory consensus about the book among most left-wing commentators, because it contradicted the explanation of economic crises that became the Stalinist dogma, while its emphasis on their inevitability was uncongenial to social democrats. Despite explicit statements to the contrary in the book, Stalinists, most council communists, as well as social democrats agreed that it expounded a mechanical theory of capitalist breakdown.[44] The controversy made Grossman more publicly prominent than any other active member of the Institute, after Grünberg was incapacitated by a stroke in January 1928.

Not inclined to passivity, Grossman drafted responses to his critics. Presumably written shortly after the appearance in 1929 of hostile reviews by Helene Bauer and Alfred Braunthal in the theoretical journals of Austrian and German social democracy, these manuscripts provided theoretical and empirical grounds for dismissing the claim that the devaluation of capital would consistently off-set the tendencies for the organic composition of capital to rise and for the rate of profit to fall.[45]

In reply to Braunthal's accusation that his theory of breakdown was concerned with the impoverishment of capitalists, Grossman reiterated that economic crises lead to intensified class conflicts and that his use of a version of

43 See Kuhn 2013, pp. 121–33.
44 Kuhn 2007, pp. 138–46.
45 Helene Bauer 1929; Braunthal 1929; Grossman n.d.a., see below pp. 210–225.

Otto Bauer's schema was designed to refute this proponent of the possibility of sustained, indefinite growth under capitalism. Marx, furthermore, quite deliberately applied the term 'law' to the tendency for the rate of profit to fall. There had been, despite Braunthal's assertion, no evidence to contradict it.

After favourably reviewing *The Law of Accumulation* in the *Chicagoer Arbeiterzeitung*, which he edited, Paul Mattick made contact with Grossman, initially through his then wife Frieda, who handled the publication's correspondence. As both men were Marxists interested in economic analysis, Grossman's letters to the German-US council communist Mattick reveal his views about both economic issues and revolutionary tactics. Mattick provided Grossman and the Institute in Frankfurt with research materials from the United States and propagated his correspondent's economic theories in the USA and European council communist circles. Grossman encouraged Mattick's development as a writer, helped him place articles, and supported his pursuit of research funding. In his letters between 1931 and 1937,[46] Grossman wrote about his own work, Marxist theory and tactics in comradely terms, despite their differences. Mattick was hostile to the political parties, conventional trade unions and the Soviet Union, and stressed the importance of spontaneous working-class action, while Grossman had a Leninist conception of Marxist politics, and consistently regarded the Soviet Union as socialist, even when he was, for a while, highly critical of Communist policies.

Grossman's essay on the plan for *Capital* pointed out the failure of Luxemburg (and many others) to appreciate Marx's method in *Capital*, which seriously undermined not only her interpretation of that work but also her understanding of capitalist dynamics. A contribution to a volume of essays celebrating Grünberg's career, 'Gold Production in the Reproduction Schema of Marx and Rosa Luxemburg', refuted a tangential aspect of her effort to discredit Marx's reproduction schemas in the second volume of *Capital*, and drew on a longstanding interest in the question of money.[47]

The essay implicitly conveyed a further argument. In the Communist press, the response to *The Law of Accumulation* had been uniformly hostile. The book had bluntly characterised Jenö Varga, from 1930 Stalin's lieutenant in economics, as an 'epigone' of Marx.[48] Since 1931, Luxemburg had been subject to another campaign of defamation by the parties of the Communist International, on the signal of its Russian leadership. But Varga's theory of crises was an

46 Grossman 1931–7, see below pp. 226–275.

47 Grossman 1924c, pp. 167–84; Grossmann 1932a, see below pp. 276–303.

48 Grossmann 1929a, p. 51.

unacknowledged appropriation of Luxemburg's arguments.[49] The mainly technical argument against Luxemburg extended the critique of the most prominent Marxist underconsumptionist in 'A New Theory of Imperialism', *The Law of Accumulation* and 'The Change in the Original Plan', and challenged the Stalinist orthodoxy in economics. In using the cover of the campaign against Luxemburg, Grossman unfortunately expressed an unwarranted, general rejection of her theoretical work that contradicted his earlier, much more generous and more accurate assessments.[50]

Luxemburg made inconsistent statements about Marx's reproduction schemas. Her proposed 'improvements' included adding a new department producing commodity money, i.e. gold, in addition to the two creating means of production and means of consumption. These improvements were, however, logically flawed and incompatible with the model's assumptions. Marx had foreshadowed that he would discuss the exchange of gold within the department producing means of production. In editing his manuscripts into the second volume of *Capital*, Engels could not find such a discussion. Grossman refuted Luxemburg's claim that this indicated that such a treatment was impossible by demonstrating that it was. He also refuted Luxemburg's criticism of Marx's conclusion that the amount of gold in circulation would build up, even under simple reproduction.[51] Gold is no longer a money commodity, as it was during the nineteenth century and into the twentieth. Marx's discussion of gold and other forms of money, nevertheless, still provides a basis for contemporary Marxist analysis of monetary phenomena.[52]

In his 1932 article, 'The Value-Price Transformation in Marx and the Problem of Crisis',[53] Grossman applied his earlier clarifications of Marx's method and the reproduction schemas in the second volume of *Capital* to Marx's discussion of the average rate of profit and the transformation of values into prices of production in the third. Competition, abstracting from monopolies, and the pursuit of higher profit rates leads to the establishment of an average rate across industries. The redistribution of surplus value, from industries with higher to those with lower rates of profit, involved results in commodities having prices of production which can be different from their values. This process

49 Day 1981, pp. 148–51, 187, 202–11.

50 Grossmann 1928a, see below p. 141; Grossman 1929a, p. 22.

51 The analysis of gold production in Grossman 1932a has attracted little attention in the literature. The objections in Sandemose 2006 are spurious.

52 See Moseley 2005. Kowalik, in his extensive discussion of Luxemburg's economic theory, endorsed Grossman's critique of her discussion of gold production, 2014, pp. 70, 173.

53 Grossmann 1932b, see below pp. 304–331.

gives all capitalists an interest in the conditions of exploitation in industries other than their own. Both Luxemburg's underconsumptionist explanation of economic crisis and accounts, particularly those of Rudolf Hilferding and Otto Bauer, grounded in disproportionality between the values produced in different departments of production, based their analyses on the reproduction schemas of *Capital*, Volume 2. These approaches were inadequate because their demonstrations, if they were to apply to the real world, should have been conducted not in terms of values but of prices of production. In failing to do so, Grossman concluded, they reverted to the pre-Marxist economic theory of Ricardo.

The problem did not arise in Marx's theory of crisis, arising from the tendency for the rate of profit to fall, as recovered by Grossman, despite allegations by some critics.[54] The tendency arose at the aggregate level and was unaffected by the redistribution of surplus value because Marx's transformation resulted in total prices of production equal to total values, total profits (in price of production terms) equal to total surplus value, and no change in the average rate of profit. Both before and after Grossman's contribution, most discussions of the value-price transformation have been preoccupied with mathematical procedures, neglecting its broader significance, that he emphasised, for the validity of Marx's economic analysis.[55]

As an exiled Polish citizen, Grossman had to be careful about his political activity in Germany. Although politically very close to the Communist movement, this and his job at the Institute for Social Research meant that he was free to conduct research and write unconstrained by a party line or the priorities of a normal academic post. He was insulated from the Stalinisation of the German Communist Party and the Communist International, completed by the end of the 1920s, that accompanied the defeat of the revolution in Russia and the rise of a new state capitalist ruling class. For the rest of his life, despite his continuing sympathy for the Soviet Union, Grossman defended his contributions to Marxist economic theory, anathematised in official Communist publications, both in periods when he supported the principle orientations of the International and when he was critical.

After Grünberg was incapacitated by a stroke, Grossman took over his task of writing entries for Elster's *Dictionary of Economics*: a standard German reference work, in three hefty volumes.[56] His distinctly Marxist entries appeared in this peculiar place. They dealt with prominent socialists, including Lenin,

---

54 Gurland 1930, pp. 79–80; Sternberg 1930, pp. 12–16; Neisser 1931, pp. 73–4.

55 See Kuhn 2016c.

56 Elster 1931–3.

socialist and communist parties, Bolshevism, the Second and Third Internationals, anarchism and Christian socialism, as well as Marxism after Marx. The editor, Ludwig Elster, allowed Grossman, as an expert, scope to express his own political and economic views in a forthright tone; the same was true of the item on 'Socialist ideas and theories (National Socialism)', written by a Nazi economist.[57]

Grünberg had written the initial sections of the item on 'Socialist ideas and theories (socialism and communism)' for an earlier edition of the dictionary. In an additional part, 'The further development of Marxism to the present', also issued separately as 'Fifty years of struggle over Marxism', Grossman provided a valuable survey of historical materialism's development after Marx's death. Published in 1932 and 1933, it examined major controversies over politics and economics, and the application of Marxist analysis, in the context of the history of capital accumulation and the labour movement. The final section summed up Grossman's own key contributions and constituted an implicit reply to his critics.[58]

Only Karl Korsch's article 'Marxism and Philosophy', which provided a shorter overview of the history of Marxism from Georg Wilhelm Friedrich Hegel to 1923, was an obvious immediate predecessor of Grossman's study. There were earlier discussions of the history of socialist ideas and Marxist organisations but none examined the development of Marxist thought, especially after Marx's death, more than superficially. Other works, the most outstanding of which was Lenin's *State and Revolution*, had dealt with particular controversies within Marxism.[59]

In his survey, Grossman condensed a huge literature by highlighting key works and arguments. He started by noting that the appreciation of *Capital*'s full significance was very limited for decades. After the Anti-Socialist Law lapsed in 1890 and the Social Democratic Party of Germany, the largest socialist organisation in the world, could operate openly, the influence and sophistication of Marxist analysis grew rapidly. But the rise of revisionism in the party challenged the revolutionary core of Marxist politics and the validity of Marx's labour theory of value. Following Luxemburg, Grossman pointed out that Kautsky, then the foremost Marxist theorist in the world who did make some telling criticisms of Bernstein, fundamentally revised Marxist politics too. Marx's understanding of the state was only 'reconstructed by Lenin over twenty five years later'.

---

57 Jessen 1933.
58 Grossmann 1932f/1933a, see below pp. 378–388.
59 Korsch 1970; Lenin 1964g.

Like Lenin, Grossman explained the rise of revisionism as the result of the emergence of a thin layer in the working classes of developed capitalist countries, an 'aristocracy of labour', that gained material benefits from the imperialist exploitation of the colonial world.[60] This was a weak argument. To the extent that imperialism improved the living standards of well-paid workers, because of more buoyant labour markets and access to cheap raw materials and foodstuffs, it did so for the rest of the working class in the imperialist heartlands too. More compellingly, Grossman associated revisionism with a period of capitalist expansion, during which the working class was able to extract concessions from the ruling class, and the rise of a layer of full-time labour movement officials, who are not by definition workers themselves, particularly in the trade unions.[61]

Grossman did not devote much space to historical materialist analyses outside the areas of politics and economics. But he mentioned studies by Kautsky and 'brilliant' writings by Franz Mehring and Georgi Valentinovich Plekhanov on philosophy, history and literary criticism. He also highlighted the work of Karl Korsch and, in particular, Georg Lukács's 'fine and valuable book' *History and Class Consciousness*. The absence of Antonio Gramsci from Grossman's survey may seem surprising to contemporary Marxists. But very few of the Italian Communist leader's works appeared in languages other than Italian during his lifetime. Gramsci's prison notebooks were still being written in 1932. It was years after World War II before his major works appeared in translation.

In the period before World War I, international tensions and domestic class struggles intensified, as economic conditions changed and capital went onto the offensive. Against this background, Marxists started to devote more attention to the issue of imperialism. There was another gap in Grossman's survey here: the theory of permanent revolution, developed by Parvus and Leon Trotsky and tacitly embraced by Lenin and the Bolshevik Party, in 1917.[62] It explained how socialist revolution was possible in a relatively backward country like Russia, because it was part of the international capitalist system and exhibited some particularly modern features, like a combative working class and advanced industry, even though the vast majority of the population was composed of peasants working with relatively primitive technologies. A socialist revolution in Russia could therefore occur but could only survive if it spread to more developed countries.[63] Contrary to the survey's assertion that the Rus-

---

60 Grossman 1932f/1933a, see below p. 335.

61 Grossman 1932f/1933a, see below p. 336; Cliff 1957; Post 2010; Bramble 2012.

62 Lenin 1964e, p. 341.

63 See Trotsky 1969a.

sian Communists did not associate the possibility of revolution with a specific level of capitalist development, the theory of permanent revolution identified *the system of global capitalism's* maturity as a crucial precondition for socialist revolution.

The theory of permanent revolution was a much more profound argument than Nikolai Ivanovich Bukharin's no doubt useful insight that in less advanced countries, ruling class power was often more fragile. Grossman unnecessarily criticised Bukharin's contention, in the mistaken belief that it was incompatible with his own understanding of the Russian Revolution as a symptom and the start of capitalist breakdown, which made developed countries vulnerable to revolution. He also misleadingly denied that Bukharin's insight was also Lenin's and was silent about the vicious repressiveness of Stalin's regime. In this way, Grossman was able to avoid alienating the Stalinist leadership of the Communist movement more than was necessary in defending his own positions. He was aided by Stalin's own contortions on precisely the question of the political implications of uneven capitalist development.[64]

Like many other Communists at the time, who remained committed, in principle, to working-class self-emancipation, the essence of Marxism, Grossman did not recognise the defeat of the Russian Revolution, which was a massive setback for the international working class, in practice.[65] He was impressed by what he saw on a visit to the Soviet Union, as the leader of an academic delegation in 1932. He did not, however, simply reproduce the Stalinist falsification of the history of the Russian revolutionary movement. His survey acknowledged contributions to the workers' movement by socialists and Communists whose positive role the Russian regime now simply denied, notably Parvus, Grigory Yevseevich Zinoviev, Bukharin and Herman Gorter and even its principal hate figure, Trotsky. Emphasising the impact that the Russian Revolution had on Marxist theory, Grossman referred to Bukharin's specific version of the revolutionary argument that the development of capitalism in the womb of feudalism could not be the pattern for the transition to socialism. The survey also noted the contribution of David Riazanov, who had a close association with Carl Grünberg and the Institute for Social Research, to the history of Marxism and his leadership of the Marx-Engels Institute in Moscow, even though he had been arrested as an anti-Soviet conspirator and dismissed from that post in 1931.

64 See Lenin 1964f; Stalin 1954.
65 See Haynes 2002; and Tony Cliff's classic, Cliff 1974.

Exile in Paris and London

Soon after Hitler became the German Chancellor in January 1933, most members of the Institute went into exile and had settled in New York by October 1934. Grossman, however, moved to Paris. From there, London and later the United States, correspondence with colleagues replaced daily contact and conversation. His letters to Leo Löwenthal[66] and Max Horkheimer, who had succeeded Grünberg as the Institute's Director,[67] provide insights into his intensely Marxist outlook, loyalty to and honesty with those he regarded as friends or close allies, and the logic of his writings for wider audiences.

The Communist movement's blindness to the significance of the Nazis' rise and the German bourgeoisie's gift of power to them jolted Grossman into a much more critical attitude towards the leadership of the Communist International for several years. The Communists' equation of social democracy and Nazism prevented an effective response to Hitler that could have united workers who were social democrats, Communists or just trade unionists. Grossman recommended Trotsky's discussion of the 'German catastrophe' to Paul Mattick and in Paris associated with the former Communists Jacob Walcher and Paul Frölich who led the Socialist Workers' Party of Germany (SAP), which was originally a split from the Social Democratic Party.

In France, Grossman wrote a critique of Franz Borkenau's study of the emergence of the scientific worldview. This very substantial review article, along with the work of Boris Hessen and unlike Borkenau's fundamentally flawed position, was a pioneering Marxist account of the emergence of modern science.[68] Its author continued to employ a Marxist approach to the history of science in book reviews and a substantial manuscript on René Descartes, first published in 2009.[69]

In early 1936, as international tensions mounted in Europe, Grossman moved to London. There, Russia's ambiguous backing for the Republican side in the Spanish Civil War seems to have prompted him to return to essentially uncritical support for Stalin's main domestic and foreign policies. This paralleled the SAP's endorsement of the Comintern's Popular Front tactic of alliances with 'progressive' bourgeois parties and, eventually, 'democratic imperialist' powers.

While Grossman was in London, Horkheimer suggested that he turn the discussion of methodology in *The Law of Accumulation* into an article for a 1937

---

66 Grossman 1933–9, see below pp. 389–399.
67 Grossman 1934–43, see below pp. 400–438.
68 Grossmann 2009a. Also see Freudenthal and McLaughlin 2009.
69 Grossmann 1938a, see below pp. 450–454; Grossman 1941d, see below pp. 549–555; Grossmann 2009b.

issue of the Institute's journal. Grossman responded with a proposal for a more original piece to mark the seventieth anniversary of the publication of the first volume of Marx's *Capital*,[70] just as the *Sotsial-demokrat* had celebrated the book's fortieth birthday.[71] The new essay would challenge the notion, shared by non-Marxists and most Marxists alike, that Marx had perfected classical political economy, arguing instead that he had revolutionised the work of his predecessors. It would identify elements that distinguished Marx's theory from those of the classical political economists and their bourgeois successors. In addition to new investigations, particularly of contemporary economics, Grossman could also draw on his previous writings, back to 1919 at the latest, research done by 1926, and courses he had taught in 1928, 'Exercises on the Question of the Relationship between Marx and Ricardo' and, in 1930, on 'Marx as a Historian of Political Economy'.[72] The essay included arguments previously intended for a sequel to *The Law of Accumulation and Breakdown*.[73]

Horkheimer liked the proposal. Hardly surprising, given that Grossman was building on and radicalising themes in his own recently published article, 'On the Problem of Truth', and an earlier letter, which in turn drew on Grossman's exposition of Marx's method.[74] These two Institute members did not exercise a major influence on one another, but did have friendly and fruitful exchanges until the late 1930s.

During the 1930s and into the 1940s, Grossman continued to keep up with the theoretical and empirical literature on economic crises and published a series of critical book reviews in the Institute's journal.[75] The most substantial dealt with Joseph Schumpeter's text on business cycles. Its concerns were closely related to those in his study of the distinction between Marx's dynamic economic theory and the static approaches of bourgeois economists, initially conceived as the *Capital* anniversary essay.[76]

70 Horkheimer 1936a; Grossman 1936, see below p. 420.
71 Anonymous 1907, see below pp. 42–43.
72 Grossman 1922, see below pp. 44–49; Universität Frankfurt am Main 1928, p. 52; Universität Frankfurt am Main 1930, p. 54.
73 Grossman 1935a, see below p. 264.
74 Horkheimer 1995c; Horkheimer 1993a.
75 Grossmann 1934b, see below pp. 444–445; Grossman 1939a, see below p. 461; Grossman 1939b, see below pp. 462–464; Grossman 1939c, see below pp. 465–466; Grossman 1939d, see below pp. 467–468; Grossman 1941c, see below pp. 546–548.
76 Grossman 1941b, see below pp. 534–545.

Reunion, Separation and Return: New York and Leipzig

After moving to New York in October 1937, the Institute's most competent economist also contributed theses and observations to its seminar series on monopoly capitalism, which included a brief recapitulation of his theory of economic crises and their implications for the class struggle and inter-imperialist rivalry.[77] A longstanding interest in slavery, which Marx regarded as the pivotal issue in the US Civil War, was apparent when he reviewed a collection of Marx's and Engels's newspaper articles and correspondence on the conflict.[78]

Grossman had completed a long draft of his examination of the relationship between Marx and his predecessors by May 1937. He considered writing it as a book, rather than an article and expanded its scope.[79] Work on the study continued in New York. Eventually titled *Marx, Classical Political Economy and the Problem of Dynamics* (henceforth referred to as *Marx and Dynamics*), its publication was delayed by the process of revision, including reductions of its length by a fifth and then a further quarter, and practical developments beyond the Institute's control. Repeated postponements of its appearance contributed to rising tensions between Grossman and the Institute, in the persons of Horkheimer and his administrative lieutenant and lifelong friend, the economist Friedrich Pollock. In 1941, relations became poisonous.

The rift had theoretical, political and financial aspects. By 1939, Horkheimer and Theodor Adorno, adopted as his closest collaborator, had truncated Marx's 'critique of political economy', validating only its negative aspect and rejecting its constructive side, the application of Marxist categories to the empirical analysis of capitalism, which they designated as 'positivism', i.e. wrong.[80]

This was accompanied by rejection of the core of Marxist politics, recognition that the working class was capable of emancipating humanity, to which Grossman was still committed; a distaste for left-wing engagement; and an even more pronounced pursuit of the apolitical, academic respectability that Horkheimer had cultivated since arriving in the USA.[81] In contradiction with his views about the working class, Grossman was again favourably disposed

77 Grossmann 1985a; and Grossmann 1985b, see below pp. 446–449.

78 Grossman 1938b, see below pp. 455–460.

79 See Horkheimer 1995c, editorial note 2, p. 164, referring to a letter from Friedrich Pollock to Grossman of 12 July 1937, and the manuscript Grossman 1937a, part of which has been published as Grossmann 2017d.

80 Horkheimer and Adorno 1985, p. 438; also Adorno and Horkheimer 2011, p. 50. Cf. '[I]t is the ultimate aim of this work to reveal the economic law of motion of modern society', Marx 1976b, p. 92.

81 See, for example, Horkheimer 1996b.

not only to the Stalinist regime in Russia but also to its foreign policies, while Horkheimer's circle recognised the reality of the violently oppressive police state there. And he resented pay cuts imposed by Horkheimer and Pollock on members of the Institute, as a result of a crisis in its finances. Through brutal behaviour, notably towards his fellow and more talented economist, Pollock also attempted to drive those regarded as peripheral to Horkheimer's higher theoretical ends off the payroll altogether.

Fed up with postponements in the study's publication as a monograph, Grossman eventually threatened to issue it as a book in English, prefaced by a statement about the Institute's two-year sabotage of its appearance, if it was not available by Christmas 1941.[82] Leo Löwenthal, who looked after the practicalities of the Institute's publications, complained that Grossman's inaccurate referencing held it up because stencils had to be retyped. As indicated in the translation below, several such errors were not picked up at that stage and it has still not been possible to identify a couple of Grossman's references to Marx.[83] Finally a mere 80 duplicated copies of the monograph, dated 1941, were issued. Since then, it has been republished at least twice in German and translated into Italian, French, Dutch (in part), Danish and English (three times).[84]

The fundamental assumptions and propositions of mainstream economics are, in the main, internally consistent and, where they are not, its usefulness as a class ideology and hence sponsorship by the capitalist class and states has ensured that theoretical doubts, conundrums and inconveniences have been concealed from broad public attention.[85] As part of the struggle against capitalism, Marx undertook a critique of its proponents' economic theories, which provided justifications for the existing order, and counterposed an alternative analysis. Grossman's study was conducted in this belligerent spirit of class warfare, not one of polite academic debate, identifying the limitations of bourgeois economics, notably the bankruptcy of then and still dominant marginalist theory, and the superiority of Marxism.

Earlier Marxists had undertaken critiques of marginalist economics.[86] Friedrich Engels began the job with a very brief comment on William Stanley

82 There is a manuscript translation into English (Grossman n.d.b) of part of the draft essay in German (Grossman 1937a), which includes material that did not appear in the published German version (Grossman 1941a, see below pp. 469–533).

83 Löwenthal 1996, p. 222; Löwenthal 1939.

84 Grossmann 1969; Grossmann 1970; Grossmann 1971a; Grossman 1972; Grossmann 1975a; Grossmann 1975b; Grossman 1977; Grossmann 2007; Grossman 2015.

85 Dobb 1936, p. 127; Varoufakis 1998, p. 352.

86 See Chaloupek 1986; and Kuhn 2014.

Jevons's theory, accurately concluding 'Vulgar Economy everywhere!'[87] While deeming marginalist economics unsatisfactory for its understanding of values and prices, Conrad Schmidt thought the approach offered insights into the behaviour of consumers faced with already established prices.[88] Henry Hyndman made telling points against Jevons's individualist perspective, its continuity with earlier vulgar economics and incompatibility with Marx's labour theory of value. As Grossman did decades later, Hyndman also noted that demand no longer drove supply. Like Schmidt, however, he mistakenly regarded the theory as incapable of explaining supply in its own terms.[89] Bernstein offered vague and eclectic suggestions that there was merit in both Marxist and marginalist theory.[90] In response, Kautsky insisted that 'Marxism's bones must first be broken' before the two could be combined.[91]

Hilferding and Bukharin also judged marginalism and Marx's labour theory of value to be incompatible. Others regarded a coherent theory of value as dispensable.[92] Otto Bauer followed Schmidt in thinking that marginalist economics shed light on demand, and advocated Bernstein's eclectic approach; Kei Shibata argued that Marx's value theory could be an optional extra; and Oskar Lange rejected it while endorsing Marx's analysis of economic institutions.[93] Later, Maurice Dobb highlighted mainstream economists' unrealistic assumptions that individuals' preferences are independent of each other, market and social relations, and are 'fairly permanent and consistent'.[94] Dobb, like Grossman, stressed the conceptual continuity between the 'revolutionary' marginalists, with their mathematical appurtenances, and their immediate vulgar economic predecessors.

Grossman did not recapitulate the arguments of earlier Marxist critics of mainstream economic theory at any length. Instead he grounded the contrast between its static approach – from the Physiocrats,[95] Smith and Ricardo through to the present – and Marx's ability to grasp capitalist dynamics in the contradiction between use value and value, and specifically the 'dual char-

87 Engels 2001a, p. 137.
88 Schmidt 1892.
89 Hyndman 1921, pp. 158–9, 261–6, 268–70.
90 Bernstein 1896; Bernstein 1993, pp. 51–2.
91 Kautsky 1899a, pp. 80, 81; Kautsky 1899b.
92 Hilferding 1949, pp. 133, 184–5; Hilferding 1912b; Bukharin 1972a, pp. 36–57.
93 Otto Bauer 1956, p. 288; Shibata 1933a; Shibata 1933b; Lange 1935.
94 Dobb 1937, pp. 136, 165, 161, 167.
95 The Physiocrats were an eighteenth-century school of French economists who stressed that productive work, which they identified with agriculture, was the source of wealth.

acter of labour'. Marx had written to Engels that this was one of the two 'best points' in *Capital*.[96]

Bourgeois economists' need to demonstrate that capitalism is rational and self-regulating resulted in the assumption that economies were characterised by a tendency to equilibrium. This approach was necessarily static and ignored capitalism's inherently wild fluctuations and crises.[97]

Disturbances came from outside, according to mainstream economics back to Smith: war, crop failure, state intervention. Later attempts to attribute crises to monetary problems, by Knut Wicksell and subsequently Friedrich Hayek, Irving Fisher and Ralph George Hawtrey were also static. Efforts to account for them in terms of technological change, disproportion among sectors, lengths of construction periods, and durability of production goods (the accelerator principle) were empirical observations divorced from theory.

Vulgar bourgeois economics had abandoned the labour theory of value and attempted to explain exchange value, understood as price, in terms of utility. Vilfredo Pareto solved the problem that it is impossible to measure the utility of commodities directly. He derived demand curves from the comparisons people supposedly make in their choices among different goods (commodities), in order to maximise their well-being. But for this 'ordinal' approach to work, Grossman pointed out in one of the first Marxist critiques of the more sophisticated version of marginalist theory that emerged during the 1930s and 1940s, further unreal assumptions had to be made: the infinite divisibility of goods, unlimited substitutability between them (ignoring the material character of commodities as use values) and perfect knowledge. He also noted the importation, without justification, of theoretical physics' conceptual and mathematical apparatus, including the distinction between statics and dynamics, into marginalist economics.[98] Pareto's equilibrium equations were only possible because he, like his predecessors, excluded the dynamic factor of the production process and dealt only with exchange.

Equilibrium theory entails 'the assumption of the simultaneous rhythm of all economic processes'. Economic processes, however, involve not just the circulation of commodities but also their production as use values. The duration of the periods of production and even the circulation of different commodities vary. Their coincidence, if it occurs at all, can only be accidental. Yet vulgar eco-

96 Marx 1987b, p. 407. On the importance and previous neglect of use value in economic processes, see Rosdolsky 1977, pp. 71–95, originally published as an article in 1959.

97 Grossman 1941a, see below p. 515.

98 For a detailed account of marginalist economics' debt to physics, see Mirowski 1989, pp. 193–395.

nomics simply assumes such coincidence or the simultaneity of transactions. It cannot theoretically incorporate time and therefore history.[99]

A long, early draft of what became *Marx and Dynamics* had included a discussion of whether Marx was the first to introduce an historical perspective into economics.[100] Extended and developed, material cut from that draft was incorporated into 'The Evolutionist Revolt Against Classical Political Economics', published in two parts by the Chicago-based *Journal of Political Economy*, in 1943. Although he had already withdrawn from many of the Institute's activities, Grossman sent a draft of 'The Evolutionist Revolt' to Horkheimer in early 1942. The Director's comments were extremely hostile, reflecting his abandonment of Marxism. Grossman made only minor changes in response to them.[101]

The study demolished the misconception that Marx, under Hegel's influence, was the first to argue that the basic structure of economies had changed over the long term. Marx's originality lay elsewhere. Grossman examined the French works of Marie-Jean-Antoine-Nicolas de Condorcet (1743–94), Henri Saint-Simon (1760–1825) and Simonde de Sismondi (1773–1842); the English writings of James Stuart (1712–80) and Richard Jones (1790–1855); and Marx's treatment of modes of production. In this way, he showed 'how dynamic or evolutionary thinking actually entered the field of economics'.[102]

The most influential works of classical political economy, including those of Smith and Ricardo, the study explained, did not recognise that economic development took the form of successive modes of production. But, from the late eighteenth century, there were theorists outside the mainstream, in both France and England, whose views were shaped by the political revolutions in America and France and the Industrial Revolution in England. They made generalisations on the basis of contemporary and historical evidence. Jones went further, using these to criticise mainstream economic theories and formulate new positions. The concept of distinct stages of economic development, widely accepted by the middle of the nineteenth century, was most precisely formulated in Marx's analysis and then disappeared from economic orthodoxy.[103]

In contrast to the earlier evolutionists, Marx shared Hegel's dialectical concept of the development of the 'cultural whole' – the totality of modern bourgeois society – as the object of his analysis. But Marx, like Sismondi and Jones,

99 See Kuhn 2015 for a more detailed appreciation of Grossman's monograph.
100 Grossman 1937a, pp. 31–3, 53–62; Grossman 1941a, see below pp. 469–533.
101 For a detailed discussion of the exchange, see Kuhn 2016b.
102 Grossman 1943a, see below p. 556.
103 Grossman 1943a. p. 562; Grossman 1943b; see below pp. 560–562, 581, 587.

saw development as 'a succession of objective economic stages of different economic structures'. For Hegel the essence of development was 'the progress within man's *consciousness* of an idea of freedom'. Without using the expressions, Grossman therefore distinguished between the materialism of the evolutionist political economists and Hegel's idealism, by distinguishing two meanings of 'development': material evolution (in the work of the political economists he discussed) and development of the 'notion' or 'concept' (in Hegel's system). Unlike the evolutionist political economists, Hegel also believed that historical change had come to a halt with the 'consolidation of middle-class society'.[104]

Horkheimer's assessment that it was 'a most rotten piece of work'[105] has not been endorsed by later appreciations of 'The Evolutionist Revolt'. The study was republished twice during the early 1990s, in a collection on Marx (in part) and another on early political economists,[106] and has been translated into at least five European languages.

After the War, three of Grossman's most intimate friends returned to Europe before he did. Oskar Kurz, a cousin who lived with him in New York, went back to Vienna. The Marxist financial trader, economist and novelist Bill Blake and his partner the Australian novelist Christina Stead, whom he had met in the United States, began an itinerant period, initially in Belgium, eventually settling in England. Grossman's letters to Blake and Stead are the only surviving evidence of Grossman's relationships with very close friends.[107] They also document his assessments of contemporary political developments and enthusiasm for research, particularly into an obscure but insightful British political economist, William Playfair. Correspondence with his admiring former student Walter Braeuer, of whose analytical abilities Grossman had no high opinion,[108] is of a different order. It contained explanations of his work, discussion of his return to Germany and details about aid packages which Grossman paid for to help sustain Braeuer, a concentration camp survivor, and his wife in eastern Germany through severe postwar shortages.[109]

'William Playfair, the Earliest Theorist of Capitalist Development' was a supplement to the project embodied in *Marx and Dynamics* and then 'The Evolutionist Revolt'. The essay on pioneering economic evolutionists had only quoted

---

104 Grossman 1943a; Grossman 1943b; see below pp. 558, 588, 589, 592.
105 Horkheimer 1943, p. 105.
106 Grossman, 1990; Grossman 1991.
107 Grossman 1947b, see below pp. 624–632.
108 Grossman 1935b.
109 Grossman 1947–9, see below pp. 633–637.

a single empirical observation by Playfair in a footnote.[110] In a letter to his friends Christina Stead and Bill Blake, Grossman wrote:

> My 'Playfair' is with [Norbert] Guterman for translation. I think that the paper itself is better than the 'content'. The point is: Sismondi went to England, to collect materials for his book on the basis of higher development of Engl. capitalism. So the English Capitalism influenced through Sismondi *French* economic literature. This must astonish, why this higher developed engl. capitalism *did not influences english* economic literature? Now, I found the missing link, the *direct* trace in english literature. If [Harold] Laski could help publish in an English quarterly, would be better, than here in Journal of Polit. Economy. If you wish, I will send you a copy of MSS.[111]

The article was written during early 1947 and appeared in the English journal *Economic History Review* the following year.[112] Playfair had anticipated Sismondi's observations about the concentration of capital, polarisation between a few in the wealthy upper class and more and more people who are poor, while the middle classes declined. He also linked the issues of growth and imperialism. Economic development transforms poor agricultural into rich industrial countries. But industrial nations have more capital than can be profitably invested at home. Moral and economic stagnation results, unless governments promote, most importantly, the 'export of commodities and of capital' but also 'decentralisation of capital, further various forms of unproductive expenditure and waste'. In Playfair's analysis of capitalism's underlying tendency to stagnate and its countertendencies, Grossman identified the first application of a methodology later employed by Ricardo, John Stuart Mill and Marx.[113] In the final two sentences of the last publication he saw into print, Grossman recapitulated an insight that underpinned many of his own contributions to the understanding of capitalism: that Marx had an original and accurate explanation, based on the long-term rise in the organic composition of capital, of the system's proneness to crises and generation of poverty.[114]

---

110 Grossman 1943a, see below p. 560.
111 Grossman 1947a, see below p. 629; editor's interpolations.
112 Grossman 1947b, see below p. 626.
113 See Grossman 1948, below, p. 618. On the relationship between Mill's and Marx's use and application of this methodology, see Grossmann 1992, pp. 73–4.
114 See Grossman 1948, below, p. 622.

The translation of Grossman's article on Playfair into English was less polished than that on the early evolutionists and its material could have been better organised. The closest it came to discussion of the relationship between Playfair's insights and working-class strategy was to mention that socialisation of production under capitalism presaged socialism. But, observing that when John Atkinson Hobson early in the twentieth century again raised the issue of the relationship between exports and stagnation, he stimulated a whole new literature, Grossman no doubt had Lenin's *Imperialism, The Highest Stage of Capitalism* particularly in mind.[115]

Although the Institute continued to pay his salary, its value severely eroded by wartime inflation, Grossman's work was now hardly of interest to Horkheimer, except as a possible source of embarrassment. They made a deal. Grossman accepted a lump-sum payment from the Institute to finance his return to Germany and in return agreed to terminate their relationship. He took up a professorial chair at the University of Leipzig, the oldest in the Soviet Occupation Zone, in early 1949. The University authorities recruited him and others exiled from Germany in the west, to replace staff who had embraced National Socialism and to raise the institution's prestige. The Stalinist authorities soon had second thoughts about this policy. But, as he died on 24 November 1950, Grossman did not suffer from the wave of persecution of these unreliable elements.

Enthused by the task of contributing to 'the construction of socialism', Grossman joined the Socialist Unity (i.e. Communist) Party, participated in the intellectual and administrative life of the University, and started to teach again. His health already weakened, particularly by Parkinson's disease, he did not undertake any new research projects but probably worked on ones already underway, including the Descartes study. He sought to have several of his essays of the late 1920s and early 1930s, now essentially inaccessible in Germany, republished together as a book. The contents would have contradicted the Stalinist orthodoxy in economics: none of Grossman's work was ever republished in East Germany. It only found a new audience when new left publishers in West Germany reissued *The Law of Accumulation* and other studies between 1967 and 1971, followed by translations into Italian, French and Spanish, during the 1970s. English translations have taken longer.

115 Grossman 1948, see below pp. 600, 612, 617, 619; Lenin 1964c.

Insights

In many of his works, including those in this volume, Grossman contributed to interlocking controversies amongst Marxists over method, the contradiction between the use value and value aspects of capitalist production, economic crisis, and the revolutionary potential of the working class. His recovery and development of Marx's analyses in these areas paralleled and were influenced by Lukács's contributions to philosophy and Lenin's to political theory and practice. They are discussed in the following sections.

Method

The sorting of the myriad aspects of the reality that impinges on us according to their importance in influencing other aspects is intrinsic to scientific research. To understand falling bodies and develop the theory of gravity, for example, physicists 'exclude the accidental and external influences of air' as a first step in their explanations. Such thought experiments, initial abstractions away from less significant factors, are also a feature of economics as a science. But not all abstractions are accurate. Although Sismondi sometimes engaged in an anti-theoretical, empiricist rhetoric, Grossman pointed out that one of his most important criticisms of the classical political economy of Smith and Ricardo was that they abstracted from '*the essential elements* which characterise capitalist society'. Contrary to the prevalent and superficial readings of his work, the Swiss economist's practice was far from empiricist. He developed François Quesnay's abstract model of reproduction, excluded survivals of previous modes of production, and concentrated on crucial relations that the mainstream economists did not include, particularly the nature of the capital–wage labour relationship.[116]

The 'method of successive approximation' – stripping away less important and relevant features that clutter our perception, by making simplifying assumptions, to identify fundamental relations, and then successively lifting those assumptions so that the abstract insights are embedded in an account closer to concrete reality – structured Marx's *Capital*. The model in the first volume abstracted, for example, from differences among the turnover times in the production of various commodities; competition amongst capitals; changes in the values of commodities; credit; changes in the value of money; systematic deviation of prices from values; differences in the organic compositions of capital among industries; and the concrete forms – industrial profit,

116 Grossman 1924a, see below, p. 65.

commercial profit, interest, ground rent – taken by surplus value. In the course of the discussions in the second and third volumes, these and other aspects of empirical capitalism were introduced progressively to generate more complicated models, incrementally closer to the reality we perceive.[117] A failure to grasp Marx's method and the reproduction schemas in the second volume of *Capital* invalidated Rosa Luxemburg's underconsumptionist explanation of economic crises.[118]

Use Value and Value

Ricardo and, before him, Smith mentioned use value, only to go on to ignore it and construct theories of abstract exchange value. Sismondi's critique of Smith and Ricardo highlighted the contradiction between the use value and exchange value aspects of commodities.[119] In mainstream economics, the neglect of use value became even more pronounced in the response to left Ricardians' employment of classical theory to justify socialist conclusions. Grossman quoted a very early text by Marx on the implications of an exclusive focus on exchange value:

> By denying the importance of gross revenue, i.e. the volume of production and consumption [which Grossman identified as 'the mass of use values necessary for the maintenance of the working nation'] apart from the value-surplus – and hence denying the importance of life itself, political economy's abstraction reaches the peak of infamy.[120]

Marx's transformation of Ricardo's economic categories was like his transformation of Hegel's dialectic. An important feature of Marx's reconfiguration was the systematic exploration, drawing on Sismondi, of the dual character of economic processes, including their material aspects, as opposed to Ricardo's one-sided concentration on them as abstract, value processes.[121] This provided a means of grasping both the real relations behind the veil of appearances and the reasons for these misleading appearances.

---

117 Grossman 1929b, see below pp. 183–209; Grossmann 1992, pp. 30–1; Grossmann 1928a, see below p. 129.

118 Grossmann 1928a, see below pp. 166–169; Grossman 1929b, see below pp. 201–209; Grossmann 1932f/1933a, see below p. 385.

119 Grossman 1924a, see below pp. 76, 96.

120 Marx 1981a, p. 421. [Marx emphasised 'infamy']; Grossman 1941a, see below p. 486–487.

121 Grossman 1941a, see below pp. 480–481, 483–484, 492; Grossman 1924a, see below p. 85.

> The point is not to eliminate the mystifying factor and substitute another but rather to demonstrate the necessary connection between the two and to explain what is deceptive in the phenomena of value. Because capitalism has a dual reality, mystifying and non-mystifying sides, and binds them together in a concrete unity, any theory which reflects this reality must likewise be a unity of opposites.[122]

The use value and value aspects of capitalist relations were not simply discussed in the first part of the first volume of *Capital* and then set aside, as many Marxist economists have assumed. Human labour is at once concrete labour that creates the use values of specific commodities and abstract labour that generates commodities' value. Human labour is the use value of the commodity labour power, while labour power's value is the amount of abstract labour required to produce it. Capitalist processes of production are at once labour processes, through which specific kinds of concrete labour are applied, and value-creating (valorisation) processes, in which quantities of socially necessary abstract labour are embodied into commodities.

Marx's method of successive approximation meant that, in *Capital*, the distinction between use value and value, gained at the highest level of abstraction, permeated the increasingly concrete analyses, progressively approaching the complex real world.[123] Capital and the organic composition of capital, for example, also have a dual character. The organic composition of capital is the ratio between the value of human labour power and other inputs into production processes 'in so far as it is determined by' 'the relation between the mass of the means of production employed on the one hand, and the mass of labour necessary for their employment on the other', i.e. the relation between the means of production as use values and living labour, 'and mirrors the changes in the latter'.[124] The contradiction between the unlimited productive potential of the development of production forces and the constraints on output imposed by capitalist relations of production also expresses that between the use value and value aspects of economic processes under capitalism.[125]

122 Grossman 1941a, see below p. 477.

123 Grossman 1941a, below pp. 480–481, 495; Grossmann 1992, p. 147. In response to criticisms of Marx by ecological economists, Paul Burkett (2004) has demonstrated that the reproduction schemas in Volume 2 of *Capital* are concerned not only with flows of values but also of use values.

124 Marx 1981b, p. 762.

125 Grossman 1992, p. 123.

The neglect of use value or its confusion with exchange value has remained a feature of mainstream economics. Much of Marx's critique of vulgar economics therefore also applies to its current, sophisticated and sophistical third, marginalist phase, preoccupied with psychology (the subjective theory of value) and mathematical technique, and popularly known as 'economics'.

There has been a long-running controversy over Marx's explanation of the way in which the values of commodities are transformed into 'prices of production' as rates of profit equalise across industries with different organic compositions of capital. The neo-Ricardian Ladislaus Bortkiewicz identified a 'problem' in Marx's failure to assume that economic processes occur simultaneously, as in equilibrium models, and 'solved' it by means of systems of equations based on precisely this assumption.[126] Paul Sweezy's very influential *The Theory of Capitalist Development* popularised this 'solution' among English-reading Marxists.[127] The acceptance of Bortkiewicz's solution to the 'transformation problem' embedded the fundamentally static, equilibrium approach of mainstream bourgeois economics in many Marxist economists' thinking. Subsequently, on the basis of a simultaneous equilibrium analysis, most cogently articulated by Nobuo Okishio,[128] not only non-Marxist economists but many Marxists also concluded that Marx's law of the tendency for the rate of profit to fall, the crux of his account of economic crises, was false. This refutation only holds if Marx's own 'temporalist' approach, which eschews the implausible marginalist assumption of the simultaneous determination of the prices of inputs and outputs, is disregarded.[129]

In contrast with the static framework of both classical political economy and its vulgar descendents, both of which assume that capitalism has a tendency to equilibrium, the dual nature of commodities, especially as applied to the commodity labour power, allowed Marx to grasp capitalism as a dynamic system. The recovery of Marx's critique of the way classical political economists and their vulgar successors assumed 'the simultaneous rhythm of all economic processes' allowed Grossman to expose many previous (and subsequent) Marxists' capitulation to bourgeois economics. They neglected the use value, therefore the time aspect of economic relations and reverted to pre-Marxist equilibrium analysis. Between the 1980s and 2010s, the temporal single system interpretation, in the process of resolving the 'transformation problem', recapitulated the

126 Bortkiewicz 1949, nb translated by Paul Sweezy; Bortkiewicz 1952.
127 Sweezy 1942, pp. 109–28.
128 Okishio 1961.
129 For a defence of Marx's approach, see Kliman 2007, pp. 113–38.

account Grossman provided of Marx's approach to capturing the dynamics of capitalism and his objections to the static methodology of vulgar Marxists.[130]

Crisis and Breakdown

Grossman subjected the crisis theories of mainstream economists and most of his Marxist predecessors to sustained criticism in the course of identifying two complementary theories of crisis in Marx's work. The first, which most commentators on Grossman's work have ignored, explained capitalism's dynamic instability. The second, based on Marx's law of the tendency for the rate of profit to fall, accounted for capitalism's breakdown logic and the cyclical nature of crises. Both were grounded in the contradictions between the capitalist production process as a labour process, creating use values, and as a process generating new values, in the form of surplus value. They were counterposed to explanations of crises and/or capitalism's tendency to break down in terms of underconsumption and value disproportion alone.

Heinrich Cunow, in 1898, offered an underconsumptionist explanation of capitalism's breakdown tendency: workers were not paid enough to buy all that they produced and export markets would only be able to absorb this excess for a limited period, until capitalism pervaded the whole world. At that point there would be no scope for exports to non-capitalist areas and the system would break down. Karl Kautsky, between 1901 and 1911, and Louis Boudin, in his widely read English-language work of 1907, also expounded this argument. Rosa Luxemburg, in 1913, provided a more systematic grounding for the underconsumptionist theory of capitalist breakdown than these earlier Marxist efforts. She drew explicitly on the work of Sismondi and argued that imperialism resulted from the pursuit of non-capitalist markets which were essential for capitalism's survival. Luxemburg recognised that, contrary to Eduard Bernstein and his reformist successors, the theory of breakdown was a key element of Marx's analysis of capitalism and the case for socialism. As she was a consistent revolutionary, who sought like Cunow to justify a theory of breakdown with inadequate arguments, her position provided Grossman with a useful foil in making the case for Marx's explanation.[131]

The reproduction schemas in the second volume of *Capital* were inadequate, according to Luxemburg, because they did not show the necessary shortfall

130 Grossmann 1932g/Grossmann 2017c; Grossman 1932b, see below pp. 304–331; Grossman 1930/Grossmann 2017b. See Kliman 2007 for an impressive account of the controversy and the temporal single system interpretation; and Moseley 2015, for a persuasive variant.

131 Grossman 1932f/1933a, see below pp. 350, 368–369, 371; Grossman 1928a, see below p. 141.

between the growth of output and its 'realisation', i.e. sale. Workers and capitalists could not buy the products embodying newly created surplus value. Those commodities had to be realised through sale to non-capitalist 'third persons' at home or abroad. But the schemas, constructed at a high level of abstraction, were designed to illuminate the process of capitalist circulation, not the much more concrete issue of realisation. The incorporation of foreign trade and investment would have undermined their provisional assumption that prices were the same as values, which was still crucial for the analysis they embodied.[132] On the other hand, incorporating them into the analysis at a more concrete level presents no difficulties.

Luxemburg's approach could not account for cyclical crises and failed as a theory of breakdown because it did not accept that the logic of capital accumulation is 'production for the sake of production', that is profit making, rather than satisfying the final demand of individuals. In addition to their own personal consumption, *if it is profitable to invest*, capitalists in different sectors will expend newly created surplus value on expanding their capacity (by buying additional means of production and employing new workers who purchase additional means of consumption, produced in other sectors). In that way, all the commodities embodying surplus value can potentially find a market.[133]

Employing a model derived from Marx's reproduction schema, Mikhail Tugan-Baranovsky, when a 'legal Marxist' in Tsarist Russia, claimed capitalist expansion could continue indefinitely, limited only by the rate of technological change. Crises, he argued, are the result of disproportional expansion in different industries. Iron ore mines, for example, periodically produce far too much for the steel industry to absorb: ore prices collapse; inefficient mines become bankrupt; new investment in mining slows dramatically or ceases; industries producing means of production for mines and the transport of ore are affected; workers in mining and sectors that supply its inputs are sacked; the demand for consumer goods falls ... Tugan-Baranovsky reproduced the harmonious conclusions of Jean-Baptiste Say, the father of vulgar political economy who contended that supply creates its own demand. 'Neo-harmonist' Marxists, such as Hilferding, Bauer and Karl Renner, embraced this approach, includ-

132 Criticisms of Luxemburg are implicit in Grossman 1922, see below pp. 44–49; and Grossman 1924a, see below, p. 62. They are explicit in Grossmann 1928a, see below pp. 166–169; Grossman 1929b, see below pp. 201–209; Grossmann 1992, pp. 41–2, 47–8, 67–8; Grossmann 1932f/1933a, see below p. 385.

133 Grossman 1932f/1933a, see below pp. 368–369 and especially 371; Grossmann 1992, pp. 41–2, 118–19, Grossmann 1928a, pp. 166–169; Grossman 1929b, see below pp. 202–206.

ing the focus, shared with mainstream economics, on the value proportions that are conditions for sustained growth and economic stability, and Tugan-Baranovsky's rejection of Marx's theory of breakdown. Their theories of disproportionality were unsatisfactory because they ignored the transformation of values into prices of production. From their analysis, the neo-harmonists drew the reformist conclusion that, if proportional investment was imposed by the state, economic crises could be avoided. While Communists like Bukharin were committed revolutionaries, their theories of disproportionality drawn from Hilferding's shared its flaws.[134]

The contradiction between use value and value in the process of production pervaded the whole of Marx's economic theory, including his treatments of crises. In contrast to neo-harmonist, value-fixated accounts of the proportions required for stable capitalist growth, his inclusion of material, use value conditions resulted in a radical theory of disproportionality with much more stringent and, in the real world, implausible conditions for capitalist equilibrium.[135]

Before September 1933, Grossman wrote that he had begun to work on a book on crisis under simple reproduction, which he described as his 'life's work'. He still referred to it as 'my chief contribution to Marxist theory' in 1947.[136] While nothing like a book manuscript has survived, his published works contain elements of the argument, built on his earlier, more general recovery of Marx's theory of radical disproportionality.

In the second volume of *Capital*, Marx dropped the preliminary assumption of equal 'production times' (the periods required for the production of commodities) of all capitals and also introduced the complication of 'circulation time' (the period commodities spend in the sphere of circulation before they are sold). Together production and circulation time constitute 'turnover time'. Differences in turnover time are conditioned by the technical (i.e. use value) characteristics of production processes and the commodities they create. Even in the model of simple reproduction (i.e. without growth) in the second volume of *Capital*, which abstracts from the credit system amongst other aspects of the real world, crises are inevitable because of the use value distinction between fixed capital (embodied in commodities, like machines, that function in mul-

134 Grossman 1932f/1933a, see below p. 340; Grossman 1992, p. 69; Grossman 1941a, see below p. 524.

135 Grossman 1922, see below pp. 44–49; Grossman 1941a, see below pp. 469–533, particularly p. 530–531.

136 Grossman 1933a, see below p. 249; Grossman 1947a, see below p. 630. Also; Grossman 1933b, see below p. 252; Grossman 1937c, see below p. 431.

tiple cycles of the labour process) and circulating capital (commodities, like raw materials or wage goods, that are used up in one cycle). In some years, more fixed capital will have to be replaced than in others. But the model assumes a consistent level of output each year.[137] Unevenness in the accumulation of fixed capital will tend to become cyclical, clumped together during some periods, generating booms, and thinning out during others, resulting in slumps.

The analysis can be extended by considering different kinds of fixed capitals, as use values, with different average life spans, to account for cycles of different periodicities. Hence there are cycles of investment in normal productive fixed capital and longer cycles of investment in larger scale fixed capital, infrastructure and buildings.[138] The existence of credit in the real world can even out fixed capital investments in different industries and enterprises, geographically, at a given time. It does not even out and may intensify fluctuations in fixed capital investment over time.

Furthermore, simple reproduction in value terms is not necessarily simple reproduction in terms of use values. Changed weather conditions in agriculture and large losses in output, due to unforeseen circumstances, in any industry can lead to a decline in the number of commodities produced while the living labour and the value of the means of production used to produce them, therefore their total value, are unchanged. Such a development will disrupt simple reproduction in other industries to which it provides inputs.[139]

When the scale of reproduction expands and there is technological change, as Grossman argued much earlier, the situation becomes even more complicated. Even if new investment is proportional across sectors, in value terms, the scope for the growth in the number of commodities produced by different sectors will vary according to the use value characteristics of their output. So, for example, 'No one who finds two tractors sufficient for the cultivation of their land will buy four simply because their price has fallen by half. Demand for tractors – *ceteris paribus* – is not dependent on their price alone but is, rather, determined by the area to be cultivated, that is quantitatively'.[140] If technological change occurs, problems of proportion will arise even when investment

137 Grossman 1937b, see below p. 272; Grossman 1941a, see below pp. 517–522, also see p. 483; Marx 1978b, pp. 264, 528–45, particularly pp. 543–5.

138 Roberts 2016, pp. 219–21. The existence and basis in Marxist theory of even lengthier 'Kondratiev' cycles or 'long waves' is more questionable, cf. Trotsky 1941.

139 Grossman 1941a, see below pp. 525–527; Grossman 1937b, see below p. 272.

140 Grossman 1941a, see below p. 533. '*Ceteris paribus*' means 'other things being equal'. The same idea, with a similar illustration, was expressed in a manuscript response to a hostile review of *The Law*, Grossman n.d.a, see below p. 216.

is not increased or increases in the same value proportions in different industries. Should technological progress leap ahead in the steel compared to the car industry, the quantity of steel will rise more rapidly than the number of cars. So, even though the car industry may have the capacity, in *value* terms, to purchase the same proportion of the steel industry's output as previously, its *technical* requirements for steel will not have kept up with the expanded production of steel. The previous equilibrium, on the basis of the previous value proportionalities, will be disrupted.

The material characteristics of the technology used in production also mean that there is a minimum amount of accumulated value that has to be invested in specific sectors. This, too, is an obstacle to simultaneous proportional expansion of production.[141] For example, surplus value accumulated over a very short period may be sufficient to expand a clothing factory by an additional number of cutting and sewing machines. But a steel mill may have to accumulate over several years before it can invest in a new furnace and related equipment.

The contradiction between use value and value also underpinned Marx's theory of capitalist breakdown, another aspect of his account of periodic crises. A tendency to breakdown was, according to Marx, inherent in the capitalist mode of *production*, but this has been denied by many Marxist economists for generations.

> It was a great historical contribution of Rosa Luxemburg that she, in a conscious opposition to the distortions of these 'neo-harmonists' adhered to the basic lesson of *Capital* and sought to reinforce it with the proof that the continued development of capitalism encounters absolute economic limits.
>
> Frankly Luxemburg's effort failed.[142]

Two circumstances facilitated Grossman's 'reconstruction of Marx's theory of crisis and breakdown': recovering Marx's method of abstraction and successive approximation that structured *Capital*; and the investigations associated with his theory of radical disproportionality.[143] Extrapolating Bauer's reproduction schema, designed to refute Luxemburg's defence of the idea that capitalism tended to break down, demonstrated the effects of the breakdown mechanism that Marx had identified but had subsequently been neglected.[144] Bauer's

141 Grossman 1941a, see below p. 532.
142 Grossmann 1992, p. 41; Grossman 1941a, see below pp. 485, 524.
143 Grossman, 1932f/1933a, see below p. 385.
144 Otto Bauer 1986; Grossman 1924b.

model broke down in the thirty-fifth cycle because of this mechanism: the tendency for the rate of profit to fall.[145]

The dual character of economic processes is apparent in this tendency, which results from the long-term rise in the organic composition of capital.[146] For there is an

> inverse movement of the mass of use values and values as a consequence of the increase in labour's productive power. The richer a society, the greater the development of labour's productive power, the larger the volume of useful things which can be made in a given labour time. At the same time, however, the value of these things becomes smaller.[147]

Capitalism spectacularly expands the number of use values produced while reducing the value of individual commodities, by channelling a progressively higher proportion of investment into new technologies embodied in constant capital, as opposed to the purchase of living labour power. The ratio between the cost of constant capital used and the wages bill increases. Driven by competition amongst capitalists, this rising organic composition of capital expresses the progressive nature of capitalism, which increases the productivity of labour because workers using more sophisticated equipment, etc. produce more commodities in a given time. But it is only living labour that creates new surplus value. The rate of profit – the ratio between the newly created value embodied in surplus value (profits) and capitalists' total outlays – falls. The requirements for the accumulation of constant capital encroach on the surplus value available for the consumption of capitalists and/or workers' wages. Eventually there is insufficient surplus value to maintain any given rate of accumulation: the model breaks down. The onset of the breakdown is accelerated as the absolute value of individual, new items of constant capital grows.[148]

This analysis captures a long-term tendency of the capitalist system. To approach the real world pattern of growth more closely, Marx continued his investigation by identifying countertendencies, also inherent in capitalism and shaped by the dual nature of capitalist production, that slow or temporarily reverse the tendency for the rate of profit to fall. These included: the cheapen-

145 Grossman 1924b; Grossman, 1922, see below 44–49; Grossmann, 1928a see below p. 169; Grossmann, 1929a.

146 Marx 1976b, p. 762; also Marx 1981b, p. 245; Grossman 1941a, see below p. 483.

147 Grossman 1941a, see below p. 484.

148 Grossman 1941a, see below p. 484; Grossman 1992, pp. 74–82.

ing of both means of production and the items workers consume, a consequence of the increased productivity of labour; reduced turnover time; increases in the variety of use values, including through foreign trade; the transfer of surplus value from less to more developed territories through unequal exchange and profits on exported capital; and economic crises themselves, which devalue means of production, sold off cheap or left idle by bankrupt businesses. The effects of the countertendencies mean that capitalism's tendency to break down takes the form of recurrent economic crises. While exploitation, the rate of surplus value, rises, and (up to a point) the mass of surplus value does increase, neither this nor the other countertendencies are sufficient to fully offset the effect of the rising organic composition of capital on the rate of profit in the long term. This is confirmed by empirical studies. Capitalism's tendency to break down and its inherent crises, grounded in the distinctively capitalist, dual nature of the production process, are both expressions of the contradiction between the forces and relations of production.[149]

Revolutionary Politics

A myth that Grossman had a mechanical theory of capitalism's collapse and the transition to socialism was fabricated by Stalinist and social-democratic reviewers of his *Law of Accumulation*. It was often associated with the implied or explicit accusation that Grossman was a proponent of political passivity. The myth was imported into the English literature by Paul Sweezy. His acolytes have continued to peddle it.[150] No act of esoteric divination was or is necessary to establish the nature of Grossman's commitment to political activity culminating in workers' revolution or that he did not mechanically apply his model of capital accumulation, derived from Bauer's schema. His positions were apparent in his political affiliations and clearly expressed, not only in unpublished responses to critics but also in his readily accessible publications, including *The Law of Accumulation*.

As a young revolutionary leader, Grossman emphasised the centrality of class struggle to both the formation of working-class consciousness and revolu-

---

149 Grossman 1992, pp. 83–5, 123, 130–200; Grossman 1941a, see below p. 496. Grossman drew mainly on US statistics. For recent empirical confirmation of his exposition of Marx's theory see, for example, Kliman 2012; Maito 2015; Basu and Manolakos 2012; Carchedi and Roberts 2013. For refutations of the criticisms of Grossman's theory of breakdown and crisis, see Grossman 1932f/1933a, below pp. 383–385; Kuhn 2007, pp. 140–5, 151–2.

150 Sweezy 1942, pp. 211, 214; Foster and McChesney 2010, pp. 52–5.

tion. Decades later he expressed the relationship between capitalism's tendency to break down and the working class as an active revolutionary subject in Lukácsian/Hegelian terms. Marx 'follows Hegel, for whom history has both an objective and a subjective meaning, the history of human activity (*historia rerum gestarum*) and human activity itself (*res gestas*)'.[151] Consequently,

> The point of breakdown theory is that the revolutionary action of the proletariat only receives its most powerful impetus from the objective convulsion of the established system and, at the same time, only this creates the circumstances necessary to successfully wrestle down the ruling class's resistance.[152]

For

> The working class's struggle over everyday demands is thus bound up with its struggle over the final goal. The final goal for which the working class fights is not, therefore, an ideal that is brought into the working class by speculative means, 'from outside', whose realisation, independent from the struggles of the present, is reserved for the distant future. Rather, as the law of breakdown presented here shows, it is a result that arises from everyday, immediate class struggles, whose realisation is accelerated by these struggles.[153]

In *Capital*, Marx commented on the importance of knowledge about the laws of economic development: society 'can neither clear by bold leaps, nor remove by legal enactments, the obstacles offered by the successive phases of its normal development. But it can shorten and lessen the birth-pangs'.[154] It is clear from Grossman's survey of the history of Marxism that events other than a purely economic crisis may trigger an 'objective convulsion'. He stressed that, in the

---

151 Grossman 1943b, see below p. 597. Sensitivity to Marx's transformed Hegelian categories and Grossman's affinities with the returns to Marx in philosophy, by Korsch and Lukács, and politics, by Lenin, was even more evident in a draft of *Marx and Dynamics*. Grossman applied this understanding to economic analysis: 'in the labour process, labour does not take the form of a tool, but rather "labour itself appears as *the dominant activity*"; here the world of objects does not control labour; rather all of the means of production are subordinate to labour', Grossman 1937a, p. 111.

152 Grossmann 1932f/1933a, see below p. 385.

153 Grossman 1929a, pp. 602–3.

154 Marx 1976b, p. 92, quoted in Grossman 1943b, see below p. 591.

context of inter-imperialist rivalry which leads to war, 'the proletariat has the task of transforming war between peoples into civil war, with a view to the conquest of power and, for this reason, of preparing strategically and organisationally for revolution'.[155]

The overthrow of capitalism by the working class is not possible at all times. In several publications, Grossman referred to Lenin's analysis of the circumstances in which revolution becomes a possibility. A revolutionary situation arises when the subordinate classes are suffering increased hardship, no longer want to tolerate the old order, and are effectively organised to act while the ruling classes are objectively unable to rule as before.[156] Luxemburg, also a proponent of capitalism's tendency to break down, had argued in the same spirit that the revolutionary position is not to passively wait for capitalism to collapse.[157] This position was counterposed to both faith in an act of revolutionary will by a minority, voluntaristic putschism, and reliance on subjectless history running its course. In suitable objective circumstances, Grossman was confident, the working class can become an historical subject capable of the revolutionary overthrow of capitalism.

> [N]o economic system, no matter how weakened collapses by itself in automatic fashion. It must be 'overthrown' ... '[H]istorical necessity' does not operate automatically but requires the active participation of the working class in the historical process.
>
> ...
>
> The main result of Marx's doctrine is the clarification of the historical role of the proletariat as the carrier of the transformative principle and the creator of the socialist society ... In changing the historical *object*, the *subject* changes himself. Thus the education of the working class to its historical mission must be achieved not through theories brought in from outside but through the everyday practice of the class struggle.[158]

The actions of the working class as an historical subject are conditioned and can be influenced by knowledge of 'the "natural laws" of capitalist production'. Looking ahead, 'The really "active", spontaneous human can only be a *species*

155 Grossmann 1932f, p. 373; also see Grossman 1928a, see below p. 138.
156 Grossmann 1928a, pp. 161–2, citing Lenin 1964a, pp. 213–14; see also Grossman 1941a, below p. 596.
157 Luxemburg 2008, p. 89.
158 Grossman 1943b, see below pp. 596–597; also see Grossmann 1929a, pp. 602–3; and Grossman 1941a, below p. 596.

being where his *species activity* is conceivable, i.e. under socialism, as the *result of history*, of real history'.[159]

Although hardly modest, Grossman's decision to conclude his 1932 survey with a summary of his own work on Marxist crisis theory, its relationship with Marxist politics and refutation of arguments made against it, entailed a sober assessment of his contribution to Marxism.[160] Grossman vindicated Marx's sustained attention to the use value and value aspects of economic processes, which underpinned his reaffirmation of Marx's theories of economic crisis and capitalist breakdown and his powerful critique of bourgeois economics' equilibrium theories. His arguments are of immediate relevance. They provide a basis for decontaminating Marxism of a range of alien, bourgeois assumptions that undermine its coherence, and they support important practical conclusions, particularly about responses to recurrent economic crises and the working class as a potentially self-conscious historical subject.

Grossman's Works in English; Structure and Conventions

This is the first volume of four containing the bulk of Henryk Grossman's publications and the most significant of his texts which he did not publish. A large proportion of them have not previously been translated into English, and those which have appear here in improved form. The second volume will bring together his primarily political writings. The third will be his *The Law of Accumulation and Breakdown of the Capitalist System: Being also a Theory of Crises*, published unabridged in English for the first time. The final volume will be a selection of Grossman's works on economic history. The series does not include works concerned with the history of science, because they have already appeared together in English,[161] nor his primarily statistical studies, nor his lecture in Polish on Habsburg economic policy in Galicia between 1772 and 1790, as much of its content was published in his later, closely related book in German.[162]

The order of the works below follows their dates of publication. The original texts quoted by Grossman have been modified to comply with this book's citation and stylistic conventions. Minor errors in his quotations, spelling of names and references have been corrected without comment. The editor has modified

159 Grossman 1937, see below p. 433.
160 Grossmann 1932f/1933a, pp. 380–385.
161 In Freudenthal and McLaughlin 2009.
162 Grossmann 1912 and Grossmann 1914.

most of the initial translations in many places, with reference to the original texts. Where they exist, published English translations are used in quotations and references. Other things being equal, editions available free on websites, such as www.archive.org, have been preferred for references. References in the bibliography include the years of publications' original editions and/or during which they were written in square brackets, where relevant. In the rest of the book, words in square brackets in quotations are the author's, unless otherwise indicated; elsewhere they are the editor's. Emphasis in quotations is the original author's, unless otherwise indicated. Explanations of abbreviations and basic biographical information about people mentioned in this book are provided in the index.

CHAPTER 1

The Fortieth Anniversary of *Capital*[*]

Translated from Yiddish by Frank Wolff

This month, 40 years ago, the most important work of scientific socialism, the first volume of *Capital*,[1] appeared. In a short newspaper article it is, of course, impossible to convey an idea of this brilliant work which established the foundations of scientific socialism. Here we only want to recall for our readers this work's most important point about the old and always new doctrine of socialism.

It is well known that the most important point of socialist doctrine lies in the 'theory of value' and in the 'materialist conception of history'. In *Capital* Marx merged these two doctrines into one complete picture. Before Marx, Adam Smith, an English bourgeois economist, had already proved that labour determines the value of commodities. But Marx explained that value is not a static category, no eternal quality of commodities but rather a social phenomenon. Exchange value is a social relation between different people which is characteristic of a particular epoch in world history. There once was a time when there was no *exchange* between people and therefore no *exchange value*. Exchange value is determined by the 'socially necessary labour time' which is expended to create a product. The labour power which determines the value of a commodity is, as Marx proved for the first time, solely determined by the sum of the products necessary for the worker's life. Because, however, people can produce more than they need for their own subsistence, the worker produces '*surplus labour*', 'surplus products'. With technological improvements, with the increase in the productivity of human labour the mass of 'surplus labour' which the worker generates for the capitalist grows, because the worker needs less and less time for his own subsistence. Due to the prolongation of the workday, because of the reduction of the worker's free time, the boss gets more surplus labour. This point thus lays bare the conflict between the entrepreneur and the worker. The entrepreneur wants more surplus labour from the worker; the worker, on the contrary, wants to keep as large a portion of his labour for himself as possible. But workers cannot keep all their labour for themselves because

* [Anonymous, possibly by Henryk Grossman, originally published as Anonymous 1907.]
1 [Marx 1976b.]

then the class of capitalists would cease to exist and this is why workers have to try to wrest production from the capitalists' hands. But, as Marx demonstrates, production has already become social, i.e. technological development requires mass production in large factories and for the whole society. The individual worker cannot take over the factory or become a small capitalist. Production must be transferred into the hands of the *whole* society which will replace the capitalist and organise production. At the same time, Marx proved that production will be more and more concentrated, small entrepreneurs will go under, the large will get still larger. The working class grows in numbers and becomes the overwhelming majority of society. Simultaneously the working class is concentrated in giant factories, unites and becomes conscious of its power and of its role in production: it strives to conquer social power, political organisation, so that, as the country's political ruler, it organises production for the whole society, in a word, it introduces socialism.

With this reasoning, Marx proved the unavoidable necessity of socialism. It is no longer a 'wish', a 'utopia', a beautiful ideal, it is a historical necessity, which *must* be realised and for which today's technological development establishes the basis.

And that is why the bourgeois world still cannot forget Marx's *Capital*. That is why it tries to prove that Marx's *Capital* is no scientific work, because in accepting his ideas as correct one must also accept the necessity of socialism. Furthermore, however, the proletariat of all countries and all nations has understood the significance of *Capital* for itself. It has already been translated into all languages, except our mother tongue. The further development of the Jewish proletariat will hopefully bring *Capital* into jargon.[2] The sooner this happens, the greater will be the progress of the Jewish labour movement.

2 [In German and Polish, 'jargon' is a derogatory term for Yiddish. It is used ironically here. *Capital* was eventually translated into Yiddish, in New York; see Marx 1917–18.]

CHAPTER 2

The Theory of Economic Crisis*

Crises in a capitalist economic mechanism occur when a certain amount of merchandise of a definite value (m) cannot be sold within the limits of the said mechanism. The problem presented by the crises consists in determining the factors which condition them, and more particularly in ascertaining whether the crises result from the very essence of the existing economic order, or whether they are the result of inessential and accidental influences.

An ineffective dispute of more than a hundred years' duration, based as it was on theoretical considerations only, has induced many investigators of the problem to try the historical method: the key to the theoretical explanation was sought in descriptions, as detailed as possible, of the reality of experience. In opposition to this tendency, the author is of opinion that naïve empiricism must be abandoned and – experiments being out of the question – logical constructions must be attempted. As a physicist investigating the fall of bodies, examines, in his desire to exclude the accidental and external influences of air, the fall of bodies *in vacuo*, under conditions created artificially, so the question whether crises result from the essence of the economic mechanism under consideration can only be explained when we make this mechanism independent in our thoughts of the disturbing influences of foreign markets and investigate it as existing for itself, as if in a vacuum. Apart from methodological considerations, this position is also recommended by an analysis, on its merits, of the hypothesis which, while establishing the impossibility of selling the total value of the year's produce within the limits of the capitalist mechanism, sees in the existence of non-capitalist foreign markets an indispensable condition for realising 'super-production'[1] (m). Since, then, the hypothesis of foreign markets leads to fictitious solutions,[2] it must be assumed beforehand that the realisation of m is bound to take place within the capitalist mechanism, and further enquiry attempts to fix the conditions under which such realisation would be possible.

---

* [Originally published as Grossman 1922. All paragraph breaks are the editor's. Some of the letters used as abbreviations in this essay have been changed to avoid confusion with their use in other works in this volume.]

1 [i.e. 'surplus value'. The translator was not familiar with the standard English terminology for Marx's economic concepts.]

2 [This is a reference to Luxemburg 1913.]

The unbroken chain of social production in an economic system based on hired labour can be schematically represented in the following manner: producers invest in production, in the course of the year, an amount of real capital – such as instruments of production, buildings, raw material, etc. – which may be indicated by the letter c, and in addition to this a sum of capital to cover the expense of workers' wages which we shall indicate by v, and thus they obtain an annual produce of $O = c + v + a$, where a indicates an average amount of profit without which they would not undertake production. For simplification, let us suppose that the real capital is entirely used up in the course of a year's production and must be renewed annually if production in the following year is not to be interrupted. Assuming $c = 4{,}000$, $v = 1{,}000$, $O = 6{,}000$, we obtain for a the figure of 1,000. From the value of $O = 6{,}000$, the capitalist is obliged, according to the above assumption, to deduct 4,000 for the renewal of real capital (c), so that the total amount of the joint income remaining is 2,000, of which $v = 1{,}000$ is in the hands of the workers, and $a = 1{,}000$ in the hands of the employers. We assume further that outside these two classes of society drawing a direct income, there is no other class: that the incomes of lawyers, physicians, artists, officials, etc. can be classified under the incomes of either the one or the other of the two fundamental classes above-mentioned.

If the capitalists consumed a entirely, social production would run along the same lines year by year, and we should have to deal with direct reproduction.[3] But experience presents to us reproduction amplified,[4] that is to say a state of things in which producers consume only part of a, for instance 600 – which we shall call k – whereas the remaining part of the profit a, that is to say 400 – let us call it the coefficient of accumulation (m)[5] – serves for the enlargement of the apparatus of production. Experience shows that the enlargement of the scale of production takes place among periodical perturbations. As long as the quantity represented by m finds purchasers in the market, the economic mechanism is in a period of 'hausse',[6] followed at more or less regular intervals, by a period of stagnation when the remainder m cannot, because of a lack of demand, be consumed by the producers. Another question: under what conditions is the realisation of $m = 400$ possible, and who realises it? Not the workers, because their purchases must move within the limits of their income $v = 1{,}000$. Not the

3 [i.e. 'simple reproduction'.]

4 [i.e. 'expanded reproduction'.]

5 [Grossman or his translator confusingly used the same abbreviation for both 'super-production' i.e. surplus value, and the part of surplus value that is not used for capitalists' personal consumption.]

6 ['*Hausse*' means 'expansion']

capitalists, because their fund of consumption amounts to k = 600, already expended. When the joint income $v + a$ amounts to 2,000, the joint fund of consumption $v + k$ amounts to 1,600. Who, then, realises the remainder m? The problem, as we see, is one of quantity, and we shall deal in what follows, with such theories only as have endeavoured to solve the problem.

Since neither the workers nor employers as consumers – and there are no other social classes in our abstract society – can be purchasers of m, it follows that only the employers as producers can be the purchasers, that is to say: super-production[7] m must be used up by the producers themselves for the enlargement of the apparatus of production. Here we approach the kernel of the problem. A crisis is the result of planless accumulation. Any enlargement of the apparatus of production can only take place, without disturbance, on condition that the coefficient m intended for accumulation be divided in strictly defined proportions: 1) Among different branches of joint production (the sphere producing instruments of production, the sphere producing goods for consumption, etc.); 2) Within each such branch among the component parts of capital $c : v$. The beginnings of a theory of proportional distribution of productive forces came from Jean-Baptiste Say, who, however, taking for the starting point of his analysis the pre-capitalist system, based on the labour of independent producers, could not explain capitalist crises.

Karl Marx was the first to work out this idea in application to the capitalist system, but he was not able to finish his work. Correct mathematical form was only given to his formulae by Professor Tugan-Baranovsky (1901)[8] and Otto Bauer (1913),[9] who pointed out that if only the proportions laid down by the formula as to the distribution of accumulated capital were observed, accumulation could be infinitely prolonged without crises. The crises, as a matter of fact, are caused by the circumstance that nobody troubles to observe the proportions demanded by the formula. Owing, however, to the oscillations of prices and wages, there takes place, *ex post*, an automatic re-establishment of the disturbed balance, and a readjustment of the apparatus of production to the proportions required by theory; for, owing to high wages or low prices respectively, the capitalist profit diminishes and the speed of accumulation slows down, causing a restriction of the apparatus of production, whilst, on the contrary, with low wages or high prices, the producer's profit grows, and with it the apparatus of production grows also. At this point the chain of ideas of the accepted doctrine breaks off.

---

7 [i.e. 'surplus value'.]

8 [Tugan-Baranowsky 2000.]

9 [Otto Bauer 1986.]

[Heinrich] Herkner pointed out as early as 1892 that the so-called 'law of wages' was 'a regulator too apt to deceive'.[10] Indeed, the basis of fact for the theory of automatic regulation here discussed is not in accord with experience. The policy of production practiced by the *trusts* teaches us that an increase of demand and prices, instead of enlarging the apparatus of production, often restricts it, if the rise in prices produced thereby secures for the trusts higher profits than they would obtain by enlarged production. Conditions are analogous in the case of a fall of prices. There is no question of an automatic re-establishment of disturbed proportion in the apparatus of production.

The super-production[11] of tonnage in Germany, the crises called forth by it and the lowering of tariffs in the period from 1892 to 1895, and again in 1909, did not cause any restriction of the production of tonnage, but, on the contrary, its enlargement, because it was decided to build new ships of a bigger type. In spite of lower tariffs these new ships were able, owing to their more economic construction, to work at a profit. The appearance of ships of the new type deprives the old ones of value: their owners go bankrupt, not being able to work at a profit. The new purchasers, however, having bought these ships very cheaply, have a new basis for making them pay. Even old ships now work at a profit. The result, then, is the following: in spite of the 'super-production'[12] of tonnage, new ships have been built. The apparatus of production, instead of becoming restricted, has been enlarged. And the crisis, nevertheless, has passed! What has been restricted is – the value of the ships. The crisis, then, is not a restriction of the real apparatus of production, but a breakdown of the accepted system of prices and values, and its reorganisation on a new level.

The above example conclusively shows that in the problem here investigated we must distinguish two sides in economic phenomena: their value, and the material foundation for the value. Now only we can take up research at the point, where the accepted doctrine stopped. If it asserts, and proves with mathematical precision, that crises would be impossible if only a definite proportion were observed in the accumulation of capital, no objection can be raised to such reasoning. But we ask: what is the proportion, which it is necessary to observe in the distribution of accumulated capital? Is it a proportional distri-

10 [The source of this quotation cannot be identified, but for a similar observation, see Herkner 1894, pp. 194–5. Critiques of wage fund theories and the 'iron law of wages' long predated Herkner, notably Marx 1985c.]

11 [i.e. 'overproduction'.]

12 [i.e. 'overproduction'.]

bution of capital as measured by its value, or by the quantity of its real bulk? Is it, for instance, the value of ships or the size of their tonnage? This question, so important for the problem of proportional distribution of the powers of production, has never yet been put. The capitalist process of reproduction, it appears, demands both kinds of proportion. A definite proportion in the distribution of capital as measured by value is indispensable in the capitalist process of production as a process of making pay,[13] a process of drawing profits from the difference in value at the beginning and at the end of production. But the process of production is at the same time a technical process of *work*. In the process of work[14] it is not value that is active, but the real and personal factors of production, which stand in a strictly defined technical relation to each other, depending on the technical development of each particular branch of work (manual labor, use of machines, etc.). Only if both proportions, viz. the proportion of capitals in the process of making pay,[15] and in the technical process of work,[16] covered each other, that is to say if they ran along the same lines, would crises be impossible. But we have seen that this is not so. The amplitude of movements of the accumulation of capital in the process of making pay[17] (as measured by value) is different from the amplitude of movements of the accumulation of capital in the process of work[18] (as measured by the real bulk of the apparatus of production). The two amplitudes cross each other. Agreement between the two movements can only be an accident, and their disproportion is a constant and unavoidable phenomenon of the economic mechanism under investigation, a disproportion resulting from the double character of its essence, which is on the one hand a process of making pay,[19] on the other, one of work. Bankruptcy of employers on the one hand, unemployment of masses of workers on the other, are met with not only in periods of depression, but in phases of fullest development as a constant symptom of our economic life. Conversely, even in periods of greatest depression the process of accumulation, of enlarging, never stops. A period of depression differs from one of *hausse* not in quality, but in quantity only, the phenomena of disturbance being more intense.

13 [i.e. 'process of creating value' or 'valorisation process'.]
14 [i.e. 'labour process'.]
15 [i.e. 'process of creating value' or 'valorisation process'.]
16 [i.e. 'labour process'.]
17 [i.e. 'process of creating value' or 'valorisation process'.]
18 [i.e. 'labour process'.]
19 [i.e. 'process of creating value' or 'valorisation process'.]

Why such intensification happens periodically, why such disturbance is not evenly distributed over all sections of a longer period of time, but embraces at certain times larger circles than formerly, that is a secondary problem in the investigation of economic crises.

CHAPTER 3

The Economic System of Karl Marx (on the Fortieth Anniversary of His Death)*

Translated from Polish by Dominika Balwin

When Karl Marx died in 1883, his economic system was just beginning to be understood. It was only after his death that the essence of his studies began to be examined in greater depth. A turning point was only possible in 1894, when the third volume of *Capital* was published. The decline and bankruptcy of bourgeois economic theory was, however, already apparent at that time in discussions and disputes about Marxism as an economic system, as stressed 20 years earlier by Father [Stefan] Pawlicki.[1] Ricardo's theory of value laid a logical basis for the recognition of the bourgeoisie and proletariat as antagonistic classes. Bourgeois science, fearing the consequences of its own assumptions, retreated into the realms of history and ethics. Instead of studying the interdependence of phenomena in terms of *economic laws*, it limited itself to the *description* of economic relations through the ages. It also attempted to escape the implications of class struggle into the sphere of ethics, by offering *ethical postulates* and reformist recommendations aimed at overcoming capitalism's shortcomings, without removing the roots and basis of the system. These were the social motivations and conditions which gave rise to the so-called historical and socio-political schools of economics. This amounted to the bankruptcy of economics as a field of study. Even the bourgeoisie, which repeatedly tried to renew and rebuild the *theory*, understood this. However, the fear of the practical consequences of a science which threatened to be a *theoretical reflection of real phenomena* resulted in the imposition of *a priori* restrictions on these attempts.[2] In this way, it was possible to construct a more subtle system than that of medieval Scholasticism, even 'laws', so long as these laws were not those of the real world. Thus a new bourgeois theoretical school emerged: having previously escaped into the realms of history and ethics, it now escapes into *psychology*. This leads us from the sphere of external economic facts to the sphere of the internal, psychological life of individuals, describing objective and accessible facts in terms of psychological facts, invisible and inaccessible to research.

---

* [Originally published as Grossman 1923b.]

1 [Pawlicki 1874. See Grossman 1923a, on Pawlick's account of socialism.]

2 ['*A priori*' means 'previously assumed, without empirical investigation'.]

Despite its own bankruptcy, bourgeois science assumes a cloak of superiority: since the appearance of Marx's *Capital* in 1867[3] it has repeatedly attempted to demonstrate that Marx's analysis has been theoretically 'defeated'. And yet Marxism, killed thousands of times by foreigners as well as home-grown Majewskis,[4] reemerges like a phoenix from the ashes and we are still only *starting* to analyse Marx's system today. This is not a coincidence.

The first volume of *Capital* enjoyed the greatest popularity and understanding, and *its contents shaped the appreciation* of what we call Marx's economic system. This is understandable. In the first volume of *Capital* the working class found an explanation of 'the secret of capitalist production', the theory that labour creates all the wealth which the bourgeoisie accumulates and, at the same time, an explanation of how this occurs. Although labour creates this wealth, the results of labour, in the form of surplus value, goes to the bourgeoisie as profit, rent and interest of all kinds. The real producer, the worker, has to be content with a modest and inadequate wage. In the first volume, workers found a theoretical explanation of everything that they *saw every day* in the factory: the tendency of the capitalist class to squeeze the greatest amount of surplus value from the worker by extending working hours and lowering pay, increasing the intensity of work with the help of machinery, through the use of the labour of women and children on a large scale. Workers found a theoretical explanation of the hopeless battle between artisanal and capitalist production, the ruin of artisanal production and the fall of independent producers into the ranks of the proletariat. Finally, at the other extreme, the concentration and accumulation of existing capital, at the expense of smaller enterprises, and ever greater expansion of production. They found an explanation and formulation of laws which encompass the disparate phenomena of the whole world in a homogeneous mechanism. These laws provide a background for the working class to understand its place and role in that mechanism. When bourgeois science proclaimed, through the lips of the Protestant priest Malthus, that the destitution of the workers is an unavoidable result of the laws of nature, since the working class reproduces itself too rapidly in relation to the available food supply which grows at a markedly slower rate, the first volume of *Capital* formulated the so-called capitalist law of population. It demonstrated that population does not grow too quickly but on the contrary that the capitalist mode of production is characterised by periodic expansion and contraction, absorbing the excess population in times of growth and throwing it out onto the streets in

3 [Marx 1976b.]

4 [Majewski 1914.]

times of depression, increasing the so-called reserve army of the unemployed – in short, that capitalism created its own law of population adapted to the needs of capital and its profitability. Again, this was not just an abstract theory; *Capital* also formulated and explained theoretical phenomena whose factual basis the working class saw in thousands of aspects of everyday life. This is why the first volume of *Capital* – the *Bible* of the working class – became the scientific explanation of all the problems which the proletariat encountered in its everyday relations with the capitalist class. At the same time it was the formulation of real tendencies of development which were confirmed by the actual development of world economic relations over the following decades. At the same time that *Capital* gave an explanation of the *genesis* of the capitalist system, it demonstrated that it is an historical and therefore temporary mode of production which will give way to a superior system, which will be the communist system, in the *future*. It also pointed beyond questions of the present moment to the direction of changes in the contemporary economic system and the end result of this development which is, at the same time, the objective of the proletariat's conscious efforts.

Nevertheless despite the enthusiasm with which the leaders of the proletariat accepted *Capital*, as expressed in a well-known letter from master tanner Josef Dietzgen to Karl Marx,[5] the grey masses of the proletariat were too oppressed by the weight of capitalist exploitation to be able to think in terms of such a distant future; they were consumed with the worries of the present moment. It could not have been otherwise.

The development of capitalism in western European countries at that time did not yet show the level of maturity which would justify raising slogans for the realisation of socialism as a demand of the working class in its everyday struggles. This is why *the whole complex of issues concerning the question of the transformation of capitalism into socialism* remained a dead letter, despite the brilliant formulations in the first and later volumes of *Capital*. Because the brilliant thinker anticipated in theory the development of the world economy over the next few decades he could not be understood. The fate of these parts of *Capital* are confirmation of the correctness of Marx's own historical materialism.

Two generations of proletarians had to pass into the arena of history and two generations had to wear themselves out in unprecedented struggle and exertions, before conditions were mature enough, before the transition to socialism was proclaimed by everyday experience, rather than just as a hazy theoretical

5 [Dietzgen 1934.]

phrase in a socialist program. Only at this moment was theory, Marx's theory, which to this point had for a decade shown the proletariat a clear path through the varied phenomena of everyday life, turned to for explanation. It became apparent, at least superficially, that this theory had, however, failed. In the course of the everyday, *practical* struggle a handful of labour bureaucrats and aristocrats, who have made peace with the capitalist system and did not see any reason to abolish it, splinter from the proletariat so that, in the *theoretical* battle, a handful of literary 'leaders' of the proletariat are reconciled with the existing system and employ their pens to extol it. With reference to the analysis in the second volume of *Capital*, where Marx considers the possibility of permanent equilibrium of production and consumption within the capitalist system, Hilferding, Kautsky and Otto Bauer hastened to reply that such equilibrium is not only possible, but that the mechanisms of capitalism – as if by the volition of Providence – are so cleverly arranged that they exhibit a tendency to *automatically restore equilibrium* if it is temporarily disrupted.[6] Despite the reality that the whole capitalist world goes through catastrophic and tragic shocks, their theory revolves around the *harmonious* development of capitalism. Marx's theory, which was 'a contribution to the *critique* of capitalism', they transformed into a pseudo-theory praising capitalism, taking it back to the level of *pre-Marxist* theory, the so-called Manchester theory of harmonists following the example of Jean-Baptiste Say, Claude Frédéric Bastiat and [Henry Charles] Carey.[7] Marx's theory indeed may have differed from the theory of bourgeois economists in a number of *partial* respects, explaining wages, profit, interest or ground rent, the law of population or the concentration of capital – but in essential points relating to the *overall mechanism* of capitalism, its stability and permanence, Marx not only differs little from these economists but rather perfects them.

Distorted in this way, Marx's theory could, of course, no longer explain reality. Thus *theoretical opportunism*, not understanding the *economic laws* governing the capitalist system, follows in the footsteps of bourgeois economics and retreats into ethics and justice. The capitalist *state*, the obedient executive organ of the propertied classes, is to be the harbinger and instrument for achieving social 'justice', and superficial Rennerism[8] is only the practical formulation of conclusions whose theoretical foundations were developed by Hilferding and Otto Bauer.

6 [See Hilferding 1981; Kautsky 1911b; Otto Bauer 1986.]

7 [See, for example, Say 1867; Bastiat 1873 and 1880; Carey 1848.]

8 [See Renner 1918.]

The so-called 'historicism' of bourgeois economics consists of describing the early forms of capitalism as it emerged from the womb of previous economic systems. This kind of economics looked only into the past. The issue of the *possible end* of this system in the future never entered the scope of its questions. The very issue sent a shiver down its spine. It preferred to write hymns of praise in honour of 'progress' and the ever greater perfection of capitalism. That is why Marxist economics *is the only scientific theory* which predicted the process that is now under way, analysed it and formulated the laws of its historical development, *the historical process of the breakdown and disintegration of the capitalist system*. The opportunist literary attempts to distort Marxist theory, constantly undertaken, must always fail when confronted with the reproach of real developments.

CHAPTER 4

Simonde de Sismondi and His Economic Theories (a New Interpretation of His Thought)*

Translated from French by Ian Birchall

This year we have the opportunity to commemorate several great economists, for it is the centenary of the death of Ricardo, the fortieth anniversary of Karl Marx's death, the 200th anniversary of the birth of Adam Smith and the 150th of that of Simonde de Sismondi. Today I propose to draw your attention to the last of these. Compared with the numerous studies devoted to the Physiocrats and the classical English[1] economists, those dealing with Sismondi are relatively few in number. And although a host of excellent authors in more or less recent times, such as Adolphe Blanqui, [Julius] Kautz, [Hugo] Eisenhart, Charles Périn, [John Kells] Ingram, Ludwig Elster, Luigi Cossa, [Alfred Victor] Espinas, Herkner, [Albert] Aftalion, [Joseph] Rambaud, Hector Denis and Charles Rist,[2] have attempted to expound Sismondi's ideas, those studies which we possess have not succeeded, in my view, in giving sufficient attention to his theoretical thinking. In fact, while they pay ample homage to this honorary professor of the University of Wilno,[3] and draw out his importance as the creator of new social policy, he is relegated to secondary status as a theoretician. It is precisely on this last point that I differ from generally accepted opinions. To set them right I will try to characterise in turn Sismondi's method, his theory and his social policy.

1 Sismondi's Method

As far as method was concerned, it previously seemed that Sismondi's viewpoint had been clearly established. It was generally claimed that Sismondi was

* [Originally published as Grossman 1924a.]

1 [The Physiocrats were an eighteenth-century school of French economists who stressed that productive work, which they identified with agriculture, was the source of wealth. Grossman's references to English economists and England conflated England and Britain: the British economists to whom he referred included people from Scotland and Wales.]

2 Blanqui 1885; Kautz, 1860; Eisenhart 1910; Périn 1880; Ingram 1915; Elster 1887; Cossa 1809; Espinas 1891; Herkner 1921; Aftalion 1899; Rambaud 1902; Denis 1907; Rist 1915.

3 [Vilnius, now the capital of Lithuania, at the time Grossman wrote, under Polish rule.]

an opponent of the abstract and deductive method and that his merit consisted solely in the fact that he had spoken out critically against the abstract and deductive method of the classical school and in particular of Ricardo, juxtaposing it to the method of historical and descriptive induction. According to Denis, 'Sismondi's basic criticism of the [classical] school is for its abstract and deductive method.'[4] Charles Rist in turn makes a very similar judgment. 'Sismondi's disagreement was not upon the *theoretical principles* of political economy. So far as these were concerned, he declared himself a disciple of Adam Smith. He merely disagreed with *the method*, the *object* and hence the *practical conclusions* of the classical school.' 'Ricardo ... is accused of having introduced the abstract method into the science ... his spirit shrank from admitting those abstractions which Ricardo and his disciples demanded from him. Political economy, he thought ... was to be based on experience, upon history and observation. Human conditions were to be studied in detail.' According to Rist, Sismondi's critique is directed against generalisation. 'It also prepared the way for that conception of political economy upon the discovery of which the German *Historical School* so prided itself at a later date.'[5]

Admittedly one can find in Sismondi many more passages similar to those noted by Rist. But we can see that the latter has stuck to a literal reading of Sismondi and has not grasped the spirit, that he has not seized the very essence of his method. Having asserted that Sismondi is an opponent of the abstract method, a few lines later he criticises him for a certain inconsistency, because 'Sismondi himself was forced to have recourse to it. It is true that he used it with considerable awkwardness and his failure to construct or to discuss abstract theories perhaps explains his preference for the other method.'[6]

If there is an inconsistency, I venture to say that it is not in Sismondi but rather in Rist's standpoint and his rather scholastic logic. According to Rist, Sismondi's methodological merit entails the critique of the abstract method and the application of the historical and descriptive method. But then Rist goes on to say that Sismondi 'was forced to have recourse' to the abstract method.

Is it true that in Sismondi we are faced with contradictions which are a sign that 'he ... creates ... confusion' and has a 'hesitating mind' – as Rist assures us?[7] To concede this would make our job a lot easier, all the more so since Sismondi is a powerful individual whose enormous influence on the development of economic thought, as well as on several great thinkers such as John Stuart

4 Denis 1907, p. 289.
5 Rist 1915, pp. 174–5. [Grossman's emphasis.]
6 Rist 1915, p. 176.
7 Rist 1915, pp. 176, 190.

Mill, [Pierre-Joseph] Proudhon, Karl Marx, Émile Laveley and so on, becomes more obvious with every passing day, as Hector Denis has quite rightly noted.[8]

If it were solely a matter of showing the need for an inductive, historical-descriptive method, Sismondi's achievement in this respect would be quite dubious. In Germany [Johann Gottlieb] Fichte, it is true, applied an abstract constructive method to his 'rational state', that is, the state as it ought to be. But where it was a question of economic relations, 'real states existing at present', he demanded an explanation of 'how everything that is came to be as it is' and it was for history to respond to this question, 'since indeed all historical research of deep penetration neither can nor should be anything else than a genetic answer to the causal question: how has the present state of things arisen and what are the reasons that the world formed itself into what we find before us?'[9] In France it is Charles Ganilh who should take the credit, albeit problematic, for having opposed the abstract method. This economist, four years before the appearance of Sismondi's book, published a program for a statistical and descriptive method. In his work he criticises Adam Smith and the Physiocrats for using an 'ambitious method' which, as a result of 'their predilection for rational and speculative theories' and 'by means of hypotheses, conjectures and analogies', aims to construct 'general laws' by a means which 'is independent of facts and experience'. Political economy is 'a practical science'. Now 'Adam Smith's system of unlimited freedom' is 'a speculative theory'. 'When one looks carefully at Smith's admirable work, one finds there only assertions which do not fit the facts, conjectures with no basis in reality and unfounded hypotheses'. To this method Ganilh contrasts the descriptive method and sees the solution in the progress of statistics.[10] It seems that he was inspired by the famous statistical treatise of Patrick Colquhoun (1814),[11] which showed the distribution of wealth among the various classes in the population of England. 'Thus it seems to me that from the table of the present wealth of a people … one can progress not only to knowledge of the *causes* of this people's wealth but even to the establishment of the principles which create modern wealth and to the *true theory* of political economy.' He defines the relationship between statistics and economics as follows: 'the former accumulates the materials and the latter builds the edifice of the science.' If the speculative theories which he criticises 'reasoned before having observed the facts … asserted instead of calculating', the method advocated by Ganilh leads *in short* to a rigorous theory, 'to math-

8 Denis 1907, p. 273.
9 Fichte 2012, p. 38.
10 Ganilh 1815, pp. 1–40
11 Colquhoun 1814.

ematical certainty'. He briefly indicates the path to be followed. 'We observe facts which can be subjected to observation and calculation and which, as a result, give economic science the right to lay claim to the same precision as the physical and mathematical sciences.'[12]

Thus it was not Sismondi who was the first to juxtapose a scientific ideal, based on the statistical-descriptive method, to the abstract and deductive method of the classical economists. However, I will not spend time discussing once more the banal question as to whether political economy should use induction or deduction. Half a century before Ricardo, James Steuart, to the great advantage of the science, applied *the two methods jointly* to economic research.[13] To employ induction and deduction simultaneously is in no way peculiar to economics but is practised in all the sciences and indeed in every non-scientific operation of thought, for it is quite simply the very nature of our mind to move from the particular to the general and from the general to the particular. And that is why I consider that reducing the problem of method in political economy to the question of induction versus deduction is to deny any *specific method of study* in economics. And this is also why I think Wilhelm Hasbach has overstated Steuart's merit, as far as method is concerned, when he claims that 'Steuart had no predecessor and until John Stuart Mill no successor who, with such clarity of thought, although it was in a less clear language, expounded *the methodological foundations* of our science'.[14] And Hasbach concludes from this that Steuart 'is the greatest economist of the eighteenth century.'[15]

I have no intention whatsoever of belittling the value of Steuart. I should simply like to show that, apart from the question of the involvement of induction and deduction in the field of knowledge and from ways of gaining knowledge as well as our mind's instruments of investigation, in short all that we understand under the name of *Denkmethode* [method of thought], the problem of method also has another aspect, not in relation to the properties of our minds but rather depending on the type of phenomena being studied – *Forschungsmethode* [method of research]. While the former problem concerning knowledge itself is *common* to all sciences and is not specific to economics as such, the latter appears differently in each science, for in each science – and hence in political economy – it is necessary to create *specific methods appropriate to the character of the phenomena being studied*. 'Every discipline', says Luigi

12 [Ganilh 1815, pp. 28–9, 38. Grossman's emphasis.]

13 Steuart 1767.

14 Hasbach 1891, p. 380. [Grossman's emphasis.]

15 Hasbach 1891, p. 381.

Cossa, 'has its own method, appropriate to its object, role and purpose, which distinguishes it from the others.'[16] If, having set aside the question of induction and deduction, we ask what constitutes this specific research method of the classical English school, applied in particular to the character of economic phenomena, we will find it very difficult to give an answer. Quesnay's 'Formula for an Economic Table' (1758) was founded on the *constructive basis* which was such a specifically economic method, effectively applied, although it was not justified theoretically. In respect of method, in relation to the problems of the totality of production and of social reproduction, the classical English school represents a retreat, a lowering of the level achieved by the brilliant creator of Physiocracy.[17] This detrimental influence of the English school becomes visible in Jean-Baptiste Say, who in his *Treatise* of 1803 criticises the Physiocrats for founding 'a principle upon some gratuitous assumption ... Political economy has only become a science since it has been confined to the results of inductive investigation.'[18] This was a return to naïve empiricism and Sismondi takes up anew the methodological problem of the Physiocrats, which entails the fact that the latter, in the study of economic phenomena, reject mere empiricism and use the *constructive method*. Sismondi develops this method in an original fashion and does so with all the expertise required of a theoretician. Sismondi's historical achievement in methodology is to have imagined and constructed this method and shown the necessity of applying it not of having supposedly applied the descriptive-historical method of induction. For, as we will soon see, not only is Sismondi not hostile to abstract analysis but he uses it on a greater scale than the classical thinkers whom he criticises, to such an extent that [Adolphe] Blanqui complains of his use of this abstraction to which, it is claimed, Sismondi was opposed: 'The principal defect in the method of M. de Sismondi lies in generalising too much, like Ricardo himself, his most illustrious opponent.'[19] The very fact that Sismondi's method has been evaluated in such diverse fashions should arouse our attention and encourage us to clarify the matter. So let us look at it more closely.

How does Sismondi proceed to analyse the phenomenon which interests him most and which, in his opinion, is 'the fundamental question of political economy', namely the problem of the 'balance between consumption and production'? Empirically there was the phenomenon of crises in the form of a glut on the market, with goods which did not find buyers at a price that would make

16 Cossa 1809, p. 77.
17 Quesnay 1972.
18 Say 1867, p. 36.
19 Blanqui 1885, p. 473.

a profit possible. Ricardo saw the phenomenon itself as transitory and saw *the cause* as lying in an erroneous commercial or fiscal policy. In a discussion with Sismondi he 'attributed this result ... to constraints imposed on the circulation of goods, and to tariffs'.[20]

At this time the effects of ruinous English competition were making themselves felt very powerfully in France. But instead of having recourse to the theoretical indication of the errors of free competition, first of all solutions were proposed in the form of *tariff protection*, as was done for example by [Jean-Antoine] Chaptal.[21]

What position does Sismondi take on this occasion? Does he follow the path traced out by Ricardo? Does he analyse 'only what is', empirical facts, the influence of taxes, of duties and of import bans on the quantity of production and exports? Does he undertake descriptive and comparative studies of the quantity of production and consumption in the countries affected by the crisis, before and after the outbreak of the crisis? Does he perhaps study the decline in demand, imports and exports as a result of changes in fashion, warfare or foreign competition? Does he try to examine the influence of the banks and of credit, or of paper money, the influence of the actual distribution of wealth, the total amount of wages, profits etc.? Not at all; instead of all that Sismondi *rejects the world of empirical phenomena* in the specific conditions of time and place and confines himself to a methodological fiction, taking his proof and his analysis into the world of *a constructed abstract example*. In fact he was perfectly well aware that the very object of his analysis was in no way empirical. We can study the level of wages, profits, prices, the quantity of production or the number of workers employed empirically. But *the problem of the economic equilibrium* of production and consumption in a capitalist society cannot be studied under the microscope of descriptive analysis; and – even if it were done by establishing as conscientiously as possible the effective state of overproduction – we would make no contribution whatsoever to demonstrating the extent to which this imbalance results *necessarily* from the very essence of the capitalist system. The object in contention in the analysis is therefore itself entirely abstract. '[T]he question I had raised was so obscure, so *abstract* that I laid myself open to the most absurd interpretations ... However, I have never believed that I must forego the defence of what to me appeared to be the truth, because *that truth was abstract*, difficult to grasp'.[22]

20 Sismondi 1991b, pp. 618–19. [Grossman's emphasis.]

21 Chaptal 1819, pp. 417 et seq.

22 Sismondi 1991e, p. 596. [Grossman's emphasis.]

While he was in Geneva in 1823 Ricardo continued orally the polemic with Sismondi that the latter had begun in 1820 against [John Ramsay] McCulloch. Once again empirical facts were put on one side. 'But a spoken discourse cannot do justice to a question which calls for a difficult reconciliation of practical *arguments* with, *in some way, metaphysical considerations*'.[23] We know what that means. In his 1824 treatise against Ricardo, where he reports the oral discussions he had with the latter, Sismondi, basing himself on certain arbitrary *a priori* principles (metaphysical considerations) constructs an abstract arithmetical example (calculations) and the polemic concerning the central problem of political economy was developed on this fictitious level.

While Ricardo, as a supporter of total freedom of exchange between nations, attributes crisis to 'constraints imposed on the circulation of goods', and the empiricists, like Chaptal, seek salvation in the defence of the internal market through tariff protection, Sismondi *excludes in advance from his argument the factor of the commercial policy of governments*. The defence of the internal market and free export to foreign markets can undoubtedly get rid of excessive production but the problem is only provisionally resolved by this means and only for one particular country, at the expense of another country. 'In that system nations are rivals to each other; industrial prosperity in one causes the ruin of industry in the others.' The export solution is likewise not viable for all nations. 'If all adopt this system at the same time, if all consign each year a greater amount of exports to foreign markets … their competition, that will embrace the world market, will be injurious to everyone'.[24] 'The immediate result of this universal battle can only be the impossibility of continuing it'[25] – and all of them in turn would have to get rid of their excess. Overproduction would then be revealed in its full extent. 'What can be done if one will not be able to sell abroad anymore?' And then 'the illusions of foreign trade' will disappear.[26] If therefore we take into consideration not a single state but 'the world market', 'for it there is no export'. Starting from these thoughts, Sismondi continues the methodological construction of Quesnay's *Tableau*[27] and admits that the economic process of the world has already reached the stage where external markets no longer exist and that is why he takes as the starting point of his theoretical analysis *an isolated nation*, without external markets, 'by either looking at the entire world market, or by postulating that every nation exists in isola-

23 Sismondi 1991b, p. 618. [Grossman's emphasis.]
24 Sismondi 1991b, p. 619.
25 Sismondi 1991d, p. 333.
26 Sismondi 1991d, p. 333.
27 Quesnay 1972.

tion from every other'. Elsewhere he expresses this thought even more clearly: 'National *expenditure* must absorb … *total national production*. In order to follow this reasoning with greater certainty, and to simplify the problems, we have, till now, completely *abstracted from foreign trade*, and we assume an isolated nation; humanity is that isolated nation'.[28]

It is only in such an isolated economic mechanism, without external markets, that Sismondi studies how the increase in production operates and in particular examines whether, as Ricardo and Say claim, an isolated nation, by increasing its production, *thereby* creates new consumers. If in fact there must be a balance 'it must be proven that it creates them itself when it increases its production'. 'To study this social mechanism', in order to analyse this equilibrium, Sismondi constructs the hypothetical arithmetical example which has already been mentioned, supposing, on the one hand, 'a cultivator who, on a given area of land' employs a given number of agricultural workers and, on the other, an industrial capitalist employing a specific number of workers. 'This is a hypothesis and an analysis presenting the least difficulty, and will force us to deal with the least detail'.[29]

It is only in a system thus isolated and simplified that Sismondi, after having established a certain specific productivity of labour and a specific wage, studies the relations of supply and demand. Subsequently multiplying one of the elements, namely the productivity of labour and modifying the sum of wages by a fixed percentage, he studies afresh the influence of these changes on the relation of production to consumption.

Can there be anything more abstract than this method? How then has it been possible to claim that Sismondi is a representative innovator of the descriptive and inductive method? Here there is a misunderstanding resulting from the fact that people have not grasped the very basis of Sismondi's critique of the classical school. In his essay against McCulloch, Sismondi says, it is true, of the English school that it 'loses itself in abstractions' and that it becomes 'to some degree, an occult science'. He requires of science 'that it finally deals with reality'. We must 'be watchful against all generalisations of our ideas that make us lose facts from sight'.[30] Seven years later in the second edition of his work he denounces Adam Smith's disciples who 'have thrown themselves even more into abstractions.' 'In their hands the science has become so speculative that it seems to separate itself from all practice … Our mind is loath to accept the

28 Sismondi 1838, p. 337; Sismondi 1991b, p. 620; Sismondi 1991d, p. 102 [Grossman's emphasis.]

29 Sismondi 1991b, pp. 620, 621. [Grossman's emphasis.]

30 Sismondi 1991a, p. 599.

abstractions they require of us'. However Sismondi rejects this abstraction, not because it is abstract but because it is an abstraction which does not fit reality, because it *does not take account of the essential elements* which characterise capitalist society. The simplification of reality must have its limits. 'The abstraction we are asked to make ... is by far too strong: ... this is not *simplification*, this is *misleading* us by hiding from our view all the successive operations by which we can distinguish truth from error'. Sismondi criticises Ricardo for having taken the state of equilibrium between independent producers as the basis of his proofs and of having, consequently, neglected such an important point as wage labour. 'We will look at society in its actual organisation, *with workers without property*, whose wages are fixed by competition, and whose master may dismiss them at the moment when he has no more need for their labour; for *it is precisely this social arrangement to which our objections apply*.'[31]

Thus Sismondi is not opposed to abstraction in general but only to abstraction which sets aside essential elements of reality. Undoubtedly Sismondi too used the inductive, historical-descriptive method. But he applied it in order to establish *facts* which were to be the starting point of his argument. He observed, for example, with the help of an empirical analysis, the struggle of large workshops against small ones, the concentration of large assets under the same management, the increase in material wealth in contemporary society, parallel to the deep poverty and pauperism of the working classes.[32] But these 'rebellious facts'[33] merely enable him to *formulate the problem*. He seeks the *explanation* of the phenomenon precisely by means of the abstract construction of a fictitious model with clearly established foundations, which enables him to draw from it conclusions which are rigorous, though for the time being hypothetical.

But Sismondi's methodological foundations are not limited to this. If science has the aim of reproducing realities in the mind and if, for this very reason, he indicts Say so vigorously for having said nothing about wage labour, he nonetheless recognises, on the other hand, that not every empirical phenomenon belongs to the domain of the reality which he wants to explain scientifically. The task that he has taken on entails discovering the laws which govern the capitalist mechanism, that is, a mechanism based on free wage labour and the monopoly ownership by the capitalists of the necessary instruments of labour. Now the empirical world showed that alongside these elements of the system

31 Sismondi 1991d, pp. 5–55; Sismondi 1991b, p. 621. [Grossman's emphasis.]
32 Sismondi 1837, 'Introduction', pp. 1–47.
33 Sismondi 1837, p. 47.

there were independent artisans and land-owning peasants. Should these survivals of former economic formations, as elements of '*empirical reality*', be for Sismondi the object of the analysis of the capitalist system?

As a historian, Sismondi is well aware of the historical variety of successive forms of the organisation of labour, as well as their *essential functional specificities*. As crises and the ills that they entail came into existence, to the extent that wage labour – that is, economic organisation based on the payment of wages – was constituted, he draws the far-reaching methodological conclusion that forms of independent labour (artisans, peasants) are absolutely irrelevant to him as a subject of his studies of the essence of capitalism.[34] But precisely these forms constituted the major part of the empirical reality of his time, while the system of wage labour which he proposed to study was still only a new phenomenon, in its initial phase, although its pernicious influence had already made itself felt and had led to disastrous disturbances. The process of the expropriation of the artisan and the peasant, recently begun, was evolving rapidly. 'We incline to separate completely any type of property from all types of labour … This social organisation is so new that it is not even halfway instituted'.[35]

Now if there exists 'the universal tendency of wealth to separate the action of capitals from that of hands',[36] it can be imagined that in its subsequent development, this tendency will reach its final objective, that is, a complete separation of property from labour. In other words it will lead to a social system composed exclusively of capitalists and workers. This will be a 'purely' capitalist system, that is, the system that Sismondi wants to study. He therefore acknowledges that this process is in fact completed, and, *mentally he cleanses* the capitalist system of all infiltrations, of all survivals of earlier systems. In fact it is only in a system stripped of elements foreign to it that the laws and properties which characterise it can appear – for example, free competition, the antinomy of the interests of the entrepreneur and the worker, as well as their struggle over the division of the social product, etc. 'To examine this battle … it will be easier to abstract from all those workers who are at the same time capitalists, and [from] all capitalists who are at the same time workers'.[37] Sismondi thus arrives at the methodological premise of an economic system based exclusively on wage

34 It is true that Sismondi devotes long passages to the description of various forms of independent labour, but he does so where, as a historian, he is comparing the former economic organisation to capitalist organisation.

35 Sismondi 1991b, p. 628.

36 Sismondi 1837, p. 241.

37 Sismondi 1991d, p. 92. [Editor's interpolation.]

labour, considered as a *universally established system* composed of capitalists and workers, excluding all third parties such as officials, soldiers, merchants and people practising liberal professions, etc.

The result of our analysis is clear. In the central problem, which for Sismondi is the most important one, that of the equilibrium of the economic mechanism, meaning the equilibrium of production and consumption, he takes as the object of his theoretical analysis and as the basis of his proof *not empirical reality but a fictitious model of capitalist society based on arbitrarily assumed foundations*.[38]

In his arithmetical schema of annual production Sismondi lists three branches of this production,

1. production of foodstuffs, represented by sacks of corn;
2. production of industrial articles absolutely essential for life; and
3. production of industrial luxury items

He subsequently assumes *in all* branches of production a specific degree of productivity of labour, equal to the value of twelve sacks of corn a year per worker and, at the same time, a specific standard of living for the workers, in other words the wage received, equal to ten sacks of corn, of which three sacks are consumed in kind by the workers and the seven others are consumed in the form of absolutely essential industrial articles. He then establishes that the whole surplus production of each worker beyond his wage, in other words, in this case, the value of two sacks of corn, accrues to the agricultural and industrial employers, and each of them shares his *indispensable* consumption in the same ratio: three sacks of corn in kind and seven in the form of indispensable industrial articles. It is only the remaining excess of their profit that they consume in the form of *luxury* industrial articles.

---

38 These are the same methodological foundations Karl Marx would adopt forty years later in his *Capital*, where, starting, like Sismondi, from the principle 'of the universal and exclusive domination of capitalist production' (Marx 1978b, p. 422), he says, clearly making the connection with Sismondi's analysis of progressive reproduction: 'Here we take no account of the export trade ... In order to examine the object of our investigation *in its integrity* free from all disturbing subsidiary circumstances, we must treat the whole world of trade as one nation, and assume that capitalist production is established everywhere and has taken possession of every branch of industry' (Marx 1976b, p. 727). Likewise: 'In *theory*, we assume that the laws of the capitalist mode of production develop in their *pure form*. In *reality*, this is only an approximation; but the approximation is all the more exact, the more the capitalist mode of production is developed and *the less it is adulterated by survivals of earlier economic conditions* with which it is amalgamated' (Marx 1981b, p. 275). [Grossman's emphasis.]

It is only after having simplified the problem by rigorously defining the data on which he is basing himself that Sismondi embarks on his subject properly speaking, namely to study the influence of each element in particular: the number of workers and their productivity, the needs of society remaining immutable. Given the *productivity* of ten agricultural workers, the problem to be resolved will entail the quantitative determination of the number of workers in both branches of industry. If on the other hand, given the *number* of workers, the productivity of labour increases and overproduction appears, then the problem is reduced to the question either of limiting the number of workers or of reducing the increase in the productivity of labour.

As we can see, Sismondi's schema is only a refined form of Quesnay's *Tableau*; the refinement entails the fact that instead of Quesnay's three classes, corresponding with the situation in the middle of the eighteenth century – productive class, class of owners and sterile class – Sismondi introduces a division more appropriate to the capitalist system: capitalists and wage-workers. *All* the branches of production are productive since they give the capitalists an income, here still envisaged in a general form and not in particular categories such as rent, profit, interest on capital, commercial profits, etc. This way of seeing things leads to the division between necessary consumption by workers and luxury consumption in which only capitalists participate. These are refinements which will later be adopted in full by Karl Marx in his reproduction schema at the end of the second volume of *Capital*.[39]

Are fictitious constructions of this sort, moving fundamentally away from Say's postulate, 'study what is', admissible from the methodological point of view? We must respond that Sismondi's premises are not arbitrary fantasies of the mind, formed without any relation to concrete existence; they are a *construction* but a *necessary* construction, resulting from the character of the materials envisaged, from the fact of the mixture and simultaneous existence in empirical reality of phenomena that are aspects of organisations having completely different historical characters. The accepted bases therefore mark a *selection* of empirical materials, a limitation of the analysis to a specific group of phenomena, to the exclusion of all other alien elements; 'they represent *positive facts, merely in the absence of disruptive causes*'. They are therefore in conform-

39 Thus when Rosa Luxemburg states that in the history of political economy there are only *two* attempts at the *exact* exposition of the reproduction of the entire social capital: at the very beginning of this history with Quesnay, founder of the Physiocratic School, and at the end, in Marx, she is, as we have seen, mistaken. Between Quesnay and Marx, Sismondi's schema constitutes historically and logically a necessary intermediary link. (See Luxemburg 1951, p. 31).

ity with the conditions of methodological analysis, defined by [John Elliott] Cairnes for the circumstance in which one uses '*hypothetical cases framed* with a view to the purpose of economic inquiry. For, although precluded from actually producing the conditions suited to his purpose, there is nothing to prevent the economist from bringing such conditions before his mental vision, and from reasoning as if these only were present, while some agency comes into operation … the economic character of which he desires to examine.'[40]

Sismondi's methodological construction, solidly ordered, is therefore, to use Cairnes's expression, 'a substitute for experiment',[41] also known as a 'hypothetical experiment' or a 'thought experiment'. Contrary to Hasbach's opinion, it accounts for Sismondi's incontestable superiority over the methodological procedures represented by James Steuart; by going far beyond the banal difference involved in the use of induction or deduction, Sismondi creates a method appropriate to the character and nature of economic phenomena, the objects of the analysis. This method is the expression of the stage of development reached by capitalism in Sismondi's day, a level it was far from having reached at the time of Quesnay and Steuart.

It is difficult to agree with Herbert Foxwell, professor at Cambridge University, who, in his 'History of Socialist Ideas in England', says that the time after Ricardo in England was 'a period of indescribable confusion', of 'sterile logomancy and academic hair-splitting' and that he saw the cause of this in the fact that 'Ricardo had adopted what was intended to be a rigorously abstract and deductive manner, but without any of those formal aids to precision and clearness which scientific, and especially *mathematical, method* provides'.[42] [Nicolas-François] Canard, who in his *Principles of Political Economy*[43] was the first to apply this method to economic problems, has shown that one could fill chapters with mathematical formulae without taking the science of economics a step further forward. That is why Sismondi, without mathematical formulae, is in my opinion more of a mathematician than those who apply such formulae in political economy. The value of the geometrical method of argument, as well as the accuracy and the effectiveness of its results, depend not on the construction of a formula but rather on the construction of a specific research method, based on clearly determined foundations which are appropriate to the character of the phenomena studied. Ricardo, despite

40 Cairnes 1875, pp. 62, 90. [Grossman's emphasis.]

41 [Cairnes 1875, p. 93.]

42 [Foxwell 1899, pp. lxxii–lxxiii. Grossman's emphasis.]

43 Canard 1801.

all the subtlety of his *method of thought*, lacked this *method of research* into the problem of the totality of social reproduction. Hence it is Sismondi who has the merit of having continued on the methodological path indicated by Quesnay's *Tableau*, which later led to Karl Marx's brilliant methodological construction.[44]

2 Sismondi as a Theoretician

A *The Problem*

The misunderstanding which we have pointed out with regard to Sismondi's methodological approach is repeated, in even more pronounced form, when this economist is considered as a theoretician. Previously the history of economic doctrines has told us that Sismondi's chief merit was being the creator of a new social policy and of a program of reforms where he

> appeals for ... the granting of the right of combination. Then follows a limitation of child labour, the abolition of Sunday toil, and a shortening of the hours of labour. He also demanded the establishment of what he called a 'professional guarantee', whereby the employer ... would be obliged to maintain the workman at his own expense during a period of illness or of lock-out or old age.[45]

On the other hand, Sismondi the theoretician has been treated lightly. Rist assures us that 'what really interested Sismondi was *not so much* what is called *political economy*, but what has since become known as *économie sociale* in France and *Sozialpolitik* [social policy] in Germany. His originality, so far as the history of doctrines is concerned, consisted in his having originated this study.' 'Sismondi thus becomes the first of the interventionists'.[46] His role is quite different as far as theory is concerned: 'Sismondi's disagreement *was not upon the*

---

44 It was only in the *Studies* published thirteen years after the essay against Ricardo that Sismondi, in his last years, revealed a certain apprehension against generalisation and insisted on the study of details (Sismondi 1837, p. iv). At this time Sismondi, reproducing his memoir against Ricardo, gives us the arithmetical schema of social reproduction as a footnote. 'Completely hypothetical calculations seem to me to have too uncertain a basis to deserve a place in the text' (Sismondi 1837, p. 81). Here, as we can see, there is a restriction of the point of view adopted in 1824 and maintained in 1827 where, in the second edition of *New Principles* these 'calculations' still figure in the text.

45 Rist 1915, pp. 195.

46 Rist 1915, pp. 172, 192. [Grossman's emphasis. Editor's interpolation.]

theoretical principles of political economy. So far as these were concerned he declared himself a disciple of Adam Smith.'[47]

> The principal interest of Sismondi's book *does not lie in his attempt to give a scientific explanation* of the facts ... His merit rather lies in having placed in strong relief certain *facts* that were consistently neglected by the dominant school of economists ... He deliberately shows us the reverse of the medal, of which others ... wished only to see the brighter side.[48]

He was 'the first to give *sentiment* a prominent place in his theory' and thought that 'political economy ... was best treated as a "*moral science*"' that must tend towards a just distribution of wealth. According to Rist, it is precisely *in this ethical conception that Sismondi distances himself from the English school*: 'That is why he gave such prominence to a theory of *distribution* alongside of the theory of *production*, which had received the exclusive attention of the classical writers.'[49]

Rist, as we can see, particularly insists on the importance of Sismondi as the creator of the ethical and socially reforming current and does not think much of him as a theoretician: 'But to imagine anything more confused than the reasonings by which he attempts to demonstrate the possibility of a general crisis of overproduction is difficult.'[50] Elsewhere Rist says that 'Sismondi ... fell into the error of ... Ricardo' (that is probably why he wrote the essay *against* Ricardo) and adds 'This shows what a hesitating mind we are dealing with'. And having attributed such a modest place to Sismondi as a theoretician, Rist diminishes it even further by claiming that Sismondi's critique, far from being determined by theoretical principles, is only the result of 'the violent reaction of humanitarianism against the stern implacability of economic orthodoxy. We can almost hear the eloquence of Ruskin and Carlyle, and the pleading of the Christian Socialists.'[51]

I will not cite the opinions of other writers here. Almost all make a similar judgment and, whether it be Hector Denis, or Eisenhart, [Werner] Sombart or [Gustav] Schmoller, they outdo each other in repeating that Sismondi inaugurated the 'ethical current' in economics. 'Sismondi's general approach', says Rosa Luxemburg, 'is predominantly *ethical*, it is the approach of the social reformer.'

47 Rist 1915, p. 174. [Grossman's emphasis.]

48 Rist 1915, p. 192. [Grossman's emphasis.]

49 Rist 1915, pp. 173, 175, 177. [Grossman's emphasis.]

50 Rist 1915, p. 176.

51 Rist 1915, pp. 189, 190, 196.

'He aspires … towards a thorough-going *reform of distribution* in favour of the proletariat.'[52] And that means Sismondi's merit consists not in a theoretical explanation of the existing economic system but in a 'normative' indication of what ought to be. He 'never tire[s] of preaching', says Sombart, 'not so much the Christian as the social spirit'.[53] In Herkner's eyes, Sismondi is a classic of social reform.[54] On the theoretical level, Denis assures us, Sismondi 'accepts the principles of Adam Smith' and he shows originality only in that 'he came to draw quite different *conclusions*'. 'The most important feature of the revolution which he brings about in economic science' consists, according to Denis, in the fact that economics 'appears to Sismondi as a science which is not merely theoretical but practical, that is, it proposes not only to illuminate the laws of what has been and of what is but of what ought to be'. Sismondi prepared or pursued 'the ethical moment of science, the subordination of political economy to morality'.[55] Böhm-Bawerk agrees: according to him, Sismondi forms the link between the classical theory of value and the theoretical consequences which the socialists were to draw from it later.[56] Even [Franz] Mehring saw in Sismondi nothing other than the 'last representative of classical economics'.[57]

Does this role attributed to Sismondi correspond with reality? This presentation is precisely intended to answer that question.

If Sismondi had only been an interventionist or a representative of the ethical current in political economy, he would have been in no way original. In England, some years before Sismondi, Robert Owen had published *A New View of Society or Essay on the Principle of the Formation of the Human Character* in 1813.[58] It called for partial reforms in order to eliminate unemployment, on the basis of rigorous statistics about the labour market and of agencies which aimed to procure work and protect such work. At the same time, from 1815 onwards, Owen put forward plans that from the outset included the principles of contemporary industrial legislation and, thanks to his persevering activity as well as the support of Robert Peel, the House of Commons in 1816 established the *first parliamentary enquiry* into the situation of children working in industry. That enquiry led, in 1819, to a law protecting children working in cotton mills. Likewise before Sismondi, under the influence of Fichte, Georg

52 Luxemburg 1851, p. 220. [Grossman's emphasis.]
53 Sombart 1909a, pp. 20–1. [Editor's interpolation.]
54 Herkner 1921, p. 48 et seq.
55 Denis 1907, pp. 276, 283, 286. [Grossman's emphasis.]
56 Böhm-Bawerk 1959a, p. 244.
57 Mehring 1913a, p. 21.
58 [Owen 1813. Grossman's original text has the wrong year, 1816.]

Sartorius in Germany published a critique of Adam Smith, of free competition and of the inequality in the distribution of wealth which it produced, while Julius Soden stated that economics was not the empirical science of what is but an ethical science laying down what ought to be.[59]

Contrary to current opinion, we do not see the historical merit of Sismondi in the field of social reform but in the first instance in that of *theory* and it is precisely to this too often neglected point of view that we should like to draw the reader's attention.

It must first of all be recalled that Sismondi himself claims a quite different role from the one historians have previously attributed to him: he considers himself above all a theoretician striving to *explain* facts which, in his view, the classical economists had not sufficiently elucidated, to explain them with the help of a new theory which he put in the place of the old one. '*I disturbed a science* which ... appeared as one of the most noble creations of the human mind', in place of which 'I had discovered new principles'. Doubtless he does declare himself the disciple of Adam Smith. But he confines this agreement to the fact that 'we declare, with Adam Smith, that labour is the sole source of wealth'. However, Sismondi complements this principle with 'the discovery of truths which he himself [Smith] had not known'.[60] Sismondi insists on 'the importance ... of the modifications' he has made to Adam Smith's system. 'When considered from *this new viewpoint* all that had heretofore remained obscure in this science, became clear'. Sismondi differentiates himself from the classical school, it is true, in his conclusions and his practical proposals. But this difference in conclusions derives from the difference in the theoretical conception. That is why Sismondi rejects classical theory, which he believes to be false. 'When the fate of millions of men *rests on a theory no experience has yet validated*, it is proper to regard it with some distrust.' That is why, being dissatisfied with the theory of the classical economists, he takes '*a path quite different from theirs*'. So here there is not only a difference in practical conclusions but in *the whole of the theory*. Classical theory, in the emerging world economy, sees harmony everywhere while reality reveals discord. To combat the criticisms made of them, the defenders of classical theory deny the facts by asserting that it is contradictory to claim 'that the increase in *wealth* can be a cause of *poverty*'. Sismondi responds, 'Since the *fact* is certain, it could not be contradictory, or rather if it presents a contradiction, it is in the *terms* used, in the definitions

59 Sartorius 1806; Soden 1815, sections 20, 138.

60 Sismondi 1991d, pp. 7, 53. [Grossman's emphasis, translator's interpolation.] Sismondi 1991d, p. 52.

adopted'.[61] And that is why he takes on the task of discovering the contradictions in the false theory. But it would be a mistake to confine ourselves to this critique of contradictory definitions. For beneath these contradictory definitions lies the contradiction of real phenomena. 'Here we have set out only to ... indicate that what seemed to be a contradiction in *terms*, growing poverty alongside abundance, could have *reality*.' So it is necessary to 'seek the fundamental principles of the science'. In reality Sismondi succeeded in explaining, as he states, the facts in whose presence the classical economists found themselves mystified. 'I have explained it *with a theory I believe to be new*'.[62]

Moreover the very title of Sismondi's work, *New Principles of Political Economy*, shows that he had the ambition of creating a new theory. In fact he says so expressly. 'This somewhat vague title might lead to the supposition that this book is merely a new manual of the basic propositions of the science. I carry my pretensions much farther; *I believe that I have placed political economy on a new foundation*'. This preponderance of theoretical considerations and purposes over practical information about economic policy is such that the writer deliberately omits any enumeration of practical means, in order not to divert attention away from the theoretical analysis of the central problem of economics. Foreseeing that he will be criticised because 'it would have been better to show what remained to do', he says 'If I presented here what I consider to be a remedy for the actual ills of society, criticism would abandon the *examination* ... of such ills, in order to judge my *remedy*, and to probably condemn it, and the question of the balance of consumption with production would never be decided'.[63] That is why Sismondi always gives precedence to *knowledge*, to *theory* over practice. 'Let us then conclude the *analysis* of the system we have taken up, before dreaming of what will have to replace it.' 'It is one of the greatest efforts to which we can force our mind to *visualise* the actual structure of society',[64] for before indicating the remedy it is necessary to make the theoretical diagnosis. If Sismondi begins by abandoning the old theory which should be 'regarded with some *distrust*', because no experience has yet justified it, if for this reason he seeks a theory which seems to him to better explain the facts, he adopts a quite different tone a few years later, in the second edition of *New Principles*. Here he rejoices that the evolution of events has confirmed his the-

61 Sismondi 1991d, p. 2; Sismondi 1991b, p. 630; Sismondi 1838, p. 210; Sismondi 1837, pp. 114, 115. [Grossman's emphasis.]

62 Sismondi 1838, p. 223; Sismondi 1991a, p. 600. [Grossman's emphasis.]

63 Sismondi 1991d, p. 12; Sismondi 1991b, pp. 634–5; Sismondi 1837, p. 105. [Grossman's emphasis.]

64 Sismondi 1991d, p. 634. [Grossman's emphasis.]

ory and says forcefully 'Seven years have passed, and it seems to me that *the facts* have victoriously fought on my side ...'. The supporters of the classical school 'are forced to seek elsewhere new explanations for events which diverge so much from laws they have believed settled' and Sismondi adds, not without pride, 'Explanations ... which I had given in advance have totally agreed with the results'.[65]

So we can see that, contrary to what has been claimed previously, Sismondi disputes with his adversaries primarily *over a theoretical conception* of the economic system of his time and not over the implementation of practical policies!

∴

What does this 'new theory' advocated by Sismondi entail? It is obvious that if we consider the social reformer and not the theoretician in Sismondi, we will not be able to elucidate this question adequately. The central point of Sismondi's ideas has been perceived as his views on the unequal distribution of wealth, on the insufficient participation of the working class in the social product of labour, in other words, as the fact of underconsumption, which Sismondi identifies as the source of social disruptions and poverty.

In fact no more clumsy misunderstanding could be imagined! If, in fact, the 'new theory' of Sismondi were to consist in opposing the unequal distribution of wealth, it certainly would not have been new. Without mentioning older writers, a host of thinkers on the terrain of modern capitalism in England and in France had, from the middle of the eighteenth century, raised more energetically than Sismondi the redistribution of wealth to counter inequality and, above all, had put forward conclusions of much greater scope than his.[66] In reality Sismondi's 'new theory' consists in something quite different!

The critical passages often found in Sismondi against the 'chrematistic or abstract school'[67] and against abstraction in general have been attributed to his methodological views. However, since we have shown in the first part of our analysis not only that Sismondi did not oppose the abstract method but that he applied it with rare shrewdness, it is hard to explain against what, in this case, his criticism of abstraction was directed. Hence we are led to conclude *that the abstraction attacked by Sismondi must entail something quite other than a prob-*

65 Sismondi 1991d, pp. 7–8. [Grossman's emphasis.]

66 See Jaurès 1924, pp. 13 et seq.

67 [Aristotle distinguished economics, gaining what is necessary for life, from chrematistics, gaining money, Aristotle 1905, Book 1 chapters 8, 9, pp. 38–45.]

lem of method. Certainly. We will try to show that Sismondi's critique strikes at the very heart of the contemporary economic organisation of capitalist society. His criticism is not a matter of the *method* of research but of the *substance* and constitutive principles of the economic mechanism of his time, as well as of the economic *science* reflecting this mechanism.

Sismondi claims that the theory of the classical economists is incapable of explaining the mechanism around us. Every economic system has the aim of creating organisations, in order to meet the material needs of humanity. The periodically repeated crises of overproduction which provoke convulsions in this mechanism (bankruptcies of employers, enforced unemployment and poverty of the working masses) are proof of some essential structural fault in the foundations of this economic system. Classical theory did not perceive this defect. Adam Smith, like Ricardo, acknowledged that the size of the productive apparatus had a spontaneous tendency to adapt to the size of the population and its needs. If the productive apparatus is too small then, thanks to a rise in prices and profits, capitals and labour will move precisely to the branch where they are most needed. By means of the mechanism of prices and profits, given free competition, that is to say the unfettered freedom of action of individuals seeking their own profit, the equilibrium of the productive apparatus with the extent of needs is therefore re-established. Free competition is thus the regulator of the economic mechanism, a regulator which maintains it in a harmonious equilibrium. It is true that in Ricardo's time it was difficult not to see facts in contradiction with this theory; but for Ricardo these were only passing disruptions, 'temporary reverses and contingencies' determined by war, by the whims of fashion, by commercial restrictions, by fiscal policy etc. Moreover 'this ... is an evil to which a rich nation must submit'.[68] But they cannot permanently disrupt the equilibrium of the economic mechanism, since equilibirum is the normal condition – the 'permanent state of things'.[69]

It is precisely against this theory of harmony that Sismondi directs his criticism. He draws out the errors in the reasoning of the classical economists and shows *that the dynamic of the real capitalist mechanism is completely different* from the movement defined by classical theory. He therefore takes on the task of discovering the reasons why the actual course of phenomena diverges from the fictitious, harmonious course depicted in the theory of the classical economists.

68 Ricardo 1912, pp. 175, 177 [English in Grossman's original text].

69 [English in Grossman's original text.]

Proceeding to the analysis of the capitalist system and the economic disruptions which are peculiar to it, Sismondi finds himself confronted by the fact that these disruptions appear and increase in time with the development of this new system, while they were unknown in earlier times. And he is led to historical comparisons. This analysis leads him to *distinguish two essentially different types* of economic system: systems without exchange and systems based on exchange. In the systems without exchange, human well-being depends directly on the *quantity* of goods obtained from production, that is foodstuffs, clothes, housing; once these needs are satisfied, people rest. In such an organisation 'wealth may exist ... *without any possibility of exchange*, or without trade. On the other hand it cannot exist without labour'. And Sismondi brings out the logic of his thought by describing to us a man on a desert island. *Ownership* of the land, woods, animals, fish and metals does not ensure his well-being and, amidst this abundance of natural goods, the man can die of hunger and cold. It is only *by labour* that man acquires the goods which enable him to satisfy his needs, to become rich. 'The measure of his wealth will not be the *price*, which he might obtain ... in exchange, but the length of time during which no further labour will be requisite to satisfy his wants'.[70] The totality of these goods acquired by labour and directly serving to satisfy his own needs will constitute true 'territorial wealth'. Sismondi does not mean thereby any agricultural product, as one might suppose, but what is called 'natural economy', which the Germans describe more precisely by the expression *Bedarfsdeckungswirtschaft* in contrast to *Marktwirtschaft* (*Warenwirtschaft*).[71]

To this organisation without exchange, to this 'territorial wealth' described in Book III, Sismondi contrasts in Book IV 'commercial wealth'. He keeps the same division in his *Studies*, where the first section (essays 3–12) covers territorial wealth, and the second (essays 13–17), commercial wealth. That the systems are identical in Sismondi's two major works is sufficient to show that here it is a question of essentially distinct economic types. If territorial wealth was not the agricultural economy, commercial wealth did not represent a separate category of commercial goods but *these same* goods which inasmuch as they serve particular needs are territorial wealth but become commercial wealth when they are taken to market and intended to be sold. 'From the moment that the products of the earth ... had left the hands of the cultivator, to the moment they came into the hands of the consumer, they constituted commercial wealth'.[72]

70 Sismondi 1991d, p. 61. [Grossman's emphasis.]
71 [Subsistence economy in contrast to market economy (commodity economy).]
72 Sismondi 1991d, p. 245.

Now, 'exchange had not in the least altered the nature of wealth: it was always *a thing* created by labour, saved for future need'.[73] But now, in the course of exchange, alongside this character of real wealth, appears a new phenomenon, the *exchange value* of these goods, in its capacity as a special kind of wealth specific to the system of exchange. The use value of goods is an intrinsic wealth residing in goods and attached to them and, consequently, it is a real wealth, serving to satisfy needs, a wealth that is independent of exchange and hence always real in every economic system and it is the product of labour. 'These goods are useful, are necessary to the very people who bring them into existence: they have an intrinsic value more legitimately than those that are commonly designated with this description; it is *independent of any exchange*, it is prior to any trade'.[74]

In opposition to this real wealth, independent of the form of economic organisation, exchange value is wealth deriving from exchange, hence exclusively linked to a certain economic organisation based on exchange.

In the exchange system, the real value of goods, their intrinsic, use value, that is to say, what constitutes the essence of real wealth – the capacity to satisfy needs – is a matter of indifference to the producer of these goods, as soon as he creates them in order to sell them. 'We come to goods which the manufacturer produces for the use *of others* ... to the goods which only start to be useful to him at the moment when he exchanges them'. The goods begin to exist for the producer of wealth if and when he sells them, for then they make real *their exchange value*. 'We have included them under the name of commercial wealth, and we designate thus all goods which are evaluated only by their exchange value'. The evolution of trade has transformed absolutely the character of the annual product of society: it has 'suppressed its character of use value, in order to leave in existence only that of exchange value'.[75] Since it is not the expression of the intrinsic value of goods, of true wealth, it is 'false riches', an 'illusion', a 'shadow without reality'.[76]

Since this exchange value plays a decisive role in Sismondi's theory, let us examine it more closely. We have seen that the exchange value of any object is distinct from and independent of the use value of this individual object: it is 'appreciation of the thing evaluated in comparison not with one thing *in particular* but with *everything*'. This fact confers on exchange value a *social character,*

73 Sismondi 1991d, p. 68. [Grossman's emphasis.]

74 Sismondi 1991d, p. 68; Sismondi 1838, p. 227. [Grossman's emphasis.]

75 Sismondi 1838, pp. 227, 230. [Grossman's emphasis.]

76 Sismondi 1991a, p. 613; Sismondi 1838, pp. 230, 234.

generalising and abstract. 'Value is therefore a social idea put in the place of an individual idea;[77] *it is an abstract idea* put in the place of a positive idea'.[78]

And we can already begin to understand what this 'abstraction' is, against which Sismondi expresses his criticism. 'The exchange price ... *is one of the most abstract ideas* presented by economic science, which is so rich in abstractions'.[79] If use value is a *thing* created by labour, exchange value is an '*abstract idea*'.

This abstract value has found its most perfect expression in capital which appears in the most abstract form. 'We touch here on *the most abstract question* ... in political economy'. In fact for society, taken as a whole, real wealth continues to be merely the mass of actual goods and services which satisfy needs. Things are different for each individual producer. For the capitalist, the natural form of capital and the continual real transformations which it undergoes in the course of the labour process are a matter of total indifference. For him the only important thing is the abstract value which he has invested in production and the increase in this in the course of production itself and of circulation. Sismondi shows that the producer never lets this value escape from his hands – whatever may be the continual modifications of the external forms of his capital. In support of his thesis he gives the example of the agricultural producer: 'the same object, passing from hand to hand, receives successively different names; while *its value, which separates itself from the consumed object* ... appears to be a *metaphysical entity* which one spends, and another exchanges, which perishes ... which renews itself and persists ... as long as circulation lasts'.[80]

For the cultivator, for example, the corn which he had harvested and used to feed productive workers 'was a *permanent multiplying value which did not perish anymore*'. This perpetual value has an independent life.

> This value separated itself from that of the provisions which had created it: it remained like a *metaphysical* and *nonsubstantial quantity*, always in the possession of the same cultivator, for whom it merely took different *guises*. First it had been corn, then an equal value of labour (wage); then

77 'As *useful activity* ... labour is ... a condition of material interchange between man and nature, quite independent of the form of society. On the other hand, the labour which posits *exchange value* is a specific *social form* of labour', Marx 1987a, p. 278. [Grossman's emphasis. German in Grossman's original text.]

78 Sismondi 1838, p. 375. [Grossman's emphasis.]

79 Sismondi 1838, p. 379 [Grossman's emphasis.]

80 Sismondi 1991d, pp. 79–80. [Grossman's emphasis.]

> an equal value of the fruits of that labour; later a credit to the person to whom these fruits were sold for later payment; then money, then again corn or labour.[81]

'*This movement of wealth is so abstract* and it demands such great concentration to understand it well.' This abstract character of capital in general likewise has repercussions on all its constituent parts and on all economic life. 'Circulating capital is an *abstract* and elusive *quantity* and cannot be grasped'.[82] 'It is the *abstract image* of all the values which commerce has at its disposal'.[83]

Following on from this analysis, Sismondi traces the properties of two different economic systems. From the dynamic point of view, he observes that effective evolution means that the system without exchange – the substance of which is the production of wealth in the proper sense, in its natural, permanent, essential form, for it belongs to every economic system – disappears more and more, under the influence of trade in its capacity as regulator of the economic mechanism. To an ever greater extent its place is taken by an accidental form of wealth, for it belongs only to a certain specific system, namely exchange value. 'Trade leads to the disappearance of *the essential character* of wealth, utility, leaving behind only their *accidental character*, their exchange value'.[84]

Now this abstract value puts its mark on the whole economic life of our epoch. If, from the point of view of essential wealth, the history of the well-being of society is nothing other than the *history of human labour*, then 'it is most important that one thinks first of showing step by step all the *actions* by which [a human] can move from penury to opulence'. Hence in the society of exchange the sole aim of every producer is not the labour process but 'the hope of profit',[85] in other words, the tendency to acquire a profit, that is to say a surplus of this exchangeable abstract value higher than the value laid out. *It is this abstract value*, in its capacity as the sole aim of production and as the regulator of it, which is the target *of Sismondi's sharpest criticisms, as he shows that it is the source of all the problems of our economic organisation*.[86] If, therefore, Sis-

81 Sismondi 1991d, pp. 81–2. [Grossman's emphasis.]

82 Sismondi 1991d, p. 84; Sismondi 1838, p. 395. [Grossman's emphasis.]

83 Sismondi 1838, p. 389. [Grossman's emphasis.]

84 Sismondi 1838, p. 378. [Grossman's emphasis.]

85 Sismondi 1991d, p. 62; Sismondi 1837, p. 59. [Grossman's emphasis. Editor's interpolation.]

86 'It contains the general possibility of commercial crises, essentially because the contradiction of commodity and money is the abstract and general form of all *contradictions*

mondi combats abstraction, abstract wealth, abstract ideas, he is thinking of wealth based on exchange value, in the same way that later Nassau Senior, Fryderyk Skarbek or Karl Marx would call exchange value abstract wealth.[87] Hence Sismondi does not attack either wealth or the accumulation of wealth in general but attacks the accumulation of wealth *in the abstract form of exchange value* and describes as 'chrematistic' economic organisation based precisely on this exchange value. As the capitalist system races towards *the accumulation of abstract value*, which finds an adequate expression in the commercial export policy, Sismondi sees only a modernised form of the old mercantilism: 'governments continue for the most part to behave according to the mercantile system, as though no argument had yet begun to undermine it'.[88]

From this brief account it appears clear that Sismondi understood perfectly the very essence of the capitalist system, the aim of which is not the production of *real goods* serving to satisfy needs but the production and accumulation of an *abstract exchange value*. And that is why it is right to consider Sismondi as the first economist to scientifically discover capitalism; that is his immortal claim to fame in economic science.

∴

The characterisation that we have just made of our *economic system* is only one of the aspects of the problem Sismondi was dealing with. This problem leads on to another: the relation of *economic science* to real phenomena. Now, according to Sismondi, the economic theory of his time was only the theoretical reflection of contemporary economic organisation based on abstract exchange value. If this organisation, as a result of its defective construction, is the source of lasting problems, this fact also has an impact on economic theory, which is likewise based on the same abstract foundation of exchange value. The real contradiction of the economic system appears in science in the form of incoherent notions and definitions and futile quarrels about words. Through a painstaking analysis of the contradictions of the economic system, Sismondi ends up

---

inherent in the bourgeois mode of labour', Marx 1987a, p. 332. [German in Grossman's original text. Grossman's emphasis.]

87 'Money is *abstract wealth* … the modes in which different individuals would employ it are infinitely diversified', Senior 1965, p. 27. [Grossman's emphasis.] 'Exchange value … can only be an abstract *idea*', Skarbek 1829, p. 138. [Grossman's emphasis.] 'Money as the end and object of circulation represents *exchange value* or *abstract wealth*', Marx 1987a, pp. 389–90. [German in Grossman's original text. Grossman's emphasis.]

88 Sismondi 1838, p. 321.

with a search for the errors and contradictions in the theory. 'This quest necessarily brings us back to the most abstract notions of the science, to the most disputed definitions, to a whole battle of words.' In both organisation and theory, the source of the problem and of the shortcomings is identical. 'It is the opposition between *use value* and *exchange value* ... which makes it impossible to give a satisfactory definition of these various terms: price, value, wealth.' The abstract character of the science based on exchange value and the contradiction between this science and the phenomena of real wealth makes it difficult to define these notions – price of production, sentimental price, monopoly price, nominal price, real price etc. – and this difficulty derives from the very nature of our system. In theory this again comes down to a battle of words, a dispute about meanings and not to the very essence of the phenomena concealed by it. So it should not be forgotten that verbal disputes about a definition do not and cannot explain what these phenomena entail. Those who think they have dealt with the phenomena through the critique of a definition are greatly mistaken. The contradiction manifested in phenomena must be eliminated from these phenomena and this cannot be done by a critique which only examines words. The classical *theory* of the spontaneous harmony of interests is not in a position to resolve this *effective* contradiction: together with the continuous increase in wealth capitalist production gives rise to 'poverty growing together with abundance'.[89] This phenomenon seems to be a contradiction; in fact it is a *real phenomenon* and hence the *idea* which expresses it is consistent with reality. So if theory has not succeeded in defining this concept adequately, that does not make it faulty; the error is in the definition, in the words. 'If a more precise analysis makes us find a contradiction somewhere, it is not the *idea* which must give way but the *word*: it is in the *definition* and not in the *fact* that we find the defect of the argument'.[90]

Sismondi was the first to present us with a deep analysis of the contradictions in theory, showing that it is not the accidental result of the incapacity of scholars but the necessary consequence of the contradictions presented by the economic system itself. That is why Sismondi uses the term 'chrematistic' to describe both the economic theory, based on the analysis of exchange value, and the economic system itself which is built on this foundation. 'The science which is commonly known as political economy, although its proper title is

89 Sismondi 1838, pp. 226, 229, 233. [Grossman's emphasis.]

90 Sismondi 1837, p. 116. [Grossman's emphasis.] In this profound characterisation of the battle of words, Sismondi anticipates the anonymous English author of Anonymous 1821, as well as his belated epigone the German Gottl, 1901.

chrematistics, has taken on the task of studying wealth abstractly.' He considers this economic science and the system itself to be 'pursuing a shadow without reality'. And he contrasts true science to this false theory. 'We reserve the name of political economy for the study of the social organisation of man in his relation with things, the man who *consumes* wealth and the man who *produces* it'.[91] Sismondi wants to consider only real phenomena, the relation of man with the real usable goods which he produces and consumes, *independently of the question of the exchange value* of these goods. And this economy which is independent of exchange and of the calculation of value, he calls the real economy, 'the rule of the house and of the community'.[92] As we will see, this problem has nothing in common with the question of the distribution of wealth which, according to the view held until now, constituted the very substance of Sismondi's doctrine.

The scientific problem which Sismondi was posing himself is hence double: critique of theory, critique of the system. Sismondi has to explain the functioning of the economic mechanism built on the basis of abstract exchange value, whose ideal aim – the aim of any economic system – is to satisfy all the needs of society but in which the aim of each particular producer is to individually accumulate an abstract exchange value. He proposes to 'seek an *explanation* for so many facts which appear *contradictory*, to discover *what is the deception of the system of industrialism*, to show how it has abandoned the *substance* to run after the *shadow*, in order finally to replace chrematistics, or the abstract science of wealth, with *true political economy*'.[93]

B *Positive Theory*

So far we have tried to show what Sismondi considered to be the true problem in his research and we have seen that this problem consisted in the dualistic character of capitalist production which, on the one hand, is the production of real goods and, on the other, the production of abstract exchange value. It now remains for us to explain why he sees this fact as the *defect* of our economic organisation and why in particular he criticises one of these elements, abstract exchange value, as being the principal source of all the upheavals which trouble our economic system. The very location of the problem no less than Sismondi's solution to it are by their depth far removed from the horizon of classical economic thought and even of contemporary economic thought in general.

---

91 Sismondi 1838, p. 234. [Grossman's emphasis.]

92 Sismondi 1838, p. 226.

93 Sismondi 1838, p. 226. [Grossman's emphasis.]

In the system producing for human needs and not for the market, for sale, an increase in production, that is, in the quantity of goods, is simultaneously an increase in wealth. 'Before the introduction of trade and when everyone thought only of supplying themselves, the increase in the *quantity* of things produced was a direct increase in wealth'. 'That is doubtless the true understanding of wealth'.[94] 'As long as men work to satisfy their own needs, *utility* is for them the true measure of values and the increase in quantity of a useful thing is a sure increase in wealth.' It is nonetheless necessary *to produce these goods within strictly defined limits*. It is true that 'the needs and desires of human beings are unlimited' but not the *concrete* needs: foodstuffs, housing, clothing etc.[95] 'One can have too much, even of the best things.' 'Consumption cannot go beyond a certain limit, difficult to indicate precisely but nonetheless definite' and which man could not go beyond.[96] 'All labour he performed *beyond that would be pointless*. Any product which he accumulated would be without value'. Nonetheless in the system without exchange 'the glut of commodities was not possible'.[97] Concrete needs gave an impulse to production, so that in practice the direction and scope of labour were adapted in advance to the extent of needs. Man, 'after having supplied his stock for consumption and his reserve stock, will stop'.[98] In these conditions one produces only as much as is necessary and the goods produced are always wealth, for they fulfil the function appropriate to them, that is, they serve to satisfy needs.

It is quite different in the system with exchange. The whole, organised for a specific purpose, which was represented by the system without exchange, has now been fragmented into distinct functions which are independent of each other, if not diametrically opposed. The independent producers, left to themselves, produce for the market, that is for other people, without knowing these people's needs and remain in contact with them only by the mediation of exchange. Each cog in the clock has made itself free and functions independently of the others; the common movement, coordinated for a particular purpose, has been fragmented into private isolated fractions.

> Trade or exchange has divided between the members of society the functions which tend toward a common purpose. Everyone, in pursuing their

94 Sismondi 1838, pp. 378, 379. [Grossman's emphasis.]
95 Sismondi 1838, p. 229; Sismondi 1837, p. 139. [Grossman's emphasis.]
96 Sismondi 1837, pp. 64, 151.
97 Sismondi 1837, p. 69; Sismondi 1838, p. 243. [Grossman's emphasis.]
98 Sismondi 1837, p. 68.

> private aims, loses sight of the general interest ... They pursue their aims without really knowing how much of this thing society requires of them.[99]

This failure to adapt the behaviour of individuals to the needs of the social whole has the necessary consequence of upsetting the whole. Society, in fact, although fragmented into specific and independent functions, nonetheless does not cease to constitute a *social whole*. If in the economic system working for the producer's own needs it was necessary to adapt every act and every function to the needs of the individual producer, this same obligation exists for the system with exchange. 'Production has limits which it is forbidden to exceed ...'. 'These rules ... are equally true in *any state* of society, even if it is no longer directed by an intelligence which understands all the relations of its members with each other, by a will which makes them all co-operate for the common good.' In a society based on the division of labour and functions, their coordination is a necessity; Sismondi compares it to a watch where all the cogs and all the motions, by the very nature of things, must be coordinated. 'All movements in society are linked together; one follows from the other, as the various movements of the gears of a watch'.[100]

However, from the time that society becomes divided into independent and even contradictory functions, this necessary adaptation can only be an objective *result* which is accomplished through the divergent interests and movements of individuals. 'Civilised society seems to be subject ... to those general laws ... which propel the whole toward a common end, by disasters that pitilessly strike the different parts.'[101] Thus it is these laws through which social union is achieved independently of the action of individuals.[102] In these conditions, economic disturbances are the natural and inevitable consequence of our economic organisation. Since each individual acts independently, producing as much as possible, without taking account of *social need*, real goods exceeding this social need cease to be wealth. 'All that is produced beyond this is useless and has no value.'[103] The defect of the capitalist system consists

99 Sismondi 1837, p. 69.

100 Sismondi 1837, p. 140; Sismondi 1991b p. 637. [Grossman's emphasis.]

101 Sismondi 1991d, p. 503.

102 'The *exchange process* of commodities is the *real* relation that exists between them. This is a social process which is carried on by individuals independently of one another', Marx 1987a, p. 282. [German in Grossman's original text.]

103 Sismondi 1837, p. 69. 'The commodity therefore has still to *become* a use value, in the first place a use value for others ... If this is not the case, then the labour expended on it was useless labour', Marx 1987a, p. 283. [German in Grossman's original text. Grossman's emphasis.]

precisely in the fact that, contrary to the law according to which all economic functions in society must be coordinated for a specific purpose, each producer tends to maximise production, thinking that by increasing the quantity of goods, he is also increasing the quantity of wealth. 'The error on which the whole system of modern chrematistics is based … confuses the increase of *production* with that of *wealth*.'[104]

And it is from this consideration, deriving directly as we will see from his new formulation of the law of value, that Sismondi starts in order to construct his theory. And over this issue Sismondi ceaselessly indicts the theory of the classical economists. 'The error into which they have fallen stems entirely from the false principle that makes the annual output, in their eyes, the same thing as the income.' This is the source of all the errors of the theory, of the confusion of concepts and of the inability to explain phenomena. 'The confusion of the annual income with the annual product throws a dense veil over the whole science.'[105]

> With this principle it becomes absolutely impossible to understand … The satiation of markets … It is equally impossible to extricate oneself from the contradictions about the meaning that ought to be given to the words *value* and *wealth* with which Messrs Say and Ricardo mutually charge each other.[106]

Here Sismondi is referring to the well-known controversy between Ricardo on the one hand and Say and Malthus on the other. The latter two identify value with wealth. Malthus claims that revenue drawn out of the earth by a landowner is an increase in social wealth, 'a new creation of riches'.[107] Ricardo is in agreement with Sismondi who regards revenue as a purely abstract value: 'rent … has a value purely nominal … consider it as no addition to the national wealth, but merely as a transfer of value'.[108] Ricardo expresses a similar opinion in chapter 20 of *The Principles*, where under the obvious influence of Sismondi, he shows that their theory has confused the ideas of value and riches. It is not value which determines wealth. 'A man is rich or poor according to the *abundance* of necessaries and luxuries which he can command … whether the exchangeable *value* of these … be high or low.'[109]

104 Sismondi 1838, p. 312. [Grossman's emphasis.]
105 Sismondi 1991d, p. 278.
106 Sismondi 1991d, p. 278. [Grossman's emphasis.]
107 Ricardo 1912, p. 272. [English in Grossman's original text.]
108 Ricardo 1912, p. 273. [English in Grossman's original text.]
109 Ricardo 1912, p. 184. [English in Grossman's original text. Grossman's emphasis.]

This way of seeing which is undoubtedly in contradiction with the whole of Ricardo's system, which is based precisely and above all on exchange value. And that is why Ricardo draws no conclusion from this difference between exchange value and wealth. In Ricardo's system chapter 20 constitutes a totally isolated point, unconnection with this system. Sismondi was the first to draw out all the implications for the economic mechanism which derive from the fact that it is precisely based on this abstract exchange value, 'value purely nominal'.[110] And in this fact he sees the cause of all the disturbances, all the disruptions of this mechanism.

∴

It now remains for us to show in a detailed analysis why and how we must necessarily end up with these disturbances if we base the economic mechanism on abstract exchange value. Sismondi asserts that if we base the economic system on this principle it is *impossible to make a proportional fit between the amount of production and the extent of needs. Disproportion becomes then and as a rule a normal phenomenon.*

In the system without exchange, composed of producers independent of each other, it did not matter whether the number of producers increased, since each was producing only for his own needs and the functions of production and consumption were dependent on each other and in close correlation; their equilibrium was thereby ensured in advance. But it is quite different in the system with exchange, where one produces for other people. Here the separation of producer and consumer came into being: 'somebody had taken the place of the producer to consume'. 'But when trade was introduced, and each no longer laboured for himself, but for someone unknown, the proportions ... between the labour and the revenue ... were independent of each other'. And then it became necessary to regulate the mutual quantitative relations between total production and total needs. But as nobody carries out this regulation, these relations are entirely random; the number of producers and the extent of their production are different and arbitrary in each branch; *need* has ceased to be the regulator of the extent of production and has been replaced by the capitalist's *profit*, deriving from [a product having] a value 'higher than the money advanced by means of which it has been obtained'. This difference, this 'surplus' is therefore itself exchange value and hence an abstract quantity. This profit, this abstract value is henceforward the aim of the whole capitalist mechanism,

110 [English in Grossman's original text.]

it is its motor, it guides all actions, independently of real needs. 'Profit making has become the first aim in life'.[111] 'The hope of profit makes capital circulate rapidly from one end of the known universe to the other'.[112]

How does the exchange mechanism function under the influence of this regulator? And thus we find ourselves at the very heart of Sismondi's theory.

Although each social function has become independent, society has not ceased to be a whole in the economic sense, an organism controlled by the law of this whole and not by the elements which make it up, something which is manifested in the law of value; Sismondi corrects the individualist theory of value of Smith and Ricardo, which determines the value of a commodity by the labour expended on producing it, with this highly significant addition, that it must be the labour *necessary* for its production. 'Mercantile value is always fixed, in the last analysis, by the quantity of labour necessary to obtain the valued thing'.[113] To tell the truth, Ricardo also seemed to define value in this way: 'I say that it is the comparative quantity of labour necessary to the production of commodities, which regulates their relative value.'[114] But, while Ricardo only speaks of the time technically necessary to produce a *unit* of a given commodity, Sismondi uses the word 'necessary', as Marx will do later, in the sense of time which is 'socially indispensible', that is time necessary to produce *the whole mass* of a given commodity necessary for society.[115] 'Value is the relation between the demand of all and the production of all'. 'Value results from the relation between the need of the whole society and the quantity of labour which has sufficed to satisfy this need'. Only the labour required to satisfy the whole need is necessary and the value of the products then corresponds exactly to the labour provided, measured by time. This condition would require the *quantitative fixing*, on the one hand, of the number of producers and the extent of their production; and on the other, of the extent of total social needs. In the end it is only under these conditions that the process of production would be in proportion *to needs*, would be *normal*, without disturbances or losses for the producer. 'To be sure of selling, he would have to know two things:

111 Sismondi 1991d, pp. 68, 254; Sismondi 1837, p. 137; Sismondi 1991b, p. 339.

112 Sismondi 1837, p. 59.

113 Sismondi 1838, p. 381.

114 Ricardo 1952, p. 149.

115 Marx himself notes this: 'Arguing directly with Ricardo, *Sismondi* not only emphasises the specifically *social* character of labour which creates exchange value, but states also that it is a "characteristic feature of our economic progress" to reduce value to *necessary* labour time, to "the relation between the needs of the *whole society* and the quantity of labour which is sufficient to satisfy those needs"', Marx 1987a, pp. 300–1. [German in Grossman's original text. Grossman's emphasis.]

the quantity of the thing he is producing that the public needs; the quantity of it that can be produced by all those who exercise the same profession as he does'. 'Whereas one or the other [wealth and population], considered by themselves, are only abstractions, and the real problem ... is to find that combination and *proportion* of population and wealth ...'.[116] Independently of the question of the unequal *distribution* of wealth between the various classes of the population, the key point is that reproduction is in proportion to the productive forces and the needs of society as a whole. 'It is *on that proportion that my* New Principles *are founded*; it is in the importance that I attach to it that *I differ essentially* from philosophers who ... have expounded the economic science of Messrs. Say, Ricardo, Malthus and McCulloch'.[117] Assuming that total production corresponds to total need, if ten garments and twenty sacks of corn are produced by the same number of days of labour, they will exchange at equal values.

But in the real world nobody adapts production to needs; that is why the course of production and exchange does not follow this normal pattern. Given the fragmentation of the social whole into distinct functions independent of each other, the number of producers and the quantity of their production are arbitrary and random. To acquire a profit the producer would like to 'produce indefinitely'.[118] Now this excessive quantity of labour, accomplished in order to generate production exceeding total social need, does not count because it has no purchasers *and hence does not create value*. 'All that is produced beyond this is useless and has no value.'[119] For 'things become wealth only at the time when they find the consumer who agrees to buy them in order to use them'.[120] Individual labour creates value only if this function is a *necessary organ of the whole*; otherwise it is a superfluous function, that is, time wasted.

If therefore the number of producers of clothing, for example, increases, although the need has not changed, the labour expended on this additional production of clothing does not create any value, the greater mass of clothes will have the same value as previously and, as a result, the price of each gar-

116 Sismondi 1838, pp. 376, 379; Sismondi 1837, p. 120; Sismondi 1991d, p. 2. [Grossman's emphasis. Translator's interpolation.]

117 Sismondi 1991d, p. 11. [Grossman's emphasis.] Rist commits a major mistake by understanding the problem of the proportionality of productive forces raised by Sismondi as a question of the *distribution of wealth* above all in the interest of the poor, that is of waged workers. Rist writes that according to Sismondi 'wealth only deserves the name when it is proportionately distributed', Rist 1915, p. 178.

118 Sismondi 1837, p. 70.

119 Sismondi 1837, p. 69.

120 Sismondi 1837, p. 30.

ment must fall. A specific producer of clothing continues to manufacture, for example, ten garments, just like the previous year, that is to say the same quantity as previously but, in view of the reduction in value of this production, he can no longer buy twenty sacks of corn but only twelve, eight or even none at all if he has not sold any of his ten garments. So, despite the claims of Say and Ricardo, it appears that it was only in the system without exchange that the quantity of the product was identical to the income and in permanent conditions sufficed from year to year to satisfy the same needs. In the system with exchange the quantity of products is not equivalent to income. This quantity of products must first of all be sold. Each producer now knows that 'by making the same quantity of products, he might earn much or little, or he might even lose'. The products of one year, identical in quantity and quality to those of the previous year, may and do represent a quite different income; *despite the identical nature of the products, the income is of a variable size*. In the exchange system, 'products are not yet positive quantities, aliquot portions of wealth, as long as they are in the hands of the producer. Only sale ... determines their value.'[121] In these conditions the manufacturer of clothing produces, it is true, the same quantity as previously but his income will depend not on the quantity of goods created by him as an individual producer but on the quantity of goods created likewise by all the other producers and hence *will depend on productive processes taking place outside of each individual producer* and independently of him, in short on competition.

> Thus, in this new condition, the life of every man who works and produces depends not ... on his labour but on what he sells. It matters little whether the work is done well ... it must be in *exact proportion* with production. The producer who cannot sell cannot live.[122]

From the point of view of society conceived as a whole, income is always a certain *given* mass of effective goods reproduced. 'Income, of which we have seen all the different sources, is a material and consumable thing; it springs from labour.'[123] But in the exchange system the producers act in isolation; for

121 Sismondi 1837, p. 65; Sismondi 1838, p. 231.

122 Sismondi 1837, p. 120. [Grossman's emphasis.] We have taken as the starting point of our argument the excessive number of producers of clothing, as a result of which some of these clothes could not be sold. But as the producers of clothing are in turn consumers of the products of other branches, the reduction of their incomes must also provoke a disproportion in other branches, namely a 'general obstruction'. Sismondi 1991a, p. 600.

123 Sismondi 1991d, p. 361.

them income is always a *variable* amount: it is an abstract value subject to fluctuations. In this disproportion of production and income, of use value and exchange value, is found the original source of the disruptions which appear in our economic mechanism. The development of this thought constitutes the first part of Sismondi's theory. It was to this that Karl Marx's penetrating observation referred: 'Sismondi founded on the *opposition* between use value and exchange value his principal doctrine, according to which diminution in *revenue* is proportional to the increase in production.'[124] Despite these words written nearly eighty years ago, Sismondi's 'principal theory' on the nature of income has not yet been understood.

The classical school considered crises as accidental phenomena provoked by mistaken commercial policy and by restrictions. Even those who are called egalitarian socialists, like for example William Thompson, saw the real source of crises only in the luxury branches of industry, as the result of the whims and changes of fashion among the rich.[125] In contrast, for Sismondi crises are the *necessary* consequence of the construction, defective in principle, of our economic mechanism, based on abstract exchange value.

Sismondi's analysis does not stop with this result. The classical school insisted that even when a crisis broke out, it could only be a transitory phenomenon, for our productive apparatus possesses a spontaneous tendency to re-establish the good order which has been disrupted. Sismondi had a quite different view. He showed that in an economic mechanism whose regulator is a variable exchange value there are causes that act permanently, that merely intensify the disequilibrium between production and needs and constantly create the tendency to enlarge production, whether or not this is required by needs.

First of all on the commodity market.

The mechanism described by the classical economists is well-known: any excess production brings down prices and profits, and has an automatic influence on the reduction in production. The tendency to equalise profits in the various branches of production brings about the withdrawal of capital from non-profitable branches and prevents disequilibrium. On the other hand Sismondi argues that in a society where the producer's aim is not the production of a specific quantity of real goods but the highest profit possible, the lowering of the selling price and income caused by overproduction in no way leads to the *reduction* of production but, on the contrary, merely *extends* it so that

124 Marx 1976a, p. 114. [Grossman's emphasis.] Also see Sismondi 1991d, p. 600.

125 Thompson 1824, Chapter II, section 2, pp. 195–210.

with a greater number of transactions the producer can recuperate his losses on prices. The producer 'always seeks to produce more, to produce cheaper, to produce all the more ... in order to regain by quantity what he loses on prices'. 'The result of the reduction of income is that he needs more capital to live, he needs more land to get the same amount of rent, he needs to lend more money to get the same amount of interest'. Overproduction by lowering prices and incomes forces the individual producer to continue overproducing even more. 'Because they had already too many goods, they have asked for more at a lower price.' That seems like a paradox. However, there is a glut on the market and there is no means of selling all the increased production, since there was insufficient demand previously for less production. But the increase in production makes it possible to reduce expenses, thanks to which the large producer wins out over his competitors and disposes of his goods at his competitors' expense. 'Each producer seeks to undercut his rival colleagues and by low prices to attract the buyer to himself in preference to someone else who cannot sell.'[126] This producer prospers even at times of general stagnation; he increases his production even when there is no increased demand. It is an artificial buoyancy: 'production is reviving', 'but this sporadic activity is more often the result of risky speculation, of misplaced confidence, and of superabundant capital, than of new demand'. 'It is a deceptive activity', 'a fallacious prosperity'.[127]

'The necessary, inevitable consequence of undercutting by some is glut for all, or the arrival on the market of a quantity of goods in excess of needs, which can only be sold at a loss.' Success in competition is conditioned by large-scale production, the purchase of cheap raw materials, the application of the division of labour, the use of machines, new inventions etc. But this success also depends on the abundance of capital and on a low rate of interest. 'A decrease in the rate of interest begins a search for a productive use of superabundant capital.' 'The capitalists, in order to employ their funds, will set afoot industries which will not find an adequate market afterwards.'[128] Finally we come to the key fact that it is not the increase in consumption which is the regulator of the extent of production but that the increases in production are 'determined, not by needs, but by the abundance of capital'.[129] All the stimuli, directions and dimensions of capitalist production today are in no way determined by

126 Sismondi 1837, p. 74, Sismondi 1991b, p. 635; Sismondi 1838, p. 232.
127 Sismondi 1991d, p. 333; Sismondi 1838, p. 329.
128 Sismondi 1838, p. 233; Sismondi 1991d, pp. 299, 332.
129 Sismondi 1991d, p. 278.

the extent of concrete need; rather, 'those who found themselves in possession of a certain quantity of accumulated wealth have in general undertaken the control of annual production'.[130]

It is obvious that, in these conditions, the increase in production 'without regard to the needs of the business world' intensifies competition 'that enriched some individuals [and] caused a certain loss to others'.[131] The increase in production is therefore parallel to the reduction of income and even to the ruin of the social whole. The increase in production, 'always tied to a greater circulating capital, and to the use of a larger fixed capital, can give an advantage to the entrepreneur, and make his manufacture flourish, without having to again conclude that this leads to a social benefit'.[132] Moreover, the source of disruptions is the same: the regulation of the extent of production by profit, that is, by an abstract exchange value. The shrinking of this abstract quantity leads to the enlargement of the real productive apparatus, as well as the mass of real products, although demand is lacking – in short, the opposition between exchange value and use value. The result is that 'the income of all is not the same thing as everyone's output ... it would be possible that the product increases and the income decreases'.[133]

⁘

In the two instances which we have just considered, since the available technology and the productivity of labour did not change, the reduction of exchange value was the result of an excessive increase, either *in the number of producers* or in the extent of their production. This reduction of exchange value may occur as a result of *technical revolutions*, in other words of progress in the productivity of labour. And here we come to the third part of Sismondi's theory. Ricardo had noticed the fact itself.[134] Sismondi develops it and shows the consequences. 'Mercantile value is always fixed, in the last analysis, by the quantity of labour required to obtain the thing being valued; it is not what it costs at present but what it will cost in the future, perhaps with improved meth-

---

130 Sismondi 1837, p. 141. 'As capitalist production develops, the scale of production is determined to an ever lesser degree by the immediate demand for the product, and to an ever greater degree by the scale of the capital which the individual capitalist has at his disposal, by his capital's drive for valorisation and the need of his production process for continuity and extension.' [Marx 1978b, p. 221.]

131 Sismondi 1991d, p. 303. [Editor's interpolation.]

132 Sismondi 1991d, p. 299.

133 Sismondi 1991a, p. 600.

134 Ricardo 1912, pp. 182–91.

ods'.[135] Whence *a constant devaluation of goods already produced* and put on the market, leading to a new source of disruptions. Moreover the old factories with their old equipment are reduced to struggling hopelessly against the competition of large factories which are better equipped. 'The old machines, even the whole factory, replaced by new inventions, lose all their value. The immense capital which had been placed in their construction is destroyed.'[136] 'Every truly important discovery in engineering, each of those that produce ... a considerable profit, immediately leads to the creation of a new factory in order to appropriate the profits exclusively.' It is a never-ending race to monopolise profit through improvement but for a very short moment, for a newcomer in turn will soon reduce the value of this improvement. 'It is in the nature of crafts that inventions succeed each other, that a new discovery comes to take away the fruits of the preceding one.'[137]

This ceaseless competition produces a constant process of devaluation of the values already accumulated, a general dislocation of exchange value and, as a result, a necessary disruption of the whole economic mechanism of which this value is the regulator. 'It has been noted that *the violent shocks suffered nowadays by manufacturing industry derive from the speed with which scientific discoveries succeed one another*.' And the effects of so many 'revolutionary inventions' are deplorable for human society. 'Not only is the value of all goods already produced diminished ... but all the fixed capital, all the machines ... are rendered useless.'[138]

In these conditions, a fortune owned is always threatened with ruin and the producer's income does not depend on labour effectively carried out. It is consequently not a positive amount, does not depend on the mass of effective goods produced but on the value he manages to obtain by selling them on the market and which he succeeds in preserving amid the continual upheavals to which this value is subject. 'His operation takes on the character of a game ... his profit depends on chance, or is based on the loss made by another.'[139]

The circumstances which we have just noted, an unlimited quantity of producers and production and technical revolutions, must and did provoke disruptions even in a system composed only of independent producers, possessing their own instruments of production. In both cases the reduction in profit and the subsequent depreciation of capital and of goods already produced, causes

135 Sismondi 1838, p. 381.
136 Sismondi 1838, p. 302.
137 Sismondi 1838, pp. 298, 305.
138 Sismondi 1838, pp. 366, 367. [Grossman's emphasis.]
139 Sismondi 1838, p. 232.

the ruin of the small producers. 'The prosperity of the producer who gets rich should not allow us to forget the poverty of the producer ruined by his competition.' It is impossible to safeguard oneself from this competition by moving into another branch of production, 'capitals leave an industry only *through the bankruptcy* of owners'.[140] The spontaneous tendency to restore equilibrium between production and consumption does not exist. In the current system there is therefore overproduction: the impossibility of selling a part of the products. 'Hence, if production increases gradually, the exchange of *each year* ought to cause a small loss ... if that loss is small and well distributed, everyone bears it ...'. But if the causes indicated act suddenly and violently 'there is a great disproportion between the new production and the previous production', and then one section of the producers get rich but only because the other one gets poor, 'capitals are reduced, there will be suffering'. 'New fortunes are built only by the overthrow of old fortunes.'[141]

Hence the *natural tendency to concentration*. 'Discoveries in the mechanical arts have always the remote result of concentrating industry within the hands of a smaller number of merchants.'[142] Obviously this goes along with the bankruptcy and ruin of others, proletarianisation and pauperism. As we have seen, Sismondi does not merely observe this tendency empirically but shows that this concentration of industry and the consequent proletarianisation are the necessary result of the current economic organisation. 'Pauperism is the state to which proletarians are *necessarily* reduced when they have no work ... This, society which gives all its support to the rich, does not allow the proletarian to work ... and condemns him to idleness.' In short the causes that we have just set out are the historic basis of the tendency which has led to and continues to lead to the *separation of property* and labour. 'We incline to separate completely any type of property from all types of labour.' Hence, on the one hand, the concentration of capital and, at the opposite pole, growth of the proletarian masses. 'Already brought into the world, that population finds no longer any room to exist there.'[143] But this excessive population 'exists today, and ... is the *necessary result of the existing order*'. When a primitive hunter dies, for want of finding any game, 'he yields to a necessity which *nature* herself presents.' Today it is a different matter for the artisan without work: 'he is still surrounded by riches ...

140 Sismondi 1838, p. 295; Sismondi 1991d, p. 487. [Grossman's emphasis.]

141 Sismondi 1991d, pp. 104, 104–5; Sismondi 1837, p. 31. [Grossman's emphasis.]

142 Sismondi 1991d, p. 561.

143 Sismondi 1837, p. 44; Sismondi 1991b, p. 628; Sismondi 1991d, p. 548. [Grossman's emphasis.]

and if society refuses him the labour by which he offers, till his last moment, to purchase bread, it is *men*, not nature, that he blames'.[144]

It is true that after the catastrophe of a crisis a new equilibrium is established at last. People have tried to see in this fact a proof that a crisis is only a passing ill and that equilibrium is restored automatically. Sismondi considers this theory of equilibrium restoring itself to be dangerous. 'A certain equilibrium will re-establish itself in the long run'[145] but the disaster nonetheless leaves a deep impression. Some of the producers go bankrupt and sink into the proletariat, while others succeed in enlarging their businesses, and a concentration of industry results. *Equilibrium is restored but on a new basis: the social structure has undergone a serious transformation.*

∴

This glance at Sismondi's conceptions enables us to conclude that economic science has previously considered the facts stressed by our writer – such as competition, the struggle between large and small industry, concentration, crises, pauperism, the reserve army, abuses committed in factories, and above all the question of the distribution of wealth – only as isolated, external facts, as *disjecta membra*.[146] Economists have not explained and have said nothing about the internal connection, the stimulus and the cause uniting all these phenomena into a set of parts of a common mechanism, in complete mutual dependence – hidden below these external manifestations. This connection is the fact *that abstract exchange value is the regulator of the extent of production.* The economic system serves to satisfy the concrete material needs of society by means of a given productive apparatus. These needs, just like the extent of the apparatus, are amounts and phenomena which can remain in mutual relations in natural conditions, without regard to value. On the other hand, our economic system, in order to apply the dimensions of the aforesaid productive apparatus to the extent of the needs, takes as its regulator exchange value, a regulator which, in a mechanism based on free competition, *is necessarily a variable standard, whose movements are the opposite of those of the effective goods which it measures*, since the *value* of a given good diminishes if the general *mass* of goods increases. So these factors, like two worlds which are impenetrable to each other, do not have a common measure and to try to har-

144 Sismondi 1991d, pp. 322, 556. [Grossman's emphasis.]

145 Sismondi 1991d, p. 487.

146 ['*Disjecta membra*' means 'scattered fragments'.]

monise them would be like measuring length in grams or weighing in metres. 'The present suffering results from the increase of quantities, while values are being reduced.'[147]

Our system is like the mechanism of a factory in which every wheel, every machine set in motion by the transmission belt, would have to experience disruptions in their movements if the belt contracted or stretched excessively. It is in this dual principle of organisation of our economic mechanism, in the fact that to control the dimensions of the real apparatus we use a changing unit of measurement, an abstract and variable value, in this contradiction between use value and exchange value that Sismondi sees the fundamental defect in the construction of our economic system, the real cause of crises, of overproduction and of economic anarchy.[148] That is why the disruptions of this system are not temporary deviations from normal equilibrium but derive from a constitutive defect and are a phenomenon which recurs ceaselessly, periodically and necessarily, to such an extent that it becomes possible to predict their regular repetition.

> The period of prosperity of any manufacture is promptly followed by a period of distress. It is enough for us to know that a manufacture is flourishing today for us to be able to foresee, almost with certainty, that in ten years, or even much less time, according to all probability, it will have had to succumb to competition.[149]

147 Sismondi 1838, p. 478. See Karl Marx: 'It is a general law of commodity production that the *productivity* of labour and the *value it creates* stand in inverse proportion', Marx 1978b, p. 227. [Grossman's emphasis.] In a distorted form, we find this theory in Wilhelm Neurath, when he criticises 'the false calculation of value', and blames the fact 'that the relation between the quantity of goods and the real need for them does not determine the estimated value of the goods'. As a result of the application of this 'false calculation of value', of this 'phantom value', 'the total value of the products can sink, even if the *quantity* … of the products increases, so that total use and total value come partially into contradiction with each other.' In Neurath's eyes this is 'something highly unusual' and 'inappropriate'. According to him factories are free 'of this calculation of value' (!) and possess 'the capacity to produce wealth and to employ heads and hands' even when they lose their value, Neurath 1892, pp. 16–18. [Grossman's emphasis.]

148 'The *continual depreciation of labour* is only one side, *one consequence of the evaluation of commodities by labour time*. The excessive raising of prices, overproduction and many other features of industrial anarchy have their explanation in this mode of evaluation.' 'Instead of a 'proportional relation' we have a disproportional relation.' Marx 1976a, p. 136. [Grossman's emphasis.]

149 Sismondi 1838, p. 306.

∴

We do not propose to give a systematic exposition of Sismondi's ideas but just to draw out the essence of his thought. So far we have done this by analysing phenomena on the market for commodities. We will complete our proof by *analysing phenomena on the market for wage labour*. And there too we will encounter what we have already indicated. Critics have previously confined themselves to external aspects without reaching the very heart of the action, to apparent symptoms and not to essential and deep causes. Hence they have obstinately repeated that for Sismondi the source of all disturbances, of all crises was to be found in the unequal distribution of wealth, in the underconsumption of the working masses. 'The disproportion between capitalist production and the distribution of incomes determined by the former appears to him the source of all evil', writes Rosa Luxemburg.[150] According to [René] Gonnard 'in Sismondi's eyes, the questions of distribution take on a preponderant importance and there are almost socialist formulations on the right of the poor to a minimum consumption'.[151] Nothing could be more wrong. Certainly nobody before Sismondi had exhaustively revealed the capitalist character of the creation and distribution of wealth and nobody before him had made such a penetrating critique of this system. In Sismondi we find in embryonic form the doctrine later developed by Karl Marx and called by him *economic fetishism*, according to which in the capitalist system there exists an objective tendency to obscure the real nature of this system, of its institutions and of the real source of its wealth. Monetary exchange is precisely the instrument whereby this process of artificial transformation is accomplished. In any economic system 'wealth ... was always a thing created by labour'.[152] 'The history of wealth is, in all cases, comprised within the limits now specified – the labour which creates, the economy which accumulates, the consumption which destroys'. But while nothing is so easy to grasp as this truth, exchanges 'blur our vision and make a positive thing into an almost metaphysical one'. Like wealth, income comes from this common origin – from labour. 'It is however usual [and this is what this metaphysics entails] to recognise three types of income under the name of rent, profit and wages, as coming from the three different sources, the earth, accumulated capital and labour.' We must lift the veil of monetary exchange to see what the phenomena really entail. 'On closer inspection one realises that these three

150 Luxemburg 1951, pp. 178–9.
151 Gonnard 1922, p. 208.
152 Sismondi 1991d, p. 68.

divisions are three different ways in which to share in the fruits of the work of man'. The worker produces by his daily labour more than his daily expenditure. But the landowner and the capitalist, thanks to the ownership of the instruments of production, have forced the worker to hand back to them the surplus 'over and above his daily needs'. The surplus constitutes the landowner's rent and the capitalist's profit. What remains forms the worker's wage. The worker has become the proletarian. 'The latter is the man for whom what he needs to work and not die has been calculated exactly'. 'The master alone profited from the increase in productive power'.[153]

Contrary to the trivial manner in which capital is identified with the material elements of the labour process, which in fact are common to all forms of production, Sismondi shows that *it is in the nature of capital that its function of exploiting the labour of others is determined*, that is, its power of taking possession of what the worker creates over and above what he has received from the capitalist in the form of wages. 'Every time the rich man obtained a gain from using labour, he was situated, in all points, exactly as the husbandman who sows the ground. The wages paid to his workmen were a kind of seed which he entrusted to them, and expected in a given time to bring forth fruit.' The capitalist knew 'that this sowing would bring him a harvest',[154] a 'commodity, *of a greater value*', namely what he would obtain in return, 'first of all a value equal to … in total the capital he had employed' and subsequently a '*surplus* of goods he called his profit'.[155] Here Sismondi opposes the idea, widespread then and later that the capitalist's profit derives *from circulation* and, as a result, from what the capitalist sells for a higher price than he paid for it; that, in a word, he sells above the value of the commodity (profit upon alienation),[156] Sismondi draws out the possibility of the capitalist making a profit even when he sells the commodity *according* to its value, that is to say, at the cost price measured by labour. 'He does not profit because his enterprise produced much more than its costs, but because he does not pay all the costs.' 'The advantage of an employer of labour is often nothing else than the plunder of the worker he hired.'[157] However, not only is the new capital *born* from the exploitation

153 Sismondi 1837, p. 22; Sismondi 1991d, pp. 62, 80, 81, 83. So Marx's critique does not apply to Sismondi: 'These bourgeois economists … instinctively and rightly saw that it was very dangerous to penetrate too deeply into the burning question of the origin of surplus value', Marx 1976b, pp. 651–2.

154 Sismondi 1991d, p. 83.

155 Sismondi 1991d, pp. 81, 83. [Grossman's emphasis.]

156 [English in Grossman's original text.]

157 Sismondi 1991d, p. 83.

of the labour of others,[158] but the already existing capital is likewise *preserved* by this exploitation. '[A]ll wealth which one does not wish to destroy, must be exchanged against a future wealth that labour must produce. Wages were the price at which the rich man obtained the poor man's labour in exchange.'[159] Thanks to that alone, capital 'employed ... to feed his productive workers ... was a permanent, multiplying value which did not perish anymore'. This value was detached from its material substratum, 'it remained like a metaphysical and nonsubstantial quantity'. Thus the real function of capital consists in the fact that, in the hands of the capitalist, it becomes a 'fruit-bearing portion of accumulated wealth',[160] an abstract value detached from its material base and constantly engendering a new value: it is a 'multiplying value'.

Here we have the theory of 'surplus value' set out with regard to both form and content, with a precision that nobody before Karl Marx had achieved. Sismondi explains here not only the particular forms of surplus value, rent, profit or interest etc., but he considers it in its general and not yet differentiated form, and seeks its origin not in the sphere of circulation but in that of *production*.

It is from this theoretical standpoint that Sismondi evaluates the ideology of unlimited labour and of endless production as propagated by the classical school. 'Modern economists ... do not cease to encourage nations to produce.' They forget that 'man does not tire himself, except to rest thereafter'. Now, in the capitalist system, things are quite different, because 'today effort is separated from reward: it is not the same man who works and then rests; but it is because one man labours that the other can rest'.[161]

So it is only in this system based on 'the cooperation of the two classes of citizens with opposing interests ... I mean the class of proprietors of accumulated labour ... and the class of men who have only their natural strength' that superfluous production is possible.[162] If everyone had to devote their own labour to their luxury items, 'there would not be one [manual worker] who would hesitate to choose less luxury and more leisure'. 'Luxury is only possible if it is bought with the labour of others'. So luxury is possible only because workers 'produce wealth, and themselves obtain scarcely any share of it'.[163]

158 As we can see, Franz Oppenheimer is mistaken when he claims that Marx is the first 'who recognised capital as a social relationship when *all his predecessors* had regarded it as a *thing*', Oppenheimer 1919, p. 92. [German in Grossman's original text].

159 Sismondi 1991d, p. 82.

160 Sismondi 1991d, p. 81.

161 Sismondi 1991d, p. 74.

162 Sismondi 1991d, p. 577 [and Sismondi 1827, p. 347. The published English translation has been modified to correct a serious inaccuracy.]

163 Sismondi 1991d, pp. 75, 285. [Translator's interpolation.]

Without any doubt, the theory of exploitation and of unequal distribution that is set out here is, by its purely objective economic argument, the product of a mature theoretical analysis, much better than the views of the contemporary English 'egalitarian socialists' such as William Thompson, [John Francis] Bray, [John] Gray and [Thomas] Hodgskin, who are not free from ethical judgement. But despite all the originality of the conceptions set out here, nothing would be more false than to claim that Sismondi saw the cause of crises in unequal distribution and in the underconsumption of the working masses and that he should be given credit for first propounding the theory which [Karl] Rodbertus took up in Germany a quarter of a century later.[164] Sismondi's analysis penetrates much more deeply into the very essence of the economic system based on exchange.

As in the capitalist system based on wage labour, labour itself (the vital force) has become a commodity that is bought and sold and at the same time the valuation of labour operates as on the commodity market, in terms of money, that is in abstract value; all the disruptions arising from the application of this *changing unit of measurement*, which we have observed on the commodity market, also appear on the labour market and thus merely accentuate the general anarchy of production. In the 'pure' capitalist system analysed by Sismondi, which is composed, as we know, solely of capitalists and workers, the former possess, at the end of the period of production A, all the product created by the latter during this period. Part of this product serves for the reproduction of fixed capital expended on this production, the remainder being given over to the consumption of capitalists and workers. Now this part of production, destined for the maintenance of workers in the future period of production B, possesses, since it results from production during period A, an exchange value determined by the labour used in producing it, and suffices to employ a specific number of workers in the given labour. But this workers' wage is a changing quantity taking into account their competition, that is to say, taking into account the fact that, just as on the commodity market nobody has fixed the number of producers required in a certain branch, so on the labour market nobody fixes the number of workers necessary for production. If in period B there are too many workers in relation to the capitalists' demand, their wage, that is the value of labour (the vital force), is lowered. 'If the value of his labour should be determined by competition, this value could diminish endlessly.'[165] Therefore this same part of the annual product of period A, destined for the maintenance of workers, is

164 [Rodbertus 1898.]

165 Sismondi 1991d, p. 321.

now, in period B, sufficient to pay a greater number of workers and by this very fact to absorb a greater quantity of labour. 'Wages do not represent an absolute quantity of labour, but only a quantity of goods which has sufficed to maintain the workers in the previous year.' Given the changed value of labour (of labour power) 'the same quantity of provisions will set in motion, in the following year, a larger or smaller amount of labour'.[166] The source of the disruption of economic equilibrium results precisely from the fact that in employing workers use has been made of an abstract measure of exchange values. The number of workers necessary to create the specific quantity of necessary products is in fact at the given moment a fixed amount, depending on the available technology and entirely independent of the level of the wage. But instead of this natural regulator, we use exchange value to establish the number of workers necessary.

> It is the income of the past year which must pay for the output of this year: it is a *predetermined* quantity which serves as a standard for the *undefined* quantity of labour *to come*. The error of those who urge an unlimited production comes from their mistaking this past income for future income.[167]

Therefore, although he does not need a greater number of workers, every capitalist who possesses a capital enlarges production in proportion to the cheapness of the labour force. 'The masters are persuaded to produce an output, not because the consumer asks them for it, but because the workers offer to them to do it at a lower price.'[168] The natural measure for fixing the number of workers necessary has been replaced by abstract value. *Wertrechnung* has been substituted for *Naturalrechnung*.[169] In total, an excessive number of workers are employed on a reduced wage; total annual production increases, although demand has not changed; the total income of the working class is reduced. Result: overproduction, crisis.

So we see that the mechanism that we have just described has nothing in common with the question of the unequal distribution of wealth, nor yet with underconsumption by the workers. Far from that being the case, intensified underconsumption is the *result* and not the *cause* of the crisis. On the other hand, the disproportion in production is the consequence of the application of

166 Sismondi 1991d, p. 93.

167 Sismondi 1991d, p. 104. [Grossman's emphasis.]

168 Sismondi 1991b, p, 635.

169 ['*Wertrechnung*' means 'calculation of value'; '*Naturalrechnung*' means 'calculation in kind'.]

a changing abstract measure to regulate the size of the productive apparatus in relation to needs – exchange value and not a natural measure: the quantity of necessary real goods, consequently the necessary quantity of labour power. '*It is the confusion between the estimation of a use value and that of an exchange value which is at the heart of the deception of modern systems of chrematistics*.'[170]

∴

The results which we have arrived at are entirely different from perspectives that have previously been accepted. Capitalism is an economic form in which all economic categories appear in the form of exchange value. But this form of exchange value is only accidental, only belonging to a certain historical period and in no way constitutes the real substance of these categories. Thus, for example, the category of income appears in the exchange system in the form of a specific exchange value. But the category of income in no way depends on this form. It is an absolute category, belonging to every sort of organisation of labour, hence also to the system without exchange. In this system, 'there is no numerical price, since there is no exchange as yet; and nevertheless the idea of income is developed there much more clearly than in our complex societies'. This income consists of 'a specific *quantity* of food, clothing and furniture'.[171] And it is only the introduction of an abstract exchange value, measured by labour, in the capacity of a regulator of production, which has brought constant disruptions and upheavals into all economic relations. Constant technical upheavals, by the very nature of things, must in fact lead to a depreciation of labour and *ipso facto* to constant changes in the size of the standard by which we measure the value of all other goods and regulate the scale of their production. Thus instead of a proportional relation between production and demand, a constant disproportion between them necessarily appears.[172]

∴

It is a curious fact that these ideas of Sismondi have not been noticed; our mind is so accustomed to the routine categories in which we think about the capitalist economy that we have not been in a position to understand a system whose conceptions unfold along a quite different course. There is, however, an exception: Karl Marx alone got to the bottom of Sismondi's system and understood it

---

170 Sismondi 1838, p. 229 [Grossman's emphasis.]

171 Sismondi 1837, pp. 137, 138 [Grossman's emphasis.]

172 ['*Ipso facto*' means 'by that very fact'.]

clearly, although he only mentioned it in very brief notes almost in the form of aphorisms. It is true that in *The Poverty of Philosophy* (1847) he calls Sismondi reactionary and in the *Communist Manifesto* the head of the school of petty-bourgeois socialism.[173] But this negative attitude of Marx towards Sismondi's proposals for reform in no way detracts from his correct evaluation of the latter's theoretical ideas. For the English socialists contemporary with Sismondi and still today for many of Marx's epigones and hostile critics, the theory of value based on labour has an ethical character. They see something ennobling in it and at the same time a revolutionary postulate: a just basis for determining the reward for future labour, that is, for the distribution of the social product among the producers.[174] But Sismondi and later Marx see in it, on the contrary, a source of all the ills of current economic organisation. They conceive labour as the source of exchange value, not for ethical reasons but because an objective analysis of the phenomena of value and prices shows, in their view, a causal dependency between labour and value. But they never go so far as to idealise and 'ennoble' labour as the source of exchange value. On the contrary, Sismondi finds in this fact the real source of all ills, of all economic crises; and Marx takes the same position in his polemic with Proudhon. 'Labour time', Marx says, 'serving as the measure of marketable value becomes in this way the law of the continual depreciation of labour ... Sismondi ... sees in this "value constituted" by labour time the source of all the contradictions of modern industry and commerce.'[175] And in agreement with Sismondi, Marx develops the former's thought. '*The continual depreciation of labour is only one side, one consequence of the evaluation of commodities by labour time. The excessive raising of prices, overproduction and many other features of industrial anarchy have their explanation in the mode of evaluation.*'[176] 'Instead of a "proportional relation", we have a disproportional relation.'[177]

173 Marx 1976a, p. 137; Marx and Engels 1976, p. 509.

174 'Marx would like to reward every working citizen, if possible, with mathematical precision and believes this goal can be reached if a quantity of goods, as wages, equal to the particular quantity of values each has contributed to the national product, is allocated to every individual.' 'Marx demands that labour will form the measure for the distribution of goods', Kleinwächter 1885, pp. 65, 68. [German in Grossman's original text.] 'Marx's great merit is having uncovered *the world of daily work* ... We are bringing [!] in a new era, an era of detailed democratic work ... social equality is founded on equality of work ... That, I would say, is the significance of Marx's theory of value', Masaryk 1972, p. 237. [German in Grossman's original text. Grossman's emphasis.]

175 Marx 1976a, p. 135. [Grossman's emphasis apart from *depreciation*.]

176 Marx 1976a, p. 136. [Grossman's emphasis.]

177 Marx 1976a, p. 136.

In our view, not enough notice has been taken of this passage, whose connection with the whole of Marx's theory has not been sufficiently brought to light. Crises and overproduction, the relations of economic disproportion, are here, in conformity with Sismondi, deduced not from the unequal distribution of wealth, nor from the fact of the underconsumption of the working class, but rather *from the fundamental fact on* which the whole edifice of the capitalist system rests: that *labour time serves as a measure for exchange value* and that as a result all relations of exchange are based on a variable measure, constantly changing and constantly devaluing. In fact 'every new invention', every perfected machine depreciates labour and, by that very fact, the measure of exchange on which the capitalist system is based. That is why, when large industry has set out systematically to apply these new inventions, these new machines, disturbances have become a necessary and constant phenomenon – hence the criticism that Sismondi directs against machines. And after him Marx: 'With the birth of large-scale industry this correct proportion [between supply and demand] had to come to an end, and production is inevitably compelled to pass in continuous succession through vicissitudes of prosperity, depression, crisis, stagnation, renewed prosperity, and so on'.[178]

Some months later, in the *Communist Manifesto*, Marx declares that Sismondi's concrete proposals are reactionary and simultaneously utopian. But with a flattering deference which is very unusual in his writings, Marx stresses the 'great acuteness' with which Sismondi analysed the contradictions of the new relations of production. Sismondi's school

> laid bare the hypocritical apologies of economists. It proved, incontrovertibly, the disastrous effects of machinery and division of labour; the concentration of capital and land in a few hands; overproduction and crises; it pointed out the inevitable ruin of the petty bourgeois and peasant, the misery of the proletariat, the anarchy in production, the crying inequalities in the distribution of wealth, the industrial war of extermination between nations ...[179]

Marx comes back to Sismondi again in his *Theories of Surplus Value*, written around 1865.[180] 'Sismondi', he says,

---

178 Marx 1976a, p. 137.

179 Marx and Engels 1976, pp. 509–10.

180 [Subsequent investigations have identified 1861–63 as the period during which Marx wrote the 'Economic manuscript of 1861–63', Marx 1988a, 1989b, 1989c, 1991b, 1994, which was the basis for the posthumously published *Theories of Surplus Value*, edited by Karl Kautsky.]

> is profoundly conscious of the contradictions in capitalist production; he is aware that … contradictions of use value and exchange value, commodity and money, purchase and sale, capital and wage labour, etc., assume ever greater dimensions as productive power develops. He is particularly aware of the fundamental contradiction: on the one hand, unrestricted development of the productive power and increase of wealth which, at the same time, consists of commodities and must be turned into cash; on the other hand, the system is based on the fact that the mass of producers is restricted to the necessaries. Hence, according to Sismondi, crises are not accidental, as Ricardo maintains, but essential outbreaks – occurring on a large scale and at definite periods – of the immanent contradictions.[181]

'*Sismondi was epoch-making in political economy* because he had an inkling of this contradiction.'[182] Likewise in *A Contribution to the Critique of Political Economy* (1859) Marx, clearly making the connection with Sismondi's analysis of the definition of 'socially necessary' labour, stresses Sismondi's conception of 'the antithesis of use value and exchange value'.[183]

Even more important than these critical commentaries by Marx is the positive theory which he formulated in *A Contribution to the Critique of Political Economy* and later in *Capital*, which for its part is only the deeper and more complete development of the conception which we already find briefly stated in Sismondi in his account of the contradiction between use value and exchange value.

In view of the preceding, [Charles] Andler's efforts to show the indirect influence on Marx of the epigones of Sismondi: [Eugène] Buret, [François] Vidal and [Constantin] Pecqueur[184] seem superfluous, since it is possible to show the direct influence of Sismondi himself.

But the problem entails defining the nature of this influence. Can we agree with Rist, when he claims that of all the ideas Marx borrows from Sismondi, the most important is that of the *concentration* of fortunes among a small number of property owners and the growing proletarianisation of the working masses? According to Rist 'this conception is the pivot of the *Manifesto* and forms a part of the very foundation of Marxian collectivism … [and is]

181 Marx 1989c, pp. 247–8.
182 Marx 1989c, p. 393. [Grossman's emphasis.]
183 Marx 1987a, p. 300.
184 Andler 1901, pp. 110, 175.

borrowed from Sismondi'.[185] Nothing could be more wrong. The concentration of fortunes and the proletarianisation of the working masses is in no way a theoretical *idea* but is an empirical observation of the effects of economic evolution frequently commented upon from the middle of the eighteenth century onwards.[186] Marx had no need to borrow from Sismondi facts which were established by the industrial statistics of contemporary England. But what Rist does not see, what he does not understand, are the deep *causes* which necessarily conditioned this concentration of wealth at one pole and the poverty of the working classes at the other. What Sismondi proposes to do is precisely to *explain* these phenomena. Just as on this point Sismondi's fundamental idea has not been understood, has not even been noticed, likewise the genetic link between these conceptions of Sismondi and Marx's fundamental conception has not been noticed.

3 Sismondi's Social Policy – Conclusions

Attention has often been drawn to the inconsistency of Sismondi's conclusions and the contradictory nature of the means he proposed: he has sometimes been seen as the representative of the illusions of the petty bourgeoisie, sometimes as a timorous reformer who aims to get rid of 'the abuses' of the present system without wishing to shake its foundations.

We have tried to show that Sismondi's strength and originality lie primarily in his theoretical analysis: he explains and understands the capitalist mechanism, while social policy has only a very modest place in his thought. Certainly, Sismondi never went so far as to make the practical conclusions drawn from his theory immediately concrete in a *clear program of action*. On the contrary he proclaimed that 'one can never rely with any certitude on even the best-established theories'.[187] This conviction made him cautious as far as programs were concerned and forced him to restrict his proposals to the directly felt needs of the time. Moreover clearly formulating programs of action for the future would have been difficult at a time when the capitalist system was only just emerging from the old organisation.

But is it true, as Andler and Gonnard insist, that all Sismondi's reforming thought could be reduced to the proposal for 'insurance legislation', for a 'pro-

185 Rist 1915, p. 198. [Editor's interpolation.]

186 'Wealth ... accumulates gradually in a small number of hands; to favour a few skilful citizens, all the rest are reduced to indigence', Holbach 1773b, p. 74.

187 Sismondi 1991b, p. 332.

fessional guarantee':[188] that Sismondi was *merely* concerned to restore to the worker protection comparable to that which the guilds had provided; that his positive program of interventionism only asked the state to intervene in order to mitigate the effects of competition, to protect the weak against the strong and in order 'that the trade and agricultural employers should be formed into compulsory insurance societies, required to meet the needs of their workers in case of unemployment or distress'?[189] In face of this opinion we nonetheless think that the position adopted by Sismondi in theory, the main feature of his diagnosis of the disease of the economic system, will facilitate our understanding of the means he proposes to cure it: perhaps then it will appear that the contradictions he is criticised for are sometimes only apparent and that in his proposals there is perhaps something more than what has been noticed thus far.

Sismondi's diagnosis has established that the disproportion of the productive apparatus in relation to demand is the inevitable consequence of the application of the abstract measure, always variable, of exchange value, as the regulator of this production. This measure is the necessary result of the present economic organisation, based on the free competition of an arbitrary number of producers who are independent of each other and remain in a social union solely as a result of exchange. In these conditions, the disturbances and conflicts of the capitalist system cannot be avoided and necessarily occur in the system, just as in the economic doctrine which reflects it there are '*insoluble questions like all those in modern political economy*'. Sometimes, for example, every effort has been made to force the worker to do excessive labour and, at the same time, 'there was no hesitation in condemning him to not working at all'.[190]

The man who characterised the disease in this way, who saw in it the defect which constituted the very foundation of the current system, who, for this reason, criticised the economic science of his time for basing itself on abstract exchange value and thus finding itself in the dead end of 'insoluble questions' – this man was bound to see a remedy in the reconstruction of the very foundation of the current system. If the root of the evil lies in organisation based *on exchange*, with its necessary consequence, an abstract measure of value, then a radical cure can be obtained only by basing the economic organisation on quite different foundations, on movement towards a system *without exchange value*.

188 [i.e. provision of income by employers to employees who are no longer able to work.]
189 Andler 1901, p. 177; Gonnard 1922, p. 213.
190 Sismondi 1837, p. 197. [Grossman's emphasis.]

Is such a program to be found in Sismondi? Did he identify all the implications of the principles which he laid down? We can only affirm one thing with certainty: that Sismondi possessed, if not the *postulation* at least the *ideal* of a better system in the future. Although he has been accused of yearning for a past state of affairs, he says 'I do not desire any part of what has been, but I want something better of what is'. He is interested in the past only as a historian and in order to draw lessons. 'I cannot judge what that is, except by comparing it with the past, and I am far from wanting to restore ancient ruins'. He is equally opposed to the present and his objections are directed against 'the new organisation of society which ... gives [the working man] no guarantee against ... competition'. In defending the ideal which he pursues he cites various sociological arguments, denounces those who consider the defects of the present system to be inevitable and who declare that things must always be the same because this present system cannot be changed. 'It is the belief in a sort of *fatality* which carries us along and a tendency to close our eyes to the precipice we are running towards, as soon as we think we cannot avoid it.'[191] These people are so accustomed to the present system that they cannot even imagine a different one. 'Our senses have become so accustomed to this new organisation of society, to that universal competition which degenerates into hostility between the wealthy class and the working class, that we can no longer imagine any *other type of existence*.'[192]

In opposition to this fatalism, resulting from the conviction that the existing system cannot be changed, Sismondi *describes the historical evolution of systems*. Society has the potential for modification, 'for the organisation of human society is our own work'. Contemporary organisation is, in fact, something very recent. 'This organisation is so new that it is not even halfway instituted'. So it would be difficult to believe that it will last indefinitely: it has scarcely emerged from former systems which themselves had been modified in their turn. Each of these former systems had become a dominant organisation because it had shown itself to be superior to the system which had immediately preceded it. 'Each of these systems had seemed ... to be an advance towards civilisation ... *Slavery* itself followed a savage condition of universal war ... [and,] following the slaying of prisoners, constituted progress in society.'[193] And it was only in the long term that this system became an obstacle to further progress and contributed to the fall of the ancient world. Then came the feudal period, based

191 Sismondi 1991b, p. 628; Sismondi 1838, p. 335. [Grossman's emphasis.]

192 Sismondi 1991b, p. 628. Sismondi 1837, p. 92. [Grossman's emphasis.]

193 Sismondi 1838, p. 372; Sismondi 1991b, pp. 628, 629. [Grossman's emphasis. Editor's interpolation.]

on *bondage* and *serfdom*. This meant 'an initial betterment in the status of the poor classes'. 'Feudalism had its shining and prosperous period' and it was only in the long term that the feudal system 'became intolerable',[194] for 'social order, threatened so incessantly, cannot be maintained except by violent means'. It then gave way to the system of *corporations* and finally to 'the system *of liberty* we have now ... The revolution is not even half completed.'[195] In face of this historical evolution can we claim that the 'wage labour system' is the final stage of progress, since we cannot imagine that anything better will follow it? 'When these three systems were dominant, likewise nobody conceived what might come next; *similarly the amendment of the existing order would have seemed either impossible or absurd.*' If we base ourselves on the fact that the former systems proved themselves to be disastrous, in short, 'because, after having first done a little good, they later imposed terrible calamities onto the human race, can we then conclude that today we have moved into the true form of society?' From the preceding argument, the conclusion necessarily follows that 'our actual social organisation ... the dependency of the worker'[196] is also historically temporary and will be replaced by a superior system in the future.[197] This will only happen when we 'discover the fundamental evil of the day labour system, as we have discovered the evils of slavery, of serfdom, of guilds'. And it was only in thinking about this future system that Sismondi could say 'A time will doubtless come when our descendants will consider us no less barbarous for having left the working classes without protection than they and we ourselves consider as barbarous those nations which reduced those same classes to slavery.'[198]

That is why Charles Rist tries in vain to interpret Sismondi's thought by arguing that the latter's criticisms are directed against the 'abuses of competition',[199] that he has shown the defects which belong to a period of transition between the old and new forms of social organisation and that the whole substance of his doctrine can be reduced to 'the *protest he makes against the indifference* of the classical school in the face of the evils of these periods of transition'. And Rist adds: 'But Sismondi was a historian. His interest lay primar-

194 Sismondi 1991d, p. 171; Sismondi 1991b, p. 629.

195 Sismondi 1991d, pp. 170; Sismondi 1991b, pp. 629–30. [Grossman's emphasis.]

196 Sismondi 1837, p. 92; Sismondi 1991d, pp. 557–8. [Grossman's emphasis.]

197 Marx rightly points out that Sismondi had 'the inkling that *new* forms of the appropriation of wealth must correspond to productive forces ... that the bourgeois forms are only transitory and contradictory forms', Marx 1989c, p. 248 [Grossman's emphasis.]

198 Sismondi 1991b, p. 629; Sismondi 1837, p. 93.

199 Rist 1915, p. 193.

ily in those *periods of transition which formed the exit from one regime and the entrance into another*, and which involved so much suffering for the innocent.'[200]

To write in these terms is to obscure the very meaning of Sismondi's thought. No, he is not criticising the periods of transition from one system to another but rather the very foundations of the present system, not the 'abuses' of competition but the very principle of competition. Overproduction with all its consequences is not a temporary phenomenon but 'the satiation of markets is on the contrary the inevitable result of a system to which everyone rushes', it is the unavoidable effect of the 'fundamental evil of the day labour system'. Hence this is not a short-term phenomenon of the period of transition between the old and new organisations but a phenomenon rooted in the defective structure of the new system which is still establishing itself and will make itself felt more and more as this system develops and becomes the dominant economic form. This is what Sismondi expresses with the greatest possible clarity in his polemic with Jean-Baptiste Say in 1824: 'For seven years I have pointed to that sickness of the body social, and for seven years it has not ceased to grow. I cannot see in such extended suffering *the frictions that always accompany change* and … I believe I have shown that the ills we experience are *the necessary consequences of the flaws of our system*, and that they are not yet at an end.' And some years later, in his *Studies*, Sismondi can claim that the disease is making fresh progress and that although we are in a period of rare prosperity, 'its only effect is to continually worsen the position of the poor classes'.[201]

If, therefore, it seems certain that Sismondi foresees, in the future, the need for a system that is better than the present one based on competition, for the particular reasons which we will set out below, he never draws a picture of this system. Anticipating the objection that he should 'show what remained to do', he states: 'We would want permission to convince the economists … that their science hereafter follows a *false* path. But we have not enough confidence in ourselves to show them what would be the *truth*.' Yet in his eyes shines the ideal of a better system in the future and he is not merely thinking of small corrections to the present social order, this omission results precisely from the fact that he insists on the *difficulty of conceiving* this future system. 'It is one of the greatest efforts to which we can force our mind to visualise the actual structure of society. Who would then be the man enlightened enough to imagine *a*

200 Rist 1915, p. 181. [Grossman's emphasis.]

201 Sismondi 1991d, p. 280; Sismondi 1991c, p. 647; Sismondi 1838, p. 334. [Apart from 'the frictions', Grossman's emphasis.]

structure that does not yet exist, to see the future where we have already so much trouble to see the present?' Conceiving of a completely different system alone is difficult, while conceiving of detailed corrections would not be difficult at all. However, anticipating the tactics of socialism in the future, Sismondi merely shows the necessity of the advent of a superior system in the future but at the same time he wants to confine himself to 'the analysis of the system we have taken up' – 'without being distracted by a comparison with an *entirely imaginary theory*' and 'before dreaming of what will have to *replace*' the existing system.[202]

What could drive Sismondi to act in this way? We have already pointed out his scientific caution about formulating a program of action which, at most, could only have been 'an entirely imaginary theory'. But Sismondi mentions another reason, an even more serious one. For him, as a theoretician, the problem is above all to explain the existing mechanism and to discover its 'fundamental evil', since as we know that is, in his opinion, the necessary condition for achieving the future system. That is why Sismondi does not want to indicate concrete means of change. 'If I presented here what I consider to be a remedy for the actual ills of society, criticism would abandon the *examination* … of such ills, in order to judge my *remedy*, and to probably condemn it, and the question of the balance of consumption with production would never be decided.'[203] This passage justifies us in concluding that Sismondi has what he considers a 'remedy' for the ills of the social system and, if he does not set it out, it is solely in order not to distract attention from his theoretical aim: to establish the diagnosis of the sickness from which the system of his time is suffering. Moreover, the fact that concrete plans for remedying the situation had little success is demonstrated by those of the reformers of this time, Charles Fourier and Just Muiron, whose works had recently been published. So it is precisely because he does not go into detail that Sismondi is superior to these utopian socialists. While they draw up fanciful plans, Sismondi *through his critique undermines the very foundations of the system of his time* and indicates that 'undoubtedly there is something wrong in the social order'. For Sismondi this critique of the elements which make up this system is for the moment the essential thing, by reason of the passivity of the human mind which is afraid of straying from principles, once they have been accepted. '[W]e have to fight against this laziness of the human mind, which, having reached the last results of a science, refuses to return to its first principles and to shake the axioms on which it is based.'[204]

---

202 Sismondi 1991b, p. 634. [Grossman's emphasis.]
203 Sismondi 1991b, pp. 634–5. [Grossman's emphasis.]
204 Sismondi 1838, p. 334.

Obviously the critique of these basic principles of the existing system, in itself, highlights in broad outline *the positive direction* of Sismondi's thought. He is thinking of an ideal organisation in which *competition* among producers independent from each other will be replaced by a *rational regulation* of the scale of production, according to the extent of need, independently of exchange and the oscillations of market prices. 'It would not suit national security if its subsistence were to depend on the fluctuations of the market', he says with reference to agricultural production. We have seen above that it is on this *proportionality of the process of production to the needs* of society that Sismondi's *New Principles* is based and that this is the key point on which he differs fundamentally from Say, Ricardo, Malthus and McCulloch. It is this ideal of a well-proportioned economic system which inspires Sismondi to this comparison, 'All movements in society are linked together; one follows from the other, as the various movements of the gears of a watch'.[205] In this well-regulated system, without free competition, human activity will find an outlet, not in the struggle of men against men but in the struggle to dominate nature. 'It is not that there is no room for the progress of human effort in the creation of wealth every time that ... man battles against nature, and not with another man.'[206]

In an ideal system without competition, in which production is organised systematically in each of its branches, any change, such as for example the extension of production, cannot be brought about in one branch to the exclusion of another but must be achieved systematically for all branches, if the equilibrium of the system is not to be upset. 'When [the progress of wealth] ... is *well-proportioned*, when no one of its parts follows a precipitous course, it spreads universal well-being; but *if any one of its gears completes its actions earlier than all the others, there will be suffering*.'[207]

---

205 Sismondi 1991d, p. 203; Sismondi 1991b, p. 637.

206 Sismondi 1991d, p. 306.

207 Sismondi 1991d, p. 306. [Grossman's emphasis.] The arithmetical diagram in the essay against Ricardo [Sismondi 1991b, pp. 621–7] is nothing but an attempt to establish in a precise manner, *exactly determined quantitative proportions* for the extent of production in each of the branches of social activity. By accepting that, given a particular technology and a level of wages, agriculture employs ten people, Sismondi concludes that, to obtain equilibrium in the system, it is necessary to determine the dimensions of production in such a way that the industrial capitalist employs 23⅓ workers in industry producing indispensible articles and 4⅔ workers in industry producing luxury articles, which together with the 10 agricultural workers and two entrepreneurs makes a total of 40 persons. It is only in these exactly determined proportions of the various branches of production and in the condition of constant value that equilibrium between consumption and production would be possible. But this constant value is not compatible with the exchange system where value, as a result of ceaseless technical revolutions, is subject to endless

Obviously this quantitative determination of the proportions of various branches of production cannot be the product of chance but must rather be the result of concerted action by the central authority: Sismondi therefore requires that the government should halt 'a *disordered* expansion'.[208] According to him 'the task of government should be to moderate these movements, *in order to equalise* them'.[209] Envisaged from this point of view and under the influence of the Italian economic tradition of the eighteenth century,[210] political economy would become 'a science of government' in the same sense as Saint-Simon understands it when he speaks of the need to replace the present system 'by an administrative system' or, again, what the German theoreticians understood by *Verwaltungswirtschaft*.[211] Chrematistics, that is the free activity of individual producers, is replaced by a systematic *regulation* of the economy according to the principle of non-exchange, in other words by 'household management' in the Aristotelian sense of *oikonomia*. 'We consider political economy, the management of the house and the community, as being essentially the science of government. It amounts to ... the *exposition of the plan of management* or influence which will be the most advantageous to society.'[212]

This general principle, which Sismondi does not set out in detail, entails the ideal he aims at and, in the system of his thought, constitutes the *maximum program*, the fundamental 'remedy' for the sickness he identifies in the economic system. If Sismondi does not indicate remedies, his caution is mainly related to this part of his ideas, to this maximum program. Should we see a contradiction if, in face of the statement that he does not want to indicate remedies, he nonetheless indicates them repeatedly and in places only a few pages apart? For example when he proposes to abolish all laws which interfere with the division of inheritances, or which protect employers' organisations against workers or

fluctuations, every time a technical improvement increasing the productivity of labour is introduced, and by this very fact this labour is depreciated in the given branch. As Sismondi shows, overproduction and disruption of equilibrium must and do in fact result, although, according to our author [Ricardo], this is not possible for the system based on exchange. Therefore, in opposition to the classical economists, Sismondi proves that in a system based on the abstract measure of exchange value a *constant disproportion* must result. That is why he attempts to fix the proportion of production in each branch according to a different principle, without having recourse to the measure of exchange value, and notably according to *the principle of the real proportions* of the extent of the productive apparatus in relation to the extent of needs.

208 Sismondi 1991d, p. 312 [Grossman's emphasis.]
209 Sismondi 1991d, p. 306 [Grossman's emphasis.]
210 Gonnard 1922, p. 206.
211 ['*Verwaltungswirtschaft*' means 'Administered economy'.]
212 Sismondi 1838, p. 238. [Grossman's emphasis.]

when he demands laws which could oblige the employer to guarantee the subsistence of the worker he employs, etc? Or again when he proposes to guarantee every worker an assured ownership of his own labour in order to put limits on competition?[213] Let us examine the question more closely.

In Sismondi's theoretical thought, the real cure for the disease is possible only through a change in the structure of the present system. For him it is the only effective means of cleansing. Sismondi does not develop this question – we have already examined why – but he is convinced that this idea will be victorious in the future and he prepares this victory by enlightening public opinion theoretically, while confining himself to posing practical conclusions for the present. 'But *for as long as the present organisation persists*, as long as the existence of the poor person is abandoned to the effects of free competition',[214] it is necessary above all to *alleviate the effects* of this system by creating obstacles to the natural tendencies originating in this system, for these obstacles 'give time ... allow to those who have been hurt the opportunity to *recover from their wounds*'. Sismondi recommends to the economists 'that they should leave the generations made superfluous time *to recover*'. For '*first, one has to think of those who suffer, and then worry about the future*'. And since, according to him, those who expand large-scale production, with a view to personal profit, are especially the big capitals, since above all 'it is colossal fortunes which disturb the equilibrium of society', he finds there a reason for 'legislation to put obstacles both to the accumulation and the amalgamation of capitals'.[215]

So we see that Sismondi's struggle against big capital is in no way inspired by the desire for a more equal distribution of wealth or by any aspiration for the organisation of medieval guilds. 'No, I do not desire any part of what has been ... I am far from wanting to restore ancient ruins.' 'It is not in any case the guilds that should be re-established.' Moreover, these could not be a solution for workers employed in mechanised manufacturing industry, because 'since the great perfection of machines, all those who worked almost like machines have had their influence diminished'.[216] Repeatedly he protests that he has no intention of giving up all technical advances, machines and inventions. If, nonetheless, as we have seen, he wants to create 'constraints' on big capital, it is because of his deep pessimism, of the conviction that as long as the system of free competition, the system of wage labour survives, economic disruptions are

213 Sismondi 1991b, p. 636; Sismondi 1991d, p. 324.

214 Sismondi 1837, p. 113. [Grossman's emphasis.]

215 Sismondi 1837, pp. 110, 113; Sismondi 1991d, p. 332; Sismondi 1838, p. 459. [Grossman's emphasis.]

216 Sismondi 1991b, p. 628; Sismondi 1991d, p. 323.

inevitable, that no cure could be found for them and that we must, by means of constraints, slow down the course of this development, only in the interests of the victims of 'a system that oppresses'.[217]

It is only when one adopts this standpoint that Sismondi becomes comprehensible when he says: 'We agree, in fact: to such extreme ills, we can offer only *palliatives* which must seem very much out of proportion'. And a little later, he insists again: 'To bring a remedy for such grave ills in the present … we know only of palliatives. The first and most important thing is *to enlighten opinion* …', and later he proposes means to delay development, that is, to attenuate disastrous effects. In this respect he says 'that the remedies we are proposing are in no way illegal, in no way revolutionary and in no way fanciful or requiring a new organisation of society'.[218] On the basis of these statements it has been denied that Sismondi had an ideal transcending the framework of the existing system. But the means he proposes can only be called palliatives by someone who assumes that no effective remedy exists or who, like Sismondi, recognises, in principle, the historical necessity of evolution towards a higher form of organisation and considers all other means as ineffective or as palliatives which are only partially effective. These palliatives are Sismondi's *minimum program*, 'for as long as the present organisation survives' and that is why from this point of view 'the first and most important remedy is to enlighten opinion'. In the first place it is therefore a question of clearly realising the causes of the sickness, of the structural defects of the present system and that is the prior condition for any future fundamental reorganisation.

It is precisely this pessimism which marks Sismondi's interventionism. Rist in fact is wrong to claim that Sismondi was the first interventionist. The mercantilists had also been interventionists. The essential difference consists in the quite distinct way of conceiving the *dynamic* of the economic mechanism. James Steuart, the most eminent representative of mercantilism in the eighteenth century, appeals at every moment for intervention by the authorities. And he does so because, he claims, government intervention can and must *maintain the equilibrium of the economic mechanism*. Sismondi's interventionism has an entirely different character. Half a century of capitalist development had dispelled these illusions and Sismondi observes that the equilibrium of this mechanism is impossible. If 'we invoke almost constantly that intervention of the government', it is merely to *protect the victims of the ills*. 'We see the government above all as the protector of the weak against the strong, the defender

217 Sismondi 1991d, p. 285.
218 Sismondi 1838, pp. 335, 363, 372. [Grossman's emphasis.]

of him who cannot defend himself.'[219] And that is where Sismondi differs from the future party of social reform.

This party demanded the reform of the existing system while preserving the foundations of that system, whereas for Sismondi these were only half-measures since for him it was the foundations themselves which were defective. The reforming school saw the state as an institution above classes, whose task was to safeguard the totality of social interests. On this point too Sismondi is pessimistic. For him *the state is the defender of the possessing class*. 'The government, which most often protects the established order without even examining the rights of the parties, [gives] at all times powerful support to the haves against the have-nots.'[220] The government gives its assistance to the capitalists against the workers. 'While these unfortunates fight for a wage on which their lives and those of their children depend ... soldiers and constables ... watch them, who await eagerly the first disturbance to hand them over to the courts and their severe retribution.' 'The greater part of the charge arising from social establishments, is destined to defend the rich against the poor.'[221]

These considerations of Sismondi on governmental power show that he was far from idealising the current state as the school of social reform would later do.

If, however, he advocates state intervention in favour of the weak he nonetheless sees in it only *a half-measure for a temporary period*. In principle these disadvantages could only be avoided in a system without competition.

∴

And now to conclude, let us summarise our analysis of Sismondi's work. Can we consider him a socialist? Certainly, if we apply to him the normal criteria for socialism: abolition of the private ownership of the means of production, abolition of the difference between rich and poor – Sismondi *was not a socialist*. It is not that he was a stubborn defender of private property. Far from it. While at this time (1818) Saint-Simon, for example, is proclaiming 'It is on the preservation of the right of property that the existence of society depends',[222] Sismondi in no way recognises the perpetual and sacrosanct right to landed property. 'It must be judged as all the rest of social institutions, by the good or bad that has flowed from them for mankind'. It is '*a gift of society, and in no way*

219 Sismondi 1991d, p. 53.
220 Sismondi 1991d, p. 446. [Translator's interpolation.]
221 Sismondi 1991d, p. 285, 446.
222 Saint-Simon 1841b, p. 265.

a natural right which pre-existed'. As a historian, he knows that many peoples did not have private ownership of land, that the institution of property is the child of historical evolution. The ownership of land is 'not based on a principle of *justice*, but on a principle of *public utility*'. Hence society can determine the conditions on which it entrusts property to individuals, it can regulate them. If the owners act against the interests of society, society 'must submit property in land to legislation which will indeed bring about *the general good*'.[223]

Yet despite these ideas about property and although, as we have seen, his ideal is a system without competition, he never goes so far as to conceive the suppression of private property; he never imagines that the disruptions caused by exchange and exchange itself are phenomena indissolubly linked to an economic organisation based on individual property.

Despite this attitude with regard to individual property and setting the question of property to one side, Sismondi *constructs the ideal of the system without competition*, consciously and systematically regulating the scale of production in relation to the extent of needs. But we will be obliged to see Sismondi as a socialist if in order to analyse socialism as an aim, we adopt a different criterion 'which characterises economic socialism: the condemnation of competition and the appeal to a rational coordination of economic elements which is systematic rather than instinctive'.[224] After having enquired on what basis a new organisation can be established, Sismondi ends up with the truly original doctrine that such a rationally coordinated organisation is not possible for a system based on the abstract measure of exchange value as a regulator of the extent of production. It is precisely on this point that the critique of the existing system and the positive economic views he opposes to it are much more profound and far-reaching than the theoretical statements of the utopian socialists of his time. These socialists, like John Gray, Robert Owen, or later Bray, and, during the 1848 revolution, Arthur Bonnard and Proudhon, attack only money and aim to abolish only the 'privileges' of precious metals, *while preserving trade based on exchange and the exchange* of commodities. They formulate plans for exchange banks where the role of metal money is replaced by a currency based on labour – for example the plans for certificates of value issued by the National Bank, devised by John Gray in 1831, or Owen's Labour Exchange in 1832, Bray's Central Bank in 1839[225] and then, during the February Revolution in 1848, Proudhon's well-known scheme and Bonnard's Exchange Bank

---

223 Sismondi 1991d, pp. 132, 138, 139. [Grossman's emphasis.]

224 Gonnard 1922, p. 25.

225 See Gray 1831; Bray 1839. [Marx 1976a, pp. 138–44; Marx 1987a, pp. 320–3.]

at Marseilles.[226] They thought that by basing exchange, not on metal money but rather on labour, they were introducing a 'fixed and invariable' measure of value[227] and were thereby ensuring that the worker received the full fruits of his labour. On this point, as we have seen, Sismondi clearly parts company with the utopian socialists and demonstrates – as Marx would later – that, since labour is the source of value, this value cannot be fixed, that it must necessarily be subject to endless fluctuations and for this reason provoke upheavals in society. Likewise, Sismondi does not confine himself to merely suppressing monetary exchange but also wants to get rid of all exchange of values. He proposes to destroy not only money as a measure but all measurement of value and to replace this regulator of production by the regulation of the extent of production in the form of real proportions, in natural conditions. In this respect then Sismondi's idea is deeper and more consistent than that of the banks of the 'exchange socialists'.[228]

This is the result of views, according to which the system which he foresees and conceives would not entail the elaboration of concrete plans for remedies, of exchange banks or small communes, as were dreamt of by certain rationalist socialists, like Owen and Fourier, but would have to be the transformation of the present capitalist organisation according to new principles of construction in the interests of the toiling classes. 'I would seek', he said, 'means to guarantee the fruits of labour to those who labour, to make the machine benefit the one who sets the machine to work.'[229] He considers the achievement of this proposition to be impossible within a system based on the measurement of exchange value and ends up with the conception of a system without exchange value. Sismondi strives to posit this new principle for constructing the future system, not by way of an arbitrary creative fantasy but through the analysis, both of the existing system and of former historical economic formations. In this regard we should see in Sismondi's analysis the first attempts at the method later applied by scientific socialism.

---

226 Gide and Rist 1915, p. 316; Knies 1885, p. 240. [In 1849, Proudhon's scheme culminated in the People's Bank, which rapidly failed.]

227 Muckle 1920, p. 53. All saw in labour taken as the basis of exchange the 'revolutionary theory' of the emancipation of the proletariat from all exploitation. Marx replied to them: 'Thus relative value, measured by labour time, is *inevitably the formula of the present enslavement of the worker*, instead of being, as M. Proudhon would have it, the "revolutionary theory" of the emancipation of the proletariat.' [Marx 1976a, p. 125. Grossman's emphasis.]

228 Aucuy 1908.

229 Sismondi 1837, p. 105.

However, Sismondi evades the problem and does not examine how it is possible to abolish all measurement of exchange value as the regulator of the extent of production without abolishing private property. It is precisely on this point that we can apply to Sismondi the legitimate criticism of Marx against the attempts of the utopian socialists to abolish metal money, that 'goods are to be *produced as commodities*, but *not exchanged* as commodities'.[230] Marx ridicules those utopian socialists who wish to retain commodities but not money,[231] and he asserts that between the commodity and money there is an '*inevitable correlation*'.[232] 'Beneath the invisible measure of value lurks hard money.'[233] So in this respect Sismondi's idea goes further than the idea of the exchange socialists but it too stops half-way. Thus Marx's criticism is quite justified when he states that Sismondi 'forcefully *criticises* the contradictions of bourgeois production but *does not understand them*'.[234]

Sismondi does not tell us who will bring about or facilitate this evolution, this economic reconstruction of society. He does not address any social class; the proletariat in whose interests he was fighting was in his day a passive mass that was merely wretched. One can apply to Sismondi what Marx said of the theoreticians of the proletariat: 'So long as they look for science and merely make systems ... they see in poverty nothing but poverty, without seeing in it the revolutionary, subversive side.'[235] In this respect Sismondi is better than Owen. Moreover Sismondi's superiority to Saint-Simon is shown by the fact that, while the latter foregrounds the struggle of 'industry' against feudal reaction – and this 'industry' includes not only the most heterogeneous spheres of agriculture and commerce but also factory owners and workers, in short, it conceals all the real contradictions existing at that time – Sismondi's opposition is completely modern. With a clarity shown by nobody before him, he draws out the antinomy of the class interests of the property owners and of the wage-earning proletariat, 'so does Sismondi denounce large industrial capital',[236] and with a penetrating critique he denounces *capitalism*, the scientific discovery of which should be attributed to him.

Certainly Sismondi often deviates from the line which we have attempted to characterise; it would be very easy to draw this out and to show contradic-

230 Marx 1987a, p. 322. [Grossman's emphasis.]
231 Marx 1987a, p. 308.
232 Marx 1987a, p. 323. [Grossman's emphasis.]
233 Marx 1987a, p. 308.
234 Marx 1989c, p. 248. [Marx only emphasised '*criticises*' and '*understand*'].
235 Marx 1976a, pp. 177–8.
236 Marx 1987a, p. 301.

tions in his fundamental conception. But these deviations merely prove that Sismondi's book is not an academic exercise but is based on living reality. From this heterogeneity of phenomena and in opposition to classical theory, Sismondi has created, in a flash of genius, a homogenous conception on which this heterogeneity of phenomena has here and there left its mark. Whether or not we call him a socialist, his immortal claim to fame in economic science is that he is the first economist to scientifically demonstrate that an economic system based on abstract exchange value, as the sole purpose of production and regulator of it, necessarily leads to disruptions and to 'insoluble questions'. It is on this point that Sismondi's doctrine constitutes one of the most important sources for the genesis of the scientific economic thinking of Karl Marx.

CHAPTER 5

A New Theory of Imperialism and the Social Revolution*

Translated from German by Geoffrey McCormack and Julian Germann

Preliminary Remarks

Outwardly, Sternberg's book, the subject of the following essay, is made up of a *theoretical* and a *historical-descriptive part*, presenting empirical facts from the development of capitalism in the English Empire and India, as well as in Germany, France and the United States of America. The *internal* structure is conceived so that a reserve army and decline in wages, then consequently imperialist war and, in order to prevent it, socialist revolution necessarily emerge from fundamental economic elements of capitalism in its imperialist phase (surplus population, wage labour, crisis), because it is impossible to realise surplus value, due to the lack of non-capitalist markets.

Sternberg describes himself as a follower of the materialist conception of history and dedicates a special chapter to it. The book, which 'is intended to be Marxist', is meant *to affirm 'decisive, fundamental Marxist ideas'* and especially the notion 'that it is necessary not to construct socialism out of one's head, but to identify the forces within capitalism itself that are destined to bring it about'. Thus the author humbly asserts that his book is 'a continuation of Marx's *Capital*'. Soon, however, he changes his mind. He does not want to merely perfect. He feels impelled by the historical situation, rather, to become a pioneer. For nothing remains of Marx's system that deserves to be carried forward. After all, Marx is said to have conceptualised his book on a premise *'that had to preclude him from recognising essential relationships'*, namely that there are no non-capitalist markets, whereas Sternberg knows that 'since capitalist production began, non-capitalist areas have played a decisive role'. It is thus understandable that Marx provided and could not but provide an absolutely false representation of capitalism. As a consequence, his whole system is false, every building block of his edifice is affected by the existence of non-capitalist areas: the accumulation of capital itself as well as capitalist

* [Originally published as Grossmann 1928a.]

crisis, the industrial reserve army, wages, the labour movement and especially revolution. The very problems that Marx dealt with 'are most strongly modified'.[1]

These statements of Sternberg already demonstrate that *Marx's name is being badly abused here*, as in Sternberg's text all of Marx's theories are declared false and are opposed. 'I abstain from agreement with the historical Marx', he declares.[2] While not one of the basic ideas of Marx remains, the living Marx is still said to be on Sternberg's side.

Now *the real structure* of Sternberg's book, its real focus, is very different from what he wants us to believe. What he envisages is assembling 'foreign policy, sociology, and economics ... into a complete system'.[3] On the basis of the materialist conception of history, this means nothing other than explaining changes in foreign policy in terms of economic changes. But there is no mention of this in Sternberg. His book is primarily a *politically* tendentious text, which places the necessity of the revolution at the forefront, not in the sense that it is a necessary final result of the historical process, dominated by class struggle, but revolution in the sense of a categorical ethical postulate, the only way to save humanity from falling into historical oblivion. The economic 'explanation' *has no internal relationship with the political thesis of revolution at all*. It is added to the latter for decorative purposes, to give it the appearance of being scientific. All the cant about the importance 'of the materialist conception of history's sociological space [!]'[4] under capitalism cannot conceal this.

It is characteristic that Sternberg is entirely under the sway of the revisionist critique of Marx's system and, although delayed by a whole historical epoch, adheres directly to revisionist lines of reasoning and critique. In a special chapter on 'the self-supercession of revisionism' he does oppose the theory of peaceful transition into socialism. This cannot, however, mislead us about his inner relationship to revisionism. Sternberg has not transcended its horizon and treads entirely in its footsteps. Nowhere even a single independent standpoint; everywhere reeling off criticisms of Marx's individual theories and findings that have been all too familiar for thirty years. These include the weakening of crises under capitalism, asserted by Bernstein; growing decentralisation of ownership as opposed to the increasing concentration of enterprises; weakening of class antagonisms; improvement in the condition of the work-

1 Sternberg 1971, pp. 7, 8, 22, 8.
2 Sternberg 1971, p. 9.
3 Sternberg 1971, p. 246.
4 Sternberg 1971, p. 306.

ing class; growing numbers of capitalist magnates; increases in the numbers of petty-bourgeois elements as well as peasant enterprises. In all these questions Sternberg follows Bernstein and delivers his judgement in favour of revisionism *ex post*.[5] 'He [Bernstein] was right, about many of his empirical findings in general, as opposed to those who adhere to Marxist orthodoxy.' *'I acknowledge all these facts unreservedly and consider it mistaken to reconcile them with the remarks made by the historical Marx himself'*.[6]

One sees that Sternberg 'acknowledges' more than simply these 'facts' alone. For while, incidentally, Marx's system might be ingenious, it cannot be reconciled with the facts of reality. However, *suum cuique*.[7] While revisionism derived a justification for its peaceful opportunistic practice from its analysis, the situation is reversed in Sternberg's case. His original achievement is to conclude from the same facts that imperialist wars are inevitable and to preach revolution as the only means to prevent war. Thus while Sternberg differs from revisionism in his conclusions and practical suggestions, theoretically he stands on the same ground and proceeds from the same assumptions. Hence his 'problems' have the same starting point and he has the same 'theoretical' attitude in his relationship with Marx's research; likewise, the same ignorance of the most fundamental premises of Marx's analysis; consequently the same adherence to the superficial; and the same ineptitude, indeed, incapacity, to integrate these empirical facts into Marx's system or into any theoretical system at all. For Sternberg also abandons Marx's system. What he 'acknowledges', apart from the facts, is Marx's method. By using it, he wants to 'systematically integrate' the facts[8] not into Marx's but into his own system. For 'through the integration, *the whole analysis of the capitalist process is shifted*'.[9] But this means nothing other than that Sternberg sets himself the task of overthrowing Marx's system by using Marx's method; beating up Marx with Marx himself. This objective of Sternberg makes it necessary to closely examine his methodical procedure as well as the facts that he cites as decisive.

5 [*'Ex post'* means 'based on past results'.]
6 Sternberg 1971, pp. 246, 255. [Sternberg only emphasised *'historical'*].
7 [*'Suum cuique'* means 'each to his own'.]
8 Sternberg 1971, pp. 246–7.
9 Sternberg 1971, p. 68. [Grossman's emphasis].

1 Sternberg's 'Facts' and Marx's Research Method

Which facts cannot be reconciled with Marx's system?

On this point Sternberg accepts the assertion of revisionism and Franz Oppenheimer, that, according to Marx, the middle strata rapidly melt away. This is Oppenheimer's well-known formulation:

> Marx's prognosis, it is well-known [sic!], rests on the assumption that under the impact of capitalist competition the middle classes rapidly melt away, that not only are artisans, petty trade and the peasantry beaten down by the cheapening of commodities produced by capitalist methods and cast down into the proletariat. The same competition also rages like the plague among the capitalists themselves and carries them off in droves, until finally only a tiny number of capitalist magnates remains.[10]

Sternberg also argues that Marx portrayed the socialist revolution as too easy, too simple, and underestimated counter-revolutionary elements. 'Their number is incomparably larger than Marx assumed, indeed could assume'.[11]

But just where and when did Marx commit this error?

For Sternberg, the evidence is Marx's reproduction schema! It is depicted exactly in the graphic form of an industrial pyramid, in which class stratification is extremely simplified and consists *of just two classes*. The small apex of the pyramid is composed of the thin layer of capitalists. The entire remaining space is occupied by the mass of workers, based on the line A – C, only receiving as wages the costs of reproducing labour power, defined as the minimum for physical existence. There is an empty space between the two classes. Revisionism, however, has discovered *a large mass of intermediate strata* between the proletariat and big capitalists: smaller money capitalists, rentiers, the 'new middle class' (white-collar employees). We know that Sternberg acknowledges these facts 'unreservedly' and inserts them graphically between the two main classes in a second, corrected pyramid, as undeniable proof of the primitiveness of Marx's system, which took no notice of them. And proud of this analysis, Sternberg explains: 'It has become apparent that between the bourgeoisie and the proletariat very important intermediate strata have persisted or arisen'.[12] This same is true, *mutatis mutandis*,[13] of Marx's 'agri-

10 Oppenheimer 1927, p. 499.

11 Sternberg 1971, p. 339.

12 Sternberg 1971, pp. 346, 354.

13 [*'Mutatis mutandis'* means 'changing what needs to be changed'.]

cultural pyramid'. In pathetic earnest, between the only two classes that Marx knows, according to Sternberg – the rural proletariat and the large landowners – he inserts the rediscovered small, medium and big peasants![14]

It has to be said in response that Sternberg's description of Marx's theory is a caricature. Marx's alleged 'agricultural pyramid' is Sternberg's invention, not only from the standpoint of 'Marx-philology', but also because it is irreconcilable with Marx's theory. In Marx's theoretical system there is no separate 'agricultural pyramid' under capitalism, nor could there be. For agriculture is completely subsumed under capital. Capitalist agriculture *is merely a branch of industry* and thus 'produces wheat, etc., just as the manufacturer produces yarn or machines'.[15] To assert this is no mere quibble over words. It is rather a matter of the important conclusion that under pure capitalism the agricultural proletariat does not confront large landowners, as Sternberg claims, but *capitalists*, entrepreneurs, i.e. that there is no separate agricultural pyramid. Only tenants fulfil an active function in the production process, and, like the other capitalists, obtain the average profit. Large landowners stand outside production and merely constitute a category of ownership, which itself has nothing to do with the workers. Modern, purely capitalist ground rent is only the excess of price above average profit, and thus presupposes *capitalist* enterprise. Marx's purpose was to distill the categories peculiar to capitalism in *pure form*: profit, ground rent, wages. Hence the reduction of the complex capitalist mechanism to its simple, *basic form*.

Marx certainly knew that empirical reality does not immediately correspond with the pure, schematic analysis, that it is extremely complex and that apart from capitalist tenant and worker, it features all kinds of intermediate classes. As well as 'pure' large landowners there are landowners who cultivate land on their own account. Everywhere there are still masses of small and micro farmers. Marx points to the peasantry in Sweden, the French and west German peasants. 'The free ownership of the peasant who farms his land himself is evidently the *most normal form* of landed property for small-scale cultivation'.[16]

In reality, therefore, the theoretical categories of ground rent, average profit, etc. never appear in pure form. Everywhere we encounter hybrid forms. It is possible that the empirical 'rent' of large landowners and what is called rent in daily life includes an element of profit and even of wages, in addition to the ground rent proper.[17] By means of his theoretical analysis, however, Marx cre-

14 Sternberg 1971, p. 346.
15 Marx 1981b, p. 751.
16 Marx 1981b, pp. 940, 943. [Grossman's emphasis].
17 Marx 1981b, pp. 756, 859.

ated the conceptual tool by means of which reality's complicated knot of facts can be understood, i.e. resolved into pure categories. The theory, the pure categories, which find simplified expression in the schema, facilitate the examination of reality 'in pure form and free from all adulterations and blurring *admixtures*'. Later, however, it is 'just as important for understanding the *practical effects* of landed property ... to know the elements from which these *obscurities in the theory arise*'.[18]

If one does that, one will realise not only the *fact* that the peasant can maintain himself alongside the large enterprise, but also *why* he could maintain himself *despite* the inferiority of his productive technology. For the large capitalist enterprise has to defray all three elements of price – wages, average profit, as well as ground rent – from the price for its agricultural goods. In contrast, 'the only absolute barrier [the small peasant] faces as a petty capitalist is *the wage that he pays himself*, after deducting his actual expenses. He cultivates his land as long as the price of the product is sufficient for him to cover his wage; and he often does so down to a *physical minimum*'. That is, the small peasant does not even receive the full, normal wage, because the soil 'appears as his main instrument of production, as the *indispensable field of employment* for his labour and his capital'.[19] Thus when Sternberg claims that in Marx's 'agricultural pyramid' *only* the worker and the large landowner confront each other, he simply demonstrates that he has not the slightest notion of Marx's research method, modern ground rent, or the agrarian problem at all; not even a purely mechanical knowledge of the content of Marx's *Capital*, which he seeks to carry forward and correct. In this connection, it should be mentioned that in Sternberg's work a Malthusian-Ricardian conception prevails. For him, 'the law of increasing returns [to scale] only' exists 'in industry'.[20] In the same way, in agriculture, he assumes *the law of diminishing returns of the soil*! One of Marx's finest and, to this day, unmatched accomplishments was to demonstrate in *Capital* and *Theories of Surplus Value*[21] that, contrary to the 'shallow conception' of Ricardo and Malthus, the supposedly 'natural' barriers to production which bourgeois economics invokes to explain the rising prices of agricultural products and the increase in ground rent (population growth and the declining fertility of the land), do not arise from 'nature' but from social institutions, that they are therefore *social limits*. Marx showed that ground rent exists *even though the land becomes ever more productive*. In industry, fixed capital inves-

18 Marx 1981b, p. 762. [Grossman's emphasis].
19 Marx 1981b, pp. 940–2. [Grossman's emphasis].
20 Sternberg 1971, p. 15. [Editor's interpolation].
21 [*Theories of Surplus Value* are in Marx 1988a, Marx 1989b, Marx 1989c, Marx 1991b, Marx 1994.]

ted in machinery is not improved through use, but is consumed and depleted. 'The earth, on the contrary, continuously *improves*, as long as it is treated correctly. The advantage of the earth, [is based on the fact] that successive capital investments can have their benefit without the earlier ones being lost.' Apart from that, the *advantage of agriculture* consists in the fact that 'the earth itself functions as an instrument of production, which is not the case with a factory, where it functions only as the foundation'.[22]

Nevertheless, the productive forces of the land are not fully utilised under capitalism. The development of industry and agriculture necessarily proceed unevenly. The backwardness of agriculture is conditioned by the fact that: 1. capital can only be used in the latter if it is capable of *paying a rent above* the customary wage and average profit. '[L]anded property is the barrier that does not permit any new capital investment in formerly uncultivated or unleased land without levying a toll, i.e. demanding a rent.'[23] 2. furthermore, large landowners have no incentive to develop the productive forces fully, even where capital has been admitted. Absolute ground rent is the excess of the value of the agricultural product over the average rate of profit. Every progress in industry *reduces the price of production* and hence *increases* the rate of *ground rent*,[24] allowing landowners to 'put away in their own private purses the result of a social development achieved without their participation'.[25] In agriculture, however, every development of the productive forces, by bringing down the *value* of agricultural products, works in the opposite direction. This means that the *ground rent declines*. These capitalist determinants of profitability evidently form 'one of the greatest obstacles to a rational agriculture'[26] – but this has nothing to do with diminishing returns of the soil. Petty already told us (1699) 'that the landlords of his time *feared* improvements in agriculture because they would cause the price of agricultural products and *hinc* (the level of) rent to fall'.[27]

Only at a relatively advanced stage of capitalist development does industry begin to penetrate agriculture with its products (machines, synthetic fertiliser, etc.). On the other hand, agriculture goes on to construct its own agricultural factories, such as sugar refineries, mills, canneries, etc. It seeks the support of the banks, which now control agriculture as well as industry. The contradic-

22 Marx 1981b, p. 916 [Grossman's emphasis]; also Marx 1982b, pp. 258–62.
23 Marx 1981b, p. 896.
24 Marx 1989b, p. 340.
25 Marx 1981b, p. 757.
26 Marx 1981b, p. 757.
27 Marx 1989b, p. 343. [Grossman's emphasis. '*Hinc*' means 'hence'.]

tions between the two branches of production disappear more and more. The commercialisation of agriculture grows and it is only in this phase, which is just beginning to take hold in Germany for example, that agriculture is forced to reduce costs more and more through mechanisation and rationalisation of production in order not to succumb to the competitive pressure of the world market. Only now 'productivity advances in both, although at an uneven pace. But when industry reaches a certain level *the disproportion must* diminish, in other words, productivity in agriculture must increase relatively more rapidly than in industry'.[28]

Sternberg knows nothing of all this and repeats the tale of the diminishing returns of the soil uncritically.[29] He has no idea of the problems and theoretical consequences that are hidden in his thesis, no idea, above all, that the proposition of the diminishing returns of the soil is irreconcilable with Marx's labour theory of value. Logically, Sternberg should have rejected it. And yet he believes (foreword), 'that I acknowledge Marx's value theory to be correct in all its essential parts'.[30]

So he acknowledges the *labour* theory of value and still lapses into the *inverted* folly of the Physiocrats, according to which human labour *only* yields increasing returns in industry, while it is increasingly unproductive in agriculture. A fine labour theory of value! As if it was not labour but the soil that produces!

But Sternberg has adopted the proposition of diminishing returns of the soil in order to conclude that competition and struggle over markets only exist in industry as opposed to agriculture, where no competition, in the specific form it takes in industry, is said to prevail.[31] But, just like the preceding proposition, so too the thesis of the absence of competition in agriculture is simply a fantasy. Has Sternberg heard nothing of tariff protection for agriculture? The agrarians of Hungary prohibited the import of Serbian pigs into Austria, which led to a long tariff war and ultimately also to real war. German agrarians were opposed to the economic union of Germany and Austria-Hungary for fear that competition from Austrian and especially Hungarian agricultural products would have an unfavourable effect on prices in Germany. Does he not know that the same agrarians today oppose a trade agreement with Poland for fear that

---

28 Marx 1989b, p. 341. [Grossman's emphasis.]

29 Consider, for instance, the fact noted by Carl Ballod that 'the costs of production, calculated per unit of product, decrease rather than increase with the size of the yield' for rye, barley, and oats as well as potatoes and sugar beet; Ballod 1927, p. 109.

30 Sternberg 1971, p. 10.

31 Sternberg 1971, p. 15.

competition from Polish pigs would put downward pressure on prices? In agriculture no competition and no overproduction is supposed to exist! Yet Swiss agriculture, for instance, is currently in crisis, indeed a crisis of overproduction because there is too much livestock. 'Oversupply led to a glut of milk, to overfull stables and cheese warehouses, to a deterioration of the meat market.' Indeed, 'Swiss agriculture is subject to the same forces as individual branches of industry, such as the watch-making industry ... While Switzerland supplied specialities to the world market for decades, foreign countries have now adopted Swiss methods of production'. Good 'Swiss cheese' is now being produced everywhere. 'The quality of butter in Denmark surpasses that in Switzerland, just as fruit processing is much more highly developed in Canada and Australia.' With the progressive commercialisation of agriculture comes dependence on exports. 'If Swiss agriculture wishes to withstand the competitive struggle on the world market, *only a cheaper price* will help'; the same cheaper price that the landowners as a class fear so much.[32]

The policy of high food prices only corresponds with a certain initial stage of agriculture. It is followed, like a shadow, by the transformation of prices for agricultural land and hence by indebtedness. High agricultural tariffs are useless when supplying the domestic market gives way to exports. In Switzerland, dumping prices are now being considered.[33]

Even in this area, apparently so remote from the actual problem of accumulation, Sternberg's absolutely Malthusian conception is revealed as the deepest source of all his errors. In agriculture he knows neither overproduction nor competition, and thus also no expansionist drive due to the law of the diminishing returns of the soil. If industrial production is dominated by crises, thus by the compulsion to expand, it is because the law of rising returns only applies in industry. The ultimate reason for all capitalist and imperialist expansion, according to Sternberg's diagnosis, lies in the natural difference between industrial and agricultural labour. Finally, we ought to be grateful to nature for endowing agricultural production more sparsely, otherwise overproduction and crises as well as expansion would be *even* more intense.

Just as Sternberg's claim that Marx did not consider any intermediate strata in his agricultural pyramid is wrong, so are all his other 'factual statements' regarding Marx's 'industrial pyramid'.

'*According to Marx's schema*', Sternberg affirms, 'an ever *smaller* number of capitalist magnates is confronted by ever larger numbers of the industrial pro-

---

32 Grimm 1927, pp. 196–7.

33 Grimm 1927. [Grossman's emphasis.]

letariat ... Finally, in the crisis-ridden economy only a few capitalist magnates remain to expropriated'.[34] And further, 'According to Marx, at the moment of revolution ... there was an empty space between the bourgeoisie and proletariat. *The intermediate strata were missing*'. Here, too, Sternberg corrects Marx's conception by observing the existence of numerous small capitalists, merchants, rentiers, white-collar employees, artisans, etc. and concludes that 'the attitude of these intermediate strata can be decisive for the success of the socialist revolution'.[35] Now, Rosa Luxemburg already asserted against Bernstein in 1899 that 'the Marxian analysis ... does not suppose, as a condition for the realisation of socialism ... the *absolute disappearance* of small capitals, usually described as the disappearance of the small bourgeoisie'.[36] And now, after a generation, Sternberg warms this absurdity over again, in order to construct his theory of the coming revolution! The path to the proletarian revolution, he writes, is thus '*infinitely more difficult and excruciating than Marx had assumed* ... the counter-revolutionary forces are too strong, ripeness for socialisation too limited'.[37] And the proof? Marx's schema, which is thus, according to Sternberg, a depiction of empirical reality! The same schema that for Marx is but a preliminary stage of cognition in his method of successive approximation.

For Marx, capitalists and workers are the only classes which function in the *capitalist* process of production and which constitute the specific character of this process, the *capital relation*. Independent bourgeois producers are remnants of earlier economic formations and remain outside the capital relation. If the essence of *capitalism* is to be understood, at first the analysis has to be limited to 'pure' capitalism, without the obscuring remnants of other economic formations, taking into account simply those two classes which *conceptually* constitute 'the *framework* of modern society'.[38] To approximate reality more accurately, this framework has to be subsequently filled with all the remaining empirical classes and strata. For, as Marx notes, 'In *the real world* the matter appears *more intricate*, since the partners who share the loot – the surplus value of the capitalist – figure',[39] '*the actual composition of society, which by no means consists only of two classes, workers and industrial capitalists*'.[40] There are

34 Sternberg 1971, p. 339. [Grossman's emphasis.]
35 Sternberg 1971, pp. 354, 355.
36 Luxemburg 2008a, p. 73. [Grossman's emphasis.]
37 Sternberg 1971, pp. 300–1. [Grossman's emphasis.]
38 Marx 1981b, p. 756. [Grossman's emphasis.]
39 Marx 1978b, p. 487. [Grossman's emphasis.]
40 Marx 1989c, p. 124. [Grossman's emphasis.]

various others at the trough of the surplus, 'therefore the way in which they spend their revenue, and the very size of the revenue give rise to *very considerable modifications ... in the circulation and reproduction process of capital*'.[41] Marx conducts this subsequent modification of the preliminary schematic analysis most diligently. All the intermediate strata, their significance and function within the capitalist mechanism, although in scattered remarks, are still characterised with stunning clarity and not from statistical compendia but the nature of this mechanism. And the entire theoretical ineptitude of revisionism was necessary in order to miss all of this and to favour the world with the discovery of 'intermediate strata'. And only Sternberg's ignorance of *the decisively important question of Marx's method of investigation* leads him to make this 'discovery' again and thus to compose a new anti-Marx book!

It would lead too far afield to point out Sternberg's *qui pro quo*[42] in all its details, to trace the methodological construction of Marx's work and to show the role accorded to elements he ostensibly overlooks in his own system. It is therefore simply suggested that the most essential component of Marx's system is the theory of breakdown, the proof of the necessary breakdown of capitalism. The classes and strata, mentioned above, only represent a weakening of the tendency to break down. These are theoretical conceptions on which discussion is possible and desirable. In dealing with these concepts, a writer of Marx's stature can demand that the most elementary results of his analysis and the readily ascertainable facts he adduces, should not be distorted or caricatured. Yet precisely on this point one cannot oppose Sternberg's method or rather his parodies sharply enough. To entirely correct them here is impossible. But there should at least be a short confrontation over those facts that, according to Sternberg, Marx did not, and, from the standpoint of his system, could not, foresee.

The existence of *small peasants* has already been mentioned. *In commerce*, Sternberg claims, Marx's tendency towards concentration is weaker. Consequently, for a period its share of the *total population* grew even faster than that of industry. The number of *self-employed* rose, and the number of *white-collar employees* grew faster than that of workers.[43] But where Marx presented the view formulated by Sternberg is not said. In the schema? Is it there, perhaps, that the decline of commerce, the self-employed, etc. is asserted? The schema demonstrates something even more appalling! It assumes '... direct sale

41 Marx 1989c, p. 124. [Grossman's emphasis.]

42 ['*Qui pro quo*' means 'this for that', and conveys misunderstanding. Grossman's original text had '*quid pro quo*', 'this for that' conveying reciprocity.]

43 Sternberg 1971, pp. 345, 441–2.

without the intervention of the merchant, since this intervention conceals various moments of the movement',[44] in a word, abstraction from the merchant! Because the schema, according to Sternberg, is a reflection of reality, it follows that, to use Sternberg's words, Marx conceptualised *Capital* 'on a premise *that had to preclude him from realising essential relationships*'[45] or, in other words, that he knew nothing about the existence of commerce and the significance of merchant capital! Of course, if one knows that the schema is only a preliminary simplification, one just as soon finds in Marx the subsequent correction – including the growing share of trade in the total population, the increasing number of self-employed and white-collar workers, a conclusion for which Marx did not need even a single empirical number. 'Commodity trade ... as a function of merchant's capital' – it is said – 'develops *ever further* with the development of capitalist production'.[46] Artisanal production produces for personal use or for a customer without the product being traded.[47] 'The extent to which production goes into trade and passes *through the hands of merchants* depends on the mode of production, *reaching a maximum* with the full development of capitalist production, where the product is produced *simply* as a commodity.'[48] '[W]ith the development of the capitalist mode of production *all* production becomes *commodity* production, and hence the whole of the product comes into the hands of the agents of circulation.'[49] But not only the relative share of trade grows. Wholesale trade develops in the same way: 'As the capitalist mode of production presupposes production on a large scale, so it also necessarily presupposes *large-scale* sale'.[50] On the one hand, concentration occurs in commerce, because '[i]n commerce ..., far more than in industry, the same function takes the same amount of labour time whether it is performed on a large or small scale. Thus concentration historically appears in commerce earlier than in the industrial workshop.' In addition, the '[t]ransport costs, which commerce is concerned with ... also grow with this fragmentation'.[51] As the number of business dealings grows, so does the number of white-collar employees: 'The more the scale of production grows, *the greater are industrial capital's commercial operations*.' This *requires the utilisation of commercial wage labourers*.[52] On

44 Marx 1978b, p. 191. [Grossman's emphasis.]
45 Sternberg 1971, p. 22. [Grossman's emphasis.]
46 Marx 1978b, p. 191. [Grossman's emphasis.]
47 Marx 1981b, p. 425.
48 Marx 1981b, pp. 442–3. [Grossman's emphasis.]
49 Marx 1981b, p. 425. [Grossman's emphasis.]
50 Marx 1978b, p. 190. [Grossman's emphasis.]
51 Marx 1981b, p. 409.
52 Marx 1981b, p. 413. [Grossman's emphasis.]

the other hand, however, *retail trade* nevertheless grows. '[N]on-functioning or only semi-functioning commercial capital also grows ... with *the increased ease of entry into the retail trade*, with speculation'.[53] With the development of joint-stock companies and the cooperative system, finally, the separation of the capitalist from the industrial and commercial manager occurs both in industry and commerce, so 'that the work of *supervision* is readily available, quite independent of the *ownership* of capital ... with the *formation of a numerous class of industrial and commercial managers*'.[54] *Regarding industry*, Sternberg writes: 'The ever-increasing size of the proletariat is confronted not by an ever *smaller* number of capitalist magnates, but by the *continually* growing stratum of small and micro *money capitalists*, who are fobbed off with interest ... In addition, ... a pure *rentier class* has emerged.' 'It is ... counter-revolutionary.'[55] These are the 'facts' that are supposed to be fatal for the implications of Marx's theory and that have failed to be reconciled with the historical Marx's explanations.

The number of capitalist magnates, then, becomes smaller according to Marx. The proof? The schema. But the schema, for the sake of simplification, shows just *two* spheres of production with giant capitals that are increasingly subject to concentration. Under this assumption, the number of capitalists does actually become progressively smaller. But Marx *shows* that reality does not simply consist of two spheres of production. In the empirical world, capital keeps penetrating into *new* spheres. 'At the same time offshoots split off from the original capitals and start to function as new and independent capitals ... With the accumulation of capital, therefore, the number of capitalists *grows*'.[56] 'The historical Marx', however, says even more. For purposes of simplification, the schema is constructed on the basis of cash payments, hence it *excludes credit*. Yet Marx does not subsequently fail to present the role of credit. This often has the effect that 'a man without wealth ... can transform himself into a capitalist'. Here, then, is another source from which the number of active capitalists is increased by a series of 'new soldiers of fortune'. This circumstance '*reinforces the rule of capital itself, widens its basis* and enables *it to recruit ever new forces from the lower strata of society*'.[57]

But what about the *rentier class*, the intermediate strata? There is certainly no mention of them in the 'schema' because in it all capitalists are initially treated as a *class as a whole*. Hence there was no room to divide off moneylend-

53 Marx 1981b, p. 426. [Grossman's emphasis.]
54 Marx 1981b, p. 511, 513. [Grossman's emphasis.]
55 Sternberg 1971, p. 343. [Grossman's emphasis.]
56 Marx 1976b, p. 776. [Grossman's emphasis.]
57 Marx 1981b, p. 735. [Grossman's emphasis.]

ing capitalists, i.e. idle from active capitalists. Subsequently, however, they are considered and their function is exactly specified. Sternberg also has to admit that Marx did not ignore them, producing a Marx quotation from the third volume of *Capital*. Ignorant of Marx's method of investigation, however, he cannot explain why these elements do not appear in the schema. Thus he concludes that they were apparently of little significance to Marx, and furnishes the quotation mentioned with a characteristic comment: the rentier class 'already started to develop in England in Marx's time and he also takes note of it.' But, Sternberg immediately adds, its 'extent is far more significant under advanced capitalism'.[58] That is to say, in Marx's time, i.e. the period during which *Capital* was drafted, i.e. in the [18]70s, this class 'began' to develop (!) and Marx only takes 'note' of it, without suspecting its later significance, thus failing to sufficiently appreciate the significance of interest-bearing and usurious capital under capitalism!

Should one still treat such claims at all seriously or rather assume that Sternberg never read the relevant chapters in the third volume of *Capital*? 'The historical Marx', however, shows us that in *France* in 1848, 'where government bonds form the most important subject of speculation and the *bourse*[59] the chief market for the investment of capital that wants to turn itself to account in an unproductive way ... a *countless* number of people from all bourgeois or semi-bourgeois classes must have an interest in the state debt, in the Bourse gamblings, in finance'; how 'with state indebtedness ... the power over the trade in state debts, the state creditors, the bankers, the money dealers and the wolves of the Bourse' emerged.[60] *Capital* shows how, with the public debt, a class of idle rentiers is created that continually enriches itself and multiplies, '[w]ithout forcing it to expose itself to the troubles and risks inseparable from its employment in industry or even in usury', that furthermore 'the national debt has given rise ... to dealings in negotiable effects of all kinds, to speculation: in a word, it has given rise to *stock-exchange gambling and the modern bankocracy*'. 'The historical Marx' teaches that a 'brood of bankocrats, financiers, rentiers, brokers, stock-jobbers, etc.'[61] already emerged in *England* at the end of the seventeenth century and attained a social significance by the beginning of the nineteenth century, two generations before *Capital* was drafted, that could not escape the attention of the economists. Already in 1836 George

58 Sternberg 1971, p. 343.

59 ['*Bourse*' means 'stock exchange'.]

60 Marx 1978a, p. 116. [Grossman's emphasis.]

61 Marx 1976b, p. 919. [Grossman's emphasis.]

Ramsay not only 'identified' this significance but portrayed it as a necessary concomitant of capital accumulation. 'For as a nation advances in the career of wealth, *a class of men springs up and increases more and more*, who ... find themselves in the possession of funds sufficiently ample to afford a handsome maintenance from the interest alone ... *This class ... has a tendency to increase* with the increasing riches of the country ... *How much more numerous ... is the class of rentiers ... in England!*' And 'the historical Marx's' 'note' does not only consist of a detailed account of Ramsay's description *twice*,[62] but even examines the role of the accumulation of money and, from the *increasing* number of rentiers and capitalists, deduces '*a tendency for the rate of interest to fall*'.[63] Those who, like Sternberg, know nothing of these matters ought first to acquire the first principles of Marxism before setting out to reform it.

Marx shows us how, with the accumulation of capital, '*those classes and subclasses who do not live directly from their labour become more numerous* and live better than before';[64] furthermore, that we can see 'from the history of 1815 to 1847 that in the battle over the corn laws, the majority of the monied interest ... were to be found amongst the *allies* of the landed interest against the manufacturing interest'.[65] And he proceeds to explain that the English take 'monied class' to mean moneylenders, those living off interest, bankers, bill brokers, etc.[66] It was Marx, finally, who reproached Ricardo for forgetting '*the constantly growing number of the middle classes* ... who stand between the workman ... and the capitalist and landlord ... and *increase the social security and power of the upper ten thousand*'.[67] And yet the same Marx is supposed to succumb to Ricardo's error?

But behind Sternberg's objections lies more than mere ignorance of Marx. For it is precisely one of the *guiding ideas* of Marx's principal work that the more the bourgeoisie is 'becoming separated from productive activity', the more it develops into a parasitic rentier class, which 'is becoming more and more ... socially *superfluous*, ... and, like the nobility in the past, becoming more and more *a class merely drawing revenues*'.[68] Sternberg has to distort the actual situation, otherwise he would have no opening for his discoveries. Hence he remarks: 'But these tendencies [the formation of middle strata, etc.] that were

62 Marx 1981b, pp. 483–4; Marx 1991b, p. 279. [Grossman's emphasis. Ramsay 1836, pp. 201–2.]
63 Marx 1981b, p. 483. [Grossman's emphasis.]
64 Marx 1989c, p. 188. [Grossman's emphasis.]
65 Marx 1989b, p. 353.
66 Marx 1989b, p. 434.
67 Marx 1989c, p. 198. [Grossman's emphasis.]
68 Engels 1987, p. 153. [Grossman's emphasis.]

only beginning to emerge when *Capital* was being drafted, are decisive for the configuration of advanced capitalism'.[69] Thus they supposedly emerged only in the 1870s, while Marx dates their emergence to the end of the seventeenth century and shows that they already played a significant role in the struggle over the Corn Laws. And as if that were not enough, a hundred pages later Sternberg carries the caricature of Marx's thought to an extreme with the graphically illustrated claim that, according to Marx's class pyramid, there are no middle strata whatsoever, but an empty space between the proletariat and the few capitalist magnates![70]

According to Sternberg, the development of Marx's schema was a necessary consequence of his false methodological premise that there are no non-capitalist areas. Only under this assumption, claims Sternberg, will the logic of Marx's schema, i.e. the disappearance of the middle strata, prevail, precisely because there are no mitigating countertendencies created by non-capitalist areas. We have demonstrated above that for Marx the number of the middle strata *grows independently of non-capitalist areas* and that this growth follows from the inner logic of the capitalist process of production itself. Thus we have demonstrated that one of the cornerstones of Sternberg's remarks is untenable; that is to say, we have demonstrated the inexcusable carelessness and superficiality of all those who, ignorant of the basic elements of Marx's method of investigation and incapable of going beyond the limited horizon of their shallow empiricism, have pointed with naive arrogance to the most primitive 'facts' that Marx supposedly failed to consider. And this fundamentally wrong but continually repeated assertion is portrayed as a long 'acknowledged' truth that irreproachably confirms the incompatibility of Marx's system with empirical reality.

2 Sternberg's Conclusions or How to Make a Revolution

The question of the reasons for Sternberg's distortions of and false attributions to Marx leads us to the main theme of the book, to Sternberg's thesis about revolution. Contrary to all expectations, it is not related to his analysis of imperialism in any internally coherent way, as the following will demonstrate.

What conclusions does Sternberg draw from the fact that middle strata exist?

69 Sternberg 1971, p. 259.
70 Sternberg 1971, p. 346.

This question concerns the *problem of tactics*, which play a large role for Sternberg. Marx is said to have misjudged this problem and its importance for socialist parties too. Sternberg is the first to correct him and teaches that it 'is of a significance that could never be derived from the historical Marx's system'.[71] Now, evidently, either Sternberg has never read the political writings of Marx or he gambles on the ignorance of gullible readers. Since the *Communist Manifesto*, since the famous *Address of the Central Authority to the League* of March 1850, and then in a series of brilliant political works such as *The Class Struggles in France, The Eighteenth Brumaire, Revolution and Counter-Revolution in Germany*,[72] as well as later writings and letters about the International Working Men's Association and the Paris Commune, Marx described the problems of proletarian tactics, the role and tasks of the proletariat in the coming revolutions, its relationship to the middle strata, and ultimately also the character of the proletarian revolution itself. The peasantry and the urban petty bourgeoisie are referred to there as the '*class* [that is] *a most important one ... in all modern revolutions*'.[73] Finally it is demonstrated how and under what circumstances 'peasants, petty bourgeois, the middle strata in general, stand with the proletariat', dissociate themselves from the ruling classes, are gradually driven to '[*r*]*evolt against bourgeois dictatorship, to change society*', and ultimately to '*group round the proletariat as the decisive revolutionary power*'.[74] And after all this, Sternberg's assertion that 'in the historical Marx's system' there is no possibility for the proper evaluation of tactics!

What, then, did Marx miss and Sternberg discover?

Sternberg's style is to crudely simplify all real problems of tactics. From the complicated and enormous complex of questions, he snatches a *single one, the question of timing*, and builds the actual content of his book upon it.

It was Bernstein who, in his time, expressed the fear that the proletariat might try to seize political power too early. Sternberg now imposes Bernstein's conception on Marx. Parallel to the growing concentration of enterprise, there was according to Marx an ascending line of development towards revolution which is 'automatically' reached at the line's endpoint. Sternberg concludes that, 'in Marx's system, revolution can come too early, never too late'.[75] His 'contrast to Marx', his discovery, consists in improving on this alleged conception

71 Sternberg 1971, p. 355.

72 Marx and Engels 1976; Marx and Engels 1978; Marx 1978a; Marx 1979a; Engels 1979.

73 Engels 1979, p. 9. [Grossman's emphasis. Translators' interpolation. Engels was describing 'The small trading and shopkeeping class'. The work was originally published under Marx's name.]

74 Marx 1978a, p. 125. [Grossman's emphasis.]

75 Sternberg 1971, p. 355.

of Marx by adding that revolution can also come 'too late'. For he predicts that, in future 'imperialist wars, the destruction of capital will assume absolutely enormous dimensions'. If this is to happen, however – and this is the start of Sternberg's brilliant achievement – '[t]hen the straightforward, simple line of development of Marx's system will not occur. Imperialist wars can have the effect of *winding back the level of ripeness for socialisation*'.[76]

In Sternberg's interpretation, the time for the revolution, according to Marx, is when the productive forces are objectively ripe for socialisation. At this moment, the proletariat would also 'automatically' possess the necessary class consciousness! Revolution '*had* to result from the ever greater concentration, according to Marx's system'! According to Sternberg, this ripeness for socialisation does not have to occur. Imperialist war can prevent the transition to the socialist mode of production, it can 'push Euramerica into *historical oblivion*'.[77] Sternberg has nowhere even hinted at just what this is supposed to mean; this despite the decisive importance of the concept in his 'system' and the pronounced threat to human civilisation associated with it. Or perhaps the reference to Rome and Egypt suffices? The development of humanity is wound back by war! Does this mean its tempo slows down? Then the victory of socialism would be delayed, but not itself be in doubt. Sternberg, however, denies the necessity of development towards socialism. It does not have to come. This, however, can only be true if it is assumed that, after a specific day, the impetus for the development of the productive forces and for this reason the entire social superstructure is disrupted *once and for all*, that there are no new tools and machines, no new methods of work and chemical processes, etc. to speak of. The contemporary level of technology would then and certainly only then be petrified, and the entire superstructure would also be brought to a halt.

Only once we have envisaged this do the consequences of completing and continuing the materialist conception of history by means of Sternberg's concept of 'historical oblivion' become clear. The continuation of Marx's materialist conception of history means, precisely, setting it aside. However, we know that the efforts of humanity as a whole to develop the productive forces cannot be stopped. The relative lag of individual nations in certain historical periods is itself only a symptom of the development of new productive forces. The economic *decline* of the countries in the area of the Black Sea from the end of the fifteenth century, for instance, is only the expression of the shift in world trade routes because of the discovery of America and the resulting massive *expansion of the productive forces*.

76 Sternberg 1971, p. 331. [Grossman's emphasis.]
77 Sternberg 1971, p. 332. [Grossman's emphasis.]

That war entails destruction is not to be denied. But Sternberg's claim that this destruction winds back ripeness for socialisation contradicts experience as well as the inner nature of capitalism. Either the destruction is so great that it embraces the basis of the productive apparatus itself, the entire capitalist mechanism disintegrates and the barricades go up between the classes. In the other case, society is impoverished by the ravages of war but this is the *impetus for the forced development of the productive forces*, for the enormous concentration and rationalisation movements of the kind we now witness in Germany. For this is the only possible way to withstand the competitive struggle with other, richer capital powers, on a capitalist basis. Actually, despite the ravages the World War, the tendencies to concentration and combination that were already present everywhere have accelerated and intensified. Lenin already noted this in 1915.[78] Within only a few years, the prewar stage of development was recovered and surpassed. The fall into historical oblivion is a naive and empty phrase. If, however, one assumes with Sternberg the possibility that humanity could be cast into historical oblivion by the next imperialist war, there is no other way to save it than to *pre-empt* the next war through revolution.

Sternberg's 'advance' beyond Marx is apparent here. The timing of revolution, Sternberg claims, was unimportant for Marx. 'In Marx's system the decisive time for a revolution could never be missed'.[79] In Sternberg's 'system', however, it may indeed be 'missed'. 'The revolution may well come *too late*',[80] at a time 'when the descent of the actively-imperialist states into historical oblivion can no longer be stopped'.[81] In other words, for Sternberg, 'problems of tactics' are reduced to the question of the timing of the revolution. 'Thus the question of the *timing* of the social revolution attains a significance that it could never achieve in Marx's system'.[82] 'The *timing of revolution therefore becomes the decisive problem*'.[83] 'Because revolution can come too late, tactics become the decisive question, for they determine the moment of the outbreak',[84] and it is therefore necessary 'that the timing of revolution ... has also to be determined *with regard to imperialist war*'.[85]

78 Lenin 1964a, p. 226.
79 Sternberg 1971, p. 333.
80 Sternberg 1971, p. 333 [Sternberg emphasised the whole clause.]
81 Sternberg 1971, p. 355.
82 Sternberg 1971, p. 333.
83 Sternberg 1971, p. 355. [Grossman's emphasis apart from '*the timing of revolution*'.]
84 Sternberg 1971, p. 358.
85 Sternberg 1971, p. 347. [Grossman's emphasis.]

If the 'choice' about the timing of the outbreak is the 'decisive task', it will be interesting to learn what, if any, conditions are attached to this timing and, finally, who is to determine it.

According to Sternberg, the counter-revolutionary forces really are too strong, the ripeness for socialisation is too low, the middle strata are numerous and growing. In short, the *objective conditions*, 'the balance of class forces in the age of imperialism is *far more* adverse than Marx could have expected',[86] and continue to deteriorate further.

But not only objective conditions. 'The horrible, the diabolical aspect of this historical situation is that the *objective* conditions that lead to imperialism, to war ... have at the same time *clouded and continue to cloud* the *class consciousness* of the one class that alone is capable of saving the world from doom'.[87]

Does this, perhaps, mean that in the absence of the objective as well as the subjective conditions for revolution, the revolution has to be abandoned? 'Surely a successful revolution is only possible when the forces of the anti-imperialist are *stronger* than those of the imperialist block'.[88] According to Sternberg, however, they are *weaker*. From his standpoint he has either to abandon revolution or demonstrate a way in which the anti-imperialist block *can grow stronger*. It is characteristic of Sternberg's logic that he opts for a *third* way. Objective conditions are becoming weaker? Sternberg abandons economic conditions and contents himself with the 'minimum' ripeness for socialisation. Still, the same objective conditions also cloud class consciousness? It is abandoned as well, to the extent that it is determined by *economic* circumstances. Still, the 'horrible situation' persists. What to do? Shouldn't Sternberg demonstrate what is to replace Marx's conception? Instead of giving a frank answer, at this point in his line of reasoning Sternberg lays the charge – which actually is an answer – that for Marx '*intellectuals*' are 'hardly of any significance in shaping the historical process'.[89] With cheap pathos he admonishes intellectuals to take the side of capitalism's opponents.[90] Yet even together with the intellectuals the numerical superiority of the counter-revolution is not overcome. 'Not only are the capitalist, the imperialist forces stronger, but the *anti-capitalist, anti-imperialist forces themselves are threatened* by the improvement in the economic condition of the working class under imperialism'.[91] According to Marx's

86 Sternberg 1971, p. 346. [Grossman's emphasis.]
87 Sternberg 1971, p. 531. [Sternberg emphasised the entire paragraph.]
88 Sternberg 1971, p. 352. [Grossman's emphasis.]
89 Sternberg 1971, p. 351. [Grossman's emphasis.]
90 Sternberg 1971, pp. 315–20.
91 Sternberg 1971, p. 353. [Grossman's emphasis.]

conception, objective conditions drive toward the necessary demise of capitalism, breakdown and revolution. 'For *it had to come*', Sternberg says.[92] Hence 'the *immanent necessity* of socialism', according to Marx.[93] And yet Sternberg denies just this necessity. His answer to the question about the path to revolution is simple and clear: *one decrees it!* 'If capitalist development had proceeded according to Marx's schema ..., the socialist revolution ... would come with 90 percent probability ... In view of the dangers of imperialist wars *a socialist revolution cannot wait for this 90 percent probability*'. It also 'has to make do with a lower probability.'[94] *Basta*! *Credo quia absurdum*.[95] Sternberg wants to replace *Marx's theory of the objective developmental tendencies of capitalism and the resultant class struggle with this!* In his subconscious, however, a shred of unease about the ridiculousness of his discovery lives on. *Stat magni nominis umbra*![96] So as not to be crushed by the force of Marx's genius, Sternberg is compelled to turn his 'immanent necessity', that is the objective, 100 percent *certainty* of socialism, into a 90 percent '*probability*' at this point and for the purpose of this comparison! By demanding a lower probability than Marx, however, he now makes the comparison with Marx easier. Both conceptions of the occurence of the revolution have, however, been reduced to the same plane. The difference now merely involves a few percent of revolutionary probability. Still, he retains the credit of being the first to realise that one can and may make do with a lower probability. *Il me faut du nouveau; n'en fût-il point au monde*![97]

Sternberg does not specify the percentage of probability required for revolution. Given that, according to him, the counter-revolutionary forces are currently *stronger*, the revolutionary elements in any case amount to less than 50 percent. Even this is enough for him, as he wants to make do with the *minimum* ripeness for socialisation. The question of the minimum may be complicated, but 'for Europe one can dare to make the assertion that the minimum ripeness for socialisation is, *determined* purely technically.'[98] What is still missing for revolution is the appropriate consciousness, to the extent that it is determined by economics, because it is – as we know – 'clouded' by objective conditions.

92 Sternberg 1971, p. 356. [Grossman's emphasis.]
93 Sternberg 1971, p. 348. [Grossman's emphasis.]
94 Sternberg 1971, p. 354. [Grossman's emphasis.]
95 ['*Basta*! *Credo quia absurdum*' means 'Enough! I believe because it is absurd', a paraphrase of '*prorsus credibile est, quia ineptum est*', Tertullian 1956, lines 24–5.]
96 ['*Stat magni nominis umbra*' means 'He stands, the shadow of a mighty name', Lucan 1962, p. 12.]
97 ['*Il me faut du nouveau; n'en fût-il point au monde*' means 'I must have something new; nothing else will do.' Fontaine 2009, p. 139.]
98 Sternberg 1971, p. 337. [Grossman's emphasis.]

As one 'cannot wait', however, one has to *create a consciousness, detached from economic conditions*. Remember the 'significance of the intellectuals in shaping the historical process'!

Overcoming consciousness clouded by economic conditions is the proper *task of the party*! 'The party has ... a far more significant function than it could have in Marx's system ... This is the enormous task of the party in the countries of active imperialism. It has ... *to overcome the clouding of the working class's class consciousness* ... to demonstrate the historically transient character of the A-D line, the reprieve.' It has 'to intervene here, *not to ... get bogged down ... in everyday politics* ... to maintain with iron necessity *that the goal is everything*'.[99] Mind you, all this is purely voluntarist, *despite the objective conditions working in the opposite direction*.

Now we consider Sternberg's materialist conception of history. Although material circumstances condition historical development, no necessity of socialism; despite it, the possibility of descent into historical oblivion, in which humanity apparently is, so to speak, left hanging in the air, independent of economic conditions; finally, class consciousness formed, independently of and in opposition to objective conditions, by the party and the intellectuals – detached, however, from everyday politics!

For Rosa Luxemburg, the economic analysis of non-capitalist markets was most intimately connected with the emergence of socialism. The full penetration of capitalism into colonial countries, the impossibility of realising surplus value in a purely capitalist area, objectively led to the necessary *breakdown* of the capitalist mode of production. Socialism emerged from the process of economic development. Because Sternberg wishes to present himself as completing Rosa Luxemburg's thought, the wicked abuse of this great fighter's name has to be asserted here too. If it is possible for revolution to occur too late and for a descent into historical oblivion to occur if, therefore, the objective necessity of socialism is denied, nothing less than the essence of scientific socialism itself is denied. 'The immanent necessity of socialism', according to Sternberg, 'does not exist as Marx and Engels conceived it'.[100] 'The socialist mode of production definitely does not arise of necessity'.[101] Yet while socialism, for Sternberg, does not of necessity *have* to come, it still *can* come. Its realisation, however, depends on the 'choice' of the timing of the outbreak, on the position adopted by intellectuals and on hammering in 'correct consciousness', detached from

99 Sternberg 1971, pp. 352–3. [All but the last emphasis is Grossman's.]

100 Sternberg 1971, p. 348.

101 Sternberg 1971, pp. 325–6.

class struggle. In other words, as Rosa Luxemburg put it, we have the justification of socialism in terms of 'pure knowledge', i.e. an *idealist* justification, straight from the writing desk; in Luxemburg's prescient words, '*positing for the victory of the class struggle a point fixed outside and independent of the class struggle*'.[102]

Having once taken the path from utopia to science, socialism has thus happily returned from science back to utopia. Independently of or, rather, in opposition to the *forces operating within capitalism*, socialism is achieved dependent on purely subjective-voluntarist aspects. Nevertheless, Sternberg still thinks 'that the point is not to construct socialism out of one's head, but to identify the forces that are destined to bring it about', within capitalism itself.[103]

Previously only the conscious enemies of Marxism have sought to refute the historical, objective necessity of socialism, that is, the essential basis of scientific socialism. Here, too, we see Sternberg simply regurgitating Bernstein. 'The question of the correctness of the materialist conception of history', Bernstein says, '*is a question of the degree of its historical necessity*'.[104] He now combats the 'iron necessity of history'.[105] '[W]hy represent socialism as the consequence of *economic compulsion*?', he asks.[106] The higher the level of development, '[t]he more that forces *other* than purely economic ones influence social life, the more the sway of what we call *historical necessity* is altered'.[107] 'The level of economic development reached today leaves *ideological and especially ethical factors* greater scope for independent activity'.[108] And Bernstein concedes further that he does not actually make the victory of socialism depend on its 'immanent economic necessity',[109] but on the 'intellectual and moral maturity of the working class itself',[110] thus on ethical factors, on the realisation that socialism *is desirable*! Kant is invoked against Marx. All this because Bernstein openly admits his *opposition* to the materialist conception of history. Sternberg's greater originality is, however, revealed when he professes the materialist conception of history and in the same breath negates it while, however, assuring that he has 'the living Marx' on his side.

---

102 [Luxemburg 2008a, pp. 47, 96.]
103 Sternberg 1971, p. 7.
104 Bernstein 1993, p. 12. [Grossman's emphasis.]
105 Bernstein 1993, p. 20.
106 [Bernstein 1899, p. 9. Grossman's emphasis.]
107 Bernstein 1993, p. 18. [Grossman's emphasis.]
108 Bernstein 1993, pp. 19–20. [Grossman's emphasis.]
109 Bernstein 1993, p. 200.
110 Bernstein 1993, p. 201.

Nothing characterises Sternberg's confusion as well as his naivety better than his belief in two conceptions of the emergence of revolution. Marx's alleged conception holds that one has to 'await' the revolution until the economic situation is ripe. To this he counterposes his 'own' conception, according to which the revolution is to occur purely voluntaristically. By way of contrast, let us quote the voice of an expert in revolutionary matters who was also a Marxist. Marxists, says Lenin in 1915, 'know perfectly well that a revolution *cannot* be "made", that revolutions *grow* out of *objectively* (i.e. independently of the will of parties and classes) mature crises and turns in history …'.[111] 'Marxism appraises "interests" according to the class antagonisms and the class struggle which *find expression in millions of facts of daily life*.'[112] 'To the Marxist it is indisputable that a revolution is *impossible without a revolutionary situation* … For a revolution to take place, it is usually insufficient for "the lower classes not to want" to live in the old way; it is also necessary that "the upper classes should be unable" to live in the old way', that an *objective impossibility* for the ruling classes to assert their rule in unchanged form develops. Secondly, that 'the suffering and want of the oppressed classes have grown more acute than usual'. 'Without these *objective changes*, which are independent of the will, not only of individual groups and parties but even of individual classes, a revolution, as a general rule, is impossible. The totality of all these objective changes is called a revolutionary situation.' It is not merely revolutionary consciousness (which, incidentally, cannot be produced outside a revolutionary situation, merely by hammering the final goal into heads) that only figures in addition as a further condition with a subjective character. It is rather something entirely different: '*the ability of the revolutionary class to take revolutionary mass action*', which presupposes an *organisation* of the coherent will of the masses and *extensive experience in the class struggles* of everyday life. 'Such are the Marxist views on revolution, views that have been developed many, many times, that have been acknowledged as indisputable by all Marxists'.[113]

And one more thing! The same Sternberg who denies the entire necessity of historical events, and thus of socialism as well, does recognise it for two events. In a certain phase of capitalism 'the thrust into non-capitalist territories is *an immanent necessity, independent of the will of the ruling stratum*';[114] and second, that 'imperialism must lead to *wars* between individual actively imperialist

111 Lenin 1964a, p. 240. [Grossman emphasised '*cannot*' and '*develop*'.]
112 Lenin 1964a, p. 228. [Grossman's emphasis.]
113 Lenin 1964a, pp. 213–14. [Grossman's emphasis.]
114 Sternberg 1971, p. 268. [Grossman's emphasis.]

states',[115] that 'war ensues with *immanent necessity*',[116] 'and that, consequently, the course of history *must differ from* Marx's prediction'.[117] Sternberg is unaware that this is inconsistent with the claim that there is no necessary development, just as he generally does not value the consistency of his own standpoint highly and prefers to say, with Lafontaine, '*Diversité, c'est ma devise*'![118] We will thus later show how this contradiction arose in Sternberg's work and how the proposition that war is an 'immanent necessity' ended up in his book.

Overall, one can describe Sternberg's theory of revolution as the attempt of an intellectual who was previously distant from Marxism to understand the *basic concepts* of the Marxist theory of the working class's final victory. While this attempt may be interesting as a symptom of the spiritual crisis of certain intellectual strata, it is nevertheless characterised by an utter lack of understanding of class struggle and appears in the grotesque form of a correction and continuation of 'historical' Marxism, which has still not been understood. Impressed by the Russian Revolution, but without understanding its necessary mechanisms, he eventually seeks to accelerate the revolution by stressing voluntarism and arrives at a mixture of old Blanquist traditions and anarcho-communist elements.

3 The Economic Rationale

We have, thus far, been able to reconstruct the essential elements of Sternberg's 'system', without having recourse to the theoretical rationale offered in the first three chapters [of his book]. This decorative pendant has no inner connection with the principle theme and can be safely disregarded in its portrayal. But Sternberg gives special weight to these chapters (surplus population, wages and economic crisis) and regards them as an essential advance over Marx. So his theory of *surplus value and wages* is also examined.

We considered above facts that Sternberg, uncritically following revisionism, considers incompatible with Marx's theory. There is, however, another fact I have not yet mentioned, which likewise disconcerts Sternberg and was also of crucial importance in the emergence of Bernstein's revisionism. 'In Marx's words', says Sternberg, 'the accumulation of capital corresponds with the accumulation of misery. *But empirical evidence shows the opposite*: the accumulation

115 Sternberg 1971, pp. 265–6. [Sternberg emphasised the whole passage.]
116 Sternberg 1971, p. 300. [Grossman's emphasis.]
117 Sternberg 1971, pp. 265–6. [Sternberg emphasised the whole passage.]
118 ['*Diversité, c'est ma devise*' means 'my motto is ever – variety', Fontaine 1896, p. 153.]

of capital entails *rising wages*'. Sternberg, who is above any 'Marx philology', apparently thinks it is only permissible when it is a matter of distorting Marx's thought. 'Marx uses the words': the accumulation of misery. This suffices for Sternberg to characterise Marx's theory of wages as a theory of absolute impoverishment, which cannot be reconciled with the empirical fact of rising wages. 'The radicals' therefore either had to deny or hush up the fact of rising wages established by the revisionists. 'Finally', Sternberg says, 'resort was made to makeshift explanations, such as the theory of relative impoverishment'. And he condescendingly adds 'Now, if one tries *to rescue* Marx *by twisting the clear meaning of his words* and speaking of the relative impoverishment of the working class ... that is not only a *distortion of Marx's unambiguous meaning*, but simultaneously the abandonment of his method'.[119]

Only ever a sounding board for other people's thoughts, Sternberg here just transcribes Herkner, who likewise merely sees a Kautskyist distortion 'when, in order *to rescue Marx's thought* it is stressed that increasing exploitation does not necessarily entail deteriorating conditions.' Herkner also opposes this 'theoretically constructed impoverishment', with arrogant scorn.[120]

That bourgeois economics has always distinguished itself by being absolutely ignorant of Marx's theory, which it combats, is not amazing. But it is astonishing to find such ignorance in a Marxist work. Instead of speaking of the distortion of Marx's meaning, Sternberg should have made himself familiar with this meaning first and gleaned the exhaustive presentation of the concept of relative impoverishment – not in Kautsky, but in Marx's 'Wage labour and capital'![121]

The concept of relative wages was, however, first developed by Ricardo, not Marx.[122] Marx considers this concept, of a wage that *grows absolutely* but falls in relation to the total value and surplus value, 'one of Ricardo's *greatest contributions* ... This is important economically, in fact it is only another way of expressing the *real theory of surplus value*. It is important, further, with regard to the social relationship between the two classes'.[123] Elsewhere he writes

> It is possible that, reckoned in terms of *use values* ... wages rise (as productivity increases) and yet *the value* of the wages may fall and vice versa.

119 Sternberg 1971, pp. 247, 63–4. [Grossman's emphasis.]

120 Herkner 1922, p. 316.

121 Marx 1977, pp. 216–21. [Grossman cited Engels's 1891 edition, the differences between this and the original publication are footnoted in Marx 1977.]

122 Ricardo 1912, chapter 1, section 7 [pp. 30–2].

123 Marx 1989c, pp. 226–7. [Grossman's emphasis.]

> It is one of Ricardo's great merits that he examined relative or proportionate wages, and established them as a *definite category*. Up to this time, wages had always been regarded as something simple and consequently the worker was considered an animal. But here he is considered in *his social relationships*. The *position of the classes to one another* depends more on proportionate wages than on the absolute amount of wages.[124]

We will demonstrate later the grave consequences that necessarily result in Sternberg's work from neglecting the 'important doctrine'[125] of relative wages, because 'relative wages' stand in the closest logical relation to Marx's 'relative surplus value.' If this is not understood, it is impossible to understand the central pillar of Marx's system, the theory of surplus value. Nothing can characterise the intellectual crisis, indeed the degeneration of bourgeois economics better than the fact that a century after Ricardo, his basic concept is stamped as Kautsky's invention in order to 'rescue' Marx.

But following Ricardo, Marx writes

> So far as the fund is concerned, out of which the capitalists and landlords draw their revenue and on the other hand the fund from which the workers draw theirs, to begin with, it is the *total product* which forms this common fund ... the important point is, *what aliquot parts* each of these groups draws from the common fund.[126]

And he demonstrates

> that the fund from which the workers draw their revenue *is* [*not*] *diminished absolutely*; only that it is diminished *relatively*, in proportion to the total result of their production. And that is the only important factor in the determination of the portion which they appropriate out of the wealth they themselves created.[127]

If Sternberg conceded that Marx's theory of wages readily explains rising wages and the improvement in the condition of the working class, then his thesis of the 'reprieve' [*Schonzeit*] and of the relationship between rising wages and cap-

---

124 Marx 1989c, p. 54. [Grossman's emphasis.]

125 Marx 1989b, p. 427.

126 Marx 1989c, p. 191. [Grossman's emphasis.]

127 Marx 1989c, p. 191. [Marx emhasised only '*absolutely*' and '*relatively*'. Grossman's interpolation does not change the sense of the whole sentence.]

italist advance into non-capitalist areas would become entirely superfluous. Thus, in order to have a field for his theoretical discoveries, he must initially misrepresent Marx's theory and, following the example of Herkner, Othmar Spann[128] and other bourgeois Marx slayers, present Marx's theory of wages as a theory of impoverishment. Now, what is Sternberg's theory of wages, this gem of his theoretical analysis?

To assess this, we must start by seeing what he has to say about Marx's theory of surplus value.

How does surplus value arise according to Marx? The answer already lies in the exact formulation of the conditions of the problem. Surplus value arises and must be able to be explained *on the basis of the law of value*, thus on the assumption of its absolute validity; i.e. that both the commodities produced by labour and the commodity labour power itself always have to be sold at their values. Both the commodity seller and the worker receive for their commodities the full value, no additions or deductions from price take place, and nevertheless the capitalist must 'at the end of the process withdraw more value from circulation than he threw into it ... *These are the conditions of the problem. Hic Rhodus, hic salta!*'.[129]

Who is unfamiliar with this passage in *Capital*! And what does it mean? It means that the formation of surplus value, 'the transformation of money into capital has to be developed on the basis of the immanent laws of the exchange of commodities, in such a way that *the starting-point is the exchange of equivalents*'.[130] Thus competition, the play of supply and demand, is eliminated from the analysis. That is to say, Marx's analysis is carried out under the fiction that prices and values coincide, or, as Marx says, that commodities are sold at their values. How could Marx arrive at such an assumption? After all, in reality we see that prices are always strongly influenced by competition. Experience shows, however, that shifting prices – depending on market conditions – always oscillate around a definite, around a relatively permanent price, which we call value. So price is expressed in the formula $Pr = v \times D/S$, where Pr = price, v = value, S = supply and D = demand. Although the value of woollen stockings, for example, amounts to 8 and can be greater than the value of rayon stockings, which merely amounts to 5, nevertheless the price of woollen

128 [For example, Herkner 1921, p. 300; Spann 2011, p. 222. Grossman wrote a scathing review of Spann's book, Grossmann 1928b, see above pp. 177–181.]

129 Marx 1976b, p. 269. [Grossman's emphasis. '*Hic Rhodus, hic salta*' literally means 'Here is Rhodes, jump here', metaphorically: 'act now'.]

130 Marx 1976b, pp. 268–9. [Grossman's emphasis.]

stockings at a time of reduced demand – perhaps half of the normal level – can be lower than that of the rayon stockings, since 8 × ½ = 4. Conversely, if at the same time the demand for rayon stockings has risen above its normal level, for example, to 2/1, the price of rayon stockings will rise to 5×2/1 = 10. Does it then make sense to analyse two commodities that are in entirely different situations on the market? If I want to measure and compare the weight of bodies, I am not permitted to observe them in *different* conditions, in air and water. The first, self-evident precondition of any scientific analysis is that *the objects being studied are investigated under identical conditions*. For our problem, this means that the analysis of prices should be carried out under the condition that demand and supply for all commodities are *equally strong*, thus S = D or 1/1, and can therefore be disregarded. That means that Pr = v × 1/1 or price = value. In fact, Marx conducts his analysis under the condition (which forms the basis of *Capital*) that the scales of supply and demand are in *equilibrium, i.e. that competition is excluded*, that the law of value, i.e. '*the exchange of equivalents is the point of departure*'. This is the only scientifically possible method. And only under this condition is it asked why e.g. the price (value) of woollen and rayon stockings is in the ratio 8 : 5. And furthermore, under *such* conditions, in which competition is excluded and all commodities, including the commodity labour power, are sold at their values as equivalents, how can surplus value arise? There is no Marxist in the world who does not know Marx's famous explanation of 'the *illusion created by competition*',[131] who does not know that competition alone, without its underlying *basis in value*, is incapable of explaining the basic phenomena of capitalism, and who does not know that the assessment of competition is the theoretical dividing line between Marxism and vulgar economics.

This does not apply to Sternberg. Rather, he explains everything in terms of competition – in doing so he believes he can deceive the reader if he relabels it and employs the well-known universal remedy of vulgar economics, 'surplus population' or 'more than off-setting the reserve army through advance into non-capitalist areas,' further divides surplus population into 'endogenous' and 'exogenous,' etc., and so replaces his lack of ideas with a wealth of words.

Let us take a closer look. How does surplus value, surplus labour, arise under capitalism, asks Sternberg. Surplus labour also existed in antiquity and under feudalism. How does capitalism differ from earlier social orders? Sternberg answers that surplus labour was previously a sociological category, because the

131 [Marx 1981b, pp. 992–1016. Grossman's emphasis.]

slave and the serf were *compelled* to perform surplus labour in excess of necessary labour. Under capitalism, however, it is an economic category, because here the 'free' worker performs it. 'But who forces the free worker to perform surplus labour?', asks Sternberg. 'Who forces him to *continue* to work once he ... has *performed* the "necessary" labour?' According to Sternberg, the answer is the industrial reserve army, surplus population, namely the fact *that due to the surplus population 'two workers chase one master'*. This is what Marx is supposed to have claimed. Surplus labour is performed under capitalism 'according to Marx through the constant reproduction of an "industrial reserve army" ... Only once a surplus population of free labourers exists is the worker coerced into performing surplus labour, does a C – B line' (i.e. surplus value) exist.[132] That the *cardinal preconditions* for the problem entirely consist of explaining the formation of surplus value, *although no competition exists and no surplus population* depresses the price of the commodity labour power – of this Sternberg has no idea and repeats in countless variants the same thing over and over again.[133] Instead of getting down to the basic elements of Marx's theory of surplus value, Sternberg's analysis remains stuck on the surface. The 'decisive question', to which he dedicates an entire chapter, is therefore for him: through which process is a surplus population of free workers created?

Of course, the question of the reserve army is 'important'. But even the first chapter, in which Sternberg discusses it, shows how he absolutely misconceives the essence and function of Marx's reserve army. Its emergence, as a result of technological progress, a *consequence* of capitalism in all of its historical phases, is confused with the *precondition* for capitalism: that independent producers are *separated* from their means of production, i.e. with the initial – if also always recurring – creation of proletarians. These are conflated under the common label of surplus population, obliterating the specifically capitalist tendency of 'setting workers free'. But, according to Sternberg, surplus population is important because it is the necessary condition for the *formation* of surplus value! Here Sternberg repeats Oppenheimer verbatim. For him, Marx's 'reproduction of the capital relation' arises from the existence of a surplus population.[134] Sternberg speaks of the decisive connections between surplus value and surplus population. 'Because ... two workers [under the pressure of the surplus population] chase after one master, the latter has ... the possibility of depressing the price of labour down to roughly the costs of reproduction, thus

132 Sternberg 1971, pp. 47, 16. [Grossman's emphasis.]
133 Sternberg 1971, pp. 50, 84, 585, 605.
134 Oppenheimer 1903, p. 28.

realising [!] surplus value'.[135] Why does the worker perform 'surplus labour'? '*Only* the analysis of surplus population can provide the answer.'[136] And here it is apparent how deeply Sternberg is bogged down in Malthusian conceptions, although he attempts to disguise this with a digression directed against Malthus. He holds that '*all theories of surplus value must be based on a theory of population*'.[137] 'Thus Malthus provides the ... foundation for every bourgeois analysis of surplus value.'[138] According to Sternberg, the entire difference between Marx and bourgeois theory, especially that of Malthus, is reduced to the fact 'that no bourgeois theory can therefore be explained without Malthus. Only once the *natural* surplus population causes two workers to chase after one master, only then is it possible to speak of surplus value.'[139] 'Malthus wants and has to show that the surplus population is a *natural* phenomenon under capitalism.' Marx's theory of surplus value, according to Sternberg, also depends on surplus population, with the mere difference that this overpopulation is not brought about *naturally*, but *economically* through the expropriation of independent producers and the formation of the actual industrial reserve army and is thus an *historical phenomenon*.[140]

Previously, it was generally understood that Marx's theory of surplus value meant that surplus value originates in the fundamental *capital relation*, i.e. the capitalist class's monopoly ownership of land and produced means of production. 'Wherever a part of society possesses *the monopoly* of the means of production, the worker, free or unfree, must add to the labour time necessary for his own maintenance an extra quantity of labour time'.[141] This monopoly, on the other hand, means that the working class, divorced from all objective conditions of labour, is forced to sell its labour power as a commodity. '*It is in fact this divorce* between the conditions of labour on the one hand and the producers on the other that *forms the concept of capital*.'[142] And the concept of capital is identical with its valorisation, with the production of surplus value.

> *The class relation* between capitalist and wage labourer is thus already present, already presupposed, the moment that the two confront each other in the act M-L (L-M from the side of the worker) ... *this relation does*

135 Sternberg 1971, p. 591.
136 Sternberg 1971, p. 585. [Sternberg emphasised the whole sentence.]
137 Sternberg 1971, p. 585. [Grossman's emphasis.]
138 Sternberg 1971, p. 593.
139 Sternberg 1971, p. 585. [Sternberg also emphasised the whole of the first sentence.]
140 Sternberg 1971, p. 597.
141 Marx 1976b, p. 344. [Grossman's emphasis.]
142 Marx 1981b, p. 354. [Grossman's emphasis.]

> *in fact exist, because the conditions for the realisation of labour power*, i.e. means of subsistence and means of production, *are separated, as the property of another*, from the possessor of labour power.[143]

In this divorce lies 'the compulsion to perform surplus labour' – and capital exercises this compulsion.[144] Capital, not surplus population! For *this separation is entirely independent of competition among workers*. It is the precondition for the existence of labour as *wage labour*. Even if two workers did not chase one master but, conversely, two masters chased one worker, the worker would at best receive a higher wage. But he would nevertheless be *forced* to perform surplus labour, surplus value would not disappear. For how can the worker live other than by selling himself, independently of the existence of a surplus population, and thus by committing himself in advance to performing surplus labour in return for permission even to be able to perform *necessary* labour for himself! Sternberg asks what compels him to do this *after* (!) he *has performed* the necessary labour for himself. But the problem consists precisely in how the worker can perform *necessary* labour for himself, given that he lacks the conditions of labour, which once belonged to the serf. The worker sells his labour power 'in order to secure the *required* means of subsistence.' His labour and surplus labour 'is for him only a means to enable him to *exist*,' asserts Marx.[145] And once again: capitalist production rests on the separation of the objective conditions of production from the personal,[146] which already *thus* determines the bases of distribution, hence also the division of the annual value product (into wages and surplus value). For 'the wage-worker has permission to work for his own subsistence, that is, *to live*, only in so far as he works for a certain time gratis for the capitalist.'[147]

In fact, we know that the assumption that no surplus population exists, that labour power is always sold at its value, and that nevertheless surplus value arises, forms the starting point of Marx's analysis.

It is embarrassing that today, 60 years after the appearance of *Capital*, it is still necessary to debate this fundamental assumption of Marx's analysis with a writer who seeks to make judgements about the most complex aspects of cap-

143 Marx 1978b, p. 115. [Grossman's emphasis. M-L is the exchange of labour power for money, L-M the exchange of money for labour power.]

144 Marx 1989c, p. 41. [Marx emphasised this phrase.]

145 Marx 1977, p. 202. [Grossman's emphasis. Marx emphasised 'means of subsistence' and 'means'.]

146 [i.e. workers not owning means of production.]

147 Marx 1989a, p. 92.

italism and Marx's theory – with reference, moreover, to the latter! – without being familiar with it in the slightest.

Is it astonishing then that Sternberg also necessarily misunderstands Marx's *theory of wages* and thus replaces it with his own 'improved' theory, which again dispenses banal *wisdom about competition* as the *only explanation for the level of wages?*

Marx's greatest merit is that he extended the theory of value – which Ricardo claimed to be valid for all commodities except labour power – to this commodity too. In this way the dangerous gap in Ricardo's theory was eliminated[148] and *all* aspects of exchange were subsumed under the *common principle* of labour value. As is well-known, the principle of value is that the value of commodities is determined by the socially necessary labour time required for their reproduction. Value may vary in time and place, but at a given time it is an *exactly determined, fixed magnitude*, determined by necessary labour time. Momentary market prices do fluctuate according to market relations, but as *prices* they are not determined by labour time. They always oscillate around *value*, as the constant centre, as the permanent price. If prices rise above value when there is a shortage of commodities, production is expanded and prices fall again to their value determined by labour time. The reverse occurs when prices fall below their value due to overproduction. Prices can only permanently rise above their value in the case of monopoly; then, however, other commodities must necessarily be sold below their values. Considered socially, the general level of prices is only explicable in terms of value, that is the magnitude of labour time. This labour time *is the necessary basis and precondition for* understanding the fluctuations and competition, *without which competition alone explains nothing*. This price and value mechanism does not literally apply to the commodity labour power (Marx precisely demonstrates the differences), but the essential components remain and the theory of wages is, for Marx, only a special application of his theory of value to the commodity labour power. Without this basis in value, Marx's theory of wages, 'the *basic proposition* of the whole system',[149] is superceded and the whole of Marx's system built on the law of value is invalid.[150]

148 Marx 1989c, p. 34.
149 Marx 1989c, p. 36. [Grossman's emphasis.]
150 [Marx 1981b, p. 398.]

The result is that the wage, i.e. the value of labour power, is and must also be determined by the labour time required for the reproduction of labour power. This wage may vary in time and place – but in each case it is permanently circumscribed by the labour time required for the reproduction of labour power, that is *exactly determined*, and independent of the market fluctuations elicited by competition, indeed it is a precondition for these fluctuations. We therefore have a double movement. On the one hand, the market prices of labour power oscillate according to the situation on the labour market, around the value or the costs of reproduction of labour power as a relatively constant centre. On the other hand, this centre itself has its own movement over shorter or longer periods. While the movement of market prices depends upon competition and is a matter of indifference for theory, the movement of the basis is determined by labour time, and is thus a constant, fixed magnitude, e.g. expressed on the line A – B by the magnitude A – C, at any given moment.[151]

A —— C —— B

Only insofar as this magnitude is fixed, in each case, and thus ends at an exactly determined point (e.g. C), measurable by the magnitude of labour time, *is it meaningful for theory*. It represents relative stability in the flood of change, because this C point defines the *permanent* price around which temporary market prices oscillate.

There is no trace of Marx's pursuit of this *fixed basis for the value* of labour power in Sternberg. What he describes as Marx's theory of wages is a banal theory of competition, which only sees oscillations and not the basis around which they take place. Sternberg asks 'What are the limits within which the *value* of labour power moves?'[152] In this formulation of the problem of wages he follows Oppenheimer literally, who likewise asks: 'How long can the *price* of labour continue to rise without its increase disturbing the progress of accumulation?'[153] Sternberg believes that, according to Marx, 'the *value* of the commodity labour power is equal to the means of consumption necessary for its reproduction'. Sternberg understands the costs of reproduction to be the lower limit, identical to the physical minimum necessary for existence or, as he says, 'the costs of reproduction in the literal sense.' 'The *upper limit* is never formu-

151 [For Sternberg A – B represents workers' daily production, A – C the labour necessary to reproduce the worker and C – B surplus labour appropriated by capitalists, Sternberg 1971, p. 63.]

152 Sternberg 1971, p. 52.

153 Oppenheimer 1903, p. 40. [Grossman's emphasis.]

lated [by Marx] with precise clarity', he does 'not say anything about the limit *up to* which wages can rise under the capitalist system'. 'The value of the commodity labour power is thus according to Marx[!] in a certain sense *elastic*.'[154] Sternberg does not once suspect that *with these words Marx's theory of value is abandoned*. The upper and lower limits between which the wage *moves* can only be spoken of in terms of the *price* of labour power, but not its *value*. Rising or falling prices, however, only ever have a transient character and are therefore of no interest for theory. At any given point of time, by contrast, the *labour time* required for the production of the necessary means of consumption for the worker is in each case a *magnitude given* by the state of technology. Consequently, the *value* of labour power is not elastic but rather, likewise, exactly determined. And the theory of value only makes sense and has any justification at all insofar as it is. For what sense would a theory of value have if the yardstick against which I measure all magnitudes itself fluctuates? If the value of labour power were at a certain moment really 'elastic' – as Sternberg claims – *then it could not be determined by labour time*, because this is fixed at any given moment, and Marx's theory of value in terms of labour time would be invalid. Marx says: 'The portion of the capital invested in the purchase of labour power is a *definite quantity of objectified labour*, a constant value like *the value of the labour power purchased*'.[155] If Sternberg rejects Marx's theory of wages, he consequently also has to reject Marx's theory of value. That he dismisses the former and nevertheless asserts that he accepts the latter in all its essential points only demonstrates his confusion!

But why does Sternberg, contradicting Marx, have to portray the cost of reproduction of labour power at a given point in time as a '*very elastic line*'? In fact wages rise, insofar as they are real wages, although not uniformly and generally. Sternberg encounters a difficulty in explaining this rise in terms of the *magnitude of labour time*, which is conceived of as fixed in each case. So he drops the theory of value and abstains from explaining the wage level in terms of the duration of *labour time*. He perceives an escape route for the explanation of rising wages in the assumption of an increase in wages above their reproduction time, thus *above the value* of labour power. In doing so, he conceives of this increase not as a *momentary* rise in the *price* of labour power above its costs of reproduction or *value* (momentary price deviations from value due to competition are irrelevant to theory), but as an *enduring* increase in wages above value (!), i.e. above the costs of reproduction. 'It must be emphatically stressed,' he

154 Sternberg 1971, pp. 54, 334 and especially 492, 53, 57. [Grossman's emphasis.]

155 Marx 1976b, p. 322. [Grossman's emphasis.]

says, 'that Marx, in the whole analysis, never goes into the case in which the working class achieves a wage increase *à la longue*, so *that its standard is above the costs of reproduction, in the long run*'.[156] Sternberg accomplishes precisely this feat! But *enduring* wage increases above reproduction costs are no longer *price* fluctuations, which oscillate around the *value* of labour power, but can only be understood as long run increases in the *value* of labour power. The result of Sternberg's contention, *therefore, is that the value of labour power can be above its value in the long run, or that the law of value* is perfect nonsense.

Nothing more banal has ever been presented so pretentiously and the confusion is only intelligible as ignorance.

1. It is incorrect for Sternberg to identify Marx's concept of the costs of reproduction with the physical minimum necessary for existence. According to Marx, they are not connected with any specific living standard. The high standard of living of the English worker only represents the *necessary* costs of reproduction for the English worker, just as the low wages do for a Chinese coolie. Living standards can rise although reproduction costs fall. These are indeed, in each case, a fixed magnitude, but vary according to place and time. Marx demonstrated that these costs of reproduction, to the extent that they represent real wages, i.e. a certain mass of means of consumption, *necessarily increase* with the progressive development of capitalism, entirely independently of any competition. That is, on the one hand, they are higher for the English worker than for the Chinese but, on the other hand, in England itself they exhibit a tendency to rise. 'The more productive one country is relative to another in the world market, *the higher will be its wages* as compared with the other. In England, not only nominal wages but *real* wages are higher than on the continent'.[157]

This increase does not mean, as Sternberg expresses it, that wages, the *value* of labour power, rise above the costs of reproduction A – C. The costs of reproduction are identical with value for Marx. Rather *the costs of reproduction themselves rise*, thus the line A – C becomes longer. D did not rise beyond point C – which could only be a momentary price deviation, but a theoretical absurdity if thought of as an enduring deviation. Rather the line A – C grew (to Sternberg's point D).[158] It did not terminate at point D, beyond the costs of reproduction C, but at the *new point* C, at the *new value* of labour power, which means nothing other than *that the labour time necessary for the reproduction of labour power changed*.

156 Sternberg 1971, pp. 62, 55. ['*À la longue*' means 'in the long run'. Grossman's emphasis.]

157 Marx 1989b, p. 252.

158 See diagram below.

2. In this situation, and from the standpoint of Marx's theory of wages, the question arises: which factors modify the *value* of labour power, i.e. its reproduction time (the distance A – C)? For Sternberg, the increase in wages from C to D on the line A – B is simply *brought about by the existence of non-capitalist countries*. For only to the extent that such areas are available is the realisation of surplus value, thus also capital accumulation, and consequently *rising demand for workers* possible. This demand can drive wages up above the costs of reproduction. Thus, non-capitalist areas are '*of decisive* importance' for the set of questions treated here. Earlier, however, we demonstrated that the attempt to explain changes in commodity prices solely in terms of the play of demand and supply eliminates the possibility of any real explanation at all. Incidentally, the explanation that a wage increase over longer periods of increased demand for labour assumes a movement in price, independent of the magnitude of *labour time*, and thus signifies the *abandonment of Marx's theory of value*. In fact, the true problem of real wages, for Marx, consists of how real wages can rise *independently* of the shifting play of supply, by the entrepreneur or the worker. That is, how can wages *rise* although the commodity labour power is always sold at its costs of reproduction, at its value! Actually, it is precisely in this formulation of the problem that the originality of Marx's theory of wages lies.

All of Sternberg's distortions presented so far have only been possible because of his failure to notice and understand Marx's *methodological procedure*. Among the many simplifying fictions in Marx's analysis is the fiction of constant *intensity* of labour, i.e. that under these circumstances the constant quantity of labour for the reproduction of labour power also requires a constant, given *mass* of means of consumption. Under this assumption, if we assume an increasing productivity of labour, the value of these means of consumption must *fall*, shift left from point C towards A. But, of course for Marx, this whole deduction has only a provisional character, in order not to complicate the analysis too much, *in the first instance*. Marx does not forget, however, to emphasise against Ricardo that this does not take into account the actually *growing intensity* [of labour], and conducts his analysis 'only on the assumption that the working day is a *constant* magnitude [both] *intensively* [and extensively]'.[159] Marx stresses that the assumption that v stays constant is made 'for the sake of simplicity'.[160] 'But in reality ... a *change in* ... *intens-*

159 Marx 1981b, p. 349. [Grossman's emphasis. He replaced the text in square brackets with elipses.]

160 Marx 1981b, p. 143.

ity' accompanies the labour process.[161] Of course, the provisional assumptions must subsequently be corrected, and that is done in *Capital* at length.

In fact, Marx shows that the increase in the costs of reproducing labour power, the wage level, necessarily *results from the consistent increase in the intensity of labour* constituted by the capitalist production process, even when competition is excluded.[162] Workers can only perform more intensive labour when their food, clothing and mental recreation improve, and live under orderly domestic conditions. Consequently the *mass* of means of consumption required is not a *given* magnitude, but grows *with the intensity* of labour. Thus, amounting to the same thing, *real wages grow* too. Point C shifts right and the line A – C becomes longer. *The tendency for real wages to rise* is therefore a self-evident consequence of the mechanism of capitalist production and, at the same time, a consequence of Marx's law of wages. No *ad-hoc*[163] theory of non-capitalist areas or any other work around is required to explain it. 'Even with given limits of the working day … *a rise of wages* may become *necessary*, if only to keep up the *old standard value* of labour. By *increasing the intensity* of labour, a man may be made to expend as much vital force in one hour as he formerly did in two.'[164]

It does not need to be stressed here that rising intensity of labour has to be sharply differentiated from rising *productivity*. And that this is not only limited to skilled workers. The modern capitalist enterprise is a mechanism whose elements are forced into an increased tempo of production. If more cotton is spun, more bales of cotton will be unloaded, and more yarn will be packaged.[165]

We have previously only considered Sternberg's theory of wages from the standpoint of the *level* of real wages. Now it must be examined from the angle *of the extent of profit*.

Sternberg borrowed the idea, also irreconcilable with Marx's theory, that wage increases occur at the expense of profits from Oppenheimer, just as he did the forumulation of the problem of wages.

161 Marx 1976b, p. 663. [Grossman's emphasis.]

162 Marx 1976b, p. 533.

163 ['*Ad hoc*' literally 'to this', means a measure adopted for a very specific purpose.]

164 Marx 1985c, p. 142. [Grossman's emphasis. Marx emphasised '*value of labour*'.]

165 This theoretical explanation for rising wages in all capitalist countries during the second half of the nineteenth century as a *general* cause does not preclude still other temporary factors from *also* operating in the same direction. 'One of the most important factors in maintaining the standard of life of the European working class', Kautsky writes, 'was *the fall in price of food products* since the [18]70s … It raised the purchasing power of their money wages, softened the effect of their fall during crises, and during the time of revival permitted real wages to rise faster than money wages.' Kautsky 1909, p. 90. [Editor's interpolation.]

It was previously shown that nothing is more misleading than Sternberg's portrayal of the growth in real wages (measured in use values) as a shift from C to D on the line A – B.

A —— C – D —— B

In doing so, capitalist *surplus value* becomes smaller, reduced from C – B to D – B. A conception worthy of a Bastiat or of his modern echo, Yves Guyot.[166] 'All factors that raise the living standards of the working class, that bring about the A – D line', Sternberg thinks, '... have the effect of strengthening imperialist advance, *because increasing wages mean falling profits*'.[167]

In this way, Marx's theory of surplus value is abandoned and Sternberg falls back far behind Rodbertus in his knowledge of the capitalist mechanism. Yet again he follows Oppenheimer, who interprets Marx's theory of wages and value to mean not only that nominal wage increases occur 'at the expense of profits'. Only on one condition, however, can rising wages mean falling profits: if the productivity of labour is *constant*. In that case, its *value* is constant and the rise in wages would mean a temporary rise in the *price* of labour power over its value, thus a reduction of profit – a temporary consequence of market competition that need not concern us, where we are speaking of enduring wage increases. But because, in speaking of the *enduring* developmental tendencies, the productivity of labour cannot be assumed to be constant, increased real wages resulting from the heightened productivity of labour, must *fall in value terms*, for they never grow in proportion with the development of the productive forces. *Consequently, profits must grow despite rising real wages*. The rate of surplus value, the degree of exploitation of labour, despite rising real wages, does not fall, but grows *with the development of the productivity of labour*. This, Sternberg's great blunder, reveals the consequences of his contemptuous dismissal of the theory of relative wages as Kautsky's invention. It therefore becomes self-evident that his graphical presentation of wages on sections of *one* line is misleading too. The value of the working day presents itself, before and after the wage increase resulting from the change in productivity, in *different quantities of use values*, and must therefore be correctly presented as *two* separate lines.

166 [Bastiat 1880; for example, see Guyot 1894.]
167 Sternberg 1971, p. 271. [Grossman's emphasis.]

Case 1: A —— C —— B
Case 2: A ——— C ——— | ——— B

In the second case, real wages A – C, as use values, have grown by half. But while in Case 1 wages account for half of the total value, in Case 2 they constitute merely a third. In the latter case, surplus value C – B has grown. *The value of labour power has fallen* and *continues to fall* with the development of the productive forces, despite *the progressive growth of real wages*. It is characteristic of Sternberg's superficiality that he does not distinguish between wages as *value* and as *use value*, and thus identifies rising wages with falling profits!

These elementary conclusions allow us to judge Sternberg's complete confusion, which expresses itself both in the question posed and in the answer. To the question, taken over verbatim from Oppenheimer,[168] 'how high can wages rise without disturbing the progress of accumulation', comes the answer, according to Sternberg 'absolutely unambiguously from Marx's system', that '[w]ages can rise as long as the worker cannot accumulate [!], i.e. as long as the denominator in the fraction capital/labour does not decline'. Thus, Sternberg thinks, again with Oppenheimer, 'that the workers can *accumulate*'! If this occurs nowhere, it is only because capital has 'prevented its labour force from crossing the boundary by continuously creating *surplus population*'.[169] Without this, according to Sternberg, the working class would increase wages so much *that capitalism would be superceded*. Overpopulation is the only reason for the existence of capitalism! Incidentally, this nonsense follows directly from Sternberg's conception of the formation of surplus value. But the facts show something entirely different. Nowhere in the capitalist world have workers successfully accumulated. The capitalist class has remained the exclusive owner of the means of production, and the power of this property has also at all times given it the power to reproduce the capital relation. For, thanks to the separation of the conditions of production from labour power, capital is always able to take *everything* that exceeds the necessary means of consumption from the worker. Workers are therefore allotted only these *in the long run*; they never receive more than what is necessary for the reproduction of labour power which, however, has nothing to do with the physical minimum necessary for existence and in no way precludes *rising* real wages. If it were different, the rise *above the necessary* means of consumption would last longer and the *price* of labour power would rise above its *value* and thus profits would fall. The capit-

168 Oppenheimer 1903, p. 40.
169 Sternberg 1971, p. 22; Oppenheimer 1903, pp. 36, 39. [Grossman's emphasis.]

alists would exclude a section of the workers from the active army by means of rationalisation, technological improvements, etc. The pressure of the growing reserve army would, in the long run, indeed cause wages to fall to the level of the *value* of labour power. Why then have these entrepreneurs not intensified the rationalisation and mechanisation of the economy and calmly let wages rise since the middle of the nineteenth century? Could rationalisation not actually more than offset increased demand for labour, due to the 'advance' into non-capitalist markets? Sternberg has no answer. In truth, however, this did not occur because the rising wage was nevertheless *necessary*. And it is 'necessary' because, in the long run, there are neither deductions from it, nor does the worker receive anything above it. Despite increasing real wages, then, the worker is *not* able to accumulate. The notion that wage increases cause *profits to fall* and that therefore rising wages are a threat or lead to the supercession of capitalism is fundamentally wrong. It does not perceive that rising real wages and rising profits are quite compatible and that, as a matter of fact, parallel to the development of capitalism in the second half of the nineteenth century, *profits rose enormously and continue to rise*.

But even more peculiar than Sternberg's theory of wages and profits is the use to which he puts it. He sees in rising real wages a tendency to attenuate the inner unrealisability of surplus value, because a 'domestic outlet is created' by the '*increased purchasing power*' of the workers of one section of capital.[170] Of course, an industrial worker who earns 8 Marks can purchase more than if he only earns 6 Marks. If he earned 6 Marks and the value of his output amounted to 12 Marks, he could purchase half of it. If the value of his output now amounts to 32 Marks, despite a wage increase to 8 Marks, he can merely buy a quarter of it, and it is misleading to claim that the purchasing power of the workforce rose in the course of capitalism's history. Even if one wanted to admit that, in the course of the nineteenth century, real wages in core capitalist countries rose by 70–100 percent, it should not be forgotten that, at the same time, productivity increased ten and a hundredfold. Even in agriculture, crop yields doubled, e.g. in Germany 1879–1913,[171] after the first two thirds of the nineteenth century when, according to Sombart's estimate, the average increase in yield amounted to 50 percent for wheat, 100 percent for rye, barley and oats, and even more for the production of meat. On the whole, Sombart assumes that in Germany during the nineteenth century it at least doubled and perhaps tripled – according to Dellbrück even quadrupled – and indeed without a corresponding

170 Sternberg 1971, p. 271. [Grossman's emphasis.]

171 Cf. Ballod 1927, p. 86.

increase in the rural population.[172] The rapidity of the growth in the productivity of industrial labour is extensively documented. In raw iron and steel works and rolling mills it doubled in the single decade 1884/85–1895/96, following the mechanisation of operations. For example, at the Phönix combine in 1884/85 each worker produced 23.9 tonnes of semi-finished and finished commodities. In contrast, by 1895/96 the figure rose to 54.1 tonnes, an increase of 126 percent.[173] According to the investigations of the US Department of Labor in 1925, productivity per worker per hour in *steel works and rolling mills* rose by two and a half times from 1899; in the *rubber industry* between 1914 and 1925 it rose by more than three times (100:311); in *blast furnace operations* it almost doubled, after production had already doubled between 1899 and 1909. In *petroleum refining* the increase amounted to 73 percent; in *cotton spinning* between 1911 and 1916, 45.4 percent and 1916 to 1925, 91.3 percent. In *weaving* the numbers are 1911 to 1916, 10 percent, 1916 to 1925, 29.4 percent; in the years 1914 to 1925 in the *cement industry*, 47.8 percent, the *leather industry* 28.2 percent, *flour milling* 39 percent, *automobiles* more than 200 percent. These numbers show the increase in the *quantity* of products without considering the substantially greater *quality*.[174] The following information illustrates the significant, stormy tempo [of growth] in *coal mining* over the last 13 years: 'the average, monthly, per capita output per shift of the coal miners and quarry workers in Ruhr coal mining amounted to: 1,845 in 1913; 1,907 in 1924; 2,100 in 1925; 2,270 in January 1926; 2, 883 in May, 1926; 2,910 in September, 1926.' 'Daily output per worker in German *pig iron and raw steel production* rose from 24 to 38 percent, between January 1925 and November 1926.'[175]

In contrast, what does a rise in the real wage of, at best, 100 percent over an entire century signify, when wide layers of the working class were excluded from this rise? Wages as a portion of total annual product *fell* despite rising wages. *Thus the purchasing power of the working class has fallen, not risen*. Sternberg's attempt to identify, in the 'increased purchasing power' of the workforce, an outlet for a part of the otherwise unrealisable surplus value rests on the same theoretical level as Henry Ford's.[176] If this is correct, it would be most advisable for the capitalists to raise wages so high that the *whole* of the otherwise unrealisable surplus value is 'realised!'

---

172 Sombart 1903, pp. 413–14. [The reference to 'Dellbrück' is presumably to the review of Sombart's book, Delbrück 1903.]

173 Cf. Kunze 1926, p. 40.

174 *Deutsche Arbeit*, 1927, p. 113.

175 Woytinsky 1927, p. 823.

176 [Ford 1922.]

During the nineteenth century, according to Sternberg, a general rise in wages occured which is, for him, identical with *falling* profits. At the same time, however, the *number of money capitalists*, rentiers, bankers, sales people and other agents of circulation, as well as other unproductive workers in the sphere of circulation (who do not *create* value), *grew*. The situation of these elements must have *become extremely bad*. Falling profits and the growth in the number of those who take a share! In one breath, however, Sternberg again claims that the number of rich in general grew.[177] Although profits fell? In contrast, Marx showed us that the layers mentioned grow with the source from which they live: *only growing surplus value* allows and makes possible growth in the number of capitalists and their fellow consumers of surplus value and allows their luxury to rise steadily.

Although the development of the productivity of labour raises wages by increasing the intensity of work, 'this does not, however, prevent [capitalists'] revenue from constantly growing, in value and in quantity ... Those classes and sub-classes who do not live directly from their labour *become more numerous and live better* than before, and *the number of unproductive* workers increases as well'.[178] It is not difficult to demonstrate that real relations confirm this. In his book on British *imperialism*, [Gerhart] Schultze-Gävernitz points out the 'expansion' of the rentier class with 'its retinues of domestic menials. The large number of servants is striking for someone from the continent'; as is growing luxury. 'In close connection ... there is, finally, the *growing significance of the domestic market*, whereas foreign markets are receding, at least relatively ... *England's exports per capita are declining*'.[179]

It is apparent that *only* Marx's theory of wages and surplus value can consistently and coherently explain the increase in real wages and the simultaneous fall in workers' purchasing power despite, however, growth in profits, consequently the number of workers who are not involved in production and who are unproductive, thus the growing importance of the domestic market. This much is certain, that those numerous theoreticians who, like Oppenheimer, characterise Marx's theory of wages as a theory of impoverishment have overlooked the methodological procedure in his treatment of the problem of wages, mentioned here, as well as the factor of the increasing intensity [of labour].[180]

177 Sternberg 1971, p. 257.

178 Marx 1989c, p. 188. [Grossman's emphasis.]

179 Schulze-Gävernitz 1906, pp. 323, 361, 324, 321. [Grossman's emphasis.]

180 It is no contradiction, however, if from a certain phase of capital accumulation on, in relation to *over* accumulation and capitalism's breakdown tendency, Marx's doctrine of wages assumes that the rise in real wages ceases and *finally they reverse to positively decline*. Marx

Sternberg is no exception. It is characteristic for him to make use of all possible quotations from Marx about the determination of wages, but not Marx's important methodological explanation. Nor does he mention Marx's explanation of the effect of the rising intensity of labour on the level of wages at all!

Sternberg's theory of wages is, however, also extremely odd in other ways. We have seen how, in his opinion, the realisation of surplus value and therefore also the accumulation of capital would be impossible without non-capitalist markets. Hence, wages also have to remain low and the reserve army has to emerge. Only imperialist advance into non-capitalist areas makes it possible to realise surplus value and to accumulate. Increasing wages are *the result* of imperialist advance. According to him, this is his great discovery, which allows him *to explain rising wages*, as these are supposedly inexplicable from the standpoint of Marx's theory of wages. But then we hear something entirely different. Workers' rising living standards, *rising wages*, have 'the effect *of strengthening imperialist advance*, because increasing wages mean *falling profits*'.[181] According to this argument, rising wages are no longer the *result* of imperialist advance, but its *cause*. Increasing wages, which are *in the first place supposed to be explained by* imperialist advance, become themselves the explanation for this advance – and so Sternberg turns in circles, like a cat trying to catch its own shadow.

Only in *one* case, according to Marx's theory of wages, could the commodity labour power *continually* obtain a *price above* its value; namely, if during the whole period over which Sternberg claims wages increased in western Europe, roughly since the middle of the nineteenth century, an insufficient quantity of labour power was available, thus if it was a *monopoly commodity*, and unemployment never prevailed. Hardly anyone would dare to claim, however, that this was actually the case. For this reason, the central pillar of Sternberg's account collapses.

3. If, meanwhile, we query the logic of Sternberg's positive account of the problem of wages, if we ask with what Sternberg replaces Marx's theory of wages, to which he objects, the answer is short: *competition!* If non-capitalist areas are available and thus the realisation of surplus value and accumulation are possible, there will be a *rising demand for labour*. If there is a lack of such

has this *end* phase of capital accumulation in mind when he says 'that in proportion as capital accumulates, the situation of the worker, be his payment high or low, must grow worse', Marx 1976b, p. 799. Despite improvements in the conditions of the working class even over prolonged periods, the tendency to impoverishment *finally* asserts itself. 'This is the absolute general law of capitalist accumulation', Marx 1976b, p. 798 [Marx emphasised the whole sentence]. It would lead too far afield to provide further justifications for this idea here.

181 Sternberg 1971, p. 271. [Grossman's emphasis.]

areas, counter-effects set in: a surplus population arises, thus an *increasing supply of labour power*. Relying on Franz Oppenheimer's false account of Marx's theory of wages, Sternberg expresses determination of wages in the fraction WG = CD/LS, in which the wage level is determined by the fluctuation of both arms of the scale – capital's demand CD and working class' supply LS, that is by *competition*. The only difference between Sternberg and the numerous other vulgar theoreticians who have taken refuge in competition to explain wage levels is just that, for him, the movement of both arms of the scale, CD and LS, are determined not merely by market relations in *capitalist* countries, but also in *non-capitalist* areas. Sternberg consciously abandons Marx's achievement compared with Ricardo, which constitutes the necessary precondition and starting point for all competition: the determination of the *value* of labour power, its costs of reproduction. 'If the *theory of surplus population* is placed at the centre' [of the analysis], he writes, 'then the result is that the debates over the theory of value are of marginal relevance to our problem'.[182] Rather than value, surplus population, competition, is at the centre! As a pupil of Oppenheimer, Sternberg believes Marx's theory really is expressed in the formula WG = CD/LS, thus in a theory of competition, which he only wants to improve. To this end he includes non-capitalist areas. For it was Oppenheimer who presented Marx's theory of wages as a wage fraction theory,[183] thus as a variant of the Smith-Ricardo wage-fund theory! According to Smith, wages are determined by capital's demand on the labour market and by the supply of labour, expressed in symbols by the fraction WG = CD/LS, whose numerator stands for total capital and denominator the number of workers. Ricardo's variant makes the numerator smaller by splitting total capital into fixed and circulating capital, and claims that only the latter exercises demand for labour, therefore fixed capital F must be separated out. Hence, WG = (CD-F)/LS. According to Oppenheimer's account, Marx goes further in the same direction by eliminating the part of circulating capital spent on raw and auxiliary materials from the numerator. Marx combines this with the fixed capital into 'constant' capital c, so only the residual capital, variable capital v, exercises demand for labour. According to Oppenheimer, therefore, Marx's formula for wages is WG = (CD-c)/LS = v/LS. Sternberg follows this uncritically when he also carelessly writes CD/LS, which we do, however, not take literally and therefore want to assume that he did not want to put total capital in the numerator, but merely variable.

182 Sternberg 1971, p. 64. [Grossman's emphasis.]
183 [Oppenheimer 1926, p. 43.]

His dependence on Oppenheimer has revenged itself on Sternberg. It is precisely Marx's achievement to have shown that competition can indeed explain deviations from a *given* [value] basis, but never the basis itself; that therefore any theory that is true must first of all determine the latter. 'It is a method,' Marx says, 'of getting from the variations that accompany competition to the limits of these variations'.[184] *Oppenheimer left out of his formula* Marx's basis for the determination of wages: *the factor of the costs of reproduction*, r. Marx's wage formula is WG = r × v/LS. Because, however, Marx begins statically and therefore sets v = LS or 1/1, he can disregard the fraction v/LS, so that wages for him are determined by the coefficient r, i.e. by the costs of reproduction or the *value* of labour power, which is entirely independent of competition. Competition, the relation v/LS, alone can explain nothing because it does not mean anything. If this relation is less favourable for workers in England than in Belgium, if in England the supply of workers is greater, e.g. 2/5, while it merely amounts to 3/2 in Belgium, i.e. supply is greater than demand, we can know nothing about the actual wage level as long as we do not know the costs of reproduction of labour to which this fraction must be related. If the factor r amounts to 10 for England and merely 2 for Belgium, wages will nevertheless be higher in England than in Belgium despite a 'surplus population.' In England it amounts to 10 × 2/5 = 4. In Belgium, in contrast and despite more favourable relations for workers, it amounts to 2 × 3/2 = 3.

We see that, initially, Sternberg denies the factor r, the basis of value independent of competition, and presents Marx's theory as purely a theory of competition, in order then to declare it so sterile as to be untenable and to replace it with an 'improved' theory of competition. But whether it is now an ordinary or an improved theory of competition, that is what it is, and it is bound to surface appearances without understanding their foundation, their basis in value.

Non-capitalist areas and the greater demand for labour generated by them are just as incapable of explaining a *general and longer lasting* wage increase as any other factor of competition. Each such longer wage increase, resulting from *increased demand* would have been easy to overcome. More vigorous rationalisation, better machines, capital equipment, etc. (applicable just as soon as the non-capitalist areas allow for the realisation of surplus value) *would have to off-set the increased demand for labour and create a reserve army*. Wages would have to sink to *the former level* or even *below* it. Why did capitalists not exploit this opportunity and 'prefer' to pay higher wages, for five decades? Sternberg cannot answer this question. On the contrary, Marx's theory of the intensity of

184 Marx 1981b, p. 485.

labour demonstrates that wages – *à la longue* – *cannot be pushed below* a certain level without also reducing the *efficiency of labour*! The level of the *value basis* of labour power is independent of the fluctuating factors of competition and hence, in the long run, of the arbitrary desires for power of the capitalist class. It is, rather, an *objectively given magnitude*, which depends upon the particular level of capitalist development, the intensity of labour, and thus also the corresponding value of labour power. Thus we observe the remarkable fact that in England, in all areas where the intensity of labour has grown[185] with factories' better technical equipment, *despite the defeat of the miners' strike*, despite the greatest defeat ever chronicled in the history of the workers' movement, wages *rose* and did not fall! The increase at Cannock Chase amounted to 5 percent, in Leicestershire 6 percent, in Nottinghamshire and north Derbyshire even 23 percent; in Warwickshire wages remained unchanged.[186] A similar pattern can be observed in Germany. Despite the rationalisation of the steel industry and the growing mass of unemployed, the pressure on the employed did not reduce their wages. In April the average monthly income of a worker at a large steel mill amounted to 163 Marks, in September to 195 Marks in December to 198.5 Marks.[187]

But, in addition to his chapter on wages, Sternberg has another, second brilliant achievement, the 'crisis chapter', which deals with the actual *problem, imperialism*, the indispensable existence of non-capitalist areas and consequently expansion or capitalist 'advance' into non-capitalist areas, and the struggle over their division. According to Sternberg, Marx did not notice the role of these areas at all, because he only analysed 'pure' capitalism, so *there are no external markets*, because he started from the assumption that capitalism is the single-ruling form of production.

It is indeed true that Marx made this assumption. But that was merely a working hypothesis, similar to the others with which we have already become acquainted. Self-evidently, Marx *subsequently* introduced the necessary correction, and thus *the role of external markets is subsequently integrated by Marx*

---

185 Rising intensity in English mining in the first quarter of 1927 compared to the equivalent period in 1926 amounts to over 13 percent. 'If one makes the average of the first quarter of 1926 as equal to 100, output has now (1927) risen to about 104, while the workforce has sunk to about 92', *Arbeitgeber* 1927, p. 191.

186 Cf. shift earnings of miners and unskilled workers (during the day) in the most important coal regions of Great Britain before and after the strike of 1926, *Wirtschaft und Statistik*, 1, 1927, p. 34.

187 *Arbeitgeber* 1927, p. 192. If according to most English newspaper reports miners' wages fell again in recent months, this can only be temporary without seriously compromising efficiency.

into his system and illuminated. In his methodological ineptitude, Sternberg has no notion of this. Rosa Luxemburg, who likewise overlooked this methodological connection in Marx, at least explained his apparent failure to observe external markets by pointing out the unfinished character of his work; Sternberg resorts to the odd idea that Marx was a blind, floundering lunatic. He asserts in all seriousness that Marx planned *Capital* under the assumption that there are no external markets, 'which [therefore] prevented Marx from knowing about *essential connections*'. And Rosa Luxemburg 'was the first to recognise the connections'.[188] Marx's fictional, simplifying assumptions are cited extensively as evidence and then he smugly states 'Marx investigated capitalism under a methodological assumption, which *has never previously existed*'.[189] Such an analysis works with assumptions, '*which are unproved*[!], more than this, whose realisation[!] is improbable'.[190] As though Marx had in mind the realisation of his assumptions! Does it once occur to Sternberg to ask which methodological end Marx pursued with his assumptions? Indeed, Marx wrote repeatedly and with emphasis that 'Capitalist production never exists without foreign trade'.[191] And elsewhere: 'Capitalist production ... is only [possible] on the basis of foreign trade and of the *world market*. This is at once the *pre-condition* and the result of capitalist production'.[192] Had Sternberg asked himself why Marx omitted the elements that he himself observed in the empirical world, he would have immediately noticed that Marx adopted this method as a conscious reaction against the predecessors of Rosa Luxemburg, against the theoreticians of 'third persons,' standing outside of capitalism, which provide a market for its [capitalism's] overproduction, *against* Malthus. In order demonstrate that solutions offered by the theory of external markets are spurious and to clarify the real role of external markets, the theory of 'third persons' is first astutely defeated and the Malthusian question, 'Whence come the buyers who relieve the capitalist of his surplus value?', is dealt with [by Marx].[193] The problem itself is then addressed positively in a two-stage method. First, pure capitalism without foreign markets is analysed and subsequently the function of these markets. Thus, what in Marx is merely a *preliminary* assumption, a stage of cognition, Sternberg presents as the *final result* of Marx's analysis. Sternberg does not,

188 Sternberg 1971, pp. 22, 23 [Sternberg emphasised the whole of this phrase].

189 Sternberg 1971, pp. 23, 303. [Grossman paraphrases here. Sternberg actually wrote 'has not previously been realised ... and cannot be realised'.]

190 Sternberg 1971, p. 301. [Grossman's emphasis.]

191 Marx 1978b, p. 546.

192 Marx 1989c, p. 388. [Grossman's emphasis. Interpolation by the editors of Marx 1989c.]

193 Marx 1989c, pp. 216–17, 233–46.

therefore, see Marx's subsequent corrections and it is, for him, Rosa Luxemburg who – a hundred years after Malthus – discovers the theory of external markets.

Sternberg's entire book is based only on the constantly repeated assertion that Marx *merely* investigated 'pure' capitalism but did not deal with non-capitalist areas. It therefore collapses, for the opposite appears to have been proved. In *A Contribution to the Critique*,[194] Marx had already designated the 'world market' as one of the six parts [of the project which became *Capital*] that he planned to deal with. And although the structure of the work changed, the object itself remained and Marx often returned to the problem of non-capitalist countries. He was also the one who argued *against* John Stuart Mill, who actually assumed that capitalist production was already dominant: 'Strange optical illusion, to see everywhere a situation *which as yet exists only exceptionally on our earth!*'[195]

Here again Sternberg only rehashes other people's thoughts and raises *against* Marx the criticism that Marx raised against Mill. This whole confusion readily explains why Sternberg never knows how to differentiate between [points] where Marx presents reality directly and where he approaches the same goal step-by-step, with the help of provisional assumptions.

Now why did Marx initially disregard foreign markets? His polemic against Malthus provides us with a precise explanation. Malthus – much more consistently than Rosa Luxemburg – allows the unrealisable surplus value which seeks new buyers to be realised by a special class of third persons – those on pensions from landed estates, the state and church – *'buyers who are not sellers'*.[196] However, if one stands on the ground of normal commercial transactions, where for each commodity of a given value sold another of *the same* value is received as an equivalent, one cannot speak of the 'disposal' of an excess quantity of products. After the transaction, one is simply back at the beginning: surplus value as well as use value and value *remain* inside the capitalist economy itself, not an atom is 'relocated' to the non-capitalist country. At most, under the assumption of the sale of commodities at their values, use values can be changed from one natural form to another. As important as this otherwise is, it has nothing to do with the problem of finding new buyers, new purchasing power. In further analysis, Marx ultimately shows that precisely in world trade the fictitious assumption of the sale of commodities at their value, which underpins the reproduction schema *does not exist*. The richer, more developed

194 Marx 1987a, p. 261.

195 Marx 1976b, p. 653. [Grossman's emphasis.]

196 Marx 1989c, p. 216. [Marx's list of such people is 'landlords, pensioners, sinecurists, priests, etc., not to forget their menial servants and retainers'.]

country always sells its commodities *above* their value and therefore draws *more value* from the world market than it cast into it. The function of non-capitalist markets is therefore according to Marx, the direct opposite of that claimed by Rosa Luxemburg and, following her, Sternberg. According to Luxemburg capitalism is threatened by breakdown as a result of the production of unrealisable surplus value, which can only flow into non-capitalist areas. Capitalism, whose sole purpose is the pursuit of surplus value suffers from having 'too much' surplus value! Can one imagine a solution more inconsistent?

In reality – and this is the basic idea of Marx's theory of breakdown – *surplus value is insufficient,* beyond a certain stage of capital accumulation, to *valorise* capital. That is absolute overaccumulation, hence the necessary *end* of capitalist production, breakdown: capital cannot exercise its sole function of valorising capital. The death of capitalism is here a logical consequence of its nature, the chase after surplus value. If capitalism is successful in selling commodities *above* their value through foreign trade, if it is at all successful in obtaining *more* surplus value from outside, then the valorisation of capital becomes possible – the breakdown is postponed, the tendency to breakdown is weakened. And Marx *enumerates a whole series of such attenuating factors.*

To cite only one of these, let us mention the *export of capital.* In Rosa Luxemburg's account as in Sternberg's, it is mentioned as a fact, but how to incorporate it into the 'system' without getting into the most flagrant contradictions is not apparent. Capitalism suffers from an excess of surplus value because no purchasers are available for it. But by exporting capital to non-capitalist countries, *new* surplus value is produced there and brought into the old capitalist countries! In reality, the export of capital has the task of rectifying the insufficient valorisation of capital, thus of weakening the breakdown tendency.

It is only this methodological connection between the breakdown tendency and attenuating factors, arising from the world market, that show us what an important role, if one entirely different from that assumed by Rosa Luxemburg, Marx accorded to foreign trade and how he described this role in its last details. It is a testament to the unbelievably low level of previous research on Marx that this central problem of Marx's system has previously been unnoticed.

Does it make sense, under such circumstances, to argue with Sternberg about problems of imperialism? These are the *most complex* phenomena of the world market, the understanding of which presupposes full knowledge of Marx's system. It was shown above, however, that Sternberg has the most confused conceptions of the most *elementary* phenomena as of Marx's *basic concepts.* What would one say about the qualities of a physicist, who argued against [Galileo] Galilei that he investigated bodies falling in a vacuum, that is 'under a methodological assumption that has never been realised', which 'is unproved and whose realisation is improbable'! Can one, after that, argue with Sternberg about whether the realisation of surplus value is possible or an unrealisable remainder is necessary? For Marx's theory of profit and wages constitutes the necessary prerequisite for the movements of profits and wages in Marx's reproduction schemas. *How, then, can Sternberg himself draw any conclusions about the development of capitalism from the schema* after he has falsely described the elements on which the schema is built?

As a curiosity, one example will be singled out from Sternberg's abundant errors:

After the revolution and the expropriation of the rentier class, it will be necessary to abolish rentier industries satisfying demand for luxuries, that is, to restructure part of industry. 'For the period of transition', Sternberg concludes, '*the productivity of labour therefore falls*'.[197] Has Sternberg given this any thought whatsoever?

The chapter on 'Imperialist war' constitutes the central point of Sternberg's theory of imperialism. Without any new ideas of his own, here too Sternberg treads in the footsteps of others. Oppenheimer does not complain without justice that he was extensively plundered without being named.[198] We have seen how Sternberg discards in turn all the essential foundations of the 'historical' Marx. What he presents as his positive theory is only borrowing from 'value-free' theorists like Bernstein, [Antonio] Graziadei, Tugan-Baranovsky,[199] who all, likewise, 'freed' themselves from value theory and attempted to explain all capitalist phenomena by means of power relations and competition. Sternberg makes similar 'borrowings' with regard to the principal point of his analyses: *imperialist war*, its historical inevitability, as well as the complex of causes that leads to it.

It was Lenin who in 1915 combatted the pacifist illusion that international or other cartels could promote peaceful development between the peoples. He showed particularly that Hobson's thoughts about the foundation of an '*alliance of Western states, a European federation of great powers*' for the division and exploitation of China and other colonial regions could not be realised. In addition to the 'United States of Europe' for the purpose of the exploitation of colonial countries, Lenin quotes another similar project of Gerhard Hildebrand for the establishment of a 'United States of Western Europe (without Russia)'

197 Sternberg 1971, p. 344. [Grossman's emphasis.]
198 Oppenheimer 1927.
199 [See Graziadei. Grigory Zinoviev attacked the book's criticisms of Marx's economic theory at the Comintern's Fifth Congress, in 1924. Tugan-Baranowsky 1905.]

for collective action against the Negroes of Africa, etc. All such pacifist illusions, Lenin believes, are shattered by the 'counteractions' that drive imperialist powers to war. To show this, he analyses the current phase of imperialism. Colonial policy and imperialism, he says, also existed before the new stage of capitalist imperialism. But he points out the characteristic aspects of monopoly imperialism and, in the chapter on the 'Division of the world among the great powers', develops the idea that the period of 1876 to 1900 is distinguished by the division of Africa and Polynesia. '[T]he colonial policy of the capitalist countries has *completed* the seizure *of the unoccupied territories* on our planet'. This does not, furthermore, mean that 'repartition is impossible; on the contrary, repartitions are possible and *inevitable*'. But they are only still possible by passing territory 'from one "owner" to another, *instead of passing ownerless territory to an "owner"*'. This means however, 'a sharpening of the struggle for the colonies': war.[200] For the division of colonial holdings 1876–1900 was very uneven. By area, France had 'almost three times as much colonial territory as the other two [Germany and Japan] combined', although the three states were quite similar in terms of area and population. But economic development is not uniform for all states:

> [A]mong the six countries mentioned we see, firstly, young capitalist countries (America, Germany, Japan) whose progress has been *extraordinarily rapid*; secondly, countries with an old capitalist development (France and Great Britain), whose progress lately has been *much slower* than that of the previously mentioned countries.[201]

So *disproportionality in the allocation of colonies* grows with economic development. Hence *wars* are *inevitable*. The division of the world will now be carried out according to no other principal than capital, strength. 'But strength,' Lenin concludes, '*varies with the degree of economic and political development*', thus disproportionality between the old allocation of territories and the new power relations can only result in war.[202]

Sternberg appropriates Lenin's fundamental ideas verbatim, although without providing the source, and merely waters them down with lavish phraseology. He states with the pathos of an apostle who, for the first time, pronounces

200 Lenin 1964c, pp. 280, 281, 202, 254, 255. [Lenin also emphasised 'repartition'. Grossman's emphasis apart from '*completed*'.]

201 Lenin 1964c, p. 259. [Grossman's emphasis.]

202 Lenin 1964c, p. 253. [Grossman's emphasis.]

a never-before-spoken truth, '*I will show* that ... imperialism *must* lead to wars between the individual active imperialist states'.[203]

Sternberg also busies himself with different forms of peaceful cooperation among capitalist states for the purpose of the exploitation and allocation of colonies, from a simple cartel to the United States of Europe – Pan-Europe – as guarantees of peace. 'It is no accident,' he thinks, 'that *a Europe Corp. for the management of the colonies* did not arise in earlier epochs'. Bourgeois pacifism believes in such possibilities. 'No wonder, given that it stands in inverse proportion to knowledge of the economy'. That is to say, 'in pacifist circles, they love to compare the *League of Nations with a cartel* in order to show that [it] can achieve a balance in the contradictory interests of the different imperialist states.' This is an illusion, and 'precisely the example of the cartel proves the total impossibility of a lasting, peaceful balance of imperialist contradictions'.[204]

Sternberg also declares that contemporary imperialism differs from that of earlier epochs in important ways, despite many similarities.[205] And, indeed, 'the epoch before the war of 1914–18 was characterised *by the transformation of non-capitalist areas without owners into colonies*, by the placing ownerless non-capitalist territories under the control of particular active imperialist states ... Such a transformation is no longer possible today'.[206] '*This phase ... approaches its end*'.[207] Like Lenin, Sternberg draws most important conclusions from this. Above all, the intensification of the contradictions among imperialist states. War is no 'accidental, unique occurrence'. Its 'necessity is grounded in the capitalist structure of states'. The division of the non-capitalist territories that took place in the epoch of early capitalism is '*in no way proportional to the necessity of expansion*'.[208] Rather, the industrial development of individual capitalist countries 'exhibit the strongest distinctions'. In the distribution of colonies, 'Germany is the worst positioned' in relation to its [level of] capitalist development and need to expand. Under capitalism this *disproportionality* cannot be remedied peacefully. Nor can the League of Nations eliminate it in the long run, by means of reallocation. It can 'do nothing but regard the status quo as decisive for the allocation' [of territories]. But 'capitalism is dynamic'. According to which principal can the League of Nations assign the individual states colonies,

203 Sternberg 1971, pp. 265–6. [Grossman's emphasis.]
204 Sternberg 1971, pp. 290, 291, 286. [Grossman's emphasis.]
205 Sternberg 1971, pp. 267–8.
206 Sternberg 1971, p. 280. [Grossman's emphasis.]
207 Sternberg 1971, p. 280.
208 Sternberg 1971, pp. 296–9. [Grossman's emphasis.]

mandates and spheres of influence? Never according to the need for imperialist expansion; rather, according to the extent of military, political and economic power. 'The crisis which welds these disparate elements together is war'.[209]

Of course, Sternberg nevertheless considers it necessary, as a precaution, to add: 'Here, too, the facts are known; some have, at times, been observed with surprising accuracy'. For his part, however, Sternberg certainly wants to do more than merely provide the 'facts'. Rather, he wants to 'systematically anchor' economic connections and their consequences.[210] So he is careful not to say who, before him, has 'observed with surprising accuracy'. For, if he were to name Lenin, the source from which Sternberg drew his *entire* wisdom and knowledge of the facts, along with their consequences, could soon be identified.

Now it is also clear why Sternberg altogether denies the *necessity of socialism* and necessity and lawful regularity in historical development, yet concedes 'the mathematical necessity' of war.[211] The contradiction is easily explained: Lenin's ideas were borrowed and mechanically grafted onto Sternberg's own tree of knowledge.

And the same applies to Sternberg's theory of social revolution.

In 1922 Bukharin, in his speech on the program of the Third International, had already opposed those who reject socialist revolution until socialism has fully developed within capitalism. Bukharin proposed that the Congress 'take up [the question of] the specific features in capitalist society that indicate its ripeness for socialism' in the program and emphasised, in contrast to the classical statement in Marx's *Capital* that 'capitalism matured fully under feudal rule', 'the [principal] difference' compared with the transition from capitalism to socialism. He shows that under capitalism 'socialism can *never* ripen in this manner, even under the most favourable conditions'. 'It is impossible', he says, 'for the working class to take production in hand within the womb of capitalist society ... [T]he proletariat ... can learn all that only when it has already achieved the dictatorship of the proletariat.' 'The revisionists, who do not want a revolution, claim that this transitional process begins already within the womb of capitalism. We hold that it begins *with* establishment of the dictatorship of the proletariat.'[212]

---

209 Sternberg 1971, pp. 291, 282, 286, 284, cf. 294 and 299.

210 Sternberg 1971, p. 266.

211 Sternberg 1971, p. 286.

212 Bukharin 2012, pp. 490–1. [The quotation attributed to Marx is actually from Bukharin but see Marx 1976b, p. 875. Grossman did not indicate his interpolation. Bukharin emphasised '*the specific features in capitalist society that indicate its ripeness for socialism*' and '*dictatorship of the proletariat*'.]

Sternberg also appropriates this idea verbatim, elaborates it into a whole chapter and again forgets to cite the source. 'The socialist revolution', he writes, 'is fundamentally different from *every other* revolution hitherto known in history'. 'An analogy between the French and the socialist revolution would only apply if the socialist mode of production already developed *within capitalism*'. But it cannot develop. Consequently, as this is not possible, the socialist revolution is fundamentally different from any previous revolution. It does not sanction a prior economic transformation but is that transformation itself.[213] The sentence: 'The socialist mode of production can never develop within capitalism' is emphasised by Sternberg. Like Bukharin, he concludes that revolution alone will lead to socialist production. Four years after the debate at the Moscow Congress of 1922, he draws the same conclusion as Bukharin and makes it his own discovery!

The same is true of Sternberg's theory of *the connection between the existence of capitalism and non-capitalist areas*. Sternberg only expands upon ideas which, almost a lifetime ago, Heinrich Cunow had already developed precisely in all details and conclusions, on a few pages, and had placed at the centre of the theoretical discussion.[214]

Marx's diagnosis of capitalism's developmental tendencies, Cunow explains, was correct. Marx merely erred in terms of *tempo*, because he considered the *markets* existing in his time to be given. But capitalism continuously managed to conquer new markets for capital and industry, which *weakened* capitalism's tendency to break down. The extension of foreign markets 'not only *provided an overflow valve for recurring glut*' – in other words, Steinberg's buyers of the unrealisable remainder – but also '*reduced the tendency for crises to develop*', just as Steinberg now emphasises the way non-capitalist areas make crises milder. Cunow continues that only thus did *workers*, in addition to employers, make gains during this period, though not to the same extent. (This then is Steinberg's 'period of reprieve'.) Without the acquisition of external markets, England 'would long have faced a conflict between the capacity to consume of its internal and external market and the enormous increase in capitalist accumulation'. '*Only the expansion of colonial possessions* in the seventies and eighties [of the nineteenth century] *with their* steadily growing consumption *made space for English capital and industrial markets*.'[215] (Sternberg's thesis of the breakdown of capitalism for lack of colonial possessions).

---

213 Sternberg 1971, pp. 322, 324, 325–6. [Grossman's emphasis.]

214 Cf. Heinrich 1898, pp. 424–30.

215 Cunow 1898, p. 425. [Grossman's emphasis. Editor's interpolation.]

Bernstein's assertions, says Cunow further, are not always incorrect, but he, like revisionism as a whole, '*generalises* the specific effects of economic tendencies … that arise during a *particular phase* of development and considers them *constant* at all stages'.[216] (Sternberg: 'revisionism's portrayal of a specific historical phase as absolute').[217] Revisionism does not ask 'whether, then, the conditions for a further moderate *extension of the world market* with the development of production are to hand.'[218] It was Cunow alone who explained why this view is false and only temporarily valid.

Already then (1898!) 'a certain end could be foreseen' to further market expansion, which Sternberg now echoes.[219] According to Cunow, serious competition with England's monopoly position on world markets emerged in Germany and North America in the [18]70s, and it crumbled further, thanks to the industrialisation of India, Japan, Australia, Russia and, prospectively, China soon as well. The possibility of extending the market 'is closely related to another: whether our economic development drives towards *breakdown*,' whose inevitability appears indisputable to Cunow. 'The only question is *how long* the capitalist mode of production can survive in particular countries and *the circumstances under which the breakdown will eventuate*.' This depends upon: 1. lack of markets and concrete relations in particular countries; 2. the degree of class contradictions in particular countries; 3. the financial situations of different states; 4. complications of the most advanced countries, e.g. wars among them, etc. Cunow even saw the possibility of a *sudden* breakdown, 'if the crisis occurred as a consequence of a European war that led to mutual exhaustion'. In the opposite case it will *not* occur *suddenly*. These are, incidentally, practical details, that are not decisive for theory. 'Whether the effective tendencies of our economic development drives towards a *general catastrophe*, that is the central point of the whole issue.'[220]

That was Cunow 30 years ago. After him, Kautsky (1901) and Boudin (1907) repeated the same argument. Rosa Luxemburg then literally adopted the theory in 1913 and merely tried to deepen it in terms of the history of ideas and at the same time to extend it theoretically. Following Tugan-Baranovsky's example, she employed a schematic analysis of the capitalist process of reproduction, to establish the necessity of non-capitalist areas. So she brought the theory to a close. Sternberg now musters the courage to repeat Cunow's and

216 Cunow 1898, p. 424. [This quotation is actually close paraphrase. Grossman's emphasis.]

217 Sternberg 1971, p. 246.

218 [Cunow 1898, p. 427. This quotation is a paraphrase.]

219 Sternberg 1971, p. 280. [Cunow 1898, p. 427.]

220 [Cunow 1898, pp. 427, 428, 430. Grossman's emphasis.]

Rosa Luxemburg's ideas as his own. In fact, he has not advanced the formulation of the problem one atom beyond Cunow and Luxemburg. Indeed, unlike Marx, his entire presentation is not based on the all-round analysis of the *real appearances* of the capitalist reproduction process in its development. Marx shows the function and role of the individual elements of the capitalist mechanism: living labour, fixed capital, money, raw materials and means of consumption in the circuit of capital, the way that these elements are replaced in value and use value terms, the flow and movement of capital within the capitalist mechanism itself and how capitalism, through all of these, *inexorably approaches its end.* Instead of this, Sternberg's analysis, his 'unshakeable position' is reduced solely to an unanalysed schematic numerical example, in which an 'unrealisable remainder' is left behind in Department 2!

We have shown that the theoretical part of Sternberg's book is a brew, concocted from all kinds of scraps that have fallen from strange tables. Sternberg's real intellectual characteristic is his assertion that it is possible for capitalism to regress into historical oblivion along with the most superficial critique of Marx that has ever been written, which he nevertheless wants to sail under the Marxist flag. Sternberg tries to spread anti-Marxist lines of reasoning in Marxist garb. What Lenin said of Russian 'Marxists' of this kind applies to him: they begin to struggle against Marxism without *openly* attacking its foundations, by supposedly *acknowledging* it, but they so leach out its content that it becomes a harmless bogeyman for the bourgeoisie.[221]

221 Lenin 1964a, p. 222. [Grossman provides a very close paraphrase of a passage in the German translation of Lenin's essay.]

CHAPTER 6

Review of Othmar Spann, *The Principal Theories of Economics**

Translated from German by Ben Fowkes

Spann, Othmar 1923, *Die Haupttheorien der Volkswirtschaftslehre*, 12th–15th editions, Leipzig: Quelle & Meyer (viii + 207pp).[1]

Othmar Spann's book under review here is widely known. The only reason for this is that it provides painless examination preparation for thousands of students, because it is short and does not go deeply into the subject. What mainly interests us here is the chapter 'A short description of the development of socialism'. Spann's basic error is that he uncritically throws together such entirely diverse phenomena as utopian and scientific socialism and therefore necessarily arrives at an incorrect determination of concepts. In the current edition he has admittedly abandoned the incorrect formulation of previous editions to the effect that socialism 'concentrated above all on the problems and tasks of *distribution*'. But one cannot say that his new formulation is any better. For Spann, socialism is not actually a *theory* of the economic process, but the *ethical demand* for a certain way of organising the economy and the state, 'the idea of giving happiness to the whole of humanity'.[2] It is evident that this is a misconception of what is most essential about Marx's socialism. One can therefore agree with Spann without reservation when he says that there is a great lack of clarity about the concept of socialism. Of course, he also failed to generate clarity. In any case, this book is marked by a complete absence of clarity. In the third edition (1918) Spann writes: 'Socialism is a *universalist* notion of the economy';[3] in the present edition, in contrast, he writes: 'Can one define socialism as a purely universalist system? This cannot succeed!'[4] The reason for this, Spann adds, is that the goal of socialism, namely the 'right to receive the full proceeds of labour', is individualistic! Spann does not know – it can be

* [Originally published as Grossmann 1928b.]

1 [There is an English translation of the later, 19th, 1929 edition, Spann 1930.]

2 Spann 1918, p. 126.

3 Spann 1918, p. 115.

4 Spann 1923, p. 127.

remarked in passing – that the right to receive the full proceeds of labour has nothing to do with Marx's socialism, and he has evidently never even heard rumours of Marx's letter about the Gotha Program,[5] with its biting critique of the right to receive the full proceeds of labour, made from the standpoint of Marx's theory of value.

Spann's complete lack of a sense of history is shown in his dilettantish remarks about socialism in the ancient world. A decade ago, in the third edition of his book – evidently relying on Grünberg's well-known article in the *Dictionary of Economics*,[6] a reference he has since then carefully eradicated – he declared that socialism in the modern sense, hence 'socialism based on the science of economics has only existed since the French Revolution'.[7] Now, under the influence of [Robert] Pöhlmann,[8] he restricts his assertion by speaking of '*more recent*' scientific socialism, as if an 'older' version ever existed, and he assures us that 'a true capitalism, and a social question of the same type as ours'[9] already existed in ancient times! Our author is evidently unaware of the fundamental difference between the world of antiquity and the modern world resulting from the lack in the former of typical free wage labour, and the consequences of this absence for the whole of economic life.

Spann's detailed discussions of modern socialism also abound in inaccuracies. Only a few examples as an illustration. It is incorrect to maintain, as Spann does, that Saint-Simon was 'the first to emphasise the innate antagonism between capital and labour'.[10] As anyone who has even half an interest in the material is aware, it is precisely this class antagonism which Saint-Simon failed to see, stressing instead the antagonism between 'industry' – the old Third Estate, i.e. the totality of all usefully active individuals – and restored feudalism. Charles Fourier (1808) and Sismondi (1819) were the first to work out the antagonism between capital and labour.[11] It is therefore completely erroneous to assert, as Spann does, that Fourier proceeds from the assumption that 'absolute harmony prevails' not only in nature but also 'in society and the economy'.[12] It was an achievement of genius for Fourier to have already seen, in 1808, the disharmonies, the basically anarchic fundamental character of industry, the

5 [Marx 1989a.]
6 [Grünberg 1911a.]
7 Spann 1918, p. 115.
8 [Pöhlmann 1912.]
9 Spann 1918, p. 127.
10 Spann 1918, p. 128.
11 [Fourier 1996; Sismondi 1991d. See Grossman 1924a, see above pp. 55–119.]
12 Spann 1918, p. 128.

crises, the misery of the industrial workers, the waste of economic forces, the annihilation and subjection of broad popular strata by a small number of the very powerful. And [Friedrich] Muckle is right to say of him 'one is repeatedly amazed by the profundity of Fourier's treatment of the peculiar social situation of the proletariat'.[13] What Spann says about Sismondi is just as misleading and it gives one the impression that he never even held a copy of Sismondi's *New Principles*[14] in his hands. Sismondi, Spann tells us, 'was an adherent of Adam Smith's system'.[15] But this is only true of Sismondi's early period. He vigorously *attacked* the views of Adam Smith from 1819 onwards and was proud of the fact. Yes, Sismondi's significance is that he shook the foundations of liberal doctrine. He limited his 'adherence' to Smith's system to his recognition, along with Smith, that 'labour is the sole source of wealth'. Incidentally, a 'historian of economic doctrines' also ought to know that Sismondi's full name was actually 'Jean Charles Léonard Simonde de Sismondi' and not 'Simon de Sismondi' as Spann writes in all editions both in the text and in the notes (!!). He also claims that the great publicist died in 1852 and not in 1842. There is nothing to be gained by picking out any further, similar blunders.

As regards Marx's doctrine, Spann's presentation displays a complete misunderstanding of its most important foundations. For Spann, Marx's theory of wages is 'nothing other than Ricardo's iron law of wages', and he adds, to the extent that the pressure of the industrial reserve army is considered, 'it would be possible for wages to fall *permanently* below the cost of subsistence. In this way Marx even outdoes the iron law of wages.'[16] In this way Spann manages to present Marx's theory of wages as a 'theory of impoverishment'. And he is naturally also unaware that heightening the intensity of labour also presupposes an *increase in wages*. In relation to Marx's theory of value, he uncritically repeats the phrase, which has been copied again and again from Böhm-Bawerk,[17] that Marx 'later', in volume 3, abandoned the theory of value presented in volume 1 of *Capital*, by conceding that 'the prices of commodities only coincide in exceptional cases with the value of the labour in them'.[18] And despite all the extensive modern literature on the subject the following point remains a book with seven seals for our critic of Marx: it is impossible to speak of a contradiction between

13 [Muckle 1920, p. 78.]
14 Sismondi 1991d.
15 Spann 1918, p. 129.
16 Spann 1918, p. 137.
17 [Böhm-Bawerk 1975, p. 30.]
18 Spann 1918, p. 137.

the first and third volumes because the third volume was written *simultaneously* with the first volume, both books contain the same ideas, and in any case the 'contradiction' can be explained very simply by Marx's methodological approach, since the investigation in volume 1 proceeds from statics, hence he makes use of extreme simplifications, while that in volume 3, in contrast, depicts concrete reality.[19]

Spann's assertion that according to Marx's theory of value only 'manual labour is productive'[20] is no less false. For Marx emphasises the productive, value-creating nature of intellectual labour, as Spann could easily have convinced himself with a glance into *Theories of Surplus Value*.[21]

Spann describes Marx's division of the value of the product into replacement of capital + wages + surplus value as 'downright primitive' and informs him in a superior manner that 'the true elements of the calculation [would be] far more diverse', adding: 'later on Marx sensed that his construction was untenable'[22] without at all divulging when and where. Marx himself showed repeatedly that surplus value is divided into a multiplicity of special forms (profit, interest, profit of enterprise, rent, commercial profit, etc.) and he analyses this diversity in volume 3. He nevertheless considered it necessary for methodological reasons to consider all these constituents of surplus value *initially in the basic form they had in common*[23] and he regarded this as 'the fundamentally new element of the book'.[24] This way of proceeding was indeed an important advance over the work of the classical economists, because this alone made it possible to formulate the law of the falling rate of profit. Let there be no misunderstanding: I do not say that Spann must be in agreement with Marx's method. But the reproach of 'primitivism', the objection that Marx fails to recognise the way surplus value is divided into different parts, can be applied more readily to the critic himself.

The necessity and the justification for such a simplification for certain purposes, and the importance of the insights into the economy it provides, is shown by the most recent investigation into national income in the United States of America, which similarly splits the value created by industry ('in well-nigh primitive fashion' to adopt Spann's expression) into no more than two

19 [Grossman 1929b deals with this issue at greater length, see below pp. 183–209.]
20 Spann 1918, p. 138.
21 [Marx 1989b, pp. 19–20.]
22 Spann 1918, p. 136.
23 Cf. 1976b, p. 710.
24 Marx 1987b, p. 514. [The letter refers to the initial consideration of surplus value as a whole to be one of 'the three fundamentally new elements of the book'.]

parts: 1) wages, and 2) income from capital (that is, surplus value), and does not carry out any further subdivision of 2).[25]

In conclusion, a short remark of a general character. Whereas the conservative Rodbertus is praised by Spann as an 'outstanding theorist'[26] and in comparison with Marx as 'a greater and more creative researcher' and as 'the true founder of scientific socialism in Germany',[27] his view of Marx is that 'every one of his theories is erroneous' and in all his fundamental ideas he is merely an epigone,[28] in short, that his talent was only 'political but not scientific'.[29]

In contrast to this, one can hardly question Spann's originality. For it is no mean feat to pile up so many inaccuracies in only 20 pages. It was only possible to pick out the most important of them here.

H. Grossmann (Frankfurt am Main)

25 Cf. Federal Trade Commission 1926, p. 189.
26 Spann 1918, p. 130.
27 Spann 1918, p. 130.
28 Spann 1918, p. 141.
29 Spann 1918, 142.

CHAPTER 7

Review of Maurice Bourguin, *Socialist Systems and Economic Evolution*[*]

Translated from German by Ben Fowkes

Bourguin, Maurice 1925, *Les Systèmes socialistes et l'évolution économique*, 3rd edition, with a preface by Arthur Fontaine, fourth printing, Paris: Armand Colin (xx + 542pp).

This, the main work of the author who died in 1910, first appeared in 1904. A second and a third edition followed quickly in 1906 and 1907, with further printings in 1913 and 1921. The present, unchanged edition also displays all the advantages and drawbacks of a book which does not claim to offer solutions for problems, in the form of a finished system, but contributions and means to construct an independent judgment, 'on the basis of a very careful application of the inductive method'. The editor of the last two printings, Arthur Fontaine, did not consider it appropriate to bring the text of the appended tables up to date in any way. The abundant empirical material in the book thus does not extend beyond the year 1907 and only illustrates conditions prevailing before the war. The relative significance of the book also results from its character: it reflects developmental tendencies in the most important capitalist countries during a particular period, and no general conclusions can therefore be drawn from the author's observations, even if they were absolutely correct (which is by no means always the case).

Two small essays from the bibliography of Bourguin's works might also be mentioned here: 'Des rapports entre Proudhon et Karl Marx';[1] and 'La valeur dans le système collectiviste'.[2]

H. Grossmann (Frankfurt am Main)

---

* [Originally published as Grossmann 1928c.]

1 Bourguin 1893.

2 Bourguin 1901.

CHAPTER 8

The Change in the Original Plan for Marx's *Capital* and Its Causes*

Translated from German by Geoffrey McCormack

As remarkable as it may seem, the set of problems concerning the structure of Marx's chief work, as well as its relation to *Theories of Surplus Value*, on the one hand, and to the earlier publication *A Contribution to the Critique of Political Economy*, on the other, has never been the subject of an investigation. One can scarcely find another book that has shaped a whole century to the same extent, theoretically and practically, and which, despite its enormous importance, has been treated more indifferently with regard to its form, the history of its genesis and the logic of its structure!

It would be superfluous to speculate here about the reasons for the unsatisfactory state of research on Marx. Suffice it to say that – despite all the discussions about Marx that we have gone through over the past three decades, in the advanced capitalist countries of Europe – we still find ourselves only at the start of scientific research on Marx. Only the publication of Marx's works announced by the Marx-Engels Institute in Moscow will decisively change this situation.[1]

Regardless, it would be an inexcusable relapse into the mistakes of historicism to remain theoretically inactive until such a time. On the contrary, the following investigation attempts to critically evaluate the problem encompassed in the title on the basis of already-known source materials and to demonstrate that important insights can be gleaned from them.

The problem that arises here is twofold. The first concerns the preliminary question whose answer must precede any scientific analysis of Marx's thought, the question of the completeness of the materials that have come down to us. That is, whether *Capital*, as it exists now – including *Theories of Surplus Value* – essentially comprises the *whole* thing, apart from individual gaps in its elaboration. Whether, consequently, *Capital* constitutes a *complete* system or whether we are dealing here with *fragments* of a larger work. The second, the real prob-

* [Originally published as Grossman 1929b.]

1 [Grossman refers to Marx and Engels 1927–41, initially published under the direction of David Riazanov, 12 of whose planned 42 volumes appeared between 1927 and 1941, when the project was killed off by Stalin's regime, as many of its German and Russian editors had been.]

lem, concerns the methodological viewpoints, which were decisive in working up the material, in the arrangement of the work and in the organisation of its elements. Both problems, it will be shown, stand in close relation to each other.

1

The first problem, of course, could only arise from the fact that Marx himself could only supervise the publication of the first volume; that the remaining volumes were published by Engels from the manuscripts left after Marx's death, and, insofar as they dealt with the theories of surplus value, by Kautsky; that the history of the origins of this work, reckoned from 1859, the publication date of *A Contribution to the Critique*,[2] the first treatment of the opening chapter of *Capital*, comprises a period of a half-century.

It is indicative of how little these problems have been considered that, on the question of the completeness of the existing materials, a cardinal and obvious *preliminary* question for all analysis of Marx, there prevails the most hair-raising lack of clarity, as the crassest example of which I want to cite the views expressed by Robert Wilbrandt. We know the material Marx wanted to deal with from the preface to *A Contribution to the Critique* (1859), where the *original plan* for the work was specified: 'I examine the system of bourgeois economy in the following order: *capital, landed property, wage labour; the state, foreign trade, world market*.'[3] The sequel to the original work, as it exists in the three volumes of *Capital*, however, followed *another plan*. Already in 1897, on the occasion of the new edition of *A Contribution to the Critique*, Kautsky wrote: 'Thus, the construction of *Capital* differed from that of the work whose first section was published by Marx in 1859. This is proved by a glance at the first lines of the preface to the *Critique* and a comparison of the plan developed there with that actually followed in *Capital*.'[4] And although this can already be seen at a 'first glance', the fact of the change in the plan for Marx's *Capital* escapes Professor Wilbrandt, despite his many bows toward this 'extraordinary work', which, so to speak, he is officially duty bound to make, as author of his own book on Marx. After going into the history of the genesis of the work and the original plan of 1859, the plan for a work of *six* parts, he then instructs the world that the only volume of *Capital* that Marx himself published has remained a

2 [Marx 1987a.]

3 [Marx 1987a, p. 262.]

4 Kautsky 1897, p. v. [The translator of the first English edition, based on Kautsky's 1897 German edition which does not include Kautsky's foreword, made the same point: Stone 1904, p. 3.]

torso in a double sense. Not only, firstly, because it is 'only the first of many volumes', but, secondly, 'it is only the first volume of a work that itself is part of a whole: *the first of six parts* of the whole work that the author envisaged would treat many problems, which he intentionally refrained from considering in the first part, in *Capital*, so as to reserve them for the later parts.'[5] According to this fantastic account, the four volumes of *Capital* that we have turn out to be merely the implementation of the *first* part of the plan of 1859, which was to be followed by another five parts! Consequently, Marx's currently available work is considered only a small fraction of a planned work that should perhaps provide just as comprehensive accounts of ground rent, wage labour, foreign trade, etc. as those on capital. So, altogether, perhaps a further twenty volumes and indeed dealing with cardinal areas, without knowledge of which what has already been said about capital, torn out of the context of the whole, would also necessarily be difficult to understand.

We must counterpose a question to this account: is it correct that Marx 'consciously refrains' from considering these problems in *Capital*; that he only intended to deal with the questions of ground rent, wages and foreign trade later? Apparently Wilbrandt has not noticed the analysis of all these questions in *Capital*. He takes the opportunity of Marx's theory of wages to highlight an alleged gap and maintains that an 'elaboration could well have been hoped for in the part on wage labour;'[6] as though Marx had not dealt completely enough with and clarified his theory of wages in *Capital*!

Wilbrandt's ignorance of the most elementary facts in his subject area should not have prevented him from being aware of the modification of the original plan for *Capital*. Not only because this modification can be seen 'at first glance' and had already been observed by Kautsky, but because Marx himself – as we are instructed in his correspondence with [Wilhelm] Kugelmann – emphatically confirmed it.

From the new draft plan, which he tells Kugelmann about and which we cite further below, it is clear to see that *Capital*, as it is presently available to us in four volumes, *is essentially complete*. In the available volumes, even though the exposition in the individual sections has gaps in places, a chapter may be missing here and there, and the logical sequence is often interrupted, on the whole not only is all of the material to be dealt with included, but at the same time, as Engels said, '*what Marx intended to say is said there, in one way or another*'.[7] This can also be seen particularly in the important letter Marx wrote to Engels on

5 Wilbrandt 1919, p. 97. [Grossman's emphasis.]
6 Wilbrandt 1919, p. 101.
7 Engels 1978a, p. 86. [Grossman's emphasis.]

30 April 1868 in which Marx tells his friend about the content of the second and third volumes in detail, and essentially enumerates the order and treatment of the material as we find it again later in the two volumes of *Capital* that Engels took care of.[8]

The example of Wilbrandt demonstrates best how the most confused views prevail, even about matters like the problem of the *external* structure of the material in *Capital*, which belongs among the preliminary questions for all analysis of Marx. Is it any wonder, then, that the *internal* structure of the work, the underlying methodological problems and solutions, which present real difficulties, is absolutely unclear?

2

If we now turn our attention to the actual object of our analysis and ask *why* the original plan for *Capital* was changed, we must emphasise that, so far, this decisive, cardinal question for the comprehension of Marx's work not only remains to be clarified, but has not even been posed! Strangely enough, people were satisfied with the statement of the facts, as was e.g. Kautsky; the 'why' was never investigated.

Understandably, Kautsky's indifference to such fundamental theoretical problems derives from his whole attitude towards Marx's principal work. According to Kautsky, '*Capital* is *essentially* an *historical* work'![9]

It is self-evident that a change in the plan for *Capital* really could not possibly be a matter of chance or a technical question of presentation, e.g. of clear arrangement, but must obviously have been the result of careful consideration and compelling reasons. This supposition appears all the more irrefutable as one is unlikely to be inclined to undertake a change in the construction of a work whose first part has already been published and that was – as Marx said in the 1859 preface – 'the outcome of conscientious research carried out over many years.'[10] Marx had been intensely occupied with studies in political economy since his anti-Proudhon, written in 1847.[11] What, then, moved Marx after sixteen years of untiring research, despite the successful publication of the first part of his work in 1859, *to revise his work anew*, which would obviously have to result in a new delay in its completion?

---

8 Marx 1987e, p. 20.
9 Kautsky 1921, p. viii. [Grossman's emphasis.]
10 [Marx 1987a, p. 265.]
11 [Marx 1976a.]

Now, if it is true that the slow progress of the work – after the appearance of *A Contribution to the Critique* – was a consequences of several unfavourable *external* causes, which Marx enumerates in the preface to *Capital* and in the letter to Kugelmann of 28 December 1862 (years of chronic illness, being overwhelmed by other work), these circumstances could only explain the *delay* in the completion of the work but not the *change* in the original plan. This consideration demonstrates to us that certain compelling *internal grounds* must have contributed to the change in plan. Indeed, Marx had already written to Kugelmann on 28 December 1862 that '*The second part has now at last been finished*, i.e. save for the fair copy and the final polishing before it goes to press'.[12] The words 'the *second* part' indicate that, at that time on 28 December 1862, Marx was still working according to the *original* plan of 1859. Thus he still thought of it as the sequel to the '*first part*', published under the title *A Contribution to the Critique*. The work was to encompass about 30 printer's sheets and would appear soon.

On 29 November 1864, however, almost two years later, Marx informs Kugelmann that he hopes that his book on 'capital' will 'at last be ready for publication next year.'[13] In the intervening time, since the letter of 28 December 1862, the already completed work was not polished and neatly copied out; it was, rather, *reworked* and extended. Its size doubled and it grew to 60 sheets. And a further year elapsed before Marx – at the beginning of 1866 – could begin the fair copy of the first volume of *Capital*.

Consequently, if Marx's work was already 'complete' at the end of 1862 and ready for final polishing, and was nevertheless reworked in the following two years, one must conclude that difficulties arose in the course of work, which led to *the necessity of revision and the change in the plan* for the work. The profound fact of the change in the plan, which had implications for the fate of the whole work, occurred between 28 December 1862 and 29 November 1864.

But we can specify the decisive point in time of the change in the plan more exactly: as is apparent from the correspondence with Kugelmann, it was carried out in the second half, namely July–August, of 1863.[14]

The nature of the difficulties, which led the implementation of the original plan of 1859 to fail, and the *methodological considerations* that compelled the change in the plan for the structure of the work, can be identified by comparing

12 Marx 1985a, p. 435. [Grossman's emphasis.]

13 Marx 1987c, p. 45.

14 He also writes, in a letter to Engels of 15 August 1863, 'When, by the by, I consider my handiwork and realise *how I've had to demolish everything* …' [Grossman's emphasis], Marx 1985e, p. 488.

the original plan of 1859 with the plan that Marx actually followed in *Capital* and had already announced in the letter to Kugelmann on 13 October 1866. Precisely there, Marx told his friend that the whole work would break down into the following parts:

> Book I: The process of production of capital
> Book II: The process of circulation of capital
> Book III: Structure of the process as a whole
> Book IV: On the history of the theory[15]

The difference between the two plans springs to the eye. While, in the plan of 1859, the work was to be comprised of six parts and was to be considered from the standpoint of the *material* – capital, ground rent, wage labour, foreign trade, etc. – the final plan of 1863 was organised from the standpoint of *knowledge* [*Erkenntnis*]. Out of knowledge-based methodological considerations, the individual *functions* of industrial capital carried out during its circuit – the production process, the circulation process, the process as a whole – are abstracted in thought and presented separately, regardless of the material. Only within the presentation of each of these functions is the whole material dealt with from the respective functional standpoints.[16]

As Engels discloses in the preface to the second volume [of *Capital*], the *first draft* of *Capital*, written from 'August 1861 to June 1863', was still 'the continuation of the volume ... published in Berlin in 1859'. Conforming to the original plan, 'The themes dealt with in Volume 2, however, as well as the many treated later in Volume 3, *are not yet grouped together. They are dealt with in passing.*' The following are *mixed up* and treated together with material that is discussed in volume 1, 'capital and profit, rate of profit, merchant's capital and money capital, i.e. themes that were later developed in the manuscript for volume 3.'[17]

15 Marx 1987d, p. 327.

16 E.g. in the *production process*: productive capital and the wage relation; commodity capital, the production of surplus value both in industry and in agriculture, etc. In the *circulation process*: the turnover time of productive capital and of money capital; the turnover of the individual constituents of industrial capital, of its fixed and circulating parts, of its variable part and its surplus value. In the *process as a whole*: the reproduction and circulation of total capital, both in industry and in agriculture, encompassing capital as well as the wage relation, division of surplus value into profit, interest, rent, trading profit, etc., equalisation of profit to the average profit, money capital, commodity capital, etc.

17 Engels 1978a, p. 84. [Grossman's emphasis. In the original the reference is, mistakenly, to the preface of the third volume of *Capital* rather than the second.]

Thus in Engels's account we also find confirmation of what emerged from the comparison of the preface of *A Contribution to the Critique* with the plan for *Capital*, as well as the analysis of the correspondence between Marx and Kugelmann: the first draft of *Capital* is organised according to the empirical material dealt with. Only a later draft, begun in the second half of 1863, sorted the variegated material, confusingly mixed together, according to the specific *functions* of the circuit of capital. That a *methodological turn* of decisive importance took place in this way is now perfectly clear. The *problem* that now arises is synonymous with the question: *what* provoked this shift? Everything suggests that it stands in the closest connection *with the discovery of Marx's reproduction schema*.

The *external* connection is readily apparent: until June 1863 the work was developed according to the original plan of 1859. On 6 July 1863, Marx sent his friend the first draft of the reproduction schema, with which he wanted to replace Quesnay's *tableau économique*.[18] Already in the letter of 15 August we hear further that Marx 'had to demolish everything'. The change in plan appears here as *an already accomplished fact*. In this way, i.e. through the chronological course of events, the relation between the change in plan and *externally* the conception of the reproduction schema appears very probable. It is the task of the following presentation to demonstrate that not only an external, but also a *necessary internal connection* exists between the change in the plan for Marx's work and the methodological construction of the reproduction schema. The methodological perspective actually followed in the structure of *Capital* – the arrangement of the empirical material *according to the functions* which capital performs in its circuit – consequently the change in the original plan of 1859 *necessarily* resulted *from the way Marx formulated the question*. As I have shown in other places, however, this question is, 'since the production of *exchange value* – the *increase* of exchange value – is the immediate aim of capitalist production, it is important to know *how to measure it*.'[19] The problem consists in the exact determination of the variations in the magnitude of surplus value in the course of accumulation, that is, in the establishment of how much surplus value a given capital can yield in its circuit.

If we formulate the problem in this way and take it as the starting point for our analysis, we can readily appreciate that the analysis of the capitalist mode of production according to the empirical material about individual, partial areas – capital, ground rent, credit, foreign trade, wage relations, etc. –

18 Marx 1985d.

19 Grossmann 1992, p. 61.

would necessarily fail in the face of insurmountable difficulties. Further, Marx nowhere commented on how he came to his ingenious conception of the reproduction schema. We are therefore compelled to reconstruct his train of thought from the conditions of the problem.[20]

Let us assume a given Capital I, e.g. of one million marks, which is invested in the textile industry. The question is: under the prevailing, exactly circumscribed conditions, how big is the surplus value realised by this capital? Initially, this problem appears to be uncomplicated. If the number of workers employed, the level of the rate of surplus value, the length of the working period and the turnover time are known, then the magnitude of yearly surplus value due is easily calculable. Upon closer examination, however, great difficulties soon appear. We know that during the circuit of capital, thanks to the specific conditions of the turnover mechanism, namely due to the inequality of the working and circulation periods, 'part of the capital successively advanced is set free.'[21] The entrepreneur does not leave this redundant capital lying idle but will temporarily lend it to the banks or invest it in easily realisable securities with a fixed rate of interest,[22] and will thus secure the enjoyment of interest, that is, surplus value. If the capital set free in our example amounts to 80,000 marks and is lent out for six months at a rate of 8%, the interest gained will amount to 3,200 marks. *From what source was this interest obtained?* Obviously not from the Circuit of Capital I, invested in the textile industry. Rather, these 80,000 marks, set free, were withdrawn from the Circuit of Capital I. They were, through

20 Rosa Luxemburg's claim that, with respect to the reproduction schema, Quesnay can be considered Marx's sole predecessor, is incorrect, Luxemburg 1951, p. 31. I have demonstrated elsewhere that Sismondi's reproduction schema forms an historical and logical link between Quesnay and Marx. Commensurate with the superior development of the capitalist mode of production in Sismondi's time compared to Quesnay's in the middle of the eighteenth century, Sismondi introduces significant improvements into Quesnay's table. The independent producers (*classe stérile*) disappear, the class contradiction between entrepreneurs and wage labourers is stressed everywhere, the production of means of consumption is divided into that of necessities and luxuries, etc. Grossman 1924a, see above p. 65.

21 Marx 1978b, p. 355. Marx demonstrates how the circuit of industrial capital is temporarily interrupted and accompanied by other forms of hoarding: because the amortisation fund of fixed capital is accumulated gradually until it is large enough to replace the fixed capital used up in the interim; because surplus value is insufficient to function independently and therefore must be hoarded until it reaches 'the minimum magnitude required for it to function actively', Marx 1978b, p. 163; or, finally, because parts of circulating capital earmarked for the purchase of raw materials or labour power are also temporarily hoarded; on hoarding, cf. Marx 1987a, p. 379.

22 Marx 1978b, p. 164, and Marx 1981b, p. 594 et seq. [The latter pages do not seem directly relevant, unlike p. 528.]

the mediation of the bank, e.g. lent out to an iron producer and included in the Circuit of Capital II, invested in the iron industry. Capitalist I, the textile manufacturer, increased his total surplus value by 3,200 marks through credit intermediation. But this additional surplus value does not originate in the Circuit of the advanced Capital I, but was obtained because the hoard of money, that came out of the Circuit of the industrial Capital I originally invested, performed 'particular capital functions *outside* the circuit of the industrial capital from which it arose.'[23] The additional surplus value of 3,200 marks was not produced by workers in the textile industry but by workers in the steel industry through the detour of credit intermediation. Had Marx adhered to the original plan for treatment according to the material, without separating out the individual functions of capital, he would have tangled himself up in irresolvable contradictions. In empirical reality, the circuits of various capitals intersect; so the exact answer to the question posed by Marx, about the magnitude of surplus value that a given capital can obtain, would be impossible without the application of the method of isolation. For a clear solution to the problem it was thus necessary to hold apart the two intersecting circuits of capital, i.e. to isolate Circuit I in thought, by first *abstracting* it from Circuit II and thus *from credit*. So we can understand why Marx was forced, by the inner requirements of the problem, to work with simplifying assumptions.

What has just been said about credit applies equally to foreign trade. From a domestic Capital I, advanced in e.g. the textile industry, a surplus value of a magnitude y is due, if the commodities – according to Marx's assumption – are sold at prices equal to their values. Now, Marx has shown[24] that in foreign trade commodities are not sold at their values; that here no equivalents are exchanged; that in fact the law of value in foreign exchange, in its international application, is thereby modified; that countries with a higher level of capitalist development exploit the less economically developed countries, 'so that the more advanced country sells its goods above their value ... The privileged country receives *more* labour in exchange for less.'[25]

It is now readily apparent that, for this reason, Marx's problematic, the question of the magnitude of surplus value that can be produced by a given capital, necessarily had to be obscured. For, through the sale of the commodities, e.g. textiles at prices above values abroad, an additional surplus value was obtained from the originally advanced Capital I, along with the normal surplus value. But

23 Marx 1978b, p. 164. [Grossman's emphasis.]

24 Grossmann 1992, p. 170.

25 [Marx 1981b, p. 345. Grossman's emphasis.]

this additional surplus value was not produced by workers in the domestic textile industry; rather this additional surplus value was created by workers *abroad* and was then *transferred* to capitalist I, by way of unequal exchange. In empirical reality, the process of production of Capital I intertwines with its process of circulation. Thus, to provide an exact answer to Marx's question – how much surplus value can a definite Capital I produce? – in order, so to speak, to maintain the sphere of production in a chemically pure state, Marx had to *isolate* the sphere of production from the disturbing influences of the sphere of circulation. The exclusion of the sphere of circulation and the consequent change in the magnitude of surplus value obtained by the originally advanced capital occurs as a result of the simplifying assumption that commodities in foreign trade are sold at their values. For, as a result of this assumption, sale at prices above values and thus the augmentation of surplus value that can be obtained domestically by means of the transfer of additional surplus value from abroad are excluded. Since values exchange for equal values, the change in the magnitude of value, and hence also the magnitude of surplus value, as a result of the disrupting influences of foreign trade, is impossible. Only now can the analysis of the surplus value that can be produced by a given capital take place in an exact way. Only in this context can we understand why Marx arrived at his assumption of 'normal' reproduction, of the sale of commodities at their values.

> If normal annual reproduction on a given scale is presupposed, then it is also supposed ... that foreign trade replaces domestic articles only by those of other use or natural forms, *without ... affecting the value ratios ...* Bringing foreign trade into an analysis of the value of the product annually reproduced can therefore only confuse things, without supplying any new factor either to the problem or to its solution. We therefore completely abstract from it here.[26]

Marx's method is nothing more than the application of the method of isolation to the process of surplus value creation, in order to obtain it in its pure form. 'The physicist,' says Marx,

> either observes natural processes where they occur in their most significant form, and are *least affected by disturbing influences*, or, wherever possible, he makes experiments under conditions which ensure that the

26 Marx 1978b, p. 546. [Grossman's emphasis.]

> process will occur in its pure state ... In the analysis of economic forms neither microscopes nor chemical reagents are of assistance. *The power of abstraction must replace both.*[27]

That is, the real experiment of natural science must be replaced by the thought-experiment in economic research, in order to maintain in pure form the functions to be investigated, unclouded by disturbing influences.

Elsewhere I have shown that, just as Marx was forced here to put aside the modifications of the magnitude of value through foreign trade, he also had to abstract from the movements of price within a capitalism conceived of as isolated. For changes in price present themselves as deviations of prices from values, where price increases on one side of society correspond to price decreases on the other side and thus cancel one another out. The task Marx set himself, *the exact measurement of the additional surplus value* over the initial magnitude of capital advanced, necessarily led him to the exclusion of *this* type of change in price. For he was only interested in the real change in value, i.e. the growth of surplus value, the increase in exchange value. In contrast, fluctuations of price are deviations from the median line of value, the result of the fluctuating configuration of supply in relation to demand. The magnitude of value, however, is not modified by changes in the relation of supply and demand. Therefore, from the standpoint of his formulation of the problem, Marx had to abstract from these changes. Thus he necessarily arrives at the assumption of equilibrium as a starting point for his analysis, where supply and demand exactly balance; hence prices coincide with values. As earlier for foreign trade, so now the assumption holds domestically that commodities are sold at their values.[28]

And, as a result of the same considerations, Marx arrived at a further simplifying assumption. In order to be able to determine the influence of changes in the productivity of labour on the creation of surplus value, he was forced to carry out the investigation on the assumption that *the value of money did not change*. The purpose was to obtain an exact yardstick for the determination of the movements of the value of industrial capital during its circuit.[29] For, if the value of money varied, it would be difficult to determine whether growth in the value (price) of commodities is only *apparent*, merely arising from a change in the value of money.

We have, therefore, demonstrated how Marx, through the requirements of his problematic, necessarily came to take not the immediately given world of

27 Marx 1976b, p. 90. [Grossman's emphasis.]

28 Grossmann 1992, p. 64.

29 Grossmann 1992, pp. 62–3.

appearances as the object of his analysis, but to work with a series of simplifying assumptions: instead of organising his analysis according to the empirically given *material*, according to partial areas (capital, foreign trade, etc.), he abstracts from credit, from competition, from foreign trade and assumes that the value of money is constant. In short, it was demonstrated how he comes to describe the particular *functions of capital* instead of the particular material areas; e.g. firstly the process of production of surplus value and subsequently the function of circulation, i.e. the transfer of surplus value. Only by the complicated means of isolating and examining the functions of capital, one at a time, was Marx in a position to explain the actually obtained, empirically given expansion of capital, i.e. to analyse exactly the sources from which it originates.

But the series of simplifying assumptions was not exhausted by the considerations already mentioned. The other simplifying assumptions that resulted from his problematic meant that Marx could not start with the empirically given *partial forms* of income without labour: industrial profit, interest, ground rent, merchant's profit, etc. He had, rather, to use their ideal aggregate in the common, fundamental form of *surplus value, as the distinctive category* of his analysis. For, to start with, the *division* of surplus value among particular groups of capitalists did not interest Marx. Instead, what interested him was the problem of surplus value itself, the magnitude of surplus value that could be obtained and its variations, i.e. its developmental tendencies, in the course of capital accumulation. If taxes are high, then the portion of surplus value remaining for the capitalists is smaller. If the interest rate is low, then the portion of surplus value remaining for the industrial and merchant capitalists, etc. is larger. The total magnitude of the surplus value originally produced is not altered by changes in the division of surplus value among the state, the banks, the industrialists, etc. From the standpoint of his problematic, Marx thus had to put aside the specific forms into which the surplus value is divided. For this reason, however, adherence to the original plan of 1859 was impossible. Where it is a matter of the *total magnitude* of surplus value, how could capital and ground rent now be treated as separate subject areas? After all, ground rent is merely *a part* of surplus value. In this way, under the compulsion of his problematic, Marx *had* to give up the treatment according to separate subject areas. Instead of the analysis of the empirically given subject areas – interest, rent, merchant's profit, etc. – he had to place *the function of surplus value creation* in the foreground; i.e. he had to make the *process of production* the chief object of analysis. For this is at the same time the process of surplus value production. Thus surplus value is grasped at its source, *before* its division into its component forms, which immensely facilitates the analysis of the magnitude of surplus value in its totality; in fact, makes this possible. 'On the other hand', says Marx, 'we treat the capitalist producer as the owner of the entire surplus value … as the representative of *all those* who will share the booty with him … The break-up of surplus value into various fragments does not affect either its nature or the *conditions under which it becomes an element in accumulation*.'[30]

Methodological implications of utmost importance for further investigation follow from this assumption. For, to begin with, the classes of landlords, big and small merchants, state officials who live from taxes, etc., i.e. all parasites, those who share in the surplus value, thus, those classes that are not involved in the production of surplus value, had to be set aside from the analysis. The whole analysis had to be reduced to the fundamental contradiction in the production of surplus value: capitalist class–working class.

Finally, it is also clear from Marx's formulation of the problem why the *independent producers*, farmers and artisans, had to be set aside from the analysis. Marx wanted to investigate the *capitalist* process of surplus value production, i.e. capitalism in a 'chemically pure' form, free of impure admixtures of non-capitalist formations. For it would otherwise not be possible to determine the exact extent to which the result of the analysis is attributable to the capitalist elements or to the non-capitalist elements blended with them. In order to obtain such a 'chemically pure' capitalism, Marx had to limit his analysis to the classes that constitute the *specific* character of the capitalist mode of production, the *capital relation*, while demonstrating that independent producers are the remnants of *earlier* economic formations and therefore remain outside the capital relation. In this way, Marx arrives at the assumption of 'the universal and exclusive domination of capitalist production'.[31] This theoretical simplification is, according to Marx, never effected in reality. 'In theory, we assume that the laws of the capitalist mode of production develop in their *pure* form. In reality, this is only an approximation; but the *approximation is all the more exact*, the more the capitalist mode of production is developed and *the less it is adulterated by survivals of earlier economic conditions with which it is amalgamated*.'[32]

---

30 Marx 1976b, p. 710.

31 Marx 1978b, p. 422.

32 Marx 1981b, p. 275. [Grossman's emphasis.] The methodologically extremely important conception of the paths that lead to the imposition of capitalism's distinctive laws, that Marx developed here, is directly counterposed to the view held by Luxemburg. According to her, the existence of pure capitalism without non-capitalist purchasers is impossible. According to Marx's conception, non-capitalist producers simply constitute the remnants of earlier economic formations, which contaminate the effect of the pure laws of the cap-

We have therefore shown how Marx, as a consequence of his problematic, necessarily had to make a whole series of simplifying assumptions, with the result that the complicated mechanism was reduced to the simple formula $c + v + s = C$.[33] This aggregate of the real parts of profit in the common, general category of surplus value as such corresponds with an analogous aggregate of the real parts of capital (industrial, interest-bearing, merchant's capital, etc.) in the common, general category of capital as such. Just as the path, once taken, had forced Marx to turn his gaze away from material to function, it also led him from the superficial, visible, partial appearances of profit and the various forms of capital to his powerful vision of the totality of aggregate surplus value and aggregate capital. *A Contribution to the Critique of Political Economy* in six parts simply becomes *Capital* and the metamorphoses of its circuit!

Marx attributed the utmost theoretical importance to the reduction of all empirically given forms of earnings without labour, like profit, interest, ground rent, etc., to 'the simple, fundamental form'.[34]

> The best points in my book are ... 2. the treatment of *surplus value regardless of its particular forms* as profit, interest, ground rent, etc. This will be made clear in the second volume especially. The treatment of the particular forms in classical political economy, where they are forever being jumbled up together with the general form, is an *olla potrida*.[35]

And in a further letter to Engels of 8 January 1868, Marx reproached Dühring for not detecting the book's 'fundamental element' in his review of *Capital*: 'That in contrast to *all* previous political economy, which *from the outset* treated the particular fragments of surplus value with their fixed forms of rent, profit and interest as already given, I begin by dealing with the general form of surplus value, in which all these elements are still undifferentiated, in solution as it were.'[36]

---

italist mode of production. Pure capitalism is not only possible, according to Marx, but its laws become all the purer the more these obscuring remnants of earlier formations disappear.

33 ['c' is 'constant capital', 'v' 'variable capital', 's' 'surplus value', 'C' the total value of commodities produced.]

34 [Marx 1976b, p. 710.]

35 Marx 1987d, p. 407. ['*Olla potrida*' is a highly spiced Spanish dish with very diverse ingredients, literally 'rotten pot'. Here it means a hodgepodge, with particularly negative connotations.]

36 Marx 1987b, p. 514.

In order to understand the whole meaning of the short formula just mentioned, one must remember that, in his analysis of the problem of equilibrium under capitalism, Ricardo neglected this essential element of the capitalist mode of production, the capital relation. He does not take the fundamental contradiction, capitalist class–working class, as the starting point of his analysis. Instead, he tries to understand and solve the problem by using the example of independent producers. Sismondi accuses him of abstracting from this class relation, the necessary characteristic of capitalist production. 'There is perhaps no other method of reasoning that is open to more errors than that of constructing a *hypothetical world altogether* different from the real one.'[37] Methodological simplifications must not go *too far*, i.e. they must not disregard the *essential* elements of the object of investigation as Ricardo does. 'To my mind the abstraction ... is too strong ... this is no *simplification*, this is *misleading* us by hiding from our view all the successive operations by which we can distinguish truth from error.'[38] And, indeed, wherever it is a matter of understanding the fundamental evil associated with capitalism, one needs to start with the class of wage labourers. 'We will look at society in its actual organisation, with *workers without property* ... because it is precisely this social arrangement to which our objections apply.'[39]

If the characteristic feature of capitalism is the capital relation, the specific relation between entrepreneurs and wage labourers, then every Robinsonade is methodologically excluded from the analysis from the outset. This applies both to the primordial Ricardian hunter with his bow and to [Johann Heinrich von] Thünen's 'tropical country' in its still undeveloped, pre-capitalist state, where the fundamental class division between entrepreneur and wage labourer does not yet exist and to which, according to Thünen's assumption, 'a people with all the skills, knowledge and craft of the civilised European nations' was relocated. And although this country '*possesses no capital and thus no tools*',[40] according to Thünen, the laws governing capitalism, the laws of capital accumulation, interest and wages should be investigated and defined among the people living there, isolated in the tropics, without capital and without a working class!

The significance of Marx's formula is much greater than the moment[41] just mentioned. In fact, Marx's method was an important advance over the classical political economists because it alone made the exact formulation and

37 Sismondi 1991a, p. 603. [Grossman's emphasis.]
38 Sismondi 1991b, p. 621. Cf. also Grossman 1924a, see above p. 63.
39 Sismondi 1991b, p. 621.
40 Thünen 1921, p. 486.
41 ['Moment' is a Hegelian term, here with the sense of 'aspect'.]

proof of the law of the tendency for the rate of profit to fall possible. The movements of the empirically visible parts of income without labour temporarily and for specific parts of surplus value run counter to the *general tendency of the movement* (or, as it is put today, the 'secular trend line') of surplus value in the course of capital accumulation, as 'the simple, fundamental form of the process of accumulation is obscured both by the splitting-up of surplus value and by the mediating movement of circulation.'[42] All those who see only the *partial* movements of surplus value, e.g. the large profits of *individual* branches of production and not the relations of society as a whole, like e.g. [Georg] Charasoff, therefore dispute the fact of the fall in the rate of profit: the law of the tendency for the rate of profit to fall is apparently a mistake.[43]

The law itself, however, is a self-evident consequence of the labour theory of value if accumulation takes place on the basis of a progressively higher organic composition of capital. 'The fall in the rate of profit thus expresses *the falling ratio between surplus value itself* and the total capital advanced; it is therefore independent of any distribution of this surplus value we may care to make among the various categories.'[44] And, in fact, if one starts with the formula c + v + s [= C] and supposes a yearly increase in constant capital c of 10 % and of variable capital v of 5 %, it follows simply and clearly that, with accumulation and as a consequence of the rising organic composition of capital, once a certain level is reached, the tempo of accumulation becomes ever smaller, despite an initial acceleration, and accumulation eventually becomes impossible. The mass of surplus value is insufficient to sustain growth at the level required by the rapidly increasing constant capital.

1 200,000 c + 100,000 v + 100,000 s
2 1,000,000 c + 100,000 v + 110,000 s
3 4,600,000 c + 100,000 v + 120,000 s

In the first case, constant capital c can be accumulated at 50 %[45] of its initial size, if surplus value is used solely for the purposes of accumulation. In the second case, with a significantly higher organic composition of capital and even though the rate of surplus value has grown, the expanded mass of surplus value of 110,000 s barely suffices to increase the initial capital by 10 %. Finally, in the third case, a mass of surplus value of 120,000 barely increases the initial

42 Marx 1976b, p. 710.
43 Cf. Grossmann 1992, p. 50. [Charasoff 1910.]
44 Marx 1981b, p. 320. [Grossman's emphasis.]
45 [The original has '40 %', which is presumably a typographical error.]

capital by 2.5%. It is easy to calculate that, as the organic composition of capital rises more, a point must come when it is impossible for accumulation to continue. That is Marx's law of breakdown – 'the absolute general law of capitalist accumulation'.[46] Its discovery was possible thanks to the analysis of the actual movement of surplus value, by means of the aggregation of the empirical parts of surplus value into the category of surplus value, that is only on the basis of the formula c + v + s [= C].[47]

The classicals, who only pursued the empirically given parts of surplus value in their particular movements, 'suspected' the law without, however, being able to formulate it. According to Marx, this law constitutes 'the mystery around whose solution the whole of political economy since Adam Smith revolves and that the difference between the various schools since Smith consists in the different attempts made to solve it.' Hence, Marx correctly says

> Simple as the law appears ... not one of the previous writers on economics succeeded in discovering it. These economists perceived the phenomenon, but tortured themselves with their contradictory attempts to explain it ... If we consider, on the other hand ... how it [previous political economy] has never presented *surplus value as something separate from profit, nor profit in general, in its pure form, as distinct from the various constituents of profit which have attained an autonomous position towards each other* (such as industrial profit, commercial profit, interest, ground rent) ... then it ceases to be a puzzle that political economy has never found this puzzle's solution.[48]

46 Marx 1976b, p. 798.

47 Marx's theory of breakdown and his famous 'negation of negation' had been regarded as merely 'pitfalls of the Hegelian dialectical method' [Bernstein 1993, pp. 29–31] and the product of a residual Hegelian dialectic of contradictions, corresponding to Hegel's three-part schema of development. This was because precisely the fact that the law of breakdown is a necessary result of accumulation on the basis of the progressively higher organic composition of capital and therefore the 'real movement' arises from the analysis of real phenomena [*Erscheinungsstoff*] had been overlooked. With regard to this law, therefore, what Marx says about the distinction between the method of presentation and the method of inquiry holds especially true: 'Inquiry ... has to appropriate the *material* in detail, to analyse its different forms of development and to track down their *inner connection*. Only after this work has been done can the real movement be appropriately presented. If this is done successfully, if the life of the subject-matter is now reflected back in the ideas, then it may appear as if we have before us an *a priori* construction', Marx 1976b, p. 102. [Grossman's emphasis].

48 Marx 1981b, pp. 319–20. [Grossman's emphasis. Editor's interpolation.]

In this account, which places the law of the tendency for the rate of profit to fall at the centre of all scientific efforts in the field of political economy since Smith, Marx links the possibility of discovering this law, which is of course identical with Marx's law of accumulation and breakdown, with the methodological simplification and condensation of the capitalist mode of production into the formula c + v + s [= C]. The fundamental idea of Marx's economic system and at the same time the central axis of the capitalist economy around which all scientific efforts since Smith turn is, according to Marx's own assessment, most intimately connected with the construction of the formula.

But, from the standpoint of Marx's formulation of the question, is the problem of leading the analysis back to the fundamental capital relation, to the formula c + v + s [= C], specified with sufficient exactitude? Was the series of simplifications exhausted? Or could and should still others have been made – and which? How far could the simplification go, which elements should not be abstracted away under any circumstances? As we have seen, Sismondi had already posed this question. With regard to the method of simplification, Hegel correctly said: 'It must be observed that in this very process of scientific *understanding*, it is of importance that the essential should be distinguished and brought into relief in contrast with the so-called non-essential. But in order to render this possible, we must know what *is essential*.'[49]

In fact, for Marx there was no doubt about the essence of capitalism. He had to recognise it before he began to present his system, even before he wrote the first page of his work. The reduction of the capitalist mode of production to the fundamental capital relation still did not exhaust the number of its necessary premises, according to Marx. That is to say, the capital relation only forms *one* necessary fundamental premise and condition for capitalism. According to the formula c + v + s = C, we are only dealing with a *single* firm; hence any commodity *exchange* and hence commodity production itself is impossible. The second fundamental condition of the capitalist mode of production, *commodity exchange*, is not taken into account.[50] For 'only the products of mutually independent acts of labour, performed in isolation, can confront each other *as commodities*.'[51] Where these conditions do not apply, commodity production, hence also capitalist commodity production, is out of the question. '[T]o consider society as a *single* subject is wrong; a speculative approach.'[52] Where no commodity exchange exists, there can also be no question of commodity

49 Hegel 1914, p. 68.
50 Cf. Grossmann 1929a, p. 607.
51 Marx 1976b, p. 132. [Grossman's emphasis.]
52 Marx 1986b, p. 31. [Grossman's emphasis.]

production, hence, of capitalist commodity production. As Marx also wanted to express commodity exchange as a necessary prerequisite for the capitalist mode of production in his formula, he necessarily had to give an account of not *one* capitalist, but at least two independent commodity producers or groups of producers, who mutually exchange their products and hence only then demonstrate their commodity character. If one does that, then instead of the formula c + v + s = C one obtains the following:

I c + v + s = C
II c + v + s = C

In this way, the parameters for the construction of Marx's schema were given, and we have shown, step by step, the chain of thought that necessarily led from Marx's problematic to this result. Now, however, if the schema is to reflect the capitalist mode of production, another element must be included in its parameters. For at the present level in the development of our thought it has merely been established that commodity exchange is a necessary, fundamental premise of all capitalist production; that therefore the schematic simplification must necessarily depict at least *two* groups of producers in enduring exchange relationships. But here another question arises: is this a matter of any two arbitrary branches of production, e.g. coal mines and steelworks? Or does the formulation of the problem here not also entail certain necessary fundamental conditions for the formation of the exchange relationships between the two branches of production? With this question we arrive at the problem posed by Rosa Luxemburg as the central point in the discussion of whether a capitalism conceived of as isolated could possibly exist and her thesis that there is a 'gap' in Marx's analysis of the reproduction and accumulation process.

We saw earlier that Marx had to exclude all foreign trade relationships from his analysis of capitalist surplus value production – not only with non-capitalist, but also with foreign capitalist countries – in order to measure the magnitude of surplus value that could be obtained by a given social capital. Now if it is true that Marx thus excluded one of the *necessary* conditions for reproduction on an expanded scale – sale to non-capitalist purchasers – from his analysis; that he demonstrated the conditions for the production of surplus value, but not the possibility of its realisation, of its sale; that, consequently, there is a 'gap' in his account, because it only depicted the process of production, but not the possibility of sales, then on-going reproduction as a continuous process appears impossible.

Rosa Luxemburg tried to strengthen her theoretical critique of Marx's analysis by pointing out 'that the second volume is not a finished whole but a manuscript that stops short half way through.'[53] Certainly a convenient method of theoretical argument. Unable to find a way out of the dead-end in which one has landed, one declares there is a 'gap' in the system. On the issue of accumulation, Marx had not, in particular, gone further than specifying certain schemas and their initial analysis.[54] Luxemburg refers to the incomplete character of the second volume of *Capital*, but she forgets that, while the *schematic* representation of the reproduction process was only carried out in the second volume, the essential aspects of Marx's theory of reproduction and accumulation are developed in the first volume, which we have in a finished form. Furthermore, it is false to claim that the specification of the reproduction schema in the second volume 'stops short halfway through'. In fact, it was already conceptualised in 1863, *before* the publication of the first volume of *Capital*, and it underlies the *whole* analysis of the first volume as well as the other volumes of Marx's principal work (and not merely the chapter on reproduction in the second volume). Luxemburg overlooks how, in the chapter on accumulation in the first volume, Marx had already anticipated the essential results of the theory of reproduction and accumulation, substantiated in detail in the second volume.

In light of these facts, it is absolutely unacceptable to claim that Marx did not go beyond the specification of certain schemas and their initial analysis. On the contrary, we have attempted to demonstrate that the reproduction schema does not merely underlie the final part of the second volume, that it is not merely important for the question of the complete sale of commodities, but that the plan for the *whole* work is intimately connected with the methodological conception of the reproduction schema. The construction of all three volumes of *Capital* was carried out methodologically on the basis of the meticulously thought-out and actually implemented method of successive approximation, which, logically, is inseparably connected with the reproduction schema. Each provisional simplification correlates with a later, corresponding concretisation. In my book *The Law of Accumulation and Breakdown* (Chapter 3),[55] I have shown that Marx's procedure of subsequent concretisation was actually carried out meticulously. So there can be no question of a 'gap' resulting from his method of simplification. Despite all the simplifying assumptions, Marx never went so far in his procedure as to abstract from the capital relationship or from commodity exchange between the two spheres of production, I and II, because both elements constitute *necessary* conditions for capitalist production. If Marx excluded foreign markets from his analysis of the process of

53 Luxemburg 1951, pp. 165–6.
54 Luxemburg 1972, p. 48.
55 [Grossmann 1992, pp. 130–201.]

reproduction this did not occur, therefore, because there is an accidental 'gap' in his account, but because the relations of foreign trade do not belong to the theoretically necessary conditions for the process of reproduction. If Marx had considered the 'realisation' of surplus value in non-capitalist countries a necessary condition for accumulation, his reproduction schema would have looked quite different, namely

I	The capital relation (capitalist country):	c + v + s
II	Non-capitalist country:	independent producers

In this schema, department I would not merely encompass the production of means of production, but would undifferentiatedly encompass the *whole* production of the capitalist country. For, once non-capitalist markets are included in the reproduction schema, what purpose would the well-known division of the branches of production according to the use values of the commodities they produce serve? What purpose would the demand for definite relations of proportionality in the size of these two branches of the production apparatus serve in the capitalist country? Even if such relations of proportionality do not exist – e.g. if the capitalist country only encompasses a *single* department and e.g. only produces means of production, and thus there is no possibility of selling its v + s parts on the domestic market of the capitalist country, reproduction and accumulation can nevertheless continue without interruption because the sale of the v + s parts can occur in foreign, non-capitalist countries. From these, on the other hand, means of consumption for workers and capitalists can be obtained through foreign trade. The division of the apparatus of production in the capitalist country into the two well-known departments – I (production of means of production) and II (production of means of consumption) – has no purpose in such a case.

If Marx combines capitalist production not into one, but into two branches of production – and not into any arbitrary branches, but in such a way that means of production must *necessarily* be produced in one, and means of consumption in the other – then this occurs *because, in his schema, Marx wanted to illustrate all the necessary conditions for the existence of a capitalism that is conceived of as isolated.* If, in capitalism conceived of as isolated, only means of production are produced, then means of consumption must be obtained from abroad if reproduction is to be conceived of as a continuous process. Conversely, if only means of consumption are produced, then the importation of means of production is unavoidable. In this way, foreign trade relations would be a necessary condition for the reproduction process as a whole. Yet, for the reasons identified above, Marx excludes foreign trade relations from his schematic analysis! If the schema of capitalist production constructed by Marx excludes foreign trade relations and is not to be an unrealistic phantom, Marx had to ensure in other ways that the schema includes all the elements that are significant, i.e. vital for the capitalist mode of production. By explaining that the division of the apparatus of production in the capitalist country was a necessary condition for equilibrium and allowing for the production of means of production and means of consumption, Marx seeks to construct a mechanism of production independent of foreign trade relations that is nevertheless viable and self-contained. Only in a capitalism thought of in this way does it make any sense to inquire about the relations of proportionality necessary for equilibrium, i.e. for the complete sale of all commodities on the domestic market. *Only in this case* do these relations of proportionality constitute a necessary condition for a course of reproduction free from disruption. Including non-capitalist markets in the schema destroys the schema's fundamental theoretical idea, the proof of the necessity of definite relations of proportionality. Thus it invalidates the real content and great significance of Marx's discovery!

3

Now we want to compare the results of our general analysis of the theoretical conditions of Marx's method in the schema, as they arose from the general requirements of Marx's problematic, with Marx's concrete presentation of the conditions for reproduction.

The process of accumulation and reproduction is dealt with first not in the second volume of *Capital*, but already in the 24th chapter of the first volume, where the 'transformation of surplus value into capital' is presented.[56] Here was the systematic place and opportunity to mention the role of non-capitalist markets, if in Marx's conception they had constituted a *necessary condition* for the transformation of surplus value into capital; if Marx considered 'pure' capitalism impossible. This even more because in the first volume Marx had not only already investigated the conditions for accumulation from the standpoint of the individual capital, but also, in the 25th chapter, developed 'the general law of capitalist accumulation' and the 'continual re-conversion of surplus value into capital'.[57] He had the *social* conditions for accumulation in mind and, in relation to them, formulated a series of social laws, such as the law of con-

56 Marx 1976b, pp. 725–61.
57 Marx 1976b, p. 775.

centration and centralisation of capital, the capitalist mode of production's distinctive law of population and the emergence of the reserve army of labour as a product of accumulation and a condition for its sudden expansion, and finally the necessary breakdown of the capitalist mode of production. Here Marx further enumerates a series of moments, which 'determine the *extent* of accumulation'.[58] Marx did *not* mention non-capitalist purchasers as a condition for accumulation! And this is supposed to be an accidental 'gap' in his account?

And further! Marx already avails himself of a series of simplifying assumptions in his presentation of accumulation in the first volume. What was the purpose of these methodological simplifications, of this abstraction from a series of empirically given moments? Marx's explanations are so clear as to be scarcely controversial: in his analysis of the problem of accumulation, Marx wants to abstract from all moments that are incidental to the problem of accumulation, even if they are otherwise important, in order to highlight all the more starkly the *essential, fundamental conditions* for the accumulation process. In the presentation of the accumulation of surplus value, i.e. its transformation into capital, Marx has to demonstrate 'the *necessary conditions* under which it [surplus value] becomes an element in accumulation.'[59] This, then, is the purpose of Marx's simplifications! Everything but the 'necessary conditions' should be abstracted away. The analysis only deals with 'the simple, *fundamental form of the process of accumulation* ... An exact analysis of the process, therefore, demands that we should, for a time, disregard all phenomena that *conceal the workings of its inner mechanism*'.[60] If Marx considered the 'realisation' of surplus value in non-capitalist markets a necessary condition for accumulation, it would be impossible for him to refrain from including the function of non-capitalist markets in his analysis of the conditions for accumulation. Marx *would have*, rather, to demonstrate this here because, according to this conception, it would constitute a necessary part of the 'inner workings' of the capitalist mechanism, its 'simple, fundamental form'. Instead of Marx's current schema, we would have had a different one, namely

I $c + v + s$
II independent producers

58 Marx 1976b, p. 747. [Grossman's emphasis.]

59 Marx 1976b, p. 710. ['Necessary' is in the original German text, Marx 1991a, p. 506, but not the Penguin translation.]

60 Marx 1976b, p. 710. [Grossman's emphasis.]

The basic fact that Marx did not do this, that he explicitly abstracted from foreign trade altogether, thus also from foreign trade with non-capitalist countries, and even counts it among '*disturbing subsidiary circumstances*', which disguise the inner workings of the mechanism 'in its purity',[61] proves the opposite of Luxemburg's claim. It proves that Marx believed that a capitalism conceived of as isolated, without external markets, was possible and he was convinced that the fundamental laws of accumulation were more sharply expressed without the 'disturbing influences' of foreign trade. Finally, it proves that one cannot speak of a 'gap' with regard to Marx's deliberate exclusion of foreign markets! The 'gap theory' is nothing other than a comfortable little cloak, which disguises the fact that Luxemburg, under the pretext of ostensible 'further development' and 'gap filling', actually, on this essential point of the structure of Marx's thought, abandoned and combated his theory of accumulation!

That one cannot speak of a 'gap' in Marx's work at this point can be precisely demonstrated by a further argument. In the chapter on accumulation, Marx considers it necessary not merely to present the conditions for accumulation positively, but to critically polemicise against the 'political economists' erroneous conception of reproduction on an increasing scale'.[62] Never and nowhere, however, had they considered the necessity of non-capitalist countries as a condition of accumulation. Was it not the best opportunity, indeed a logical requirement, to demonstrate their theoretical 'mistakes' and to point out the necessary function of non-capitalist countries precisely here? But one does not find a trace of this in Marx. The same Marx who refutes the erroneous conception of accumulation of bourgeois economics, namely that of Smith, and uncovers Smith's 'stupid blunder'[63] which claims that surplus value in accumulation 'is laid out exclusively in the payment of wages'.[64] The same Marx who in the chapter mentioned above polemicises against the iron law of wages and further against the theory of compensation in relation to workers displaced.[65] Would this Marx have silently ignored that other theory of all previous economics, that accumulation *without* non-capitalist markets, that 'pure' capitalism is possible? That would be highly unlikely for another

---

61 Marx 1976b, pp. 269, 727.

62 Marx 1976b, p. 734.

63 Marx 1978b, p. 449.

64 Marx 1976b, p. 737.

65 [Marx 1976b, on the possibility of higher wages, pp. 768–72; against compensation theory, 'that all machinery that displaces workers simultaneously, and necessarily, sets free an amount of capital adequate to employ precisely those workers displaced', pp. 565–75.]

reason. Engels mentions in the preface to the second volume of *Capital* that 'It is sufficient to enumerate the manuscript material that Marx left to show the incomparable conscientiousness and severe self-criticism with which he strove to bring his great economic discoveries to the utmost degree of perfection.'[66] In fact, we know that all the more important problems are mentioned by Marx at different points in his work three, four and often more times, and Marx never missed the opportunity to point out the errors of his predecessors. To give just one example: the 'erroneous conception of increasing accumulation' on the part of bourgeois economics, namely that of Smith, mentioned above, is already refuted in the first volume,[67] and then combated again in the third part of the second volume.[68] Finally, for the third and fourth times, Marx deals extensively with this problem in his critical analysis in *Theories of Surplus Value*.[69] The same is true for a series of other problems. Would it not be odd, then, that Marx should repeatedly uncover all the errors of bourgeois economics but fail to mention, even with one syllable, in any place in his works and manuscripts over a period of 30 years, the cardinal error that a capitalism conceived of as isolated, without a non-capitalist 'milieu', is possible?

The previous indications suffice to license us to conclude that the convenient 'torso' – or 'gap' theory – that takes the path of least resistance is absolutely insupportable and that it must be discarded once and for all.[70] Rather, it is

66 Marx 1978b, p. 84.

67 Marx 1976b, pp. 734, 736. [Grossman is paraphrasing Marx's words, already quoted above, rather than quoting them.]

68 Marx 1978b, pp. 438 and 442.

69 Marx 1989b, p. 25 et seq.; Marx 1989c, p. 49, and especially p. 52.

70 This also applies to Georg Lukács, who advocates the 'fragment' theory criticised here and who rejects the conception that 'Marx's formulae were arrived at on the basis of a hypothetical society (posited for reasons of method) which consisted only of capitalists and workers.' On the contrary, L. emphasises 'that Marx posited this society for the sake of argument, i.e. to see the problem more clearly, before pressing forward to the larger question of the place of this problem within society as a whole.' Up to this point, we can agree with L. His mistake lies in his view that Marx himself never completed this task. That is, Marx – to use Marx's language – made the journey from the conception of the concrete totality, from the 'conception of the whole' analytically, by means of simplifying methodological assumptions, until he arrived at 'more and more tenuous abstractions', i.e. to an abstract capitalist society, which consists only of capitalists and workers, without foreign trade. But that he did not retrace the journey back to a concrete 'rich totality of many determinations and relations', to the 'living whole'. [Marx 1986b, p. 37]. According to L., the result is 'that *on this issue* Capital *is an incomplete fragment* which stops short at the point where this problem should be opened up. In this sense what Rosa Luxemburg has done is precisely to take up the thread where Marx left off and to solve the problem in his

imperative for the analysis of Marx, in all theoretical respects to start with the opposite, basic premise: that the material left to us by Marx is essentially finished, apart from the details of exposition. Consequently, when dealing with difficulties that arise for the problematic of the individual partial areas and partial theories of Marx's system, the highest principle must be that the difficulties are *to be overcome* not by means of mechanical, superficial additions and completions but *within the given material*, in accordance with the logic of the system as a whole. This means nothing more than that one must hold to the idea that Marxist economics, as it has been bequeathed to us, is not a 'fragment' or a 'torso', but constitutes a finished, i.e. complete, system.

In constructing his schema to present only the 'necessary conditions', the essential, fundamental form of the process of reproduction and accumulation, Marx had to know what was essential about capitalist production in order to separate it from the non-essential, to use Hegel's language. Marx already has these essential, fundamental conditions in mind when he approaches the composition of *Capital*, the presentation of the *first* chapter of his work. In the first chapters of the first volume, Marx is already concerned not with immediately given empirical appearances, not with profit, interest, ground rent, etc., but with their ideal aggregate, with surplus value. He is not concerned with the empirically given appearance of price but starts with the fictitious premise that commodities are sold at their values, which includes further assumptions: that the apparatus of production is in a state of equilibrium; that the commodity labour power is likewise sold at its value; that no reserve army exists; and, finally, that no competition takes place. In short, Marx already had all the simplifying assumptions of his reproduction schema in mind before he even wrote the first page of his work or could write it.

It is certainly one of the greatest misunderstandings and distortions of Marx's thought to associate Marx's reproduction schema with only the last chapter of the second volume of *Capital*, with only the problem of the *complete sale* of the year's product; and, finally, to see only the simplifying assumptions, but not the subsequent corrections. As was shown here, Marx's reproduction schema is intimately connected with the methodological procedure that underlies all three volumes of *Capital*. For this reason, the change in the plan

spirit', Lukács 1971, p. 31. Elsewhere Lukács writes of Rosa Luxemburg's 'admirable extension of Marx's theory of capitalist reproduction', Lukács 1970, p. 41. In my book, *The Law of Accumulation and Breakdown*, I have shown that Lukács's assertion is incorrect and indicated 'that in the methodological construction of the system each of the several fictitious, simplifying assumptions is subsequently modified.' 'These considerations mean that the abstract analysis comes closer to the world of real appearances', Grossmann 1992, pp. 30 and 131.

for Marx's life's work and the construction of the reproduction schema arose from the same fundamental idea. Marx's method is, in its general principles, the true expression of his formulation of the problem. Only in relation to the latter can the real reasons for it also be understood.

CHAPTER 9

Notes for 'Response to Criticisms of the Principle Work'*

Translated from German by Rick Kuhn

Manuscript Starting 'Die Entwertung sollen ...'

Devaluation overcomes the tendency to break down and not, as Marx argued, only weakens it temporarily? How is that possible? *That* through the rising productivity of labour, the elements of constant and variable capital are devalued, so that in part the rate of surplus value, in part the rate of profit temporarily rise; this I argued myself, drawing on Marx.[1] As a consequence, the objection that I neglected the weakening tendency of devaluation cannot logically be raised against me. If Helene Bauer's objection concerning devaluation has any meaning at all, it can only be understood that through devaluation the original, existing tendency to breakdown, conceded as possible, is always, time after time *overcome* and not simply weakened.[2]

The question of the *conditions* under which it is possible to permanently abrogate the tendency to breakdown must, consequently, be considered. The simplest reflection shows that this would only be possible if, through devaluation, in value terms total social capital *does not grow* in relation to living labour (unpaid labour, that is surplus value included) but declines or at least remains constant! Helene B's and Braunthal's proposition that devaluation of capital abrogates the tendency to breakdown necessarily entails the proposition that there is no development of an ever higher organic composition of capital in contemporary capitalist society![3]

The Marxist concept of a progressively higher organic composition of capital entails two different conclusions. On the one hand, the development of the productivity of labour means that the same mass of living labour (L) can set in motion an ever larger mass of means of production, that, as a consequence, the progress of the human economy is expressed in a progressively higher *technical composition*, in the relative increase in MP in relation to L.

* [Selected from Grossman circa 1929–32.]

1 [Grossmann 1992, pp. 139–40, 144–7.]

2 [Otto Bauer 1929.]

3 [Braunthal 1929.]

On the other, with this technological progress, which is just another expression of the increase in the productivity of labour, the products of human labour (means of production and consumption) are *devalued* and thus become cheaper. So we have two counterposed movements. On the one hand an ever *greater mass* of MP,[4] on the other hand a *cheapening* of this mass of products. Considered purely abstractly, one can imagine that the devaluation is *greater* than the increase in the *mass* of means of production. In that case, despite the ever larger mass of MP per worker, there would be a progressively *declining value* of this larger mass; then not a progressively higher organic composition but merely a higher technical and a declining value composition would be possible. A higher organic composition of capital implies that the means of production grow in both their mass *and their value* compared with living labour. Both will move in the same direction (even if not at the same rate). The question arises, how do things develop in reality? Is the *pace* of these two counterposed movements, growth in mass and decline in value, equal so that they *paralyse each other*? Or does the movement of one or the other predominate? Let's look at an example. A worker, whose labour creates a value of 100 Marks and receives half as wages, serves two machines whose value, including necessary raw and other materials is 600 Marks. The value of living labour = 100 i.e. 50 v + 50 s.[5] Thanks to technological progress, this worker is capable of servicing 4, that is double the mass of MP with the same amount of labour, 100. But, thanks to the same technological progress, the machines and raw materials and similarly the worker's necessities of life are made more cheaply, *devalued*. As a consequence, the MP do not represent a value of 1200 Marks, but a *smaller* value. If the worker's necessities are devalued by 1/5, that is to 40 Marks, and similarly the machines and raw materials to 960 Marks, then there would be *no change in the value composition of capital*: 1200 : 50 = 940 c : 40 v [should be 1200 c : 50 v = **960** c : 40 v = **24**]. Only in such a case, when despite the higher productivity of labour there is *no change in the value composition of capital*, is the decline in the rate of profit excluded and a *constant* rate of profit possible. For

600 c + 50 v + 50 s, p = 50/650 = 14.28 %[6]
480 c + 40 v + 60 s, p = 60/520 = 14.28 %[7]

4 [MP is means of production.]
5 [v is variable capital i.e. the value of labour power, and s is surplus value.]
6 [p is the rate of profit, s/(c + v).]
7 [These numerical examples are both mathematically wrong and inconsistent with Grossman's preceding assumptions.]

Here there is *no* development to a higher organic composition of capital. Admittedly, there is a higher technical composition of capital. But not a higher value composition. According to Marx, a [higher] *organic* composition of capital can only be spoken of where the higher technical composition also expresses a higher *value* composition ([even] if they do not have to grow in the same proportion).

The proposition that the devaluation of capital overcomes the breakdown, that no tendency to a relative decline in the mass of living labour compared to capital is apparent *thus means the negation of the Marxist doctrine of the progressively higher organic composition of capital* in the course of capitalist development, means that there is a tendency for the value composition of capital to *decline*, or at best remain *constant*.

Now the question which of the two tendencies, growth in the mass or devaluation is stronger, that is the question of whether devaluation is of the same extent as the growth in the mass of the MP and thus the growth in mass is paralysed by the decline in value, or rather whether devaluation is not as great and consequently that despite the devaluation of the MP, *its value in relation to L grows*,[8] cannot be abstractly, deductively decided and has to be decided through *empirical observation*. *Experience*, indeed experience of more than one hundred years, teaches that the *value* of constant capital, thus also of the total capital, in relation to variable capital grows *more quickly* than variable, i.e. that in the relationship c : v, c grows *faster* than v. This can be expressed more exactly when we consider not simply the *paid* part of labour but the *entire* living labour (including the unpaid part) as it is incorporated into the product and the part of the constant capital that is, in the same way, used up in a product. Then the new value created by living labour, or *value product* W,[9] constitutes a progressively *smaller* part of the annual *value of production* Y (the living and the dead labour, i.e. the part of constant capital used up). That is, the size of W/Y declines and can, for example, be presented by the series 10/12, 9/12, 8/12, 6/12, 4/12 etc. The *living* labour, presented in the numerator is an ever *smaller* part of the total labour (living and dead).

That has been the *experience* of our proposition since Marx. Braunthal, who constantly refers me to observed reality, to experience, does not notice that precisely my *assertion of the falling rate of profit has as its precondition the proposition based on the experience* of the rising organic composition of capital and that he ends up precisely contradicting this proposition based on the experience of more than a hundred years, by asserting a tendency for the rate of profit

8 [L is labour power.]
9 [W is v + s.]

to *rise*! Just this long experience, this repeated empirical confirmation of the fact that living labour is progressively replaced by the work of machines and that despite the devaluation of the machines the total mass of value per worker rises, that is the *organic composition rises* and hence the value component of living labour in the product declines,[10] In his polemic against Tugan-Baranovsky's assertion of a tendency for the rate of profit to rise, Otto Bauer also proceeds from the *empirical fact* that the total social capital grows *more quickly* than the *living* labour which sets it in motion: 'As a consequence of the progress of a higher organic composition of capital, the *social value of production* [that is the denominator] grows *faster* than the social value product [numerator] ... so we can *assert the tendency for the size of W/Y to decline*.' Indeed, obviously in view of the experience of all countries under the capitalist mode of production, he speaks of a '*law*' of the decline of W/P.[11] I cite in my book on the tendency of accumulation and breakdown, on p. 453, statistics from which it is apparent that the census results from the United States of America for the thirty years 1889–1919 show that the capital per worker more than *tripled* and indeed the capital per worker grew from 1889 to 1904 by 55% and from 1904 to 1919 by 111%.[12]

	Capital $ million	Workers	Capital per worker	Wage $
1889	6,525	4,251,613	1,535	445
1899	9,814	5,310,598	1,855	
1904	12,675	5,468,383	2,310	
1909	18,428	6,615,046	2,780	
1914	22,790	7,036,247	3,230	
1919	44,466	9,096,372	4,888	1,157

In this period were there no crises, no devaluation in the United States? Did a crisis in 1893–96 and the crash of 1907, to name only these two examples, happen? But *despite this devaluation*, value per worker from 1889 more than tripled. From this the only conclusion to be drawn is that *without* devaluation, the organic composition would have been *even* larger.

10 [This sentence was left hanging by Grossman's deletion of its final clause, whose concept is worked into the next sentence.]

11 Otto Bauer 1907, pp. 822, 823. [Grossman's emphasis].

12 Grossmann 1929a, p. 453.

Wherever examinations of the organic composition of capital have so far been available this empirical tendency has *always* been apparent. Despite capitalism's manifold devaluations, this tendency has not been overcome but only weakened. Stronger or weaker, but it remains, despite the actual devaluations.

Share of wages in the value of the product:[13]

1849	23.23%
1859	20.46%
1869	18.30%
1879	17.65%
1889	20.18%
1899	17.85%
1904	17.67%
1909	16.56%
1914	16.85%
1919	16.88%

In 1889 there were 4,251,613 workers, the wage was \$1,891 million = \$445 per head. 1919 there were 9,096,372 workers, wage \$10,533 million = \$1,157 per head.

And no-one has previously proved the incorrectness of this empirical tendency or had a stab at a proof. It was reserved for Helene Bauer to disprove this tendency, which has been continuously confirmed over a hundred years, with her assertion that devaluation is the basis for overcoming the tendency to break down, without providing even a shadow of proof and without being aware of the consequences of her assertion. From this uncontested empirical tendency, following Marx, I derived the crisis tendency; from the fact that living labour continuously declines compared with the capital outlaid and thus, in this sense, is eventually exhausted, being insufficient to sustain accumulation on the basis of the organic composition of capital: the system therefore blows apart.

If, then, Helene Bauer wants to contradict the tendency to break down and show that, through the devaluation of capital the mass of surplus value in relation to this total capital is *not* exhausted, does *not decline* she has to demonstrate the *incorrectness* of the empirical fact of the progressively higher organic composition of capital or, to speak with Otto Bauer, she has to demonstrate that the *law* of the 'decline of V/P is incorrect'.[14]

13 Grossmann 1929a, p. 453.

14 In his polemic against Tugan-Baranovsky, Otto Bauer 1907, p. 823.

It is an impermissible contradiction, a lack of awareness to speak on the one hand of the fact of the progressively higher organic composition of capital and at the same time to assert that *devaluation* overcomes the tendency to break down, to deny the fact of the higher organic composition of capital. Only when there is no progressively higher organic composition of capital does living labour not decline in relation to capital outlaid and therefore cannot be exhausted.

But if the tendency to a higher organic composition of capital, thus to a relative decline in living labour, exists then the tendency to breakdown results from the progress of capital accumulation and at a certain level a *continuously larger part* of the newly created value product will be accumulated as additional capital.

c	v	m	Living labour	a_c[15]
200,000	10,000	100,000	200,000	12,000
212,000	105,000	105,000	210,000	12,720
224,720	110,250	110,250	220,500	13,482

The a_c part grows relative to the total mass of living labour and with correspondingly large growth of constant capital entirely swallows the *mass of value* created by living labour, surplus value and the wage fund.

It is *not every* increase in productivity that increases the *rate of surplus value*. Only in so far as commodities which are *consumed by the working class* are produced more cheaply (Ricardo). Hence not through increased productivity in *luxury industries*, indeed the mass of these articles increases and their value declines but the *rate of surplus value* is *not* increased.

It is in *part* similar with the *means of production*. The rate of surplus value in Department I is *not* increased as they are cheapened. Only in so far as they go into Department II, and indeed at cheaper prices, are the necessities of life consumed by workers pro rata cheaper, hence the rate of surplus value also rises.

One can finally speak of devaluation in the discussion of individual branches of production under the real assumption that the development of productivity in individual branches of production occurs unevenly. (Of course one has

15 [a_c is surplus value that is accumulated, i.e. reinvested in constant capital.]

to show why this development of productivity takes place so unevenly.) But in the schema we assume that in all branches of production

[large gap on page]

In addition when one does not start with the *individual commodity* but considers the *total mass of commodities*, devaluation has indifferent consequences. The 100,000 workers in the schema indeed produce a tremendously greater mass of use values with the same amount of labour, as the total outlay on labour has not changed. *The total mass of value is unchanged* even if the *individual* commodity is cheaper. There are now *more things* that the value (v + s) represents, but the amount of new value produced by the same number of workers has not changed. And the same is the case with the c part in Department II. It incorporates *more* commodities, useful things. Each *individual* commodity is cheaper, but the size of the total mass of commodities nevertheless, has the same value which is consumed and carried over to the annual product.

If the objection that devaluation is not considered is to have any sense at all, then it is only that one's starting point is *useful things*. Let us assume that the entire rural economy uses 1000 electric ploughs (each with a value of £80 = £80,000) which are sufficient to work the available land. If productivity now doubles so that with the same labour 2,000 electric ploughs can be produced, then the rural economy will not therefore be able to buy them as they are superfluous. Devaluation must have the consequence that the rural economy now only buys 1000 ploughs each with a value of £40 = £4000. Consideration of devaluation shows the unsaleability of the product, the disruption of all the proportions worked out so arduously by Otto Bauer.

Manuscript Starting 'Br. verweist …'

Braunthal refers with an ironic smile to the fact that Marx foresaw an intensification of *proletarian suffering*, whereas I on the other hand deduced the breakdown of capitalism 'from a kind of *impoverishment of the capitalists*'. From Otto Bauer's numerical example, I deduce the 'amazing result' that the entrepreneur's revenue not only declines relatively, but after the 21st year declines absolutely and finally in the thirty-fifth year disappears entirely. That is, 'in brief, the idea underlying' my theory of so-called overaccumulation.[16] There is not a trace of this in my work. Nowhere did I say that capitalism will go under due to the impoverishment of the capitalists. I showed, rather, that an increasingly large part of surplus value (a_c) is, under the assumptions of Bauer's schema, devoted

16 Braunthal 1929, p. 294.

to accumulation. The remainder available for the consumption of the capitalists and workers does not suffice. As a consequence an increasingly sharp struggle between workers and entrepreneurs over the level of wages necessarily flares up. *If* workers continue to receive the same wage, then nothing *remains* for the entrepreneurs. If, however, the latter maintain and, where possible, even increase their living standard then they forces down the level of wages, i.e. from this point on the *impoverishment of the workers* necessarily sets in. That, however, drives the workers to revolution and, as a result of this impoverishment of the workers, and [sic] capitalism will go under.

Braunthal's theoretical position cannot be particularly strong when he uses such means of distorting my argument and fails to mention with a single little word the entire chapter on the theory of wages, where I develop this idea and which is an important component of my theory of breakdown!

The ridicule of my 'mathematical persistence' in continuing Otto Bauer's numerical example over 35 years does not help. I thoroughly justified my approach and provided a logical and mathematical proof. For those who prefer a concrete illustration I also gave an arithmetical example of Bauer's schema.

Such a process is not only required, it is *necessary* and arises from the nature of accumulation. Accumulation is a successive expansion of the productive apparatus through the successive transformation of surplus value into capital. If one wants to determine 'the *historical tendencies*' of accumulation, to understand capitalism's 'law of motion' then it is obvious that one must consider the *course* of accumulation *over time*. 'Historical tendencies' are precisely tendencies which only emerge *à la longue*[17] in the course of capitalist accumulation and are not always observable over short periods of time.

Admittedly, nothing has yet been said about the *length of time* over which this tendency becomes apparent. The critique of Otto Bauer's equilibrium theory was made using his example and this showed that the tendency to breakdown emerged in 35 years. But the *length* of this period in itself has nothing to do with the idea I demonstrated and is a *coincidental* result of Bauer's concrete numerical example which should go down onto Otto Bauer's debt account, not mine. Further, if Bauer's schema is intended to illustrate contemporary capitalism, it shows an *entirely insufficient organic composition* of capital. It assumes as the social average a composition of 200,000 c : 100,000 v, constant capital comprising only twice the value of yearly wages. Now *Engels* already gave 'an example of the *actual* composition of capital in modern large industries', from a cotton-spinning factory in 1871 where a total capital of £12,500 was divided

17 ['*À la longue*' means 'in the long term'.]

into £12,182 constant and £318 variable capital. In percentage terms, the organic composition was 97½ c + 2½ v = 100 C.[18] The constant capital is 39 times larger than the variable. It is clear that today there is an even higher organic composition in large industries. For precisely this reason, Bauer's numerical example, with its unusually *low* organic composition is not a reflection of contemporary capitalism but expresses the low organic composition of capitalism in its early phases. And the long cycles of Bauer's schema are precisely a consequence of this low composition, hence the necessity of calculations over 35 years. This is because the tendency to break down only takes effect in the late phase of accumulation when the organic composition is high; as a consequence *long* periods are necessary before Bauer's schema with its slow rate of accumulation develops a high organic composition. With a higher organic composition assumed as a basis for the enquiry from the start, which would express reality, the cycles and with them the necessity for 'mathematical persistence' would be diminished. For this too Otto Bauer is responsible, not I. I undertook my proof under circumstances which Otto Bauer dictated.

Let us assume that Braunthal does not hide behind the hardly valid proposition that Bauer's schema is calculated 'indeed only for a short period', namely a period of four years.[19] In my critique of Bauer's equilibrium schema, I give a variation of Bauer's schema.[20] It shows that, with a higher organic composition of capital, the reproduction process will definitely not [be viable], even for this 'short period'.[21]

But the indication that my theory of breakdown, in contrast to Marx's, is a theory of the *capitalists'* impoverishment also does not help. I conducted my proof under the *most favourable conditions* for the survival of capitalism, that Otto Bauer, not I, laid out in his schema; I merely showed the consequences which result. Actually B assumed that the entrepreneurs are such altruists that they think foremost about unconditionally employing all workers who are already active, as well as the annual new generation of workers and that, to the extent necessary and taking into account the latest technological progress, the extension of the productive apparatus necessary for this purpose is secured and that surplus value is employed first of all for this purpose and only the *remainder* of surplus value that is left over remains as the capitalists' revenue, for their individual consumption. Thus Otto Bauer assumes precisely that the

18 [C is total capital outlaid.]
19 Braunthal 1929, p. 300.
20 Grossman 1929a, p. 225.
21 [The manuscript seems to break off in the middle of 'viable', at this point.]

accumulation rate of constant and variable capital has a fixed, constant magnitude and that the consumption part is a variable magnitude.

If Braunthal finds this assumption absurd he should take it up with Bauer.

However absurd the *content* of this assumption may be, methodologically there can be nothing against it. Surplus value is divided into three parts, $a_c + a_v + k$. In order to prove the idea I propose, that the mass of surplus value at high levels of capital accumulation becomes insufficient for the continuation of accumulation, it is irrelevant which part of the surplus value is assumed to be constant and which to be variable. For the sake of completeness, in order to encompass all consequences, one should go through all possible cases one after the other and proceed on the basis of Marx's example:[22]

1) a_c and a_v constant, k variable
2) a_v and k constant, a_c variable
3) a_c and k constant, a_v variable[23]

All cases lead to the same result; they show that limitless accumulation on the basis of a progressively higher organic composition of capital is impossible because the mass of surplus value at high levels of accumulation is insufficient. If the rate of accumulation of the constant part is assumed to be constant, it is apparent that there is a deficiency in the capitalists' revenue part. If the rate of the k part and the a_v part are assumed to be constant then it is apparent that the part of surplus value that is destined for the accumulation of constant capital is insufficient. It is just as when a blanket is too short, if it is pulled over the head then the feet are uncovered, and vice versa. Consequently it is methodologically irrelevant which of the three possible cases is taken as the starting point of the analysis and, for those who are not content with sticking with the concrete individual case but rather are capable of grasping its significance *in principle*, the essential side, that arises from the fact of the insufficient amount of surplus value for accumulation, would be immediately intelligible.[24] If Braunthal, instead of belittling my 'mathematical persistence' had the scientific curiosity to examine all the possible variations of the amount of surplus value in the course of accumulation he would have immediately realised that he would achieve nothing, by this means, but merely a reprieve.

As, however, Braunthal proceeds lazily, namely lazily in thought, for him we must implement the changes in the proof he postulated. Let us assume the

---

22 Marx 1981b, pp. 145–6, 147–8.

23 [a_c is surplus value that is accumulated, i.e. invested in additional constant capital.
a_v is surplus value that is used to purchase additional variable capital, i.e. labour power
k is surplus value that is used for the personal consumption of the capitalists.]

24 [This sentence includes some garbled repetition in the original manuscript.]

second of the possible cases, namely that the rate of growth of variable capital a_v and of the revenue of the employers k is constant, while the rate of growth of constant capital, which constitutes the remainder of surplus value, that is left after the a_v and k parts are deducted, is variable. Let us therefore assume that variable capital, corresponding to the growth of the population by 5% a year, likewise rises by 5%. Let us assume further that the employers appropriate 20% of the total surplus value for their personal consumption and that the rate of surplus value is 100%. How will accumulation proceed under these conditions?[25]

The Kautskyite school lags a further 10–15 years behind leading revisionist thinkers. 1901 Tugan-Baranovsky's equilibrium theory, 1902 Kautsky polemic [against it] – 1910 Hilferding already accepts; 1913 Otto Bauer.[26] 1901 Tugan-Baranovsky combats falling rate of profit, 1907 Boudin, Otto Bauer combat [Tugan-Baranovsky] – so that 1929 Braunthal accepts.[27] [1910] Conrad Schmidt drops the law of value,[28] Kautskyites combat [him]. They will also give it up and are already on the road to doing so.

Just as in real life and in its practice, the task of Marxism as a *movement* consists of accelerating and thus foreshortening real tendencies of development, through practical intervention, the task of Marxist theory is to accelerate intellectual development through *critique*.

The task [is] to force Braunthal [to concede] that, as he has given up the falling rate of profit, he will give up the Marxist theory of value and surplus value, that he also has to give up the Marxist theory of the tendency for the development of a progressively higher organic composition of capital.

Manuscript Starting 'Nach Braunthal …'

According to Braunthal, Marx started with the observation that

> the rate of profit shows a tendency to decline and derived his law from that. *This observation* was correct *for that time*. But it really must be

25 [Two tables employing these assumptions follow in the manuscript, with numerical examples of accumulation over 96 years, starting with a low organic composition of capital; and over six years, starting with a high organic composition of capital. There are calculation errors in the table which, in any case, do not advance Grossman's argument, which is presumably why he did not elaborate on them.]

26 [Tugan-Baranowsky 1901; Kautsky 1902; Hilferding 1981; Otto Bauer 1986.]

27 [Tugan-Baranowsky 1901; Boudin 1907; Otto Bauer 1907; Braunthal 1929.]

28 [Schmidt 1910.]

> renewed for the present before such a broad conclusions as Grossman's are drawn from it. This observation is missing from his work … After all the symptoms, which can be surveyed, it seems that the conclusion has to be drawn that the decline in the rate of profit has been brought *to a halt for several decades* by counter tendencies – intensified technological rationalisation in association with organisational rationalisation in the form of the concentration of capital. So no prediction should be made for the distant future.[29]

What Braunthal understands as a 'law', according to this presentation, is absolutely unintelligible. The decline in the rate of profit was only Marx's one-off observation 'for that time'. This observation does not apply to the present; the tendency to decline has come to a halt and in the future can hardly be different, as no prediction can be made. A fine conception of 'laws', whose validity only extends to the period of observation, whose efficacy, however, then immediately ceases. A 'law' whose validity only extends over the period of observation is really nothing other than another expression of the observation, thus a contentless and superfluous phrase. The facts that underpin the observation disappear, and the 'law' loses validity.[30] Previously something different was understood by law, namely that the course of events runs according to the law, the law dominates the events and there is here an imposed course, not only during the period of observation but also during later periods and, from this imposed sequence, *prediction* of the course of phenomenon in the future is possible. A law that is 'derived' from observation but is only valid at the time of the observation is identical to the observation, is only a statement of the observation, is, therefore, not a law.[31] Saying of a pile of stones, 'here are 8 stones' is an observation and not a law. A law implies that where **A**, necessarily also **B**. 'Where the organic composition of capital rises, there the rate of profit *must* decline in the long term.' The circumstance that Marx did not speak of the 'fact' of the declining rate of profit already shows that it was impossible that he only made a one-off observation 'for that time' but was rather thinking about a *necessary causal* connection. Here we have a little test of Braunthal's intellectual level. He, who wants to instruct others about methods of investigation, in this is unable to make the most elementary distinction …

---

29 [Braunthal 1929, p. 302.]

30 [At this point there is an annotation in the margin: '(Riazanov *Zur Krit*)', presumably a reference to Marx 1987a.]

31 [At this point there is an annotation in the margin: '(Marx investigates capital in *general* in contrast to concrete movement)'.]

On the contrary Smith and Ricardo observed the fact. They were disturbed by it. Marx did not claim the discovery of the fact for himself but rather only the development of a law, i.e. a principle which explains the course of events as a necessary connection.

⟨But this position on Marx's law of the tendency for the rate of profit to fall is no accident. If it is a *law* of capitalist development then it has, precisely, an absolute validity. But then the consequences which I demonstrated were immanent in this law also have validity. If these consequences are denied and combated then the assumptions that underpin them must be presented as unreal and false. 'We will establish, *that the decisive assumption for Grossman's entire theory of breakdown,* namely the assumption that the rate of profit declines in the long term, even if with interruptions, is *invalid*. For this reason, naturally various conclusions which Grossman draws also collapse.'[32] (p. 302). The intention is clear, blabbed openly.⟩

Before we confront the proof of Braunthal's thesis of a rising or at least constant rate of profit, we have to ask him: who, when and where has someone noted this new tendency in the movement of the rate of profit? It is important to know since when the new tendency has come to the fore and who first determined this. Did it come to the fore during the nineteenth century, at the start of the twentieth century before the War, or is it the product of the period after the War? Braunthal cites no work that can inform me. He cannot do so because *such a book does not exist*! Perhaps Braunthal will write it. If it was already here and if I had not considered its results then his accusations along these lines would be justified. Obviously, I cannot consider a book that Braunthal still wants to write. And there are also no other works. And Braunthal, who refers to reality, instead of crushing me with the results of observations and casting the '*facts*' before my eyes – nor does Braunthal know such impressive 'facts' – only speaks about 'conclusions', which he has to draw from 'all the symptoms which can be surveyed'.[33] Thus he does not want to combat and falsify Marx's law of the tendency for the rate of profit to fall and all that follows with the *facts* of reality. He only does so with 'conclusions' that he believes he has to draw from 'symptoms'. So it is necessary to compare the power of Braunthal's conclusions with Marx's conclusions before we decide in favour of Marx's law of the falling or Braunthal's 'law' of the constant or rising rate of profit.

32 [Braunthal 1929, p. 302.]
33 [Braunthal 1929, p. 302.]

No one should doubt that *experience* is the source of new knowledge and that without and outside experience knowledge is impossible. But this truth has nothing in common with insipid empiricism. 'It is not sufficient merely to *observe*', says Henri Poincaré, 'we must use our observations, and for that purpose we must *generalise*.'[34] We can only know *isolated* facts through experience, observation. But, for science, isolated observations have no value. 'The circumstances under which one has operated will never be reproduced simultaneously. The fact observed will never be repeated.' The only thing that can be asserted is that, under similar circumstances analogous facts will occur. That means, however, taking refuge in analogy or generalising beyond the single observation. 'Without generalisation, prediction is impossible.'[35] And the most important task of science is prediction of sequences in the course of phenomena. All observations are not, therefore, of equal value and it directs its attention particularly to those observations that permit generalisation. Observation only establishes isolated factual points. It *ties them into a line* and in this way reads off the *direction of development*. In this way, a 'law' arises from 'observation'. Observation only comprises of isolated facts, a law extends beyond the isolated facts and is the product of generalisation. Of course, the validity of such laws can only remain uncontested so long as they do not contradict experience. If, for example, new facts arise which cannot be accounted for by the law that has been formulated then it is apparent that the generalisation was premature. If we accept this, Braunthal's depth is immediately apparent: according to him, Marx's law of the tendency for the rate of profit to fall derived from observations that were only correct 'at that time'. 'Laws' that are only valid for the period of their derivation are evidently not laws. They are, rather, identical with observation, only another expression of them, i.e. they are temporary formulations. Laws are generalisations of not merely observed cases but also extend to many other cases that have not been observed and that may arise during a later period. This general validity of a generalisation is already expressed in the word 'law'. Braunthal does not have a notion that he tangles himself in unbridgeable contradictions by speaking of a 'law' which is only valid for observed cases 'at that time'. Braunthal's actual intention becomes apparent here: to debase Marx's *law* into an insignificant one-off *observation* in order to dispose of it.

But if the tendency for the rate of profit to fall was not, for Marx, merely an observation but a *law* of fundamental importance, it is nevertheless possible that, by means of *new facts, new observations*, the short-sightedness of Marx's

34 Poincaré 1905, p. 140 [Grossman's emphasis].

35 Poincaré 1905, p. 142.

generalisation could be demonstrated. 'Every age', says Poincaré, 'has scoffed at its predecessor, accusing it of having generalised too boldly.'[36] The task of Marxist theory consists in showing that it is still possible to account for 'new facts' in terms of the law formulated by Marx; that, therefore, this law is still active.

Before we move on to examine the *facts* of reality itself, we will first consider the *views* of the best known Marxist theoreticians of the previous period. The altered tendency of the rate of profit should have been apparent for 'several decades'. Then it would have been odd if this tendency had not been noted by them. It is indeed only my narrow-mindedness to insist on individual theories and statements of Marx, without being concerned with reality. Braunthal does not raise this accusation, however, against Kautsky, Boudin, Otto Bauer, Hilferding, who are, for him, the real luminaries of science and have their eyes open for new facts.

We have seen that, according to Braunthal, the tendency for the rate of profit to decline came to a standstill 'several decades' ago. As he has not provided the work which served as the source of his knowledge, we have to take a look back into the relevant Marxist literature. The decline or rise in the rate of profit depends on both factors in the profit fraction $s/(c + v)$, i.e. on whether, in the course of capitalist development, the numerator in this fraction grows *faster* than the denominator.[37] ⟨How can that be determined? Are we directed to the empirical, statistical results of their extent in different periods? We know, however, that the calculation of s comes up against almost insurmountable difficulties. The entire art of hiding and obscuring the real extent of surplus value is employed, just out of tax considerations, and different, significant components of profits are disguised under various rubrics as 'expenses', open and hidden reserves, bonuses, excessive deductions.⟩

Conrad Schmidt's derivation of the *tendency for the rate of profit* to fall in 1889, that is before the appearance of the third volume of *Capital*, on the one hand, demonstrates his enormous perspicacity; on the other hand, that these consequences are already, undeniably contained in Marx's law of value (accumulation on the basis of the organic composition of capital). 'If it is apparent that … [the total capital advanced], $c + v$ in the real course of capitalist development *necessarily* swells *faster* than [the mass of surplus value] then it is demonstrated that, in the case that the faster growth of $c + v$ is not matched by the *long term* rise of s/v, a *continuous decline in the rate of profit* must occur.'[38]

---

36 Poincaré 1905, pp. 140–1.

37 [At this point there is an annotation in the margin: 'Magnitude of profits *Bogdanov*' perhaps a reference to Bogdanov 1923.]

38 Schmidt 1889, p. 63. [Grossman's emphasis.]

Conrad Schmidt's mathematical proof of the growth of the individual components of constant capital (fixed capital, circulating capital) at a faster tempo than the rise in the sum of wages led to the proof 'that the *total capital* advanced in any case grows faster than the sum of wages in the course of capitalist development'[39] and shows 'that such a faster growth of c + v compared with [the sum of wages] ... *necessarily* results from the course of economic progress'.[40]

Five years later, in 1894, the third volume of *Capital* appeared, in which the 'law of the tendency for the rate of profit to fall' was developed by Marx. This volume was greeted with jubilation by the entire socialist world and the deepest and most mature thought of proletarian science was evidently not out of date at the moment it appeared. The law of the tendency for the rate of profit to fall was evidently still valid in 1894 and not merely 'at that time', when Marx wrote it down in 1863.

At the end of the nineteenth century, the validity of this law was not doubted by anyone on the Marxist side. And the era of the rising rate of profit, of which Braunthal speaks, therefore occurs, at best, at the start of the twentieth century.

In April 1902, Karl Kautsky began a series of articles on 'Crisis theories'. Right at the start of the second part is the heading 'The falling rate of profit'. For the time being, what interests us is not his polemic and critique of Tugan-Baranovsky but his positive statements. Kautsky speaks there about the 'law of the tendency for the rate of profit to fall following on from' Marx's theory of surplus value. Tugan-Baranovsky denies but Kautsky accepts and defends the law.[41] Even more: [he] refers to the empirical fact that the fixed part of constant capital not only steadily grows absolutely but relatively. Kautsky says 'The more, however, fixed capital (buildings, machines and similar) predominates... *the more the law of the falling rate of profit prevails*.'[42]

Thus, after the start of the twentieth century, in 1902, no trace of Braunthal's transformative discovery is apparent. Kautsky, who he deifies and honours with tasteless phrases, obviously also belongs amongst those blind people who are not concerned with reality and accept the continued relevance of the theory.

---

39 Schmidt 1889, p. 78 [emphasised the entire passage.]
40 Schmidt 1889, p. 78. [Grossman's emphasis.]
41 Kautsky 1902, p. 38.
42 Kautsky 1902, p. 42.

CHAPTER 10

Letters to Frieda and Paul Mattick*

Translated from German by Ben Fowkes, Tom O'Lincoln and Rick Kuhn

14 April 1931[1]

Mrs Frieda Mattick[2]
Chicago Ill.
822 W. North Ave

You have been friendly in sending me the March issue of the *Chicagoer Arbeiter Zeitung*, which includes the review of my book by P.I.C.[3] under the title 'An important book'. I am very grateful for this and see that the author has, with great understanding, laid principal weight on Marx's method of inquiry, reconstructed by me. For that reason, I want to draw the writer's attention to my further important essay, which appeared in Grünberg's *Archive für die Geschichte des Sozialismus und der Arbeiterbewegung* volume 14 (1929). 'The change in Marx's original plan for *Capital* and its causes' has the same theme as the object of its analysis. The *Archiv* is published by Hirschfeld Verlag of Leipzig. Unfortunately, I have already given away the few off-prints that I had, so I cannot send you the essay. To me, it appears exceptional to see how the *Chicagoer Arbeiter Zeitung*, is interested in the theoretical problems of revolutionary Marxism.

At the same time I turn to you with a request. The Institute at which I work is the only one in Western Europe which collects all material on the situation of

* [The original letters, apart from that of 18 July 1937, are in Grossman 1931–38; a selection, including that of 18 July 1937, was published in Grossmann 1969, but some lacked passages and contained transcription errors.]

1 [Ben Fowkes translated the letters of 30 June 1932, 6 March 1933, 16 September 1933, 24 November 1934, 31 January 1935, 22 October 1935, 19 December 1935, 29 October 1936; Tom O'Lincoln, the letters of 21 June 1931, 16 September 1931, 7 May 1933, 17 June 1933, 1 November 1933, 2 October 1934, 19 February 1935, 18 July 1937; Rick Kuhn, the letter of 15 April 1931.]

2 [Frieda Mattick handled the correspondence of the *Chicagoer Arbeiter Zeitung*, which her husband Paul Mattick edited. The newspaper was the monthly organ of the federation of German socialist associations in Chicago, Arbeiter Kultur- und Sport Kartell Chicago, and was only published in 1931.]

3 [Probably Henk Canne Meijer, Roth 2014, p. 92. The review was of Grossmann 1929a.]

the working class in all the important countries of the world, in order to make them accessible for research. We have our own building, a large reading room, an archive and a library with about 40,000 volumes in all languages including, further, 450 newspapers and scientific journals. We cannot buy everything. Much is sent to us by our friends in all countries. We would be pleased if you could send the first issues of the *Chicagoer Arbeiter Zeitung* for our library. We also desire, in addition, any material on the condition of American workers. We collect posters, constitutions of workers' associations, appeals etc. In short everything that is concerned with the economic, political and cultural condition of the working class (e.g. dramatic pieces that have been performed by workers' theatres).

As an expression of my appreciation, I am sending you several contributions, that I have published in Elster's well-known *Dictionary of Economics*. Unfortunately, I no longer have the important essays on 'Anarchism' and 'Bolshevism'.[4]

I remain, with Marxist greetings
your faithful
Henryk Grossman

21 June 1931

Frankfurt am Main

Dear Comrade

Many thanks for your letter and for the information you are giving me. If I am only replying to you now, it is because, as a contributor to the fourth edition of Elster's *Dictionary of Economics*,[5] that has a very wide distribution in Europe, I am heavily burdened with urgent *deadlines*. Most recently I had to deliver essays on Jules Guesde, Alexander Herzen and [Henry] Hyndman, and I am working on an important essay on 'the Internationals' (First, Second, Two and a Half, Third).[6] It is an important task. In this bourgeois but widely

4 [Grossmann 1931a; Grossmann 1931b.]

5 [Elster 1931–3.]

6 [Marx and Engels played leading roles in the First International, the International Working Men's Association, of unions and workers societies, which existed between 1864 and 1876. Second, Socialist International of political parties, 1889–1914. Second and Half International, the International Working Union of Socialist Parties, of left social-democratic parties, 1921–3. Third, Communist International of Communist parties, 1919–43.]

read publication I am the only representative of the revolutionary, proletarian standpoint. The publication is read by thousands of editors, students, officials etc. for information and reference. I cannot neglect this opportunity to exercise influence.

A few more words about our Institute. It is a *neutral* institution, at the University [of Frankfurt am Main] to which all have access. Its significance lies in the fact that, for the first time, it collects everything concerning the labour movement in the most important countries of the world, above all [primary] sources (minutes of congresses, party programs, statutes, newspapers and journals). We can of course only collect the most important works about America and the United States. We orient ourselves according to the title and scope of a book, the reviews it has received and its publisher. If someone wants to study American conditions they have, in any case, to travel to America. Nevertheless, we place particular weight on *important pamphlets* and we would be particularly grateful if you could help us with that and could possibly send us the *catalogues of second hand bookshops*. To make a compilation of everything we possess would be too big a job. We have much, though only in the form of large books; we lack pamphlets, placards, factory newspapers, photos of significant personalities in the labour movement, their letters (which we particularly collect in our manuscripts department). Anyone in western Europe who wants to write about currents in the labour movement today *must* come to us, because we are the only collection point.

And now I turn to what is the most important thing for me: my theoretical work. I was delighted by what you wrote to me about my book and the audience it has found in America. I am especially pleased to know that it aroused interest in *workers'* circles. It goes without saying that I have a strong interest in an Anglo-American translation. Finding a translator is easy; it is much more difficult to find a publisher for a book dealing with the collapse of capitalism. I would personally forego any royalties etc., just in order to make the rapid appearance of the English translation possible. I would only want a certain small number of copies. I would also make changes insofar as I would like to deal critically with the book by Mitchell in the English edition.[7] After all, for America a discussion of this well known representative of bourgeois American theory is important. Secondly, I wanted to ask you whether it would not be advisable to translate my small *programmatic* work on the 'The change in the original plan for Marx's *Capital*' *first*.[8] The second printing of 'The plan' (*expan-*

7 [Mitchell 1927.]
8 [Grossmann 1929b, see above pp. 183–209.]

ded to 4–5 printer's sheets, i.e. 70–80 pages) will be published by Hirschfield in Leipzig in October. It is a methodological investigation, but one which is fundamentally important for understanding Marx's principal work; and it would arouse interest in that great book.

And now to theory. The essay in English that was sent to me correctly emphasised the key points. But I would not like to create the impression that I derive the tendency to collapse *from Bauer's schema.* I emphasised in my book that Bauer's schema is unrealistic. That conclusion emerges clearly from my methodological text about the plan [for Marx's *Capital*]. Bauer makes unrealistic, false assumptions, and I just wanted to reduce *ad absurdum, his thoughts about* his own schema. Someone has ironically said, in criticism of me, that in my book capitalism does not break down because of the misery of the workers but rather because of the misery of the capitalists.[9] This objection does not affect me but rather Bauer. It arises from *his* schema, because he *assumes* that capitalists accumulate *at most* by 10% annually, and that workers' wages increase at most by 5% a year. In reality these assumptions do not apply. There is, in fact, a struggle between workers and capitalists over the division of surplus value. It is insufficient to ensure *both* a satisfactory wage level *and* the required level of accumulation. One can only occur at the expense of the other. Hence class struggles become more acute. The situation in the United States, England and Germany over the past two years, directly confirms this 100 percent. I do not claim that surplus value becomes smaller. It can become larger. And still it is insufficient because accumulation (as it requires an ever greater organic composition) swallows up *an ever larger part* of the surplus value. This idea is best illustrated *graphically*:

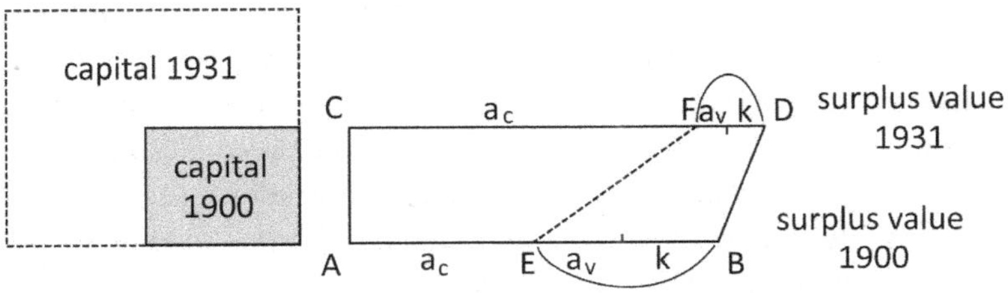

The size of capital in 1900 (small square) has grown by 1931, and so has the organic composition. The surplus value in 1900 (line A–B) has also *grown*, by

9 [Braunthal 1929, p. 296; the joke was also told by Helene Bauer 1929; and repeated by Karl Muhs 1931, pp. 9, 13–14.]

1931, to C–D. In order, however, for the organic composition of the expanded capital to rise, *a relatively larger and larger part of the mass of surplus value must be used for the purpose of accumulation* [a_c]. Therefore the *consumable* portion of the surplus value, the part available for additional workers (a_v) and that available for the consumption of the capitalists themselves (k), becomes smaller and smaller both relatively and absolutely. In 1900 it is E–B but in 1931 only F–D. If the workers receive the previous amount, a_v, not enough would remain for the capitalists. If they secure their portion, k, then not enough remains for the workers. An *objectively revolutionary* situation arises: the system shows it can no longer secure the living conditions of the population. As a consequence of and *through* this *objective* situation the *class struggle* becomes more acute, i.e. in this phase of development, the objective situation is now joined by the *subjective* factor: the working class is capable of bringing down the system through class struggle. Of course, I am far from thinking that capitalism must break down 'of itself' or 'automatically', as Hilferding and other socialists (Braunthal) assert,[10] in criticising my book. It can only be brought down by the class struggle of the working class. But I wanted to show that the class struggle alone is *not* enough. The *will* to bring it down is not sufficient. In the *initial phases* of capitalist development such a will cannot even arise. It would also be ineffective *without* a revolutionary situation. Only in the final phases of development are the objective *conditions*, which create the *precondition* for the *successful*, victorious intervention of the working class, present. Of course, as a *dialectical* Marxist, I know that both sides of the process, the objective and subjective elements influence *each other*. In the class struggle these factors merge. One cannot wait until, *eventually*, the 'objective' conditions are present so that, only *then*, the 'subjective' ones can operate. That would be an inadequate, mechanical perspective, which is alien to me. But, *for the purposes of the analysis*, I have to use the process of abstracting and isolating individual elements to show the essential functions of each element. Lenin often speaks of the *objectively* revolutionary situation that must be present as the precondition for the active, victorious intervention of the proletariat. My breakdown theory is not intended to exclude this active intervention but rather aims to show when and under what conditions such an objectively revolutionary situation can and does arise.

Bauer's schema is inadequate for many reasons: it assumes an *annual* relationship of constant capital (c) to variable capital (v) of 200,000 : 100,000,

---

10 [Braunthal 1929. Rudolf Hilferding did not himself write about Grossman's book, but edited *Die Gesellschaft*, which published Braunthal's critique and another by Hans Neisser 1931.]

whereas in reality the constant capital per worker is eight or ten times his annual wage. If we insert into Bauer's schema all the elements that he neglects, the concept of breakdown becomes *even clearer*. I wanted to show that even this erroneous schema gives rise to breakdown and not equilibrium. *But in no way do I want to associate myself with this schema of Bauer*!

For Germany, my book is already relatively cheap. With a 'prestigious' bourgeois publisher, one printer's sheet (16 pages) costs 80 pennies, i.e. 32 marks for 40 sheets. On my insistence Hirschfeld reduced this to 22 marks (naturally, my royalties suffered as a result), but by ordering five or more copies from the *library* of our Institute you can get a discount of (I think) 30 percent. You have to write directly to the library and ask how to transfer the money. I do not have anything to do with this.

Regarding the questions put to me, I want to establish first that I do oppose Hilferding's concept of 'finance capital' but *not* Lenin's concept. The two are *fundamentally different*. Hilferding understands finance capital to be *bank capital*; he does not ask who stands *behind* this bank capital. I oppose this conception of the decisive role of bank capital. Lenin, on the other hand, understands finance capital not as bank capital, but as the merging of monopoly capital, primarily *industrial* capital, with state power and policy, which is a tool of this capital. That is something quite different. That the banks are *facilitators* of the expansion of capital is clear. But one has to ask whether, for example, the American bankers play the chief role in America's economic life, *deciding the direction of expansionist American policy*. Or are they mere *organs* of the industrial magnates, who have their representatives in the bank administrations? In my book I have tried (admittedly only briefly) to show how, in the early stages of industrial development, bank capital has autonomous influence. In the advanced stage, the industrial magnates have the decisive influence. I affirm the mighty role of finance capital in Lenin's sense, because he does *not* speak of 'bank capital' dominating industry any more than I do, but rather of industry dominating the state and its policies.

This letter has already grown too long. I must conclude. In a further letter I will answer your other questions. But I have just received issue 5 of the *Chicagoer Arbeiter Zeitung* with the second review of my book, and I am pleased to see that in the headline you already express the *correct basic proposition* of the book, in connection with my chapter on the *theory of wages*.[11] There Comrade Kristen Svanum also takes up the question of *countervailing tendencies* that

11 [Mattick 1931, p. 4.]

I discuss. Are they capable of overcoming crises again and again? I have not evaded this question. In part, I already take it up in my book; in part it belongs in the second volume.[12]

1. So, for example I mention *wage cuts* as means to mitigate or overcome the crisis. But at the same time I emphasise that this countertendency cannot last 'forever'. I say that it has *narrow limits*; and I even quote John Stuart Mill, who saw this as early as 1848.[13]
2. I treat 'the elimination of *commercial* profits' as a countertendency.[14] I show that in many sectors the elimination of wholesale trade in Germany has reached 50 percent and more. This countertendency is *temporally limited*. One can reduce the profits of *wholesale* commerce by 60, 80, even 90 percent. *More than 100 percent* cannot be eliminated. Once this limit is reached, *the countertendency ceases to be effective*.
3. I deal with the shortening of turnover times as a countervailing tendency; and particularly with reductions in *inventories*. By reducing the stocks of goods on hand, profitability improves. But this reduction has its *limits*. If they are too small, then the *continuity of the production process* suffers. Marx demonstrated this in the second volume of *Capital* in the sections on inventories and, during the current crisis, this was precisely confirmed in Germany. The organ of heavy industry, *Deutsche Bergwerks-Zeitung* (Düsseldorf) in an essay titled 'Inventory problems' (10 November 1929) draws attention to the *limits of rationalisation* by reducing stocks. If stock holdings are too small, when there is immediate demand, industry goes *backwards* rather than operating continuously, etc.

These *limits* of the countertendencies were ignored by Comrade Svanum. I will treat this problem more fully and systematically in the second volume. In doing so, I need to take into account the theoretically very difficult problem, which the Marxist literature has not dealt with so far, namely the derivation of *prices of production* from values (as a result of the formation of the *average* rate of profit) and the influence of prices of production on the breakdown tendency.

With best regards
Henryk Grossman

---

12 [Grossman intended to write a sequel to Grossman 1929a.]

13 [See Grossman 1929a, p. 190.]

14 [See Grossman 1929a, p. 348.]

16 September 1931

Frankfurt am Main

Most esteemed Comrade

Before anything else, I have to thank you very much for the valuable material you sent for our Institute. It is exactly what I meant, the shorter pamphlets, the leaflets etc. that are otherwise lost and can no longer be obtained and that are still important for the American workers' movement. Many thanks! But you must have had additional expenses in doing this, you have to let us know how much!

I have sent you the offprint of my 'International' essay.[15] At the same time I am sending another three copies for our comrades over there, which you can dispose of. Before I get onto theoretical things I want to deal with your observations in a few words. You say you are 'anti-parliamentary'. Dear Comrade, I do not want to 'work on' you or 'agitate' you – to begin with because from this distance I cannot get an overview of political circumstances in America in all the detail that is required. Nevertheless, I consider that the term 'anti-parliamentary' under *present* capitalist circumstances has lost its justification and is out of date. We should and must revise it. There was a time when the workers' movement and social democracy wanted to use parliamentarism, in fact for *propaganda* purposes, as a means to the end of liberating the workers. Then they grew so deeply into parliamentary cretinism that they sought to achieve the resolution of social problems and the liberation of the working class *only* through 'democratic' parliamentary means. In the face of this fraudulent, parliamentary cretinism, 'anti-parliamentarism' was for the most part justified.

Today, however, when the proletarian movement only wants to engage in parliamentarism for agitational purposes, when it clearly knows that the bourgeoisie can only be defeated in the streets and the workplaces through forceful revolution, it would be irresponsible to refuse to make use of the parliamentary tribune. You can already see the completely transformed situation of capitalism from the fact that today it is *dangerous* for the representatives of the proletariat to appear in parliaments. In Poland, for example, Communist deputies are handed over to the courts and sentenced to four or six years in prison. *The bourgeois, possessing classes today are* 'antiparliamentary' and fascist; they want a dictatorship, whether open or hidden. And it is the task and the duty of the

15 [Grossmann 1932c; Grossmann 1932d.]

revolutionary workers' movement to brand this reversal in orientation, to show that the bourgeoisie was for 'democracy' so long as it had a large majority in the parliaments. Now that in Europe the working class has 40 percent and more of the seats and democracy could work *against* the bourgeoisie, the possessing classes betray their principles and their past. They answer the demands of the workers with dictatorship and machine guns; they abolish freedom of the press and freedom of assembly.

If you want to be consistently 'anti-parliamentary', you should not publish any *legal* newspapers, such as the *Chicagoer Arbeiter Zeitung* because, after all, freedom of the press is an aspect of bourgeois parliamentary democracy. So you should only have an *illegal* press. But, in fact, you make use of *legal* freedom of the press, *as long as it lasts* – and rightly so. And the same applies to 'freedom of assembly'. That too is a right guaranteed by parliament. But it would be a nonsense not to make use of it, as *long as it lasts*. The difference between us, in the revolutionary movement, and the parliamentary fraudsters consists in the fact that we know it *will not last forever*. Eventually, the time will come when the ruling classes *abolish* freedom of the press and assembly. We are prepared for this and will respond with an *illegal* press and illegal meetings. In Germany, over the last few months, 73 Communist newspapers have been banned under emergency regulations.

But enough of this!

What you told me about the debates at the Proletarian Party[16] congress in Chicago was extremely interesting to me, and I will follow further developments with close attention. I will also be indebted to you for further information!

In my book I have attacked Varga over an important issue. (It concerns Marx's 'absolute rent' which V had completely misunderstood. I have demonstrated his error.) *He has nothing to say in reply*. So he preferred to *abuse* me in a Communist journal.[17] In response to my arguments and objections, he has not said a single word. As soon as I have more time, I will write a critique of Varga, and cast a closer light on this puffed-up statistician.

And now to theory and to many of the questions you raised in your *first* letter. First: Otto Bauer has not written a book about accumulation. Rather, in 1913, he wrote two articles against Rosa Luxemburg's book, in *Neue Zeit*, edited by Kautsky.[18] It was in these articles that he presented the schema which I

16 [The small Proletarian Party was formed by a Michigan based group expelled from the Communist Party of America in 1920.]

17 [Varga 1930.]

18 [Otto Bauer 1986.]

have reproduced. The comrade who posed the questions to me has *correctly* observed that Bauer *transfers* a residual amount from department II to department I, so that in department I beyond its own portion of surplus value of 10,000 destined for accumulation, a further 4,666 is accumulated: 14,666 [in total]. Conversely department II accumulates *less* than the 10,000 earmarked for accumulation, i.e. 10,000 – 4,666: *only* 5,334.

The question arises as to *why?* Rosa Luxemburg and her supporter Fritz Sternberg maintain that these 4,666 in department II *cannot find a market*, that they represent an *unsalable remainder*, which proves that equilibrium is impossible, i.e. *complete* realisation is *impossible*.[19] That was their strongest argument.

And how did Otto Bauer reply? He *was silent*. But his wife Helene Bauer, who plays a large role in Vienna, especially in editing the theoretical organ of Austrian Social Democracy, *Kampf*, and yet is a shallow woman, answered that these 4,666 had been shunted *by way of credit* (!) from department II to department I!![20]

Such an answer is identical with Otto Bauer's theoretical bankruptcy and Sternberg had an easy success. For, if you make the *assumption* that the transfers in the schema take place *without credit* (and Marx does in fact make such an assumption), you cannot later, when you have found yourself in difficulties, change the assumption in order to get out of trouble.

Rosa Luxemburg and Sternberg, in his book *Imperialism* (I sent you my *critique* of Sternberg's book),[21] drew the conclusion that under capitalism this unsalable remainder can only be disposed of in 'non-capitalist areas', i.e. that capitalism cannot exist at all *without* non-capitalist colonies! Marx had not seen any of this, so there was an important gap in his system. Indeed he had failed to say the *most important thing* and Rosa Luxemburg was the first to fill this dangerous gap!

I regard refuting this dangerous distortion of Marx's teachings by Rosa Luxemburg and her supporters and repeatedly showing, from different sides, that it is untenable as one of my most important tasks. In my big book and my critique of Sternberg ('A new theory') as well as in my work on the 'The change in the original plan for Marx's *Capital*' I illuminate this theory from different sides.[22]

---

19 [See Luxemburg 1951; Sternberg 1971; and Grossman's detailed critiques in Grossmann 1929a; and Grossmann 1932a, see below pp. 276–303.]

20 [Helene Bauer 1929.]

21 [Grossmann 1928a, see above pp. 120–176.]

22 [Grossmann 1929a; Grossmann 1928a, see above pp. 120–176; Grossmann 1929b, see above pp. 183–209.]

Here I want to present still *further* arguments, taken from a chapter on the *average rate of profit* that I have not yet published.[23]

In Bauer's schema (on the assumption that commodities are sold *at* their *values*), department I yields *a different rate of profit* from department II. Take a simple example:

I	4000 c + 1000 v + 1000 s = 6000	Profit rate p = 5000 : 1000 = *20 %*
II	2000 c + 1000 v + 1000 s = 4000	Profit rate p = 3000 : 1000 = *33.3%*

In department I, the profit rate is 20 percent, in department II p = 33.3 %. In the capitalist system, such large differences in the rate of profit cannot be sustained *in the long run*. There is a *tendency for profit rates to equalise*. In what way can this equalisation occur? I cannot go into the details here in a letter. One thing, however, is clear and certain: by whatever *route* or in whatever *manner* this equalisation takes place, the *result* of the equalisation process is that *the same rate of profit* prevails in both departments, i.e. *25 %*.

Department I	From 5000 capital advanced, 25 % profit = *1250*
Department II	From 3000 capital advanced, 25 % profit = *750*

That is, for the purpose of equalising profit rates, department I must sell commodities *above* their value, while department II must sell them *below* their value. Thus at *prices* which *deviate* from *values*. Through these deviations in prices, a portion of the *excess* surplus value in department II is *transferred* to department I, where the surplus value is *too small*; and not by means of credit but rather by means of the normal sale of commodities. And this is the explanation of why *a part of the surplus value* from department II must migrate to department I. Because, if this migration, this transfer did *not* occur *rates of profit would be unequal*; yet Marx says, and capitalist reality confirms it, that the tendency to equalise profit rates is the *driving factor* of the capitalist system.

In passing, I also have to mention an important circumstance that casts an impressive light on the whole discussion in the Marxist camp (Tugan-Baranovsky,[24] Hilferding,[25] Rosa Luxemburg, Otto Bauer, Sternberg), to date.

The *whole discussion* has been based on a schema that only took *values* into account and not *prices*. Insofar as we are dealing with the individual depart-

23 [Grossmann 1932b, see below pp. 304–331.]

24 [Tugan-Baranowsky 1905; Tugan-Baranowsky 1908.]

25 [See Hilferding 1981.]

ments of the schema, i.e. with individual spheres of production, this is a *fictitious, false* assumption which contradicts reality and which is also *incompatible* with Marx's teaching. For, according to Marx, *prices of production must deviate from values in individual spheres*. Precisely because of the drive to establish an equal rate of profit. The whole discussion to date has not concerned itself with this. Consequently all the conclusions drawn from a schema that *only recognises values and not prices of production* in the individual spheres are false! Indeed worthless. Worthless quite apart from whether one wants to demonstrate the existence of *equilibrium* in the schema (Hilferding, Bauer) or one demonstrates necessary *disequilibrium* (Luxemburg). The whole discussion was misleading, unmarxist thinking.

Something entirely different holds in my schema. As you see from my book, the *individual spheres* are unimportant for me. I also concentrate only on the *sum* of the two departments. Naturally, since I want to determine the *tendency of accumulation*, its dynamic for society *as a whole*, without regard to the division of accumulated capital between the individual spheres. For me, only *the fact of capital accumulation and its consequences* are important. According to Marx, however, for society as a whole, *values and prices are identical*! Therefore I can and must deal with *values* alone.

Those who stand on *proportionality theory*, however, regarding the relationship of the two departments to each other as the most important problem of the schema, should *not* neglect prices. But that is just what has been done for decades! As a result:

1. If, in the schema, *only* values are considered, the individual spheres will have different rates of profit. The schema is *unrealistic*. Only in such a schema do we find an 'unsalable remainder'.[26]
2. If the same profit rate is generated in all spheres, part of the surplus value has to be transferred from II to I. Rosa Luxemburg's whole argument collapses. In Marx, the value schema is only a *provisional* assumption. Subsequently one has to re-calculate the values into prices, and thereby approach concrete reality. In this problem, too, one can see the importance of Marx's method of successive approximation, which I have reconstructed!

And now the question of my collaboration. As you can see from my 'International' article, I am accustomed to expressing my revolutionary opinions openly – which has provoked much bad blood here in Germany in university circles. But collaboration on a left-revolutionary newspaper in America is

26 [Luxemburg 1921, p. 339.]

something different. I plan, in about two years, to make a fairly long *study tour* of the United States and there are indications that if I were to collaborate on left wing newspapers, the authorities would deny me a *visa* or entry permit. For this reason I must be careful. It is my opinion that a Marxist theoretician absolutely must become acquainted with the most developed capitalist society, i.e. American capitalism, and not just from books but through personal experience. I do not want to squander this opportunity.

On the critique of [Anton] Pannekoek, let me say that what he has to say about these things is known to me, from his polemic 20 years ago against Tugan-Baranovsky in *Neue Zeit*, volume 28, 1910.[27] That was unconvincing and weak. But I would still like to hear his arguments against my book and, if I have time to reply immediately. As you know, my collaboration on Elster's *Dictionary* robs me of all my free time. There are genuine, urgent *deadlines*, determined by the alphabetical order of the work already in print. If I did not reply immediately, it could easily give rise to the impression that I have nothing to say in reply. For that reason any prospect of a polemic must be postponed for another year.

I wanted to write more but just received a telegram from my publisher, so I have to break off. I will write again soon!

With best regards
your
Henryk Grossman

30 June 1932

Frankfurt am Main, Victoria-Allee 17

Dear and valued Comrade Mattick

I send you my warmest thanks for your repeated shipments to our library and archive. These pamphlets and other printed matter are of very great value to us. They are absolutely unavailable in Europe, unless they can be sent by friends over there, as in this case.

But I want to thank you particularly for the things you have sent that are of special concern to me, as they relate to matters I follow with the greatest attention. An example is the Draft Program you sent me just recently.

Please also excuse my long silence, and please do not misinterpret it. I am *very* busy, but my work on Elster's dictionary is approaching its end. I will then

27 [Pannekoek 1910.]

be a free man again. I will also reply fully to Krist's[28] objections to my theory – objections which are somewhat naive. In the middle of July I will send you my latest theoretical essay, 'The value-price transformation in Marx and the problem of crisis'.[29] At the end of August I will travel for 4–6 weeks to the Soviet Union (a study trip). Whether there will still be any possibility for Marxists to work here after the July elections is uncertain. The Nazis have a significant chance of victory owing to the cleavage in the working class. So far, the German working class has failed to unite – at least at the moment of mortal danger to it – against the common enemy! The victory of the Nazis would mean the destruction of the workers' movement for 10 to 15 years, and it would immensely increase the danger of a war against the Soviet Union! The German working class understands everything, knows everything, but it *does* almost nothing! Yet again we see that insight and perceptiveness alone are not sufficient – if the will to fight is not there.

With sincere regards

Your

H. Grossman

P.S. The *Japanese* translation of my accumulation book[30] came out in April in Tokyo, 814 pages long, with my preface (in facsimile). There is a prospect that a *French* translation will also appear, in Brussels.

6 March 1933

Trianon Palace Hotel, 4bis et 3, Rue de Vaugirard, Paris

Dear Comrade Mattick

First of all, please excuse me for my failure to respond to the letters and parcels you have sent in the course of many months. Before my trip to Russia, I had to work for months on the Elster dictionary. The essay on 'Socialist and Communist Parties' demanded a great deal of work and research into the subject – although the essay was in itself a boring task for me. I worked 15 to 18 hours a day, for 6 weeks on the essay entitled 'Fifty years of struggle over Marxism',[31]

28 [Possibly Kristan Svanum.]

29 [Grossmann 1932lb, see below pp. 304–331.]

30 [Grossman 1932.]

31 [Grossmann 1933b; Grossmann 1932f/1933a, see below pp. 332–388.]

so as to finish writing before my departure. That completely took the stuffing out of me. After the five-week trip to Russia, which was also not relaxation, I returned feeling ill and I then caught influenza. The political upheaval then made its contribution. I had a good idea of what was coming, so I had a lot of things to organize, both for the Institute and for myself.

Two weeks before my departure I spoke in favour of Soviet Russia (despite everything!)[32] in a big meeting attended by over 2000 people, which was held in Frankfurt (in the Saxophone Hall). As a result, the whole of the reactionary press up to and including the Social Democratic *Volksstimme* came down upon me in a most vulgar manner. They will probably want to deprive me of my professorship.

Here, I am for the moment incapable of working, apart from reading ten to fifteen newspapers a day.

I must point out, in connection with your work against Sternberg,[33] that it is definitely not 'worthless', as you write. On the contrary: it contains a number of valuable thoughts and arguments. Its main shortcoming – if I may be frank – is that, purely *from the stylistic point of view* it is *not sufficiently focussed*, hence the main line of reasoning does not find expression sufficiently clearly. But your argument is to the point and I intend to refer to it in my counter-critique (which I am considering at present). Of course, I do not yet know when I will be able to do this.

You provide very interesting material in your essay on unemployment.[34] I have my doubts about whether it is suitable for our journal. I will correspond with Professor Horkheimer and Pollock about the matter, which is the more uncertain because we do not yet know whether it will be possible for the journal[35] to appear any longer, under the present state of emergency in Germany.

32 ['Trotz allem': this phrase recalls Ferdinand Freiligrath's poem, 'Trotz alledem', written in early June 1848 after a conservative turn of events during the 1848–49 revolution and published in Marx's *Neue Rheinische Zeitung*. For Freiligrath's poem in German and English see Robb and John 2011, pp. 29–30. 'Trotz alledem' was also the title of Karl Liebknecht's famous article in the Communist Party of Germany's newspaper after the suppression of the January 1919 Spartakus uprising, on the day he was murdered, Liebknect 1919.]

33 [There is no work on Sternberg in the comprehensive bibliography of Mattick's publications, Buckmiller 1981. See Grossmann 1928a, above pp. 120–176, a long critique, of Sternberg 1971. Sternberg had responded to Grossman in two further books, Sternberg 1929; and Sternberg 1930.]

34 [Eventually published as Mattick 1969.]

35 [i.e. the *Zeitschrift für Sozialforschung*, the organ of the Institut für Sozialforschung.]

My sincerest thanks for your kindness in sending your novella in the collection *Thirty German Storytellers*.[36]

It is good to know that the book has come from you. Because Malik Verlag are obliged to send me a copy, but they usually fail to do this unless reminded. I have not yet read the novella, but friends to whom I have lent the book have read it with the *greatest* interest, and they describe it as very worthwhile!

My special thanks for the many books you have sent to the Institute.[37] Do not send *any more* for the present as it is not yet certain whether the Institute will be closed or raided by the Nazis!

What is of greatest interest to me is what you report about the crisis on the basis of the American economic literature, which I cannot chase up from here. I would therefore be *very grateful* if you, or someone else who has an overview and an understanding of these things, were able to send me regular *excerpts* (with precise references, i.e. titles, pages etc.) from the relevant overaccumulation literature. I will naturally provide compensation for the time taken to do this. But under my present circumstances, as an emigrant, I do not have very much money at my disposal and I would need to know how much it would cost.

In bourgeois European literature, too, the theory of overaccumulation is increasingly coming into its own, *unconsciously*. Not of course in its true, essential form, but in a *distorted*, derivative form, namely that of *excessive indebtedness*, hence an inability to make *interest payments*. Overaccumulation comes most conspicuously into view in its *derivative* form. The debtor is not capable of discharging interest payments. What is not seen is that this form is only a special case of a general phenomenon, namely inadequate valorisation with respect to the overaccumulated mass of capital.

To begin with I am collecting all expressions of the above kind in scientific journals, the daily newspapers and books. It is therefore *very important* for me to have extracts from the American literature as well. I hope to find the time to shed theoretical light on the present crisis, in its latest phase, on the basis of the new material.

During my trip to Russia, my book was repeatedly described as the most important piece of Marxist literature of recent decades. This was said by, for example, Professor [Sergei Mitrofanovich] Dubrovskii, the director of the International Agrarian Institute in Moscow. When I asked why in that case my book had been torn to pieces so unfairly by Varga, D. replied 'My dear Comrade Gross-

---

36 [Mattick 1932.]

37 [i.e. the Institut für Sozialforschung (Institute for Social Research).]

man, here we do not take Varga seriously.' But I will of course have to come forward now with a counter-critique, which will not simply abuse the opponent, but answer his arguments scientifically and, going beyond this, make genuine understanding of the present crisis possible.

I will now close these remarks, thrown together hastily in my hotel: I have no patience at present for theoretical discussion, in view of the upheaval in Germany. The KPD[38] has certainly committed major errors, for which the 'leaders' installed by Moscow – in reality mere marionettes – bear the main responsibility. But: despite everything![39] The party, forced into illegality by Hitler and compelled to engage in a fight for its life, will come out of this struggle *purified* and strengthened, and bring forth new, better leaders. The way things are in Germany, the KPD *alone* can be the point of crystallization for a serious struggle for power and for the overthrow of Fascism! Anything other than this is a criminal utopia!

I intend to come back to all these questions again. But for the moment, enough.

Most sincere regards
from your
Henryk Grossman.

P.S. I have found a very important and clear confirmation of the *theory of overaccumulation in Marx* as early as 1845, in the new *Marx Collected Works*.[40]

---

38 [*Kommunistische Partei Deutschlands* (Communist Party of Germany).]

39 [Here Grossman uses Freiligrath's exact phrase.]

40 [A reference to Marx 1981a, pp. 416–17, not previously translated into English:

'Ricardo therefore explains the decline in profit on capital or interest the more capitals grow, although the *kinds of application* proliferate as capital does, in terms of the greater difficulty of procuring the *first* and *most necessary* means of life. He leaves competition entirely out of play. If capitals – understood on the assumption of private ownership – were not too numerous in relation to the application of capital then *competition* would be entirely inexplicable, as competition is not possible unless there are 20 instead of 3, therefore an excess of capitals in relation to their application.

'Further, in the place mentioned in Smith, 2 points, which Smith confounds under the assumptions he makes, should be differentiated:

1) Accumulation in the sense that one and the same capital expands

2) Accumulation as a *distributed* action, as a result of many capitals.

'Competition lies in the latter point. That a capital can still be so big and always find application is self-evident. The disproportion does not result from the disproportion between the huge size of the capital on the one hand and the number of possible applications on the other. It arises from the *multiplicity* of capitals, their division and mutually hostile action. Smith can regard 1 and 2 as the same thing because he assumes one country, experiencing progressive prosperity. And, under the assumption of private property, the first

7 May 1933

6 rue de Huysmanns, 6th
Paris

Respected and dear Comrade Mattick

My sincerest thanks for the two letters dated 16 March and 21 April, along with the two items you sent (two copies of the IWW pamphlet and issue number 2 of the *Freidenker*).[41] First on the meeting with your wife. She is an unusually bright, clever and pleasant person and I am truly pleased to have become acquainted with her. Now I hope that I will also meet you too and in the not too distant future. We really have a lot to talk about!

I have read your novella 'The bees' now. A gripping episode from working class life, which through its plain, unadorned simplicity enhances the artistic effect and forces us to confront the question: what are all these sacrifices for? They can only gain meaning if they point to a realm beyond today's world!

---

stage of rapid *accumulation* and the *multiplication* of capitals are the same. It is understood that if accumulated capitals are concentrated in a few hands, competition ceases and, despite accumulation, profits – as monopoly profits – rocket.

'Economics not only has the miracle of over-production and extreme poverty but also of growth of capitals, in the forms of their application, on the one hand, and lack of productive opportunities due to this growth, on the other hand.

'In the current situation Ricardo's theory only shows the most important thing: how competition amongst capitalists, which occurs during progressive accumulation, and the decline in their profits, does not, as Smith assumes, determine the necessity of a rise in wages. The *number of workers* is now higher in all countries than demand for them and more can be recruited daily from the *unemployed* proletariat, as they are, for their part, daily recruited. Conversely, the consequence of accumulation with competition is that the wage is depressed further and further.

'What Ricardo and, just as little Mr Say (who agrees with him and first raised the principle that demand for products is only limited by production), cannot answer is: where do *competition* and the consequent bankruptcies, trade crises etc. come from, if every capital finds its appropriate employment? If employment is always in proportion to the number of capitals? In this one sentence, the chief principle of the masters of competition, is revoked, as is the *basis* for this principle and their entire wisdom, namely that every individual (understood as an individual who is not without money) best knows what is appropriate for his interest and consequently (the content of this "consequently" is difficult) for that of society. How did these *wise* individuals come to ruin themselves and others, if there is profitable, available employment for every capital?']

41 [The *Freidenker* was published by the Free Thought League of North America.]

Your 'Unemployed' essay is *very* good.[42] The material is very interesting and unknown in Europe. The work gives us a living picture of the currents in the working class – an extremely interesting cross section of the sociological layering of individual strata – *in flagrante*[43] so to speak. In this sense I have also written to Geneva. Nevertheless ... 6–8 months ago I could be sure of getting it published. Now everything has changed. We do not ourselves know whether and where our journal will be able to appear. The first issue of the second volume was printed a long time ago, but could not appear. But even if it can continue to be published in Switzerland, it will have to avoid anything to do with practical political questions and just confine itself to 'heavenly realms' – since Fascism is also making great strides in Switzerland and our Institute is threatened with new dangers there as well. The labour movement is everywhere knocked out cold on the floor. Reaction is growing rapidly everywhere. Where else your essay could be taken I don't know. [Emil] Lederer's *Archiv für Sozialwissenschaft* [*und Sozialpolitik*] no longer appears (L himself is in London). The other scholarly publications will willingly submit to the Nazi Regime ...

My publisher, Dr Kohlhammer in Stuttgart, owner of Hirschfeld in Leipzig and known as a publisher of 'left books' was arrested on the pretext of some sort of 'embezzlement' ...

Here in Paris (in France generally) we lack foreign books – it is difficult to work in my field here – it will never be possible to work as comfortably anywhere as in our Frankfurt Institute. That concerns me, since I have just been negotiating with Alcan here,[44] concerning a French edition of my crisis book – which after four years should really be a second edition. That is, it must be reworked (shortened in many places). Above all, the French edition must answer the most important criticisms, and then work through American empirical material. But it is not here – and it is difficult to get. The *Bibliotheque Nationale* has a reactionary management – 'left' literature is not bought or only bought after many years – as long as things are topical and they are needed, they just are not there.

I owe you special thanks for your efforts to disseminate the theory of accumulation in America. I'm especially pleased that my concept of crisis has been accepted into the programmatic IWW pamphlet as the theoretical basis of the program. The pamphlet is clearly written and particularly suitable for propa-

---

42 [This may refer to an early version of an essay in 1936 accepted by but never published in *Zeitschrift für Sozialforschung* that eventually appeared as Mattick 1969.]

43 ['*In flagrante*' means 'caught in the act'.]

44 [A publishing house which issued left-wing literature.]

ganda among the broad masses. The section about the role of the *trade unions* is very good – their functions under rising capitalism and in the final phases of the system.

On the other hand the section about Germany has turned out to be rather thin. You have not experienced it in direct proximity as we have. In principle you are right. But the situation must be presented *more concretely*: the KPD masses were ready to fight but, unaccustomed to any spontaneous activity, they *waited* for the leaders' orders. The orders did not come. Many, many organisations, especially of youth, in their disappointment have gone over to Hitler ... they speak of the 'betrayal' of the leaders ... And here, with this example, the 'bottom up' principle, in contrast with the 'top down' approach that prevailed in the KPD, could be elucidated. I am convinced that the KPD was not destroyed by individual policy errors. Every party makes mistakes – one only learns through one's own mistakes – which can be corrected. The 'Nazis' made many, many mistakes and yet they were finally victorious. But the fundamental mistake of the KPD was that at its head stood figures without responsibility, who were not capable of taking independent decisions at the decisive moments. All the independent ones, who were capable of thinking for themselves, were thrown out of the party. What remained was a bureaucracy, which submitted slavishly to the Muscovites. But a revolution cannot be made on command from Moscow.

The essay in *Modern Monthly*[45] is important to me, because every such essay can later lead to finding an English publisher for my book. Last year a long essay about me appeared in the *Revue internationale de sociologie* ('L'économie politique d'Henryk Grossmann' by Prof [Mohand] Tazerout, May–June 1932).[46] I hope that this will help me to finalise a contract with Alcan soon.

I received *Der Proletarier* today. As the essay[47] is not finished, I must refrain from criticism. But I will say this much now: the fact that I want to determine the phase length of the conjunctural cycle theoretically by means of mathematics, leads me – according to the critic – 'directly into the camp of bourgeois conjunctural research'. Why? Not one little word about why. Mathematics is nothing but a form of exact thought. Just because one investigates the phase length of crises, e.g. the fact that they become more and more frequent, i.e. why they

45 [*Modern Monthly* was a political and cultural journal, founded and edited by independent Marxist Victor Francis Calverton.]

46 [Grossman's citation was not accurate, see Tazerout 1932.]

47 ['Ko' i.e. Karl Korsch, Korsch 1971. The first and only issue of *Der Proletarier* was published in February 1933 by a small group of council communists in Berlin, after the Nazis took power.]

succeed each other in shorter periods of time – this makes one a bourgeois researcher? The critic apparently understands nothing of what he writes about. He would have to reject Marx's way of posing the question, as Marx too, in a letter to Engels, specifically speaks of his efforts to mathematically determine the trajectory of crises on the basis of its components ...

For Marx – the critic assures us – it is not a matter of *explaining* capitalist reality (as I maintain). Yet the same critic wants to offer a 'theory' of crises. But what does theory mean other than that the facts of the capitalist mechanism are not simply *described* but also understood in their functional context, that is, *explained*! Here critique is nothing but a thoughtless word game!

On pages 15–16 the critic cites the countertendencies that mitigate the breakdown. In doing so he does not mention at all that I was the first to bring these tendencies into a meaningful relationship with the breakdown tendency. No work known to me, appearing *before* mine, has even mentioned this relationship, not to speak of concretely elaborated the foreign trade theory of capital exports etc., as a means of *producing* additional surplus value, in contrast with Rosa Luxemburg's theory of the *realisation* of surplus value.

I will write to you again about this in a few days.

Many thanks for the addresses in Amsterdam. It is uncertain when I will go there.[48] I cannot come to America. That is a question of money. My material circumstances have become significantly worse. Whether I will somehow succeed in establishing a new basis for existence in Paris is problematic.

For today, that's enough, so the letter can be sent off!

Sincere regards to you and your wife from

your

Henryk Grossmann

I have just received the Japanese translation of my work '50 years of struggle over Marxism' from Tokyo. Some passages were struck out by the censor![49]

---

48 [A postcard to Leo Löwenthal indicates that Grossman was in Amsterdam on 31 July 1933, Grossman 1933–9.]

49 [Postscript, written at the top of the letter and in the margin.]

17 June 1933

6 rue Huysmanns, 6th
Paris

Dear Comrade

I am only getting around to writing you the promised letter today. You already know that in Frankfurt two chests with valuable manuscripts – the fruit of ten years' work – were confiscated from me by the police. I just succeeded in having the two chests freed, through diplomatic intervention. I await their arrival here in about two weeks. So I have a clear head for my work.

Firstly could you please put me in contact with your friends in Germany. After the collapse of the KPD in Germany, the official leadership has *learnt nothing* from events. Mr [Willi] Münzenberg continues to publish *Unsere Zeit*[50] in Basel – from volume 2, number 7, you would not notice that something has happened in the mean time, such a minor matter as the collapse of the KPD. Not only is that fact not analysed and no lessons are drawn for the future but the fact itself is denied and turned into a lie about a 'victory'. A call by the Central Committee of the KPD, dated 15 March, says 'Our party has *acquitted itself brilliantly*.' Likewise, in Moscow they make similar assessments of the situation. 'The policy of the KPD was right.' Only the lower level Party organs are at fault. The outrage in working class circles is great. And, nevertheless, we must take account of the fact that the great majority is not willing to break with the Third International. It is likewise a fact that the KPD cadres represent the main contingent in the resistance to the fascists. The situation in Germany is difficult. I would like to be in contact with all active groups – and also be *as well informed as possible* about the movement there. If your friends could keep sending me whatever publications they have, I would be grateful. At the same time I'm sending you an essay by Trotsky in the *Neue Weltbühne*.[51] Publications sent to me will be industriously studied by groups here.

For the time being, nothing has come of the French edition. I want to completely rework the book, i.e. remove all polemics against German professors. And on the other hand, introduce much new material – about developments over the last four years in America and other countries. For a translation after four years must count as a second edition and hence consider the latest facts.

---

50 [Fortnightly publication of the previously Berlin based Workers International Relief, which was a Communist front organisation.]

51 [Trotsky 1975.]

The publisher is now ready to issue the book, once I provide the complete French manuscript. But the translator is demanding a thousand francs, which I cannot pay. This is the sticking point!

From Yugoslavia (Belgrade) I have received the news that, despite the dictatorship there, volume 1 of Marx's *Capital* will appear in a month. In this connection, my views about Marx and method are being written about (in preparation [for publication]). My supporters, the Marxist intellectuals, believe that the events in Germany have made me destitute and have offered to send me regular monthly subventions, money that they want to collect by means of voluntary deductions from their incomes. I am really very moved by this noble offer but have turned it down as my basic subsistence is secure, at least for the time being.

You have offered to send me material for the theory of crisis. Many thanks. I believe that we must all work together on developing the theory. I do not claim to be infallible and am ready to correct any errors I am proven to have made. But the question is: *what* should constitute the starting point for the corrections? And here I believe that my theory is, in principle, superior to others. By the way, the theory of overaccumulation is not my invention. The new *Collected Works* of Marx, volume 3 (1932) contains Marx's excerpts from Ricardo; they brilliantly demonstrate that the young Marx (the excerpts are written around 1844–5) already wrote explicitly about the overaccumulation of capitals and saw it as the cause of crisis!![52] These new publications brilliantly confirm my conception. (Sadly, I cannot find the *Collected Works* here, anywhere – my own were confiscated in Frankfurt am Main along with other books.)

But, quite apart from whether I am consistent or not, it must be stated that the theory of overaccumulation stems from Marx. I have reconstructed it. Whereupon I am told that I have failed to consider disproportionality. A fine logic. A doctor is investigating lung disease. In answer, he is told that kidney disease also exists. Marx never denied that disproportionalities can cause disruptions and yet throughout his life he fought the Frenchman Jean-Baptiste Say, the founder of disproportionality theory with a special hatred, as a fathead ('the insipid J.B. Say').[53] The *most important* result of my research so far is the reconstruction of the method of successive approximation. The critic in *Proletarier* simply denies the existence of this method in Marx.[54] Does he believe that, with this bald assertion, he can refute the evidence that I have provided?

52 [Marx 1981a, pp. 416–17. See note 40.]
53 [Marx 1987a, p. 399.]
54 [Korsch 1971.]

All Marxist research to date has debated, and continues to debate, whether there is equilibrium in the 'schema' or not. But what is the sense of the reproduction schema if it is torn out of the [context of] the method of successive approximation, the method which Marx employs? None at all! The schema *without* this method, i.e. torn out of this methodological unity, makes *no* sense, it is meaningless. With the assertion that there is no method of successive approximation in Marx, not much is achieved. I have proven this briefly in my book, then in 'The change in the original plan' and finally in 'Gold production in Marx and Rosa Luxemburg' (part 1).[55] Those who deny the method of successive approximation will and must find *Capital* incomprehensible. In hundreds of places, after all, Marx mentions simplifying assumptions: we abstract from credit, from money, from prices, from the merchant, from ground rent, etc. The reproduction schema is the result of this method of abstraction. And then Marx always immediately says: but in reality there are only prices (and no values), in reality there is credit, money, ground rent, the merchant, etc. What sense does any of this make, if one simply denies the method of successive approximation?

My critics all pounce on various details of my theory, wanting to prove its internal contradictions or contradictions with the facts but none has ever dealt with and disputed this most decisive aspect of my methodological position.

For this very reason, all Marxists to date have had a 'little' accident, in that they have not noticed *simple* reproduction in Marx, have not noticed its real meaning. All engage only with *expanded* reproduction as a problem. In the schema of simple reproduction everything *works*. And it is precisely the opposite that Marx wanted to demonstrate. Even under simple reproduction, crises are unavoidable. This, precisely, is why Marx is a really *dynamic* thinker, in contrast to bourgeois economics, which is essentially static ('tendency to equilibrium' which is automatically produced – the crisis must therefore come from *outside* the system as a *deus ex machina*).[56] In Marx, disequilibrium is bound up with the nature of the system. In the work that I am now preparing (second volume), I want to demonstrate precisely *this* characteristic of simple reproduction in Marx. If the method of successive approximation is rejected, the meaning of simple reproduction in Marx will never be grasped. For Marx explicitly says that all the important problems arise *here*. Having once solved these, expanded reproduction presents *no difficulties*.

---

55 [Grossmann 1929b, see above pp. 183–209; Grossmann 1932a, see above pp. 276–303.]

56 ['*Deus ex machina*' means 'god from the machine': in the plot of a play, an improbable, unexpected resolution of a problem.]

And now turning to the materials that I need.

1. The results of the latest American census concerning the accumulation of capital per worker. In my book on pp. 289 and 453, I give census figures only *up to* 1919, because I did not have access to more recent census results. It would be important to establish (from the volume on 'Manufactures') the number of workers, total capital, capital per worker. I am convinced that a prodigious per capita increase has taken place.
2. For the theory it is important to work out how the 1929 stock exchange crash came about. Capital that is *superfluous* and does not find *sufficient* outlets, according to the theory, will flow to the banks and from there, further to the stock exchange. I have read repeatedly that in the USA, even *before* the 1929 crash, industrial production was contracting. One of my students, Dr [Julian] Gumperz, an American who has written a book about the American agrarian crisis[57] and who on my prompting will be sending you the book, maintains that this is not the case, that no contraction in industrial production took place before 1929. The facts of this matter need to be clarified.
3. From the census data it should be possible to reproduce the *organic composition* in the most important industries. That is very important for the theory. I have been accused of not taking into account that the rate of surplus value rises in reality. My answer is that, if I am to present *reality*, then the organic composition must also reflect reality. In Bauer's schema it is 2:1. I believe that in the most advanced industries the relationship is 10:1 or even 12:1. That is, the capital invested per worker is 10 or 12 times greater than the worker's annual wage. It should be noted that the census data often only counts fixed capital. But it is important to consider the capital which is not fixed but is still constant capital, for example raw materials. And note that *credit* relations must be taken into account. For example, the factory owner has a fixed capital of a million dollars and spends $50,000 per week on *raw materials*, which is $200,000 per month. But before his goods are sold, he gets bank credit for each $50,000. As a matter of actual fact, he spends 52 × $50,000 = $2,500,000 on raw materials. His constant capital is therefore not $1,050,000 but rather $3,600,000. If we take into account the *rising* rate of surplus value (it was asserted) the breakdown is postponed into a remote, very remote future. I reply: if we look at examples that resemble reality, both in regard to capital and the rate of surplus value, nothing in the result is decisively changed. Break-

57 [Gumperz 1931.]

down emerges as a tendency in a foreseeable period. I will show this to you in my next letter, with an example that is closer to reality than Bauer's abstract schema.

I finish with that, so the letter does not become an essay.

With sincere regards

your

Henryk Grossman

To your wife best regards and greetings.

P.S. if it is possible for you, it would be desirable to send the IWW pamphlet to Belgrade (Yugoslavia). Address: Miss Mara Fran, Beograd, Milosâ Velikoja 29. I am now in contact with Spanish Marxists. Friendly greetings to Comrade Wendelin Thomas!

16 September 1933

Impérial Hotel
45 Rue de la Victoire
Paris

Dear Comrade Mattick

I have a bad conscience: I owe you a reply to numerous letters! But now, after my return, I am doing a lot of work in libraries – and other ongoing matters have also prevented me from writing. But your endeavours on my behalf have really placed me under a great obligation to you. Entirely irrespective of whether it will yield a positive result, please accept my deepest and sincerest thanks. My prospects of coming to the USA are slight, I believe. Professor Emil Lederer (from Berlin) is over there. He is a 'socialist', that is to say a member of the German SPD,[58] with the support of which he has made his career. But he wants to correct Marx by using Böhm-Bawerk! He was a member of the group of professors who studied the economy of the Soviet Union, under my direction last summer. I gained this impression: he is a bourgeois liberal through and through, who uses a few 'socialist' phrases to conceal his bourgeois essence. Now he is setting up a university in the USA for the refugees – but of course he would rather invite 10 bourgeois professors

58 [*Sozialdemocratische Partei Deutschlands* (Social Democratic Party of Germany).]

or lecturers to be his colleagues than call upon such a dangerous person as myself! Never mind![59] If people are scared of me, this is something I am used to.

And now the matter of your review of [Sidney] Hook.[60] Our journal is due to appear soon (second issue for 1933 – but the *first* issue to be printed in Paris, by Alcan). It is already in press. The review cannot therefore appear until the February issue. We only publish *very short* reports, or rather simple 20 to 25 line indications of the contents of books. In this case, however, we will make an exception. I have written a very energetic letter to Geneva. But your 9 typed pages will have to be cut down by about half – if you are in agreement – not only for reasons of space but also on *factual* grounds. To judge by your report, H's book is *weak*, that is to say it presents things *which have long been known* and are therefore of no interest to a scientific journal. After all, we want to push forwards! It is better to make mistakes than to chew over old stuff again and again. We pay a fee of 5 Swiss francs per page. For 3 printed pages you would receive 15 francs – or, if you wish, a year's subscription to the journal (which costs more). Your purpose, to direct attention to H's book, will have been achieved in any case with the publication of the report.

Despite prudently anticipating future events, our Institute has suffered financial losses. Our building in Frankfurt has been confiscated and converted into Nazi student accommodation (they have seized my library, which contained roughly 2,000 rare volumes – economic theory starting with Aristotle, Plato, Xenophon, and passing through the Physiocrats right up to the present day). Our Institute's funds which we were unable to liquidate (mortgages) have also been confiscated. And we now regard it as our principal task to help the numerous, unfortunately very numerous scholars who had to flee from Germany and are literally without any means of support, at least for the initial period, with payments, albeit very modest ones.

The ground is shaky here in France. It smells very much of war. This is being prepared behind the scenes, as Hitler's Germany is also arming furiously. If it actually comes about, all the refugees from Germany will be arrested and sent to concentration camps. I want to make use of the *intermission*, i.e. to finish my book on *simple* reproduction as quickly as possible. I regard this as my life's work. In it, the whole wealth of the Marxist problematic will be demonstrated for the first time. The present discussion, in which people only talk about the proportion between departments I and II of the reproduction schema, is noth-

59 ['Refugees' and 'Never mind!' in English in the original text.]
60 [The reference is to Mattick 1934a.]

ing but intellectual masturbation. I must make haste to finish writing the book, as I cannot foresee what will happen or where history will drive me next.

Karl Korsch is still in Berlin. It is not possible to correspond with him directly, without endangering him. You have to write to the address of his student: Mrs Dr Hanna Kosterlitz, Berlin, Nollendorfplatz 7. But one must be *very cautious* about the content, and also the form of address, e.g. 'Dear Karola' in the letter etc.

Arthur Rosenberg is in Zürich. I will find the precise address.

The few remarks – actually suppositions – you made about the crisis under simple reproduction are not correct. But you will have to wait patiently until my book comes out. Here in France a book by Jean Duret (actually Koral, a former member of the Communist Party and a notable),[61] entitled *Marxism and Crises*, has been published by Gallimard. Superficial, completely unsystematic, and preoccupied with appearances. In his chapter on 'Theories of imperialism' he devotes 6 pages to Rosa Luxemburg, 4 to Pavlovich, 2 to Kautsky, 1½ to Hilferding, 4½ to Lenin, 3 to Sternberg, 12 to me. But I have the impression that he has *not* read my book on accumulation, and only draws on 'Fifty years of struggle'.[62]

So far, I have *not* received Professor Hook's letter.

While I was uncertain about my chest of manuscripts I did not have the patience for correspondence. Now that this matter has been settled satisfactorily I will gradually give my responses to the scientific problems you raised in earlier letters.

For now, though, I will close, so that the letter finally gets sent.

Sincere regards to you and your wife

your

Henryk Grossman.

P.S. In the issue of our journal which is currently in press, there is an article by Professor Horkheimer on 'Materialism and morality'.[63] Horkheimer is a philosopher and sociologist. It would be desirable if Hook contacted him – after all, they have things in common. Draw Hook's attention to Horkheimer's 'Materialism and metaphysics' in the *previous* issue of the journal. The article is very good and, equipped with all of modern philosophy, makes new arguments in favour of materialism and against metaphysics, which it severely embarrasses.

---

61 [Duret 1933.]

62 [Grossmann 1932f/1933a, see below pp. 332–388.]

63 [Horkheimer 1993a.]

1 November 1933

45 Rue de la Victoire
Paris

Dear Comrade Mattick

Most sincere thanks for your last two letters. They were really interesting, especially what you reported about the strike wave. Your enclosures were also very interesting. The school project – one can see that serious work is going on to educate workers. This is one of the most important tasks. We see how the KPD – even leaving aside its tactics – did not and could not fulfil this most elementary duty because its leaderships, rather than work for clarity, knowledge and insight, *just hurled abuse*. All independent thought had become impossible because 'deviation' was immediately scented in it and the best, most self-sacrificing and battle-tested comrades were marked as lackeys of the bourgeoisie. If the bourgeois revolution in France sent its own fighters to the guillotine, killed them physically, the proletarian fighters, who think for themselves and *seek* the right path, are currently put to death in a moral sense. The program of the University in Exile[64] is really interesting. The whole clique that I fought against here has assembled there: Lederer, [Arthur] Feiler, [Eduard] Heimann. Lederer, the specialist in the capitalist planned economy. One only needs to control *credit* – and thereby the economy will gradually grow *beyond* capitalism.[65] Lederer has not even gone as far as Hilferding's idea of controlling the banks. Because for Hilferding taking over the banks is the *first* act of a parliamentary *socialist* majority, the 50% + 1 deputies, which should be secured, one day, at an election. Ah, almighty God and Hitler have destroyed that beautiful dream. Lederer wants to put controls on credit today, *within capitalism*, and then achieve economic controls as well, at some time in the future. A pity that he went to America *too late*, now that every nook and cranny of Roosevelt's plans for a controlled economy are crashing. In April he could have dramatically promoted himself.

And Feiler? Read his 1925 book *America seen through German eyes* now.[66] It *is* worth reading. Not the slightest inkling that a crisis could arrive – not a *trace*. 'Prosperity' has solved the social question, the labour question. The fairy stories about the high salaries *of the* working class were repeated and spread

64 [The University in Exile was set up as a graduate division of the New School for Social Research in New York in 1933.]

65 [See Lederer 1925.]

66 [Feiler 1974.]

uncritically. Only the 'peripheral' layers of the working class, Negroes or immigrants, had 'not yet adapted' to the American standard of living. The reader will think: sure, you cannot turn a Polish Jew or Ruthenian[67] or Italian into a Yankee overnight. But within a couple of years 'adaptation' will take place. That is what the 'socialists' *à la* Feiler are like, the types who work in the business section of the financial press like the *Frankfurter Zeitung* and, when they get thrown out, put it about that this happened due to their socialist 'disposition'. They quickly join the SPD so that, with help from an SPD Minister, they can quickly snare a professorship in Königsberg! And Heimann? He wants to take the whole money economy, with all its consequences, disruptions, crises, over into the 'socialist' economy.[68] But really, the pity is the young brains that Heimann has confused with his mish-mash!

Your essay in the *Freidenker* was very interesting. You have made great progress (when I compare it with the Sternberg essay). For a start, your style. As is necessary in such a popular presentation, it is moderately humorous, spirited, not watered down, particularly the *first* part, which is much better than the ending. The material that you mention is also interesting, particularly the newspaper review of Hugh S. Johnson on 25 July 1933, 'that too much of profits are used for entirely new factories and too little for consumption'.[69] Has he not read my theory of overaccumulation? I almost suspected it.

The article in *Modern Monthly*, which had been announced, has *not* arrived. I assume that it has not appeared. Our journal has appeared and you should receive the current number, 2 (as you have written that you already have number 1). If I have misunderstood, please write to me and number 1 will be sent to you.

I wanted to say a few words more about the first edition of the *Proletarier*, sent to me on your initiative. The authors put on a 'radical' face – but we know from past experience ([Gustave Hervé) and such examples are legion in Germany – that those who make the loudest radical noises will later be the first to defect to the other side, as class enemies. All they want to do is criticise. In the discussion, the writer 'Ko'[70] makes me out to be a supporter of Luxemburg's theory and arrives at the conclusion that *crisis theories* are completely superfluous as instruments for achieving *knowledge*. So he ends up praising

67 [i.e. Ukrainian.]

68 [See, for example, Heimann 1932.]

69 [As President Franklin D. Roosevelt's head of the National Recovery Administration, Johnson made a national radio address on 25 July 1933.]

70 [Grossman closely paraphrases Korsch 1971.]

[Georges] Sorel's theory of myths, which is to replace crisis theory and any sort of *knowledge*. At the same time (!) the good fellow spouts empty phrases about a 'thorough *empirical* investigation of the present capitalist mode of production and its recognisable immanent tendencies of development'. As if a crisis theory was anything but the theoretical summing up and result of this research!

How far one can get with myth alone and what one can achieve with it, Hitler has precisely shown us. The whole petit bourgeois demagogy, which works with promises that it cannot keep, is the practical application of the theory of myth. The bourgeois will always be superior masters in this field. If the petit bourgeois layers had *knowledge* of tendencies of development, they would not have lined up with Hitler. He *must* deceive them and will deceive them. Disillusionment will be the result. We, however, do not want to deceive others or ourselves. Accordingly, our actions must be based on theoretical knowledge of the tendencies of development, i.e. how things work out objectively. And Ko wants to sacrifice this. Shouldn't people on such a level be excluded from the discussion from the start? Do we always have to start the discussion with Adam and Eve? Isn't it necessary to hold the discussion only among people who have a certain common basis, on which controversial consequences and problems can then be grappled with? If one questions every fundamental assumption, one will *never* get to clarify important contemporary problems. Apart from that, Rist in his history of economic theories makes fun of the myth-notions of the French syndicalists and sees in them the abandonment of Marxist materialism in favour of French utopianism. He quotes Sorel's remark that 'You rarely meet with a pure myth without some admixture of utopianism'.[71] But to let myths lead you, isn't that the same as climbing to the stars on the pattern of the great Magi or following the pillar of fire, which led Israel to the promised land? And with this hope, this belief which is borrowed from the early church, haven't we ended up with utopianism, a long way from historical materialism?

So much for a bourgeois historian. I have very carefully presented everything that is really valuable in Sorel in my essay on Sorel in Elster's dictionary.[72] But I likewise ridiculed the myth theory in my book on crisis. To preach myth to today's working class as a substitute for knowledge and a scientific crisis theory, that is a retreat to the standpoint of around 1848–67. And *Proletarier* aspires to be and calls itself the organ of the *most advanced* elements of the workers' movement! It would make me laugh, if it didn't make me cry!

---

71 [Rist 1915, p. 483. '[T]here are very few myths which are perfectly free from any Utopian element', Sorel 1925, p. 32.]

72 [Grossmann 1933c.]

Apologies for my scribble. My little book on the Physiocrats will be ready early in the year.[73] You will see that it deals with important contradictory problems (questions of method).

With sincere regards
your
H. Grossman

2 October 1934

12 Rue Victor-Considérant, 14th
Paris

Dear friend Mattick

I have not shown any signs of life for a long time, until your latest card compelled me to write. As I told you at the time, I have begun to write a critique of the Borkenau book. In the meantime the problem of the origins of mechanical thinking absorbed me and claimed my attention, so much so that for months I have been spending almost all my time in the Bibliothèque Nationale reading the literature of the sixteenth and seventeenth centuries. In particular, I am investigating the origins of all manner of mechanisms (clocks, cannons, industrial devices, transport and architecture, machines etc.), and have collected some very nice material. When I finish writing this, it will become – I hope – a nice contribution to the materialist conception of history, not like the general chatter *à la* Bukharin, but rather through *concrete* research into the historical material. Such work calls for such a massive amount of reading, in economic, historical and philosophical fields, that I forgot everything else as a result and interrupted and neglected my correspondence. In addition to interest in the content of the work, I was driven by the feeling that perhaps soon, owing to anticipated international complications (war, etc.), I will have to leave France. Accordingly I wanted at least to completely draw together all the *material* for my book.

Naturally, I still followed with the greatest interest the powerful stirrings of the US workers' movement and its new forms, both in San Francisco and now in the textile strike. One can see the obvious weaknesses of the movement – and yet one feels what a giant the American working class is, when once it strikes a

73 [It is not known to what this refers.]

blow. One has the impression that it is now going forward rapidly in giant steps, that perhaps the new centre of revolutionary events is maturing in the USA.

By contrast, on our old and senile continent there is still, *for the time being*, inconsolable misery. The collapse of the Third International, as a result of events in Germany in January 1933, is being followed by even greater misery, with the Communist movement subordinated to the Soviet Union's foreign policy and need for peace. The result: an unprincipled opportunism in the daily politics of all countries.

Nevertheless, in my opinion the awakening of the workers' movement will come. A new world war is approaching at a rapid rate. It will end in a series of revolutionary upheavals. Admittedly: rather than waiting consciously for events and preparing themselves to actively intervene, the Communist Parties of every country pursue a policy very similar to that of the KPD before Hitler's seizure of power, one that can only be called a politics of bluff.

As you well know, Gumperz is in New York, and recently Professor Horkheimer too. I recently wrote an essay for our journal: 'Capitalism of the Renaissance period and the origins of modern mechanics'.[74] In Belgrade a translation of 'The change in the original plan for Marx's Capital'[75] was already in press – it was to appear simultaneously with the translation of the third volume of *Capital*. In addition the manuscript of 'Fifty years of struggle' was ready and was to appear in September. Well, this week there was a raid on the home of Miss Mara Fran. She was not arrested, but my correspondence with her was confiscated along with the proofs and manuscripts.

From Holland, I have been sent *Rätekorrespondenz* (numbers 1–4), where I read with great interest a critique of my book and an anti-critique.[76] Judging by the style and method of argument I surmise that you are the author. The philosophical engagement with Hook[77] has deepened your perspective, and made the language and expression more concise and the content richer. In other words, the anti-critique is lively and quick-witted. Indeed it took your arrival to show the contributors to *Rätekorrespondenz* that breakdown, in my view, is identical with revolution. For my part, I must thank you for this courageous intervention *for the cause*!

74 [Published with a different title, Grossmann 2009.]

75 [Grossman 1929b, see above pp. 183–209. The Serbo-Croatian translation was eventually published as Grossman 1938c.]

76 [Pannekoek 1977; and Mattick 1973. *Internationale Rätekorrespondenz* was published by council communists in the Netherlands.]

77 [Mattick 1935a.]

I have still much, very much more to report. Sadly I have to break off as someone is coming.

Most sincere regards to you and your wife
from your always faithful
Henryk Grossman

Pass on my friendliest greetings to [Max] Nomad. He promised to send me his book.[78] I do not know his financial situation. Remind him about it if you think that he can do so without difficulty.

24 November 1934

Dear Comrade Mattick

You gave me a pleasant surprise with your photo. I am glad to get to know you finally, at least from the picture. I am sending you a photograph which has just arrived here from Vienna, from a comrade who visited me in August and wanted to talk about programmatic matters. My referee's report about your review was brief, and it read 'Short but absolutely to the point' and I sent it off *immediately*. Pollock wrote to me about the conversation you had with him. You are right to say that Pollock's point of view does not entirely coincide with mine. There is a whole history behind my relationship with Pollock in the theoretical field. In 1925, when I was invited to join the Institute, Pollock was a supporter of Sternberg; they had become friends when they were both students under [Franz] Oppenheimer at the university. I then began my fight against Sternberg and for a while there were tensions between Pollock and myself on account of this.

I gradually managed to win Pollock over theoretically, to the extent that he abandoned Luxemburg's market theory and in principle adopted my views. Pollock's article 'Remarks on the economic crisis', published a few months ago in the *Zeitschrift* (volume 2, issue 3, 1933)[79] stands in principle on the ground of my view of the tendencies of capital accumulation. The difference consists in this, that Pollock does not emphasise the tendency towards collapse as much as he does the *countertendencies*, and he therefore still considers that present-day capitalism has a number of possible ways out of the crisis. On the other hand, he is certainly no optimist and in a letter I received from him just yester-

78 [Presumably Nomad 1932.]
79 [Pollock 1933.]

day he expresses the conviction that the difficult situation for capitalism will lead the capitalist states of Europe (France, Germany, England) to bridge over all their *temporary antagonisms* in the interests of their *enduring* class interests by engaging in a general crusade against the Soviets.

I look forward to your work on the American workers' movement. Only I cannot entirely agree with you when you speak of the 'betrayal' of the workers' interests by their current leaders. The word 'betrayal' has often been misused and applied simply when the situation did not develop in the expected direction. But it *explains* very little. The 'betrayal' itself is, for me, a symptom and an index of the *immaturity* of the workers' movement, an indication that the working class's objective situation makes a betrayal profitable, a sign that the traitors (leaving aside all the weaknesses of their character) have not yet seen the objective possibility of a proletarian victory. As such a possibility draws closer, the 'traitors' will become scarcer and scarcer.

Warmest thanks for your efforts to find a publisher for my work. The fact that the publisher of the *Modern Monthly* wanted modifications, as indicated, is perhaps useful in this respect. Firstly, because a shorter article works better because it is clearer. Then, because you yourself, as it seems to me, have made great advances in your power of expression. I observed this in your polemic against Pannekoek. Of course, you will have to sacrifice your valuable time once again.

With best regards to you and your wife
your
Henryk Grossman.

P.S. My picture looks as if it had been taken somewhere in the sunshine of the 'Midi'. But I was simply snapped in front of the building in the Rue Victor Considérant.

31 January 1935

Dear Comrade Mattick

I have been wanting to write to you for a long time, above all to thank you for the numerous items you have sent. I have, however, been pursued by telegrams from New York about the delivery of the manuscript. That has now happened, so at present I have somewhat more time. I wrote a sharp critique of Borkenau's book, supplementing it with a small contribution on Descartes's mechanistic conception and the history of machinery. Now the work has a defect: it is too small for a book, and too big for an article in our journal. I do not know what

Pollock and Horkheimer will do. But I could not cut it any shorter. The section on Descartes will interest you, I hope. I have, it seems to me, offered extensive and convincing material demonstrating that Descartes arrived at his mechanistic conception by observing the machines of his epoch.

Many thanks, too, for sending your reportage on 'The strike wave' in the USA (in *Neue Deutsche Blätter*).[80] Reading it was a real pleasure for me. The articles demonstrate your remarkable literary gifts. One senses that they are written with deep commitment, and they display a certain dramatic verve.

I gave one of the articles to an artist, who has no interest in politics, and she told me that it gripped her and she had to read it right to the end without taking breath.

Nevertheless, I will again stress my doubts in relation to the passage about 'betrayal by the leaders of the strike'. I certainly agree with you that these people must be labelled traitors *in the day-to-day struggle*. On that point we are agreed. But from the point of view of *comprehending* the events, what is explained by giving them such a name? Nothing! *Why do these people betray?* That is the problem.

To the KPD, for example, the whole of social democracy was nothing but 'betrayal'. Instead of asking why the masses in their millions followed social democracy, the Party reassured itself by branding them as 'traitors'.

And the same thing is true not only of the KPD and the SPD but generally; of the USA as well. They have there on the one hand such small groups as, previously, the IWW and now the Workers' Party[81] and the most recent formations. Their principles are more or less fine and good, but they remain small and sectarian. On the other hand you have broad mass movements, which are far removed from these sects with their pure principles. Why? Is that accidental? I do not think so. One should and must analyse why the most progressive elements of the workers' movement do not know how to overcome their character as sects so as to become a movement of the masses. That is the most important task of the moment. Indeed, it was just the same in Germany. First Spartacus, then the KAP[82] etc. up to the KPD – all of them were small groups without any

80 [Mattick 1934b.]

81 [Industrial Workers of the World, a syndicalist organisation, was the largest revolutionary group in the USA until 1920. The Workers Party of the United States was established in December 1934, through a merger of the American Workers Party, led by A.J. Muste, and the Trotskyist Communist League of America.]

82 [*Kommunistische Arbeiterpartei Deutschlands* (Communist Workers' Party of Germany) was established in 1920, by expelled members of the left wing of the KPD. It splintered during the 1920s.]

influence as long as they remained revolutionary. The KPD became a million-strong party when it accustomed itself to parliamentary cretinism on the model of the SPD, and *acted* the same way as the SPD, only employing a few more radical words in their dictionary.

At my place for some time, there have been weekly meetings of workers and former members of the KPD etc. – such as Paul Frölich, Jacob Walcher etc. – and we discuss these *same* problems, in order to learn and to understand why in 1918/19, 1920, 1923 etc. all the objectively given revolutionary opportunities were squandered! Why the revolutionary elements always remained isolated.

I am reading *The Inevitability of Communism*[83] at present and I thank you for your friendly gesture in sending it. I already know the ideas it contains from the German text, which I received when it was first published. Similarly, I am also reading 'One step forward'[84] etc. in *Modern Monthly* (I was prevented from doing this until now by the need to sort out various domestic worries).

I have now been interrupted while writing. I will nevertheless send the letter, and I will definitely write again *this* week. My most sincere regards to you and your wife

your
Henryk Grossman

19 February 1935

12 Rue Victor-Considérant, 14th
Paris

Dear Comrade

I have wanted to send you the letter I promised for a long time. I was busy: most modestly and without the usual carry-on, an international workers' conference representing eleven countries met here. Those assembled were delegates from the left wings of the social democratic parties and independent (communist) parties. It did not address theoretical issues, but rather attempted to determine whether, with the *given* circumstances and groupings (leaving completely aside whether we like them or not), a common platform for *action* is possible with which one could take *practical* steps against the fascists and against the warmongers. Although the conference was not entirely fruitless, it

83 [Mattick 1935a.]
84 [Mattick 1934c.]

was still clear that the differences are still too great. In particular, the left of the French Socialist Party ([Jean] Zyromski) operated with lavish radical phrases, but it was apparent that behind the radical words there was no serious will to revolutionary action. The same was true of the left of the Socialist Party of Poland, as well as the Jewish Bund, etc. On the other hand several other groups showed they had learned much from the events in Germany, Austria, Spain etc. In general the need for the workers' movement to break away from the Third International was recognised as a necessity. I am touching on only some declarations, but I cannot tell you anything concrete, because the conference decided that only official statements to the public are permitted.[85]

In the *Kampfsignal*, of 15 November 1934, I read your article 'The communist economy'[86] and I agree with it in principle, apart from the minor matter in which you, apparently relying on Borkenau, maintain that manufacture realised the immanent principle of all capitalist econom[ies], calculability; and further that you reduce all qualities of labour to general human, purely quantitatively determined labour. In our journal, I offer a critique of Borkenau, which shows that not a single sentence of his claims hold water.

But in addition this side issue, which is peripheral to your essay, I also cannot agree with your assessment of the planned economy in the Soviet Union. You must judge this planned economy not on the basis of the current degeneration, but on the ideas that in principle underlie it. I was in the Soviet Union in 1932 and did not limit myself to the theoretical declarations of the various theoreticians, but also asked the practical planners how the plan is 'made'. I gained the impression that over there they make calculations in *use values*, insofar as it was a matter of the duration of production (annual or five yearly). That these *volumes* of use values are expressed in money at the same time in fact changes nothing. Because money here only plays the role of *an index for the purpose of exact comparisons*, since you cannot compare 10 tonnes of potatoes + 2 wagons of coal in 1934 with 8 tonnes of potatoes + 1 wagon of wheat + 1 wagon of coal in 1928, if all the quantities are not reduced to value indices. But money has changed its function in the sphere of production as well as in the sphere of circulation. One has to see that. If things happen in Russian planning *nowadays* which have nothing to do with a socialist economy, still the *basis* of the five year

85 [The conference was a meeting of the International Working Community, known as the IAG (Internationale Arbeitsgemeinschaft). In Paris, Grossman associated with Paul Frölich and Jacob Walcher, leaders of the Socialist Workers Party (SAP), which was affiliated with the IAG.]

86 [Mattick 1934d. *Kampfsignal* was an independent, German language, Marxist publication in New York, issued for two years.]

plan was *right* at the time and I am convinced that every other economic plan in coming communist economies, whether in Germany or in England, will be unable to take a path that is different in principle, making allowance for the historical fact that these countries will be able to begin a planned economy on a *higher* level. But that is a consequence of the higher level of development of German and English industry compared with the industry of Russia.

I agree with your critique of the American Workers Party (*Modern Monthly*, December 1934).[87] In our country we also hear from younger comrades that we should 'learn something' from Hitler. You are correct when you write that we cannot and must not compete with fascist demagogy. But I will not hold forth any longer about that. The most important problem, which we have all been studying for months, is the source of the mistakes that have been made, for example in the German workers' movement. Every revolutionary movement must *begin* as a tiny minority, since it is its task to oppose the status quo. But why didn't this minority, despite the favourable objective conditions, succeed in overcoming this sectarian character and winning the *masses in their millions*. That is the central problem: what use is it if various carping critics constantly watch over the 'purity' of the revolutionary program, like old school-mistresses over their virtue. The point is rather to set the masses *in motion* and a step of real revolutionary practice is more important than half a dozen virtuous theoretical programs.

You know I wanted to write an essay criticising Borkenau and, beyond that, a short book about the history of mechanics. Now something between the two has been published, a study of 80 printed pages, where I, as I believe, convincingly identify the social origins of the mechanistic philosophy of Descartes and, in addition, [Thomas] Hobbes and [Gottfried Wilhelm] Leibniz. I have, indeed, assembled a *gigantic amount of material* that I was not able to use in this essay. But now I finally want to return to my second volume, dealing with *simple* reproduction. In it, I will not examine systematics, so much, and in the appendix I want to 1) go into the world crisis; 2) discuss a number of important critiques of my book. I observe, in passing, that for example in Louis Segal's *Textbook Political Economy* there is a note: 'A social democratic theory of the automatic breakdown of capitalism'.[88] Grossmann, the theoretician of 'left social democracy' has claimed there is an automatic breakdown because of a falling rate of profit and tried to attribute this foolishness to Marx. The title of my book is not mentioned; the author has not, apparently, read it.

87 [Mattick 1934c.]
88 Segal 1934, p. 207.

I have a request for you: in November 1933, I was asked for an essay on Simonde de Sismondi for the *Encyclopedia of the Social Sciences*[89] (I wrote a book in French about S. in 1925,[90] which Mr [Jean-Rodolphe] de *Salis*, the author of a large biography of Sismondi, that appeared in 1933,[91] regarded as the best economic book about S). I sent the essay off in January 1934. I was sent the honorarium but not the minimum of 30 offprints that are normally regarded as necessary, not even a single one. I would like to ask you to look in a library to see if the article has appeared yet (under 'Sismondi'). The *Encyclopedia* reaches Europe after a long delay. Today, I regret that I provided the article for the *Encyclopedia*.

With most sincere regards to you and your wife
your
Henryk Grossman

22 October 1935

Paris

Dear Comrade Mattick

And now I want to reply to your letter of 26 August 1935, with apologies for the lateness of the response. I have been in London in the intervening period, in connection with my intention to emigrate there.

First of all, about Vera Buch. She made a wretched impression on me. Worse than that: a complete nullity. If one comes to Europe with the grandiose intention of coordinating the various political tendencies, one must surely have a plan, a program or a tactic. But to come here with absolutely nothing amounts to regarding all of us as idiots. Moreover, she herself knows very little about American policy (e.g. in the Pacific) and she denied the imperialist character of that policy (under Roosevelt). Comrade [Paul] Wassermann (whom I invited for this purpose) confirmed my impressions. We took note of her information, without getting into any sort of discussion. Incidentally, I have the impression that her journey was a 100% failure, and as a result was a tourist trip.

I am really sorry that you are in such a miserable situation. It would be in vain to expect any help or offers of employment from Europe. Here the situation for

89 [Grossman 1934, see below pp. 439–442.]

90 [Grossman 1924a, see above pp. 55–119.]

91 [Salis 1932.]

the exiles is very grave, particularly in France. Anyone who can leave does so. The number of exiles has melted down by half in two years. There are comrades who are actually starving, etc. I would really be overjoyed if the Guggenheim Committee[92] gave you the chance to do scientific work.

I wanted at least to refund you the postal expenses you incurred in sending your letters and various publications.

Now there are no obstacles, in relation to the failure of an essay to appear in the *Modern Monthly*. Thank you, however, for your efforts in this direction. I very much regret that there is no journal where I can place the kind of articles I am writing, e.g. my critique of attempts to stimulate the German economy through war industry. Here I develop Marx's reproduction schema, and show – in contrast to Rosa Luxemburg, who views war as an *investment opportunity*[93] – that according to Marx there are very *definite* and narrow quantitative limits to *unproductive* accumulation. If these are overstepped, tremendous dislocation results.

Indeed, here many Marxists regard the German 'boom' as a *normal* boom in accumulation. As against this, I demonstrate that war industry does not represent any enrichment of society. Individuals enrich themselves, the whole is impoverished. Not accumulation, rather a regression.

These seem to me – as a Marxist – to be simple, primitive truths. In the present theoretical confusion a demonstration of them, particularly when it is presented in a clear and convincing formulation with the aid of a reproduction schema, is important. This confusion was brought into Marxist ranks by Sombart, in particular, in his book on war and capitalism, where he said that war *accelerated* accumulation.[94] That was then simply taken over by Rosa L. I show, in contrast, that war always restricts the tempo of accumulation, which would proceed more quickly, perhaps much more quickly, without war.

And with this I come to your friendly invitation to collaborate with you on C[ouncil] C[orrespondence].[95] I cannot do this, for two reasons. Firstly, because I am dependent on the Institute, I want to come to the USA, and the Institute now keeps its distance from all *practical* political movements, and would take amiss such an involvement on my part. I now want to move to London, and for the last four months I have been making endeavours to do this, so far in vain, because the Home Office has collected information about me, and

92 [Refers to a committee of the John Simon Guggenheim Foundation, established by the industrialist Simon Guggenheim in 1925 to provide grants to scholars and artists.]

93 [Luxemburg 1951, pp. 460–5.]

94 [Sombart 1913, p. 61.]

95 [*Council Correspondence* was founded and edited by Mattick.]

knows that I have written a book about the collaps of capitalisme. This gives the gentlemen a heart collaps.[96] Leaving all this aside, there are, however, reasons of principle why I cannot join CC. This is because of CC's position on the Soviets. I believe that CC's analysis of Soviet policy is fundamentally false. The Soviets are not, like capitalist countries a surplus value producing state entity. I too dislike the Stalinist bureaucracy, I too feel there is much, very much, to criticise. But in principle I consider that there are no private property-owners nor private accumulation in the S[oviet] U[nion], and, furthermore, many of the deformations there were unavoidable, given the constraint of the threat from the external enemy. Your opinion that the capitalist states do not fear Russia today is fundamentally wrong. Sooner or later the Western Europeans will enter into a coalition against the SU, which Japan will also join in from the East. I am convinced that your point of view towards the SU is un-Marxist. You reject the SU because it does not correspond with your abstract, theoretical idea of a socialist entity. This is the standpoint of a sectarian. In such cases, the danger is that the sectarian is 'right' in abstract terms, but he remains a sectarian with few supporters – and will always remain apart from the great mass movement. I am convinced that if you yourself were able to exert decisive influence on developments in Russia, you would not, under the pressure of objective conditions, in the economic sphere, in *essential* points, pursue a different economic policy from that of the SU. To be sure, I write 'if' and 'but'. The above remarks are not intended as a critique of your standpoint, or as a subject of discussion. They are only meant to indicate *my* standpoint. I believe that in the USA you are too far away from things. Here in Europe everyone knows that a defeat of the SU would throw the workers' movement back 50 years. So one cannot *fight against* the SU as a state that produces 'surplus value'; we have rather to *defend* the SU from its external enemy.

Your reports about the books by Ralph Epstein, and [H. Parker] Willis and [John M.] Chapman,[97] are extremely interesting. Here these books can hardly be found. A scientific atmosphere is missing here. That is why I want to go to London. Perhaps I will succeed in overcoming all the difficulties and move there at the end of December.

With best regards to you and your wife
your
Henryk Grossman

---

96 [The original, 'collaps of capitalisme' and 'Herz collaps' are presumably attempts to use English terms.]

97 [Presumably a reference to Epstein 1934. Mattick reviewed Willis and Chapman 1935, Mattick 1935b.]

19 December 1935

Dear Friend Mattick

I am in the midst of packing books etc., as I am moving to London in two weeks. I have finally succeeded in obtaining a travel permit, after a wait of six months. But I would like to reply to your last letter from here.

Your situation must be really difficult, if you have to lay aside all theoretical work. Your presentation of conditions in the factory has made a profound impression on me. You undoubtedly possess great literary talent for graphic description, so that one almost sees what you are depicting before one's eyes. You will yet become a great novelist (which does not mean that I underestimate your scientific gifts).

I was already aware of the questionnaire you sent me, as the Guggenheim Foundation sent your request along with the other documents for my inspection. The recommendation I sent to Horkheimer for the Guggenheim was even more energetic than the one you saw, since I could express my opinion more freely in a document for internal circulation only. I would be delighted if you were successful in your endeavours. But one shouldn't count too much on this. In any case, you should approach Dr Julian Gumperz. Perhaps you know him. He is an American and has far more connections than Pollock and Horkheimer. He is the author of a book on the agricultural crisis in the USA,[98] a clever and pleasant fellow; mention my name. Perhaps he can be useful to you, by recommending you somewhere. His address: 610 Fifth Avenue, Room 519, New York City.

What I wrote to you about your and my attitudes to the USSR was not meant to be a discussion but a characterisation of my position. It is difficult to reply by letter to long disquisitions, misunderstandings always come up and one would have to write a dissertation rather than a short letter to explain everything. I will just make one remark. You say, among other things: you have given up on the workers' movement; you prefer the movement of workers. I regard such an answer as insufficiently serious; indeed I see it as self-deception. What is one to understand by your remark? Do you want to become the leader of a sect, who will admittedly be in the 'right' in private but who will have absolutely no influence on events? After all, we want to change the world and in another place you say indeed that you do not want to work for your children, but to experience socialism yourself. Good. But in what manner, with what means? And will the great proletarian masses not be concerned with this?

98 [Gumperz 1931.]

Your comment on my analysis of the role of war also seems to me to introduce a dangerous lack of clarity. The distinction between productive and unproductive labour is after all an elementary part of Marx's theory. War belongs in the latter sphere. The fact that one can exact tribute after victory does not prove that war is productive. It is just the same as when a bandit in the forest gains a substantial income from his gains, yet you would not call his profession 'productive'. Great confusion has been created in this area (by Sombart, for example) and it has crept into socialist circles. My objective here is to restore clarity. With such presentations, everything depends on the how they are conducted. I hope to find peace and quiet in London, so that I can finally finish off my work!

You have, I hope, received my work on Descartes. Of course, if you do not read French you will miss out on the most important ideas. Perhaps someone will be able to translate them for you.

For the moment, I just have *one* further observation: Professor Henri Sée, the most distinguished bourgeois economic historian in France, who is himself an opponent of the materialist conception, has written to me expressing his vigorous and enthusiastic agreement with my comments on economic history, questioning only my *factual* presentation of the genesis of capitalism and confirming that I am on the right road.

Please accept my best wishes to yourself and your wife for the coming New Year

your
Henryk Grossman

29 October 1936

9 Belsize Avenue, London NW3

Dear Comrade Mattick

Since receiving your letter of 5 October I have been waiting for the request which the Guggenheim Foundation advised it would send. So far nothing has arrived. It goes without saying that I will support your selection. Unfortunately that has had little success. The members of the guild do not like outsiders, because they lay greater stress on superficial, scholastic systematisation of presentation (which is generally lacking in autodidacts) than on originality of thought.

You must not misinterpret my long silence. Nothing has changed in my relations with you. I have been silent both because conditions in general are oppressive – here in Europe one senses this more strongly than where you are – and because the events in Spain but also in France are psychologically debilitating, to which several unpleasant personal experiences must be added.

I am doing a lot of work but so far nothing has yet crystallised out or is ready for publication. The Blum 'experiment' has now demonstrated the bankruptcy of the 'theory of underconsumption' *in practice*, if such a proof were still needed. I would like to write an occasional article on this subject – but where? The *Zeitschrift* is, after all, more sociological than economic. It would be good to draw up a balance of the experiences of the world crisis in relation to this theory, which is popular and rampant, particularly in trade-union circles. Insofar as the crisis has been 'overcome', this has nowhere occurred through an expansion of mass consumption but always and everywhere through a *reduction* in the level of wages, either openly or in the disguised form of devaluations, price-fixing etc.

Now that the theory is absolutely dead, it would be appropriate to arrange a solemn funeral procession to the cemetery.

You have sent so many parcels to me that I venture to enclose 10 shillings as compensation for your expenditure on postage. I am also sending you the review of my work on Descartes in *Der Kampf*.[99] I am amazed that little Helene allowed something like that to be published! She is ill-disposed towards me.

Sincere regards to you and your wife

your

Henryk Grossman

10 February 1937

9 Belsize Avenue
London NW 3

Dear Comrade Mattick

I have read through your work on unemployment with great pleasure, the last part on the movement of the unemployed was particularly interesting for me, because I gained graphic insight into the American workers' movement. A very *detailed* referee's report already went to Horkheimer on 3 February. If what

99 [Grossman 2009a, reviewed in the theoretical journal of the Austrian Socialists, with Helene Bauer edited, l. d. 1936.]

Horkheimer wrote is true, that the Guggenheim Foundation's referee recognises my scientific authority, then it must succeed this time and it would please me a lot if you had the possibility to devote yourself, without worries, to scientific work.

I was asked whether you employ modern statistical methods, etc. My professional opinion – for your private information – is: no modern statistical methods. You *make use of* statistics in wise, mature selection but do not master statistical material to the extent necessary. The value of your work and your appeal lies elsewhere. In short, summarised in headings:

1. The work is a synthesis of all possible aspects of the problem. You provide a multifaceted illumination.
2. The principal value of the work is that it is not limited to the empirical description and presentation of the facts, rather that it illuminates the material theoretically and demonstrates the *limits* of social policy.

To where should I return the work and the other material that has recently been sent to me? New York or Chicago?

On the occasion of the seventieth anniversary of the appearance of the first volume of *Capital*, I have written a study for the journal, under the title 'Marx and classical political economy or the theory of value fetishism'.[100] Only *part* will be able to appear in the journal. The whole will be about 100 printed pages. It deals with the central problem of Marx's conception – and I think in a new way.

Sincere regards to you and your wife
from your
Henryk Grossman

18 July 1937

London

Dear Comrade

For a long time I have wanted to thank you for the materials you sent me, which I have read with great interest, for example both of your articles about unemployment in the USA in the *Sozialistische Warte*.[101] Today, on the

---

100 [Grossman 1937a.]

101 [*Sozialistische Warte* was published in exile by the Internationale sozialistische Kampfbund. (International Socialist League of Struggle), a small split from the German Social

anniversary of the outbreak of the Spanish Revolution, I wanted to make some theoretical observations on the essay in *Council Correspondence* 5/6 (June 1937) 'Nature and the significance of overproduction',[102] presumably written by you.

There is no argument that without accumulation capitalist production is unthinkable in actual, concrete reality. Nonetheless, the notion of *simple reproduction* without accumulation has taken on great meaning for the theory. What is it? Marxist theory has not previously revealed this. For it, simple reproduction presents no problem. The portrayal of simple reproduction is dispensed with in five lines: between Department I and Department II of the schema there is a nice equilibrium; the entire problematic concerning the stability of capitalism only begins with expanded reproduction, as the title of Rosa Luxemburg's book[103] already indicated and as a dozen other authors have repeated.

You also tend to reduce the whole problem of crises to the accumulation question *alone*, namely the *interruption* of accumulation. You say: 'Overproduction is nothing but the interruption of the expansion process (of accumulation). Looking at the situation superficially, it conveys a picture of unbalanced production and consumption. The equilibrium seems suddenly disrupted and production now exceeds consumption.'[104]

That the interruption of expansion can be *one* cause of crisis should not require an argument either. Is it the exclusive cause? That I contest. For what purpose did Marx introduce simple reproduction into the theory? He showed that crisis is already possible in simple reproduction. Accordingly, factors are present which cause crisis features independently of any accumulation (and its interruption). Read Marx's account of the reproduction of fixed capital within simple reproduction. 'There would be a crisis – a crisis of production – despite reproduction on a constant scale.' 'This example of fixed capital – in the context of reproduction on a constant scale – is a *striking one*.'[105] That the clique of neoharmonists, Hilferdings and Otto Bauers, tried for decades to systematically distort Marx, that passages such as the ones cited above were systematically concealed and that there is no trace of them to be found in the Marxist literature, is not a reason for *us* to go along with the neoharmonists. Once you

---

Democratic Party, that existed between 1934 and 1940. It was valued for its sober accounts of developments in Germany.]

102 ['Overproduction' in English in the original text. Mattick 1937.]

103 [Luxemburg 1951.]

104 [Mattick 1937, p. 24.]

105 [Marx 1978b, pp. 543, 545.]

think through Marx's concepts consistently to the end, how can a crisis arise at the level of simple reproduction in which such a harmonious equilibrium appears to prevail? Then you will find in Marx many more theoretical concepts of which the 'philosophers' have not dreamed, even those such as Karl Korsch, who imagine that they understand something of Marxist economics.

And you can read another example of crisis at the level of simple reproduction in the second volume of *Capital*: 'Exchange within department II. Necessary means of subsistence and luxury items'.[106] Why were these passages concealed for decades, effaced, where otherwise every comma is quoted and used by the literary Marxists as a weapon in battle? Because here, if we think these examples through to the end, we encounter a Marx who does not fit into the traditional interpretation which arose under the influence of bourgeois economists (Werner Sombart).[107] We find that simple reproduction has great methodological tasks to fulfil, that there are huge problems in simple reproduction and that only previous, two-dimensional Marxist theory could pass over these problems – indeed dance past them – without an inkling. One fancies oneself so uncommonly clever, by having enriched the world with so much 'material', thanks to the experience of the previous crisis; while in reality one ought to start afresh with the ABC of Marxist theory, if one is to understand this material.

But enough for today, dear Comrade Mattick. You know, perhaps, that in October I am coming to New York for about three months. I hope to have the opportunity to see you and to develop a more extensive exchange of ideas about the problems that interest us both.

In the latest issue of the journal there was a particularly good essay by Horkheimer, with a sharp, principled critique of the new (logical) empiricism.[108] Very much worth reading because, precisely in socialist circles, Marxist materialism is often confused with empiricism, because people express sympathy with this empiricism as an ostensibly anti-metaphysical current.

With best regards to you and your wife
your
Henryk Grossman

106 [Marx 1978b, pp. 478–87.]
107 [Notably, Sombart 1913.]
108 [Horkheimer 2002, pp. 132–87.]

5 November 1937

New York

I have been here for 3 weeks, only able to write to you today. I arrived here ill. In summer I blundered out of the sun in France into London's rain, caught a severe flu, with a high temperature, lay in bed for 4 weeks and lost 7 kg. Despite the doctor's warning I came up against a fixed deadline, as I did not want to postpone the trip any longer. I arrived much weakened, stumbled into severe theoretical struggles (within the Institute) and, at least to this point, only make slow progress and it will require still more effort before I win the people over to my standpoint!

On the other hand, I was celebrated and received a friendly welcome here, am invited out almost daily and wander, so to speak, from one hand into another – this, altogether, the explanation of my silence.

Now my health is significantly better. *Voilà*,[109] I am getting in touch and, if you do not come here, I definitely hope to go to *Chicago* in order to visit you, in any case at a later time.

I am writing now because I have just received a communication from Guggenheim's [sic] Foundation and did not want to answer before I received the apparently necessary information from you.

With sincerest greetings
I am your
Henryk Grossman

I had a visit from a gentleman from a Californian university,[110] who wants to write a doctoral dissertation about Rosa Luxemburg and brought me your greetings. I gave him the information he wanted and declared myself ready to help him in the future.

109 ['*Voilà*' means 'there you are'.]

110 [Charles Easton Rothwell's PhD thesis acknowledged Grossman's assistance, Rothwell 1938.]

19 November 1937

New York

Dear Comrade Mattick

After receiving your letter of 8 November, I went to Mr [Henry Allen] Moe straight away and conferred with him for almost an hour, during which I particularly emphasised that I do not know you personally, that is, for on my part, there are exclusively *objective* concerns. I believe that I influenced him favourably, at least in the moment; later other influences may indeed turn him in the other direction. In any case, *he* suggested to me that when I am back from Chicago and have made your acquaintance he would be pleased to see me again and to hear my impression. I said, perhaps I will only be in Chicago at the end of December or the start of January. Moe thought that there was enough time; it would not be decided before then.

On the other hand, I heard hear that the Foundation prefers to support *rightwing* people

If they make grants to leftists, from time to time, it is only *already well-known* people, in order to be able to boast: see how objective we are. These friends do not think you have much of a chance of receiving the grant. I write this so that you do not become too optimistic. In any case, you should set everything that may be useful in motion.

I am over-extended here. There are always lectures, discussions, seminars etc.

Sincere greetings to you and your wife
from your
Henryk Grossman

CHAPTER 11

Gold Production in the Reproduction Schema of Marx and Rosa Luxemburg*

Translated from German by David Meienreis

Marx's account of gold production in the framework of his two-part reproduction schema has been most harshly criticised by Rosa Luxemburg. Despite the importance of this very controversial problem and the far reaching implications of Luxemburg's criticisms for Marx's system, if they were true, the question Luxemburg raised has received no further attention in the Marxist literature. The following is an attempt to resolve the problem.

1 Luxemburg's Position on Marx's Research Method

Marx's method, the method of successive approximation, consists, as I have shown elsewhere,[1] of three elements which together form an *indivisible whole*: namely, an abstract *reproduction schema* as a tool of theoretical analysis; further of hypothetical, *simplifying assumptions* which form its basis; and finally, *subsequent corrections* that have to be made to the preliminary theoretical results achieved by these means. These three elements of Marx's method, then, constitute only parts of a *single* methodological tool in our thinking. Without the other two, none of the elements contributes to understanding the truth. Hence Marx's reproduction schema alone and the process of production and distribution it describes make no claim to represent concrete capitalist reality. The schema does not *immediately* represent the empirically given mechanism of production but merely describes a 'normal' process of reproduction under fictitious, simplifying assumptions. It is, therefore, only a *preliminary* stage of understanding, the first step in the cognitive method of successive approximation toward the *real* process of reproduction.

This method of step-by-step approximation, which *Marx* elaborated precisely and is of such crucial importance for the understanding of the Marx's entire system, is not recognised by Luxemburg. She disregards this context,

---

* [Originally published as Grossman 1932a.]

1 Grossmann 1929a; Grossmann 1929b, see above pp. 183–209.

tears the reproduction schema out of its logical connections with the other elements of Marx's method of successive approximation, so that it loses its methodological value and necessarily leads to a distortion of the results of Marx's research. That Luxemburg herself senses that her appraisal of the reproduction schema is inadequate is demonstrated by the circumstance that she – without being aware of it – repeatedly altered her opinion of the schema and offered no fewer than *three* different and mutually exclusive interpretations of it.

She begins her book with an accolade for Marx's reproduction schema. Not only because it '*posed the problem* of the reproduction of the entire social capital', the formulation of the schema belongs among Marx's 'lasting services to economic theory'. 'The problem of capitalist reproduction contains a number of *precise relations* ... whose combination, both in its contradictions and congruencies, presents the underlying problem.'[2] 'In the history of economics', RL continues, 'we find only two attempts at an exact exposition of this problem: one by Quesnay, the father of the Physiocratic school, at its very inception; and in its final stage this attempt by Marx.'[3] But Marx's great historical achievement was not merely *to pose the problem*. 'Marx's schema is *the scientific solution of the problem*.'[4] Marx showed that the two departments are 'interdependent' and therefore must have 'certain *quantitative relations*'[5] and indeed 'their mutual relation is derived from an *exact value-relationship*', namely I (v + s) = II c.[6] 'The figures in this schema express quantities of value ... which are chosen arbitrarily, *but their ratios are exact*.'[7] But there is more! Luxemburg is not content to state that, under the assumptions specified, Marx's schema reveals the solution to the problem of reproduction, i.e. that it shows the necessary fictitious conditions under which reproduction can proceed 'normally'. Instead of regarding Marx's schema as what it actually is, a *theoretical tool for the analysis* of concrete reality, Luxemburg *hypostatises* it and attributes an objective validity to it! The exact proportions of Marx's schema, she writes, form the 'general and absolute

2 Luxemburg 1913, p. 76.
3 Luxemburg 1951, p. 31. [Grossman's emphasis. This translation, by Agnes Schwarzschild, of Luxemburg 1913, is unsatisfactory in places. Where that is the case, new, more accurate translations from the German original have been provided. Where Schwarzschild's translation has been used and her terminology diverges from Marx 1978b, her texts have been modified. The term 'diagram', for example, has been replaced with 'schema'.]
4 Luxemburg 1913, p. 76. [Grossman's emphasis.]
5 Luxemburg 1913, p. 55. [Grossman's emphasis.]
6 Luxemburg 1913, p. 57. [Grossman's emphasis.]
7 Luxemburg 1951, p. 84. [Grossman's emphasis.]

foundation of social reproduction',[8] and not only for *capitalist* production 'but also – *mutatis mutandis* – for *every* regulated and planned economic order, for instance a *socialist* one.'[9] The question RL raises of whether an 'objective social existence' can be attributed to the schema is answered in the affirmative: 'This proves the schema to have *objective* social validity.'

We are not interested here in the odd conclusion Luxemburg reaches, namely, the assertion that this isolated and unrealistic schema already immediately reflects economic reality. In fact, however, the preliminary simplification in Marx's schema extends so far that it does not take into consideration *fixed* capital, which plays such an important role in the real economic process, *commercial* or *bank* capital, and, just as little, is *ground rent* encompassed. It includes *no average rate of profit*, rather there are *different* rates of profit in the two departments; consequently, it is not *prices of production* but abstract values that appear in the schema. And *such* a schema is to definitively represent capitalist reality?

What primarily concerns us about Luxemburg's confusion of a preliminary methodological fiction with reality is her *glorification of Marx's schema* with its exact proportions, as presented by Marx. For the hypostatisation of the schema, the objective existence attributed to it, expresses the fact that Luxemburg regards it as real *in the strongest sense*. Its numbers may be fictitious and arbitrary, Luxemburg believes, but their relations are nevertheless exact and retain their validity not only for a capitalist but even for a socialist society.

But what a different picture of the significance of the same reproduction schema Luxemburg paints when she proceeds to critically 'develop' Marx 'further'!

In the study of 'The change in the original plan for Marx's *Capital* and its causes', already mentioned, I have shown that the schema, if it is to incorporate the essential conditions of capitalist reproduction, must not encompass arbitrary branches of production but necessarily a *two-part division* of the apparatus of production: I the production of means of production, II the production of means of consumption. This two-part division forms the basis and the starting point of Marx's polemic against Adam Smith, David Ricardo and their successors in the nineteenth chapter of the second volume of *Capital* ('Former Presentations of the Subject').[10] In the third volume of his lifework, Marx also returns to the question and says: 'In volume 2 we divided all capital into two

8 Luxemburg 1913, p. 56.
9 Luxemburg 1951, pp. 103, 128–9. [Grossman's emphasis.]
10 Marx 1978b, pp. 435–67.

great classes: department I, which produces means of production, and department II, which produces means of individual consumption.' And finally Marx spoke of the '*absolute validity of this division*. It is in no sense a hypothesis, but simply the expression of a fact'.[11]

The reproduction of the money material does nothing to compromise the validity of this division, as Marx identifies the production of gold with metal production in general and, consequently, allocates it to department I of the schema: 'The production of gold belongs, along with metal production in general, to department I, the category which comprises the production of means of production.'[12]

Marx seldom expressed himself so definitely and unambiguously about any other result of his research as here. And yet Luxemburg attacks precisely the 'absolute validity' of the schema's division, which Marx asserts so emphatically. Despite her initial apotheosis of Marx's schema she now believes she has found a fundamental flaw in its construction, which induced her to 'deviate from Marx' at this point.[13] To treat money as an element of department I of the schema is a mistake. Marx committed the sin of '*confusing* means of exchange with means of production', which led him to inexcusable 'inconsistencies'.[14] Money should be regarded as neither means of production nor means of consumption. As a means of exchange, it fulfils a *special* circulatory function within the mechanism of reproduction. 'So [Marx's] schema actually has to appear incomplete ... [A] third department, producing means of exchange whose characteristic is that it serves neither production nor consumption, has to be added to it.'[15]

One is astonished at the kind of objections Luxemburg makes. Did Marx really confuse such elementary categories as means of exchange and means of production?! Once Marx had mistaken this elementary truth, as Luxemburg assures us, the more complex insight that 'to include the production of money in department I would *violate all material and value proportions of Marx's schema* and would rob it of validity'[16] was bound to escape him.

In contrast, Luxemburg claims that only separately accounting for the production of money as a third department in its own right and describing it 'in its

11 Marx 1981b, p. 975. [Grossman's emphasis.]
12 Marx 1978b, p. 546.
13 Luxemburg 1951, p. 99.
14 Luxemburg 1951, p. 100. [Grossman's emphasis.]
15 Luxemburg 1913, p. 72.
16 Luxemburg 1913, p. 73. [Grossman's emphasis.]

intricate organic interconnection with the other departments ... would result in a *comprehensive* [!] schema for the whole capitalist process in its *essential* points.'[17]

What, then, remains of Marx's schema after this criticism, with its admirable dialectics? Nothing but a heap of rubble! What demonstrates these dialectics? Initially, Luxemburg praises the 'exact' proportional relationships of Marx's schema as the greatest scientific contribution to economic theory since Quesnay, regarding the schema as real in the strongest sense, namely, as objectively existing. Subsequently these 'exact' ratios prove illusory, they do not and – without a third department in the schema – cannot exist at all! The schema is incomplete and misleading because a two-part division would run counter to all 'material and value proportions' causing it to lose 'its validity'. Thus Luxemburg topples the schema from the pedestal of the ingenious 'scientific solution' of a problem into a scientific nothingness, declaring it incapable, in the form Marx gave it, of comprehensively portraying the capitalist mode of production in its '*essential points*'. In order to preserve Marx's schema, therefore, one has first to surrender it in its old form and then, to save the dilapidated building from collapse, add a third department. In the face of the heap of rubble that remains of Marx's schema, one asks in amazement of what, after all, does Marx's ingenious 'scientific solution' of the problem of reproduction consist? One is reminded of the poet's words: 'How beautiful the mare, sadly she is dead!'[18]

However scathingly the above criticism repudiates the foundations of Marx's schema, the fact that Luxemburg considers improving it and seeks to complete it by the adding a third department proves that she ascribes to the schema great significance in principal, as an instrument for the understanding economic phenomena: the schema is an *immediate theoretical reflection of reality*. Indeed, it may, in this respect, exhibit great, even fundamental flaws – and Luxemburg makes efforts to overcome these flaws by suggesting improvements. But she seems to have no doubts about the possibility, in principle, of an immediate congruence between a schematic formula for reproduction and empirical reality. Her suggestions, after all, are intended to bring Marx's schema into a greater degree of *conformity with reality* than Marx achieved!

Rosa Luxemburg is, however, not content with these results of her criticism of Marx's schema. Her utter failure to appreciate the scientific function the schema fulfils in Marx's analysis, her belief that the schema is and should be

17 Luxemburg 1913, p. 71.
18 [Grossman paraphrases lines from Chamisso 1842, pp. 194–5.]

an immediate reflection of reality, even when isolated from the other elements of Marx's method of successive approximation, soon had to convince her that the schema does not accord with experience and that there is a gaping contradiction between the schema and the real course of economic events. So she begins to doubt whether the schema is an appropriate means to understand reality at all. After initially crediting the schema with an 'objective social existence', she now turns to a diametrically opposite – third – view and claims that the schema (the 'paper schema', as she says, the empty mathematical formula) contrasts with, even contradicts real life. According to the *mathematical formula*, according to the schema reproduction proceeds smoothly. But '*how does the matter appear in reality*?'[19] She now speaks ironically of the 'astonishingly smooth results' of Marx's schema 'because we always simply did certain mathematical exercises in addition and subtraction ... because mathematical equations can easily be put down on paper'.[20]

Still RL hesitates to draw the *conclusion* and to repudiate the schema. The three assessments of the schema, described above, stand side by side in her book: a crass demonstration of her philosophical and methodological ineptitude.

But later, when she is cornered by her critics, especially by Otto Bauer and by his schema, which seems to demonstrate unlimited accumulation, she opts for the third view and accuses her critics of 'prejudice ... in favour of the schemas'.[21] The schemas, she now writes, are worthless as tools for understanding reality because the economic problem of accumulation 'does not have anything to do with mathematical formulae'.[22] The accolade for Marx's schema with its 'exact ratios' is forgotten. Now the schema's admirer turns into its sharpest opponent, *who denies it any scientific value*! This turn is certainly obscured by the fact that Luxemburg fought in the first line against the *harmonist conclusions* of the schematic analysis of the process of reproduction drawn by Tugan-Baranovsky, Hilferding, Eckstein, and Bauer. The way in which she conducts her anti-critique, however, demonstrates sufficiently that, in fact, she disputes not only the harmonist results of her critics' schematic presentation but the very *possibility of a schematic representation of reality*.

---

19 Luxemburg 1913, p. 76. [Grossman's emphasis.]

20 Luxemburg 1913, p. 92.

21 Luxemburg 1921, p. 6.

22 Luxemburg, 1972, p. 48. [This translation by Rudolf Wichmann of Luxemburg 1921 is unsatisfactory in places. Where that is the case, new, more accurate translations from the German original have been provided. Where Wichmann's translation has been used and his terminology diverges from Marx 1978b, his texts have been modified.]

She now speaks scornfully of the '*orthodox cult of formulae*'[23] and of schemas 'that can be continued forever on paper'.[24] Instead of soberly demonstrating the faults in the construction of Bauer's schema – and these are the only criticisms that she makes of the structure of Bauer's formulae as such – she is content to raise the objection that he added to the Latin letters c and v, 'that Marx used ... as abbreviations of constant and variable capital', some Greek letters: 'four tables, with wide, lengthy, round bracketed and four storeyed formulae'[25] which made his tables 'seem *even more intimidating* [!] than all the schemas in Marx's *Capital*'.[26] The question of whether capitalists can 'find a continually expanding market for expanded production, and *where* such a market is to be found ... *no arithmetical operations with fictitious numbers* on paper can answer, but *only* the analysis of the economic social *relations of production*.'[27] She ridicules 'the most amusing *qui pro quo*',[28] i.e. the mistaking of schemas for reality, 'The naive notion that mathematical formulae are the main point here' rather than the economic reality which is being investigated. Luxemburg finally comes to the conclusion 'that, on the question of accumulation, *mathematical schemas can prove absolutely nothing*, since their premise is untenable.'[29]

In this way Luxemburg introduces a cleavage between the scientific methods of presentation and the economic reality which is to be represented: reality is juxtaposed to paper formulas whereas, on the contrary, this formula – the schema – is merely meant to serve as a tool for the reproduction of reality in thought! The analysis of economic social relations is *counterposed* to the schema's arithmetic operations, even though, on the contrary, the schema is claimed to be an instrument for the analysis of social relations that has been called for!

By laughing at the 'orthodox cult of formulae' and speaking of Marx's 'intimidating' schema, RL lands on methodological territory in questionable proximity to Robert Liefmann and Robert Wilbrandt, whose utterances about Marx's reproduction schema may be mentioned here as curiosities, as documents characteristic of the level of bourgeois economics in its relationship with Marxism. 'It seems hard to believe', Liefmann writes, 'that such equations ... should

23 Luxemburg 1972, p. 65. [Grossman's emphasis.]
24 Luxemburg 1921, p. 58.
25 Luxemburg 1972, p. 67.
26 Luxemburg 1972, p. 66. [Grossman's emphasis.]
27 Luxemburg 1921, p. 32. [Grossman's emphasis.]
28 Luxemburg 1921, p. 32. ['*Qui pro quo*' means 'confusing this for that'.]
29 Luxemburg 1921, p. 30. [Grossman's emphasis.]

be discussed as economic theory on page after page and no one notices that they are *nonsense*.'[30] Wilbrandt, in turn, sees in the 'junk formulas', which Marx and Engels so valued, and in Marx's 'characteristic' but 'overestimated external forms of presentation' one of the reasons why '*vigorous practitioners* [!] entirely reject Marxism'.[31]

What would one think of a physicist who wanted to juxtapose the 'junk formulas' of theoretical physics with its 'fictitious numbers' (to use Luxemburg's words) to the 'relations in nature' which are being investigated? Would these 'junk formulas' perhaps lead 'vigorous practitioners' (to borrow Wilbrandt's pretty words) to reject the science of physics? Science in any case would not lose much.

Luxemburg, by the way, failed to see that in criticising the schema, she not only struck a blow against the neo-harmonists Hilferding, Tugan-Baranovsky and Otto Bauer, but also completely invalidated her own case.

If, then, only an analysis of living reality, but not arithmetic schemas with fictitious numbers, can shed light on the relations of production, if the schemas are of no value in this analysis, then it makes no difference whatsoever whether these fictitious schemas feature only two departments (as, for example, Marx suggested) or three – as Luxemburg proposes. It is impossible to see, then, how separating out the production of gold into a third, department (in addition to those for means of production and means of consumption) can provide 'a *comprehensive* schema of the whole capitalist process in its *essential points*[!]' Rosa Luxemburg has entangled herself in irresolvable contradictions.

2 Two-Part or Three-Part Division of the Schema?

While we have thus far shed light on Luxemburg's research *method*, her relationship with the reproduction schema, it is now time to investigate her own *achievement*. For the purpose of our investigation, let us assume Luxemburg's position in criticising Marx and examine the positive content of objections she raises against the two-part division. Is it true that subsuming gold production under department I of Marx's schema destroys all of its material and value proportions? That, therefore, a special third department for gold production must be separated out in the schema and that only in this way can we achieve a reproduction schema comprehensive in its essential points?

30 Liefmann 1923, p. 19. [Grossman's emphasis.]
31 Wilbrandt 1919, p. 97. [Grossman's emphasis.]

Has Luxemburg provided evidence for her serious objections? She says: 'Besides, a mere glance at the schema of reproduction itself shows what inconsistencies must result from confusing means of exchange with means of production.'[32]

The 'questionable results' of Marx's two-part division are portrayed as follows: 'with the money (5 v) received as wages from the capitalists, workers in department I g buy means of consumption from department II'.[33] As, however, having received these I g (5 v),[34] the capitalists of department II 'do not know how to use it, because it cannot be employed as constant capital, Marx allows this amount of money to be hoarded! But in order to *avoid a deficit* in the constant capital of II from occurring' Marx finds a way out by transferring the deficiency in II c to II s. Hence, according to Marx, '"The result is that a part of the surplus value is stored away as a money hoard."'[35]

Luxemburg then turns mockingly on Marx and says:

> The result is strange enough. To the extent that we have only considered the reproduction of the money material annually *worn out*, suddenly a *hoard* of money arises, that is an excess of money material. One does not know how this excess came about – *at the expense of the capitalists in the department producing means of consumption*, who have to mortify themselves, not in order to expand their own production of surplus value but so that there are enough means of subsistence for workers producing gold.
>
> The capitalists of department II, however, get poor reward for this Christian virtue ... As part of the product of I now consists of *money* which cannot be used as a means of production, so [the capitalists of department II], in spite of abstinence, cannot renew [their] *constant* capital on the old scale.[36]

---

32 Luxemburg 1951, p. 100.

33 Luxemburg 1913, p. 73.

34 ['g' is 'gold'. I g (5 v) is the gold equivalent of the value of variable capital used in department I. Luxemburg, following Marx, actually stated that 3 v (rather than the whole 5 v, as Grossman implied) became a money hoard. She wrote 'Now, however, Marx allows the capitalists of department II to buy gold "as a commodity material" worth 2, with the 5 in money from I g. He therefore leaps out of money production into the industrial production of gold, which has as little to do with the problem of money production as with the production of boot-polish. As, however, of the I g (5 v) there are 3 left over, which the capitalists in department II do not know how to use because it cannot be employed as constant capital, Marx allows them to hoard this amount!' Luxemburg 1913, pp. 73–4.]

35 Luxemburg 1913, p. 74 [quoting Marx 1978b, p. 548. Grossman's emphasis.]

36 Luxemburg 1913, pp. 74–5. [Grossman's emphasis.]

Luxemburg reaches the conclusion that:

> As our schema presupposes *simple* reproduction, its conditions are thus violated in two directions: surplus value is being *hoarded*, and constant capital shows a *deficit*. Marx's own results, then, prove that the production of gold *cannot possibly be accommodated in either of the two departments of his schema* without overturning the schema itself.[37]

This, then, is Luxemburg's revolutionary 'proof'. One does not read this kind of criticism of Marx, which comes close to treating him as a 'dead dog', without feeling pain because even leading spirits of socialist theory are accustomed to dismissing problems whose importance they acknowledge with a few, cheap, mocking phrases! Luxemburg herself senses, however, that this proof of the 'inconsistency' of Marx's schema is insufficient. A further proof is needed. She seeks and finds it soon enough: the well-known fact that one page is missing from Marx's manuscript on gold production so that 'the analysis of the exchange of newly produced gold within the *constant* capital of department I' (i.e. I c of gold production) which Marx announced was *not* carried out.[38] From this Luxemburg constructs a further basis for her own position and says that if the announced investigation was found, 'it would have [!] increased the insupportability [of Marx's schema] even further.'[39]

There is something repellent to scholars in Luxemburg's baroque way of thinking: rather than thirst for knowledge and understanding, this line of argument merely expresses the will to crush her opponent in the dispute. Hence the one-sided emphasis on points favouring her argument and silence about inconvenient ones. Hence calling not only witnesses who are present but also ones who are *absent*. They too are to testify for Luxemburg and against Marx! Instead of reconstructing the missing page on the basis of an analysis and thus delivering proof of the correctness of her thesis, she demands that we have faith in her assertion that the page would have confirmed her criticism. This scholastic mode of disputation explains why, at the end of her biting critique of the Marx's schema, she invokes no one else to support her case but – Marx himself! '*The point of view we advocate is confirmed by Marx himself* when he gives an exhaustive answer to the question, as striking as it is brief: "money in itself is not an element of real reproduction"'.[40] Since Marx appreciated that

37 Luxemburg 1913, pp. 74–5. [Grossman's emphasis.]
38 Marx 1978b, p. 548.
39 Luxemburg 1913, p. 75.
40 Luxemburg 1951, p. 103, quoting Marx 1978b, p. 566.

gold *per se* was not an element of real reproduction, he thereby conceded, according to Luxemburg, that his two-part schema was faulty and that the reproduction of gold should not to be incorporated in department I but should rather to be presented in a third department! She regards this as proof that Marx did not want to say what he actually said, which constitutes his title of scientific greatness, but rather *what* he did not say and, rather, contested! With this 'analysis' Luxemburg has scaled the peak of the art of sophistic interpretation. The conclusion she reaches is deduced from a single sentence of Marx's: she values two innocent words of his more than the whole of Marx's analysis of the process of reproduction of gold and commodities, and more than all the schema's 'exact ratios' and the 'absolute universal validity' of the two-part division. Despite Marx's line of argument for the correctness of the two-part division, finally he supposedly concedes that not he but Luxemburg is right!

Luxemburg's way of thinking reveals itself in yet another very important respect. One would not expect that she would end with the purely *negative* results of her criticism of Marx. *If* incorporating gold production into department I of the schema violates all its proportions, if only the introduction of a third department comprising gold production would result in a '*comprehensive* schema' of the capitalist reproduction process, then it is obvious that it would be worthwhile to take the effort to reconstruct such a comprehensive schema. *Paris vaut bien une messe*.[41]

These are Luxemburg's three departments:[42]

I	4,000 c +	1,000 v +	1,000 s =	6,000	means of production
II	2,000 c +	500 v +	500 s =	3,000	means of subsistence
III	20 c +	5 v +	5 s =	30	means of exchange

How do the turnovers proceed in such a 'comprehensive' schema? Here we encounter something surprising: Luxemburg's voluminous book of 450 pages affords plenty of room for long historical debates, which take up nearly a third of the volume. Yet, she found neither time nor space for the cardinal task she set herself, for the *demonstration of the organic interconnection* between gold production and the two other departments of production! In fact, there is *not*

41 ['Paris is worth a mass', comment about his acceptance of Catholicism in order to take the throne of France attributed to Henry IV.]

42 Luxemburg 1951, p. 100.

a single word of enlightenment on *how the exchange relations of a three-part schema would interact* and would be realised. This fact alone shows the unfruitfulness of Luxemburg's critique, it proves that her criticism is purely verbal and formal and is not sustained by any profound thought. She not only proved herself incapable of presenting any positive proof of the deficiency of Marx's schema but she never even tried to provide it! If she had, the mere attempt would have been enough to show her – and we will argue this in more detail below – that her three-part schema is fundamentally false.

In order to reduce the problem of gold production – as a subordinate problem in the general problem of capitalist reproduction – to its simplest and clearest expression, our analysis must focus exclusively on gold production for *monetary* use (Marx, too, makes this a premise of his analysis),[43] because the production of gold in its capacity as material commodity *for industrial use* in no way differs from the production of any other metals (which belongs in department I of the schema) and is, therefore, *not a problem*. Only the production of gold for use as money is problematic. Luxemburg only raised her critical objections against Marx in this regard. And this is also what we will have to investigate.

One thing should be 'conceded' from the start: incorporating gold production into department I does produce *difficulties*. If we assume that gold production of the scale 20 c + 5 v + 5 s = 30 is included in department I of the schema above, then at the end of the year there is 30 of the product of department I (means of production) *in the form of gold* and only 5,970 in the form of means of production. Meanwhile, since the consumed means of production of both department I (= 4,000 c) and department II (= 2,000 c) have to be replaced out of the annual product of department I, it clearly follows that a deficit in constant capital arises, i.e. 30 constant capital of both departments cannot be replaced since no means of production (machines, buildings, etc.) can be made out of gold, or as Marx says 'Money is not an element of real reproduction'. It was not Luxemburg who first discovered this difficulty; rather Marx himself pointed it out and announced its *solution*. Since, as Engels stated, this solution is not to be found in the manuscript, the real task of Marxists is to reconstruct the missing page of Marx's manuscript on this point. Luxemburg, by contrast, *denies* the possibility of solving the problem on the basis Marx announced, and prefers instead to annihilate that basis, i.e. the two-part reproduction schema!

But like all her other formulations of problems and solution, the 'solution' she presents in this case is also purely *extrinsic, mechanical*. If it appears to

---

43 Marx 1978b, p. 400.

her that commodities cannot be sold within capitalism, she simply amends the capitalist world by adding, from outside, non-capitalist territories and thus 'solves' the problem. Her approach to our problem is similar. If difficulties regarding gold production arise on the basis of a two-part schema for the problem of reproduction, instead of attempting a solution, a third department for gold production is simply added and the difficulty is thus 'dealt with'.

Can, however, the difficulty mentioned above be resolved by merely mechanically and formally allocating gold production to a third department? Will the above-mentioned *deficit of constant capital* disappear because of a change in the technical mode of presentation? Why? In what way? RL does not spare us so much as a syllable on these questions.

For Marx's problem of the reproduction process, the formal dispute over whether the schema has two or three parts is quite irrelevant. The point is not to invent classifications but to achieve conceptual clarity about the *essence of the problem*. Once the differing functions of gold in its capacity as a commodity and as money (means of exchange) are understood, it is easy to master the problem in either a two-part or a three-part schema. The problem itself, the 'difficulty', is much greater than Luxemburg believes and must be resolved by taking as a starting point the *character of money as a means of exchange*, and not a two-part or three-part mode of presentation.

3 Gold as Commodity and as Means of Exchange

Before we approach the presentation of gold production, let us first examine the preliminary question: what relative amounts of gold does the problem of the reproduction of the money material involve? The answer follows from Marx's law of circulation:[44] at a *given* velocity of circulation, the amount of money necessary for circulation is determined by the *mass of commodities* and the *commodity prices* to be realised, minus the mutually balancing payments and those postponed (credited) to a later period. Moreover, the mass of money must suffice to cover the *fluctuations* in circulation which result in part from fluctuations in the average velocity of circulation, and in part from the differing and varying proportions in which money functions in cash or credit transactions.[45]

---

44 Marx 1987a, pp. 341–2.
45 Marx 1978b, p. 400.

In Marx's schema of simple reproduction, shown above, the annual product of both departments to be sold amounts to 9,000 value units. If these were to be sold all at once (e.g. abroad), the foreign buyer would need to have money capital of 9,000. With ten turnovers, the necessary amount of money would be reduced to 900.

For the purpose of our analysis, let us assume that four turnovers take place a year in the schema so that, for the *sale of commodities*, a *mass of money* of 2,250 suffices. However, a *reserve fund* is necessary to deal with fluctuations in the circulation of money, already mentioned. If we assume this to amount to a ninth of the total amount of circulating currency (this is an arbitrary choice), then the total amount of money needed is 2,500. For the sake of simplicity, let us further assume that the annual loss of money due to abrasion is 1 percent = 25 (the actual rate of abrasion is considerably lower). So gold production only has to *replace* this annual loss of 25 – on the assumption of simple reproduction, where the *same* quantity of annual production is circulated using the *same* mass of money every year.[46]

From the standpoint of gold production the question now arises as to which amount of gold belongs in the reproduction schema: 2,500 g or 25 g? Does the whole existing mass of money, gradually accumulated over the course of centuries or only the amount of gold newly produced in the last year to replace money that has worn out belong in the schema?

Luxemburg speaks generally of 'money' or 'means of exchange' that belongs in a third department of the schema.[47] This proves that she was not clear about the fundamental purposes and functions of Marx's reproduction schema. Since Luxemburg raises the objection that Marx's schema deals with gold production only as metal production (in department I) and fails to account for the specific function of gold as *means of exchange*, she should logically have included in the schema not only the newly produced mass of gold (25 g) but *all* of the money amassed over the course of centuries (2,500 g) *because, precisely this entire mass of money functions as means of exchange*. From her own standpoint, the reproduction schema should logically appear as follows (fractions in department III have been omitted):

I	4,000 c +	1,000 v +	1,000 s =	6,000 means of production
II	2,000 c +	500 v +	500 s =	3,000 means of consumption
III	1,668 c +	416 v +	416 s =	2,500 money

46 Marx 1978b, pp. 400, 410.

47 Luxemburg 1951, p. 100.

Luxemburg recoils from this conclusion, and contrary to her own demand, includes in department III only the *newly* produced gold:

III 20 c + 5 v + 5 s = 30

Hence gold not *as a means of circulation* but gold as a *commodity*, as a component of the newly produced annual product seeking an outlet. And rightly so. For the purpose of Marx's schema is, like Quesnay's *Tableau économique*, to provide a picture of the *annual product* and its *sale*.[48] Only the *newly* produced gold (25g) is a *commodity* that seeks to be sold. In this respect it does *not* differ from the other commodities produced annually.[49] Things are different, however, when it comes to money as *means of circulation*. This mass of money, which has been piled up over the course of centuries, is not the product of the last year; it does not function *as a commodity* and is therefore *not sold*. It only *mediates* the sale of newly produced commodities and *therefore does not belong* in the schema.[50] *Hence, Marx did not incorporate 'money resources' in his schema at all*, neither in department I nor department II. And, as we will soon see, Marx could not and should not have represented them as *components* in the schema.[51] Money resources are needed but are not consumed; consequently, they are not *reproduced* but only *piled up*. The only gold encompassed in Marx's reproduction schema is therefore the quantity of gold (indeed in department I) necessary to *replace worn out* (abraded) money resources.

48 Marx 1976b, pp. 737–8; Marx 1978b, pp. 435, 468.

49 'As far as obtaining the money material (gold and silver) from its source of production is concerned, this is reducible to direct commodity exchange, exchange of gold or silver *as a commodity* against other commodities, and is thus just as much *an aspect of commodity exchange* as obtaining iron or other metals', Marx 1981b, p. 436; cf. Marx 1978b, p. 546.

50 Marx 1978b, p. 412.

51 Money, by the way, even to the extent that it functions as means of circulation cannot be allocated to a third sphere of equal rank, *alongside* the other two spheres of production. This is because the circulation of money is not a *special*, independent sphere, it is rather a *function* also exercised *within* the said two spheres. The capitalists of both these spheres must have a certain money capital, aside from their productive capital.

I	4,000 c + 1,000 v = 5,000	in productive capital and	1,668 in money
II	2,000 c + 500 v = 2,500	in productive capital and	832 in money

Marx does not include the existing money capital of 2500 in his schema because the means of circulation *mediate* the turnovers of commodities not only between I and II but also *within* them, i.e. they circulate 'in the two spheres of the reproduction process.' Marx 1981b, pp. 575, 578. [Grossman's emphasis.]

If Luxemburg now introduces only the *newly* produced gold (25 g) into the schema, she deals with gold only as a commodity and not *as means of circulation* (2,500 g). Once she does that, however, *the only economic reason she gives* for allocating gold to a *special*, third department of the schema is no longer valid. For gold as a commodity does not need to be separated out from the other commodities in the schema and belongs in department I with the production of other metals.

4 Impossibility of Exact Quantitative Determination of the Proportions between Money Resources and the Other Two Departments of the Reproduction Schema

Let us now prove that Rosa Luxemburg's demand that money resources be separated out into a third department contradicts the logical premises that form the foundations of the schema. As we know, the scientific purpose of the schema is to illuminate the quantitative and qualitative proportions between the individual elements *of the annual product*, proportions which are preconditions if reproduction is to proceed undisturbed. Now, it is clear that such quantitative proportions are only to be found between the c, v, and s elements of the *annual product of the last production cycle* of both departments I and II and, consequently, also in relation to the *newly* produced gold *as a part of this annual product*. Such proportions do not exist and are impossible between the elements of the schema on the one hand and the total amount of *money resources* necessary for circulation on the other. After all, Marx's law of circulation means that '[it in no way follows …] that the *scale of production*, even on the capitalist basis, has its absolute limits *determined by the volume of money capital in operation*',[52] i.e. that the apparatus of production on a *given* scale can be set in motion by a *larger* or *smaller* amount of money depending on the velocity of circulation or the organisation of the settlement of accounts.[53] We have seen that the annual product of our schema, which has a value of 9,000, can be disposed of with 9,000, 2,500, or 900 in circulating money, depending on the number of transactions. In other words: the mass of money resources required for circulation – although *calculable* on the basis

52 Marx 1978b, p. 431. [Grossman's emphasis. Marx emphasised 'absolute'. For reasons of style and to conform to the standard English translation, Marx's words in brackets have been included rather than Grossman's paraphrase.]

53 Marx 1978b, pp. 400, 418, 433; cf. Sismondi 1992, pp. 349–51.

of the particular scale of production, velocity of turnover etc. – in its *absolute size* stands in *no fixed proportion with the total volume of the annual product.* It is *variable,* and this is precisely why Marx did not incorporate and should not have incorporated money resources in his reproduction schema with its exact quantitative relations, if he wanted to avoid violating the *logical foundations* of the schema, those exact proportions.

5 Money Circulation as *Faux Frais*[54] of Commodity Production

In addition to a society's *productive capital,* part of the total social capital always has to function as *money capital.* This mass of money naturally depends on the scale of production and the velocity of money which in turn is conditioned by the length of the turnover period, i.e. the ratio between the period during which labour is done and the actual circulation period. 'But whatever this ratio may be, the portion of the capital value in process that can function at any one time as *productive* capital is always restricted by the part of the capital value advanced that must always exist alongside the productive capital in the *money form.*'[55] In our schema, for example, total social capital is 10,000. The part that exists as money, 2,500g, *restricts* the *productive,* i.e. the total surplus value producing, capital to 7,500, namely 4,000 c + 1,000 v in department I, and 2,000 c + 500 v in department II.

What has been said here about the total amount of circulating money also applies to the gold *newly produced* each year and to the mass of gold that replaces money that has been abraded: *gold production means a restriction of the scale of commodity production.* If gold production is 25g, then productive capital has to be further *reduced* from 7,500 to 7,475, i.e. a capital of 25 must be transferred from productive industry to gold production for the *unproductive purposes of circulation.* If the extent of gold production was 200, then that of commodity production would have to decrease from 7,500 to 7,300. Or, as Marx put it, 'A part of the social *labour power* and a part of the social *means of production* must therefore be spent each year in the production of gold and silver.'[56]

54 [*'Faux frais'* means 'incidental costs'.]
55 Marx 1978b, p. 430. [Grossman's emphasis.]
56 Marx 1978b, p. 410. [Grossman's emphasis.]

The application of a part of productive capital to gold production occurs in reality – since not all countries have gold mines of their own – through the direct and indirect *exchange* of a part of a country's annual product, e.g. German chemicals, coal, etc., for the product of gold producing countries. The international character of this transaction disguises its simple core. So as not to complicate the problem and to reduce it to its most transparent expression, let us assume with Marx *that gold production takes place in each country* and constitutes a part of the social production of each country.[57] Such an assumption does not in any way modify the real conditions of reproduction, as Marx explicitly states, it expresses, rather, the actual situation.

In fact, it can be asserted *that each country acquires its own gold reserve* – if not in a technical, then in an economic sense – *through its own gold production.* As it has to employ an *additional* part of its means of production and labour power in the production of chemicals, machines, coal, etc. above the overall need for such goods – be it for the domestic market or for export – for the sole purpose of acquiring or enlarging, through this *additional* export-oriented commodity production, an equivalent supply of gold.

The above assumption of *domestic* gold production in all countries which use gold currency allows us to immediately grasp the characteristics of this production. It has already been emphasised that the schema relates to gold not in its capacity as money but merely as commodity. But newly produced gold differs fundamentally from the other commodities produced annually. In the course of the production of any other commodity (coal, machines, etc.) the capitalist entrepreneur – by casting his annual product onto the market at the end of the production period – *increases* the *mass of commodities* circulating at the beginning of the [next] production period by the volume of the newly produced surplus value and at the same time *withdraws* from circulation an equivalent *amount of money.* The opposite is true in gold production. Here the *entire annual product* (and not just the surplus value part but also c and v parts) exists in the form of gold and at the end of the year all of these components are cast into circulation in order to withdraw *commodities* in exchange for the entire annual production of gold.[58] Gold production, like hoarding generally – although it is a necessary and constitutive element in the mechanism of capitalism – signifies the *loss* of a part of the society's available productive elements, a '*reduction* in the scale of social production'.[59] *This is precisely why*

57 Marx 1978b, p. 400.

58 Marx 1978b, pp. 402, 410, 553.

59 Marx 1978b, p. 433. [Grossman's emphasis.]

Marx counts *money* among society's unproductive costs of circulation, 'They are *faux frais* of commodity production ... This is a part of the social wealth which has to be *sacrificed* to the circulation process.'[60] 'It *withdraws* from social use a corresponding sum of possible additional means of production and consumption, i.e. of real wealth.'[61] This explains the capitalists' efforts to reduce – if not absolutely, then at least in relation to the volume of transactions – the mass of money necessary for circulation, i.e. this dead fund, by increasing the efficiency of the existing mass of money.

6 The Source of the Mistakes in Luxemburg's Schema: Addition Instead of Subtraction

Luxemburg is also not unaware of the fact that gold production *restricts* the volume of total social production.[62] She copies this principle, however, mechanically from Marx without drawing the slightest conclusion from it when it comes to its practical application in the schema. With regard to our schema, the expenditure of

$$20\,c + 5\,v + 5\,s = 30\,g$$

in *gold* production would mean truncating the extent of social *commodity* production. Consequently (as soon as gold production is separately accounted for in a separate department) this production or rather Marx's schema illustrating it,

$$6{,}000\,c + 1{,}500\,v + 1{,}500\,s = 9{,}000$$

would have to be reduced to

$$5{,}980\,c + 1{,}495\,v + 1{,}495\,s = 8{,}970$$

that is, by the value of the productive forces expended in gold production. If, as we assumed 1 percent = 25 g of the existing means of exchange of 2,500 are worn out annually, then every year society has to withdraw an equal portion of

60 Marx 1978b, p. 214. [Grossman's emphasis.]
61 Marx 1978b, p. 420. [Grossman's emphasis.]
62 Luxemburg 1951, p. 101.

productive capital from commodity production and apply it to the production of gold to make up for this loss.

By contrast, Luxemburg leaves the initial volume of social *commodity* production unchanged and – despite the separation out of gold production – *adds* gold production to commodity production:

$$\begin{array}{rrrr}
6000\,c + & 1500\,v + & 1500\,s = & 9000 \\
20\,c + & 5\,v + & 5\,s = & 30 \\
\hline
6020\,c + & 1505\,v + & 150\,s = & 9030
\end{array}$$

In this way total social production is not actually *restricted* but is *expanded* by the contribution of gold production!

On the basis of Marx's assumption that the social scale of production is *given* and that the total annual product is 9,000, gold production can commence – as long as we assume simple reproduction – only by *withdrawing* a portion of labour and means of production from the production of other *commodities*, e.g. coal mines, and transferring it to *gold* production. This does not and cannot violate the proportional relations of the schema since the total volume of social productive forces remains *the same* and only its *distribution* among the individual branches of production has changed: less coal is produced but more gold in its stead.

In Luxemburg's schema, in contrast, *the growth in social productive forces within the parameters of simple reproduction* is an unsolved mystery, a creation *ex nihilo*,[63] labour power and the means of production apparently fall from the sky!

It is clear that the schema's proportions are disturbed precisely through the addition of a third row. The 'inconsistencies' of the schema do not stem from its two-part division, which Luxemburg criticises. On the contrary, it is only Luxemburg's procedure, which we have described here, adding where she should have subtracted, that is the source of all her errors and contradictions in dealing with gold production.

63 ['*Ex nihilo*' means 'from nothing'.]

7 Gold Production in the Transition to Socialism

Luxemburg presents another 'weighty reason' for separating out gold production into a separate, third department, which we will now assess. Gold production for the purpose of circulation, whose character as a 'false cost' results only from the anarchic economy of capitalism, 'finds its most exact expression as a separate department'.[64] Since gold production for monetary purposes will be discontinued in the transition to a planned socialist economy, Marx's schema of simple reproduction will remain valid for a socialist economy if we simply delete the third department!

This reasoning is another striking example of Luxemburg's mechanical 'solutions' that were discussed earlier. The schema of capitalist production requires *three* departments, the third department (gold production) giving expression to the *specifically capitalist* aspect of reproduction. After the transition to socialism, it apparently suffices to decree the deletion of department III in order to make the old schema, which now only has two departments left, applicable to the new, socialist economic order. The 'weighty reason' for separating gold production out lies then … in the comfort of not needing to devise a new schema for socialist reproduction!

Can such mechanical-formal reasons for a specific mode of presentation be taken seriously? Obviously, Luxemburg proposes nothing concrete in terms of the 'discontinuation of gold production', because this discontinuation elicits no *visible effects* in the world of real phenomena. In reality, the discontinuation of production would have to *free up means of production and labour power*, which would find other employment. If the transition from the fiction of a moneyless economy to gold production means *reducing* the scale of commodity production from 7,500 to 7,475, then, conversely, the discontinuation of gold production would lead to an *extension* of in the production of goods in two ways. First, the liberated productive forces formerly bound up in gold production would now be deployed in the production of goods[65] and would raise its volume from 7,475 to 7,500. Secondly, the complete discontinuation of the circulation of money would deprive the money capital of 2,500, accumulated over long periods, of its function – unless it was needed as *world money* for international transactions.[66] Through its transformation into elements of production by way of exchange with other, capitalist countries the scale of production of

64 Luxemburg 1913, p. 75.
65 Marx 1978b, p. 433.
66 Marx 1978b, pp. 390, 433.

goods could be expanded from 7,500 to 10,000. While, then, in reality the discontinuation of the circulation of money would have to *entail the expansion and planned reorganisation of the entirety of commodity production*, according to Luxemburg, the scope of commodity production remains *unchanged* in both the cases mentioned, of the transition to gold production and its discontinuation under socialism.

8 Accumulation of Money Despite Simple Reproduction

There is an almost paradoxical ring to Marx's claim that a gradual *accumulation of gold* takes place despite the fact that we assume only *simple* reproduction in the production of both *commodities* and *gold*, i.e. although it is presupposed *that the scope of gold production* remains *unchanged* from year to year. It is exactly these results of Marx's analysis that Luxemburg has attacked. Still, we want to show not only that such accumulation does take place in the schema but also that it must, necessarily, take place under the given assumptions.

The loss of money by both departments of commodity production is 25g: 16 ⅔ in department I and 8 ⅓ in department II. Given the fundamental assumptions of Marx's schema, that commodities are sold and bought *at their value*, capitalists in commodity production have to exchange an *equivalent amount* of means of production[67] with the entrepreneurs in gold production to purchase the 25g of money that has been missing.

The capital invested in gold production as 20 c + 5 v yields – since the *surplus value* of gold production is added – an annual product of 30g so that 5g of gold piles up over and above the replacement of 25g worn out. This happens despite the assumption of simple reproduction, i.e. despite the assumption that surplus value is consumed. There is nothing surprising about this result, however 'strange' it may appear to Luxemburg. She has obviously forgotten that from the viewpoint of society and despite all the assumptions of simple reproduction, the surplus value from gold production *cannot be consumed* and therefore must necessarily pile up. The gold producers may 'consume' their surplus value. Since this is not possible in kind, they have to exchange it for means of consumption from department II. This, however, increases the money supply of the *commodity* producers from 2,500 to 2,505. Luxemburg believed she had to object that

67 [Logically, 'means of production' here should be 'commodities' or 'means of production and means of consumption'.]

Marx deviated from his own assumption of simple reproduction. She failed to grasp that the genius of Marx's achievement is apparent precisely here. With a rare insight, he recognised that this assumption is *historically impossible to uphold*. Even if we speak of simple reproduction – as a intellectually permissible approximation – in gold production in the ancient world and during the middle ages because of the lack of large fixed capitals and *relatively static technology* even over long periods of time, still over the course of centuries the *amount of gold* would have to *build up*, forming one of the *preconditions* for the capitalist mode of production:

> *It is clear … that even simple reproduction*, which excludes accumulation in the strict sense of the term, i.e. reproduction on an expanded scale, necessarily involves the *storage of money*, or hoard formation. And since this is repeated anew each year, it explains the assumption from which we proceeded in considering capitalist production, namely that at the beginning of the reproduction process, the capitalists in departments I and II must each already possess a quantity of the monetary medium which corresponds to the amount of commodity exchange. There is even storage of this kind after deduction of the gold lost by the abrasion of the money in circulation.[68]

9 The Organic Interconnection between Gold Production and the Two Departments of Commodity Production

Once we are clear about the categories and interrelations discussed above, identifying the relation between gold production and commodity production is no longer difficult. And it does not matter in this regard whether we formally allocate gold production to a third department, separate from commodity production, or not. This becomes a question of *technical presentation*. What matters are the *real conditions* under which the separation takes place, i.e. the modifications in the volume of commodity production in departments I and II due to gold production.

For the sake of clarity, we will first examine gold production separately. Once its interrelations with commodity production are understood, our analysis will

68 Marx 1978b, pp. 548–9.

not be changed in the least by the subsequent presentation of gold production as a component of department I of our schema.

The starting point for our account is the familiar schema at the point when the turnover of commodities has been completed and the initial money capital of 2,500 has been worn down to 2,475. This loss is shared by the two departments in proportion to the respective sizes of their capitals and amounts to 16 ⅔ in department I, and 8 ⅓ in department II. This gives us:

I	4,000 c +	1,000 v +	1,000 s =	6,000 (in commodities) and	1,650 (in money)
II	2,000 c +	500 v +	500 s =	3,000 (in commodities) and	825 (in money)
					2,475

Since, according to our assumptions, a mass of money of 2,475 is insufficient for circulation, the commodity producers are forced to replace the missing 25 g through gold production. Both departments of commodity production make *money advances* to the gold producers of 16 ⅔ g, by department I, and 8 ⅓, by department II, so that the commodity producers' money capital is temporarily reduced by another 25 g to 2,450.

As the gold producers purchase, with these 25 g, means of production and means of consumption from the commodity producers, these 25 g immediately flow back to them, restoring their money reserve to 2,475. This reflux, however, is distributed *in a different proportion* to the earlier advances. Since the organic composition of capital in gold production is, by our assumptions, the same as the average ratio between c and v in department I (according to our example 4 to 1), of the 25 g they received the gold producers must spend 20 c on the purchase of means of production from the commodity producers of department I and 5 v on the purchase of means of consumption from department II. These commodity producers can *only* satisfy the requirements of the gold producers for means of production and consumption *from their surplus value*, if they are not to encroach on the volume of their own production. Their surplus value is thus reduced through the gold producers' purchases to 980 s in department I, and to 495 in department II. Through these sales department I has received 20 g *in money* back while it initially only advanced 16 ⅔ to the gold producers. It thus receives 3 ⅓ g *too much*. Things are the other way around in department II. It initially advanced 8 ⅓ g *in money*, but it receives only 5 g in return, 3 ⅓ g *too little*.

As a result, the capitalists of department I, who have amassed 3 ⅓ too much surplus value as money, must *consume* these 3 ⅓ g, since we assume *simple* reproduction. To this end they buy means of consumption from department

II, thus channelling the excess 3 ⅓g back to the capitalists of department II. The latter use this income to cover their money deficit of 3 ⅓g; in the same act, they yield out of their surplus value an equivalent amount of commodities (means of consumption) to the capitalists of department I, thus decreasing their own surplus value to 491 ⅔.

These turnovers which are meant to *lay the basis* for gold production have modified the schema in the following way:

A. Commodity production
I 4,000 c + 1,000 v + 980 s (means of production) + 3 ⅓ s (means of consumption) + 1,650 money
II 2,000 c + 500 v + 491 ⅔ s (means of consumption) + 825 money
B. Gold production
20 c + 5 v (in commodity form)

The schema shows us that the capitalists in commodity production have arranged for the replacement of the worn out gold. To this end, they have given means of production and means of consumption from departments I and II to the capitalists in gold production, in proportion to the size of their respective capitals. We see, however, that these transactions have *disrupted the proportional relations of the schema of commodity production*. For a complete exchange between I (v + s) = 1,980 and II c = 2,000 is now no longer possible. Does this not tend to confirm Luxemburg's objections?

If Luxemburg believes identification of the *deficit* of *constant capital* in *commodity* production contradicts Marx's assumption of simple reproduction, she only proves that, for her, the concept of simple reproduction has actually become contentless, 'stupid formulas'. None of the premises of simple reproduction can make the *deficit* in constant capital in *commodity* production disappear, so long as we assume *that this constant capital is transferred to the gold producers*! One cannot become two. The deficit of constant capital in *commodity* production is a logical and necessary consequence of its investment in gold production.

What interests us here and what is important for an understanding of reproduction are the consequences of this deficit. The reduction in I (v + s) = 2,000 to 1,980 must – since and as long as we maintain the assumption of simple reproduction – necessarily entail a corresponding *reduction* in II c – likewise from 2,000 c to 1,980 c – because a complete exchange could otherwise not take place. Correspondingly, the 500 v in department II must be reduced to 495 v. Altogether, the volume of reproduction in department II must be reduced by 25, i.e. means of consumption to a value of 25 must be

consumed by the capitalists of department II, because no other buyers are available. Of course! The next and *one-off* consequence of the commencement of gold production – which is only made possible by a withdrawal of constant capital from I s – is an increase in the consumption of means of consumption in department II. By the same token, a *lasting consequence* – in accordance with the earlier presentation under heading 5 – is a *restriction* of the scope of production in department II from 2,000 c + 500 v to 1,980 c + 495 v.

After the completion of these adjustments, during a transition period, the process of production can proceed without disturbance. We have:

A.	Commodity production					
I	4000 c +	1000 v +	1000 s =	6000 +	1650	(in money)
II	1980 c +	495 v +	495 s =	2970 +	825	(in money)
				8970	2475	(in money)
B.	Gold production					
	20 c +	5 v +	5 s =	30 +	30	
				9000	2505	(in money)

Afterwards, as before, the aggregate volume of production is 9,000. The assumption of simple reproduction has not been violated. But *as a consequence of* the commencement of *gold* production the volume of *commodity* production has been *reduced* to 8,970.

At the same time, we see that gold production is only apparently undertaken at the expense of the capitalists in department II. The restriction of the volume of production in department II was only a *one-off* effect of the transition to gold production. *In the long run*, however, the worn out money is not replaced at the expense of only *one* of the two departments in the schema, as Luxemburg asserts. Rather, the capitalists of both departments in the schema share the expenses of making up for the abrasion of money *equally*, i.e. in proportion to the size of their capitals. Thus the capitalists of department I annually cede 20s means of production out of their surplus value of 1,000 s, and the capitalists of department II cede 10 s out of their 495 s for the purpose of gold production, without disrupting 'material and value proportions', i.e. *equilibrium.*

Finally, the *hoarding of money* appears as a necessary consequence of gold production even under the assumptions of simple reproduction. Instead of the actual abrasion of [their] money by 16⅔, the capitalists of department I have got back 20g, i.e. 20/6 [= 3⅓] *more* money. The capitalists of department II have received 10 g instead of their consumption of 8⅓ g, i.e. 10/6 [= 1⅔] more money. In this way, society's total money supply has been increased from 2,475 to 2,505.[69]

---

69 Nothing in the results of our analysis will change if, having initially described gold production separately, we now represent it as a component of department I. We then obtain the following schema:

I	4,020 c +	1,005 v +	1,005 s =	6,030	money reserve 1,650 g
II	1,980 c +	495 v +	495 s =	2,970	money reserve 825 g
	6,000 c +	1,500 v +	1,500 s =	9,000	money reserve 2,475 g

First, it is important to establish that the whole annual product of 6030 of department I does not consist of *means of production*: of these only 6000 available; the remaining 30 consists of *gold* and is therefore not suited to replace c in either department I or II. Hence, we have to partition department I into two sub-departments, one for gold production and one for actual commodity production. The schema then takes the following form:

I {	20 c +	5 v +	5 s =	30	(in the form of gold)
	4,000 c +	1,000 v +	1,000 s =	6,000	(in means of production)
II	1,980 c +	495 v +	495 s =	2,970	(in means of subsistence)

The turnovers in this schema can now be briefly explained. The II v = 495 consume their own means of subsistence. The II c = 1,980 (means of consumption) need to be exchanged for means of production I (v + s), namely for I v = 1000, consisting of means of production (the remainder, of I v = 5 consists of gold) and I s = 980 which also takes the form of means of production. In I s there remains 20s (means of production) and 5 s (gold). As, according to our assumption, I v = 5 (gold) and I s = 5 (gold) are, in the first instance, *consumed*, i.e. exchanged for means of subsistence, these means of subsistence have to come from II s = 495, because in neither II c nor II v are there freely available quantities of means of subsistence. Hence the surplus value to be consumed by the capitalists of department II sinks to 485, but in exchange 10s in the form of gold remains in their hands. The outcome is that the 15 v + 5 s of gold production are *not exchanged for II c*, as would normally be the case in the schema of commodity production. We see, rather, that the means of subsistence for the workers and the capitalists who undertake gold production have to be taken *from the surplus value of department II of commodity production*.

But how is the I c = 4,020 replaced? According to the schema of simple reproduction, the value of the I c that is consumed is transferred to the annual product, and the I c which is consumed can normally be renewed *in kind from the annual product* of its own department. In our schema, which incorporates gold production, the I = 4,020 cannot, however, be fully replaced from the c component of the annual product since, as we know, only I 4,000 c takes the form of means of production, while the remaining I 20 c takes the *form of gold*. Hence there is no way of replacing the 20 c means of production involved in gold production. Consequently, the capitalists [involved in department I gold production] buy the necessary means of production, I c, for gold production with 20 c in the form of gold, in return for I s from capitalists of department I *commodity* production, in whose hands

So the outcome of our analysis confirms that the account of the reproduction of money as presented by Marx in the second volume of *Capital*[70] is completely valid and that Luxemburg's criticism of it has proved to be completely mistaken.

---

as we know, there is still an unsold remainder of their surplus value, 20 s. In this way, the constant capital of department I, in both production of commodities and production of gold, is fully replaced. But, at the same time, the capitalists of department I (commodity production) retain 20 s, in the form of gold, the value equivalent of the means of production they exchanged with the gold producers. Here too, with regard to the renewal of I c of gold production, we see a *difference* from the normal schema of commodity production. The I c of gold production is not replaced out of the corresponding c component of the annual product of its own [sub-]department, but *out of the surplus value of commodity production in department I*.

The result of the turnovers is that there remains in the hands of the capitalists of department I (commodity production) surplus value of 20 in the form of gold, in the hands of the capitalists of department II surplus value of 10 in the form of gold, so that the existing amount of money increases from 2,475 g to 2,505 g. We have, finally, here reconstructed the account of the *specific movements* in the replacement of both constant capital in gold production, I c, and its I (v + s) component, that Marx announced but which is missing from his manuscript. We have therefore fulfilled the task we set ourselves.

70 Marx 1978b, p. 545.

CHAPTER 12

The Value-Price Transformation in Marx and the Problem of Crisis*

Translated from German by David Meienreis

1 Concrete Reality as the Object and Goal of Marx's Research

The task of all science is the exploration and understanding of the concretely given totality of phenomena, of their interconnections and their mutations. The difficulty of this task is that phenomena are not immediately identical with the essence of things. The exploration of the essence constitutes a precondition for understanding the world of appearances. Marx, in opposition to vulgar economics, seeks to identify the 'hidden essence' and the 'inner connection' of economic reality;[1] this is not to say that he is not interested in concrete appearances. On the contrary! Only appearances present themselves to consciousness, which means that – purely methodologically – their hidden, essential 'core' can only be accessed through the analysis of appearances.[2]

But the concrete appearances are important to Marx not only because they are the starting point and the medium for understanding the 'real movement'. They are, rather, the very objects that Marx ultimately wants to identify and understand in their interconnection. By no means does he simply want to restrict himself to the exploration of the 'essence' while ignoring the phenomena. In fact, the essence, once identified, has the function of enabling us to comprehend concrete appearances. This is why Marx strives to find 'the law which governs these phenomena', i.e. 'the law of their variation'.[3]

Only phenomena *in themselves* and without the context of the 'hidden essence of things' are, according to Marx, incomprehensible and '*prima facie* vulgar'. But it would be a disastrous mistake – falling into the opposite error of vulgar economics – if economic science contented itself with the 'hidden essence' of the things that has been discovered, without finding the *way back to concrete appearances* with whose explanation we are, after all, concerned, that is, without reconstructing the *many mediations* between the essence and

* [Originally published as Grossmann 1932b.]

1 Marx 1981b, p. 956.

2 Marx 1981b, p. 311.

3 From a Russian review quoted by Marx 1976b, p. 100.

the form of appearance! Marx therefore regards this path from the abstract to the concrete as 'obviously the correct scientific method'. Here 'abstract determinations' lead, '*by way of thinking to the reproduction of the concrete*' because 'the method of advancing from the abstract to the concrete is simply the way in which thinking *assimilates the concrete* and reproduces it *as a mental concrete*'.[4]

By using a concrete example, Marx shows that it is not enough to reduce the values created in industrial production to the general law, i.e. to state 'that commodity values are determined by the labour time they contain'. This is because empirical processes in the sphere of circulation, e.g. the influence of commercial capital on the commodity prices, which are visible in practice, show 'phenomena which, in the absence of a very far-reaching analysis of the intermediary stages of the process, seem to presuppose a purely arbitrary determination of prices' so it appears that 'the circulation process as such determines the prices of commodities, and that this is within certain limits independent of the process of production', that is, of labour time. Therefore, in order to demonstrate the illusion of this appearance and to establish the 'inner connection' between the phenomenon and the 'actual process' – which is 'a very intricate thing and a work of great detail' – 'it is one of the tasks of science to reduce the visible and merely apparent movement to the actual inner movement',[5] 'just as the apparent motions of the heavenly bodies are intelligible only to someone who is acquainted with their real motions, which are not perceptible to the senses.'[6]

The decisively important 'task of science' is thus to find the 'mediations', the 'intermediary stages', which lead from the essence to the concrete phenomenon. Without these intermediaries the theory, i.e. the 'essence' of things, would be in contradiction with concrete reality. Marx rightly scorns those 'theorists' who lose themselves in unrealistic constructs. Only '[t]he *vulgus* has therefore concluded that theoretical truths are abstractions which are at variance with reality.'[7]

The structure of Marx's *Capital* and the method of successive approximation he applies there, as I have shown,[8] also conform to Marx's basic methodological idea, which finds its most concise expression in the construction of his reproduction schema. Applying numerous simplifying assumptions, the

4 Marx 1986b, p. 38. [Grossman's emphasis.]
5 Marx 1981b, p. 428.
6 Marx 1976b, p. 433.
7 Marx 1989c, p. 72. ['*Vulgus*' means 'vulgar', 'economists' is understood.]
8 Grossmann 1992, pp. 29–31; Grossman 1929b, see above p. 202.

'journey' from the concrete towards the abstract is undertaken there. The given world of appearances, the concrete partial forms in which surplus value appears in the sphere of circulation (profit of enterprise, interest, commercial profit, etc.) are ignored and the entire analysis of volumes 1 and 2 of *Capital* focuses on *aggregate* value and surplus value, on their creation and their changes in size, in the processes of production and circulation. The 'mere semblance belonging only to the process of circulation' is thus excluded.[9] While the purpose of the analysis in volumes 1 and 2 of *Capital* was to research the *creation of* surplus value as the essence of the total economic process, the following task – and, as Marx expressly emphasises, this constitutes the purpose and the content of the third volume – was to construct the 'inner connection' between the 'essence', which had been discovered, and the form of its appearance, the empirically given forms of surplus value. That is, '[o]ur concern is rather to *discover and present the concrete forms* which grow out of the *process of capital's movement considered as a whole*. In their actual movement, capitals confront one another in concrete forms.'[10]

Here, in the third volume, the simplifying assumptions previously made (e.g. the sale of commodities at their value, the exclusion of the sphere of circulation and competition, treating surplus value in its totality, excluding the partial forms into which it divides itself) are dropped. Subsequently, in this *second stage* of the method of successive approximation, the mediations thus far neglected are taken into consideration, step by step, and the concrete forms of profit (ground rent, interest, commercial profit, etc.) are dealt with. Only in this way is the circle of Marx's analysis completed and proof is provided that the labour theory of value is not an unrealistic construct but that it indeed constitutes 'the law of phenomena', i.e. the foundation which enables us to *explain the real world of appearances*. Marx formulates this basic methodological idea with unmistakable clarity when he says: 'In volumes 1 and 2 we were only concerned with the *values* of commodities. Now [in the third volume] ... the *price of production* of the commodity has also developed, as a transformed form of value.'[11] 'The configurations of capital, as developed in this volume, *thus approach step by step the form in which they appear on the surface* of society, in the action of different capitals on one another, i.e. in competition, and in the everyday consciousness of the agents of production themselves.'[12]

9 Marx 1981b, p. 729.
10 Marx 1981b, p. 117. [The first emphasis is Grossman's.]
11 Marx 1981b, p. 263. [Editor's interpolation.]
12 Marx 1981b, p. 117. [Grossman's emphasis.]

2 The Contradiction between the Value Schema and Reality

If, as we have shown, the reproduction in thought of concrete reality is the goal of Marx's research then the function of Marx's reproduction schema within Marx's research method is readily apparent: *it does not claim that, by itself, it is a representation of capitalist reality*. It is only an element in Marx's method of successive approximation that together with simplifying assumptions (which are the basis of the schema) and subsequent *modifications* (giving rise to progressive concretisation) constitute an indivisible whole. Without the other two, each of these three parts by itself consequently loses all significance for understanding the truth and can therefore only constitute a preliminary stage of understanding, the first step in the method of successive approximation of concrete reality.

Once this character of Marx's reproduction schema is clear, it is apparent that it is only an aid to our thought and is not a representation of concrete processes. There can, then, also be no doubt about the character of the individual elements out of which the schema is constructed – value, surplus value, different profit rates in the individual spheres of production. As I have shown elsewhere, surplus value is *a real quantity*.[13] This is only true, however, for *society as a whole* in which values and prices, and therefore surplus value and profit, are quantitatively identical. Matters are different as regards *individual spheres of production*. Within these, in capitalist reality, we do not have values but prices of production which diverge from them. There are not quantities of surplus values but of profits. In short, the values and surplus values that figure in the reproduction schema are, from a quantitative perspective, not categories of reality; they are not immediately given in the world of capitalist reality. They are, rather, assumptions which initially contradict reality, that are chosen arbitrarily for the methodological purpose of simplification. Let us examine *values* first. Is it still necessary to recall that for Marx the sale of commodities at their values only has the character of a preliminary theoretical *assumption* but that Marx did not claim anywhere or at any time that this assumption accords with reality? In the first volume of *Capital*, he explicitly says 'We *assume* here that the capitalist sells the commodities he has produced at their value.'[14] – 'I *assume* ... that commodities are sold at their value.'[15] In the second volume too, Marx emphasises the *theoretical* character of this premise when he writes

13 Grossmann 1992, p. 103.
14 Marx 1976b, p. 710. [Grossman's emphasis.]
15 Marx 1976b, p. 655. [Grossman's emphasis.]

'In volume 1 … it was assumed … that the capitalist sells the product at its value.'[16] But nowhere is it claimed that this assumption accords with reality. Rather, the opposite is said, that this assumption diverges from and is, *prima facie*,[17] in apparent contradiction with reality. With exceptional clarity Marx even states in the first volume of *Capital* that the circulation of commodities at their values is an assumption that holds true only in the theoretical, 'normal course' that he assumes, 'in so far as' and 'provided' that the phenomenon proceeds 'in its purity'. 'In its *pure* form, the circulation process necessitates the exchange of equivalents, *but in reality processes do not take place in their pure form*.'[18] Here, then, the 'pure' process is counterposed to reality. Only in the former but not in the latter are the commodities exchanged at their values. So, in a letter to Kugelmann of 11 July 1868, Marx with his typical sarcasm flagellates the confusion of theoretical assumptions for experience that is frequently apparent in bourgeois economics. 'The vulgar economist has not the slightest idea that the *actual*, everyday exchange relations and the value magnitudes *cannot be directly identical*.'[19]

On innumerable other occasions in all three volumes of *Capital* as well as *Theories of Surplus Value*, Marx reiterates that in reality commodities are *not* sold at their values but at *prices of production* while 'the prices of production of *most commodities must differ* from their values.'[20] For this very reason, he polemicises against Ricardo's claim that commodities are sold at their values: 'This is the first *erroneous assumption* … Only in exceptional circumstances are commodities exchanged at their value'.[21] And, against Adam Smith, he says 'as I shall show later, even the average price of commodities is *always different from their value*'.[22]

What has been said here about value is true of *surplus value* too. We have surplus values in the reproduction schema but not in reality. Surplus value is

16 Marx 1978b, p. 428.
17 ['*Prima facie*' means 'at first sight'.]
18 Marx 1976b, p. 262. [Grossman's emphasis.]
19 Marx 1988b, p. 69. [Grossman emphasises 'actual'.]
20 Marx 1910c, p. 91. [Grossman's emphasis, quoting accurately from this, Karl Kautsky's edition of *Theories of Surplus Value*. Kautsky here and in the other relevant passages Grossman quotes from *Theories of Surplus Value* had changed 'cost prices' in Marx's original manuscript into 'price of production'. This was because Marx used the term 'cost price' in *Theories of Surplus Value* for what he termed 'price of production' in *Capital*, volume 3, where 'cost price' meant the cost of inputs, i.e. c + v. For the literal translation of the original text, see Marx 1989c, p. 272; see also note 6, p. 548.]
21 Marx 1989b, p. 266. [Grossman's emphasis.]
22 Marx 1988a, p. 400. [Grossman emphasises 'from their value'.]

'invisible' while in the reality of capitalism only different *forms of profit* such as profit of enterprise, interest, commercial profit, ground rent, occur. The surplus values represented in each sphere of production of the reproduction schema are therefore only preliminary assumptions which do not correspond with reality. The same is finally true of the profit rates visible in the schema. In a reproduction schema based on values, in other words, on the assumption that commodities are sold at their values, there have to be *different profit rates* in each of the departments. The *experience* of the capitalist system, conditioned by competition, shows that in reality a *tendency for the different profit rates* in the individual spheres *to equalise*, to form a *general* i.e. *an average rate of profit*, prevails. This process is immanent to the concept of prices of production: 'the existence and concept of price of production and the *general rate of profit* it involves rest on the fact *that individual commodities are not sold at their values*'[23] as, conversely, 'the mere existence of a general rate of profit necessitates prices of production that differ from values.'[24]

Hence the reproduction schema, in which only values, surplus values and different profit rates in the individual spheres of production feature, initially *contradicts concrete reality*. The theoretical, preliminary character of the reproduction schema and particularly the assumption that commodities exchange at their values is thus clear. *Real processes* play out quite differently to those in the reproduction schema. And it is not, indeed, a matter of their accidental or temporary deviations from the processes represented in the schema, which can be disregarded by science. Rather, the real process of reproduction is *fundamentally* different from that represented by the schema. The deviations of prices from values as they occur in reality are not merely *temporary* fluctuations, as is the case, e.g. with market prices; on the contrary, the transformation of values into prices of production that actually occurs 'creates *permanent deviations from values*.'[25] In the schema, the *surplus values* produced in the individual spheres are realised in them. It is very different in reality. In the long run, it is not the surplus values that are realised but the *average profit*, which continuously deviates from them. '[A]ll capitals, whatever the surplus value they themselves produce, tend to realise in the prices of their commodities not this surplus value, but rather the average profit.'[26]

23 Marx 1981b, p. 895. [Grossman's emphasis.]
24 Marx 1989b, p. 402.
25 Marx 1989b, p. 435. [Grossman's emphasis].
26 Marx 1981b, p. 274.

'The theory of value thus appears incompatible with the actual movement, incompatible with the *actual phenomena of production*, and it might seem that we must abandon all hope of understanding these phenomena.'[27]

3 Prices of Production and the General Rate of Profit as 'Regulators' of Capitalist Reproduction

To understand the capitalist mechanism, however, it does not suffice to state that the value schema of the reproduction process and the categories of surplus value as well as the particular profit rates in the individual spheres of production do not correspond with reality. We have to ask: which categories, then, determine the character of capitalist reality and are of decisive importance for the 'real movement' of the capitalist mechanism? Marx's answer to this question – and it constitutes the content of the third volume of *Capital* – is well-known. It is not values, assumed in theory, but the empirically given prices of production which form the objective centre of gravity around which everyday market prices oscillate. For concrete movements of capital, the empirically given general average rate of profit is decisively important, rather than the theoretically different profit rates assumed in the schema.

'There is no doubt, however', Marx says, 'that in *actual fact*, ignoring inessential, accidental circumstances that cancel each other out, no such *variation* in the average rate of profit exists between different branches of production, *it could not exist without abolishing the entire system of capitalist production*.'[28] Marx says that this *general* rate of profit is '*the driving force* in capitalist production'.[29] 'This average profit' should be understood '... as is the case in the capitalist mode of production, as the overall *regulator* of production'.[30] It is 'the law ... governing capitalist production'.[31] For the same reason, for Marx, 'the basic law of capitalist competition ...' is 'the law that governs the *general rate of profit* and the so-called *prices of production* determined by it'.[32] Finally Marx believes that '*the movement of this equalisation* [is the foundation] *on which the whole of capitalist production depends*'.[33] For not values but prices of production

27 Marx 1981b, p. 252. [Grossman's emphasis].
28 Marx 1981b, p. 252. [Grossman's emphasis].
29 Marx 1981b, p. 368. [Grossman's emphasis].
30 Marx 1981b, p. 918. [Grossman's emphasis].
31 Marx 1981b, p. 959.
32 Marx 1981b, pp. 127–8. [Grossman's emphasis].
33 Marx 1981b, p. 566. [Grossman's emphasis].

'are the actual averages governing market prices', i.e. they are the point around which real market prices oscillate: 'Market prices rise above these *governing production prices* or fall below them'[34] since 'it is not values but rather *prices of production* differing from them that form the *governing average prices* in each sphere of production.'[35]

'Regulating average prices', however, means nothing else than that, in the long run, production price and not value constitutes the *condition for reproduction*. As Marx explicitly states, it 'is in fact the same thing that ... Ricardo [calls] "price of production" or "cost of production", and the Physiocrats "*prix nécessaire*" ... *because in the long term it is the condition of supply, the condition for the reproduction of commodities*, in each particular sphere of production.'[36]

But there is more! The practical importance and relevance of the general rate of profit will become even more clearly apparent when we consider that it forms the basis of *the community of economic class interests among entrepreneurs*. For if commodities were exchanged at their values, each entrepreneur would only be interested in the exploitation of the workers he personally employs and his profit would be identical to the surplus value that 'his' workers produce. Only the transformation of surplus value into the general rate of profit ensures 'that each individual capitalist, just like the totality of all capitalists ... *participates* in the exploitation of the entire working class as a whole, and in the level of this exploitation; not just in terms of general class sympathy, but *in a direct economic sense*, since ... the average rate of profit depends on the level of exploitation of labour by capital as a whole.'[37]

If we remain in the schema, where commodities are sold at their values and hence there are *different* profit rates in individual spheres, then competition and its result – the fact of regulation by prices of production – are not considered.[38] And the average rate of profit, which is the 'driving force' – 'on which the whole capitalist production depends' – is lost!

---

34 Marx 1981b, p. 1000. [Grossman's emphasis].

35 Marx 1981b, p. 1013, cf. Marx 1981b, pp. 302, 308, 967, 1000, 1009, 1022. [Grossman's emphasis].

36 Marx 1981b, p. 300. [Grossman's emphasis].

37 Marx 1981b, pp. 298–9. [Grossman's emphasis].

38 The objection of Fritz Sternberg (1930) to my conception of value, that it 'neglects the importance of competition under capitalism', turns matters on their head. It is not I who has overlooked competition. It was, in fact, not considered in the course of the entire 30-year debate over the problem of accumulation and crisis. Mr Sternberg *indeed speaks of the necessity* of taking competition into account *but does it* just as little as other authors, from Tugan-Baranovsky to Bukharin, since all of them operate with a schema that only knows values. The *very concept of value*, however, includes *diversity of*

Since, however, such a value schema does not and cannot tell us anything about prices of production and the average rate of profit as a whole, it is obvious that it can explain just as little about the individual *partial forms of profit*, which arise from the division of surplus value. It is not suited to 'present *the concrete forms* which grow out of the *process of capital's movement considered as a whole*.'[39] The existence of all these forms of profit is inconsistent with the value schema and therefore not immediately explicable from the standpoint of the value theory which underlies it.

That is to say, the value schema only encompasses *productive* capital, that engages in the production of value and surplus value, but not money and merchant's capital that operate in the sphere of *circulation*. Hence, if industrial producers sell commodities at their values, i.e. at '*value prices*'[40] quantitatively identical to values (as happens in the value schema), the existence of *commercial profit*, i.e. the profit of *merchant's* capital that does not engage in production at all, becomes an insoluble riddle. 'At first appearance, pure and independent commercial profit seems impossible so long as products are sold at their values.'[41] 'The principles about value formation, profit, etc. derived straight from

---

profit rates in individual spheres and, therefore, also the exclusion of competition since '*it is only the competition* of capitals in different spheres that brings forth the production price that *equalises* the rates of profit between those spheres', Marx 1981b, p. 281 [Marx only emphasised 'different']. If one treats *crises primarily* as partial, resulting from disproportionality between the individual spheres – as in the works of the authors mentioned – then it is absolutely necessary to consider competition, i.e. the tendency of profit rates to equalise. This is not the case in my book, which attempts to explain the *primarily general* crises of over-accumulation that affect all spheres. For society as a whole, 'the distinction between values and prices of production loses all significance', since here the dimensions of the two are identical, cf. Grossmann 1929a, pp. 107, 211.

Just as incorrect is the further objection that the effects of competition are already contained in values, because competition determines value, i.e. socially necessary labour time. This conception is absolutely irreconcilable with the essential foundations of Marx's theory of value. In fact, the function competition fulfills for values is not constitutive but merely declaratory. It does not determine socially necessary labour time but only registers it after the fact. Competition, after all, plays out on the *market*, i.e. in the sphere of circulation. Values, however, are created in the sphere of *production*, they therefore precede all competition. 'The value of a commodity', Marx says, 'is expressed in its price *before* it enters into circulation, and it is therefore a *precondition of circulation and not its result*', Marx 1976b, p. 260 [Grossman's emphasis]; similarly Marx 1987a, p. 350. The Physiocrats Quesnay and [Pierre-Paul] Mercier de la Rivière already knew that commodities have an exchange value before they enter the market to be exchanged, cf. Marx 1981b, p. 260, and Oncken 1902, p. 370.

39 Marx 1981b, p. 117. [Grossman emphasises 'concrete forms'.]

40 Marx 1981b, p. 275. [Grossman's emphasis].

41 Marx 1981b, p. 447.

the examination of industrial capital *cannot be applied directly to commercial capital*.'[42] As long as we restrict ourselves to the investigation of *value*, a large and important portion of the phenomena of capitalist reality – the profit of commercial capital – particularly in its international form, i.e. the *appearances of the world market and global trade*, remain inexplicable.

However, the transformation *of values* (value prices) of the schema into prices of production and also the equalisation of the different profit rates in the individual spheres of the schema into the general rate of profit would by no means suffice to explain the existence of commercial profit. We would merely be taking into account productive capitals, i.e. those contributing to the *creation* of surplus value in the formation of the general rate of profit and the transformation of value prices into prices of production. Such a process of equalisation would therefore only be 'our *first* consideration' of the general rate of profit but by no means its '*finished* form'.[43] Commercial capital, which has no part in the creation of surplus value, still remains to be considered. To explain the existence of commercial profit yet another stage in the method of successive approximation would be necessary, to 'supplement' the first process of equalisation of *productive* capitals alone with 'the *participation of commercial capital* in this equalisation', i.e. by a second-order equalisation.[44] Only in this way can the 'finished form' of the profit rate be attained, after *prices of production* have been given a 'more accurate definition'[45] and been modified into '*commercial prices*'[46] which presents the original average profit rate 'within more closely defined limits than before'.[47] We see that if the concrete, empirically given form of commercial profit is to be understood, the value schema has to be modified by the method of successive approximation in a number of ways. Under the premises of the value schema, i.e. without these intermediary steps which lead from 'value prices' via 'prices of production' to the phenomenon of 'commercial prices', the existence of commercial profit would be neither possible nor comprehensible.

But that is not all! There is the further circumstance, that the *course of the accumulation process*, as presented in the value schema, is powerfully *modified* by the existence of commercial profit, i.e. by the transformation of values into prices of production and then commercial prices.

---

42 Marx 1981b, p. 441. [Grossman's emphasis].

43 Marx 1981b, p. 459. [Grossman's emphasis].

44 Marx 1981b, p. 460. [Grossman's emphasis].

45 Marx 1981b, p. 398.

46 Marx 1981b, p. 429. [Grossman's emphasis].

47 Marx 1981b, p. 336.

For it is evident that the portion of the surplus value shown in the value schema which accrues to commercial capital as profit and is accumulated in the sphere of circulation (the commercial buildings of trading companies, office fittings, operating capital, etc.) constitutes a 'deduction from the profit of industrial capital'[48] and 'proportionately reduces the scale on which the capital advanced functions productively.'[49] This portion of surplus value is excluded from future accumulation of productive capital, as presented in the value schema, and is no longer involved in the *creation* of surplus value. It does, however, participate in the *distribution* of profit. Both facts, the reduction in the active side and the increase in the passive side, slow down the pace of the accumulation of industrial capital *pro tanto*.[50] 'The bigger commercial capital is in comparison with industrial capital, the smaller the rate of industrial profit.'[51] At the same time, it is clear that the existence of commercial profit transfers a portion of surplus value – from Rosa Luxemburg's standpoint part of the 'unsaleable remainder'[52] of surplus value – from the sphere of production to the sphere of circulation. The conversion of value prices into prices of production and commercial prices consequently disturbs of all the ratios calculated in the value schema!

What has been said here about commercial capital is literally true, and for the same reasons, of *money* and *bank* capital. This capital, too, functions exclusively in the sphere of circulation, and *indeed* participates in the distribution but not in the production of surplus value. If commodities were sold *at* their values, i.e. if industrialists retained *all* of the surplus value they initially appropriated, then 'upon that supposition, merchant's capital and banker's capital would be impossible',[53] since it would make no profit.

Finally, on the basis of the value schema, not only is the existence of interest impossible but *interest rate* movements also cannot be understood.

The rate of interest is related to the profit rate in a similar way as the market price of a commodity is to its value. In so far as the rate of interest is determined by the profit rate, this is always through the *general* rate of profit and not through the specific profit rates that may prevail in particular branches of industry ... The general rate of profit, *in fact, reappears in the average rate of interest as an empirical, given fact.*[54]

48 Marx 1981b, p. 400.
49 Marx 1978b, p. 211.
50 ['*Pro tanto*' means 'to that extent'.]
51 Marx 1981b, p. 400.
52 Luxemburg 1913, p. 308.
53 Engels 2001c, pp. 228–30.
54 Marx 1981b, p. 487. [Grossman's emphasis.]

'In this sense', it is stated elsewhere, 'interest is governed by profit, and more precisely by the general rate of profit.'[55] In a value schema with different profit rates in the individual spheres of production and its aggregate surplus value, neither the existence of an interest rate nor its movements can be explained, nor can bank and financial capital, to which Hilferding ascribes a decisive significance in capital's most recent development.[56]

And the same is true of *ground rent*, in its modern, capitalist form which 'only exists in a society the basis of which is the *capitalist* mode of production.'[57] The existence of ground rent is impossible to explain on the basis of a value schema, i.e. under the assumption that commodities are sold at their values.[58]

The discussion above has made it sufficiently clear that the categories presented in the value schema, value, surplus value and different rates of profit are not of immediate, decisive importance for understanding the *concrete* process of capitalist production. On the contrary, the important categories are *those not encompassed by the schema: prices of production, profit* and *its partial forms*, and finally the general *average profit rate*. These categories must be awarded primacy for the immediate understanding of concrete capitalist production, precisely because the average rate of profit is the 'regulator' and the 'driving force' of this production and because the whole capitalist movement rests on the *equalisation* of different profit rates.[59]

---

55 Marx 1981b, pp. 481–2.

56 [Hilferding 1981.]

57 Marx 1991b, p. 322. [Grossman's emphasis.]

58 Because *absolute rent* is merely a 'surplus profit', i.e. an 'excess over and above the average', Marx 1991b, p. 332; also Marx 1989b, p. 271; Marx 1981b, pp. 297, 918.

'If then the value of agricultural produce is higher than the price of production determined by the *industrial average* profit would be, the excess of this value over the price of production constitutes the absolute rent. But in order that this excess of value over price of production can be measured, the price of production must be the *prius*; it must therefore be imposed on agriculture as a law by industry' 'Rent ... cannot possibly be explained if industrial profit does *not* regulate agricultural profit', Marx 1989c, p. 289. ['*Prius*' means 'prior element'.] 'If we are to speak of an excess over the average profit, this average profit must first be established as a measure and, as is the case in the capitalist mode of production, as the overall *regulator of production*', Marx 1981b, p. 918. The existence of an absolute ground rent cannot, therefore, be explained by a value schema in which this regulator does not exist.

59 Marx 1981b, pp. 368, 918.

If one recalls this state of affairs, it becomes clear that a value schema that lacks all of these real categories, on which real capitalist movement rests, allows us to recognise the tendencies of historical development, in other words 'the *general law* of capitalist accumulation' as Marx already presents it in the first volume of *Capital*.[60] But it is not at all suited to reproduce in thought the *concrete forms of the movement* of capital. This is precisely why deductions based on the *value* schema regarding proportionality or disproportionality of individual spheres of production are not conclusive and at least premature.

4 The Value Schema as an Historical and Theoretical Point of Departure

If we allocate the role of the regulator and driving force of capitalist production to the categories provided by experience – prices of production, average profit and general rate of profit – this raises the urgent question: what function, then, do values fulfil? Isn't a reproduction schema based on values irrelevant if it does not provide an adequate depiction of capitalist commodity production and does not immediately apply in the real world? Such a conclusion would be mistaken. Despite the reality of prices of production, values retain their central significance, indeed, as Marx stresses, in *two* respects:

1. They are an *historically primary form*, valid for the epoch of simple, i.e. *pre*-capitalist commodity production of independent producers – artisans, peasants – 'as long as the means of production involved in each branch of production can be transferred from one sphere to another only with difficulty',[61] i.e. as long as there are legal or material barriers to the movement of capital which hinder the formation of a general rate of profit.[62] *Only in this period* of simple commodity production is the exchange of commodities at their (market) values not only a theoretical assumption but an *actual occurrence*, in the sense that *values form the centre of gravity* for the daily fluctuations of market prices.[63]
2. Under *capitalist* commodity production, on the other hand, the previous function of values in the exchange is modified. Commodities now exchange at *prices of production* which differ quantitatively from values, while values only fulfil the function of a *theoretically primary factor*, from

60 Marx 1976b, p. 762. [Grossman's emphasis.]
61 Marx 1981b, pp. 278–9.
62 Marx 1981b, p. 298.
63 Marx 1981b, p. 279.

which prices of production are derived. *Prices of production* are the *regulator* of the scope of production under capitalism, they determine the movement of capital, i.e. the steady injection and withdrawal of capital in individual spheres of production and, therefore, of the distribution of aggregate social capital. They and not values are therefore *responsible for the proportionality or disproportionality of this distribution.* While bourgeois economics accepts prices of production as a fact without investigating their origins any further, Marx proves that prices of production must be derived from values, that without such a derivation 'the general rate of profit (and hence also the price of production of the commodity) remains a meaningless and irrational conception.'[64] If average profit is to be discussed, then the components from which the average is calculated must be known. 'Without this, the average rate of profit is the average of *nothing*, pure fancy.'[65] Only in this sense does the *law of value* govern the movement of commodity prices under capitalism. In *individual spheres of production*, that does not prevent *prices of production rather than values* from constituting the *centre* around which daily market prices fluctuate[66] and 'at which they are balanced out in definite periods'.[67] Furthermore, prices of production and *not values* regulate production, its scope and the distribution of capital. They, therefore, directly determine the very elements that are of crucial significance for understanding *crises*, insofar as these can be attributed to disproportionality in the distribution of capital.[68]

---

64 Marx 1981b, p. 257. [Grossman also cited Marx 1989b, p. 416, which should have been the reference for the next quotation from Marx.]

65 [Marx 1989b, p. 416; Marx 1989c, pp. 273–4. Grossman mistakenly cited Marx 1981b, p. 277 for the quotation and included the next sentence in it. The next sentence is, however, a paraphrase of text on that page. The additional reference, to Marx 1989c, pp. 273–4, seems more relevant to the previous quotation.]

66 It is, consequently, incorrect when Karl Diehl, in what seems like a concession to Marx, acknowledges that, within Marx's schema, *incongruence between the values and the prices* of individual commodities is justified and necessary, yet then claims 'Marx decisively assumes that labour value is *the gravitational centre* of *average market prices*', Diehl 1898, p. 6, and likewise as late as Diehl 1921, p. 96.

67 Marx 1981b, p. 280.

68 'The entire capitalist production process, moreover, is governed by the prices of products. But the *governing prices of production* are themselves governed in turn by the equalisation of the rate of profit and the *distribution of capital* among the various spheres of social production which is appropriate to that equalisation. Thus *profit* appears in this case as the principal factor not just of the products' distribution but also of their actual *production*', Marx 1981b, p. 1022.

We see that the sale of commodities at their values does not occur in capitalist reality. 'The exchange of commodities at their values ... thus corresponds to *a much lower stage* of development than the exchange at prices of production, for which a *definite degree of capitalist development* is needed.'[69] Capital accomplishes the equalisation of different profit rates in the individual spheres of production more easily 'according to *how advanced capitalist development* is in a given national society'.[70]

What has been said so far makes it clear that the line of argument of Rosa Luxemburg and her followers but likewise that of Hilferding and Otto Bauer had to fail from the outset, because they undertook to demonstrate (or to refute) the capitalist law of crises by means of a schema that only knows the sale of commodities at their values and which is therefore, according to Marx, only the expression of a '*lower stage*' of development, namely that of precapitalist commodity production. For this reason, they ignored the production price schema that governs *developed* capitalist production, and thus the very elements, such as prices of production and average profit, which are decisive for the proportionality or disproportionality of capital distribution in developed capitalism. The real categories which regulate the whole mechanism are disregarded; attention is only given to categories which are unreal (different profit rates) and which – if they were realised – would inevitably 'abolish ... the entire system of capitalist production'![71]

The deficiency of such a procedure is clear. If the contradiction, discussed earlier, between value theory and 'actual phenomena of production', i.e. between the value schema and capitalist reality, is to be resolved, then the analysis of the capitalist reproduction process cannot remain at the level of the value schema with its different profit rates. Then it actually has to be regarded only as 'theoretically prior'. Using value theory and therefore the value schema merely as a *starting point* for an analysis, with the help of a *series of intermediary stages*, we can find the bridge that leads us to real phenomena, i.e. to prices of production and the average profit rate. In short, the value schema must be transformed step by step, through multi-level, successive approximations into a *production price schema*. 'It is evident that the emergence, realisation, creation of the general rate of profit *necessitates the transformation of values into prices of production that are different from these values*.'[72]

69 Marx 1981b, p. 277. [Grossman's emphasis.]
70 Marx 1981b, pp. 297, 281. [Grossman's emphasis.]
71 Marx 1981b, p. 252.
72 Marx 1910b, p. 161. [Grossman's emphasis. Cf. Marx 1989c, p. 69.]

In the second volume of *Capital* Marx *does begin* his analysis of the crisis problematic with a value schema. But his line of argument at this level of abstraction, removed from and initially in contradiction with reality, is not and cannot be conclusive. It has a merely *preliminary* character and will be completed by the theory of the third volume of *Capital*, the theory of the transformation of values into prices of production. In Marx's analysis, the *value schema* constitutes only the embryonic form, the *first stage* in the method of successive approximation, which can only mature into the price form through a series of metamorphoses!

Marx's value schema restricts the analysis to only the *creation of* value and *surplus value* as a whole, i.e. the form in which they emerge from the *process of production*, so that competition and the *influences of the sphere of circulation on the distribution of this surplus value* are not considered at this stage. Subsequently, however, the elements previously excluded must be considered. Thus the analysis of the creation of surplus value in the process of production must be supplemented by the analysis of its *distribution in the process of circulation* by means of competition.

The following conclusion for the crisis problematic – insofar as it relates to the mutual relations of dependency and proportionality among the individual spheres of production – which also indicates the course of further research, emerges from what has been said above.

If the analysis of the law of crisis is to be conclusive about *capitalist reality* then it must not be restricted to the *value schema*, the first stage in the method of successive approximation, but must occur at *all* stages and also be demonstrated through a *production price schema*.

5 The Crisis Problematic and the Lessons of the Third Volume of Marx's *Capital*

The research agenda formulated so far, however, stands in blatant contradiction with the actual history of the treatment of the crisis problematic in the Marxist camp. '[E]mpty tradition', Marx says, 'is more powerful in political economy than in any other science'.[73] We will see that this is true not only of bourgeois economics but also, just as much, of the political economy of Marx's epigones. At first, the significance of the reproduction schema developed in the second volume of *Capital* for the crisis problematic was not recognised at all.

73 Marx 1991b, p. 259.

In a review of the second volume published in *Neue Zeit* in 1886,[74] Karl Kautsky identifies the reasons why, in his estimation, this volume was of *less interest* to the working class *than the first.* Only the production of surplus value in the factory was important. The further question of how this surplus is *realised* is of more interest to the capitalists than to the working class. And, on the occasion of the publication of the third volume of *Capital* ten years later, Eduard Bernstein uncritically repeats the same judgement, even in part using the same words, in a summary of the whole of Marx's principal work which was then concluded.[75] The practitioners of the movement have often only read the first volume and for decades have not laid hands on the other volumes. 'As you want to have a grind in prison at *Capital* 2 and 3', Engels wrote to Viktor Adler, as late as 16 March 1895, 'I will give you a few hints to make it easier'.[76] Hilferding speaks accurately of the 'analyses in the second volume of *Capital*' being 'largely ignored' until the publication of Tugan-Baranovsky's book in 1901,[77] and adds: 'Tugan-Baranovsky deserves credit for calling attention to the significance of these investigations for the problem of crisis in his *Studies on the Theory and History of Industrial Crises in England.* The curious thing is that this needed to be pointed out at all'.[78]

With the publication of Tugan-Baranovsky's book, there was a turn to the opposite extreme. Whereas the significance of the reproduction schema for the problem of crisis had not been recognised at all until then, now – as I have shown elsewhere[79] – it is exalted in the most effusive manner, ascribed 'objective social existence' and regarded as an *exact representation of the capitalist reproduction* process. Conclusions about processes in capitalist reality are now drawn directly from the relations in the reproduction schema! So Rosa Luxemburg, for example, says 'we now have to ask ourselves what significance the schema of reproduction, that has been analysed, has for reality'.[80] Her answer is that the exact ratios of Marx's schema form the 'universal and absolute foundation of social reproduction', not only for a capitalist but also for a socialist and in fact any planned economy![81] In a planned socialist economy production would

74 Kautsky 1886, p. 164.
75 Bernstein 1894–5.
76 Engels 2001d, p. 468.
77 Hilferding 1981, p. 243.
78 Hilferding 1981, p. 420; Tugan-Baranowsky 1901, part of which had been translated: Tugan-Baranowsky 2000, pp. 53–80, 81–110.
79 Grossmann 1932a, pp. 153–4, see above pp. 276–303.
80 Luxemburg 1913, p. 76.
81 Luxemburg 1951, pp. 85, 103–4, 130.

correspond exactly to the ratios of the schema. Rosa Luxemburg states, further, that 'a *capitalist* economy lacks such planned organisation of the total process. *Consequently*[!], *nothing runs smoothly according to a mathematical formula, as it appears in the schema.* On the contrary, the circuit of reproduction proceeds with continual *deviations* from the relations of the schema'.[82] 'With all these deviations, however, *the schema presents a socially necessary average, around which these movements occur and which they time and again approach* after they have moved away from it'.[83]

The matter is no different according to Otto Bauer. For him too, the value schema presents a state of balanced equilibrium between capital accumulation and population around which the circuit of real reproduction oscillates. In reality there may be continual cyclical *deviations* from the schema's state of equilibrium because the apparatus of production exhibits overaccumulation or underaccumulation in relation to population growth. At the same time, however, there is a tendency inherent in the capitalist mode of production which – if 'only through great crises' – 'automatically [cancels out] overaccumulation and underaccumulation, with the accumulation of capital adjusting again and again to the growth of population'[84] *i.e. the real movement tends towards the theoretically calculated state of equilibrium represented by the schema.*

In striking contradiction with Marx's theory of the regulating function of the average rate of profit and prices of production, developed above, and with the theory that it is not values but their transmuted form, *prices of production*, which constitute the *gravitational centre* for fluctuations in market prices, Rosa Luxemburg and Otto Bauer ascribe this function to values. Unlike Marx, they both regard the relations of the schema not just as a first stage in the method of successive approximation *but* as an immediate reflection of reality.

This divergence in the understanding of the value schema, by Marx on the one hand and Rosa Luxemburg and Otto Bauer on the other, has further ramifications for the analysis of the crisis problematic. The reproduction schema developed in the second volume of *Capital*, with its values and, in the absence of competition, unequalised, different rates of profit, does not correspond with

82 Luxemburg 1913, p. 76. [Grossman's emphasis.]
83 Luxemburg 1913, p. 77. [Grossman's emphasis.]
84 Otto Bauer 1986, pp. 106–7. [This translation has been modified, as indicated by the square brackets. In its original form it seriously distorted the meaning of Bauer's text by rendering 'aufhebt' as 'generates', see Otto Bauer 1913, p. 872.]

reality. If value theory is not to contradict but to explain real phenomena, then – in accordance with Marx's theory in the third volume of *Capital* – values must be transformed into prices of production with the help of competition, i.e. a 'number of intermediary stages'[85] must be developed which lead to the general rate of profit and, finally, to the empirically given forms of profit (interest, ground rent, commercial profit). By ascribing real world validity to Marx's preliminary, methodological assumption that commodities are sold at their values and thus by regarding the value schema as a reflection of reality, Rosa Luxemburg and Otto Bauer *from the outset exclude the necessity of transforming values first into prices of production and, further, into commercial prices from the circle of their problematic*. They disclaim the *method of successive concretisation* of the relations presented in the schema, the *method of increasing the accuracy of the reproduction schema*. According to Rosa Luxemburg and Otto Bauer, there is no need to approximate the understanding of reality, step-by-step, since the schema already reflects reality!

It is therefore only a logical consequence of this disastrous error that, for Rosa Luxemburg and Otto Bauer, not only the problem of the value-price transformation but also the connected problem of the *general rate of profit* and the problem of the transformation of surplus value into the *specific forms of profit* (commercial profit, interest, etc.), that is, *the whole theory of the third volume of Capital, do not exist*! They remain within the 'embryonic form' of the value schema, at a stage of abstraction far removed from reality, without entering into the 'metamorphoses',[86] i.e. the path which leads to the approximation of concrete capitalist reality. It is self-evident that, as a consequence of this fatal misconception of Marx's method, the connection between the problem of the value-price transformation and the problem of crisis can be neither seen nor dealt with.

What then is this connection and the specific function of the calculation of prices? To show this, we turn to Rosa Luxemburg's formulation of the problem. Her critical analysis of Marx's reproduction schema led her to the result that within such a schema – insofar as there are different organic compositions of capital in its two departments – the complete sale of commodities, i.e. equilibrium, is not possible because 'with every year ... a growing *excess of means of consumption* must arise'.[87] This *unsaleable remainder of surplus value* in depart-

85 [Marx 1989b, p. 401.]
86 [Marx 1976b, p. 154.]
87 Luxemburg 1913, p. 306. [Grossman's emphasis.]

ment II is even greater in view of the rising productivity of labour, because this indicates 'a much larger excess of unsaleable means of subsistence than arises from the extent of this excess, in terms of value'.[88]

Let us assume that Rosa Luxemburg had succeeded in proving this. *What* would she have demonstrated? Only the circumstance that an 'unsaleable remainder' arises in department II *of the value schema* – i.e. under the assumption that the commodities are exchanged at their values. But we know that this assumption does *not* accord with reality. In the value schema, which is the foundation of Rosa Luxemburg's analysis, there are *different rates of profit* in the individual spheres of production. In the absence of competition, these do not equalise. This, too, contradicts reality where, as a consequence of competition there is a tendency for different rates of profit to equalise to the general rate of profit. How cogent are Rosa Luxemburg's conclusions – the demonstration of an unsaleable surplus of consumer goods – in relation to reality, when they are deduced from a schema that has no validity in the real world? *Since competition leads to the transformation of values into prices of production and thus to a redistribution of surplus value among the individual branches of industry in the schema, which necessarily results in a modification of the previous relations of proportionality between the individual spheres of the schema*, it is extremely possible and likely that a surplus of unsaleable consumer goods in the value schema subsequently vanishes in the *production price schema* and that, conversely, an original equilibrium in the value schema turns into disproportionality in the production price schema. The deficiency of the line of argument which is restricted to analysis of merely the value schema and which operates with values and different profit rates instead of prices of production and the general rate of profit is evident. Rosa Luxemburg herself says 'Thus social capital and its counterpart, the whole of social surplus value, are not merely real quantities, having an objective existence, but, what is more, the relation between them, *the average profit, guides and directs the whole process of exchange ... by the mechanism of the law of value* which establishes the quantitative relations of exchange between the individual kinds of commodities *independently of their specific value relationship*.' The average rate of profit is, after all, the guiding force so that 'every capital is in fact treated only as part of a common whole, the whole of social capital, and assigned the profit to which it is entitled, according to its size, out of the surplus value wrested from society, *regardless* of the quantity which this particular capital has *actually* created'.[89]

88 Luxemburg 1913, p. 308.
89 Luxemburg 1951, p. 79. [Grossman's emphasis.]

According to Rosa Luxemburg's account, the average profit rate governs all commodity exchange. Nevertheless, she investigates the question of whether complete exchange is possible by using a schema which knows no average profit. Can one imagine a greater contradiction? Furthermore, if, as Rosa Luxemburg states, the relations of exchange among individual commodities in reality takes place 'independently of their special value relations', if each capital realises not the quantum of *surplus value* it produced but merely receives the average *profit* in proportion to its size, then Rosa Luxemburg concedes indirectly that her theory of the necessity of the realisation of *surplus value* is wrong. So she indirectly admits that commodities are exchanged *not at their values* but at prices, namely prices of production, which permanently deviate from their values since, according to Marx, 'the average rate of profit ... alone determines the prices of production'.[90] After all, in Marx's system equal average profits and prices of production, which deviate from values, are correlative concepts! It is therefore self-evidently a logical contradiction that Rosa Luxemburg *identifies no consequences* for the subsequent course of her own analysis from her own assertion of the empirical fact of average profit and its central governing role; that she does acknowledge the existence of the average rate of profit rate but equally insists on the proposition that commodities are exchanged at their values! The section of her book quoted above is also the *only one* where she speaks of average profit and, in a disguised form, of prices of production. But nowhere is this insight put to use in the analysis of the problem of crisis.

Rosa Luxemburg herself apparently sensed that the *value schema* is a construction distant from reality, when she wrote about the relationship between the third volume of *Capital* and the theory of value in the first volume, in her *Anti-Critique*: 'For the doctrine of *average profit, one of the most important discoveries* of Marx's economic theory, is central to its argument. This *alone* gives *concrete meaning* to the *theory of value* in the first volume.'[91]

She insists here that not the *value theory* of the first volume but rather only the prices of production and the average profit of the third volume have 'meaning in reality'. In her book on *Accumulation* as well as in her *Anti-Critique*, however, prices of production are not mentioned once, and the false premise is maintained that the exchange of commodities between I (v + s) and II c at their values is not merely a methodological *assumption* but *actually occurs* in capitalist reality! So she says, for example, that the need for means of consumption in department I of the schema, as expressed by the variable capital

90 Marx 1910b, p. 78 [cf. Marx 1989b, p. 444].

91 Luxemburg 1972, p. 73. [Grossman's emphasis except for 'average profit'.]

and the surplus value of this department, can only be met out of the produce of department II, 'indeed can only be obtained in exchange *for the value equivalent* of the produce of department I'.[92] Even in her last book, published posthumously, she claims that '[a]ll commodities are exchanged *at their values*.'[93] This self-contradictory statement of Rosa Luxemburg, which causes her to fall into the worst errors of vulgar socialism, is no coincidence. It stems from her false conception that the *natural form of surplus value* is given once and for all and determines its function either as means of production in department I or as means of consumption in department II. These predetermined functions make, according to Rosa Luxemburg, any *transfer of surplus value* (in total or in part) from department I to department II impossible. Rosa Luxemburg believes that transfers of surplus value fail for another reason, namely the *equivalence* of exchange relations between the two departments.[94]

This claim inevitably leads Rosa Luxemburg to negate the whole content of the third volume of *Capital* and specifically the theory of prices of production and the emergence of a uniform rate of profit. Her verbal concession that the theory of average profit, 'one of the most important discoveries of Marx's economic theory', is the centrepiece of the third volume cannot conceal the truth that she has abandoned the theory of average profit; rather, this abandonment is underlined when Rosa Luxemburg identifies the only *means* by which a uniform, average profit can emerge as impossible. Let us recall the circumstances of Marx's schema of simple reproduction:

I	4000 c + 1000 v + 1000 s = 6000 profit rate = 20 percent
II	2000 c + 1000 v + 1000 s = 4000 profit rate = 33 percent

We therefore see that if we abide by the value schema, with its exchange of equivalents, in other words the *equivalent* exchange of 1,000 v + 1,000 s from department I for 2,000 c from department II, then Marx's theory of prices of production is ignored and there *must* be *different profit rates* in the two departments. The profit rate in department I is 20 percent, that in department II is 33 percent. How can the *same* rate of profit rate – in this case, 25 percent – emerge in both departments of Marx's schema? It seems almost banal to point out that this is only possible through the emergence of prices of production, that is the circumstance that the commodities of department I are sold to depart-

92 Luxemburg 1951, pp. 128, 340–1; Luxemburg 1913, p. 311. [Grossman's emphasis.]

93 Luxemburg 1925b, p. 239. [Grossman's emphasis.] Similarly, Eduard Heimann says: 'On the market, quantities of commodities *of equal value* are exchanged', Heimann 1922, p. 10.

94 Luxemburg 1951, pp. 340–1.

ment II *above* their values whereas the commodities of department II, insofar as they find their way to department I, are sold *below* their values. Only because department I *receives more* for the (v + s) = 2,000 value units which it sells to department II, namely 2,250 value units can there be the same rate of profit in both departments. In this way, *part of the surplus value of department II is transferred to department I in the process of exchange*. Only thus can department I attain a larger profit (namely, 1,250) than it initially generated (1,000 s), which results in a profit rate of 25 percent on the 5,000 C outlayed.[95] In department II instead of the initial surplus value (1,000 s) only a profit of 750 remains, which results in a profit rate of likewise 25 percent on the 3,000 C outlayed.

From what has been said, it is without anything further clear that the tendency for profit rates to level out, through the transfer of a part of surplus value from department II to department I, shakes the foundations of Rosa Luxemburg's theory of the 'unsaleable surplus of consumer goods' in department II. Her 'unshakeable position' (Sternberg)[96] proves to be a soap bubble that bursts on contact with reality. If Rosa Luxemburg had really wanted to prove her idea of an unsaleable remainder of consumer goods then she would have had to demonstrate her proof not only on the basis of the value schema but also within the production price schema. She would have also had to show that such an unsaleable remainder would result *after* the average rate of profit emerged.[97] She never demonstrated nor even attempted to demonstrate such a proof.

---

95 [[Here, C = c + v.]]

96 [Sternberg 1971.]

97 In Otto Bauer's well-known reproduction schema, *each* department makes 10,000 c and 2,500 v from its surplus value available for the purposes of accumulation in the first year of production. The actual accumulation is a different matter. In department I it amounts to *more* – namely, 134,666 c and 53,667 v – and in department II to *less* – namely, just 85,334 c and 51,333 v. This means that Bauer *reallocated* a share of surplus value earmarked for accumulation in department II to department I, without, however, having been able to give any scientifically plausible reason to justify this *reallocation*. Helene Bauer's attempt to save this procedure by indicating that such a reallocation occurs by means of *credit* must be considered a naive excuse [Helene Bauer 1929]. Reallocations by means of credit – however great their role may be in *reality* – are impermissible in the *theoretical* analysis of the reproduction process. After all, it is one of the many simplifying assumptions of the Marx's reproduction schema that it *abstracts from credit*. The very purpose of the schema is to show the *exchange* relations between its two departments and to investigate whether *complete sale* is possible. It is not permissible to change the initial assumptions after the fact, once one has encountered difficulties in solving the problem. This is why Fritz Sternberg could claim an all too easy triumph over Bauer. Even if the reallocation of a share of surplus value from department II to department I was an inexplicable difficulty for Otto Bauer, over which he stumbled, from the conception advocated in the text it is not only permissible and justified but necessary. The fact that there are different *profit rates* in the

The tendency for profit rates in different branches of production to level out is an *observation* confirmed by experience, that has been unanimously recognised by theorists from various scientific schools over the course of a century. It was already regarded as a fact by Ricardo and Malthus. Marx, too, refers to it as an 'empirical, given fact',[98] a 'practical state of affairs'.[99] 'Observation of competition – the phenomena of production – shows that capitals of *equal* size yield an equal amount of profit on average.'[100] Nor has this levelling tendency of capitalism, conditioned by competition, been disputed by more recent theorists like Böhm-Bawerk and others.[101]

The schools only disagree over nature of the explanation for this fact and the post-Ricardian school, specifically, collapsed on the challenge of this explanation, because it could not reconcile the *fact* of the uniform rate of profit with the labour *theory* of value. This is the point at which Marx's historical greatness became apparent. Through his theory of the divergence of prices of production from values, he was able to explain the fact of the uniform profit rate, which *prima facie* contradicts the law of labour value, on the basis of this law of value. Rosa Luxemburg, in defiance of all experience, denies the possibility of the transfer of a part of surplus value from department II to department I, consequently the possibility of the establishment of prices of production, and insists that commodities exchange *at* their values within the individual spheres. She is consequently incapable of explaining the average rate of profit on the basis of the labour theory of value. Although she rigidly adheres to the law of value, in fact she abandons the foundation of Marx's theoretical system at this point. It is impossible to account for a uniform rate of profit on the assumption that commodities exchange at equal values between the spheres

---

departments of Bauer's schema (in department I p = 29.4 percent, in department II p = 38.4 percent) has been overlooked in the previous discussion. If the *same*, i.e. average, rate of profit of 33.3 percent is to be constructed, then the amounts transferred from department II to department I must not be, as Otto Bauer holds, 5,833 (4,666 c and 1,167 v) but 6,667. And this transfer is facilitated *by means of exchange*! Certainly this is an unequal exchange where the commodities of the two departments are not exchanged at their values but at their *prices of production*. [Otto Bauer 1986. Grossman did not copy Bauer's figures in the second sentence of this note accurately. They are corrected here.]

98 Marx 1981b, p. 487. [Grossman's emphasis.]

99 Marx 1981b, p. 270.

100 Marx 1989c, p. 258.

101 So Böhm-Bawerk, says the assumption 'which is indubitably corroborated empirically, is that earnings on capital are subject to an averaging process', 1959a, p. 303. Likewise, Siegfried Budge: 'Experience shows that profit rates ... tend to equalise, that they are balanced in the imaginary equilibrium state of economic activity, *equalised* in the "static" economy', 1920, p. 6.

of production. But instead of dismissing the false assumptions that 'exchange at equal values' takes place between the two departments of the schema and, further, that a transfer of surplus value from department II to department I is impossible, in order to be able to explain the facts, Rosa Luxemburg sacrifices the facts and prefers to uphold the false assumption of exchange of commodities at 'equal values'! With a stroke of the pen the whole of Marx's theory of uniform average profit, according to Rosa Luxemburg herself 'one of the most important discoveries of Marx's economic theory', is wiped from the face of the earth.

6 Instead of Advance beyond Marx – Regression Back to Ricardo

What we have said above about Rosa Luxemburg's treatment of the crisis problematic is quite literally true of all Marxist theorists who have engaged with the problems of crisis and accumulation. However strange this may sound, it is nevertheless a fact that in the course of the entire debate over the possibility of the uninterrupted development of the capitalist process of production, inaugurated 30 years ago by the publication of Tugan-Baranovsky's book, no one has so much as posed the essential problem: to demonstrate the crisis problematic at all stages of the method of successive approximation. Whether it is the neo-harmonists Kautsky, Hilferding and Otto Bauer, or Rosa Luxemburg and her followers, or finally Bukharin[102] and other theorists of communism, all have treated the problem only at the level of its inception, by means of the value schema, which knows values, surplus value and different profit rates. Instead they should have substantiated their analyses and conclusions on the basis of a *production price schema*, which presents the regulating categories of prices of production, competition, and the average rate of profit. Whether one argues for the necessity and inevitability of crises under capitalism, or, as the neo-harmonists do, for the possibility of crisis-free progress, it is clear that any deductions drawn from a value schema must be premature and inconclusive. What could the analysis of a value schema possibly tell us about the necessary proportionality or disproportionality of commodity exchanges under capitalism when the proportional relationships so meticulously calculated in the value schema are later *overturned* by the tendency for profit rates to equalise and by the necessary redistribution of surplus value this causes! None of the theorists named above has identified, even mentioned in

102 [Bukharin 1972.]

a single word, let alone engaged with the importance and consequences for the crisis problematic of the transformation of values into prices of production.[103]

Bourgeois economics since Ricardo and Malthus has acknowledged the 'practical state of affairs'[104] of the uniform rate of profit. But neither the classical nor the post-Ricardian school have been able to reconcile this fact with value theory. They strayed into a theoretical dead-end as they were forced either to sacrifice the theory to the facts or the facts to the theory.[105] This contradiction between theory and facts, the impossibility of deducing the general rate of profit from the abstract labour theory of value eventually led to the demise of the post-Ricardian school, and Marx correctly indicates the cause of the school's dissolution in his epitaph, 'Elaboration of the *general rate of profit* ... *Failure to understand the relation between values and prices of production*.'[106] He raises the specific accusation against Ricardo that he 'postulated' a general rate of profit, in accord with reality, without inquiring 'how far its existence is in fact consistent with the determination of value by labour time', while in fact '*prima facie*, it *contradicts* it, and that its existence would therefore have to be explained through a number of intermediary stages'.[107] This is why Marx stresses the 'scientific inadequacy' of Ricardo's method, because it leads him

103 This is even true of Isaac Ilych Rubin who concedes: 'Thus the labour theory of value and the theory of production prices are not theories of two different types of economy, but theories of one and the same capitalist economy taken *on two different levels of scientific abstraction*', 1973, p. 253. Although, according to Rubin, prices of production are a more *concrete* level of abstraction than values, he investigates neither the problem of the transformation of values into prices of production nor its implications for the crisis problematic. The same is true of numerous other authors, such as Diehl 1898; Tugan-Baranowsky 1905, particularly p. 174; Bortkiewicz 1952; and Bortkiewicz 1907; and more recently Hans Zeisl 1930; as well as Emil Walter 1930. They all centre their interest on the problem of the calculation of values and prices. But they deal with it exclusively in order to find out how far Marx's deduction of prices of production from values is correct and compatible with his labour value theory. None of these authors have recognised the importance of the value-price transformation for the crisis problematic.

104 Marx 1981b, p. 270.

105 According to Marx, '[t]his confusion on the part of the theorists' is that

'all economics up til now has either violently made abstraction from distinctions between surplus value and profit, between rate of surplus value and rate of profit, so that it could retain the determination of value as its basis, or else it has abandoned, along with this determination of value, any kind of solid foundation for a scientific approach, so as to be able to retain those distinctions which obtrude themselves on the phenomenal level.' (Marx 1981b, pp. 268–9.)

106 Marx 1910c, p. 280 [Grossman's emphasis. Cf. Marx 1989c, p. 373.]

107 Marx 1989b, p. 401.

to 'erroneous results'. It consists of Ricardo 'begin[ning] with the determination of the magnitude of the value of the commodity by labour time and then examin[ing] whether the other economic relations and categories' correspond with or contradict that value. The inadequacy of this method therefore arises 'because it *omits some essential links and directly* seeks to prove the congruity of the economic categories with one another'.[108]

By reconstructing these 'intermediary stages' and reconciling the labour theory of value with the facts through his theory of the formation of a general rate of profit and of the transformation of values into prices of production and commercial prices, Marx advanced economic theory beyond the point at which the post-Ricardian school collapsed.

And precisely this specific result of Marx's theoretical research vanishes from the entire previous discussion of the problem of crisis and accumulation. It exists just as little for Rosa Luxemburg as for Otto Bauer, Hilferding or Bukharin. All of their analyses remain in the sphere of the value schema which is removed from reality, without being concerned that this schema is only the first approximation of reality, which does not represent this reality itself. They fail to see that, without the 'intermediary stages', the schema is not an appropriate means for the investigation of the developed *capitalist* mode of production and of those *concrete forms*, in which capitals confront each other 'in their actual movement'. As Engels correctly says in his preface to the second volume of *Capital*, the 'investigations of this volume 2 ... are *simply premises for the material of volume 3*, in which the *final results* of Marx's presentation of the process of social reproduction on the capitalist basis are developed.'[109] The presentation of the process of reproduction on the basis of the value schema in the second volume of *Capital*, therefore, contains only the premises of a line of argument whose *conclusions* only follow in the third volume of *Capital*, in the theory of the transformation of the value schemas into production price schemas. Only this theory completes Marx's chain of thought and concludes the method of successive approximation, after it has passed through all its stages and arrived at concrete reality. It is, needless to say, peculiar that the discussion of Marx so far has been guided not by an understanding of the totality of Marx's line of argument in all its stages but only by '*premises*', i.e. the value schema, ripped out of this coherent chain of thought. Instead of developing Marx further, as the theorists named above believed they were doing, they all

108 Marx 1989b, pp. 390 [Grossman emphasises 'omits some essential links and'. Editor's interpolations.]
109 Engels 1978a, p. 102. [Grossman's emphasis.]

return to the point at which the post-Ricardian school stalled and finally collapsed around 1850, the '[f]ailure to understand the relation between *values and prices of production*.'[110]

110 Marx 1910c, p. 280. [Grossman's emphasis. Cf. Marx 1989c, p. 373, where Marx's earlier term 'cost prices' is used.]

CHAPTER 13

Fifty Years of Struggle over Marxism 1883–1932*

Translated from German by Rick Kuhn and Einde O'Callaghan

1 Marxists of the Early Period

Until the end of the seventies of the last century, the circumstances for understanding Marx's ideas were not very favourable, even within the socialist camp. A particular difficulty was that *Capital* was initially only available as a torso, as only the first several volumes. Almost another three decades passed before the volumes completing the system appeared (the second volume in 1885, the third in 1894).[1] And a further 15 years passed before Karl Kautsky brought out the last of the volumes of *Theories of Surplus Value* (1910). These, intended by Marx as the fourth part of *Capital*, are a magnificent history of political economy from the end of the seventeenth century, one that bourgeois historical writing has been unable to equal.

During the first decade after the founding of the German Empire it was hardly possible to speak of 'Marxism' in Germany (and still less in other countries). There was only a very loose connection between the workers' movement and the theories of scientific socialism. Many years after [Ferdinand] Lassalle's death the German workers' movement was still under the influence of Lassalle's theories and activities. Apart from that, it drew its ideas and sentiments from memories of 1848, from Proudhon, Rodbertus and Eugen Dühring.[2] Many socialists justified their demands by appealing to ethics and humanity or oriented themselves on the publications of the International Workingmen's Association.[3] When the two tendencies in the German workers' movement (the so-called the 'Lassalleans' and the Marxist 'Eisenachers')[4] united at the Gotha Congress (1875), Lassalle's ideas and demands were in

* [Originally published as Grossmann 1932f and Grossman 1933a.]

1 [Marx, 1978b; Marx 1981b]

2 [From February 1848, a wave of revolutions, starting in Paris, swept east across Europe. Marx wrote critiques of Proudhon, Rodbertus and Dühring.]

3 Cf. Grünberg 1932. [Marx played a vital role in the leadership of the International Working Men's Association, later known as the First International, between 1864 and 1872, when it moved its seat to Philadelphia. It was shut down in 1876.]

4 [The Social Democratic Workers' Party, led by August Bebel and Wilhelm Liebknecht who were influenced by Marx, was founded at a congress in Eisenach in 1869. After its fusion with

large part incorporated into the newly agreed Gotha.[5] Initially workers in large-scale industry were not organised in either party, rather the bulk of the movement consisted of workers, such as shoemakers, tailors, book printers, tobacco workers, etc., who still retained close ties with the *petty bourgeoisie*. Lassalle's pamphlets and demands, his woolly conception of the state, his complete lack of clarity about the party's goal evidently expressed much more the labour movement's lack of maturity at that time than the cohesive and magnificent edifice of Marx's theory. Even the leading figures in the labour movement were, for a long time, unable to grasp key aspects of Marx's theory. Characteristic of this is the request, in 1868, (by Wilhelm Liebknecht, who during his stay in London had had a close relationship with Marx) that Engels make the actual differences between Marx and Lassalle clear in an article for the party organ.[6] From correspondence between Marx and Engels it is apparent how distressed Marx felt about the fact that German party circles were almost unbelievably indifferent to *Capital*.

Only gradually and in constant struggle against other views that were widespread in the labour movement (the struggle against Proudhonism and Bakuninism in the First International, Engels's polemic against Dühring in 1878, etc.)[7] did Marxist ideas permeate the workers' movement. From 1883 Karl Kautsky (born 1854) sought to spread Marxist ideas, as the editor of the party's theoretical organ, *Neue Zeit*. However, the period of the Anti-Socialist Law (1878–1890) was quite unfavourable for the theoretical consolidation of Marxism.[8]

The great popularity that Marx's lifework achieved was initially due to those sections of the first volume [of *Capital*] that describe the *immediate process of production* within the factory and thus make the situation of the working class, its exploitation by capital and everyday class struggles taking place before everyone's eyes intelligible. So this volume became the *Bible* of the working class for decades. The fate of the parts of the work which present the *historical tendencies of capitalist accumulation* and the tendency towards the breakdown of capitalism that follows in their wake was quite different. Here Marx was so far in advance of his epoch intellectually that these parts of his work, at first, necessarily remained incomprehensible. Capitalism had not yet achieved

---

the Lassallean General German Workers' Association in 1875, it became the Socialist Workers' Party of Germany, renamed the Social Democratic Party of Germany in 1890.]

5 Cf. Marx's criticisms in Marx 1989a.

6 [Wilhelm Liebknecht 1963, p. 88.]

7 [Engels 1987.]

8 [The Anti-socialist or Exceptional 'Law against the public danger of social democratic endeavours' banned social democratic organisations, publications and trade unions in Germany.]

the maturity that would have made its breakdown and the realisation of socialism an immediate reality. So it is understandable that in a review of volume 2 of *Capital* (1886) Kautsky explained that, in his opinion, this volume had less interest for the working class than the first, that for them only the production of surplus value in the factory was of importance.[9] The additional question of how this surplus value is realised was of more interest to the capitalists than to the working class! Kautsky's well-known book *The Economic Doctrines of Karl Marx* also exclusively confined itself to describing the contents of the first volume of *Capital*. Only an extremely deficient outline of the theories in the second and third volumes was added to later editions.[10]

Two generations had to pass after the appearance of *Capital* before capitalism, as a result of capital accumulation, matured to its current heights and conflicts developed in its womb that translated the problem of the realisation of socialism from the domain of a programmatic demand, only appropriate for the remote future, to the sphere of daily political practice. The understanding of Marx's ideas has also grown, in correspondence with the changed historical situation.

The situation was different after the end of the Anti-Socialist Law (1890), when the socialist movement started to develop rapidly from a small, persecuted group into the largest party in Germany and its appeal encompassed broad layers of intellectuals and the petty bourgeoisie, far beyond the working class. Outwardly, the strength of Marxism grew rapidly during this period. In the Erfurt Program (1891) it achieved a victorious expression. But, precisely at the time when the appearance of the third volume of *Capital* (1894) publicly concluded Marx's theoretical system, with the rapid blossoming of international capitalism and with the strengthening of an opportunist labour aristocracy inside the working class, a change occurred which was to be of the greatest significance for the further development of Marxist theory. Sooner or later social differentiation in the working class had to be expressed not only in politics but also in its theoretical conceptions of the goals and tasks of the labour movement.

9 Kautsky 1886, p. 164.
10 Kautsky 1925a.

2 The Advance of Reformism

a) *Revisionism*

The victory of opportunism, initially in England, then in France and Germany, as well as a series of smaller European countries is necessarily connected with the *structural transformation of world capitalism*, which exhibited extremely powerful development and increasingly showed its imperialist face, during the last decade of the previous century. Its fundamental economic traits are the replacement of free competition by monopoly and colonial expansion combined with bellicose entanglements. Through capital exports, monopolistic domination and exploitation of huge regions that supply raw materials and provide outlets for capital investment in Central and South America, Asia and Africa, the bourgeoisie and the financial oligarchy of the capitalist great powers acquire billions in superprofits. These make it possible for them to win over an *upper layer of the working class* and the petty bourgeois following of the socialist parties with higher wages and various other advantages, so that they take an interest in colonial exploitation, are politically bound to them and enter a community of interests with them against the broad masses and other countries. These upper layers were the bourgeoisie's channels of influence into the proletariat. The emergence of the labour aristocracy, which found expression politically in the formation of 'bourgeois workers' parties' on the model of the Labour Party in England, is typical of all the imperialist countries.[11]

These layers, which found the revolutionary tenets of Marxist theory inconvenient and a hindrance to their practical efforts to cooperate with the bourgeoisie and the organs of the state, soon went onto the offensive against Marxist theory, with the argument that it was *contradicted by capitalism's real tendencies*. Their main difference with Marxism was that it denied the possibility of a lasting improvement in the conditions of the working class under the current economic order (apart from temporary improvements for shorter periods) and advocated the opposite point of view: that when capitalism reached its full development, its immanent powers would necessarily lead to a worsening of workers' conditions. In contrast, the representatives of reformism pointed out that, even under the existing economic order, a lasting improvement in the situation of the workers – whether by means of *state legislation* (pensions, accident and unemployment insurance) or by means of self-help (by founding and expanding trade unions and consumer cooperatives) – was possible and already occurring. Here the rather slight improvement, confined to a narrow

11 Cf. Grünberg and Grossmann 1933.

upper layer only, was overvalued and generalised and its character was misjudged, to the extent that it was not considered temporary but the start of a transformation that was consistently expanding in breadth and depth.

The rising strength of the trade union movement was, undoubtedly, the most effective lever for the enforcement of antiradical attitudes. For the leaders of the trade unions – the typical representatives of the labour aristocracy – reformism was tailor-made. For these men, conducting the small-scale war for entirely gradual improvements in the situation of the workers that were again and again threatened by setbacks, all radicalism represented a threat to the positions they had conquered, their organisations and trade union funds. They therefore sought to nip every intensification of the methods of struggle in the bud. Under the Anti-Socialist Law, there was no room for such efforts as the trade unions then hardly suffered less than political social democracy. With the strengthening of the trade union movement, after the repeal of the Emergency Law, particularly from the foundation of the *General Commission of the Free Trade Unions* which was connected with the tight centralisation of the movement, the relationship of the trade unions to the party changed. The initial dependence on the political movement was soon transformed and, at both the Köln Trade Union Congress in May 1905 and the Mannheim Party Congress in September 1906, the trade unions and their leaders knew how to impose their demands – often on decisive questions too – against the will of the Party authorities.[12] Now their influence on the theoretical conceptions of the socialist workers' movement was also increasingly apparent. Gradually certain – essential – elements of Marxist theory were eroded by the practical trade union negotiators of wage agreements. In the hands of the trade union leaders the concept of '*class struggle*' experienced a gradual transformation, so that little of its original content remained. Under the same influences, the attitude of the trade union leaders to the state also changed. They pointed out the benefits they saw for the working class in the state institutions of social insurance, a system they hoped to be able to expand further. Thus these circles felt compelled to revise the ideas previously inherited from Marx ('revisionism'). During the nineties and after the turn of the century, a question was often raised as to whether a *special trade union theory* that would justify reformism – the perspective of a gradual 'socialisation', 'drop by drop' within the existing order – ought to be compiled for the socialist inclined trade unions. But it never came to such a trade union theory. All the friendlier was the trade union welcome for efforts emerging within the political party that accommodated their desires.

---

12 Cf. Grossmann 1932c, pp. 436–8.

Revisionism is inseparably linked with the name Eduard Bernstein (born 1850). He was the first to systematically demand a revision of Marx's theory, arguing that it did not correspond with the actual development of capitalism, even though the former radical Georg von Vollmar had earlier developed similar ideas, in his famous Eldorado speeches in Munich (1891) and in the pamphlet *State Socialism* (1892), and advocated reformist tactics.[13] Eduard Bernstein, who seemed to be a true disciple of the theory while Engels was still alive, emerged as a critic only after the death of the master, in his *Neue Zeit* articles of 1896–7, on 'Problems of socialism' (published in book form as *The Preconditions of Socialism*). Other writings by Bernstein are relevant: *How is Scientific Socialism Possible?, Guiding Principles for a Social Democratic Program, On the Theory and History of Socialism*.[14]

Bernstein never openly described Marxist theory as a whole as false. It is an essential feature of revisionism that it neither had the intention of nor succeeded in constructing a *complete theoretical edifice* to replace Marx's. Its historical significance lies primarily in the *influence of trade union and political practice*. Theory was only of concern to the extent that it was an obstacle to this *practical reformism*. This was to be disposed of through the revisionist critique that adapted theory to practice so that inconsistency between inherited revolutionary theory and reformist activity could be overcome. For this purpose, in his critique of Marx's theoretical edifice, Bernstein used the convenient procedure of sharply separating the enduring, generally valid elements of the theory – fundamental theoretical propositions – from its *variable* elements, because they are propositions of applied science. Under the cover of this distinction, however, the fundamental propositions of the theory were also incorporated, albeit on the pretext that they were now reinterpreted as not fundamental. The goal of revisionism was never declared to be the defeat of Marxism; it was, instead, supposed to be a matter of rejecting certain remnants of 'utopianism' that Marxism still allegedly carried in its baggage.

Bernstein's 'purification campaign' was an attempt to liberate socialism from Marx's *theory of value and surplus value*. Value is a construct in thought and not a phenomenon. Whether Marx's theory of value is correct or not, Bernstein argued, is superfluous for the demonstration of surplus labour, as surplus labour is an empirical fact which suffices alone as a rationale for socialism. Bernstein never offered such a rationale, a positive theory of capitalism, built on the fact of surplus labour, that led to socialism. He remained negative.

13 [Vollmar advocated a program of reform and alliances with bourgeois parties, in two speeches in Munich's Eldorado pub, Vollmar 1891; Vollmar 1892.]

14 Bernstein 1993; Bernstein 1901b; Bernstein 1909; Bernstein 1901a.

Bernstein concedes the accuracy of Marx's predictions about *increasing centralisation and concentration of capital,* increasing concentration of enterprises, a rising rate of surplus value (exploitation) and the fall in the profit rate but he maintains that the overall picture of capitalism in Marx's work is one-sidedly distorted. Marx supposedly neglects the countertendencies in the principal matter. Divisions among already concentrated capitals counteract the tendency to concentration. Income statistics show *growth in the number of shareholders* and the average magnitude of their shareholdings. Undeniably the number of property owners is growing both absolutely and relatively. And the employment statistics, for their part, prove that the *middle classes are expanding.* Finally enterprise statistics irrefutably demonstrate that in a whole series of branches of industry small and medium-sized firms are quite viable alongside large concerns. This applies not only to industry but also to commerce. To the extent that large enterprises are concerned, developments in agriculture demonstrate either no change at all or a decline in the scale of operations. After Bernstein, Eduard David attempted to show that in agriculture a development in the size of operations had begun that was diametrically opposed to Marx's prediction. His thesis contended that small-scale operations were not only viable but were even a superior form of production.[15]

Bernstein regards the Marxist *theory of crisis and breakdown* as an *a priori* construct in accordance with Hegel's scheme of development. In various ways, actual developments have taken a different course than they would have if breakdown were unavoidable for purely economic reasons. Bernstein concedes the possibility of *local* or particular crises but the huge territorial *expansion of the world market,* the *reduction* of the time required for communications and the transport of goods, combined with the elasticity of the modern credit system and the emergence of cartels have created the possibility that local disturbances will cancel each other out. The occurrence of general crises should, therefore, be considered unlikely. Bernstein does not treat breakdown from the perspective of whether it was the necessary result of the immanent development of capitalism, whether with the existing level of economic development and the degree of maturity of the working class a sudden catastrophe might be to the advantage of social democracy. Bernstein answers these questions in the negative because there is a greater guarantee of enduring successes in a steady forward march than in the possibilities offered by a catastrophe. It is precisely in the theory of breakdown that Bernstein sees the quintessence of 'utopianism' in Marxism, because this makes the victory of socialism dependent on its

15 David 1903.

'immanent economic necessity'.[16] Bernstein combats the 'iron necessity of history'[17] and the *materialist conception of history* as a theory of historical necessity and emphasises the increasing effectiveness of ideological and ethical factors. Against Marx he appeals to Kant. The victory of socialism does not depend on economic necessity but on the moral maturity of the working class, i.e. its realisation that socialism is desirable.

Ultimately, Bernstein *conjures away the final goal* of socialism, ('[T]he final goal ... whatever it may be, is nothing to me, the movement everything.')[18] The final objective is subordinate; instead, the attention and energy of the working class should be concentrated on 'immediate goals', on 'daily, detailed work' which will lead to an advance in cultural development, higher morality and legal conceptions. It is apparent that such a formulation of the tasks of the workers' movement has nothing at all to do with socialism and coincides with the conceptions of bourgeois liberalism. The general perspective that in all individual goals there is always a pointer to a further goal, yet to be achieved that has to be pursued later only leads to '*progression to infinity* and that is diametrically counterposed to the essence of socialism, which at a particular stage of development, wants to and should replace one definite system with another'.[19]

It was only consistent that when Bernstein gave up the final goal he simultaneously abandoned the revolutionary tactics necessary to achieve it. In contrast to Marx's *theory of class struggle* and his conception that force is the midwife of every society that is coming into being, Bernstein emphasises *parliamentary* activity as the means for emancipating the working class. The idea of conquering political power through revolutionary action is supposedly a foreign body in Marxism, a remnant of Blanquism[20] from which Engels parted towards the end of his life.

From his critique, Bernstein drew the conclusion that it was false and disastrous to count on great social catastrophes and to focus the party's tactics on them. The utopia of a coming revolution had to be given up. Development blunts class antagonisms and democratises society. It is appropriate to promote this development. In order to gain influence social democracy has to find the

16 [Bernstein 1993, pp. 199–200.]

17 [Bernstein 1993, p. 20.]

18 [Bernstein 1898, p. 556; Bernstein makes a very similar statement in Bernstein 1993, p. 190.]

19 [Brauer 1929, p. 142. Grossman's emphasis.]

20 [Blanquism is a political approach influenced by or similar to that of Louis Auguste Blanqui who regarded revolution as the product of the efforts of a small group of dedicated conspirators which would establish a temporary dictatorship in the interests of the masses.]

courage 'to make up its mind to appear what it is in reality today: *a democratic socialist party of reform*'.[21]

From all this it is apparent, as Brauer correctly emphasises, that Bernstein is no socialist in the Marxist sense, because he is caught up in political categories.[22] For Marx, the proletarian revolution is not just a 'political act' that replaces the old power, based on parliament, with a new one, but is simultaneously a 'social' revolution insofar as it abolishes the whole of the previous form of society to replace it with a new one. Class struggle – just like its highest form, civil war – is not, for Marx, the product of the good or bad will of the people and cannot be replaced at discretion by parliamentary activity. Instead, class struggle and revolution are inevitable concomitants of the immanent economic necessity with which development drives towards socialism.

The considerable influence Bernstein exercised on intellectuals can be explained by the fact that the boldness of his approach was initially captivating because, in contrast to the fear that Marxism was being petrified, it in seemed to pave the way for the further development. At the same time, he won over those who, for opportunist reasons, did not wish to 'commit' themselves and found in Bernstein's limited determinations and qualifications the bolt holes they desired for their own indecision.

Among the critics of the Marxist theory of crisis and breakdown who, like Bernstein, proceed from an ethical perspective, the Russian Professor Mikhail Tugan-Baranovsky particularly excelled, with arguments that were later used extensively by revisionists.[23] According to Tugan-Baranovsky, crises and the ultimate breakdown of capitalism cannot be due to a lack of markets since, in the course of the expansion of production, the individual spheres of production reciprocally create new market opportunities. Tugan-Baranovsky seeks to prove this, using a reproduction schema based on Marx's. Nor need the [relative] reduction of social consumption as a result of technological progress and the replacement of human labour by machines lead to overproduction. With the expansion of production, *human* consumption is replaced by *productive* consumption, i.e. stronger demand for means of production. According to Tugan-Baranovsky, these results of abstract theoretical analysis are confirmed by the empirical facts. Recent capitalist development shows a strong expansion

21 [Bernstein 1993, p. 186. [Grossman's emphasis.]]

22 [Brauer 1929, p. 148.]

23 Tugan-Baranowsky 1901; [Tugan-Baranowsky 2000, a translation of chapters I and IV in Tugan-Baranowsky 1901]; Tugan-Baranowsky 1905; Tugan-Baranowsky 1910.

of the industries producing means of production, such sectors as coal and steel, mechanical engineering, chemicals, etc., whose products do not flow into human consumption, while those sectors directly serving human consumption, such as textiles (cotton) have almost reached a standstill.

The absolute *limit for the expansion* of production is constituted by the productive forces that society possesses at any time. *Capital can never reach this limit* to the extent that this expansion of production occurs *proportionately* in all branches of production. Capitalist crises are thus exclusively the result of disproportional investment in individual spheres. With proportional investment, the productive forces of capitalism can develop without limit. 'The capitalist economy cannot break down for *economic* reasons.'[24] Marx's theory of value is superfluous for the demonstration of surplus labour. Surplus product is not the product of the wage labourer employed and exploited in production alone but is the produce of the whole of society as a unit. Capitalist society's defect is that the propertied class appropriates this surplus product. The end of this unjust system can thus only be the result of ethical causes. 'There is, therefore, no occasion to suppose that capitalism will some day die a *natural death*; it will be destroyed by the *conscious will* of people, by that social class which has been the foremost object of capitalistic exploitation – the proletariat.'[25] For this reason, Tugan-Baranovsky praises so-called utopian socialism, which was far more scientific than Marxism, to the extent that it did not attempt to provide untenable objective justifications for its ethical demands that the existing economic order be reorganised.

In addition to those mentioned, Conrad Schmidt, the author of a valuable book on *The Average Rate of Profit on the Basis of Marx's Law of Value*, which was praised by Engels, ought to be mentioned. Yet he soon became one of the fiercest opponents of Marx's theory of value and surplus value. He was not, however, content to criticise and reject Marx's conception, but himself undertook a systematic analysis of the capitalist economy and its laws.[26] Here Schmidt reached the same conclusion that Marx deduced about the capitalist economy: with the purchasing power in the form of wages, to which he is entitled, the worker can only buy an amount of value for whose production only a fraction of the labour that he performed was necessary. In other words, if the commodities he produced are to be profitable for the employer, he must

24 [Tugan-Baranovsky 1904, p. 304 et seq.]

25 [Tugan-Baranovsky 1910, p. 96.]

26 See Schmidt 1889; and his articles on the theory of value and crises: Schmidt 1899; Schmidt 1901; Schmidt 1910; in particular, Schmidt 1915.

always perform *surplus labour*. But, according to Schmidt, this basic result was achieved without having to use Marx's untenable law of value. In this way many contradictions associated with this law of value can be avoided.

b) *The Neo-Kantians*

In addition to the revisionist movement, which sought to undermine the economic and political foundations of Marxism, a stronger revisionist current in the *field of philosophy* also arose within social democracy, towards the end of the last century. The entry of broad intellectual layers into the workers movement soon led to a discussion about the *meaning and validity* of the '*materialist conception of history*'. Engels already made certain modifications, in letters to socialist university graduates who asked him for information (see, in particular the letter of 21 September 1890 to Joseph Bloch). In these letters, Engels warned against exaggerations and observed that 'some younger writers attribute more importance to the economic aspect than is due to it'[27] and that the economic situation was not the *only* but merely the determining moment[28] of socio-historical development in the *last instance*. These intellectuals imported *secondary idealist currents* into the workers' movement, that abandon the materialist conception of history or seek to combine it with idealism. This is particularly so in France, where Jean Jaurès in his Latin dissertation of 1891[29] develops an idealist conception of history according to which it is the product of the human spirit – a conception that he also retained later as a socialist. The idealist current is assisted by some supporters of the materialist conception of history such as, for example, Paul Lafargue (1842–1911) whose crude interpretations helped discredit it.[30] In Germany a current, initially arising in *university philosophy departments*, seeks to justify socialism idealistically and to link it with Kant. It originates with Hermann Cohen (1842–1918), the founder of Neo-Kantianism, the so-called 'Marburg School' who, in his 'Introduction' to Friedrich Albert Lange's *History of Materialism*,[31] attempted to prove that socialism is 'based on the socialism of ethics' and to this extent Kant was 'the true and genuine initiator of German socialism'. In his book *Economics and Law According to the Materialist Conception of History* Rudolf Stammler (of

27 Engels 2001, p. 36.
28 ['Moment' is a Hegelian term, here with the sense of 'aspect'.]
29 See Grossmann 1932e. [Jaurès 1891.]
30 Cf. Lafargue 1909.
31 Cohen 1896.

Halle) recognised this as, so far, the best and most consistent method for *causal* research into economic development but demanded that it be supplemented by *goal-setting* ('teleological') considerations. Only by means of the latter is it possible to achieve the highest social goal, which Stammler regards as the 'community of people who want to be free', where 'everybody makes the objectively justified purposes of the other his own'.[32] Franz Staudinger (1849–1921) attempted even more in his writings, to reconcile the Marxist standpoint with Kant's epistemological critique and ethics.[33] Each Kantian had to come to Marx by logically developing his own basic ideas. And vice versa: 'As soon as Marxism no longer merely pursues social development scientifically in accordance with the causal viewpoint but makes *conscious and planned transformation* of the given into its goal, it arrives at Kant, as a result of consistent pursuit of its own principle.'[34] Along similar lines to Staudinger, Karl Vorländer in his writings[35] advocated a combination of 'Marx' and 'Kant', i.e. a combination of an economic, historical with an epistemologically critical, ethical justification for socialism.

This current, which initially arose outside the socialist movement, soon also created an echo within it, particularly in the ranks of the revisionists: Eduard Bernstein, Conrad Schmidt and Ludwig Woltmann, who also attempted to undermine Marxism through philosophy, but also in the ranks of the then radical, younger Viennese Marxists, such as Max Adler and Otto Bauer, who ultimately deviated into the camp of reformism.[36] They all demanded a stronger consideration of 'ideological' moments, epistemological critique and ethics in socialist theory. Similar attempts by Russian revisionism in the field of philosophy evoked the resolute resistance of Plekhanov and Lenin.[37] On the whole, revisionism remains negative philosophically and proves itself to be just as infertile here as in the field of economics. With the victory of reformism in German Social Democracy during and after the War, however, these currents succeed in coming into their own. It is characteristic of the completely altered attitude of socialism in this period that the article on the

32 Stammler 1896, pp. 575–6.
33 Staudinger 1899; Staudinger 1907. [Grossman's emphasis.]
34 [Staudinger 1899, p. 159.]
35 Vorländer 1900; Vorländer 1926.
36 Woltmann 1900; Adler 1904; Adler 1908; Adler 1913; Adler 1925; Otto Bauer 1906, directed against Kautsky; Kautsky 1906.
37 See Grossmann 1932i; Lenin 1962b.

philosophical foundations of socialism in *The Program of Social Democracy: Suggestion for its Renewal*, which appeared before the Görlitz Party Congress, was written by the above-mentioned Kantian Karl Vorländer, at the request of authoritative party circles.[38]

As far as revisionism as a whole is concerned, it is not only the circumstance that both Bernstein and Tugan-Baranovsky subscribe to the theory of marginal utility[39] that lends it an *individualistic aspect* but also, as was shown, its attempt to replace the Marxist materialist dialectic with Kantian ethics and epistemological critique. For, in contrast to socialism insofar as it is a fundamental socialism, Kant's starting point, it must be insisted, is the *autonomous personality*. Here, however, there is a fundamental contradiction with socialism in general and Marxist socialism in particular, which only knows and explains individuals as conditioned by the social environment.

Revisionism as a whole has not been able to replace Marxist theory with one of its own that in any respect grasps the economic mechanism with its social interconnections. It remained stuck in critique and therefore the question of whether, in principle, revisionism should be pronounced to be socialism has to be answered in the negative. But also as pure critique the standpoint of revisionism has proved to be false. One only needs to compare its critique of the Marxist account of how artisanal production and the middle classes are prone to crises and concentration, and finally its conception of the superiority of small-scale operations in agriculture with the *experience of the postwar period*,[40] in order to see that history has proved that not revisionism but Marx is correct. Anyone who delves into *Capital* today, after seven decades, has to concede with astonishment how correctly, indeed prophetically, Marx understood the large-scale tendencies of capitalist development.

Over the two decades before the World War, reformism became an *international phenomenon*. Much earlier than in Germany, it appeared in *England*. There, the first mass movement of the proletariat, the Chartist movement, was defeated in the 1830s and 1840s. But its struggle had shown the English bourgeoisie the danger that threatened it. Subsequently, it knew how to calm the dissatisfaction of the working class by means of concessions and the timely grant of real benefits to its upper layer, which its supremacy on the world

---

38 Vorländer 1920.

39 [i.e. mainstream neoclassical economics, as opposed to Marx's labour theory of value.]

40 See Pollock 1932 and Gumperz 1931.

market permitted. In this manner over a long period, it successfully prevented the English proletariat from combining to create an independent political party. The whole energy of the working class turned to developing trade unions, mutual funds and cooperatives. The great reorganisation of local government gave workers the opportunity to represent their interests, through autonomous local authorities, in the field of municipal economic and welfare services. The trade unions developed a purely reformist practice. The revolutionary traditions of Chartism were forgotten. The reformist-socialist Fabian Society, founded in 1883–4 and consisting of a few hundred intellectuals, gained considerable influence in bourgeois circles and the trade union bureaucracy, under the leadership of Sidney Webb (born 1859) and George Bernard Shaw. The report they wrote for the International Socialist Congress in London (1896) provides a clear insight into the essence of the Fabians.[41]

The Fabians do not want to be a party; instead they want to permeate all existing organisations and movements with Fabian ideas. The 'tactic of permeation' is one of the specific characteristics of the Fabians. 'The Fabian Society endeavours to rouse social compunction by making the public conscious of the evil condition of society under the present system.'[42] Apart from the Fabian Society's numerous pamphlets (tracts), English reformism found its theoretical expression above all in the works of the couple, Sidney and Beatrice Webb, and of James Ramsay MacDonald.[43] The Labour Party, which was finally founded in 1900, immediately adopted the reformist principles and practice of the Fabians and the trade unions.

In *France* one already finds reformism in the pamphlets that Paul Brousse published in Paris in 1881–2.[44] Brousse was the founder of the party of the so-called 'Possibilists', which existed until 1899. Subsequently, reformist ideas were most strongly promoted by the activity of Jean Jaurès, who also advocated participation in a bourgeois government (ministerialism) in 1899.[45] In the Socialist Party of *Italy* too – despite the weak industrial development of the country –

41 [Shaw 1896.]

42 [Shaw 1896, p. 7.]

43 Webb and Webb 1895 [German edition with an afterword by Eduard Bernstein, original edition Webb and Webb 1894]; Webb and Webb 1897; Webb and Webb 1911; Webb and Webb 1920; Webb and Webb 1923; MacDonald 1912 [German edition with a foreword by Eduard Bernstein, original edition MacDonald 1905].

44 [Brousse 1882.]

45 See Grossmann 1932e. [Ministerialism was the participation of socialists in bourgeois governments as ministers.]

strong reformist currents appeared, essentially represented by petty bourgeois intellectuals who participated in all the theoretical controversies about impoverishment and concentration that were fought out from time to time in the party's theoretical organ *Critica sociale* in the period 1895–1905, after the publication of volume 3 of *Capital*. The syndicalist Professor Arturo Labriola (son of Antonio Labriola), in his *Study of Marx*, was the foremost critic of the theory of impoverishment and breakdown.[46] In *Economic Speculation* and *The Dictatorship of the Bourgeoisie*,[47] he dealt with the problem of imperialism. With the stronger industrial development of the country after 1905, the related intensification of class struggles and the advance of reaction within the bourgeoisie, numerous intellectuals abandoned socialism. Émile Vandervelde in *Belgium* worked with the same orientation as Jaurès in France.[48] Reformism took a specific form in Russia. Its most notable theoretical representatives were Tugan-Baranovsky and Petr Berngardovich Struve who, however, soon swung over to liberalism. It achieved mass political influence in the workers' movement in Menshevism.[49]

c) *The Radicals on the Defensive*

The efforts of revisionism were soon countered by the so-called 'radicals' or 'orthodox Marxists', Karl Kautsky, Franz Mehring, Heinrich Cunow, Parvus, but above all Rosa Luxemburg, in *Neue Zeit* and in specific polemical writings, while the revisionists used the newly founded *Sozialistische Monatshefte*.[50]

Kautsky's *Agrarian Question* targets the revisionist critique of Marx's presentation of developmental trends in agriculture.[51] This is Kautsky's most significant and independent economic work, although even here the historical-

46 Labriola 1926.

47 Labriola 1907; Labriola 1924.

48 Vandervelde 1906; Vandervelde 1901; Vandervelde 1908; Vandervelde 1902; Vandervelde 1925.

49 Cf. Grossmann 1931b, p. 423.

50 [Kautsky 1899b. When editor of the daily *Sächsiger Arbeiter-Zeitung*, Parvus wrote a series of articles, Parvus 1898. Mehring's articles appeared in another daily party newspaper, Mehring 1898a, Mehring 1898b, Mehring 1898c; Cunow 1898; Luxemburg 2008a. [For writings by major contributors to the debate and an introductory overview, see Tudor and Tudor 1988. The contents of *Neue Zeit*, the official theoretical journal of the German Social Democratic Party, and *Sozialistische Monatshefte*, the organ of the right wing of the Party, for the period are accessible online from http://library.fes.de/inhalt/digital/zeitschriften.htm, accessed 20 June 2013.]

51 Kautsky 1988a.

descriptive element crowds out the purely theoretical aspect. In his anti-critique directed against Bernstein's critique,[52] Kautsky deals with the questions of *method, program* and *tactics*, particularly the tenets disputed by Bernstein: the theory of breakdown, developmental trends with regard to enterprise size (large and small enterprises), the increase in the number of property owners and the middle class, the theory of impoverishment and crisis. Here Kautsky seeks to refute Bernstein's claims about the alleviation of capitalist contradictions, by means of philological interpretation of Marx's texts and comprehensive company, tax and other statistics, and to defend the thesis that class contradictions are intensifying. In the course of doing so, he relaxes or completely abandons important fundamentals of Marxist theory. Even the Erfurt Program (1891), which was drawn up by Kautsky and signified the high-point in the Marxist development of German Social Democracy, portrays the decisive point of the political program very vaguely. The process of capitalist development seems to be the result of blind social forces. The *conquest of power* is wrapped in total darkness. The *dictatorship of the proletariat* is not even mentioned. As a result, the political aspect of Marxism was virtually decapitated, until Lenin reconstructed it over 25 years later.[53] Engels's critique of the draft program of 1891 was disregarded and ineffective, just as Marx's critique of the draft Gotha program had been in 1875.[54] In the dispute with Bernstein, Kautsky now intensified the reinterpretation of Marx's original theory even further. Compared with Bernstein's demand that the Party should become a democratic socialist party of reform, he emphasised that Social Democracy 'had to become a party of *social revolution*'.[55] Here, however, Kautsky added that it was not a matter the concept of revolution 'in the sense of an armed uprising' but of 'every large-scale *political convulsion* that accelerated the political life of the nation and made it pulsate most energetically'. Admittedly 'extra-legal use of violence' could form an episode in such a convulsion but could never be the revolution itself. In this reinterpretation of the concept of 'political revolution', its real content – the transfer of power into the hands of a new class – was clearly lost. At the time, Engels's 'political testament', his famous introduction to *The Class Struggles in France*, written in 1895, played a not unimportant role in the debate over tactics. He allegedly revised the tactics of the workers' movement and supposedly counterposed barricade struggles – violent revolution – to purely legal struggle –

52 Kautsky 1899b.

53 [This is a reference to Lenin 1964c.]

54 [Engels 1990a; Marx1989a.]

55 [Kautsky 1899b, pp. 181–3, Grossman's emphasis.]

parliamentarism. It emerged 30 years later, thanks to David Riazanov who uncovered the correct text, that the 'Introduction' was published by the Party executive in an abridged form which significantly distorted its meaning.[56]

Kautsky also reconstructed the economic side of Marxism in important points, by interpreting his own conceptions into Marx's text. Initially, this was not sufficiently recognised by the socialist public, since he appeared in the role of the defender of Marx's theory against Bernstein and adhered to Marx's traditional terminology. That was particularly the case for Marx's theory of breakdown and crisis. Instead of maintaining Marx's theory of breakdown, the theory of the objective necessity of the demise of capitalism, in its genuine form against the distortion in the revisionist critique, that the breakdown could happen 'automatically' without the active intervention of the proletariat, Kautsky denied this decisive position of Marx's system altogether and portrayed the theory of breakdown as Bernstein's invention. At the same time and in contradiction with this, he maintained in relation to crises that, while production could expand practically without limit, external and internal markets had their limits. Consequently, '*from a specific historic moment onwards the capitalist mode of production would become impossible*'. Not only a temporary crisis but 'incurable chronic overproduction' would then set in, as the 'final limit' on the maintenance of the capitalist regime. The significance of this '*utmost limit of the viability*' of today's society was that socialism [would emerge] from the sphere of nebulous ideas 'to become a *necessary* goal of practical politics'.[57]

That Kautsky's unclear and contradictory attitude to important elements of Marx's theory was unsatisfactory is clear and all the more so when Kautsky's theoretical confusion increased in his later writings. Three years later in a series of articles, on 'Crisis theory', directed against Tugan-Baranovsky's critique he combats Tugan-Baranovsky's view that crises arise from lack of *proportionality* in production and argues against his assertion of the possibility that capitalism could expand without limit: 'the capitalist mode of production has its limits which it cannot transcend'. Yet, after a [further] quarter of a century, in his preface to the popular edition of the second volume of *Capital* he embraced Tugan-Baranovsky's theory of disproportionality as the cause of crises, which he had earlier combated, without any reservations.[58] In his last large work, in the autumn of his life, Kautsky finally abandoned the Marxist theory of the

56 Engels 1990b. [This edition indicates the abridgements made when the 'Introduction' was first published.]

57 [Kautsky 1899b, pp. 142, 145. [Grossman's emphasis.]]

58 Kautsky 1902; Kautsky 1926.

impassable limits of capitalist development and based himself on Tugan-Baranovsky's theory of the possibility of the unlimited expansion of capitalism, which he had criticised 25 years earlier, and with that disowned his lifework. The pattern that every mode of production ultimately survives to become a fetter on production during its decline does not apply to capitalism. Industrial capitalism does not lead to decline, but 'to an ever *more rapid development of the productive forces*'. Kautsky claims that post war capitalism has 'demonstrated in practice in the most impressive fashion its ability to survive and to adapt to the most diverse, even the most desperate situations. *There are no arguments of economic theory* that could call its *vitality* into question.' Although he – Kautsky – had anticipated a chronic crisis of capitalism three decades earlier, this proved to be false. 'Capitalism … is today, considered from the purely economic standpoint, *more solidly established* than ever.'[59]

If one bears in mind Kautsky's later development, already present in nascent form at the time of his disputes with Bernstein in his unclear and vacillating position on important points of theoretical principle, it is comprehensible that the controversy between these two theoreticians did not and could not result in the clarification of fundamental questions of Marxist theory. Both had abandoned Marxist theory in decisive points and conducted the struggle only over less important points, sometimes merely over words. At the time only a few (Rosa Luxemburg) noticed this. However great Kautsky's service was in popularising Marxism, the real *revolutionary character* of Marxism remained alien to him. In Kautsky's struggle with Bernstein, ultimately Bernstein was the victor.

The arguments advanced by Parvus (Israel Lazarevich Helphand), an enthusiastic social patriot during the War, in a series of writings against revisionism were more effective.[60]

Most impressive and enduring were Rosa Luxemburg's essays, the highpoint of which, on the theoretical side, is her *Social Reform or Revolution*, published against Bernstein's *Preconditions* (now assembled with the essay against French Ministerialism and with Rosa Luxemburg's speeches at party congresses, under the title *Against Reformism*).[61]

If Bernstein was expecting the transition to socialism [to result] from the progressive development of the bourgeois *legal system*, from *statutory social reform*, Rosa Luxemburg explains, then he was committing a fundamental error with regard to the essence of capitalist class rule. This rests, in contrast

59 Kautsky 1988b, pp. 421, 424–56. [Grossman's emphasis.]

60 Parvus 1901; Parvus 1908; Parvus 1910; Parvus 1907.

61 Luxemburg 1925a. [*Social Reform or Revolution*: Luxemburg 2008a.]

to earlier class societies, not on legally anchored 'acquired rights' but on *real economic forces*. 'In our juridical system there is not a single legal formula for the class domination of today.' 'No law obliges the proletariat to submit itself to the yoke of capitalism. Poverty, the lack of means of production', which are taken from it not by law but by economic development, 'obliges the proletariat to submit itself to the yoke of capitalism'. The exploitation of the working class as an economic process cannot, therefore, be abolished or moderated by legal provisions within the framework of bourgeois society. 'Social reform', factory laws, health and safety regulations, do not indicate an element of 'social control' in the interests of the working class, they do not constitute 'a *threat* to capitalist exploitation but simply the *regulation* of exploitation' in the interests of capitalist society itself. In fact, development leads to an accentuation and intensification of the contradictions of capitalism. From the standpoint of *individual* capitalists, *credit, business associations* and other means that allegedly serve to overcome these contradictions and to regulate production are only suited to adjust their insufficient means to the demands of the market, to raise falling profit rates in cartelised branches of industry at the expense of the others. Cartels cancel out their own effectiveness when they extend to *all* the more important branches of production. From the standpoint of the economy as a *whole*, credit helps increase production beyond the limits of the market and promotes the most reckless speculation. Far from being means to moderate the contradictions of capitalism, business associations and credit, on the contrary, powerfully aggravate and promote crises and must accelerate its downfall. The breakdown of bourgeois society – says Rosa Luxemburg not only against Bernstein but evidently against Kautsky too – is the cornerstone of scientific socialism. The historical necessity of socialist upheaval is based 'First, on the growing anarchy of [the] capitalist economy, leading inevitably to its ruin'. If, however, the progressive moderation of contradictions is assumed, if it is assumed 'that capitalist development does not move in the direction of its own ruin, then socialism ceases to be *objectively necessary*'. Then its justification is only possible by means of 'pure reason', that is an 'idealist explanation', while 'the objective necessity of socialism, the explanation of socialism as the result of the material development of society, falls to the ground.'[62]

With the same acuity, Rosa Luxemburg also develops her principal tactical ideas about the class struggle. Radical Marxism too desires everyday social reform work, a tactical orientation to current questions – the trade union struggle over wages, the struggle for social reform and the democratisation

62 [Luxemburg 2008a, pp. 45–7, 61, 90–2. Grossman's emphasis. Editor's interpolation.]

of political institutions – just as much as reformism. 'The difference is not in the *what*, but in the *how*.' Because it starts from the assumption that the political seizure of power is impossible, reformism wants, through 'trade union and parliamentary activity [to] gradually reduce capitalist exploitation itself. They remove from capitalist society its capitalist character. They realise *objectively* the desired social change'. By contrast, for Marxism trade union and political struggle is significant only as necessary preparation of the *subjective factor* in socialist upheaval – the working class – for the decisive revolutionary battle, first organising the workers 'as a class' and effecting the emergence of *understanding*, of united proletarian *class consciousness*. The socialist transition will not come of its own accord by fatalistically waiting for it to occur. It results, instead, from understanding, won in the everyday struggle of the working class, that the supersession of capitalism's objectively intensifying contradictions through social upheaval is indispensible. Thus for Rosa Luxemburg, as later for Lenin, *reforms are only by-products* of class struggle oriented on revolution. Revisionism, by contrast, makes everyday work independent of the final socialist goal. It separates reform from revolution and, by raising the movement to an *end in itself*, changes its character. It is no longer a means to achieve that goal – social upheaval – but, instead of this upheaval, has itself become the goal. This undialectical attitude sees only mutually exclusive opposites – either/or, reform or revolution – but not the subsumption of these opposites in the totality of the social process.[63]

As we see, only with these explanations is the concept of the 'final goal', neglected in the *Erfurt program*, defined. Rosa Luxemburg does not understand the 'final goal' as the ideal state of the future, to be erected after the socialist upheaval, but as the conquest of political power, the *revolution* itself. If the future state is understood as the 'final goal' then *every* democratic or economic achievement can be considered to be a step on the path to this goal. But if the conquest of political power through revolution is regarded as the final goal, a sharp boundary is drawn with reformism, which replaces the strategic task of *developing people's revolutionary capacity* with current, opportunist work or the propagation of a more or less vague final goal to be awaited fatalistically. So Rosa Luxemburg's interpretation of Marxism assigns the decisive role to working class political activism, through the orientation of current work towards the final revolutionary goal, even though the seizure of state power is dependent on the objective course of material social development and 'presupposes ... a

63 [Luxemburg 2008a, pp. 66–9. Editor's interpolation.]

definite degree of maturity of economic and political relations'.[64] Marxism is therefore sharply distinguished from both fatalism and pure voluntarism.

For the fate of the dispute between reformists and radicals, see the article 'Internationals'.[65] Reformism was defeated in all *theoretical* skirmishes, condemned by resolutions of party conferences and international congresses, refuted again and again anew by the prevailing intensification of class contradictions in the course of *actual development*. But, maturing on the basis of the aristocracy of labour, it nevertheless made a triumphal procession through the daily practice of the workers' movement. The growing power of Marxism was, however, demonstrated by the fact that, of all the socialist tendencies in all European countries during the first half of the nineteenth century – Saint-Simonism, Proudhonism, later Blanquism,[66] etc. – it alone dominated the masses intellectually and that reformism, in order to be capable of winning over the masses, had to sail under the flag of Marxism.

d) *Reformism in Marxist Disguise (the Neo-harmonists)*

Here we refer primarily to 'Austro-Marxism', a group of Viennese intellectuals – Rudolf Hilferding, Otto Bauer, Max Adler and Karl Renner – grouped around the newly established theoretical review *Kampf* (from 1908). They attempted to provide theoretical formulations for reformist practice. The most important book from this tendency, one that strongly influenced later theoretical development, is Rudolf Hilferding's *Finance Capital*. Its two components have to be distinguished. On the one hand, Hilferding strives to integrate the latest phenomena of economic life – trusts, cartels, export of capital, imperialist expansionism – in short *monopoly capitalism*, which has replaced competitive capitalism, into the system of Marx's economics. On the other hand, following Tugan-Baranovsky's theory of crisis and renouncing the Marxist theory of breakdown, Hilferding endeavours to reinterpret the Marxist theory of breakdown in the harmonistic spirit of the limitless possibilities for capitalist expansion. Reviving Jean-Baptiste Say's old theory, which Marx always combated, that *primarily general* overproduction is impossible because individual spheres of production create markets for each other, Hilferding reaches the conclusion that crises are not necessarily associated with the essence of capitalism. They arise simply from disproportion in growth among individual spheres, i.e. only

64 [Luxemburg 2008a, p. 95.]

65 Grossmann 1932c; and Grossmann 1932d.

66 [Saint-Simonism was the theories of the French utopian socialist Henri de Saint-Simon and his followers. Proudhonism, drew on the writings of Pierre-Joseph Proudhon. Blanquism was inspired by the revolutionary actions and writings of Louis August Blanqui.]

from '*unregulated* production'. If the distribution of capital among individual branches of industry is proportional then there is no limit to production, 'production *can be expanded indefinitely* without leading to the overproduction of commodities'. In short, if production, even on a capitalist basis, can be regulated, crises can be avoided.[67]

The foundation of the work is Hilferding's theory of money and credit, which departs from Marx's theory of money and distorts it in the spirit of [Georg Friedrich] Knapp's 'chartalism'.[68] Certainly, for this purpose, Hilferding has to breach the general validity of Marx's law of value for the money commodity, which Karl Kautsky correctly asserted meant 'the suicide of Marxism'.[69] The theory of finance capital is built on the foundation of this theory of money. The characteristic feature of the most recent developments is the *dominant role of bank capital compared with industry*. With capitalist development, the total sum of money made available to the banks by the non-productive classes and through the banks to the industrialists, i.e. the role of bank capital in the form of money that is transformed into industrial capital, constantly grows. A particular role falls here to the type of enterprise known as a *joint stock company*. With shares so-called *fictitious* capital, detached from productive capital functioning in factories, arises. It enables banks to rapidly *concentrate ownership*, independently of the concentration of factories and is accelerated by speculation on the stock exchange and the accumulation of promoter's profit[70] by the banks. By means of this 'mobilisation of capital', an ever growing portion of capital in industry becomes finance capital, i.e. it no longer belongs to the industrialists working with it. The direction of capital invested in industry falls more and more to banks. '[T]hey become founders and eventually rulers of industry.' The tendency towards *concentration in banking*, towards progressive elimination of competition among banks, 'would finally result in a single bank or a group of banks establishing control over the entire money capital. Such a "central bank" would then *exercise control over social production as a whole*.'[71]

A parallel tendency towards combination is also at work in production. In a section on 'the historical tendency of finance capital', probably intended to be a counterpart to Marx's famous chapter on 'The historical tendency of capitalist accumulation', Hilferding presents the course of historical development

---

67 Hilferding 1981, p. 241. [Grossman's emphasis.]

68 ['Chartalism' is a theory of fiat money, issued and backed by law rather than precious metals, elaborated in Knapp 1924.]

69 [Kautsky 1911b.]

70 [The profits made by floating shares in a new joint stock company.]

71 [Hilferding 1981, pp. 105 et seq., 226, 180. Grossman's emphasis.]

quite differently from Marx.[72] The latter depicted the limits of capitalist accumulation that, in a dialectical shift at a definite stage of development, ultimately leads to the 'expropriation of the expropriators'.[73] Hilferding wants to demonstrate the peaceful and gradual growth of capitalism into a regulated economy. The cartelisation of industry, in order to raise prices and profits, lowers the rate of profit in the non-cartelised industries, intensifies competition in them and thus the tendency towards concentration. This leads to further cartelisation, in these industries too. So a tendency towards the continuous extension of cartelisation emerges. The result of this concentration movement, its ideal, theoretical endpoint, will be the complete cartelisation of all branches of industry not only in the national but also in the world economy, a universal or *'general cartel'* which consciously regulates the entirety of capitalist production in all its spheres, sets prices and also undertakes the distribution of products. With the advance of the concentration movement in industry, production is *increasingly planned* ('organised capitalism') and finally reaches its highest expression in the general cartel. The anarchy of production disappears, crises are eliminated and replaced by production 'regulated' by the general cartel, even if still on the basis of wage labour. 'The tendencies towards the establishment of a *general cartel* and towards the formation of a *central bank* are converging',[74] hence a peaceful and painless transition from capitalism to socialism becomes possible. 'The socialising function of finance capital *facilitates* enormously *the task of overcoming capitalism.* Once finance capital has brought the most important branches of production under its control, it is enough for society, through its conscious executive organ – the state conquered by the working class – to seize finance capital in order to gain immediate control of these branches of production.' 'Even today, taking possession of six large Berlin banks would mean taking possession of the most important spheres of large-scale industry.'[75]

After the war (1927), Hilferding declared that he had always 'repudiated every theory of economic breakdown', that Marx had also considered them to be false. The *overthrow* of the capitalist system would *'not happen because of internal laws of this system'* but had instead 'to be *the conscious act of the will of the working class*'.[76]

72 [Hilferding 1981, pp. 227–35; Marx 1976b, pp. 927–30.]

73 [Marx 1986a, p. 335.]

74 [Hilferding 1981, p. 234.]

75 [Hilferding 1981, pp. 367, 368. Grossman's emphasis.]

76 [Hilferding 1927, p. 2. Grossman emphasised *'not happen because of internal laws of this system'*. Hilferding also emphasised 'repudiated every theory of economic breakdown'.]

During the postwar period, the other neo-harmonists, such as Otto Bauer and Karl Kautsky, also derive crises simply from disproportion in the distribution of capital among individual branches of industry. They consider crises to be avoidable even under capitalism, if the distribution of capital is regulated, and the unlimited development of capitalism to be possible. Bauer's assertion that the capitalist mechanism automatically enforces this proportional distribution of capital – even if it is mediated by periodic crises – gives his harmonistic interpretation of Marx's theory of crisis a specific colouration. '[T]he mechanism of the capitalist mode of production *automatically* generates overaccumulation and underaccumulation.' While Marx had maintained that the progressive growth of the industrial reserve army of labour was necessary, Bauer tries to prove the opposite: 'There exists, in the capitalist mode of production, *a tendency for the adjustment of capital accumulation to the growth of population*.'[77]

3 The Resurgence of Revolutionary Marxism

a) *The Decay of Revisionist Theory*

As already shown, reformism was the result of the relatively peaceful period of capitalist development between 1872 and 1894. Revolutionary Marxist theory, itself the product of the revolutionary period of 1848, no longer seemed to suit this peaceful period. The reformist attempt to divest Marxism of its revolutionary character, in order to adapt it to the reformist practice of peaceful constructive work, was ultimately doomed to theoretical failure. Economic development at the end of the previous century experienced a decisive shift, once more demonstrating that the 'practice of the peaceful work of construction' was entirely questionable.

The policy of imperialist expansion, which in the most advanced countries was temporarily able to secure advantages for the upper layer of the working class, at the turn of the century led to a *sharpening of all antagonisms* in both domestic and foreign policy. The imperialist era of heightened colonial policy, of feverish military and naval arms build-ups, and finally of bellicose collisions that led to the outbreak of the World War began.

A sharpening of domestic class antagonisms in all capitalist countries ran in parallel with growing tensions in foreign policy. The great advances of the

77 Otto Bauer 2012, pp. 740, 739. [Bauer emphasised the whole of the first sentence above.]

socialist workers' movement accelerated the process of the combination of employers into powerful associations for struggle, which forced workers onto the defensive in all economic struggles. Kautsky demonstrated in 1908 'that the factors which had resulted in increased real wages over previous decades were all already going into reverse'. The period of rising real wages was replaced by one of falling wages and certainly not merely during periods of transient depression 'but even in periods of prosperity'.[78] The fact of the deteriorating conditions of working class life over this period has been demonstrated by private and public investigations in a series of advanced capitalist countries (America, Germany). [The advance of] state protection for workers also came to a halt under the pressure of employer associations. More and more, in this context, the trade unions' old methods of struggle proved to be insufficient. The period of *isolated strikes* in individual enterprises was past. Development drove on to large mass economic struggles in whole branches of a country's industry. On the other hand, the bourgeoisie became protectionist and reactionary. Political liberalism began to die out. There could no longer be talk of the further extension of democracy, which had been promoted earlier by a certain [degree of] cooperation between the liberal bourgeoisie and the working class. This entire development was strengthened and accelerated even more by the impact of the Russian Revolution of 1905. The development, predicted by the reformists, of progressive improvement in the condition of the working class and the weakening of class struggles did not occur. Instead, class struggles intensified. Since it was apparent that the old trade union and parliamentary methods were no longer capable of achieving further gains, the working class was forced to look around for new methods of struggle, that took into account rising economic and political pressure from the bourgeoisie. This was the significance of the *discussion about the political mass strike*.[79]

In such circumstances, during the era of bellicose imperialism and colonial expansion as well as reactionary domestic policies, reformism of the old kind was a typical product of epigones: repetition of dated lines of thought, diametrically counterposed to reality. As an example of this oversimplified popularisation of socialism that spread throughout the workers' movement at the beginning of the twentieth century and, despite its Marxist phraseology, retained nothing of the genuine content of Marx's socialism, mention should be made of a book by Morris Hillquit, the current leader of the American

78 [Kautsky 1908b, pp. 546, 549.]

79 See Roland-Holst 1905; Luxemburg 2008b; Branting 1909; Kautsky 1914.

'Socialist Party', *Socialism in Theory and Practice*.[80] In the chapter on 'Socialism and the state' Hillquit settles accounts with two dozen definitions of the state, starting with Aristotle and Cicero, through [Anne Robert Jacques] Turgot and [Jeremy] Bentham to [Pierre Paul] Leroy-Beaulieu and Anton Menger, according to whom the state is the organised humanity of a given territory. To this definition, designated as faulty, Hillquit counterposes the 'entirely correct' 'socialist definition of the state', according to Marx and Engels, and shows that the 'state, as a product of class [divisions]' arose at the same time as the institution of private property and 'has at all times been the instrument of the propertied classes' and, 'as an organisation of the ruling classes', necessarily 'keeps the exploited classes in a condition of dependency'. From this 'entirely correct' definition, however, Hillquit draws no conclusions for working class policy. In relation to the 'present-day', 'modern state', Hillquit nevertheless allows the validity of the bourgeois definition and asserts that it has experienced 'deep inroads made in its substance and functions by the rising class of wage-workers'. 'Under the pressure of the [socialist and] labour movement, the state has acquired new significance as an instrument of social and economic reforms.' 'The state which came into being solely as an instrument of class repression, has gradually, and especially within the last centuries assumed other important social functions, functions in which it largely represents society as a whole, and not any particular class in it.' Its exploitative function in the interests of the ruling classes are 'curbed' more and more, while its 'generally useful' functions claim its attention more and more, as it protects 'workers from excessive exploitation', so it 'is gradually coming to be recognised by the [workers] as a most potent instrument for the modification and ultimate abolition of the capitalist class rule'. The ruling capitalist class will, indeed, never voluntarily give up its property and the supremacy that results. Hillquit draws the conclusion not that it has to be expropriated economically and politically but instead that the process of transformation will come to pass gradually through 'a series of economic and social reforms and legislative measures tending to divest the ruling classes of their monopolies, privileges and advantages, step by step'. Violence does not, consequently, have to be employed. That would be 'but an accident of the social revolution ... [violence] has no place in the socialist program'. Through these reforms, a 'period of transition' will be entered, in which the state, although not yet socialist, is no longer an organ of the capitalist class but instead a 'transitional state'. 'Definite lines of demarcation', where it begins and where it ends cannot be specified but

80 Hillquit 1909.

today a 'number of municipalities and states are already wholly or partly under socialist control'. Many of the political or social 'transitional reforms' of socialism have, to a certain degree, been realised in countries in Europe, America and Australia and the 'conceded tendency' of all modern law-making is directed towards the extension of such reforms. In this sense, it may well be said that we are in the midst or in any case at the start of the 'transitional state'. Hillquit, logically, recommends tactics that are confined to 'electoral tactics' and the 'positive work of parliament', 'without violating the principle of the class struggle'.[81]

If such theories were strongly utopian during the period before the War they completely lost any connection with reality after its outbreak. In order to avoid shipwreck on this contrast with reality, reformist theory was forced to adapt to it. In pure logic, this correction was possible in two ways. From the proletarian standpoint: through a return to revolutionary Marxism. In a further, consistent development of its nature, reformism chose the other way and placed itself entirely on the ground of bourgeois society and the capitalist state. Karl Renner already drew this conclusion, contained in embryo in Hilferding's book, with great clarity in articles published in the Viennese *Kampf* and *Arbeiter-Zeitung* (which appeared in book form as *Marxism, War and the International*).[82] Extending the conclusions of Hilferding's book, he seeks to portray the upheaval that has taken place in the fabric of the economy, the state and society, the mutual relations of classes, the character of ownership and the external relations of economic territories, finally also in the tasks of today's proletariat, since Marx's death. Although Marx and he posit different developmental tendencies in all these areas, and although he abandons all the fundamental components of Marx's theoretical edifice and finally identifies different goals and tasks for the workers' movement from those of Marx, he does not forego a Marxist disguise for his theory. Instead, he claims to be a proponent of genuine Marxism who struggled against the 'reactionary misconstrual' of Marx's thought against the 'vulgar orientation … of Marxism', against the 'ossification' and 'oversimplification' 'of the [Marxist] theory of class struggle'. Not he but rather the supposed Marxists had distorted the theory of the master. In the short period since Marx was active, class relations have often, 'almost

81 [Hillquit 1909, pp. 97–105, 174, 181, 189. Grossman wrote 'class struggles' where the original had 'class divisions'; and left out 'socialist and' from the quotation starting 'Under the pressure …'; Hillquit took the quotation 'without violating the principle of the class struggle' from Kautsky 1901, p. 37, who in turn quoted his own letter, Kautsky 1899c.]

82 Renner 1918.

every decade and a half', been transformed. Instead of lugging around the old 'catechistic propositions' of Marx's system as 'old goods', it is necessary to revise the theoretical baggage in all areas. So his book is a 'Marxist examination' of the new material of social development, a draft of a 'study program for Marxists'.[83]

Marx's entire period of activity falls, according to Renner, into the liberal social epoch, with its individualistic-anarchistic economic mode, for which the power of the state was a bogyman. Marx researched this epoch and described it in *Capital*. In order to expose its laws in their pure, logical form, every state intervention had to be conceptually disregarded. This 'capitalist society, which Marx experienced and described, does not exist any more', something that Marxists have so far overlooked. The essential feature of the fundamental changes in the structure of society, which were completed between 1878 and 1914, consists of the 'statification' of the previously stateless economy, that is, precisely 'what Karl Marx's system logically and practically excluded', what Marx did not experience or describe. There were important consequences of this statification because 'the *economy* more and more exclusively serves the capitalist class, the *state* more and more predominantly the proletariat'. Consequently, the state is the tool, with the help of which the historical overthrow of capitalism into socialism will be carried out. But it is a 'crazy conception' to think that the conquest of political power by the proletariat can be carried out through a sudden overthrow of the system, through a political surprise attack. Those are conceptions that have been smuggled from the political history of the bourgeoisie into the world of socialist ideas. The state will, instead, be conquered step by step in daily struggles. Its transformation is carried out through the *gradual socialisation of all economic functions*. Marx was far from condemning and negating the state, from 'state nihilism', 'with which contemporary Marxism coquettes'. Through the state all economic categories are fundamentally transformed. The *competitive price* of the private economy is transformed into *cartel price*. Finally, during the period of high protection and under the influence of the state, *regulated price* develops into national price, whose form and extent differs from state to state. 'It is only one step further to state legislation directly prescribing the price': '*tax price*' or 'political price'. 'The economy is not sufficient to explain such pricing', overall 'deviation from the natural laws of the economy' is determined by the process of statification. 'An *extra-economic law* … imposed itself over the basic economic law. And that is now the new problem of Marxism', because the deliberate allocation of goods,

83 Renner 1918, pp. 61–2, 70, 90, 97.

that is the exclusive *mode of circulation of a socialist society*, is today already merged into the system of automatic commodity circulation.[84]

What can be said of commodity prices can also be said of the category of wages. The wages system is being fundamentally reorganised by the state. Today the worker's wage is already comprised of an individual and a collective wage. The state socialises variable capital, i.e. capital spent on wages, through compulsory contributions by workers and employers for health, accident and old age insurance, after individuals are paid. Basically, the state has already long done this through certain public outlays, e.g. public schools, that contribute to the maintenance and renewal of the working class. 'The working class, consequently, already receives a part of its wages collectively.' 'Development is towards the collectivisation of an ever larger part of wages.' To an increasing extent, the worker becomes the subject and object of 'public institutions'. 'The process of socialisation integrates him as an element into the state.'[85]

This *'process of socialising the worker's wage'* has not yet been analysed by Marxists. But large transformations of the individual components of the wage also take place. The *individual wage* is replaced by the *trade union wage* and finally by the *regulated wage*. 'These institutions ... transform the worker from a serf into an economic citizen. The leap from the free wage contract to the regulated system is of the same significance as that from manorial subjection and patrimonial justice to the bourgeois court.' 'But the regulated wage is still not the highest point of development. Giant capitalist enterprises construct service programs for their white collar employees and, to an extent, their workers', with 'a wage scale that is calculated over their whole lives, including their deaths', in short, forms of wage payment which Renner calls the *'pragmatic wage'*. 'From this it is only a step to the direct setting of wages by the state, to a *tax wage*.' Through statification, 'today the working classes find themselves in a different social situation from Marx's period'. Ownership becomes a 'public institution', work a 'public job'. A 'regrouping of classes' takes place. Industrialism is no longer the predominant form of enrichment in contemporary society. The factory owner of the old kind is no longer counterposed to the proletariat. Rather the dominant powers within the capitalist class have become *agrarianism* and *finance* capital. An upheaval in the economic function of land ownership occurs. While the process of statification and socialisation is very extensive in agriculture, landownership, encompassed economically as ground rent, has

84 [Renner 1918, pp. 7–12, 28, 41–3. Grossman's emphasis. According to Renner, the regulated price was a consequence of the interaction of cartels and protective tariffs.]

85 [Renner 1918, pp. 46–7.]

become more and more parasitic. The question of ground rent will become the principal social question over the next five years and decades.[86]

Loan capital has also experienced massive transformations. Loan capital of the old kind was usury, a merely parasitic economic function. The usurers were, however, defeated. 'Credit capital' of the new kind is not parasitic and is 'generally felt to be a blessing'.[87]

The purpose of Renner's arbitrary construct, which cannot be fully itemised here, is the justifications that his conclusions provide: the working class must *affirm* the contemporary *state* and, through the 'policy of changing alliances' with individual bourgeois classes, painstakingly, step by step work its way up and 'take power over bourgeois society intellectually', positioning itself everywhere on the basis of the state and bourgeois society. Such an alliance policy is 'not a watering down of class principle but its fulfilment'. As the proletariat affirms the state it must also affirm state policy. There is no 'amorphous internationality' but internationality, which is 'specifically new' in our period, is rather only the result of the actions of groups of nation states. 'Capital is not international but national'. '*National capital* organised by the state has become the active agent on the tribune of the world.' Marx's categories are *universal*, Marxists start with the category of the *stateless world economy*, but for the time being this unit is still not a single state. For the time being development has achieved the level of national-political, territorial states. Hence there is also no 'world proletariat', which is only a 'mystical unit'; in reality only *national proletariats* within state territories exist. The world economy is only coming into being, promoted by the tendency of individual states to extend their economic territories. 'In terms of specific states, expansionist tendencies appear as colonial policy and colonial exploitation, domination and servitude.' But this 'moralistic standpoint' lies 'deep below Marx's mode of thought', as behind these 'mundane complaints about colonial policy' the 'secular greatness of the economisation of the world' should not be overlooked.[88]

'In this way, to be an opponent of the colonial system means being an opponent of world history.' So long as capitalism persists in the economy and the anarchistic antagonism of states in politics, wars are unavoidable, because *competitive struggles among economic territories* take place in two ways: peacefully through states' trade agreements and aggressively through conquest. Imperialist war should not be judged ethically but should be accepted as a fact, just like trade policy. It is nothing other than the turning of 'price

86 [Renner 1918, pp. 47–55, 61, 64–5, 67. Grossman's emphasis.]

87 [Renner 1918, pp. 82–3.]

88 [Renner 1918, pp. 63, 65–6, 101, 106, 112–13, 123. Grossman's emphasis.]

competition' 'into arms competition'. At most, there should be efforts to 'civilise war' and the extension of the organisation of the world into a 'peaceful association of nations', through international law. So long, however, as such a 'future, supranational organisation of the world' has not been achieved, war remains 'possible and, in certain circumstances, necessary', because it concerns the existence of a state and its economy. Since methods of struggle in trade union work rest *'on the basis of this capitalist order'*, trade unions must act positively in the struggle. No union desires the destruction of industry. 'The existence, continuation and future of this capital' also affect the working class positively. 'In bellicose periods the working class also struggles for that continuation.' If there is war, the proletariat also has to take the path of war: this path is also 'a path of history' and, 'as the proletariat cannot absent itself from history, it has to travel this path'. From the moment of the outbreak of war, there is no other possible attitude than 'alignment with its own state'. The stand of the proletarian parties on 4 August 1914 was justified.[89]

Obviously Renner's theorems cannot be reconciled with proletarian socialism. They should be evaluated as an attempt to divert the proletariat from its tasks as a class and to bring it into the train of the imperialist bourgeoisie. In his works, reformism sank from the level of social criticism to apologetics for bourgeois society. It was therefore unavoidable that reformism, having come to power after the war and the outbreak of revolution in the defeated states, was incapable of fulfilling even one of the tasks posed by proletarian socialism.

Eclecticism and the tendency to turn away from Marxism are characteristic of reformist theory during the postwar period. Emil Lederer restricts the applicability of Marx's labour theory of value in two ways. In his *Outlines of Economic Theory*,[90] he restricts it to the terrain of *competitive* capitalism. He regards it as insufficient to explain *monopoly prices* and hence tries to construct a fusion of the labour theory of value with marginal utility theory. He regards Marx's labour theory of value, secondly, as only suited to the explanation of *static* economic processes but not of *dynamic* conjunctual cycles.[91] Lederer's explanation of crises is in essence an *underconsumptionist* theory – on a detour through monetary theories of crisis (extension of the labour process 'only through additional credit')[92] – with all its attendant deficiencies.

89 [Renner 1918, pp. 281–2, 331, 360–1, 328–9, 353. [Grossman's emphasis.]]
90 Lederer 1922.
91 Lederer 1925, pp. 355–413.
92 [Lederer 1925, p. 387.]

Alfred Braunthal's *The Contemporary Economy and its Laws* is intended to be a textbook of socialist economics, 'faithful to the idea of Marxism'. In fact, Braunthal combats Marx's theory with arguments borrowed from bourgeois criticism of Marx: it provides 'no information about the laws according to which the social product, in fact, is divided into wages and returns to capital'. The (bourgeois) theory of productivity is, in this respect, 'without doubt superior to Marxist theory'. He refers further to the 'secure results' of marginal utility theory. His account of the contemporary economy is essentially a simplified compilation of Hilferding's thoughts about the progressive *organisation* of the economy and Renner's ideas about *statification* and the ever stronger influence of the *state which is being proletarianised*. Through its growing *regulation* of the organisation of the whole economy, finally through 'cold socialisation', i.e. through the encroachment of the public economy, the free economy with its market mechanism is more and more superseded. For this reason, Braunthal thinks, we stand at the beginning of a social revolution, 'a society which is changing from capitalism into socialism'.[93]

With the transition in the leadership of the world economy from Europe to the United States of America and under the impression of American 'prosperity' after the World War, a flush of uncritical admiration for American methods of organisation and work ('rationalisation') arose in bourgeois Europe. The emulation of these methods by German capitalists found the fullest approval among the proponents of trade union theory and practice. A typical product of this current is the work of the chairperson of the German Woodworkers' Association, Fritz Tarnow, *Why be poor?* 'The old economic theories about the social question', Tarnow thinks, 'originated primarily in England ... The new theories are being shaped in America'. America has shown that poverty is no economic necessity but a social illness, 'whose curability, even within the framework of the capitalist economy, is undoubted'. Wages, as a cost factor, have declined in significance but as a factor in purchasing power they have gained importance. *Increasing consumption* and, above all, mass consumption is the 'key to the development of production'. In view of the enormous development of the productive forces, from now on waste is a blessing and restraint a curse. Not only is labour dependent on capital but capital is also dependent on the purchasing power of worker consumers. High wages are in the well-understood interests of the employers themselves. Countries with high wages have accumulated most strongly and can compete most successfully. American employers are advancing along the track of this knowledge which is the basis of the secret of the

93 Braunthal 1930, pp. 62–3, 241, 63, 46, 220.

continuing boom in the United States of America. Henry Ford's book *My Life and Work* is 'certainly the most revolutionary text of all economic literature to the present'.[94]

In addition, the various sub-species and currents of reformism as they appear in individual countries or internationally should also be mentioned briefly. First *'municipal socialism'*, which is concerned with reformist activity in the area of local politics – amongst other things, also the effort to municipalise water, gas and electricity services for the urban population in the general economic interest, without reference to their private sector profitability.[95]

A current in the English workers' movement is known as *'guild socialism'*. It aspires to the control of production and the supersession of the wages system through the organisational unification of all manual and intellectual workers, not according to profession or trade union groups, but in associations (guilds) of whole industries. It seeks to achieve this goal possibly through a general strike. Guild socialism differs from syndicalism in that it does not oppose the state but instead allocates it certain functions outside the sphere of production.[96]

On *'religious socialism'* see the article 'Christian and religious socialism'.[97]

So-called 'liberal socialism' stands outside the workers' movement and has less to do with socialism than liberalism, i.e. capitalism. Represented by the isolated efforts of Franz Oppenheimer, drawing on the theories of Eugen Dühring, it seeks to maintain the mechanism of exchange.[98]

b) *The Development of the Materialist Conception of History*

The materialist conception of history, sketched by Marx with Engels's collaboration in a series of youthful writings (1842–59) in inspired outlines, was never systematically developed by them. It was only Marx's students who undertook to extend it philosophically and epistemologically, deepening it, above all, through fruitful, specialised research, in various areas of social, economic and cultural history. Karl Kautsky dealt with it philosophically, above all in *Ethics and the Materialist Conception of History, Class Antagonisms in the Era of the French Revolution, Thomas More and his Utopia* and *Foundations of Chris-*

94 Tarnow 1928, pp. 10, 19, 70, 71; [Ford 1922.]
95 See Lindemann 1906a; and Lindemann 1906b.
96 See Taylor 1921; Cole 1920a. [The German edition, referred to by Grossman, Cole 1921, was introduced by Rudolph Hilferding]; Cole 1920b; Cole and Mellor 1918.
97 Grünberg and Grossmann 1931.
98 Oppenheimer 1932.

tianity.[99] In his last large work, *The Materialist Conception of History*, Kautsky revised his earlier conception of the driving force of historical development just as he had in relation to his economic and political conceptions.[100] Franz Mehring (1846–1919) in his *The Lessing Legend* chose the literature and the history of [Gotthold Ephraim] Lessing and Friedrich II as his field of application. In brilliant essays in *Neue Zeit*, he dealt with the most diverse areas of history and literary history. In his consummate, broadly conceived *History of German Social Democracy*, that admittedly only extended to the beginning of revisionism, he illuminated the economic and social context of the growth of the socialist workers' movement and combined this with a presentation of its theoretical developments.[101] Georgi Plekhanov, the creator of the materialist sociology of culture and art, entered the struggle against revisionism as one of the most brilliant proponents of dialectical materialism.[102] From the postwar period: the fine and valuable book, *History and Class Consciousness: Studies in Marxist Dialectics*, by Georg Lukács,[103] and Karl Korsch's *Central Points of Historical Materialism* and *Marxism and Philosophy*, should be mentioned, above all.[104] Finally, in addition to the works by Max Adler, already mentioned, also Heinrich Cunow's *Marx's Theory of History, Society and the State*.[105]

Significant Writings on Historical Materialism in Particular Countries

France

Sorel, Georges 1925 [1901], *La ruine du monde antique: conception materialiste de l'histoire* (*The Collapse of the Ancient World: the Materialist Conception of History*), Paris: Rivière.

Rappoport, Charles 1925 [1901], *La philosophie de l'histoire comme science de l'évolution* (*The Philosophy of History as an Evolutionary Science*), Paris: Rivière.

Italy

Croce, Benedetto 1915 [1901], *Historical Materialism and the Economics of Karl Marx*, London: George Allen & Unwin.

99 Kautsky 1906; Kautsky 1908a; Kautsky 1927; Kautsky 1925b.

100 Cf. Kautsky 1988b; Korsch 1929.

101 Mehring 1938; Mehring 1913a; Mehring 1913b; Mehring also published many hundreds of articles in *Neue Zeit*.

102 See, above all, Plekhanov 1976b; Plechanow 1908; Plekhanov 1976a; Grossmann 1932i.

103 Lukács 1971.

104 Korsch 1922; Korsch 1970.

105 Cunow 1920.

Croce, Benedetto 1913 [1909], *Philosophy of the Practical: Economic and Ethic*, London: Macmillan.

Mondolfo, Rodolfo 1912, *Il materialismo storico in Federico Engels* (*The Historical Materialism of Friedrich Engels*), Genova: Formiggini.

Mondolfo, Rodolfo 1932, *Il concetto marxistico della 'umwälzende Praxis' e suoi germi in Bruno e Spinoza* (*The Marxist Concept of 'Revolutionary Praxis' and its Origins in Bruno and Spinoza*), in Max Adler et al., *Festschrift fur Karl Grunberg: zum 70. Geburtstag*, Leipzig: Hirschfeld, pp. 366–76.

Labriola, Antonio 1908 [1896], *Essays on the Materialist Conception of History*, Chicago: Kerr.

Labriola, Antonio 1912 [1898], *Socialism and Philosophy*, Chicago: Kerr.

Poland

Brzozowski, Stanisław 1990 [1910], *Idee: wstęp do filozofii dojrzałości dziejowej* (*Ideas: introduction to the phlosophy of historical maturity*), Kraków: Wydawnictwo Literackie.

Russia

Bukharin, Nikolai 1925 [1921], *Historical Materialism*, New York: International Publishers.

Deborin, Abram 2012 [1916], *Vvedenie v filosofiiu dialekticheskogo materializma* (*An Introduction to the Philosophy of Dialectical Materialism*), Moskva: Librokom, 2012 [1916], Georgi Plekhanov's preface to the original edition is in 1976 [1916], 'Preface' to Abram Deborin, *Vvedenie v filosofiiu dialekticheskogo materializma*, in Georgi Plekhanov, *Selected Philosophical Works. Volume 3*, Moscow: Progress Publishers, pp. 577–99.

Holland

Gorter, Hermann 1919, *Der historische Materialismus* (*Historical Materialism*), with a foreword by Karl Kautsky, Stuttgart: Dietz.

Writings about Particular Areas of Application of Historical Materialism

Law

Pashukanis, Evgeny 2002 [1924], *Law and Marxism: A General Theory*, New Brunswick: Transaction.

Stutschka, Peteris 1991 [1922], *Das Problem des Klassenrechts und der Klassenjustiz* (*The Problem of Class Law and Class Justice*), in Eugen Paschukanis, *Allgemeine Rechtslehre und Marxismus*, edited by Hermann Klenne and Leonid Mamut, Freiburg: Haufe, pp. 233–68.

Compare with: Kelsen, Hans 1931, 'Allgemeine Rechtslehre im Lichte materialistischer Geschichtsauffassung' ('The general theory of law in the light of the materialist conception of history'), *Archiv für Sozialwissenschaft und Sozialpolitik*, 66 (3): 449–521.

Szende, Paul 1932, 'Nationales Recht und Klassenrecht, Beiträge aus der ungarischen Rechts und Wirtschaftsgeschichte' ('National law and class law: contributions from Hungarian legal and economic history'), in Max Adler et al., *Festschrift für Carl Grünberg – Zum 70. Geburtstag*, Leipzig: Hirschfeld, pp. 445–78.

Economic History

Cunow, Heinrich 1926–31, *Allgemeine Wirtschaftsgeschichte. Von der primitiven Sammelwirtschaft bis zum Hochkapitalismus* (*General Economic History: From the Primitive Gatherer Economy to Advanced Capitalism*), four volumes, Berlin: Dietz.

The process of transition from the feudal state of the eithteenth century to the modern capitalist state is dealt with, using the example of Austria and Poland, in:

Grossman, Henryk 1925, 'Struktura społeczna i gospodarcza Księstwa Warszawskiego na podstawie spisow ludnosci 1808–1810 roku' ('The social and economic structure of the Duchy of Warsaw on the basis of the results of the censes of 1808 and 1810'), *Kwartalnik Statystyczny* 2: 1–108.

Grossmann, Henryk 1914, *Österreichs Handelspolitik mit Bezug auf Galizien in der Reformperiode 1772–1790* (*Austria's Trade Policy with Regard to Galicia in the Reform Period 1772–1790*), Wien: Konegen.

Grossmann, Henryk 1916, 'Die Anfänge und geschichtliche Entwicklung der amtlichen Statistik in Oesterreich' ('The beginnings and historical development of official statistics in Austria'), *Statistische Monatsschrift*, new series, 21: 331–423.

Hartmann, Ludo Moritz 1919, *Römische Geschichte* (*Roman History*), Gotha: Perthes.

Hartmann, Ludo Moritz 1910 [1903], *Der Untergang der antiken Welt* (*The Fall of the Ancient World*), Heller, Wien.

Wittfogel, Karl August 1931, *Wirtschaft und Gesellschaft Chinas* (*China's Economy and Society*), Leipzig: Hirschfeld.

Sociology of Knowledge

Horkheimer, Max 1993 [1930], 'A new concept of ideology?' in Max Horkheimer, *Between Philosophy and Social Science*, Cambridge, MA: MIT Press, pp. 129–50.

Szende, Paul 1922, 'Verhüllung und Enthüllung: Der Kampf der Ideologien in der Geschichte' ('Masking and unmasking: the struggle of ideologies in history'), *Archiv für die Geschichte des Sozialismus und der Arbeiterbewegung*, 10 (2–3): 185–270.

c) *The Problems of Imperialism and War*

We pointed out earlier that, towards the end of the previous century, the development of capitalist states took on more and more imperialist features and was distinguished by arms build-ups and colonial expansion. Socialists schooled in the Marxist approach to history very early recognised the significance of these processes. From the start of the new century, in a series of writings, Karl Kautsky predicts the approach of a '*new epoch of revolution*' as a result of colonial policy and imperialism. Particularly in the east, an age of conspiracies, coups and constant social upheavals, he explained, was beginning in east Asia and the entire Muslim world. Eventually the west would be caught up in these. 'A world war is brought within threatening proximity.' In all these writings, Kautsky describes the *features of capitalism that had changed* during its imperialist period, its inclination to arm for war, acts of violence and conquest in the struggle over the world market. At the time, these developments did not appear to him as consequences of the whims of individual power-holders but as bound up with the inner nature of capitalism. '[T]he iron necessity of economic requirements drives modern industrial nations towards ruin.'[106]

This conception of capitalism's developmental tendencies, until then generally widespread in the workers' movement, could not be reconciled with Tugan-Baranovsky's and Hilferding's theories of the unlimited possibilities for the development of capitalism, already mentioned. The harmonist conception of capitalist development obviously contradicted the reality of its steadily growing competition and the escalation of struggles among the advanced capitalist countries over markets and spheres of investment; it also contradicted the fundamental notion of historical materialism that explains politics on the basis of the economy. In her book *The Accumulation of Capital: A Contribution to the Economic Explanation of Imperialism*,[107] Rosa Luxemburg set herself the task of resolving this contradiction. If the neo-harmonists' conception of capitalism's unlimited possibilities for development was right, then the imperialist features which were appearing with such intensity could not be explained in terms of the nature of capitalism. They were instead to be evaluated as merely accidental phenomena. On the other hand, as Rosa Luxemburg correctly emphasises, 'the theory of capitalist collapse … is the cornerstone of scientific socialism'.[108] And this is the great historical significance of Rosa Luxemburg's book: that, in conscious opposition to the attempted distortions of

106 Kautsky 1903; Kautsky 1909, p. 107; Kautsky 1911a, p. 94.
107 Luxemburg 1951.
108 [Luxemburg 1951, p. 96.]

the neo-harmonists, she adheres to the fundamental idea in *Capital* of an *absolute economic limit* to the development of the capitalist mode of production, even though the concrete justification that she provided for the theory of breakdown, today, has to be identified as mistaken. In her critique of Marx's analysis of the accumulation process, which assumes a society that consists solely of capitalists and workers and does not engage in foreign trade, she came to the conclusion 'that Marx's schema of accumulation does not solve the question of who is to benefit in the end by enlarged reproduction'. Purely abstractly, assuming the relations of dependence and proportions of Marx's schema, his analysis gives the appearance that capitalist production can by itself realise all surplus value and employs capitalised surplus value to satisfy its *own requirements*. That is, 'capitalist production *buys up* its entire surplus product'.[109] For example, coal mining is extended in order to make the expansion of the iron making and then machine building industries possible; the latter are expanded to make the extension of the production of means of consumption possible. This extension of industries producing means of consumption, however, creates markets for the extended production of the coal mining, iron making and machine building industries. Individual branches of industry thus *create markets for each other*. Setting out Marx's analysis, which Rosa Luxemburg regards as mistaken, in this way, production can be extended '*ad infinitum* … in circles', without it being apparent 'who is to benefit … *who are the new consumers* for whose sake production is ever more enlarged'.[110] Such accumulation does not serve consumption but is 'production for production's sake'.[111] Actually workers can really only consume a part of the enlarged product, the part which expresses the value of their wages. Part of the product serves to replace means of production that have been used up; the remainder that is left, surplus value, consistently grows in the course of accumulation. Who realises the consistently growing surplus value? The capitalists themselves only consume a part of it, while they employ an ever-growing part of it for further accumulation. But what do they do, then, with the even larger annual product, with their surplus value? Rosa Luxemburg comes to the conclusion that 'the realisation of the surplus value for the purposes of accumulation is an *impossible task* for a society which consists solely of workers and capitalists', that is, such a capitalism cannot exist. The capitalist mode of production requires for its existence 'as its prime condition … that there should be *strata of buyers outside capitalist society*',

109 [Luxemburg 1951, p. 330. Grossman's emphasis.]
110 [Luxemburg 1951, p. 330. '*Ad infinitum*' means 'to infinity'.]
111 [Marx 1976b, p. 742. Grossman's emphasis.]

that is, social layers, 'whose own mode of production is not capitalistic' and realise the capitalist surplus value. But capitalism does not only require non-capitalist 'milieus' to realise surplus value, even more in order to obtain a large part of the means of production, in particular raw materials (constant capital); and finally: 'Only the existence of non-capitalist groups and countries can guarantee such a supply of additional labour power for capitalist production'.[112] It is therefore apparent that the 'process of capital accumulation is connected with non-capitalist forms of production in all its value and material relations: constant capital, variable capital and surplus value.'[113] Capitalist accumulation 'as an historical process' is, in practice, dependent on 'the *given historical setting*' of non-capitalist countries and layers: artisans, peasants. Without this milieu it is 'in any case unthinkable'. The result is capital's aggressive drive to bring non-capitalist territories under its sway. In this way, Rosa Luxemburg believes that she has explained not only accumulation and the conditions under which it takes place, but also the *driving force behind imperialism* and the tendency to colonial expansion. Military occupation of colonies, the violent theft of their means of production and labour power, 'planning for the systematic destruction and annihilation of all the non-capitalist social units', the struggle of capitalism against the natural economy and the ruin of independent economies of artisans and peasants, all result from the drive to realise surplus value. In contrast to the 'crude optimism' of Ricardo, Say and Tugan-Baranovsky for whom capitalism can develop without limit, 'with the logical corollary of capitalism-in-perpetuity',[114] her own solution, seems to be in the spirit of Marx's theory of the final breakdown of the capitalist system of production, which is founded on 'the dialectical contradiction that the movement of capital accumulation requires non-capitalist formations as its context … and *can only exist as long as this milieu is present*'.[115] As natural economies are subordinated to capitalism, the situation which Marx predicted in his analysis draws nearer, namely capitalist production as 'the exclusive and universal domination of capitalist production in all countries and for all branches of industry'.[116] 'But this is the start of a dead end. Once the final result is achieved … *accumulation becomes impossible*.'[117] The *historical limits* of accumulation, the impossibility for the

112 [Luxemburg 1951, pp. 350–2, 361. Grossman's emphasis.]
113 [Luxemburg 1913, p. 337.]
114 [Luxemburg 1951, pp. 365–6, 370. Grossman's emphasis.]
115 [Luxemburg 1913, p. 392. Grossman's emphasis.]
116 [Luxemburg 1951, p. 417.]
117 [Luxemburg 1913, p. 393. Grossman's emphasis.]

productive forces to develop further, is apparent here. The consequence is the end of capitalism. Its imperialist phase is thus the final period in its historical career. So the economic analysis of non-capitalist markets has the closest inner connection with the emergence of socialism. Socialism is not merely dependent on subjective-voluntarist factors but results from the economy's course of development, connected with the forces within capitalism that objectively work towards its necessary breakdown.

This theory, which places emphasis on the problem of markets, on the question of the realisation of surplus value, is not capable of satisfactorily explaining the characteristic feature of capitalism's imperialist period, the export of capital (see Lenin's theory of imperialism, below). Furthermore, these ideas were not new; they have a history of more than a hundred years. In essence, they were already developed by Simonde de Sismondi in his *New Principles of Political Economy* of 1819 and Robert Malthus in the chapter on accumulation in his *Principles of Political Economy* of 1820.[118] These ideas were later extended by socialist theorists to explain imperialism by Heinrich Cunow, Louis B. Boudin and Kautsky himself (see above).[119] Luxemburg's achievement was new in that she used Marx's reproduction schemas to demonstrate the necessity of non-capitalist areas.

This is not the place to offer an extensive methodological and material critique of the theory. In this regard, refer to the works of Henryk Grossman, discussed further below.

Directly opposed to Rosa Luxemburg's is the position of Vladimir Ilyich Lenin, who already argues against the Russian Narodniks[120] in his *A Characterisation of Economic Romanticism* (*Sismondi and Our Native Sismondists*). The Narodniks adopted Sismondi's theory of external markets as the condition for the existence of capitalism in full. Lenin repeatedly criticises the theory that it was impossible to realise surplus value under 'pure' capitalism, in his principal work against the Narodniks, *The Development of Capitalism in Russia*.[121] The contradiction between the limits of consumption and limitless expansion

118 [Sismondi 1991d; Malthus 1836, pp. 308–438. Grossman wrote two studies of his work, Grossman 1924a, see above pp. 55–119; and Grossman 1934, see above pp. 439–442.]

119 Cunow 1898; Boudin 1907a. [Kautsky's foreword to Boudin was only published in the German edition, Boudin 1909; Kautsky 1902.]

120 [The Narodniks were populists who opposed Tsarism and identified with the peasantry in late nineteenth-century Russia.]

121 Lenin 1960a; Lenin 1960b.

of 'production for the sake of production'[122] does exist. But this is not a contradiction in a theory but a real contradiction in the capitalist system. Nothing would be more vulgar, however, than to conclude from the contradictions of capitalism, i.e. from its irrationality, that it is impossible. This contradiction is not capitalism's only one. It can neither exist nor develop without contradictions. 'Nothing could be more senseless than to conclude ... that Marx did not admit the possibility of surplus value being realised in capitalist society, that he attributed crises to *underconsumption*, and so forth.'[123] Instead, different branches of industry constitute markets for each other. Since, however, they *develop unevenly and overtake each other*, because there is no regulation to impose consistency on individual branches, *'the more developed industry'* necessarily *'seeks a foreign market'*.[124] This uneven development of individual branches of industry is, therefore, the final cause of crises and capitalism's expansionist tendencies. After the outbreak of the World War, as the problem of imperialism naturally attracted greater attention, Lenin undertook to lay bare the nature of imperialism, its economic and social roots, in his book *Imperialism: The Highest Stage of Capitalism*.[125] He identified these in the *structural transformation of world capitalism*, in the displacement of competition by monopoly, which opened the phase of capitalism's decline. Its characteristic feature is no longer the *export of commodities* but of *capital*. The monopolistic character of capitalism explains continuous colonial expansion and the division of the world among monopolist associations of capitalists, dominated by the financial oligarchy. Capital export, through the domination of enormous territories in Asia and Africa that supply raw materials, secures colossal super profits for the bourgeoisies of the ruling capitalist countries. The essence of imperialist expansion does not lie in the sphere of circulation (the realisation of surplus value) but in the sphere of production (raising profits).

The emergence of imperialism opened a *period of constant war and threat of war*. Wars are a product of imperialism, an unavoidable result of the antagonisms of the epoch of decline. In this respect, the character of wars has changed; the formal distinction between wars of defence and offence has lost any meaning. For, in contrast with the wars of national liberation during the rising phase

122 [Marx 1976b, p. 742; Lenin 1960a, pp. 161, 182.]

123 [Lenin 1960b, p. 58. Grossman's emphasis.]

124 [Lenin 1960b, p. 66. Grossman's emphasis.]

125 Lenin 1964c.

of capitalism, wars in the period of decline are predatory wars amongst imperialist countries and against less economically developed nations and states. As a consequence, the working class has special responsibilities in questions of war, civil peace, defence of the fatherland and approving war credits.[126] During the phase of capitalism's decline, the proletariat has the task of transforming war between peoples into civil war, with a view to the conquest of power and, for this reason, of preparing strategically and organisationally for revolution. Grigory Zinoviev, Leon Trotsky, Nikolai Bukharin and Hermann Gorter take similar stances on the problem of imperialism and war.[127]

d) *The Problem of the Proletarian Seizure of Power. Marxist Theory and the Soviet Union*

The establishment of the Soviet Union is, in principle, not simply a turning point of great importance in the political and economic history of capitalism but also in the field of Marxist theory. The outbreak of the Russian revolution confirmed the correctness of the prognosis of Marxists who had predicted its advent and thus based their strategy and tactics on it for decades. Further, it proved the correctness of those who, like Lenin in 1905, had already predicted on the basis of Marxist theory that the coming revolution would be an upheaval of a new kind – *proletarian revolution* which, in its *goal*, *organs* and *tactics* would move beyond the bourgeois world.[128] The international significance of the October Revolution[129] and its historical meaning from the point of view of Marxist theory is, moreover, that the *sole* rule of the capitalist system has reached its end. With the October Revolution, the bourgeois mode of production, before this turning point the dominant and the most progressive

126 Cf. Grossmann 1931b, pp. 427–9.

127 Sinowjew 1924 [a section of the book is in English translation, Zinoviev 1952–3]; Lenin and Sinowjew 1921 [a collection of 74 articles, the longest articles available in English are Lenin 1964a and Lenin 1964d]; Trotsky 1971; Bukharin 1929, introduced by Lenin; Gorter 1915.

128 [In 1905 Lenin did argue that the working class would play a leading role in the revolution against the Tsar in Russia and in the establishment of a 'revolutionary-democratic dictatorship of the proletariat and the peasantry', Lenin 1962a. This would clear the way for capitalist development. But he maintained that the coming revolution was definitely not a socialist revolution, Lenin 1962a, p. 28. Only in 1917 did Lenin conclude that socialist revolution was on the immediate agenda, Lenin 1964e, p. 341.]

129 [i.e. the Bolshevik Revolution, which took place in November 1917, according to the modern Gregorian calendar.]

mode of production, lost its aura of permanence and indestructibility, proving to be an historical, i.e. a transitory, category. Previously only remnants of social formations that have gone under and are in comparison more backward (artisans, peasant, the primitive economies of colonial people in Africa and Asia) have survived alongside it. In contrast to capitalism, socialism was previously only a demand for the future arrangement of society. Now – as experience seems to confirm – a superior economic system in the Soviet Union confronts capitalism, which has been convulsed by the world economic crisis. Through the formulation of the first Five Year Plan of 1928–32 it is on the best path to realising, for the first time in history, the idea of a socialist, planned economy, after initial, transitional difficulties are overcome. In a sixth of the world, particularly in the previously most backward areas of Asiatic Russia, the Soviet Union knew how to construct a socialist economy on the basis of the most advanced technology at a gigantic tempo in the areas of economics and culture, for which there is no historical analogy and boldly leaping over whole historical stages of development. The great *popularity of the planned economy's configuration*, in almost all the highly developed countries of Europe and in the United States of America, expresses the shaken faith in the justification for and adequacy of the capitalist market economy. Capitalism's difficulties seem to have become more acute because of the fact of the very existence of the Soviet Union alone, as a consequence of its successful socialist construction. Social contradictions and class antagonisms are no longer, as earlier, contradictions between reality and a hoped-for socialist future but rather the ever more pronounced contradictions between two social and *state systems, that exist side by side*. The foundation of the *Marx-Engels Institute* in Moscow, under the leadership of the well-known Marx researcher David Riazanov, is of the greatest significance for the scientific deepening and development of Marxist theory. It took on the monumental task of [producing] the *Marx-Engels Collected Works* (in more than 40 volumes) which will publish fundamentally important parts of Marx's and Engels's world of ideas that were previously unknown.[130] *Marx-Engels-Archiv*, which also appears in German, is the organ of the Institute.

Research into the particular conditions of the existence and development of the *peasant economy* plays a specific role in the socialist literature of the Soviet Union. From the extensive literature only the following are mentioned:

130 [Marx and Engels 1927–41. This project was terminated under Stalin. Riazanov was dismissed as the head of the Institute in February 1931.]

Alexander Vasilyevich Chayanov, *The Optimal Size of Agricultural Enterprises, The Theory of the Peasant Economy, The Theory of Peasant Co-operatives*; Nikolai Pavlovich Makarov, *The Peasant Economy and its Evolution*. Further, the *International Agrarian Institute* in Moscow and its journal deal with these problems.[131]

Russian socialist literature, however, engages above all with the *theory of socialist upheaval and the period of transition to socialism*. In his speech on the program of the Third International, in 1922, Bukharin criticised those who want to delay the socialist upheaval until socialism has ripened within capitalism. In contrast to the classical statement in Marx's *Capital* that 'capitalism matured fully under feudal rule' until the new order was able to fully develop after the conquest of political power, the Russian Communists, especially Bukharin, insist that this theory does not apply to socialism. Under feudalism, the *bourgeoisie* could already possess a monopoly over industrial means of production, achieve leading roles in industrial production and, drawing on its economic power, also overtake the feudal class culturally. In contrast, the *working class* cannot become the owner of the means of production and control production under capitalism. Nor can it rise to a higher cultural level than the bourgeoisie within the framework of capitalism. 'Socialism can *never* ripen in this manner, even under the most favourable conditions ... It is impossible for the working class to *take production in hand* within the womb of capitalist society ... [T]he proletariat ... can learn all that only when it has already achieved the dictatorship of the proletariat.'[132] '*Socialism does not arise*, it must be *consciously constructed*.'[133]

Accordingly, for the Russian Communists, the possibility of a proletarian revolution is not tied to any *definite developmental maturity* of capitalist soci-

131 Chayanov 1930; Chayanov 1966 [the Russian edition published in 1925 was based on an edition published in 1923, to which Grossman refers]; Chayanov 1991. Makarov 1920. [The International Agrarian Institute, Mezhdunarodnii Agrarnii Institut, published its journal *Agrarprobleme* in German, from 1928 until 1934.]

132 Bukharin 2012, p. 491. [Grossman's emphasis. Bukharin emphasised 'dictatorship of the proletariat'. The first quotation is from Bukharin rather than Marx, but see Marx 1976b, p. 875.]

133 [This quotation does not appear in the English edition, Bukharin 1979, or the German edition, Bucharin 1929, to which Grossman referred. Its sense, however, is apparent in Bukharin 1979, p. 99: 'the bourgeoisie did not build capitalism, but it was built. The proletariat, as an organised collective subject, is building socialism as an organised system. If the creation of capitalism was spontaneous, the building of communism is to a marked degree a conscious, i.e. organised, process.']

ety. Only a sufficient concentration of production is required to make the planned organisation of the economy possible and a correspondingly advanced union of proletarian atoms into a revolutionary class, to guarantee the overthrow of the bourgeoisie in the revolution and the construction of the apparatus of the proletarian dictatorship. In addition to these two objective moments, two subjective moments are required: the revolutionary enthusiasm of the proletariat and its desire to end the capitalist order, and the incapacity of the bourgeoisie to effectively resist the proletariat. All these moments, however, are compatible with the most diverse economic conditions. The breakdown of capitalism, according to this conception, can just as easily take place at a high or a relatively low level of capitalism's inner maturity. A country does not necessarily have to be amongst the *leading* capitalist countries in terms of its general level of economic development. On the contrary, since the capacity of the bourgeoisie is, *ceteris paribus*, directly proportional to the economic maturity of capitalism, it is likely that 'the collapse of the entire system ensues, beginning with the organisationally *weakest* links of that system'.[134] Later we will see that this theory of breakdown, which constitutes nothing other than a formulation of the specific Russian situation during the War, neither corresponds with Lenin's conception of the overthrow of capitalism nor does it apply at all to the advanced capitalist countries of western Europe.

The *problems of socialist economic construction* in industry and agriculture is of immediate, current significance and at the same time present the greatest theoretical difficulties. No doubt the expropriation of the means of production has long been a fixed component of all socialist programs. But the question of the extent of the expropriation of industrial and commercial capital, the nature and extent of the connection between the socialist elements of the economy without markets and the remainder of the capitalist economy, i.e. the question of the extent to which the market economy is to be retained and an economy without markets and money is to be introduced, now had to be answered. The problem of the socialist restructuring of the village had to be solved: whether a state monopoly over agricultural products should be introduced or private peasant production and private sales, only burdened with a tax in kind, should remain. Likewise the question of whether collective agricultural production should be introduced and, finally, to what degree. Everywhere, the first tentative attempts at proletarian economic policy had to be made.[135] These problems

134 Bukharin 1979, p. 65. [Grossman's emphasis.]
135 See Grossmann 1931b, pp. 433–43.

eventually achieved a preliminary resolution with the formulation of the First Five Year Plan and of rules for a planned economy, which also laid the foundations for a *new science*.

Until the October Revolution, it was almost only within the *Russian* workers' movement that the problems of the proletarian seizure of power were discussed concretely. With this event they moved, most strongly inspired by Lenin's *The State and Revolution*,[136] to the centre of discussions within the workers' movement of the entire world, particularly *Western Europe*: the question of whether the conquest of power by the proletariat would take place by parliamentary or extraparliamentary means, that is, through the revolutionary action of the working class; the question of the choice between the dictatorship of the proletariat – the council system – as the realisation of proletarian democracy and parliamentary democracy as the form of appearance of the dictatorship of the bourgeoisie; the question of the choice between spontaneous proletarian revolution and conscious organisation through a party and thus the fundamental relationship between party and class; the problem of the organisation of a new proletarian international, whether it should be organised according to the principles of democratic centralism as a unitary world party with the task of practically preparing for the world revolution; the task of conquering the middle strata in the towns and countryside as allies of the proletariat; the question of colonial peoples' struggle for freedom and the right of nations to self-determination, that is the problem of mobilising the oppressed masses of the entire world against imperialism.[137]

The *assessment of the tendencies of economic development of world capitalism* is, naturally, of decisive importance in answering these questions. At present, those like Kautsky and the speakers at the Brussels Congress of the Second International in 1928 are of the view that capitalism stands at the outset of a further era of upswing. Others, on the contrary, assume that it is in a *period of decline*, which is indeed punctuated by short periods of *temporary stabilisation*, but that on the whole a continual sharpening of class antagonisms is apparent, which must finally lead to the decisive struggle for power.[138]

The experiences and lessons of the Russian revolution are a current problem for Western European capitalism, if it is in the midst of decline, placing the question of the Western European revolution on the agenda for the next period.

---

136 [Lenin 1964g.]

137 See Grossmann 1931b, pp. 430–3; Grossmann 1932d, pp. 440–2.

138 See Grossmann 1932d, p. 445.

This is the significance of debates over the conquest of state power inside the left wing of the Second (Socialist) International, e.g. the debates at the *Linz Congress* of Austrian Social Democracy (30 October–3 November 1926),[139] at which the new Party program was adopted. The core problem was the question of whether civil war and the use of force should be avoided by the working class in its struggle for state power and socialism. The result of the discussion can be summarised thus: the working class should in principle make use of the legal means of democracy in its struggle. It should not, however, ignore the fact that it is probable that the bourgeoisie will have recourse to force against the working class and its state if the proletariat conquers political power by means of democracy, if therefore democracy is decisively deployed *against* the bourgeoisie itself, as no ruling class gives up its power without a struggle. Under such circumstances, the working class for its part cannot abstain from the use of force.

e) *The End of Capitalism*

While the sole rule of the capitalist system was convulsed by the victory of the October Revolution in Russia, it did not resolve the question of the end of capitalism in socialist *theory*, given the concrete circumstances in which this victory was possible. With the October Revolution, the breakthrough from the capitalist system took place at its weakest point, namely where the revolutionising effects of capitalism had hardly begun at the moment of the social explosion. For the *technological backwardness* of old Russia was still more characteristic of feudalism than of capitalism. The Russian example is not, therefore, to be regarded as typical of the breakdown of capitalism in the *industrially most developed countries*. Their capacity to resist, as Bukharin says, is in direct proportion to their economic maturity, thus significantly greater than was the case in Russia, whose capitalist development was just beginning. If the October Revolution was a symptom and also the *beginning of the breakdown of the capitalist world system*, the immediate concrete causes of this event are still to be found in factors other than the likely causes of the breakdown of capitalism in *fully* capitalist countries, like England, Germany, and the United States of America. After as before it, the *breakdown of capitalism* therefore remains a problem, from the standpoint of Marxist theory and the labour movement.

During the postwar period, Henryk Grossman undertook to reassert anew the validity of this highly disputed but basic concept of Marx's system. Previously, there were two variants of the theory of breakdown. One (for example,

139 [Sozialdemokratische Arbeiterpartei Österreichs 1926.]

Bukharin, *Imperialism and the Accumulation of Capital*) only speaks generally about the 'limit ... given to a certain degree by the *tension* of capitalist contradictions' which 'will unavoidably lead to the collapse of capitalist rule',[140] without proving this 'unavoidability', i.e. without providing the theoretical explanation of why these contradictions must culminate in the final impossibility of balance. Just as little does this interpretation provide *concrete indicators* by which the 'degree' of critical tension in the contradictions that make breakdown 'unavoidable' can be identified in advance. This can only be determined *ex post*, after the advent of the breakdown. Then, however, the theory of breakdown is superfluous as an instrument of scientific knowledge. Such a 'general' explanation of breakdown must be considered to be unsatisfactory because of its scientific indeterminacy, as it really does not fulfil the 'Marxist requirement of concreteness' (Lenin).[141]

The other variant of breakdown theory, represented by Cunow, Kautsky (in writings of the period 1901–11, cited above), Boudin and Rosa Luxemburg, sought to derive the necessity of the downfall of the capitalist system from the limitations of the market, thus from processes in the sphere of circulation ('the realisation problem').

In his 1898 article, already mentioned, Cunow investigates the core problem of 'whether our economic development ... drives towards a *general catastrophe*'. Previously, the steady expansion of colonial possessions functioned to weaken the tendency to break down, resulting from insufficient markets. As such an extension of markets has its limit, however, the 'unavoidability of breakdown' is also a given. Without gaining external markets, 'England would long ago have faced a conflict between the capacity of its domestic and foreign markets to consume and the gigantic escalation of its capitalist accumulation'. For Cunow, breakdown is not in doubt; rather [it is] simply [a matter of] '*how long* the capitalist mode of production ... will survive and *under what circumstances* breakdown will take place'.[142]

After Kautsky's endorsement in the preface, Boudin's book deals with 'the decisive points of Marx's system'. Boudin also sees in the sale of surplus value 'the great problem' on which the existence of the economic constitution of capitalism depends. 'It is the inability to dispose of that product that is the chief cause of the temporary disturbances within its bowels and which will lead to

140 Bukharin 1929, p. 265. [Bukharin emphasised all of 'a certain degree by the *tension* of capitalist contradictions'.]

141 [Lenin 1964b, pp. 308–9, similarly p. 316.]

142 Cunow 1898, pp. 425, 427, 430. [Grossman's emphasis.]

its final *breakdown*.' Indeed if crises have previously ended and further accumulation has been made possible again, it is only because 'capitalistic countries ... had an *outside* world into which they could dump the products which they could not themselves absorb'. But this solution was only temporary. The thorough capitalisation of the territories of agrarian markets signifies the '*the beginning of the end of capitalism*' and will lead to 'the inevitable *breakdown* of the capitalistic mode of production'.[143]

In contrast to all previous breakdown theorists, Henryk Grossman treads a new path in his principal work *The Law of Accumulation and Breakdown of the Capitalist System* and numerous methodological and critical essays.[144] He explains the decisive cause of the inevitable demise of the capitalist system in terms of the *overaccumulation of capital in highly developed countries* and the resulting *insufficient valorisation* of capital, thus in terms of the process of production itself ('the valorisation problem'). With new proofs taken from modern economic relations, Grossman seeks to support the theory developed by Marx, today almost forgotten but already present in John Stuart Mill and Adam Smith in an embryonic form.[145] It holds that once a nation's capital *exceeds a definite scale, its accumulation finds no further profitable opportunities for investment* and consequently either lies idle or has to be exported. Since Tugan-Baranovsky's book on crisis, the problem of crisis and breakdown in the Marxist literature of the last 30 years has simply been dealt with from the point of view of *disproportionality* between individual spheres of production. Grossman demonstrates that, for Marx, the decisive problem was not *primarily partial crises* arising from disproportionality but rather the *primarily general crisis*, 'general glut', which is caused by 'parallel production ... which takes place simultaneously over the whole field'.[146] 'Precisely the possibility of such primarily general crises and not primarily partial crises arising from disproportionality is the object of Marx's dispute with the Say-Ricardo conception.'[147]

That an ever growing mass of means of production (MP = machines, buildings, raw materials, instruments of production) can be set in motion with a progressive decline in the expenditure of labour (L) is an empirical law charac-

143 Boudin 1907a, pp. 150, 235, 244. [Grossman emphasised '*breakdown*'.]

144 Grossmann 1929a; Grossmann 1928a, see above pp. 120–176; Grossman 1929b, see above pp. 183–209; Grossmann 1932a, see above pp. 276–303; Grossmann 1932b, see above pp. 304–331.

145 Mill 1900, book 4, chapter 4, pp. 481–91; Adam Smith 1910, book 1, chapter 9, pp. 77–89.

146 [Marx 1989c, pp. 115, 136. 'General glut' in English in Marx's and Grossman's original texts. Marx emphasised 'simultaneously'.]

147 Grossmann 1929a, p. 211.

teristic of the capitalist mode of production, as ever-expanding reproduction. On the basis of capitalism, the law is expressed in the constant growth in the amount of constant capital per worker in relation to variable (wage) capital (c : v, as the Marxists say, the organic composition of capital), which American census figures also confirm. As a result of the progressively higher organic composition of capital, because of the associated rising productivity of labour, wages do account for an ever smaller portion of total production. To the extent that the surplus value generated by a given working population grows absolutely (the rate of surplus value increases), however, it falls in relation to the continuously expanding total capital (c + v). This is the fact that underlies the *law of the tendency for the rate of profit to fall.*

The classical economists (Ricardo) already correctly identified the tendency for the rate of profit to fall as a phenomenon but mistakenly attempted to explain it *as a law of nature*, resulting from the decline in the productivity of the soil. Ricardo drew pessimistic conclusions for the future of capitalism from this phenomenon, as without profit 'there could be no accumulation'. He consoled himself that 'happily', from time to time, industrial and agricultural inventions (mechanical engineering and agronomy) can break through this pernicious tendency, so that it will only have an impact in the distant future.[148]

Many earlier theorists, like Boudin but above all Georg Charasoff,[149] felt that Marx also connected the breakdown of capitalism with the fall in the rate of profit. They could not, however, demonstrate the content of this connection and 'the *great importance that this law* has for capitalist production'.[150] That is easy to explain, as they only ever pointed out the fall in the rate of profit alone. The rate of profit, however, only expresses a proportional relationship, nothing other than a numerical concept. It is apparent that this cannot lead to the breakdown of a real system. For that to happen, *real causes are required.*

Moreover, the tendency for the rate of profit to decline has been a constant, concomitant phenomenon of capitalism from its beginnings until today, that is, during the whole process of its development. Where, then, does the sudden *shift* to breakdown come from? Why can't capitalism survive with a rate of profit of 4 percent just as well as with one of 13–15 percent, as the declining rate is offset by a rising mass of profit? Indeed, the growth in the mass of profit, as a consequence of the even faster growth in total capital, would be expressed in ever smaller percentages. The rate of profit would approach zero, that is the

148 [Ricardo 1912, pp. 71, 73.]
149 Charasoff 1910.
150 [Marx 1981b, p. 319. Grossman's emphasis.]

boundary point in the mathematical sense, without reaching it and yet the capitalist class could nevertheless feel comfortable as a consequence of the growth in the mass of profit.

Grossman was the first to point out that breakdown cannot be derived from or explained by the *rate* of profit, that is by the index number of profits, but must be understood in terms of what is concealed behind it: the real *mass* of profit in relation to the social mass of capital. For, according to Marx, 'accumulation depends not only on the *rate* of profit but on the *amount* of profit'.[151] If accumulation proceeds as a continuous process, the surplus value of the capitalists must be used for three purposes, be divided into three parts. First, one part must be used as additional constant capital (a_c); a second part as additional variable capital (a_v) – for the application of additional labour power; the remaining, third part can be used as a fund [(k)] for the capitalists' consumption. Now, the mass of surplus value does grow absolutely with the development of the capitalist mode of production. If, however, the organic composition of capital grows – as is necessary for capitalist production and is also assumed in the theoretical analysis – then *a relatively ever larger part of the surplus value* must be deducted for the purposes of additional accumulation (a_c). As long as the absolute mass of total social capital – with a low organic composition – is small, surplus value is relatively large and this leads to a *more rapid* increase in accumulation. For example, with a composition of 200 c + 100 v + 100 s, constant capital c can be increased by 33⅓ percent of its initial size (assuming the employment of all the surplus value for the purposes of accumulation). At a higher level of capital accumulation, with a significantly higher organic composition of capital, e.g. of 14,900 c + 100 v + 150 s, the expanded mass of surplus value is only 1 percent, when it is employed as additional capital a_c. It is easy to calculate that with continuing accumulation on the basis of an ever higher organic composition, a point must come when *all accumulation ceases*. This is all the more true because it is not any arbitrary fractional amount of capital that can be employed but rather a definite minimal amount is required, whose scale consistently grows with increasing accumulation of capital. With the progress of capital accumulation, therefore, an ever larger part, not only absolutely but also relatively, must be deducted from surplus value for the purposes of accumulation. So at high levels of accumulation, when extent of the total social capital is great, the part of surplus value required for additional accumulation, a_c, will be so large that it finally absorbs almost all of the surplus value. A point must be reached at which the part of surplus value destined

151 [Marx 1989c, p. 165. Grossman's emphasis.]

for the consumption of the workers and the capitalists ($a_v + k$) declines absolutely. That is the turning point at which the previously latent tendency to break down begins to take effect. Now it is apparent that the conditions required for the continuation of accumulation can no longer be entirely fulfilled, that the mass of surplus value, although it has grown absolutely, *is not sufficient for the three functions*. If, as previously assumed, the additional constant capital (a_c) is deducted from surplus value to the required extent, then the revenue part is not sufficient to cover the consumption of workers and employers to the previous extent. *An intense struggle between the working class and the employers over the division of revenue*, rising pressure from employers on the level of wages becomes unavoidable. If, on the other hand, the capitalists are forced, under pressure from the working class, to maintain the previous level of wages and consequently the part destined for additional accumulation a_c is reduced, the tempo of accumulation would slow down. This would signify that the productive apparatus cannot be renewed and expanded to the extent required by technological progress. A relative *technological backwardness* in the productive apparatus would set in. Any further accumulation must in such circumstances increase the difficulties, because the mass of surplus value can only be increased to an insignificant extent, with a given population. Surplus value flowing from previous capital outlays must therefore lie idle; an *excess of inactive capital searching in vain for investment opportunities must eventuate*. In this way, Grossman explains the technological backwardness of older capitalist countries, like England, with a higher level of capital accumulation and the tendency apparent there for the level of wages to stagnate or decline.

In 'pure', i.e. isolated, capitalism, these tendencies must soon prevail, i.e. lead to the breakdown of the system, under the pressure of intensifying class antagonisms.

In capitalism which is interdependent with the world economy, numerous *countertendencies* operate to *weaken* the tendency to break down, which is then only expressed in temporary *crises*.

Valorisation (the rate of profit) is repeatedly improved and increases the mass of profit by reducing the cost of producing constant capital and variable capital (the level of wages), shortening turnover time, improving the organisation of transport, reducing stocks and commercial expenses and the periodic devaluation of available capital. The advantages derived from the *domination of the world market* operate in the same way. *Unequal exchange* takes place in foreign trade – the technologically advanced countries receive a higher value in exchange for the value of their commodities – which also increases profits. This also applies to the export of capital. Capital export occurs because an overaccumulation of capital predominates in the highly developed capitalist countries and thus there is a lack of opportunities for investment. As a consequence, the capital exporting country receives an additional injection of surplus value, that improves the insufficient valorisation of capital and weakens or temporarily suspends the tendency to break down. This explains the *intensity of imperialist expansion during the late phase of capital accumulation*. Imperialism is an attempt to improve currently insufficient valorisation and hence to extend the lifespan of the capitalist system, by weakening tendencies to break down, through the transfer of surplus profits from colonial territories to highly developed capitalist countries. In this way, Grossman combines the theory of breakdown with the theory of crisis. *Crisis is an expression of breakdown that has not fully developed, because it has been mitigated by countertendencies*. But soon it is apparent that, because of the nature of the above countertendencies, they are only temporary and only able to counteract the tendency to break down to a certain extent. Stocks can only be reduced to a definite lower limit, breaching which would disrupt the continuity of the production process. Wages can only be depressed to a definite limit, breaching which would mean that the labour power of the working class was not fully reproduced; instead the intensity and quality of labour would decline. The reduction of commercial profits can only improve the profitability of industry to a limited extent. The more commerce is reduced, the smaller the mitigating effects of a further reduction will be. The counter-effects of capital export can also only be temporary. To the extent that the number of countries with excess capital and consequently seeking to export increases in the course of accumulation, competition on the world market, *the struggle over profitable spheres for investment*, increases. For this reason too, the tendency to break down must become more intense, at a definite point. The increase in fixed capital does not have a different effect. At higher levels of capital accumulation, at which fixed capital accounts for a larger component of constant capital, the contraction of production during the crisis has ever smaller significance: a firm's burden of depreciation and interest payments for fixed capital does not decline when production is reduced.

So it is apparent that the immanent laws of capital accumulation themselves progressively weaken the countertendencies. Overcoming crises becomes ever more difficult, the tendency to break down more and more holds sway. The periods of upturn become ever shorter, the duration and intensity of crisis periods rises. In his formula for crises Grossman attempts to determine the phase length of the economic cycle theoretically, by means of mathematics, and to identify the factors on which the extension or contraction of the economic cycle depend. If crisis is, for him, the tendency to breakdown which has not fully developed, *the breakdown of capitalism is nothing other than a crisis that is not checked by countertendencies*.

So capitalism approaches its end as a result of its inner economic laws.

From the standpoint of a Marxist theory of crisis and breakdown, it is obvious to Grossman from the start that the question of perhaps fatalistically awaiting the 'automatic' breakdown without actively intervening, does not arise for the working class. Old regimes never 'fall' of their own accord, even during a period of crisis, if they are not 'toppled over' (Lenin).[152] According to Grossman, the point of a Marxist theory of breakdown is only to demarcate voluntarism and putschism, which regard revolution as possible at any time without considering [whether there is] an *objectively revolutionary situation* and as dependent only on the subjective will of the revolutionaries. The point of breakdown theory is that the revolutionary action of the proletariat only receives its most powerful impetus *from the objective convulsion* of the established system and, at the same time, only this creates the circumstances necessary to successfully wrestle down the ruling class's resistance.

Grossman could achieve these results, which he regards as a reconstruction of Marx's theory of crisis and breakdown, because he had previously researched and recovered Marx's method and the plan which underlies *Capital*.

Rosa Luxemburg assumed that there was a gap in *Capital*, namely that Marx had not considered foreign trade; the only explanation of this assumption is that the method which underlies the structure of *Capital* had not previously been recognised as a specific theoretical problem. For this reason, however, it was not possible for Luxemburg to fully understand of Marx's solution.

If the process of *isolation* served the classical economists, Marx – according to Grossman – employs the so-called *method of successive approximation*. In order to research causes in the complicated world of appearances, Marx, like the classical economists, makes numerous simplifying assumptions by means of which he departs from the concrete totality of appearances, although this is precisely in order to explain it. The understanding achieved [in this way] can *only have a preliminary* character, can constitute only the *first stage of acquiring knowledge* in the method of successive approximation, which must be followed by a further, definitive stage. To each simplifying assumption there corresponds a subsequent correction, which in the final result takes into account the elements of actual reality that were initially neglected. All phenomena and problems are dealt with at least twice in this method: first under simplifying assumptions, then in their final form. This method underlies Marx's analysis in all three volumes of *Capital*. Those from whom this remains hidden must encounter continual 'contradictions' between the individual components of Marx's theory.

---

152 [Lenin 1964a, p. 214.]

Literature

Older literature is identified in the previous edition of this dictionary;[153] it is expressly referred to here. Of the more recent literature see:

Ashcroft, Thomas 1922, *An Outline of Modern Imperialism*, London: Plebs League.

Bauer, Otto 1931, *Kapitalismus und Sozialismus nach dem Weltkriege* [*Capitalism and Socialism after the World War*], Wien: Wiener Volksbuchhandlung.

Beer, Max 1957 [1922, 1929], *The General History of Socialism and Social Struggles*, two volumes, New York: Russell & Russell.

Bober, Mandell Morton 1927, *Karl Marx's Interpretation of History*, Cambridge MA: Harvard University Press.

Brauer, Theodor 2012 [1929], *Der moderne deutsche Sozialismus* [*Modern German socialism*], Paderborn: Salzwasser.

Graziadei, Antonio 1927, *Capitale e colonie* [*Capital and Colonies*], Milano: Casa editrice sociale.

Heider, Werner 1931, *Die Geschichtslehre von Karl Marx* [*Karl Marx's Theory of History*], Stuttgart: Cotta.

Heimann, Eduard 1922, *Mehrwert und Gemeinwirtschaft: kritische und positive Beiträge zur Theorie des Sozialismus* [*Surplus Value and Social Economy: Critical and Positive Contributions on the Theory of Socialism*], Berlin: Engelmann.

Heimann, Eduard 1931, *Kapitalismus und Sozialismus: Reden und Aufsätze zur Wirtschafts- und Geisteslage* [*Capitalism and Socialism: Speeches and Essays on the Economic and Intellectual Situation*], Potsdam: Protte.

Heimburger, Karl 1928, *Die Theorie von der industriellen Reservearmee* [*The Theory of the Industrial Reserve Army*], Halberstadt: Meyer.

Jenssen, Otto, 1927 *Der Kampf um die Staatsmacht: Was lehrt uns Linz? Verhandlungen des Linzer Parteitages der deutsch-österreichischen Sozialdemokratie* [*The Struggle over State Power: What Does Linz Teach Us? Proceedings of the Linz Congress of German-Austrian Social Democracy*], Berlin: Laub.

Jostock, Paul 1928, *Der Ausgang des Kapitalismus: Ideengeschichte seiner Überwindung* [*Capitalism's Exit: the History of Ideas of Overcoming it*], München: Duncker & Humblot.

Laidler, Harry Wellington 1927, *A History of Socialist Thought*, New York: Crowell.

Laurat, Lucien 1932, *Un système qui sombre* [*A System That is Sinking*], Paris: l'Églantine.

Lenin, Vladimir Ilyich 1960–8 [from 1920], *Collected Works*, Moscow: Progress.

Leubuscher, Charlotte 1921, *Sozialismus und Sozialisierung in England: Ein Überblick*

153 Grünberg 1911b.

über die neuere Entwicklung der sozialistischen Theorien und über die Probleme der Industrieverfassung in England [*Socialism and Socialisation in England: an Overview of Recent Developments in Socialist Theory and the Problem of the Industrial Constitution*], Jena: Fischer.

Lewin, David 1913, *Der Arbeitslohn und die soziale Entwicklung* [*The Wage and Social Development*], Berlin: Springer.

Liebert, Arthur 1931, 'Materialistische Geschichtsphilosophie' ['The materialist philosophy of history'], in *Handworterbuch der Soziologie* [*Dictionary of Sociology*], edited by Alfred Vierkandt, 360–70, Stuttgart: Enke.

Louis, Paul 1931, *Les idées essentielles du socialisme* [*The Essential Ideas of Socialism*], Paris: Rivière.

Luxemburg, Rosa 1972 [1921], 'The Accumulation of Capital – an Anti-critique or What the Epigones have made of Marx's theory', in Rosa Luxemburg and Nikolai Bukharin, *Imperialism and the Accumulation of Capital*, 44–153, London: Allen Lane.

Luxemburg, Rosa 1919 [1916], *The Crisis of Social Democracy*, New York: Socialist Publication Society.

Mallock, William Hurrell 1918 [1917], *The Limits of Pure Democracy*, London: Chapman and Hall.

Nakhimson, (Spectator), Miron Isaakovich 1929, *Mirovoye khozyaystvo do i posle voyny. Tom 3* [*The World Economy before and after the War. Volume 3*], Moskva: Kommunisticheskoy akademii.

Pollock, Friedrich 1926, *Sombarts 'Widerlegung' des Marxismus* [*Sombart's 'Refutation' of Marxism*], Leipzig: Hirschfeld.

Ralea, Mihai 1923, *Révolution et socialisme: essai de bibliographie* [*Revolution and Socialism: Bibliographic Essay*], Paris: Presses universitaires de France.

Rosenberg, Arthur 1934 [1932], *A History of Bolshevism: From Marx to the First Five Years' Plan*, Oxford: Oxford University Press.

Sée, Henri 1982 [1927], *Matérialisme historique et l'interprétation économique de l'histoire* [*Historical Materialism and the Economic Interpretation of History*], Genève: Slatkine.

Seligman, Edwin Robert Anderson 1967 [1902], *The Economic Interpretation of History*, New York: Columbia University Press.

Seydewitz, Max et al. 1931, *Die Krise des Kapitalismus und die Aufgabe der Arbeiterklasse* [*The Crisis of Capitalism and the Tasks of the Working Class*], Berlin: Verlag der Marxistischen Büchergemeinde.

Sorel, Georges 1990 [1911], 'The Economic Interpretation of History', in Georges Sorel, *From Georges Sorel: Hermeneutics and the Sciences*, 191–208, New Brunswick: Transaction.

Sozialdemokratische Arbeiterpartei Österreichs 1926, *Protokoll des sozialdemokratischen Parteitages 1926, abgehalten in Linz, vom 30. Oktober bis 3. November* [*Minutes*

of the Social Democratic Party Congress, held in Linz, from 30 October to 3 November], Wien: Verlag der Wiener Volksbuchhandlung.
Stalin, Joseph 1934 [1924–6], *Problems of Leninism*, New York: International Publishers.
Trotsky, Leon 1975 [1922], *Between Red and White: A Study of Some Fundamental Questions of Revolution, with Particular Reference to Georgia*, Westport, CT: Hyperion Press.
Trotsky, Leon 1970 [1928], *The Third International after Lenin: The Draft Program of the Communist International: A Criticism of Fundamentals*, New York: Pathfinder.
Trotsky, Leon 1977 [1930], *History of the Russian Revolution*, London: Pluto.
Turgeon, Charles 1932, *Critique de la conception matérialiste de l'histoire* [*Critique of the Materialist Conception of History*], Paris: Recueil Sirey.
Wilbrandt, Robert 1919, *Sozialismus* [*Socialism*], Jena: Diederichs.

Journals

Die Gesellschaft: Internationale Revue für Sozialismus und Politik, since 1924.
Unter dem Banner des Marxismus, since 1925.
Archiv für die Geschichte des Sozialismus und der Arbeiterbewegung, 1911–30.

See, further, the literatures identified in the articles 'Bolshevism', 'Internationals', 'Social democratic and communist parties' and also the biographies of [individual] socialists.[154]

154 Grossmann 1931b; Grossmann 1932c; Grossmann 1932d; Grossmann 1932d; Grünberg and Grossmann 1933b.

CHAPTER 14

Letters to Leo Löwenthal*

Translated from German by Rick Kuhn

10 December 1933

Paris

Dear Mr Löwenthal

In answering your friendly letter of 29 October I only want to return briefly to your essay. You write that you do not want to identify with LdN [Richard Lefebvre des Noëttes][1] in all questions of detail, 'as you are not competent in them'. This is where the source of the problem lies. Instead of confining yourself to a mere *report*, you have entered an area that you have not mastered. Consequently you have made mistakes, not only in questions of detail, rather the whole article is rife with short-sightedness, factually false statements etc., from the start to the finish. Mr LdN's discoveries about 'power' during the Middle Ages did not have to be awaited. Twenty others had made them before him.

But I only want to touch on the principal problem: *slavery*. 'Why did slavery arise?' The answer you give on p. 202, following LdN, is the pure dilettantism of a cavalry officer, who does not understand anything about history: inadequate mastery of the harnessing of draft animals was the cause!

If what Mr LdN [wrote] about harnessing was correct, what would then be proved? That, as a consequence of bad harnessing of horses, much human labour is necessary for transportation. Why must this labour be specifically *slave* labour? Neither you nor LdN go into this. You just stand there, where, for historical materialists, *the problem begins*, namely [with] *class* relations!

But I do not want to discuss [this]. I only want to emphasise Mr LdN's obvious ignorance: before something can be transported it must exist, i.e. it has to be *produced*. The *principal areas* of antique (as more recent) slavery are not *transport* but *production*, agricultural production, mining production (the slaves in Greece's silver mines are well known), industrial production. Only a dilettante like LdN could centre the problem on the question of transport.

---

* [A selection of the original letters in Grossman 1933–9.]

1 [Grossman is referring to Löwenthal 1933, which deals with Lefebvre des Noëttes 1931.]

LdN's book should be sharply criticised in the journal.[2] Instead you glorify the book as a scientific achievement of genius!

Pollock requested that I write a correction for the journal. Apart from lack of time, the mere correction of the facts would require entire pages and that alone would be very compromising for you, dear Mr Löwenthal, even if I did it ever so gently. I will deal with Mr LdN in my book on the 'critical history of slavery', which I have just received back from Frankfurt am Main with the manuscripts.[3] I do hope to be able to do this in two to three years.

But the most important thing in your presentation is the 100 percent abandonment of the materialist conception of history and its reinterpretation into its direct opposite.

If it was only deficient harnessing that was *the* cause of slavery, why did slavery still *advance* in the nineteenth century, when we not only knew how to harness properly but had railways! In my crisis book I show that, according to the first census in the USA there were 752,000 slaves – in 1861, however, there already were 4 million.[4] And there had to be a *war* before slavery could be abolished! What do all these class relations have to do with 'knowledge' of the art of harnessing? What does it have to do with [Charles Maurice de] Talleyrand who, as the representative of France at the Congress of Vienna in 1814 was *against* the abolition of the slave trade[?] We know, however, that Le Havre and Nantes, as great slave ports, demanded Talleyrand take this stance, in the interests of their profits.

Dear Mr Löwenthal, I hope that you will not misunderstand my lines. I have considered whether I should make my critical comments for a long time. I believe that the *real duty* in friendship is not to flatter but to tell the truth, otherwise you will be in danger of making further mistakes.

I feel, here, the lack of the kind of collaboration that existed in Frankfurt am Main. Collaboration has decided advantages and I could have guarded you against many an [error] through my critical comments *before* publication. That is the value of the friendly exchange of ideas before the final formulation, through publication.

Many thanks, dear Mr Löwenthal for your friendly dispatch of the books I needed, which I received yesterday. Mattick in Chicago has issue 1/2 of *1932*.[5]

---

2 [i.e. *Zeitschrift für Sozialforschung*, the journal of the Institut für Sozialforschung.]

3 [The Nazis confiscated material in Grossman's office at the Institute in Frankfurt am Main. Thanks largely to the intervention of the Polish consul, some of it was returned to him.]

4 Grossmann 1929a, p. 412.

5 [Issue of *Zeitschrift für Sozialforschung*, for which Löwenthal had some editorial and administrative responsibilities.]

As payment, please send him a year's worth, starting with the current, second issue. *In addition* also number 3 of 1932 and issue 1 of 1933 and, indeed, on *my* account. He sent me some literature from the USA so, as compensation, I will pay for these two issues.

Sincere regards to you and your wife from your

Henryk Grossman

31 December 1933

Paris

Dear Mr Löwenthal

Your letter with New Year wishes from you and your wife genuinely gave me pleasure and I respond most sincerely. I would really be pleased to see your wife again – she is the only one in our circle who I have not seen since the March events.[6]

Concerning your factual statements, today only a few words, as I have had a severe cold for several days (as a casualty of the bad heating in the small hotel). So, despite the kind invitation to New Year's Eve with Eduard Fuchs, I have to stay at home.

You did not interpret my letter correctly when you assessed it as an 'attack'. There is no occasion for this in it. We have already known each other quite long and are close enough to express our views to each other unadorned. As an historian who has long engaged with economic history and also especially with the history of slavery in Europe, I wanted to convey some experience to you, as a younger colleague whose area of work has previously been different, in order to guard you too against some mistakes.

I hope to have recovered enough in eight to ten days to be able to present you with some materials. E.g. I will contest and refute the statement that only a few traces of slavery were passed on from the Middle Ages along four lines.

1) The *fact of (white) slavery in Europe*, particularly in *Italy, as a mass phenomenon* from the thirteenth *until the end of the sixteenth* century. Likewise in *southern France*, i.e. French Catalonia, (Roussillon, Provence) in the thirteenth to seventeenth centuries. In some areas of France it was still present *in the eighteenth century*.

6 [The events leading up to 24 March 1933, when the Nazis obtained full control over the German state.]

2) The Catholic Church still regarded slavery as a recognised institution in *numerous works* in the sixteenth century and sought to incorporate it into the totality of its doctrine.
3) Extensive *contemporary literature*, particularly *comedies*, in Italy and France still reflect slavery in the sixteenth and seventeenth centuries.
4) *Recent historical research*, which has unearthed all of this.

Why does Mr Lefevbre dN know nothing at all about this? Similarly, almost every one of your statements is contestable. But more about that later. For today, affectionate regards from your

Henryk Grossman

Also best regards to Horkheimer and wife, Pollock and Mrs Rabes.

29 January 1934

Dear Mr Löwenthal

Affectionate thanks for your letter. You have given me great pleasure by sending Borkenau's book to Mattick. Not for personal reasons. I do not know Mattick personally. But I appreciate proletarians like him, who through their own efforts elevate themselves. The man is hardly 31 years old and in the worst material circumstances. Long unemployed. But he engages to an uncommon extent in intellectual labour, without rest, and *develops* himself. He will rapidly overcome his lack of income etc. I am convinced that he will yet play a role in the future of the workers' movement in the USA. He deserves to be supported in his intellectual activity. (He cannot afford to buy Borkenau's book.)

Coming back to your letter, I have to say that you really do not know me, even though we have known each other for years now, if you think that I am irritated because of the delay in your reply. I am not that petty. All these personal motives are alien to me. What interests me is the matter itself. Here too there are no grounds or motives for annoyance. The letters which we have exchanged in intimate friendship do aid mutual understanding. Since we are no longer concentrated in the same city, we cannot clarify much through the verbal exchange of views. That is the ideal form. So we are left with correspondence which, however, always gives rise to misunderstandings. If I criticise your statements so openly and without unnecessary obfuscation I evidently claim *no privilege for myself*. On the contrary, I count on you to criticise my output with the same severity and openness and would be grateful for this. Any sensible person has to prefer such criticism to banal praise.

Mr Horkheimer suggested that I review Borkenau's book (in its economic and economic history contexts) for the journal. The task attracts me and, if I had my library here, I would not have hesitated for an hour. Now, as the books are so hard to access here, I fear that the review will rob me of much time and divert me from rapidly finishing my Quesnay book.[7] Nevertheless, I realise that I do still have to write the review of Borkenau.

I am looking for a new place. Here in the hotel I am constantly catching something new. I was coughing severely for two months with a kind of flu. That had hardly passed and now I have back pain and can only move my neck with difficulty.

With most sincere regards
your personally faithful
Henryk Grossman

12 February 1934

La Coupole
Restaurant, thés, soupers dansants
Montparnasse[8]

Dear Mr Löwenthal

Only today, the day of the general strike, as businesses are closed, do I find time to answer your kind letter. I have been running about dealing with my accommodation. I want, at last, to be able to work in peace, which is impossible in the hotel. My new address, from 16 February: 12 rue Victor Considérant (14th [District]).

Concerning our discussion, I see that a major misunderstanding has actually arisen between us. Concerning my objection that, despite the discovery of harnessing in the tenth century slavery existed in the USA until the second half of the nineteenth century, you think this fact is favourable for your and Lefebvre's argument. How? Because the abolition of slavery in the USA in the nineteenth century was also only the effect of some changes in technology. As if I would have denied that! But the discussion is not about that. It is rather about what slavery in the sixteenth or nineteenth century has to do with the improvement in harnessing in the tenth. For Mr L's *generalised* conclusions, that are absolutely untenable, do not accord with the facts, which is why I call his theory 'dilettantish'. That *other* changes in technology played a role in the

7 [This project does not seem to have made much progress.]
8 [Printed letterhead.]

abolition of slavery and constituted its precondition is clear. But here too class relations have everywhere to be analysed and demonstrated. For it is not simply the forces of production and changes in them that are the essence of the materialist conception of history but [also] the relations of production associated with them. Whoever tears this connection between the two apart and one-sidedly demonstrates development only through changes in technology, that is forces of production, lapses into idealism.

13 February

I wanted to continue but today, as yesterday, I have been in about ten junk shops after a few pieces of furniture, with Mrs Lotte Schneider. The sad news from Vienna, that is oppressing me psychologically, has now come. It is apparent how its mistakes and indecisiveness have revenged themselves on social democracy. 'Too late!' Months ago the working class as a whole should have struck and not left the action to the Schutzbund.[9] If only the social democrats had taken the *initiative* and not left it to Mr [Engelbert] Dollfuß! First of all, there should really have been a *battle plan* to disperse the regime's troops and draw them out of Vienna, so that workers could take the city into their hands. Nothing of the kind! This fight is nothing more than an act of desperation, without a plan; merely saves the honour of the Viennese working class, that goes under because of its little 'leaders', *à la* Otto Bauer. Will this lesson at least be useful in the future?

Concerning your request about Mr [Alexandre] Koyré, I want to advise you in the matter, namely not to take his silence too tragically. He is in Cairo; before departing he did not have much time to write and it is understandable that he forgot to justify himself. The French are *not* excessively polite, despite the opinion to the contrary. Their politeness is calibrated according to the *advantages* that they expect from someone. Perhaps, in your correspondence with K, limit yourself to his editorial communications, with an official, polite close, without any personal references. Correct, polite but cold.

If it was possible for you [to] get hold of or just borrow Engels's book *The Peasant War*, likewise Olschki's *Galileo and His Times*, Leipzig 1927,[10] I would be most indebted. It is hard to find German books here. Also the book by Arthur

9 [On 12 February 1934, the paramilitary Heimwehr (Home Defence) associated with the Christian Social Party of the Austrian Chancellor Engelbert Dollfuß, who had assumed dictatorial power on 4 March 1933, raided a building belonging to the Social Democratic Workers' Party in Linz, which was defended by the Schutzbund (Republican Defence League), its armed paramilitary organisation, triggering a civil war that lasted until 16 Feburary 1934.]

10 [Engels 1978b; Olschki 1927.]

Salz about mining in Bohemia 1912 (or 1913).[11] I do not know the exact title, Horkheimer thinks the Olschki that might be purchased for the Institute.

If you come to Paris again I hope to see you at my new place. Then we can continue our discussion. I am looking forward very much to that.

With sincere regards to you and your wife
your devoted
Henryk Grossman

26 February 1936

60 Belsize Park
London NW 3

Dear Mr Löwenthal

Your letter of 13 February came as a surprise to me: I made my address known on all sides, in Geneva, Paris and to have forgotten New York! I have to beg for forgiveness. I am happy that I finally have the move behind me. It cost a lot of time, bother and money! I have also lugged many books with me to London, at the same time leaving 10 cartons of books in Paris with acquaintances in order to save money! Hopefully they will not go missing.

After arriving here I was quite depressed because, for a long time, I could not find a room for the money I can afford. And I simply cannot live in the run-down student rooms around the British Museum, because I am simply incapable of working under such conditions. After a long search, I finally found a large, beautiful room in a guesthouse, where I can install my library. The food is certainly poor (the owner does have to have a source of profit somewhere). But I do not place any great weight on food. The main thing: properly presented and cultured accommodation, into which I can sometimes invite someone for tea. So I feel really good and have immediately thrown myself into work. For weeks I have been sitting daily from 9:30 (I leave home around 9:00) until 4–4:30 in the British Museum. This week I also began to visit the library of the London School of Economics. I have not had such an atmosphere for work as that prevailing in the reading room of the British Museum since the period in Frankfurt. When I compare that with the difficulties in Paris, a real struggle for every book, I regret that I did not come here earlier! In addition: the pleasantness of the people. Professor Tawney and his wife are unusually charming people; he placed his

---

11 [Salz 1913.]

large private library at my disposal (naturally, I will not make any use of it but the noble gesture is in itself of value!) and both make efforts to be helpful to me in some way. After the calculating politeness of the French, this warm atmosphere is enchanting.

With these conditions for work, I hope to create something really good. Sadly, sadly, I have to work a great deal!

And now to [Max] Beer's essay, which I have not read (because I have no time to do so) but the content of which I know! In principle, I do not like to burden you with essays. In this case, I believe, the essay warrants it. I do not write to you because I want to influence your decision in some way. But I want set my motives out to you.

It is not a matter of [Numa Denis] Fustel de Coulange the person nor of an historical essay. Likewise you could say: why do we pay attention to Descartes: we are interested in theory. It seemed to me that the Institute is interested in the problem of dialectical materialism, the social conditionality of the 'superstructure', quite independently of the material that illustrates the problem: the ancient world, the philosophy of the Middle Ages or the modern period. Once my crisis book is finished, I also want to use material on the historical development of the ancient world myself, to present the inevitable changes in the *whole* superstructure (law, state, literature, religion) from the sixth century until the great breakdown, as the consequence of the penetration of capital, in short as the consequence of changes in the relations of production. I recently wrote to Pollock about this.

Thus it seemed to me that, just as a good, backwater businessman will not disdain occasional profits that [come] to him in another branch, the journal will also carry good essays on this principal theme.

The *problem of primitive communism*, set out by Max, is of unusually great significance for the sociological consideration of the law of the family, customs etc. The entire history of the late Middle Ages is simply unintelligible without the clarification of this problem. Is the institution of primitive communism in Germanic areas (including Franconia)[12] a Marxist fantasy or an historical fact? The facts here are clear. But bourgeois 'research' has been concerned to distort them for decades, through daring interpretations; making it suspect, by sleight of hand, and inspiring the impression that this Marxist 'fable' was long ago refuted and exposed.

Remember that the problem was also dealt with in our Institute in Frankfurt, because the same thing always happens. And the source of this entire bourgeois

12 [Franconia is an area in what is now central Germany.]

campaign of distortion is Fustel! By criticising him, Beer destroys the idol, the source of the entire falsification!

In addition, also consider this: in the ranks of Marxists, who is today capable of dealing with this problem with such knowledge and with such diligence? There is in the essay, the work of many, many months. It has a rare value and I believe that this essay will always be read and sought after. Beer himself told me that he is prouder of this short work than of his two-volume work on British socialism, that was itself a great achievement and has had the justifiable success of a two-volume work going through five editions in ten years!

Perhaps you automatically underestimate the old man, as a result of his failure with the work in Frankfurt. But the failure then was understandable. Such work, like my essays for Elster, requires *systematic* training and education and Beer, like every autodidact, lacks precisely that. Where, however, Beer deals with a topic that he has mastered through his *own* research, he can accomplish much.

You have no idea of how much the man is appreciated by the English. I will not speak about things such as a baronet, who he did not know, sending him a cheque for £20 as an expression of his appreciation, after reading his autobiography. But despite his apparent poverty, he is invited with great piety into elegant circles with his young (16 year-old) daughter. The 'Lords Passfield'[13] (Sidney and Beatrice Webb) recently sent him their large two-volume work on Soviet Communism with the warmest dedication from him and her etc. etc.

His autobiography has sold out. Just in New York 250 copies were sold and a second edition (which is much to be desired as the man and his daughter live in poverty [on the royalties] from it) is very likely.

Apparently he is going to New York in May where his married and well-off sister will take him up, 'until the end of his days'. Alvin Johnson has offered him a professorial post at the so-called emigrant university (Emil Lederer etc.).[14] (I do not believe that Beer is suited to something like that.) I thought it might sometimes be useful for the Institute to have, in Beer, a well-disposed contact. Finally, Beer is one of the best-known authors, read in almost all cultured languages. Entirely independently of how you assess the value of his work, this fact stands. Thanks to the great popularity of this man, an essay by him in the

13 [English in the original.]

14 [Johnson was the founding director of the New School for Social Research in New York, whose Graduate Faculty of Political and Social Science began in 1933 as the University in Exile a program which employed exiled German and Italian academics. Lederer was its first dean.]

journal would attract new readers, particularly now that problems of socialism in the USA, it seems, have become fashionable.

Another question is *when* you want to publish the essay. Beer is not concerned if, considering that my, in part historical, essay[15] was recently published, you would prefer to have two issues between them. He will be happy if he has the assurance that the thing will appear soon.

One further matter, given his reputation and connections here, he could easily have placed the essay in an historical review here. But one wanted to soften some 'poisonous' statements against Fustel, out of bourgeois solidarity. And that is precisely what he did not want: the value of the work lies precisely in the demonstration of Fustel's art of distortion! *Dixi et salvavi animam meam*![16]

And now there remains only a little room for private news. I want to write to Pollock on a scientific matter.

Sincerest regards to you and your wife
from your
Henryk Grossman.

Today sensational news: the supporters of a war against [the] Soviet [Union] in the Japanese army have murdered several ministers.

Undated (Early August 1939)

Tallwood, Maranacook, Maine[17]

Dear Mr Löwenthal

Many thanks for your friendly and detailed letter. I knew in advance, as I do not believe in miracles, that the appearance of my essay in the next issue was impossible. Nevertheless I directed my question to you, in order not to have to blame myself for having neglected something. I regard the appearance of this essay (which will certainly not bring me any laurels but only hostility) as my debt to Marx and a heavy burden will fall from my heart if the essay appears in the winter issue. It is the most important thing that I have to say about Marx's economics.

15 [Grossmann 2009.]
16 [*'Dixi et salvavi animam meam'* means 'I have spoken and saved my soul'.]
17 [Letterhead. Tallwood was a rural resort hotel.]

In relation to the postage stamps for Daniel, you are mistaken. I lie often and with pleasure. If, however, I once tell the truth, I am not believed.[18]

In relation to my summer experiences in Timberland[19] and here, I have seen and experienced really interesting things but I do not want to write about them. It is the tragic end of a cult, particularly insofar as it concerns women. At the next opportunity, in our closer membership circle of the Institute – with your wife – I will give a short talk about it, at my place one evening. You will see that it concerns very serious questions.[20]

My stay here is purely [a case of] falling for it. The countryside is, indeed, lovely – I am in a boat two or three times a day and row 5–6 miles along the lake. There are fine horses here and I ride a lot. But the people! The dictatorship of the petty bourgeois. We are conducting a war. That stimulates me, so I have stayed.

Warm greetings to you and your wife
from your
Henryk Grossman

18 [A reference to foreign stamps which Grossman had sent to Löwenthal, for his young son Daniel. Grossman was denying having purchased the stamps.]

19 [A rural resort in upstate New York.]

20 [Presumably, Grossman is referring to the attitudes of young women towards love, which he raised in his letter to Max Horkheimer of 6 August 1939, see below pp. 436–7.]

CHAPTER 15

Letters to Max Horkheimer*

Translated from German by Nick Reynolds and Rick Kuhn

24 August 1934[1]

Paris 14
12. r. Victor Considérant

Dear Mr Horkheimer

Thank you very much for the letters you so graciously sent me. I am happy that you and your wife are well again and wish you a rapid recovery.

I received your telegram on 12 August and your letter of 30 July, just a week later, because it was delivered to me late through [Paul] Honigsheim, following summer festivities at the Rue d'Ulm.[2] I sent a card to you in Lake Placid – and now, after talking to Pollock today, I would like to discuss matters relating to the essay that I gave him.

I already began to write a critique in March. I had to deal with all important aspects of the book, constitutional law, morals, philosophy, history, not just to limit myself to critique but rather – as objectivity demands – to emphasise the good aspects too and ultimately to deal with [Franz] Borkenau's method.[3] The result: the work became too great and quite unsatisfying, because I could only devote a small amount of space to each problem. Consequently I could only hint at everything, instead of being able to convince the reader by presenting material. I therefore decided on different, more effective means: instead of writing a proper, conventional critique of the book, I would rather single out two central points and concentrate the force of critique on them. I hope that you will agree with me. Borkenau's book is based on two principal ideas: 1) The origins of modern mechanics, which creates the prerequisites for the emergence

* [The original letters are in Grossman 1934–43, most were published in Horkheimer 1995a; Horkheimer 1995b; Horkheimer 1996a.]

1 [Nick Reynolds translated all letters apart from those of 23 August 1935 and 14 April 1938.]

2 [The École Normale Supérieure, an elite research and higher education institute, housed the Paris branch of the Institute for Social Research and was in Rue d'Ulm.]

3 [Horkheimer had commissioned Grossman to write a critical review of Borkenau 1971 in order to distance the Institute from the book which it had published.]

of a mechanistic worldview, date back to the mid-seventeenth century. 2) They are to be explained in terms of the industrial division of labour. Now one cannot imagine a more serious, forceful attack than the one I undertook, insofar as I show that neither 1) the phenomenon to be explained nor 2) that with which it was to be explained exists. Both are illusions, based on ignorance of the facts. That is to say, the origins of modern mechanics reach back not to the first half of the seventeenth century but rather to the beginning of the sixteenth. Secondly, the industrial division of labour existed just as little at the beginning of the seventeenth century and first emerged in the second half of the eighteenth century. Borkenau placed the origins of the mechanics of the sixteenth century too late, in the seventeenth century, and placed the division of labour of the eighteenth century too early, in the seventeenth century. In doing so he created an artificial temporal coincidence of the origins of mechanics and the much later division of labour.

You will appreciate the scope of my critique. I believe that in opening the discussion just such a critique can be fruitful, because it transplants the discussion into the correct historical period from the outset.

Moreover, in the essay on the capitalism of the Renaissance period, I provided more. Beyond pure critique, I posed the question that Borkenau should have answered: how were the origins of mechanics possible at the beginning of the sixteenth century? I believe that I offer interesting and new material that can also have a fruitful effect on the discussion.

For that reason I would ask you to initially allow the publication of the first essay, 'Capitalism of the Renaissance period', with a short introductory note by you. I sent the second essay on 'Manufacturing from the sixteenth to eighteenth century' for the purpose of orientation but I would still like to change the beginning of the essay somewhat, i.e. adapt it to the specific purpose of an essay for the journal.[4]

I believe that both of these essays provide what is essential for a critique. Later, if you like, I can still write an essay about Borkenau's method or another aspect of the book.

I would be happy to get a message from you soon. With best wishes to you and your wife

your devoted
Henryk Grossman

4 [Eventually only one article by Grossman, criticising Franz Borkenau's book, was published in the *Zeitschrift für Sozialforschung*, Grossman 2009.]

16 October 1934

12 Rue Victor-Considérant
Paris (14e)

Dear Mr Horkheimer

Many thanks for your letter and the friendly greetings from your wife.

I will begin by assuring you that it will be a pleasure to take part in the collective labour on the family[5] and that it would not occur to me to think of it as a 'waste of time'.

With regard to the article on the Renaissance, I would like to have the proofs in good time, because – aside from grammatical corrections – there are still a few factual revisions to be made.

With regard to the other article, I am in a quandary: I am suffering from *embarras de richesse*:[6] I have here, in particular, *several* essays that provide new material and in *essential* points show the fundamental untenability of Borkenau's construct. For example, the chapter on the new ethics. Borkenau follows Max Weber here uncritically;[7] Calvinism had created a capitalist ethic before capitalism existed. The emergence of capitalism is religiously and morally conditioned. Borkenau concedes Max Weber's assumptions and only from within this problematic does he polemicise against Weber. He wants to show that, in spite of the reality of these assumptions, the materialist basis should not be abandoned. This is a convoluted demonstration that, in the face of so many trees and details upon which it turns, forgets the forest, i.e. the great historical context. Namely:

1. It is a fact that capitalism already existed in *Italy*, from the fourteenth century and in *Flanders* in the thirteenth (the putting-out system, *decentralised*, large-scale industry).
2. But even if we leave the older developments aside, on German soil a powerful industrial capitalism already existed at the end of the fifteenth and beginning of the sixteenth century – German-Tyrollean-Hungarian *mining*. Only the Fuggers' *financial* business is generally mentioned,[8] but today it has been established that mining (thanks to technological improvements, mechanical devices to pump water, etc.) was the *found-*

5 [Published as Horkheimer 1936b, which does not include a contribution from Grossman.]
6 [*Embarras de richesse* means 'embarrassment of riches'.]
7 [Weber 1968.]
8 [The Fugger family was a very powerful dynasty which engaged in trade, banking and mining across Europe and in Spain's American empire during the fifteenth and sixteenth centuries.]

ation of the Fuggers' fortune, which they guarded as the apple of their eyes. *Industrial capitalism* with machines was a major power on German soil before Calvin or even Luther appeared on the public scene. Fugger corrupted the entire administration of Germany, bribed the Emperor's advisors in Spain. Since [Leopold von] Ranke, it has been known that he actually decided the election of Karl V as Emperor in 1519.

Weber's entire problematic – which Borkenau accepts uncritically – bursts like a soap bubble! But the presentation of all this requires space: the historical material has to be provided; otherwise explanations like the one above are mere words.

The same applies to manufactured goods. I have an essay here that shows year by year, *using the example of France*, that until [Jean Baptiste] Colbert's administration (1661) *absolutely no manufactories* were large enterprises; consequently the mechanical worldview that arose in 1615–40, according to Borkenau, could not have been influenced by manufactories.[9] I will send you this essay within the next week and let you decide which essay you want to be published. My original thought was trichotomous. a) The Renaissance article shows that modern mechanics arose around 1500, indeed in connection with the development of *machinery* of the period. b) Using the example of France to show historically that, in France before the end of the seventeenth century, there was *no division of labour characteristic of manufacture*. c) The article about the phases of development of manufacture (which you now have) shows theoretically that labour under manufacture is, in principal, unsuited to form the basis of mechanics. Here I also struggle at every step with *space* because all these essays are otherwise already finished, they are just too long.[10]

I send affectionate regards to you and your wife and remain your faithful

Henryk Grossman

May I ask you to deliver the enclosed letter to Pollock.

G.

9 [A manufactory is a workplace where the labour of multiple workers using craft technology, i.e. does not involve use of complicated machinery, takes place under the supervision of overseers.]

10 [One of Grossman's essays from this period, criticising Weber and Borkenau, has been published as Grossman 2006; also see Kuhn 2006.]

26 October 1934

12 Rue Victor-Considérant
Paris (14e)

Dear Mr Horkheimer

Your letter of 8 October with the news that the Renaissance article will now not be published was distressing for me. Certainly, I can write the desired article by 15 December and you will receive it in a timely fashion. I believe, however, on practical grounds, that it would be better if it appears earlier. It would seem to me more effective if one study was counterposed to the other, so that the critique is exercised positively. In that case, the Institute stands above as a neutral centre, which allows a problem to be worked on from different standpoints. Otherwise the Institute will suffer, whether or not this is what you want; the more important are the errors, indeed *factual* errors, that I have to demonstrate, the more it will be asked why such a book was published by the Institute. That was my impression.

I do not know if you have read my article on the Renaissance in my manuscript or in the clean copy produced in New York. In the latter case, I want to correct a typographical error that slipped through, which unfortunately distorts the meaning of the essay at a decisive point. (Perhaps this error already slipped past me in the manuscript.) There it reads: 'This is how, e.g. Leonardo da Vinci, investigates the work of a wheel propelled by water'. It should read 'This is how, e.g. Leonardo da Vinci, calculates … etc.' This sentence shows that the concept of mechanical work did not arise in connection with division of labour in manufacture, around 1620, but already around 1500, and that it was born in connection with hydraulic mechanisms.

I have now received my library from Frankfurt and I am very happy; sadly [a] valuable part of it is missing.

With best regards
your faithful
Henryk Grossman

I have not received back the article on manufacture.

4 January 1935

12 Rue Victor-Considérant
Paris (14e)
The manuscript leaves tomorrow (5 January).[11]

Dear Mr Horkheimer
Dear Pollock

Please both accept my warmest and most sincere thanks for your telegram. It was a pleasant surprise to have the feeling that I am not isolated in the world and that friends are thinking of me from a distance. First and foremost, please thank Mrs Horkheimer. I will write another letter to you, dear Pollock, concerning your charming letter.

And now I will move on to the question of my essay and will explain to both of you why I have not answered your letter or telegram until today.

For years I have not done any work that has given me so much to do, neither my book on crisis, nor the Elster articles (which had to be written rather quickly), as the Borkenau essay.[12] I was immediately sick and nervous. For various reasons. First, I feared that I would not be finished *on time*, although I have been working 12 or more hours per day over the previous two months. The increasing scope of the essay made me even more nervous. You will recall that I wrote repeatedly about this matter. Months before, when I received the first request to write the critique, I already tried to squeeze the essay into two or three printer's sheets. It did not work. For that reason I had the idea of writing the article about the Renaissance, i.e. instead of a complete critique, to present a specific problem. I am now trying again to subsume the entire critique into two printer's sheets. It is not working. *It is an impossible task that you have set me*.

Of course I can fit a couple of critical remarks against Borkenau into one printer's sheet or just six pages. *But what will the result be?* You called upon me to open up a dignified *discussion*. I understood, i.e. I resolved to present material and to show the path that Borkenau should have taken, but did not.

Soon the *essay became long*. So I addressed only the relationship between the mechanistic view and the division of labour in manufacture, and by contrast the *new morality*, and did *not* treat the connection between capitalism and Calvinism. It would have had to become yet another section.

11 [Added to the top margin of the page.]
12 [Grossmann 1929a; Grossmann 1992; Elster 1931–3.]

You will see the enormous amount of work that went into the essay. Borkenau is finished off by the essay. But for me he was a secondary issue. I not only offer a critique but also show *positively* how the solution to the problem is to be found.

It would be a mistaken conception to believe too great an honour for Borkenau results from the length of my essay. You have conferred on him the honour of his book appearing as a publication of the Institute.[13] As you have conferred the great honour on him of placing his book next to your book, dear Pollock, next to [Karl August] Wittfogel's book and finally next to mine, you can also grant him the smaller honour of a more extensive critique devoted to his book.[14] The result of my critique already ensures that Borkenau will not reap much honour. I do not believe that my critique of Sternberg, despite its scope, brought Sternberg many laurels.[15]

Moreover, my Borkenau essay is an independent presentation of the problem, conceived as a kind treatment in parallel with Borkenau's book that has the task of preparing the discussion. I go beyond critique. In section IV, I treat the sources of Descartes' mechanistic conception (and, for the first time, assemble the relevant texts by Descartes). In section V [there is], I believe, the first outline or sketch of the historical genesis of theoretical mechanics. This small section is the result of many months of research work in the Bibliothèque Nationale. I did the work of three people and even worked during the summer heat because I knew that a huge amount of material had to be dealt with and that there was pioneering work to be done here. These few pages emerge from a huge amount of material on the history of mechanics that I have collected and that would be enough to fill a volume all by themselves.

For these reasons, give me satisfaction for my difficult labour and print the essay in this form or in another. Print it in the smallest font and at the end of the journal – the formalities do not mean much to me – but print it. Grünberg, who actually hated theory, nevertheless printed almost four printer's sheets of the Sternberg essay. It is no misfortune if a couple of reviews are dropped.

If you believe that the essay is still too long, then leave out section VI ('Borkenau's Method').

Or, alternatively – you might decide to print the work as a supplement to the journal. In that case I will still write a further chapter on Calvinism and

13 [The original German is not grammatical.]

14 [Grossmann 1929a; Pollock 1929; Wittfogel 1931. Horkheimer 1936 was the fifth and last volume in the series.]

15 [Grossman 1928a, see above pp. 120–76.]

capitalism. Furthermore, I already have a part in which I devote myself to the Nominalism[16] of the thirteenth and fourteenth centuries and give hints about its relationship with the social conditions of the time. Finally, a further part examines the Renaissance, the beginning of irreligiousness [i.e. secularism], etc.

I will send to you both these parts (Scholasticism, Renaissance) in about a week; they only come into consideration in the case that you want to publish the work as a supplement. In both these parts I show the real emergence of natural science, i.e. the development from the feudal to the bourgeois worldview. Only that it occurred in the thirteenth and fourteenth centuries and not in the seventeenth!

Now you understand my concerns. Do not believe that I have acted frivolously or arbitrarily. I wanted to fulfil the task that was given to me as well as possible. But it could not be done any other way. The various shorter drafts were not satisfactory and I became convinced it was just not possible. Think of how much space the second section 'The reality of historical development' took up. And still the section is a summary in 12 theses and encompasses the minimum that had to be said about actual historical development. Moreover, it is incidentally – as far as I know – the first summary of the results of the discussion of capitalism's genesis and therefore has, in turn, its own distinct value, independent of Borkenau's critique. And the same is true of what I say about French manufacture, its emergence, its technical backwardness, etc. In printing such an essay, you are not making any propaganda for Borkenau, rather just the opposite.

But you will read and judge for yourself.

With most affectionate regards to you both

your

Henryk Grossman

P.S. I will write to Löwenthal separately.

P.S. [Alexander] Koyré, with whom I get together quite often, told me that he was in London during the summer holidays. [Raymond] Klibansky told him there that Borkenau delivered a lecture on the theme of his book. Klibansky thinks '*C'est un fou*!'[17]

16 [Medieval Nominalism denied the existence of universal categories.]

17 ['*C'est un fou*' means 'He is crazy'.]

5 January 1935

Paris

Dear Mr Horkheimer

Yesterday I wrote you a letter in which I announced the dispatch of the manuscript[18] and today your telegram came. The manuscript is finally finished.

Sections I–III conform to your desired scope of about two printer's sheets, if you set the essay in a small font. Of course, then Section IV on 'Borkenau's Methods', which, it appears to me, includes important explanations, will be missing. For example, my critique of Borkenau's characterisation of the 'gentry', which I depict as a conservative caste, whereas Borkenau makes it a 'champion' of the bourgeoisie.

Likewise, if you only allow the publication of two printer's sheets, Sections IV and V, which I regard as the most important results of my work, will be dropped. Both sections, which are related to Descartes, will particularly interest you, as a philosopher. They are not just mechanically connected to the Borkenau critique but rather form an organic whole with it. Indeed, for the following reasons:

1) Every critique that remains purely negative, without positively showing the path that should be taken, I regard as a failure.
2) In the concrete case of Borkenau, some people will say: well then, Grossman proved this and that historical error in his critique of Borkenau; granted that in the area of economic history Borkenau is an ignoramus; but what follows from this? Although he establishes his case with false arguments, his conception is nonetheless ingenious and correct, despite all of Grossman's great erudition.
   This line of argument is annihilated by the Descartes section, in which I positively show that Borkenau's thesis is pure invention, using texts by Descartes. For that reason it is very important to me that the entire work be published.
3) Finally, I believe that the best method of distancing [the Institute of Social Research] from Borkenau's book is precisely not to *merely criticise* it; then people will ask: why was the book allowed to appear in the first place, only then to be criticised? On the other hand, if you publish *new research findings* then it can be understood that the Institute approaches the problem from different sides.

18 [A manuscript of Grossmann 2009.]

I touch on important problems, namely the *beginnings* of the natural sciences in the thirteenth and fourteenth centuries, in Part II (on Scholasticism and the Renaissance), which I will send next week: the whole work is caste from one mould.

Naturally, I can do no more than repeat this suggestion. But, if you only print two printer's sheets, my main conception, that the slow maturation of the natural sciences over centuries, parallel with the development of cities and of the bourgeois element, will demonstrate that Borkenau's conception of science suddenly emerging between 1620 and 1640 is vulgar nonsense.

I repeat once again: the historical presentations cannot be shortened. When Borkenau claims that the 'gentry' was radical and I that it was conservative, one claim is counterposed to the other. One can prove *any* claim by citing *some* source. In order to show that the gentry was in fact conservative and that it led to the destruction of the bourgeoisie, I give 1) *factual* evidence. I show how bourgeois accumulation was slowed down by the sale of offices and prove this with quotations from [Charles] Normand and [Georges] D'Avenel. 2) Further, I show how the real champions of the bourgeoisie, Diderot and Voltaire, combatted and criticised the *parlaments*.[19] 3) I finally show how one of the best modern economic historians, Henri Sée, judges the *parlaments* to have been a conservative caste.[20] 4) I show analogous situations in Spain.

All of this requires *space* and none of it can be left out because only in this way can I prove that my characterisation captures *what is typical*. Logical argumentation alone is insufficient in history.

Of course it is up to you. If you want to limit it to two printer's sheets, then publish only the first three sections. Then omit the first short introductory essay, which I put in red parentheses.

With sincere regards to you and your wife

Henryk Grossman

May I ask you to give the enclosed letter to Mr Löwenthal?

19 [The *parlaments* were courts in prerevolutionary France.]

20 [Sée 1933.]

30 January 1935

12 Rue Victor-Considérant
Paris (14e)

Dear Mr Horkheimer,

After sending off my essay[21] I wanted to indulge in a bit of a rest, after previously having worked so hard. It was not to be: various 'domestic' concerns, which I have never lacked, left me no leisure. But the one thing that really gave me joy and genuine satisfaction was your splendid essay in the journal, 'On Bergson's metaphysics of time'. It is the most profound work that I have read in the Marxist philosophical literature. In a dignified form, you not only criticise Bergson but also show the source of his errors and offer positive perspectives for a correct theory of thought. In the most skilful way, you erect a bridge from the theory of abstraction to Marx's standpoint of totality.[22] In short, the essay is what Marxist literature has needed for a long time: a critique, from Marx's standpoint, of the newest and 'highest' products of bourgeois philosophical thought. I admire how much you were able to express in so few pages, as well as the subtlety of your uncontrived and *simple* language.

It is to be hoped that you will compile and extend your essays in a small *book* so that your philosophical work will accessible to wider circles.

I have long since given up the hope that the Muscovites would fruitfully point the way in the area of philosophy. Over there Stalin must be praised as the greatest philosopher, greatest economist, greatest thinker ever.[23]

And now a few more lines about my essay or, actually, not the essay but the problem originally posed by Borkenau: the transition from the feudal to the bourgeois worldview.

If it is established that the *beginnings* of capitalism reach back to the fourteenth and thirteenth centuries then one must conclude, *a priori*, that relevant traces of this can be demonstrated in the thought of these centuries. And, in fact, that can be proved *a posteriori*[24] from the history of philosophy – which you know better than I. The philosophy of [Robert] Grosseteste and Roger Bacon, in the thirteenth century, then [Jean] Buridan and Nicole Oresme in the fourteenth century, like all Nominalism in general, are the products of this current. Whoever wants to investigate the transition from the feudal to the

21 [Grossmann 2009.]
22 [Horkheimer 2005, p. 16.]
23 [The ellipsis replaces a word that cannot be identified.]
24 ['*A posteriori*' means 'on the basis of empirical investigation.']

bourgeois worldview has to engage with *this* thought and not with Descartes, because Descartes represents a stage of bourgeois thought that is already *highly developed*. In my essay on Scholasticism, (which I wrote following the critique of Borkenau) I attempt to correlate this philosophy with the two most important economic centres of the period, northern Italy and Flanders, where this philosophy, formally associated with Averroism, arose, and from which spread the *theory of the double truth*, which corresponds with the needs of the bourgeoisie.[25]

I cannot correct the deficiencies of previous investigations; but the purpose of my essay was and is to arouse interest: I confine myself to showing the general direction to be pursued. Perhaps the Institute can find a gifted young person who would examine the material of the period more closely. I am already convinced that the results will be along the same lines as I have indicated: that all of these '*moderni*' of the thirteenth and fourteenth centuries were *originally* within the radius of these two industrial and commercial centres. Paris as the capital of France was merely the *centre* where people from Flanders and the border region (Artois) *came together*.

These two industrial centres radiated out capitalism to France and England. Rudiments of capitalist development are also found in these two countries in the thirteenth and fourteenth centuries. Of course, in the fifteenth century there was a large secular *setback*: development was interrupted and reversed. Only from the end of the fifteenth and during the sixteenth centuries [was there] new capitalist development. Hence the *illusion*. If you do not know about the first stage of bourgeois development, you believe that both capitalism and bourgeois thought began at the same time, only in the sixteenth century. For the *beginnings of bourgeois thought*, precisely the thirteenth and fourteenth centuries are important.

And now something else about Borkenau: Max Beer wrote to me – after a two year break – from London (without knowing that I was writing a critique of Borkenau) and said, word for word: 'I met Borkenau a few times here. An insufferable renegade. A careerist and a crawler. Disgusting!'

Best regards and greetings to you and your wife.

Henryk Grossman

P.S. Paul Mattick's pamphlet, *The Inevitability of Communism*, (a critique of Sydney Hook), that just came out, New York 1935, cites your essay on *prévi-*

---

25 [The work of the Spanish Muslim philosopher and medical doctor Ibn Rushd, known in Latin as Averroës, formed a basis for Scholasticism. The theory of the double truth argued that philosophy and religion are distinct.]

sion in the journal on page 43.[26] Mattick, by the way, wrote a *splendid* essay, 'Die Streikwelle', in *Neue Deutsche Blätter*, October/November and December 1934,[27] which is proof of his great *literary* gift.

7 February 1935

12 Rue Victor-Considérant
Paris (14e)

Dear Mr Horkheimer and Mr Pollock,

Your letter from 26 January crossed over one from me, that you have since received. Your friendly words and your decision made me very happy. I am aware of their value and I am indebted to you both.

I would appreciate receiving suggestions on cuts and, for my part, will also suggest cuts and then coordinate them. A rearrangement will also be undertaken and smaller errors will be corrected.

I do not want to write in more detail today. I only want to say one thing again: your kind words really made me happy. Ultimately, we all fight for the great proletarian cause. But as a result of the disruption of the worker's movement, there is no longer any possibility of the satisfaction every fighter previously – before the World War – had of acknowledgement from within the movement. So one is therefore happy that one can find satisfaction within the narrower circles in which one is involved and has the incentive to work on from this.

With sincerest regards to you and Pollock, as well as regards to your wife
Henryk Grossman

I have come back to your Bergson essay: what you say about the *role of the historian*, is fine, deep; a real rehabilitation of history writing's role, so often underestimated by theoreticians![28]

26 [Mattick 1935a; Horkheimer 1933. *'Prévision'* means 'prediction'. Following Duprat 1932, Horkheimer made the distinction between the French terms *prévision*, prediction in the form of abstract laws, and *prédiction*, concrete prediction.]

27 [Mattick 1934b.]

28 [Horkheimer 2005, pp. 18–19.]

20 July 1935

12 Rue Victor-Considérant
Paris (14e)

Dear Mr Horkheimer

First on the matter of Emil Grünberg.[29] By coincidence he was just in Paris (he was working as an interpreter at the Congress of the International Chamber of Commerce with good pay, 5,000 French francs for a week). To me, his essay seems, in principle, to be correct and interesting, judging by the summary before me. Of course, everything depends on the way that he carries it out in detail and documents it. In particular, I found his explanation of the larger role of the middle class in France to be unsatisfactory, especially the sentence 'The middle class was not preserved in France in spite of the old capitalist tradition, rather France's economic development lagged from the beginning of the Industrial Revolution.' I have offered a few hints to Grünberg with regard to this problem. Otherwise, I read him a few sentences from your letter, which he found correct and self-evident. With this, the matter is provisionally settled. He needs about two months to flesh out the essay.

Now I want to return to Borkenau. It puzzles me how you could come to the idea that I avoid discussion with Borkenau. Anyone who makes such criticisms as I have must be prepared for a response and I regard forwarding the proof sheets as a matter of course. If I identify Borkenau as 'dangerous', it is not a matter of him, in a scientific sense, as an opponent in a discussion, but rather in the sense of his character. Judging on the basis of the political examples that he has provided, he is capable of anything. I am afraid that if he gets to see my *manuscript* from Rue d'Ulm, he can turn it into a weapon in the discussion, in the following way, for example: the editors of the journal thought certain explanations untenable and nonsensical, and therefore deleted them, etc. etc. I know you would not approve of such a polemic, but Borkenau could publish his reply in another journal and, with help of such a ploy, squirm out of providing a *real reply* to my objections. Now, since my original manuscript is not going to the printing press at all, the matter is closed.

You do not know my past and do not know that I have fought through in many discussions with success, I believe. My book on the emergence of the Austrian population census[30] was, for example, directed against Professor Gürtler

29 [Horkheimer had sent Grossman the abstract of an essay by Emil Grünberg; the *Zeitschrift für Sozialforschung* never published an article by him.]

30 [Grossmann 1916.]

of Graz (I was a young, unknown doctor at that time). My book had the honour of being published by the Statistische Zentralkommision Österreichs,[31] through which it almost received an official character. My critique was devastating for Gürtler. He could not prove a single sentence wrong and for this reason he was finished as scholar. He turned to politics and became an Austrian minister!

And just one more matter that may interest the editors in general, but Pollock in particular. The doctoral student Leif Björk from Stockholm wanted to speak with Pollock here, with regard to his dissertation on the planned economy in Soviet Russia. He is 28 years old, was in Russia for about two years, knows exactly what the circumstances there are, is – as far as I can judge from two conversations – *extremely gifted*, sharp-witted and has a talent for *theoretical* analysis. He has devoted himself to the problem for the past five years. In short, to me, he seems to be just the man to write a theoretical work about these things that is nevertheless based on rich materials. I advised him to contact Pollock and to assemble his results in a draft of four to five pages and perhaps to write an essay of about 30 pages for the journal. I believe that Björk's results, as well as his clear, theoretical method are very interesting: the best I have seen on the planned economy!

I read an essay here in the *Manchester Guardian*, in which the charms of Mexico were praised. The author related that he did not know how to spend his money. It is that cheap there! A well-furnished room with the family of a bankrupt large landowner in the city, including delicious meals (he describes all the meals), $15 = 220 French francs *per month*! Every convenience: taxi, cafes, bars, etc., $10. Along with it, the interesting area with reminders of Montezuma's time! In your position, I would go to Mexico![32]

Because it is cheap, I will go to Belgium or Spain for a few weeks around 1 August.

With best wishes to you and your wife, and also to Pollock and his wife
from your faithful
Henryk Grossman

31 [Austrian Central Statistical Commission.]

32 [This is a suggestion for a summer holiday.]

23 August 1936

Valencia

Dear Mr Pollock, dear Mr Horkheimer

I write to you, as I suspect that you are near each other and that you will, perhaps, find these lines interesting. I was warned about the heat before the trip to Spain. I underestimated these warnings somewhat. Actually, it is often 35° in the shade here! The organism suffers from this. I drink a lot of soda water, lemonade etc. which upsets the stomach, in short I am not well disposed and several times wanted to break the trip off; particularly as travel here is no pleasure; although it is cheap: I paid 147 pesetas = 300 French francs for 3,000 kilometres, but third class is only good in Germany. Here, there is no water etc., uncultured people throw everything on the floor of the carriage in which they spend several hours. Because the train generally only makes 30 km per hour. Despite all these unfavourable aspects, I am happy that I had the opportunity to travel across the whole of Spain, not only out of pure curiosity but because I have learnt much in the most diverse connections! Because you know that my recreational trips are also, in part, study trips, which I could otherwise never undertake. The plague of begging is nowhere else as widespread as here. But what is interesting is that beggary is 'statised' here! Namely, in the conduct of the Lotteria Nacional, the state is served by beggars – the lottery tickets are 5 and 3 pesetas, i.e. 10 or 6 francs – and tens of thousands of beggars harass the public everywhere: in cafes, on trains, etc. Apparently the commission contributes more than income from beggary!

But I want to return to the actual purpose of my letter, in connection with my last work. The problem still exercises me, because it is still not completely solved, as long as *one* aspect of it is not clarified. It does not suffice to show – positively – why mechanics, e.g. arose around 1500. It is necessary to prove negatively why it e.g. could not arise in *antiquity*.

I am not, therefore, entirely happy with my journal article; but, in the end, it was conditioned by polemical-critical considerations and under these circumstances, I could not develop the underlying thinking enough.

Now, to the question of why no scientific mechanics could emerge in antiquity, the answer since Marx has been that there is no reason to save human labour and replace it with machines in a society based on slavery. Henri Hauser (*The Origins of Modern Capitalism*)[33] also agrees with this conception. Now,

---

33 [Grossman conflated the titles of two books by Hauser: Hauser 1927 and Hauser and Renaudet 1929.]

Marx's answer is in general correct but is not *concrete* enough. Marx was a visionary who correctly grasped the result, without showing us the way in which he arrived at this result! I also present this view in the essay 'Der Kapitalismus der Renaissancezeit', which I gave you in Paris, dear Pollock, before your trip to America; but this answer did not fully satisfy me.

Now, the trip to Spain has enabled me to answer this important question *much* more concretely, thanks to a real *trouvaille*,[34] which I made in the Museo Arqueólogico Nacional in *Madrid*! Treasures of rare historical value are there, like e.g. Maya manuscripts, which look like the finest *illuminated* manuscripts of the early Middle Ages and are documents of the great culture of the indigenous people of the Americas, who were annihilated by bandits *à la* [Francisco] Pizarro. These manuscripts are real miracles of the arts of writing and painting, genuine miniatures!

Now, to say that machinery could not emerge in antiquity due to slavery is not entirely precise; there was machinery in antiquity. You certainly remember 1) the giant *catapults* at the Roman settlement, whose name escapes me, near Frankfurt am Main. Giant, 25–30 kg stone projectiles could be catapulted great distances. 2) The Romans likewise had *scales* with unequal arms and in French-speaking regions scales with unequal arms are called *romaine* (*romana*); the Romans knew the most important relations of balance for a lever with unequal arms.

They therefore knew that the longer the arm, the smaller the weight has to be to hold the load on the other arm in balance. 3) And, finally, I found a proper *water pump* in the museum!! A suction and expulsion pump, that was capable of spraying water a great distance! That is, a hand pump. A pump is a complicated machine and it must be declared that in antiquity machines, 1) catapults, 2) levers, 3) pumps, were known.

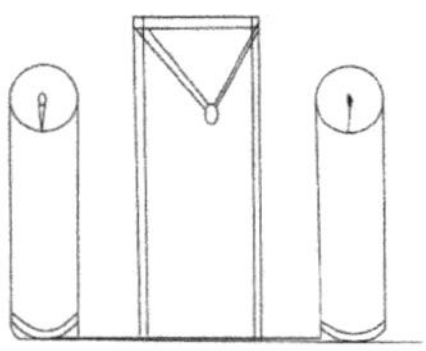

34 ['*Trouvaille*' means 'discovery'.]

People like [Paul] Tillich or his intellectual relatives therefore say that it was only a *coincidence* that mechanics arose during the fifteenth century and that it could just as well have arisen under the Romans.

Now, however, a closer examination of these machines allows the precise demonstration of why theoretical mechanics could not emerge in antiquity.

1. Catapults did not have the task of replacing slave labour but of casting heavy stone missiles over enemy ramparts into enemy encampments, to inflict damage. Slave labour could not help; it was not a matter of its replacement.
2. The scales in Madrid are, e.g. from a *saliteria*, i.e. a saltpeter mine, in Temblegue (near Toledo). Here too, it was not a matter of replacing slave (human) labour but of *exact measurement* in the sale of saltpeter.
3. Finally, the circumstances in which the pump was found are interesting. Namely 80 meters below the earth, in the iron pyrites *mine* in Valverde (Huelva province), i.e. in southern Spain near Gibraltar. It was a *fire extinguisher* in the mine. And here the purpose was not to replace slave labour; because of the great heat and danger of explosion, people could not approach the seat of the fire. The fire had to be overcome from a distance.

In all three of these cases, it is a matter not of *replacing* human labour but the *specific issue* that induced the construction of the machines. The fundamental principle of mechanics, the idea that machines were concerned with the replacement of human labour, could not therefore arise. I believe that my presentation of three cases demonstrates this clearly and allows an answer to the question posed, that is much more concrete than has been the case in the previous literature.

In contrast, in Sagunt, however fine and otherwise informative the Roman and Carthaginian remains and ruins are, I found nothing to do with this problem.

But enough of this. Apologies for my long letter. But the joy which it gave me to extend my theory in relation to antiquity impelled me to much scribbling.

But I also learnt much in many other connections. Discussion of the modern idea of tolerance, for example, usually involves referring back to predecessors of the French Revolution, like Turgot. That's fine, if others refer back to the English revolution. Now, I have been convinced that the *Arabs* were the genuine *practical* representatives of tolerance, *tolerating* the Catholic cult after the conquest of Spain, while after the Arabs were expelled, their mosques were destroyed or transformed into churches.

But it is time to finish the letter. My trip is at an end, as I have spent more money than I expected and am also tired. I return to Paris via Tarragona and Barcelona.

I wish you both the best holidays and my best greetings to the ladies.
Your
Henryk Grossman

P.S. From London I learn that inquiries are being seriously made in all directions about who I am, what I have written, the extent of my income, etc. because of the permit.[35] It is taking time but I hope that the result will be *positive*.

3 July 1936

9 Belsize Avenue
London NW 3

Dear Mr Horkheimer,

I am hurrying to tell you, since you may not find out elsewhere, that a review by Hans Honegger of the Institute book appeared in the arts section of the *Neue Zürcher Zeitung* (number 1116) of 28 June, page 4, under the title 'Väterliche Gewalt und Familie'. I cannot avoid the impression that the man is a little crazy. He *takes pains* to be friendly and praises you, Fromm and Marcuse abundantly. In doing so, the critique as a whole gives an *unpleasant*, perhaps unintended ironic impression. After he has praised you, he continues 'H. is just as much a philosopher as a sociologist and psychologist. Moreover, he is *rather poetic*'. That would be fine and good, if he had not immediately tacked on 'secondly, an eminent psychologist takes the floor: Erich *Fromm*. His observations are *somewhat* more expertly but no less brilliantly and inspirationally expressed ...'[36]

About Marcuse, he says, among other things, that he is 'a bit too profound, too serious, too – unrealistic. The subheadings of his essay on the "history of ideas" already come across as almost weird, like blows from a hammer [!]: "Luther and Calvin", "Kant", "Hegel", "counterrevolution and restoration" "Marx" ... What Marcuse offers is a kind of "history of the idea of the problem of authority"; there is no discussion of the family in the long essay at all. But the effect of this compilation of names is arbitrary, sometimes ... on the other hand, too one-sided – German – caught up in Marx.'

35 [i.e. Grossman's British residency visa.]
36 [Honnegger 1936, review of Horkheimer 1936.]

Crude malignities are directed at 'individual studies'. Irony is again used against Honigsheim; H. (!) [Richard] Meili from Switzerland is praised.

Finally the work as a whole is identified 'as an astounding achievement'. As far as I know, H. and you are friends. I would understand if he offered a *serious engagement* with the book.

As it is, the review makes an unpleasant, ironic impression – in spite of specific praise, so that I thought of the adage: God protect us from our friends; we can take care of our enemies!

Answering Marcuse's communication concerning the plan for a book on forgotten authors in the area of historical materialism, allowed me to express some critical doubts. To me, the formulation of the inquiry is not clear enough: by which criteria should it be judged whether a given writer is to be included? 'Materialism' is a complex term, which represents a synthesis of many moments. 1) General, i.e. philosophical materialism. 2) The fundamental significance of the economy for the transformation of the superstructure. 3) The theory of the revolutionary significance of praxis. 4) The moment of the dialectic, etc. What then is meant[?] *Which side* of materialism should be considered? Or should one rather assume that *as much* material as *possible* should be sent and that the editor reserves the right to critically examine and select it? Perhaps posing the question in a more specialised way would make answering it easier?

I am completely stuck in 'money' here, i.e. merely in the literature on money.

I will only go on holidays in August. Since you are already going to the countryside I wish you and your wife pleasant recreation and I remain with

sincere regards
your faithful
Henryk Grossman

1 October 1936

9 Belsize Avenue
London NW3

Dear Mr Horkheimer,

Many thanks for your friendly letter of 9 September. The news that several favourable reviews[37] have already appeared pleases me. I have not read the

37 [Horkheimer 1936.]

American Sociological Review and I do not get to see the international newspapers here. As always, I read your important and valuable observations on 'Egoism and the liberation movement'.[38] By contrast – quite frankly – the essay by Rottweiler[39] (with whom I am not familiar) to me seems to completely miss the point. Too much uninteresting, technical shop talk, behind which there is almost no sociological analysis. We all knew that jazz did not come from Africa but was a product of capitalist centres.

In relation to your observation that 'a *satisfied* mood' is consciously maintained: [it] only applies – as you stress – to the *masses*.[40] It is otherwise in relation to 'creative intellectuals.' Here the nastiness of the world will not be so easily forgotten, with a few jazz notes or festivals. Consequently, 'painfulness' is an ideology of the necessity of this sadness about the real world for the formation of a creative individuality. I therefore draw your attention Julien Teppe's book *Dictature de la douleur ou précisions sur le dolorisme* and at the same time send you the review from *Le Temps*[41] which is just as interesting. At the same time, you will be interested in the report on the conference of the Deutsche Philosophische Gesellschaft, which I have included as well.

Now, concerning my essay for the journal, I would like to make the following two suggestions. In 1937, 70 years will have passed since the first volume of *Capital* appeared. I can write a fundamental essay on Marx. The first part is literary-historic; I show, by way of a survey of the literature, that friends and foes of Marx regard him as a follower of Ricardo. I ask: is that right? I show that Marx regarded Ricardo as completing bourgeois economics; consequently, there was nothing more to 'complete' here. That Marx drew a few *conclusions* from Ricardo that were inherent in the Ricardian theory of value, which he himself had not articulated, is *in principle* nothing new; they are just conclusions. But Marx – as I prove – wanted to *revolutionise* this economic science from the ground up (not, then, to 'complete' it). He wants to pioneer – not to complete.

Did he do this? What is *essential* in his scientific achievement as an economist?[42]

In the second part, which is purely theoretical, I want to demonstrate what is *new* in Marx's achievement, *through which* he distinguishes himself from his predecessors and followers and characteristically advances beyond them.

38 [Horkheimer 1993c.]
39 [Hektor Rottweiler was a pseudonym for Theodor W. Adorno. Adorno 2002.]
40 Horkheimer 1993c, p. 58.
41 [See Teppe 1936. Rageot 1936.]
42 [Eventually published in duplicated form as Grossman 1941a, see below pp. 469–533.]

The second suggestion is that the journal – *without* a lot of to-do – as a modest contribution brings two, three, or four essays to the seventieth anniversary of this remarkable book. You would probably also write one and perhaps Pollock – or if he is too busy with finances, perhaps Dr Gumperz?

I believe that this would be a worthy form in which to celebrate this anniversary – precisely today – with the general decline of theory. Unfortunately such an article with the evidence – as I mention above – is already extensive. And it is this literary evidence that is important. You will be astounded at *what* has been written about Marx. Only thus does the problem posed gain perspective and importance, and become understandable.

I will impatiently await your reply. Until then, sincerest regards to you and your wife as well as to the Pollocks.

Henryk Grossman

6 November 1936

9 Belsize Avenue
London NW3

Dear Mr Horkheimer,

I am pleased that you have agreed with my thoughts and I will endeavour to do everything so that my essay reaches you by the middle of January.

In the meantime, I have specified the content of an additional article to Pollock. It deals with a sociological problem, namely the problem that scientific *theories*, completely independently of their scientific correctness, are denatured by followers under the pressure of *political* requirements and are distorted away from their original meaning. I illustrated that with the reproduction theories of Quesnay, Ricardo and Marx, which all succumbed to this fate with astonishing regularity, despite all the clarity one could hope for in the texts! These texts are not to blame for the debate over Marx; it is rather the product of a definite (reformist) phase of the worker's movement. Independently of the main argument, I believe that what I say about Quesnay's *Tableau*, namely the demonstration that he already used the method of successive approximation – his *Tableau* incorporated preliminary, simplifying assumptions and subsequent, progressive concretisation – I believe that this *methodological* side of Quesnay's *Tableau* is very important for Marxists. It shows that the method of successive approximation that I have asserted in relation to Marx's reproduction schema is not *my* invention (as some assert) but that it was taken over from Quesnay and perfected by Marx.

You mention that there have been 'no *fundamental* economic contributions' in the issues [of the *Zeitschrift für Sozialforschung*]. That is correct. But how often and how many 'fundamental' problems can now be raised? I believe that economics is now in a stage at which there have been enough theoretical *constructions*, from which nothing results. Now the *examination* of the correctness of these theoretical constructs is more necessary than *research*! That is my conviction. For one hundred years *all* positions have been adopted and then repeatedly asserted with new variations. The results of the great experiments of the last five years should now be examined.

I am ready to write a short essay for an issue later in 1937, on the *failure of underconsumptionist theory*. The contents in brief: 1) Marx's position on *underconsumptionist theory* (i.e. his theory of wages considered from this point of view). 2) The attempts at stimulation in all countries (United States, England, Germany, etc.) did not anywhere begin by *raising* the purchasing power of the working class but, on the contrary, devaluation, in an open or in a disguised form, reduced the *level of wages*. Empirical data. In Germany the wage level was brutally held down. 3) The Blum experiment[43] led to a general rise in prices and the inability of French industry to compete. Briefly, the failure of stimulation. He had to openly withdraw the wage increases. Since this was impossible, he stumbled into devaluation, i.e. an escape route which in a disguised form meant *wage reduction*. 4) Marxist conclusions.

Of course in such an essay there would have to be some *statistics* on wage levels in relevant countries. I believe that an embarrassing funeral for underconsumptionist theory is important!

Finally, it seems to me that a purely theoretical article about shifts in the distribution of capital across individual spheres, in which I deal with the problem of the *possibility* of the shifts of capitals from department II into department I of the reproduction schema, is very important.[44] I want to emphasise that this problem is of fundamental importance. Rosa Luxemburg's theory, her entire book,[45] proceeds from the contrary assumption that, according to Marx, as a consequence of the once and for all, *fixed* natural form of commodities (either as means of production or as means of consumption), such a shift is *impossible*.

43 [The economic policies of the French Popular Front Government under Socialist Prime Minister Léon Blum, under the pressure of massive working class struggles, in 1936.]

44 [For detailed discussions of related issues, see Grossmann 1929a/Grossmann 1992; Grossmann 1929b, see above pp. 183–209; Grossmann 1932b, see above pp. 304–331; Grossmann 1932a, see above pp. 276–303.]

45 [Luxemburg 1951.]

It is, therefore, an unsaleable remainder in department II and then exports are the only way out!

This is contradicted by 1) the facts, and 2) the theories of all economic schools, that depict such a shift as possible and extant. I want to limit myself to only a few of *Marx's texts* and show how Marx's thoughts on the elasticity of capitalism, which corrects such disproportions, are turned into their opposite! Rosa L.'s entire theory stands and falls on the possibility or impossibility of such a shift!

I show that Marx explicitly taught that an entire series of commodities can be used in I *just as much* as in II and therefore that a shift is possible.

It will interest you perhaps to hear a few things about Borkenau. He gave up the position in Panama (I do not know if this was voluntarily). In the summer he was in Spain for 6 weeks. After his return, presented a lecture at the Sociological Society, where he took a position *against* the Madrid government. In short, a dangerous fellow, an outspoken fascist![46]

To me, exceptionally sweet and polite. Apparently he belongs to the type of person who is only polite once they have received a few thrashings!

I read the review in the *American Sociological Review*[47] with pleasure. The program of your lectures in Colombia is extraordinarily carefully elaborated and makes the best impression. Showed it by chance to [Fritz] Heinemann in the British Museum, he lapsed into sheer 3G (grey-yellow-green)[48] out of jealously!

Recently Dr [Ernst] Schoen and wife, and Matthias Seiber visited me. He expressed himself rather critically about the jazz article.

I want to draw your attention to a book written by a lecturer at Göttingen, Dr [Nikolaus] Pevsner: *Pioneers of the Modern Movement: From William Morris to Walter Gropius*.[49] Deals with a very important problem which imposes itself on everything: why England has *no art* (not painting, nor architecture, nor music). As far as I can tell from a review in *Reynolds News*, it links the question with capitalism and machine production [*Maschinismus*]. In this the answer is misdirected. I have another answer, that also seemed very probable to Dr Schoen. I believe that this book should be more extensively (critically) reviewed because of the importance of the question with which it deals.[50]

46 [Franz Borkenau was critical of the repression of the revolutionary left by the Republican regime and particularly the Stalinist Spanish Communist Party. He was in no sense a supporter of Franco's 'fascist' Nationalist regime. See Borkenau 1938.]

47 [Dollard 1936.]

48 ['3G' stands for 'grau-gelb-grün', meaning 'grey-yellow-green'.]

49 [Pevsner 1937.]

50 [The book was reviewed, Schapiro 1938. The journal had already published Benjamin 2008, on related questions.]

Unfortunately, I have no time to do this, am not a specialist, even if the question interests me very much, as it does everyone who sees that all of the art here is imported from the continent!

I have become acquainted with Professor [Eduard] Westermarck (of *Marriage*) here.[51] [He] invited me to his lecture on marriage (probably the thousandth) at the Anthropological Institute of the Royal Society. I ended up at a celebration there. Men in evening attire. It was an ovation organised on the occasion of the small man's 50 years of activity and W. was celebrated as 'the greatest world-authority' in the area of marriage. In this milieu, I first understood the reason for this adoration. Engels already writes, in the preface to *The Family*, of the deliberate *silence* about [Johann Jacob] Bachofen and [Lewis Henry] Morgan in England.[52] Westermarck is the antipode. He saved biblical, monogamous marriage and proved that 'even' higher animals like the chimpanzee and the gorilla live monogamously, that promiscuity in the sexual life of primitives is therefore a fable.

Given this opportunity, I looked through Wittvogel's[53] essay in the *Authority and Family* book and noticed how he carefully ... avoids all of these important but awkward problems. Westermarck's lecture was miserable. The whole evening – brilliant wretchedness! Westermarck received a medal from the Royal Society!

With sincere regards to you and your wife, I remain
your,
Henryk Grossman

19 December 1936

9 Belsize Avenue
London NW3

Dear Mr Horkheimer

Thank you very much for both your letters of 27 November and, on the Mattick matter, of 8 December. I was in the process of writing to you when the news of the New Year bonus reached me from Geneva, for which I am much obliged to you and our finance minister, Pollock. Not only is this of much practical significance for me but I am also especially pleased that you thought of it!

51 [Westermarck 1921.]

52 [Bachofen 2003; Morgan 1877. Engels 1990c, p. 131. In the preface Engels mentions Morgan but not Bachofen, who is referred to later.]

53 [Wittfogel 1936.]

Your outline of the operations of the Institute's activity and planned work is interesting and instructive for me. I will come to that again below. Now, before anything else, I would like to divest myself of the mental weight that has been burdening me over the past weeks: I see that I will not be able to finish my essay by 15 January, in spite of my efforts. I ask you to please forgive this and for an extension of the deadline until the end of February, when you will definitely receive the essay. By way of excuse, an anniversary essay is no ordinary essay; it has to offer something special and I must place the highest demands on myself. Now, from the abundance of material, I have to choose only the most important aspects.

You know that the main difficulty for me is not the *content* but *giving it form*, in the clear, logical presentation, which can also convince opponents. Moreover, I have technical difficulties here; as good as the libraries are, there is not much German socialist literature. Much that is essential for me (e.g. Kautsky's anniversary essay on Marx, Korsch's *Turning-points*, etc.)[54] is missing here. What is here, I had to excerpt in the library, which eats up a lot of time (earlier, each of us had such publications of their own). Now I am far enough along that I hope that the essay will become good and really show Marx in a new light but I must have time to polish. The time limitation would make me nervous and frustrate my work. I am writing to Pollock right now concerning the content. But I ask him and also you, dear Mr Horkheimer, not to place too much weight on such a description of the content. It always depends on *how* the schema is actually carried out. I am afraid, specifically, that you will not like the description of the content!

Naturally, my task cannot consist in characterising the *results* of Marx's research. I would, rather, like to illuminate how his *way of thinking*, which starkly distinguishes him from the classical political economists and thus show what was original, through which he *enriched* the science of political economy, that has, however, previously been unnoticed.

What you report about Wittfogel is interesting and gratifying. I have never received news from him. As long as I was in Frankfurt, we maintained quite a brisk correspondence. And now to your account of the work of the Institute. It would be unfortunate if the philosophical-historical book that was prepared by Mr Marcuse were *completely* shelved. I only mean that such a work, as a *principal* activity, requires too much time. By contrast, as a task *on the side*, it offers the possibility of slowly obtaining the material – as the by-product of other work, so to speak. So, for example, I would like to draw attention to

54 [Kautsky 1919; Korsch 1922.]

the following books: for the chapter on the sociology of literature, Bachofen's *Mother Right* (1861)[55] and particularly the sections in which he points to Aeschylus's *Oresteia* as a dramatic depiction of the struggle between the right of the mother and the emerging right of the father. An inexhaustible wealth of viewpoints for the same chapter can be found in Aristophanes. So, for example in *Peace*, in which the army suppliers and weapons-manufacturers are against peace because of their private interests – in contradiction with the interests of the entire nation. A real treasure-trove is *Plutus* in which it is shown, for example, that the power of the gods is actually dependent upon the wealth of humanity, because only the rich can make sacrifices.[56] Without money, there is an end to worship of the gods and thus of the power of gods! Etc. etc.

Another more recent book, which will especially interest you, is Gaston Boissier's *The Opposition under the Caesars* (second edition, Paris 1885),[57] written 50 years ago. In it Seneca's old *stoicism*, his recommendation of an ascetic, modest, withdrawn life, of sleeping on a hard floor, modest meals, etc. are explained in terms of the political circumstances of the period of terror, under such Caesars as Caligula, Nero and Tiberius.

For another chapter, that is for the problem of *praxis* in its *significance for knowledge*, dealt with by Marx in the 'Theses on Feuerbach',[58] a precursor could surely be seen in [Jan] Ludovicus *Vives* (1492–1540). Unnoticed on the Marxist side, mishandled by Borkenau, he is, *before* Francis Bacon, one of the great critics of Scholasticism. He demands not only *observation* of nature but also emphasises the importance of active engagement, underscores the significance of *manual skills*, the great role of the *tool* and of the *hand* as a *tool*. ('Technology reveals the *active* relation of man to nature.')[59] A Marxist could extract much from these works. Complete edition in VIII volumes; Folio, Valencia 1782–90. Previously it has only been taken up *pedagogically*.

Once I receive Mattick's manuscript,[60] will report on it as soon as possible.

I am under the impression of an incident. A couple of weeks ago I was invited to a cocktail party by some English people, where I met one Mrs Holand [sic]. She told me that her husband had just left for Madrid as a pilot. (He was a cap-

55 [Bachofen 2003.]
56 [Aeschylus 1906 pp. 42–173; Aristophanes 1913; Aristophanes 1907.]
57 [Boissier 1885.]
58 [Marx 1976c.]
59 Marx 1976b, p. 493 [Grossman's emphasis. Vives 1979.]
60 [Presumably the manuscript submitted to but not published in *Zeitschrift für Sozialforschung*, eventually published as Mattick 1969.]

tain of British Air Force).[61] I asked whether he is a socialist. 'No, but he hates the fascists.' On the sixteenth the papers brought the news that Holland had been shot down in his bomber! His daughter is orphaned!

You have probably heard about the coup in Barcelona (by closest liberal friends of [Lluís] Companys). There were open street battles. The anarchists defeated the uprising. But the tensions persist!

Excuse the long letter and I wish you and your wife my best wishes for the holidays and the new year.

I remain
your
Henryk Grossman

P.S. At the same time I send you *Der Kampf* with a longer – if not very inspired, sympathetic discussion of my Borkenau article. I am surprised that little Helene [Bauer] allowed it to be published![62]

25 May 1937[63]

9 Belsize Avenue
London NW3

Dear Mr Horkheimer!

I have wanted to write to you for a long time now; I have been expecting Pollock's promised letter day after day, which has delayed my writing. You will certainly understand my psychological state, because I have tensely expected Pollock's opinion about my work and now I am worried. Is Pollock really so busy or ultimately unwell that his writing is hampered?[64]

At the same time these comments should serve as an apology, for only now thanking you for the friendly invitation to come to New York in autumn. I do not need to assure you at length about how glad I am about this; not just for practical reasons, although I hope the discussions will greatly advance my work. I am, rather, very happy that I will again to be in the circle of old Frankfurt friends.

61 ['Of British Air Force' is in English in the original.]
62 [l. d. 1936. Also see Helene Bauer 1929.]
63 [In the original Grossman mistakenly has 1935, at which point he was still living in Paris.]
64 [Grossman was working on the project, the bulk of which was eventually published as Grossman 1941a, see below pp. 469–533.]

I have not heard anything from you in a long time but I assume that you and your wife are well. I also miss the long-overdue issue of the journal with your essay.[65]

Concerning my work, I knew that I would not obtain agreement so easily.[66] In judging a conception like Marx's in its totality, it is not enough to select only certain aspects, that please me but pass over others, which do not please me, in silence. I have made the effort to single out these aspects of the system, deliberately *passed over in silence*, and to inquire into their meaning.

Are they of such subordinate significance that they can be passed over? Or do they constitute an *essential* part of Marx's economic conception? Then one must indeed demonstrate their position in the whole system.

What has previously been disastrous and still persists in Marxism is that only quotations from Marx which are of use have been sought out, without making the slightest attempt to bring them into accord with other passages that openly contradict them. Under the influence of the bourgeois economics, Marx's theory of value *only* has been one-sidedly emphasised and analysed and value phenomena have been regarded as being the real expression of the social; that Marx declared that *all* forms of value are deceptive and misleading is passed over in silence.

This central point of my conception cannot be refuted at all, even though I know that my explanations will have a shocking[67] effect on those who, for 70 years, have been accustomed to seeing only the value side of Marx's theory …

I read Mitchell's book, *Gone with the Wind*,[68] with great interest. She knows the milieu of slaveholders and plantation owners and she correctly showed that the loss of the war against the Yankees meant a real social revolution for the plantation owners. What she portrays entirely falsely, however, is the situation of the Negro. What she portrays are just the *house* Negroes, who are personal servants, and here too (even though the situation of these Negroes was better) she has idealised the situation too much. Slavery demoralises not only the enslaved but also their masters. It was not so 'nice', as Mitchell would have it, everywhere. It was not so seldom that, when guests came into the house, when saying 'good night', they were offered not merely a candle but also an attractive woman slave as an expression of hospitality …

65 [Horkheimer 1972.]

66 [Grossman refers in what follows to the project that became Grossman 1941a, see below pp. 469–533.]

67 ['Shocking' is in English in the original.]

68 [Mitchell 1936.]

But the main issue in the problem is not house slaves, but the *plantation slaves*. On this, Mitchell does not offer a word – and only the faint recollection that the house slaves rejected work in the fields, on the grounds that they were not 'field-hands'[69] … The honour of their rank was high above this despised level, even despised by house Negroes.

And foremost the supply of slaves: the slave *trade* and slave *smuggling* with all their horrors, finally the breeding of slaves. Slave breeding factories existed, where slaves were produced, as today pigs or horses are raised on farms. Sweet Mitchell does not breathe a word about any of this.

Not to mention the peculiar morality that Mrs Mitchell justifies: shooting a vagabond marauder, just because he *wanted* to steal something. Of course Captain Butler immediately gives her absolution. As Scarlett did not have *any other alternative!*

Where it is a matter of maintaining the elevated social position of a landowner, any ruthlessness is justified to avoid being declassed!!

And this same Scarlett, who wanted to sell herself for 300 dollars, just to save her plantation, looks with disdain at the red-haired prostitute, who sells herself in order to save her *bare life* and the life of her illegitimate child! The book is interesting, in places exciting – it has no artistic value.

Here it was cold until Pentecost and I still had to turn on the heat at night. Only in the past three days have we had the sun that I wanted so much!

The Blum 'experiment' – even though I do not want to underrate some of its results, especially the 40-hour week – suffered a sad, total breakdown. It would, in particular, be interesting to demonstrate the fiasco of *purchasing power theory*. Nowhere in the world has the crisis been overcome by means of *wage increases*. In reality wages were lowered openly (as in Germany) or in concealed form – mainly through manipulation of money. Blum was also subsequently forced to take back the wage increases he had initially conceded, through devaluation of the franc.

After these experiences, it is high time for underconsumption theory to disappear from Marxist discussion.

I would be very pleased to hear something from you again.

I remain, with sincere regards

your

Henryk Grossman

69 ['Field-hands' is in English in the original.]

30 June 1937

9 Belsize Avenue
London NW3

Dear Mr Horkheimer,

Before anything else, I hurry to inform you that, after taking care of a few formalities, I have received the tourist visa. With this, the formal side of my trip to America is taken care of and I look forward to seeing you in October in New York.

And now a few words about my function there. Pollock wrote to me about a few 'important tasks' that are intended for me. I would be glad to know what they are in advance, so that I can comply with expectations.

In connection with this, I have a favour to ask of you. Pollock wrote to me about the compilation of the work program for the autumn. I would be very pleased if a discussion about the roll of *monetary* factors (money and credit) in the economy could take place within the framework of this program. Not only because this is what I am working on now. But it seems to me that this decisively important and current problem has been completely neglected in Marxist literature. Yes, a few *critiques* of monetary conceptions ([John] Strachey,[70] etc.) have been written. But this is absolutely insufficient. The role that money and credit play has to be *positively* demonstrated, i.e. the capitalist mechanism, taking into account the element of credit in its real function, has to be presented. But this is entirely lacking. It is only with such a positive account of reality that a critique of opponents can usefully be written. It will be very important for me if a discussion about *theories of credit creation*, about the possibility of regulating the economy through open-market policy, equalisation funds, etc. can take place. If these monetary theories are proved correct, Marx's theory can be buried. The example of a young theorist here in London showed me how the problems can be approached purely scholastically. He was able to conclude from utterly ingenious theoretical constructions – a pure, *a priori* theory of money – that, according to Marx, money is a '*universal* commodity'.[71] By contrast, I emphasise again and again that what money is cannot be stated *a priori*, rather only through analysis of reality – and only then can the results be formulated generally.

70 [Strachey 1935; review, Mattick 1935c.]

71 [Marx 1976b, p. 184, Grossman's emphasis.]

My second point, which seems important, very important, to me, would be the internal discussion of my work 'Marx and classical economics'. The problem is not purely academic, as might appear at first glance. I would begin, as a point of departure, with the discussion on pages 119–23, i.e. Marx's immensely important assertion, that *crises* are already inevitable in the notion of simple reproduction.[72] There has not previously been a single word about this, during 40 years of discussion. On the contrary, it was asserted that an account of simple reproduction posed *no problems*. If the facts that I present, i.e. the possibility of crisis under simple reproduction, are thought through to the end, then the common conception of Marx's theory must by drastically modified. And that is the point of my work.

Finally, the third point that I would like to offer for discussion – or if the theme suits you, I would like to write an essay of about 2 printer's sheets for the journal – is the *Blum experiment*, I mean the economic side of his politics, his purchasing power theory as a means to stimulate the economy and overcome crises. At this moment, after Blum has fallen and indeed in an unprecedented financial crash, it seems important to me to summarise the most important phases and stages of his experiment and draw out a few *theoretical* conclusions that are of general significance for crisis theory. Theory is no unworldly, scholastic rumination; it should create from experience! In light of the facts, this experiment shows that purchasing power theory, i.e. underconsumption theory, has suffered a scandalous bankruptcy.

I am very much looking forward to America. The English mentality – I have not seen anything so narrow-minded in a long time – is *à la longue* unbearable. For me, the brilliance of French thought is entirely missing here. Once I happened to be in the company of an intelligent man who spoke in a very interesting way about art. Soon it was evident that he was no full-blooded Englishman and that he had spent his youth abroad. A small clique of conservatives has been able to impose their mannerisms, way of life and thinking onto the great mass of people. Everyone only wants to be and becomes a 'gentleman' by wearing white flannels and playing tennis on Sunday and speaking only in short, disjointed words but, when possible, by being silent. The peace of the cemetery!

People of intelligence like, for example, [David] Lloyd George are not really Englishmen – his speeches are the sole recreation in the extremely boring reading of parliamentary debates.

---

72 [Eventually published as Grossman 1941a, see below pp. 525–527.]

Summer is approaching and you will probably be on holiday soon. So I wish you and your wife, as well as Pollock, who will probably be near you, good and pleasant recreation and remain, with best wishes

your
Henryk Grossman

1 August 1937

9 Belsize Avenue
London NW3

Dear Mr Horkheimer

I read both the essays by Marcuse, on the affirmative character of culture, and by you, with the critique of new positivism,[73] in the last journal with genuine pleasure. Marcuse's essay is very important and useful in its critique, because he does not begin with an arbitrarily constructed conception or definition of culture to which the critique is subordinated. He rather demonstrates, with skilfully chosen, important, characteristic examples, i.e. with historical material, that the bourgeoisie had such a conception of culture during its phases of emergence as well as decline. The demonstration of the identity of the content of the totalitarian states' cultures, despite the completely changed form, is especially fine.

Concerning your fine essay, I regard it as your best and deepest accomplishment so far. When I remember the first year of my stay in Frankfurt and your Cornelian[74] beginnings, I am amazed by the maturity of your development and the great accomplishment of the labour that finds expression in your essay. The essay is highly topical and important because of the confusion that the 'Vienna School',[75] in particular, induces in the heads of younger socialists. Your principal critique, with its great logical precision, combined with elegant irony and, when necessary, a blunt fist (e.g. where you reproach their superficiality and presumption or their ignorance of dialectics),[76] will have a beneficial effect. So it is even more regrettable that the article, because it is published in a journal,

73 [Marcuse 2009; Horkheimer 2002.]

74 [A reference to the early influence of Hans Cornelius, the neo-Kantian philosopher, on Horkheimer.]

75 [The 'Vienna Circle' was a group active in the 1920s and 1930s, which advocated a logical positivist/empiricist philosophy of science.]

76 Horkheimer 2002, pp. 174, 177.

is not accessible to the general public. Precisely from the standpoint of activism, you should have an interest in addressing broader layers of youth. It should never be forgotten that the triumph of Cartesianism, in its time, was not simply promoted in university halls by the force of a pure idea but by the fists and sticks of the Dutch students, who answered the brutal power of the scholastics with the same kind of power, of their fists!

I have noted various points for myself that I find particularly fine. But the letter itself could develop into an essay. I will therefore forego that and, just in case you should indeed decide to issue your essay in book form, want to draw your attention to one point that you overlooked in your essay and seems very important to me.

For the scientist too, you emphasise the necessity of 'definite goals', constructive decisions,[77] as opposed to mere functions of registration and calculation. And rightly so. Against *these* people, this emphasis was extremely necessary. But with this, the inner Marxist problematic is not exhausted. Conscious decisions are imbued with spontaneity; they are connected with the conscious will of the relevant decision-making subject. But in a class divided society there is no general subject, societal subject; there are merely classes and class interests that influence decisions. So several subjective decisions are counterposed: one will, with definite goals, stands opposed to another will, with other goals. On what does the actual historical process and the final victory of just *one* definite goal depend?

In the preface to the first edition of *Capital*, Marx speaks of the 'natural laws' of capitalist production, 'working themselves out with *iron necessity*'.[78] And the postface to the second edition states that Marx 'treats the social movement as a process of *natural history*, governed by laws *not only independent* of human will, consciousness and intelligence, but rather, on the contrary, determining that will, consciousness and intelligence ... If the *conscious element plays such a subordinate part in the history of civilization* ...'[79]

I know very well that these sentences do not contradict activism. But this is, therefore, precisely a problem that deserves to be treated in an essay like yours.

The really 'active', spontaneous human can only be a *species being* where his *species activity* is conceivable, i.e. under socialism, as the *result of history*, of real history.[80]

77 Horkheimer 2002, p. 181.
78 [Marx 1976b, p. 91. Grossman's emphasis.]
79 [Engels 1976, p. 101. The first ellipses are Engels's. Grossman's emphasis.]
80 Marx 1975b, pp. 333–4.

But we do not have history because there is no species being in a class divided society. We are in the *prehistory* of humanity, where, thanks to class division and private property and thus *alienation*, humans do not decide freely, because of the existence of the domination of production relations over the producers; a human is not a subject but *a component of the rest of calculable nature*.

Consequently, the decisive role of the economic, which makes historical development a 'natural-historical', calculable process, in which the conscious element has previously played a subordinate role and will only come into its own in the real history of the future.

Again, my best regards and wishes to you are your wife, as well as to the Pollocks

your
Henryk Grossman

P.S. I would like very much to hear your opinion on this point.

14 April 1938

Sevilla-Biltmore
Habana Cuba[81]

My dear Mr Horkheimer

My wonderful trip has not turned out as I expected. I had hoped to be able to send you a telegram today, saying that the matter had been successfully resolved. Unfortunately, my Polish passport has worked against me. While Germans immediately get visas, in my case a telegram had to be sent to the Polish Foreign Ministry in Warsaw (at my expense) with the response paid for, to find out if an immigration *number* is free. The consul believes that the answer, according to his experience, will be affirmative. Since Monday, now that I have passed the medical examination, I have been going to the consul at 10 am and 5 pm to ask if the answer has arrived. Today, Thursday, and tomorrow, Friday, are holyday [sic]. So I have to wait for the answer until Saturday *and* can only then deal with the other formalities. Yes, the Poles work slowly in Warsaw. In the meantime, I bathe at the pretty, unfashionable, small provincial beach, while everything is still developing. The city is beautifully laid out and kept clean;

81 [Letterhead.]

the authorities seem to work very well. Transport (buses) works excellently, a single fare of 5 cents for a very great distance! A typical southern city, in relation to architecture and life-style. The tropical fruits and fantastically beautiful colours of the sea. Here you can understand the splendid colours of a [Paul] Gauguin. One is bewitched by this natural splendour.

If I look not only with an artistic but also with a social eye, then the 'other side' is immediately apparent.

The whole island is in the orbit of the big brother to the north. Not only that US dollars circulate alongside Cuban dollars. All of life here is only a pendant of the USA. I had to come here to hear 'Bei mir bist du schön' in Spanish.[82]

What applies to musical hits applies to the rest of life. Woolworth and its imitators are the 'bearers of culture'. *The same* colours that you see in New York in Woolworth are here too. Cuban or Negro women buy everything from stockings and handkerchiefs to lipsticks and girdles in the large department stores. Never original, indigenous costumes; all Woolworth material. In passing both Negro and Cuban women on the street, I recognise the same cheap eau de cologne. On the one hand, it's gratifying that these Negroes are able to do this, on the other hand ...

All that remains of originality are the few baskets, straw hats, castanets, etc. – as a 'souvenir' export industry!

However, another *large industry*, which does not go into the statistics, is blossoming. While I sat for *half* an hour on the 'Prado' (the main promenade street) I was made four offers by Negroes (who were very well dressed): very 'fine' young girls[83] of 17–19, black or blond, or do I prefer *younger* girls or perhaps boys – or else perhaps I would like three girls *at the same time*: 'One will ... the other, the third ...'

What is more, I can *watch* various productions; it does not cost anything to look![84]

One thing must be insisted on. In this [population of] half a million, [there] is an *active intellectual life*. Not only many Spanish newspapers, an immense number (about 25) of different magazines. Including translations from German, English and French into Spanish. Many are published in Mexico by Universidad Obrera. But a huge three-volume work *History of Slavery*[85] was

---

82 'Bei mir bist du schön', by the Andrews Sisters, sung in English and Yiddish was a number one hit in early 1938.

83 ['girls' in English in the original.]

84 ['look' in English in the original.]

85 [Presumably either Saco 1932; or Saco 1938.]

even published in Havana. Many bookshops. The layer which reads all these new publications may be small but it is there, interested in everything.

Spain, South and Central America taken together – that is indeed a great power, politically divided, but culturally alive.

The ship was very favourably/badly occupied, only 100 passengers instead of 500. But there were two women from New York, one very attractive. Because of the holiday … the casino is shut! I try to dispel my worries on the beach, where I have come to know several women from New York. Perhaps I will do 'tour number 3' – into the countryside, to see a few tobacco and pineapple plantations.

A policeman earns 20 dollars *a month*. The people live in great poverty – I have not seen such worn-out suits for a long time.

The Cubans an attractive race. Cuban women exceptionally beautiful in the splendour of their bodies and the rhythm of their walk.

I close this report which explains my longer stay here and wish you and the other ladies and gentlemen the best for the Easter holidays

Your faithful

Henryk Grossman

The normal evening dancing is not happening because of the holiday![86] On the same basis the church of Jesus Christ was full!

6 August 1939

Tallwood
Maranacook, Maine[87]

Dear Mr Horkheimer

I am sitting here at the beautiful, seven mile long Maranacook Lake (an Indian name). The people – typical petit bourgeois – no Jews. (The few Jewish types turned out, without exception, to be Italians.) One can hardly imagine a stronger contrast to Timberland, where there were only Jews. I wanted to send you a longer report – but it was too long, so I did not send it. But perhaps there will be an opportunity to discuss it in New York, at a tea evening at my place. Here flirting and the sexual question play only a subordinate roll – in the tradition of flirting in summer places. What I saw in Timberland is an organised

86 ['Dancing' and 'holiday' are in English in the original.]
87 [Letterhead.]

market – supply and demand – no flirting, no 'romance', as it is portrayed in the film *Have a Nice Time*.[88] Everything 'rationalised' to the extreme. The specific economic circumstances under which such an organised market of sexual life comes about: the era of the secretary, who has no prospect of marriage. Nor does she wait for a husband – she is determined, rather, to completely devote her youth to amusement. No old-fashioned 'romance', no. She is beyond that. No more longer ties, that last for a few days! She wants to have free reign: she seeks another for the afternoon and yet another for the evening. Intellectual qualities play absolutely no role: the girls look at the men with the gaze of a slave trader: the man must be big and strong.[89]

You can imagine the future if these tendencies generally ruled! Twenty year-old girls[90] are sarcastic or completely cynical where 'love' is concerned. They do not know anything about it. They only know sex. That is very convenient for the man. Seen from a social standpoint, that is a catastrophe. I believe it is the symptom of a capitalist world that is going under.

I hope that you and your wife are doing well, in spite of the heat. Here in Tallwood, a provincial idyll.

With best regards
your
Henryk Grossman

30 April 1943

New York

Dear Mr Horkheimer

My most obliged thanks to you and your wife for the friendly thoughtfulness and the birthday wishes, as well as the attached bottle of scotch whiskey.

From your letter I had the impression that you intend to be here over the coming weeks in connection with the Jewish Project.[91] Löwenthal informed me, however, that your visit is not planned until the autumn.

---

88 [Presumably Alfred Santell's 1938 *Having Wonderful Time* set in the Catskills, with Ginger Rogers and Douglas Fairbanks Jr.]

89 ['Girls' and 'big and strong' are in English in the original.]

90 ['Girls' is in English in the original.]

91 ['Jewish Project' is in English in the original, referring to a project on anti-semitism, for which the Institute of Social Research (as it was known in the United States) had attempted to attract outside funding since 1938. The American Jewish Committee took it on in

I do not know if you read the New York press. Moreover whether the Jewish Project interests you only in so far as it can earn a few thousand dollars. If your interest goes further than this it will interest you to know that over the past months here in New York State, in New York, etc., millions of antisemitic flyers (*à la* Hitler), were repeatedly distributed to workers, women and youth in all war industry factories. The authorities – and that leads one to think – look on idly. The FBI[92] has not intervened, no one has been imprisoned, the Dies-Committee[93] is silent about it.

From the enclosed newspaper clipping, you can see how far the antisemitic propaganda has penetrated. Under these circumstances, it is my deep conviction that now is not the time for theoretical studies of antisemitism. It is a time for swift *political* action by the Jews. We are sufficiently informed as to the motives that lie at the base of fascist, antisemitic agitation. One can and one must *act*. If Jews do not do this, no theoretical projects will help at all (even if they are the best conceivable) and Jews will have to expect many evil experiences.

With best regards
Your
Henryk Grossman

1943, eventually issuing a series of five publications, Horkheimer and Flowerman 1950, authored by members and associates of the Institute and others.]

92 [Federal Bureau of Investigation, domestic US intelligence agency.]

93 [The Committee Investigating Un-American Activities of the US House of Representatives, was initiated and then chaired by Martin Dies Jr between 1938 and 1944. While rhetorically concerned with right- and left-wing subversion, it was preoccupied with the activities of leftists.]

CHAPTER 16

Sismondi, Jean Charles Leonard Simonde de (1773–1842)*

Swiss economist, historian, historian of literature and publicist. Sismondi, a Genevan descended from an old French family, emigrated to England in 1793 and to Tuscany the following year but in 1800 settled in his native city, where from 1809 on he lectured at the Academy of Geneva on ancient and literary history and economics. His development, particularly as historian and historian of literature, was profoundly influenced by his friendship with Madame [Germaine] de Staël and by the prominent personalities whom he met in her cosmopolitan salon at Coppet.

Through his *History of the Italian Republics in the Middle Ages*[1] Sismondi was the first to awaken general interest in the mediaeval history of Italy. But while he was a pioneer in the reclamation of the Middle Ages from the contempt of the eighteenth-century rationalists, he shared the tendency of the latter to use history for didactic purposes: he wrote his history of the Italian towns as an anti-Bonapartist republican who wished to remind an enslaved nation of its glorious past. He was one of the first to understand that the liberation of the mediaeval Italian cities enabled them to take precedence in the development of a bourgeois society. His descriptions of currency, trade, manufactures, agriculture and the role of productive capital often reveal technical precision, although he had little inkling of the interdependence between politics and economic drives. His subsequent *History of the French*[2] without transcending the limitations of the earlier work won recognition as the earliest comprehensive survey of the subject based on original research and as a suggestive synthesis of varied currents particularly in the mediaeval period.

As author of *On the Literature of the South of Europe*,[3] a revision of his lectures on the evolution of Arabian, Provençal, Italian, Spanish and Portuguese literature, Sismondi became cofounder with Madame de Madame de Staël of the 'philosophy of literature', which paved the way for the sociological approach to the subject. Just as his investigations of the mediaeval history of Italy had

* [Originally published as Grossman 1934.]
1 [Sismondi 1807–18.]
2 [Sismondi 1821–44.]
3 [Sismondi 1852.]

convinced him that national character was determined by social and political institutions rather than by racial or climatic peculiarities, so he now presented literature as the natural if sometimes belated refection of the same forces. His use of the comparative method enabled him to show the universal parallelism in the stages of intellectual development of different nations and his defence of national art smoothed the path of romanticism especially in France.

Sismondi's general political outlook, as represented, for instance, by *Études sur les constitutions des peuples libres*, was liberal but anti-Rousseauistic and antidemocratic.[4] Believing that both the proletariat and the lower middle classes were not yet ready for democracy, he offered an apologia for the privileges of minorities, particularly of the urban bourgeoisie and the intellectuals, whom he regarded not only as the progressive elements but as the representatives of national tradition.

Although in his earliest economic writings, *Table of Tuscan Agriculture* and *On Commercial Wealth*, he had defended Smithian liberalism and popularised it before Jean-Baptiste Say, his *New Principles of Political Economy*,[5] which reflects his observation of the economic crisis during his second trip to England (1818–19), constitutes a devastating criticism of the basic axioms upon which the classical economists built their idealised and static conception of capitalism. He showed clearly the untenability of the doctrine that competition always tends to establish an equilibrium between production and consumption. More specifically he emphasised that general crises, or gluts, are not only possible – a fact denied by the classical economists, although they admitted the possibility of partial gluts arising from an occasional disproportion between individual branches of industry – but an inevitable periodic concomitant of the prevailing economic structure. The direct cause of such crises he found in underconsumption on the part of the working classes, whose purchasing power is insufficient to absorb the annual national output. The second inherent characteristic of capitalism overlooked by the classical economists was the necessity of continuous expansion and of new outlets, resulting from the restriction of the internal market. While Sismondi was incorrect in limiting demand to consumers' demand and in other aspects of his argument, the essential validity of his conclusions makes him the scientific discoverer of capitalistic dynamics.

The deeper cause of underconsumption, that is, of the simultaneous decline in income and increase in the volume of production, Sismondi attributed to

4 [Sismondi 1836. Sismondi was hostile to the work of Jean-Jacques Rousseau.]
5 Sismondi 1801; Sismondi 1803; Sismondi 1991d.

the fact that in a capitalistic society the extent and direction of economic activity are determined by exchange value, which by reason of the unevenness of technological advance within each branch of production is in a constant state of flux. The only possible basis for a harmonious and stable adjustment is the social need measured in terms of the quantity of useful commodities. Since the latter has no determining effect in a capitalistic system, Sismondi denied categorically the possibility of regulating economic activity in such a system. His various reform proposals, including his demand for public protection of workers, were consciously advanced merely as palliatives, which he realised could not correct the evils inherent in the existing order.

Among his contemporaries Sismondi was recognised chiefly as historian and historian of literature and subsequently fell into oblivion, except in Italy, where his work as a national historian influenced the spiritual revival during the Risorgimento.[6] After 1850 the protagonists of social reform, frequently exaggerating Sismondi's really limited faith in reform measures, rediscovered him and hailed him as a precursor. Today he is famous especially as a theorist of crises, whose ideas were taken over not only by his contemporaries Malthus and Rodbertus but under the disguise of Marxist terminology by such socialists as Heinrich Cunow, Louis Boudin, Karl Kautsky and Rosa Luxemburg.[7] Since the outbreak of the present world crisis this underconsumption theory, which Lenin justly attacked as non-Marxist, has become the official doctrine of numerous socialist parties and trade unions in Europe and America.[8]

Henryk Grossman

Works

1807–18, *Histoire des républiques italiennes au moyen âge*, 16 volumes, Zurich: Gessner, Paris: Treuttel et Würtz; 1840–1, new edition, ten volumes, Paris: Treuttel et Würtz; 1832, abridged edition as *Histoire de la renaissance de la liberté en Italie*, two volumes, Paris: Treuttel et Würtz; 1832, translated as *A History of the Italian Republics*, London: Longman, Brown, Green and Longmans, reprinted 1907, London: Dent.

6 [The Risorgimento was the movement which culminated in the unification of Italy in 1870.]
7 [See, for example, Malthus 1836; Rodbertus 1898; Cunow 1898; Boudin 1907a; Kautsky 1902; Luxemburg 1951.]
8 [Lenin 1960a.]

1821–44, *Histoire des Français*, 31 volumes, Paris: Treuttel et Würtz; 1839, abridged edition as *Précis de l'histoire des Français*, two volumes and a third volume by Edmond Robinet 1844, Paris: Treuttel et Würtz.
1813, *De la littérature du midi de l'Europe*, four volumes, Paris: Treuttel et Würtz; 1837, fourth edition, two volumes, Bruxelles: Dumont; 1852 [1823], translated by Thomas Roscoe as *Historical View of the Literature of the South of Europe*, two volumes, London: Bohn.
1836–8, *Études sur les sciences sociales*, three volumes, Paris: Treuttel et Würtz.

Consult

Salis, Jean R. de 1932, *Sismondi: 1773–1842*, two volumes, Paris: Champion.
Aftalion, Albert 1899, *L'œuvre économique de Simonde de Sismondi*, Paris: Pedone.
Grossman, Henryk 1924, *Simonde de Sismondi et ses theories économiques*, Warszawa: Bibliotheca Universitatis Liberae Polonae, 2.[9]
Tuan, Mao-Lan 1927, *Simonde de Sismondi as an Economist*, New York: Columbia University Press.
Festy, Octave 1918, 'Sismondi et la condition des ouvriers français de son temps', *Revue d'économie politique*, 32: 46–72, 118–36.
Lenin, Vladimir Ilyich 1960a [1897], *A Characterisation of Economic Romanticism* (*Sismondi and our Native Sismondists*), in *Collected Works. Volume 2*, 129–265, Moscow: Progress.
Jeandeau, René 1913, *Sismondi: précurseur de la législation social contemporaine*, Bordeaux: Cadoret.
Pellegrini, Carlo 1926, *Il Sismondi e la storia delle letterature dell'Europa meridionale*, Geneva: Olschki.
Gooch, George Peabody 1913, *History and Historians in the Nineteenth Century*, 165–8, London: Longmans Green.

9 [See above pp. 55–119.]

CHAPTER 17

Review of Élie Halévy, *Sismondi**

Translated from German by Ben Fowkes

Halévy, Élie 1933, *Sismondi*, Paris: Félix Alcan (146pp, 15 French francs).

This little volume – the tenth in the series of texts edited by Célestin Bouglé under the title *Social Reformers* – is a solid selection of texts illustrating Sismondi's intellectual world. It consists of a small number of clearly arranged chapters (*Contribution des peuples libres; Critique de la chrématistique*; *Vices de la société économique moderne*; *Vue d'histoire économique et sociale*; *Les remèdes*).[1] Halévy's short introduction succinctly demonstrates the relationship between Sismondi's doctrines and classical economics, in particular Jean-Baptiste Say's doctrine of harmonious equilibrium, as well as the growing present-day significance of Sismondi's theory of crisis. What is perhaps missing is any reference to the fact that the various *theories of underconsumption* prevalent in the working-class movement at present (e.g. those of Louis Boudin, Heinrich Cunow, Karl Kautsky, Rosa Luxemburg and the CGT[2] in France), which have also spread widely beyond it, in reality signify a renaissance of Sismondi's theory of crises, despite their Marxist terminological disguise.

Henryk Grossmann (Paris)

---

* [Originally published as Grossmann 1934a.]

1 ['Contribution of free peoples; Critique of chrematistics; Defects of modern economic society; Economic and social perspective on history; Solutions.']

2 [*Confédération Générale du Travail*, the largest trade union federation.]

CHAPTER 18

Review of Robert Bordaz, *Marx's Law of Capitals in Light of Contemporary Events*[*]

Translated from German by Ben Fowkes

Bordaz, Robert 1933, *La loi de Marx sur les capitaux à la lumière des événements contemporains*, Paris: L. Rodstein (200pp, 36 French francs).

The title of the book is erroneous. In the text too, the author speaks of a 'law of capitals', as if there were a single 'law of capitals' in Marx! Which law is he referring to? The law of the falling rate of profit, perhaps? This fundamental law, which lies at the centre of Marx's doctrine of crisis, is *not* examined by the author. Instead he dismisses it in a couple of words, as 'not confirmed by experience', in a footnote on page 175! The book discusses the changing organic composition of capital, that is to say the law of the increasing growth of the constant part of capital in proportion to its variable part in the course of accumulation. Marx, he says, offered no conclusive proofs for his law[1] because statistics of industrial production did not exist in his time. The author therefore intends to demonstrate the correctness of the law on the basis of extensive modern material.

The material he draws on, however, is fragmentary and unsystematic; the tables (leaving aside cases of evident negligence in their compilation, as on page 106) are often incomprehensible.[2] The table for the period between 1899 and 1919 in the USA, on page 123, is supposed to show the *rising* share of wages in the value of the product but actually shows the opposite (the share of wages falls from 36 percent in 1899 to 20 percent in 1919).

The author does not, however, restrict himself to statistical demonstrations. In the first part of his book he enters into the area of theory, and out of the law of the rising composition of capital he constructs – a theory of crises! Rising productivity, as a consequence of a higher organic composition of capital, is accompanied by a fall in the share of wages, hence a fall in the purchasing power of the working class. 'At a certain moment', a disturbance of equilibrium

* Originally published as Grossmann 1934b.

1 Bordaz 1933, p. 69.

2 Bordaz 1933, p. 119.

must result from the contradiction between the two developmental tendencies.[3] In this simplistic manner, therefore, Marx's doctrine of crisis is presented as a theory of underconsumption which is merely a paraphrase of Sismondi's doctrine.[4] It has escaped the author that, in the theory he has constructed, a boom would be absolutely impossible, while crisis would inevitably be *permanent*. The author is unaware of both earlier and more recent discussions conducted both in Germany and in Russia over the last 35 years concerning Marx's theory of crisis, in which Tugan-Baranovsky, Kautsky, Pannekoek, Louis Boudin, [Sergei Nikolaevich] Bulgakov, [Georg] Charassoff, Lenin, Rosa Luxemburg, Bukharin and Henryk Grossmann participated.

Admittedly, he does mention[5] that the workers rendered unemployed by technological progress could again be absorbed into the labour process where there is an *accelerated* rhythm of accumulation but he says at the same time 'that this becomes ever more difficult'. With this empty phrase he silently passes over the decisive aspect of the problem and the *proof* of this impossibility.

Adam Smith's optimism, the author thinks, is understandable, since he could not in 1776 foresee the harmful effects of the introduction of machinery.[6] The author really ought to have been aware that, 30 years before Smith, [Charles] *Montesquieu* had already emphasised that machinery had the harmful effect of making workers unemployed (*The Spirit of Laws*, book 23, chapter 15).[7] If he studies more deeply, Bordaz will presumably be able to achieve better results in later publications.

Henryk Grossmann (Paris)

3 Bordaz 1933, p. 55.
4 Bordaz 1933, pp. 55, 59.
5 Bordaz 1933, pp. 53–9.
6 Bordaz 1933, p. 14.
7 [Montesquieu 1873, p. 144.]

CHAPTER 19

Contributions to a Seminar Series on Monopoly Capitalism*

Translated from German by Ben Fowkes

1. While countries with recent capitalist development, in the initial stages of capital accumulation, can profitably invest more capital than their own creation of surplus value provides, it is apparent that in countries with very advanced capital accumulation an *over-saturation* occurs, which finds expression in a progressive reduction in profitable investment possibilities for the capital which has been accumulated and seeks investment. The result of this is a fall in the rate of profit, a relative reduction in the amount of profit in proportion to the capital invested.
   The restriction of the possibilities for productive investment means that booms (considered apart from unproductive investments in armaments) remain *short-lived*, i.e. that crises follow each other at shorter and shorter intervals.
2. From the point of view of the world economy, the over-saturation of the highly capitalist countries with superfluous, unemployed capital means there is a *compulsion* to *export capital*. Hence the number of capital-exporting countries grows with the progress of development while, by that very fact, the number and extent of areas for investment, hence *debtor countries*, declines. The necessary result of this is a sharpening of the struggle for *spheres of investment* or the piling up of large quantities of unemployed capital, which eventually seeks valorisation in the unproductive spheres of the stock exchange and land speculation. This speculation occurs at the expense of the broad mass of the participating public. On the other hand, it is precisely the struggle for spheres of investment which has led to wrongly directed capital investments, where no account has been taken of the given level of profitability, and which leads to collapses of the debtor countries.
3. The increased export of capital leads to rapid capitalist penetration of backward regions and the emergence of many new national econom-

* [Originally published as Grossmann 1985a, written 1937; and Grossmann 1985b, written 1937. Other participants in the seminars included Julian Gumperz, Max Horkheimer and Karl August Wittfogel. There was no title or date on Grossman's theses.]

ies, which make the bulk of goods from the sector that produces finished commodities. Thus there is a *structural change* in exports: relatively, ever fewer finished commodities and more means of production (machines etc.) are exported. That, however, requires ever more external markets.

4. Since an ever *greater* portion of the value of the relatively falling mass of profit must be employed in order to accumulate this increased amount of constant capital,[1] a *progressively smaller* portion of the amount of profit remains is left over as the *revenue* of the classes of capitalists and workers. Consequently there results a *sharpening of the class struggle* over the distribution of the revenue portion between wages and profit, with the result that the *value share* of workers' wages in the total social product progressively declines, which is only somewhat alleviated by the fact that, in terms of [the number of] products, the mass of commodities consumed by the workers does not fall, or may even rise temporarily, owing to the higher productivity of labour.
5. The struggle between the capitalists and the working class over the distribution of the reduced revenue share is made still sharper by the struggle over distribution within the working class, with the result that the class becomes divided into two different groups: a minority of organised workers succeeds in securing for itself an above-average standard of living at the expense of the vast majority, whose standard of living thereby necessarily falls below its previous level.
6. The reduction in the profitability of the economy as a whole, which prevails in the long run, has the effect that the *long-term debts*, taken on at a time of greater profitability, become an ever more unbearable burden and lead in increasing measure to a *revolt of the debtor countries* and the *debtor strata* against the creditor countries (and the creditor strata). Bankruptcies occur on a mass scale, demands are raised for moratoria and other interventions by the state, such as periodic *seisachtheia*[2] (debt relief), but the impossibility of direct state intervention to the detriment of the creditors leads to the use of an indirect method of debt reduction: *currency devaluation*.[3]

1 Level A 200,000 c + 100,000 v + 100,000 s 10% of constant capital is 20,000, i.e. 1/5s
Level B 1,000,000 c + 110,000 v + 110,000 s 10% of constant capital is 100,000, i.e. 10/11s
Level C 4,600,000 c + 100,000 v + 120,000 s 10% of constant capital is 400,000, i.e. the total surplus value is merely sufficient for an accumulation of 2.6%.

2 [Transliteration of the Greek 'σεισάχθεια'.]

3 Long-term private indebtedness in the USA:

7. The reduced profitability of the economy as a whole has led to movements of centralisation and concentration and the creation of *large monopolistic enterprises* in production and transport, which endeavour to improve their profitability at the expense of the vast mass of consumers through *excessively high monopoly prices* (within the country and also on the world market). They also seek to reduce their own costs by exerting pressure on the prices of the raw materials and semi-finished goods they obtain from others.
8. The reduction in the profitability of the economy as a whole produces a sharpening of the competitive struggle on the *world market*. This particular sharpening is indicated by the following: though this struggle was previously carried on by well-known means (cost reduction through concentration and large-scale production, establishment of cartels, tariff wars, dumping, wage cuts, improved technology, the control of cheap raw materials etc. etc.) it remained limited to the *commodity aspect* and was conducted on the basis of a gold-backed currency, which was regarded as the *noli me tangere*,[4] the holy of holies.

   The sharpening of competition, after all the previous means of struggle prove to be insufficient, is shown by the fact that now currencies are also brought into the conflict. The struggle among currencies, as the last available means of securing a price advantage in the competitive struggle, led to the abandonment of the gold standard and the automatic international balancing mechanism bound up with it; led to the *splitting up of the world economy* into individual, isolated regions, segregated from each other by tariff walls, compulsory currency regulations and quotas; led to the destruction of the international *credit* system and of capital exports, and indeed to an inappropriate distribution of gold. The automatic international balancing mechanism was replaced by artificial balancing funds in individual states (currency manipulations).
9. These currency manipulations should 'theoretically' contribute to *price stabilisation*, by raising prices, if prices are falling, and by reducing prices, if prices rise too steeply. Their actual meaning, however, is shown by the fact that in practice they function *only one-sidedly, in an inflationary direction*. At advanced levels of accumulation where further open, direct pressure on wages meets with great resistance in countries with strong

---

1900 $15 billion; interest burden $800
1914 $332 billion; interest burden $1,742
1930 $856 billion; interest burden $4,882.

4 ['Do not touch me', in the Latin *Bible*, Jesus's words to Mary Magdalene after his resurrection.]

trade unions, these inflations and devaluations have the task of pushing through wage reductions in an indirect way and thus restoring profitability which has been falling.

10. A chronic excess of unemployed capital and a progressive increase in the unused capacity of heavy industry leads, despite all technological advances, to the destruction of great masses of capital and commodities and the reduction of the area under agricultural cultivation, and this at a time when vast numbers of unemployed people are not even sure of receiving the minimum required for existence. Capitalism has moved from its rising to its declining phase, in which the expansion of the productive forces of the economy is held back in the interests of the profits of a small minority of owners and to the detriment of the great mass of the people.

20 November 1937

Grossmann gives a schematic presentation of the phase of monopoly capitalism with regard to the average rate of profit, namely that the dominant group of entrepreneurs (A) appropriates a share of surplus value greater than the average rate owing to its monopoly position. They are confronted with a group of entrepreneurs (C) who are not yet organised as a monopoly, who stand in increasingly sharp opposition to the first group and who appropriate less than the average rate of profit. Meanwhile Group B, standing in the middle, and receiving roughly the average rate of profit, tends to become smaller and smaller and can be disregarded.

CHAPTER 20

Review of G.N. Clark, *Science and Social Welfare in the Age of Newton*, and George Sarton, *The History of Science and the New Humanism**

Translated from German by Rick Kuhn

Clark, G.N. 1937, *Science and Social Welfare in the Age of Newton*, New York and London: Oxford University Press (159pp, $2.50, 6s); and Sarton, George 1937, *The History of Science and the New Humanism*, Cambridge, MA: Harvard University Press, London: Oxford University Press (xx + 196pp, $2.00, 8s. 6d).

Clark's little book, the fruit of extraordinary erudition and great expert knowledge, is a valuable contribution to the problem of the social determination of inventions and sciences, in which the author's attitudes to these two are fundamentally different.

The general social preconditions for scientific research in England and France during the seventeenth century are set out in the introductory essay 'Science and technology'. The main interest in the period was directed towards technology and mechanical inventions. Many wealthy aristocrats had their own laboratories; technological literature expanded; finally societies like the Royal Society (1622) and a few years later the Académie Royale des Sciences, were established in England and also France. In them, organised technological studies, often in collaboration with industry were pursued. Against this background, C in a further essay ('Economic incentives to invention') masterfully sketches the importance of the economic drive for inventions and the greater application of inventions which were already to hand. Even more important are the impulses to invention, which arise from the form of social organisation of labour and particularly from the pursuit of profit. Inventions, C thinks, are entrepreneurs' answer to depressions, during which profitability suffers from falling commodity prices. Labour costs are lowered through improved mechanisation and profitability thus restored. The relative backwardness of mechanisation in agriculture is, according to C, not to be attributed to the lack of appropriate inventions. Rather, because there is an overabundance of cheap

* [Originally published as Grossmann 1938a.]

labour power, machines are not needed: small farmers could make use of the labour of their family members. Where large firms producing for export and using expensive wage labour arose, machines were invented and introduced early or else the social form of the organisation of labour was altered. Thus sugar and tobacco plantations went over to the use of cheap slave labour. In severely depopulated Spain, where wage labour was particularly dear, the *sembrador*, a combined machine for ploughing, sowing and harrowing was already used around the middle of the seventeenth century.

But C goes even further and attempts to demonstrate the regularity of the uneven technical development of individual historical periods. Using the analogy of the economic cycle, he attempts to explain the unevenness of technological development during these periods in terms of the great historical periods of boom and slump. The long period of currency devaluation after the discovery of America signified the devaluation of all fixed returns, harming creditors and favouring debtors, particularly industrial debtors. This naturally promoted the rise of the new capitalist entrepreneurs and their exports. The palpable scarcity of wage labour and rising prices then gave impetus to the introduction of many inventions, particularly in export industries, which faced strong competition on the world market. The overwhelming majority of inventions consisted of 'labour saving' machines.

But the impetus to introduce technical improvements was even more powerful in the following period of downturn as, from the middle of the seventeenth century, prices moved in the opposite direction. The fall in prices intensified competition, led to the protectionism and wars over foreign markets, that were characteristic of the mercantilist era. During this period of practical and intellectual Colbertism,[1] technological activity and the number of mechanical inventions significantly grew.

The fourth essay, 'Social control of technological improvement' describes, with numerous examples, the obstacles to the introduction of technical improvements that set in during the sixteenth and seventeenth centuries, whether on the part of workers threatened with unemployment or on the part of guild organisations. The latter defended their monopoly domination of markets by excluding any competition and in this way significantly slowed technological progress and capitalist development.

Despite the effective exposition, some deficiencies are apparent in the book. C presents the connection between technology and social history factually but

---

1 [Policies designed to increase a country's reserves of gold and silver through a favourable balance of trade, pursued by Jean-Baptiste Colbert, French minister of finance, 1665–83.]

has not mastered it theoretically. He asserts, for example, that we are little informed about the class structure of early capitalism. So, he thinks, the introduction of machines led to the transition to mass production of cheap and necessary, everyday commodities, in contrast with earlier manufacture,[2] which merely satisfied luxury requirements. Against this, it has to be emphasised that mass production is not the simple result of growing technical capacity, as a consequence of the introduction of machines. It is, rather, made possible only by the emergence of broad layers of a prosperous bourgeoisie in the sixteenth century, in contrast to the earlier period when production had been limited by the requirements for luxuries of the small circle of the nobility and higher clergy.

The weakness of the author's standpoint is even more apparent in the book's central essay, 'Social and economic aspects of science'. While C concedes that technical inventions are socially and economically determined, his attitude to science is completely different. It is outside the economic sphere of influence and in relation to it, *spiritus flat ubi vult*[3] applies. The external impulses to scientific research are not exclusively economic; they can arise, in part, from four further sources, culture, religion, medicine and war, which are radically independent of economic influence. The development of medicine, for example, is not determined by any kind of social, specifically economic conditions but is rather an expression of the general human tendency to prolong life. Above all, however, the disinterested drive for knowledge, independent of all utilitarian intentions, operates here. On this basis, C argues against Russian Professor Boris Hessen's essay, which undertook to explain the specific character of [Isaac] Newton's mechanics in terms of the social and economic conditions of his time.[4] Despite C's assurance that he only wants to deal with Hessen's principal thesis, he becomes lost in polemical details and consequently, as will be demonstrated, Hessen's principal thesis is not even mentioned. If science is independent of economic and social influence and is merely to be explained by the drive for the truth then it is hard to grasp why classical mechanics only developed during the two hundred years from Leonardo da Vinci to Descartes, Galileo and Newton and did not already arise with the high level of development of ancient Greek philosophy and mathematics. C raises the objection against Hessen that he indeed cited the names of many weighty authors but did not give more than a general illustration of the proposed connection between the scientific view of Newton's physics and mechanics and the practical problems of mining, transport and war industries. It can be answered

2 [i.e. capitalist production on the basis of craft technology.]
3 [The spirit blows wherever it wants.]
4 Hessen 2009. [Grossman referred to an earlier, flawed translation of Hessen's study.]

that the proof of this connection does not lie at the centre of Hessen's analyses. For the connection between the mechanistic conception of Descartes and Galileo and industrial development during the sixteenth and eighteenth centuries, I may be permitted to indicate my work where a more detailed case is attempted.[5] Hessen's principal thesis goes much further, however, something that C seems to have missed. Hessen attempts to understand the general character of classical mechanics and physics in contrast to the later development of these sciences.

In nature we encounter various forms of motion of matter (mechanical, thermal, electromagnetic), which are linked and convert into one another. In nature pure forms of motion, isolated at such, are never found. It is nevertheless characteristic for the whole of classical mechanics, from Leonardo da Vinci through to its completion by Descartes, Galileo and Newton, that it only deals with the theory of a single form of motion, mechanical motion, and never the transformation from mechanical motion into other forms of energy.[6]

Now Hessen explains this circumstance in terms of the fact that during the period of classical mechanics the machines employed in industry (hoists, water-driven machines, etc.) only transmitted precisely this single, i.e. mechanical form of motion. Only with the development of large-scale industry, immediately after Newton, particularly the invention and further application of the steam engine, led to a shift, in that it gave the impetus to the study of new thermal forms of motion of matter (Watt's investigation of the thermodynamic properties of steam) and thus led to the foundation of thermodynamics as a specific branch of physics. The further development of thermodynamics by [Sadi] Carnot (1824) was also most closely connected with the observation of steam engines. While, in the machines of classical mechanics just one form of mechanical motion was transformed into another form of the same mechanical motion (e.g. motion in a straight line into circular motion), the essence of steam engines consists of the conversion of one, that is thermal, form of motion into an entirely different, namely mechanical, form. In this way and conditioned by new technical developments, the entirely new problem, of which no trace can be found in classical mechanics, the conversion of energy arose.[7] With the invention of electromagnetic machines – on the basis of experience with them – electromagnetism, as a specific branch of physics was constructed, in addition to those previously mentioned, mechanics and thermodynamics, and the general theory of the conversion of energy and its particular forms

5 Grossman 2009, pp. 133–45.
6 Hessen 2009, pp. 81.
7 Hessen 2009, pp. 79–81.

was completed. It is thus apparent that science is in no way independent of social development, moreover that precisely the economic-technical development of bourgeois society is in a position not only to make the content of the development of individual sectors of science intelligible but also that it allows us to grasp the historical sequence of the individual stages in this development.

Sarton's book contains diverse contributions of uneven value. The essay 'The new humanism' is a reform program for history teaching. In the introductory, methodological chapter S provides a confrontation, from his standpoint of his idealist conception of history, with individualist history writing, not because it is individualistic but because it singles out the 'wrong' heroes. S wants to replace the kings, great dignitaries who conduct war with the real 'creators' of history, the creative architects, craftspeople, thinkers, social reformers or saints. S refutes the economic determination of science and culture. On the other hand, he makes certain concession to the opposing conception when he admits that there is a 'certain determinism in the sequence of discoveries'[8] and when he emphasises the great significance of practice. The most valuable part of the book is the essay 'East and west', which briefly summarises the results of the author's research. In contrast with many authors who – like Max Weber – glorify modern science as the exclusive product of the 'western European' spirit, S shows the strength and important influence of the orient, the great scientific achievements of the ancient Egyptians, Babylonians, Persians, Indians, Phoenicians, later the Jews and Arabs. Not only the Greek but also the Arab 'miracle' can be spoken of. The superiority of e.g. Arab as opposed to western European culture until the middle of the thirteenth century cannot be disputed. Western European science of the past 500 years was only possible on the basis of the orient's efforts over 5,000 years.

Henryk Grossman (New York)

8 [Sarton 1937, p. 20.]

CHAPTER 21

Review of Karl Marx and Friedrich Engels, *The Civil War in the United States**

Translated from German by Joseph Fraccia

Marx, Karl and Friedrich Engels 1937, *The Civil War in the United States*, edited by Richard Enmale, New York: International Publishers (325pp, $2.50).

The book contains the first reprint of seven articles by Marx on the American Civil War that appeared in the *New York Daily Tribune* from 18 September 1861 until 11 January 1862, a further 35 articles from the *Wiener Presse* and excerpts from the famous correspondence between Marx and Engels from 1860 to 1866. The second part, from the *Wiener Presse*, is by far the most interesting and the most valuable theoretically and historically.

From the very beginning, Marx stood on the side of the 'bourgeois republic' of the North against the slave oligarchy of the South because of his conviction that the complete abolition of slavery was the precondition for the emancipation of the American working class: labour in a white skin cannot achieve dignity as long as it is despised in a black skin.[1] Moreover, slavery and its inherent expansionist tendencies limited the possibilities for northern industrial capital and hence the development of the industrial proletariat. For these reasons, Marx attached the highest hopes for the future of the workers' movement to the victory of the North.

The content Marx's reports in both newspapers deals with three topics: the political, the military, and the economic dimensions of the Civil War.

1. The largest part, perhaps two-thirds of the space, is devoted to daily political questions, to England's relationship with the Union: daily journalism. But what journalism! The reader is astonished by the wealth, the speed and the precision of the information of the London correspondent who assesses all opponents' arguments on the basis of the facts, consular reports, the movement of stock market prices and statistics; corrects false reports; in a period of pending international legal conflicts assesses the positions of the English gov-

* [Originally published as Grossman 1938b.]

1 [Cf. Marx 1976b, p. 414.]

ernment according to the literature on international law and, in doing so, uses information from the whole range of large and smaller presses of the American North as also from numerous secessionist papers of the South; and portrays the motives behind the actions of all the personalities stepping onto political and military stages with extraordinary knowledge.

Marx attacks 'English humanity' particularly sharply. In contrast to the 'real people of England' who regard the cause of the American Union as their own, as a matter of freedom, the London press maintains that it cannot sympathise with the North because the North does not advocate the emancipation of the Negroes seriously enough![2] At the same time, however, this same press condemns the proclamation of the emancipation of the Negroes by the North as a 'desperate expedient' and attacks the 'repulsive and dreadful' call for a general insurrection of slaves against their masters particularly sharply.[3]

2. For Marx, slavery was the central question. It was not only the immediate cause of the war, but for more than half a century had determined the inner history of the Union and the parliamentary battles that finally culminated in the Civil War. Thanks to their alliance with the Democrats of the North, the slavocracy of the South succeeded in opening more and more areas to slavery, beyond the boundary that was legally established in the first Constitutional Congress of 1789–90. Thus in the so-called Missouri Compromise of 1820, also in 1854, and finally in 1857, as a Supreme Court interpretation of the Constitution made it possible to introduce slavery even into previously free States, against the will of the settlers. In this way the slavocracy of the South succeeded in making the Union serve itself, so that it became the 'slave of 300,000 slaveholders'.[4] The question of democracy in relation to centralism became simply a veil for the advocacy of the interests of the slavocracy.

Because of the pressure of the South, similar tendencies to those in domestic policy were apparent in foreign policy. In 1851, the land-hungry slavocracy already demanded the acquisition and, if this was rejected, the armed occupation of the Spanish island of Cuba. It was the driving force behind the occupation of Northern Mexico in 1857–9 and also the 'piratical expeditions' against Nicaragua and other Central American regions.[5]

2 [Marx 1984a; pp. 209–11; Marx 1984b, p. 140.]
3 [Marx 1984c, p. 14.]
4 [Marx 1984d, p. 38.]
5 [Marx 1984d, p. 37.]

It is understandable that this tyranny of the South called forth opposition from the North to an ever-growing extent, then led to the formation of the Republican Party and, finally, [Abraham] Lincoln's victory in the presidential campaign of 1860, in which one of the main demands of the Republicans was the limitation of slavery to the territory originally determined by the Constitution. At that moment, when there was no further prospect of transforming new free territories into slave regions, the Union lost its value for the South. The immediate consequences were the South's secession from the Union, the proclamation of independence, finally the opening of the war against the North by the secessionists.

What did this war mean? What the secession called the 'South' comprised three quarters of the previous area of the Union and encompassed – as Marx shows in a detailed analysis of population relations in the individual States – many regions, the so-called border States, in which slavery had not at all or only sporadically existed and where the large majority of the population stood on the side of the Union. In these circumstances, the secession and the war against the North was not a defensive war for the status quo but rather a war of conquest over hitherto free regions, suited for settlement by small farmers, in order to transform them into slave regions. Still more. The secession of the South, once accomplished, would cut off the most fertile agricultural regions of the North from the Atlantic as well as the Pacific Oceans and force them, under the pressure of their economic interests, to join the secessionists too. The secession of the South would thus lead to the *de facto* dissolution of the entire Union and to the reorganisation of its entire area on the basis of slavery and under the control of the Southern oligarchy. It was not difficult to predict that, in this case, the living standard of the white working class of the North would gradually be forced down to the level of the slaves.

Against this state of affairs Marx's formulation of the question centred on the following primary problem:

What was the reason for the constant expansionist efforts of the slave territories? Marx sketches *the economic law of motion of the capitalist slave economy*. It is, to be precise, not simply identical with the slavery of antiquity but is rather built into the capitalist system of profit making in which production is not for one's own consumption but for the world market. Negro slavery in the USA is a product of the capitalist development of North America, especially of the growth of the cultivation of cotton, tobacco, and sugar on plantations.[6] The

6 Until 1660 slavery existed only in fact, but not legally, and was numerically small. By 1715, black slaves already made up one third of the population.

slave trade, which had been legally forbidden since 1808, existed in fact and made great advances precisely in the years immediately before the Civil War.

The slaveholders of the South knew that if the slave economy were to remain limited to its legal borders, that is to the 15 States in which it existed, and if there existed no possibilities for expansion, it would eventually but with unavoidable necessity die out. The cultivation of cotton, tobacco, sugar, etc. on plantations for export was only profitable because of naturally fertile land, cultivated by means of *extensive farming*, i.e. only on the basis of slave labour. After a few years of such extensive farming, the land is exhausted and the States are forced to move from the cultivation of agricultural export goods to the breeding of slaves as export items. Once this point is reached, the recruitment of new territories as export markets, where these slaves could be used in plantation agriculture, was unavoidable. In this manner, for example, Maryland and Virginia rapidly transformed themselves from regions which exported agricultural goods into regions which exported slaves. The economic law of motion of the slave economy is that the steady expansion of its area is the vital condition of its survival. The establishment of new slave States was not simply the basis of the *economic* power of the Southern oligarchy but also, at the same time, of its *political* influence in the Senate and thus its hegemony over the entire Union. Forcing slavery back into the original region determined by the Constitution – the principal programmatic point of Lincoln's Republican Party – would necessarily have led to the extinction of slavery altogether and hence to the breakdown of both the economic and the political hegemony of the Southern oligarchy.

According to Marx's presentation, all struggles between the South and the North revolved exclusively around the slave question! Not only whether the Negroes in the existing slave States should be emancipated, but also whether the 20 million free people of the North should continue to be subjected to the 300,000 slaveholders of the South! It was an unavoidable struggle between two social systems that could no longer peacefully coexist, because the continued existence of the one was only possible by virtue of its victory over the other!

3. The purely military side of Marx's reports, with which Engels assisted and exhibited his expertise as a theoretician of military affairs, can be omitted here. It is interesting, however, that while Engels harboured doubts about the victory of the North, after the initial defeats of the Union armies, Marx, in his evaluation of the situation – with regard to the higher degree of development of the forces of production in the North in general and particularly because of the individual superiority of each individual man – did not for a minute doubt the military superiority of the North.

Marx's views about the political prosecution of the war follow (letters in the *Wiener Presse* of 3 March and 9 August 1862).[7] Military action cannot be separated from political aspects: the military and political prosecution of war are inseparably linked. If this is valid for every war, it is even more the case for civil war. This could only be won through the application of revolutionary methods that annihilated the opponent, not only militarily but also economically and socially, as a class. Instead, the North strove, initially and for a long while, to hold fast to 'legal', constitutional means and, indeed, out of consideration for the 'loyal' slaveholders of the border States who remained true to the North. It did not want to force these elements into the ranks of the secession by abolishing slavery. The indecisive stance of the government also coloured the military course of the war. The border States succeeded in ensuring that the runaway-slave laws would be enforced, which rendered it impossible for Negroes to enter into the ranks of the Northern armies.

On the other hand, the army was also robbed of its revolutionary soul by the indecisive stance of the government. Its movements were for the most part inhibited by the political stance of the officer corps. Many Northern officers were bound to Southern officers by friendship or family ties. Apart from a great defeat, [George B.] McClellan, who was named commander-in-chief as a result of the influence of the Democratic Party, feared nothing so much as a great victory, according to Marx. He did not desire the defeat of the South or the abolition of slavery but envisaged rather the restoration of the Union on the old basis, as it existed before the Civil War.

Only consideration for the slaveholders of the border States prevented Lincoln from using more radical means. He attempted to avoid an open break with the border States and strove at first to move them to abolish slavery voluntarily. It was only the defeats suffered by the Union army and growing pressure from the Abolitionists that contributed to convincing Lincoln of the necessity of using more radical measures. On the other hand, the War itself brought about forceful structural change in the social composition of the border States. With every Northern victory, the most active slaveholders emigrated with their slaves to the South, in order to preserve their assets. In the border States, only the 'moderate' slaveholders remained, which rendered all consideration of them superfluous. This brought about the end of the 'constitutional' phase of the war's conduct, which was in fact replaced by revolutionary measures that sought to shatter the opponent economically and strike its social base. First (June 1862), slavery was abolished in all the 'territories' of the Union. Then the

7 [Marx 1984e; Marx 1984f.]

partial abolition of slavery in the rebel States followed, when the proclamation promising freedom to all Negroes in rebel States, as soon as they fell into the hands of the Republican armies, was issued in September 1862. Finally, emancipated Negroes were permitted to fight in the Union army against the South, in self-contained military units, with weapons in their hands. Through the Confiscation Act of 1862, Congress empowered the President to confiscate the lands and other assets of Confederates.

These revolutionary measures in fact accelerated the outcome of the Civil War. The Union ended the war victoriously. But the principal problem, over whose solution the Civil War was fought, was not solved. Negroes fought for their freedom in Union armies with weapons in their hands. At the end of the Civil War, 200,000 Negroes were active in the Union army. Four million Negroes in the South expected that the government would distribute the land on which they had worked for so long or, at least, sell it to them cheaply. The South could have been developed into a region of small farmers. These hopes were quickly dashed. After the assassination of Lincoln, during the presidency of his successor [Andrew] Johnson, there was a regrouping of class relations, which prevented the realisation of a radical program and imposed reconstruction on the basis of an alliance between the petty bourgeoisie of the North and the oligarchy of the South.

Henryk Grossman (New York)

CHAPTER 22

Review of F. Grandeau, *The Theory of Crises**

Translated from German by Ben Fowkes

Grandeau, F. 1937, *Théorie des crises*, Paris: Éditions A. Pedone (33pp, 10 francs).

The succession of booms and crises is apparent in the succession of rising and falling prices. The removal of these oscillations in prices were removed would remove or alleviate crises. Hence the great significance of speculation ('honourable' speculation, of course). Reducing high prices and raising depressed prices contributes to the alleviation of crises. Speculation is thus the great counterweight to the social inertia of the masses, who have the habit of buying during a boom and selling during a depression, which leads to catastrophic results. The intelligent speculator should buy exactly when the others are selling.

To the author, ordinary language seems too poverty-stricken to express these thoughts. He therefore provides a series of mathematical equations, which give us 33 pages of '*une solution complète*'[1] not only to the problem of crises, but also to the general law of social development derived from the law of supply and demand, which 'clearly shows us where we came from and where we are going'. In addition, he provides an historical and geographical proof from the French Revolution to the present day (if we leave aside a few prophecies). Napoleon I [Bonaparte], for example, came to power during a crisis – in 1805 (!) – and ten years later he lost power owing to another crisis (and not as a result of military defeat, as is commonly assumed). The author demonstrates trivialities of this sort with the help of mathematical equations, thereby forgetting his own correct remark that '*les mathématiques ne sont qu'un langage commode et l'on ne trouve jamais à la fin d'une démonstration que ce qu'on a mis au départ*'.[2]

Henryk Grossman (New York)

---

* [Originally published as Grossmann 1939a.]

1 ['*Une solution complète*' means 'A complete solution'.]

2 ['Mathematics is only a convenient language, and one never finds at the end of a demonstration more than one has put in at the beginning.']

CHAPTER 23

Review of Cleona Lewis, *America's Stake in International Investments**

Translated from German by Ben Fowkes

Lewis, Cleona assisted by K.T. Schotterbeck 1938, *America's Stake in International Investments*, Washington D.C.: Brookings Institution, London: Faber and Faber (710pp, $4, 18s).

The problem of capital export has concerned public opinion more and more over the last two years. The Midland Bank examined the possibilities for international capital investment in its report for May–June 1936.[1] In 1937 the Royal Institute of International Affairs, Oxford, concerned itself with this question in a lengthy report with the title *The Problem of International Investment* (373pp.),[2] as did a publication of the International Chamber of Commerce, *The Function of Foreign Lending* (22pp.) by Oscar R. Hobson.[3] The question has also been dealt with repeatedly in America, for example in the annual report of the Foreign Bondholders Protective Council, which provides exact material on 589 different foreign loans at the end of 1937 – although this is limited to the dollar loans contracted by foreign public debtors.[4] Among private foreign loans only those currently in default are taken into account.

Lewis now gives an exhaustive and careful presentation and critical analysis of all the available factual material relating to capital movements to and from foreign countries for the 160-year period from the American War of Independence to the present day. The book is divided into three parts, the first of which[5] examines America's foreign debts, the second[6] America's foreign investments, while the third part[7] analyses the experience of the USA in its character as a creditor and debtor. Finally, in the Appendix,[8] detailed stat-

* [Originally published as Grossman 1939b.]
1 [*Monthly Review* 1936.]
2 [Royal Institute of International Affairs 1937.]
3 Hobson and Dacey 1937.
4 Foreign Bondholders Protective Council 1938.
5 Lewis 1938, pp. 7–170.
6 Lewis 1938, pp. 173–437.
7 Lewis 1938, pp. 439–509.
8 Lewis 1938, pp. 513–710.

istical tables and estimates and other available materials are laid out. While its balance sheet revealed that the USA was still $3.6 billion in debt in 1914, it developed into a creditor country in the course of the War. Its foreign loans reached a maximum of $8.07 billion in 1929, falling to $7.36 billion by 1935 as a result of the world crisis (the government debts of European countries to the USA amounting to a total of $11.68 billion are, it is true, not included in these figures).

Valuable as the book is in the area of the pure presentation of the *facts*, it fails completely where it is a matter of investigating the economic laws that govern the export of capital. The book is entirely *untheoretical*, although at every step the author stumbles upon facts which call for theoretical consideration. She herself presents a number of examples of the unbearable *oversaturation of capital* that prevails in the USA in the section on the pre-crisis period between 1925 and 1929, which is headed 'The scramble for investment opportunities'. The lack of domestic investment opportunities led the representatives of American banking and financial houses to directly compel foreigners to take out loans. American financial agents forced three million dollars on a small Bavarian town, for whose needs a loan of $125,000 would have been sufficient, while 36 banking houses competed to give a loan to the city of Budapest!

But the author presents these and other facts without drawing any kind of theoretical conclusion. Is it an accident that one nation is a creditor, another a debtor? Or can domestic or foreign investment be regulated arbitrarily, for example from the point of view of the distribution of the risks of investment over as many fields as possible? Does the export of capital perhaps result from the higher interest rate abroad or is the export of capital a necessary phase in the capitalist development of every country, namely at higher levels of capital accumulation, when there are no investment opportunities, or not enough, for the mass of capital that has accumulated domestically?

If the author has done very little to clarify the investment problem for the domestic economy theoretically, she has done just as little along these lines in relation to international outlays of capital. Do unlimited possibilities exist for capital export and are the present difficulties only temporary hindrances connected with the worldwide depression, as the above-mentioned report by Hobson assumes? Or does this demonstrate a barrier which arises from the essence of capitalist accumulation? Cleona Lewis limits herself to establishing empirically that present conditions on the world market for the export of capital from the USA are very different from what they were a century ago, when English capital export was in its infancy. She sees that there will be far fewer profitable investment opportunities in the future. She identifies the reason for this in a series of burdens which all tend to reduce profitability – foreign tariffs, moves towards autarchy, legislation that protects workers, government control of railways and public utilities – instead of regarding all these facts as merely superficial manifestations of a deeper cause, namely the limit of saturation which results from the advancing accumulation of capital.

Henryk Grossman (New York)

CHAPTER 24

Review of Jürgen Kuczynski, *Hunger and Work**

Translated from German by Ben Fowkes

Kuczynski, Jürgen 1938, *Hunger and Work*, New York: International Publishers and London: Lawrence & Wishart (xii + 132pp, $1.50, 3s. 6d).

Although Great Britain is the oldest industrial country and wage statistics were gathered there from an early period, the last few decades have seen an astounding degree of neglect in this area and, in gathering wage statistics, the country has fallen behind not just Canada, the USA and Germany, but also a number of small countries such as Czechoslovakia, etc. The specific method the author utilises is this: he proceeds from the so-called Rowntree minimum income as a basis for comparison and asks how many adult workers (men of 21 and over, and unmarried economically independent women of 18 and over) earn a wage which does not even reach this minimum, which was calculated by [the Joseph] Rowntree [Foundation] in October 1935, on the basis of a detailed budget for living costs, of 53s a week for a married industrial worker, 41s for an agricultural worker, and finally 31s 3d for an independent woman. In order not to be accused of exaggeration, the author mainly uses – along with other sources – the results of the government inquiry of October 1935, adjusted to apply to the year 1937. This inquiry arrived at exaggeratedly high average values, which can be explained by the fact that the government investigation, while it covered all the larger enterprises (employing 10 or more workers) which pay higher wages, only took into account 20 percent of the smaller firms, where pay is lower. On the basis of a detailed analysis of the available data for almost all the major branches of industry as well as for agriculture the author has calculated how many workers either completely fail to reach the Rowntree Minimum of Existence or only attain it by doing overtime or 'in theory', i.e. on the assumption that they are 'fully and normally employed', whereas in fact they fall below the minimum as a result of short-time work.

Here we shall pass over a number of interesting results for specific industries and confine ourselves to the overall results. These establish that, in the oldest industrial country in the world and one of the wealthiest, during the period

* [Originally published as Grossman 1939c.]

of the greatest industrial boom of the postwar epoch, 2 million adult females and 4 million adult males, amounting altogether, if we include wives and children, to roughly 10 million human beings, hence more than one fifth of the total population of Great Britain, had a standard of living below the Rowntree minimum.

In the final part of the work, somewhat too summarily, Kuczynski attempts to give some insight into the development of wages during the seven-year economic cycle from 1931 to 1937. During this period the wages of employed workers rose by 13 percent in money terms, while weekly real wages merely rose by 7 percent up to 1936, but then began to fall owing to the rise in food prices, and in 1937 the improvement in comparison with 1931 merely amounted to 5 percent. This happened during an economic cycle in which dividends and real profits rose by between 200 and 300 percent. The overall income of the working class rose more than the earnings of individual workers, because it was not just money wages that increased. The number of workers employed rose by 21 percent so that the monetary income of the working class as a whole rose by 37 percent, between 1931 and 1937, that is to say from £1,365 million to £1,871 million. Nevertheless, the share of the working class in national income did not grow and, at 36 percent, was exactly the same in 1937 as in 1931. This can be explained by the fact that the number of workers increased not just in absolute terms but also relatively, i.e. the number of workers increased more rapidly than the total population. If one takes this into account, it turns out that while real wages rose by 5 percent, the relative share of the working class in total national income fell by 6–7 percent, that is from a baseline of 100 in 1931 to 94 in 1937, and the employed workers' share fell still more steeply from 100 to 85. This discrepancy is yet more striking in industrial production: production per worker employed rose by 21 percent, while the worker's share in the social product fell from a baseline of 100 in 1931 to 75. The author rightly remarks that this development is not at all peculiar to the last seven years: it can be witnessed throughout the last 150 years.

Henryk Grossman (New York)

CHAPTER 25

Review of L.P. Ayres, *Turning Points in Business Cycles**

Ayres, L.P. 1939, *Turning Points in Business Cycles*, New York: Macmillan (214pp, $2.75).

The author's investigation is deliberately empirical. He does not construct a theory of the business cycle, the assertions and results of which would then be compared with reality, and in which statistics would be merely auxiliary. Instead, he tends to impute to statistics the role of a decisive source of proof. From statistical tables and diagrams covering a period of 109 years, and representing changes of five factors assumed to be characteristic of the course of the cycle (business activity, interest rates, bond and stock prices, capital issues), he attempts to read off a theory of economic crises as one reads off the time from the position of the hands on a clock. By using a purely statistical method, he hopes to find the regulating principle that is responsible for the decisive turning points in the course of the economic process, from depression to prosperity and back to depression. The main inadequacy of the book is clear: it will never be possible to explain a casual *propter hoc* by an empirical *post hoc*.[1] Ayres pursues his program with great faithfulness. In the first seven chapters he gives a graphic presentation of the individual histories of 26 cycles in the period from 1831 to 1939. He does this in order to show, in chapter 8, on that historical basis, the course of a 'typical cycle.' In chapters 10 to 12, he examines and rejects consumers' purchasing power theory, the pump-priming recovery theory, and, finally, the purely monetary theories of the cycle, not because of any theoretical inadequacy, but because they do not agree with the empirical data obtained by him. In direct contrast to this criticism, the author arrives at his main conclusion that the real cause of the long series of crises in the United States has been the specific structure of the monetary mechanism in operation here, particularly the regulation of credit expansion by the bank reserves. Ayres starts with the fact 'that in our highly industrialized economy the cyclical fluctuations in

* [Originally published as Grossman 1939d.]

1 ['*Propter hoc*' means 'before this'; '*post hoc*' means 'after this', i.e. developments cannot be explained simply by what happens after them.]

the production of *durable* goods are much more regular and of greater amplitude than are fluctuations in the production of *non-durable* goods'. But he is unable to trace these fluctuations to non-monetary causes. In the last analysis he derives the fluctuations from the structure of an automatic mechanism which periodically produces the upward and downward movement of bond and stock prices. The expansions and contractions of the flow of new capital in the production of durable capital are a result of sales of new issues, when 'market conditions' have become favourable or unfavourable for floating new issues. This mechanism has broken down in recent years, and ceased to function. It has been replaced by government regulations, on which the course of the cycle now depends.

The novel feature of this study is the detailed and clear description of a typical 'normal' cycle of three and a third years (40 months), of which about 27 months is taken by the upward movement and 13 by the downward movement. Both movements are dissected into more detailed, precise time phases. The author underestimates the whole problem. 'The difficulties', he says, 'involved in locating turning points of business cycles ... are rather matters of the inadequacy of the available statistics than of the complexities of the process'. When the rate of interest is low, the bond and stock markets are high, and there is a 'favourable market' for new issues, new capital is invested in industry, and the volume of production increases. But the primary causes of all these movements are not shown and cannot be shown with the help of purely statistical methods. Moreover, if the intensity and duration of prosperity is solely dependent upon the extent of the increase in capital, as Ayres maintains, how is the 'saturation' of enterprises possible and explainable? How, too, can we explain the fact that the increase in capital is excessive, so that part of it remains 'idle'? The author himself shows that this already happened in the so-called 'rich man's panic' of 1903. It is impossible to educe the true relationships on the basis of monetary theories of crises and with purely descriptive, statistical methods. The favourable or unfavourable market for securities, and the consequent increase and useability of capital are evidently not dependent upon the structure of the monetary mechanism but on the fluctuating prospects of the profitability of industry. But Ayres does not tell us what causes these fluctuations.

Henryk Grossman (New York)

CHAPTER 26

Marx, Classical Political Economy and the Problem of Dynamics*

Translated from German by Rick Kuhn

1

In the dominant view, Marx is merely a student of the classical political economists, someone who completed their work, or their successor.[1] A precisely delineated conception is thus erected: the labour theory of value, developed by Adam Smith and Ricardo, in its innermost essence, leads to socialism. This consequence was not, however, articulated by its founders. Marx was the first to think Ricardo's theory through to its end, as it were, providing its previously unarticulated final word.[2] This conception must certainly already appear to be extremely questionable from the general position of the critique of political economy, if 'the development of political economy and of the opposition to which it gives rise keeps pace with the real development of the social contradictions and class conflicts inherent in capitalist production'.[3]

---

* [Originally published as Grossman 1941a.]

1 Pareto 1902, p. 340; Croce 1914, p. 138; Schumpeter 1954, p. 15; Wilbrandt 1919, p. 101; Engländer 1928, p. 380. 'It was Karl Marx … who, as a value theorist, was indeed the last great figure in the classical school', Douglas 1927, p. 65. The socialists, Franz Mehring, Conrad Schmidt, and above all Rudolf Hilferding, however, are no different. See Mehring 1913b, p. 250; Mehring 1920, p. 557; Schmidt 1889, p. 112. Hilferding not only regarded Marx as an opponent and conqueror of but also as perfecting 'Classical Economy which begins with William Petty and finds its supreme expression in Marx', Hilferding 1981, p. 21. Maurice Dobb does not go beyond this traditional view in his new book. If Marx offered no adequate 'proof' of his theory of value, this was because he was not dealing with a new or unknown theory. 'Marx was adopting a principle', 'The essential difference between Marx and classical political economy lay, therefore, in the theory of surplus value', Dobb 1937, pp. 67–8, 75. [Grossman indicated that the author of Croce's book was Antonio Labriola, who, however, fell into the category of Marxist proponents of the notion that Marx's economics were essentially Ricardian, Labriola 1910, p. 79.]

2 'Smith's formulation of the problems of exchange value and of the distribution of the national product … was such as almost inevitably gave rise to the doctrines of post-Ricardian socialists and to the labour theory of value and the exploitation theory of Karl Marx', Douglas 1927, p. 53. Similarly, Frank H. Knight (Chicago): '[Marx] is certainly the thinker who above all others worked out the classical (Ricardian) theory to its logical conclusions', Knight 1940, p. 105.

3 Marx 1989c, p. 500.

Marx distinguishes four phases in the development of political economy: the first embraces the period of 'classical economics' and the remaining three the various stages of 'vulgar economics'. According to Marx, the identity of the historical situation combines the representatives of classical political economy into one consistent intellectual school, despite their sometimes great individual differences (e.g. between [William] Petty, [David] Hume and the Physiocrats, and between these and Smith or Ricardo).[4] This was the period during which modern capitalism and consequently the modern working class emerged, thus the 'period in which the class struggle' between the proletariat and the bourgeoisie 'was as yet undeveloped'.[5] Classical economics is the expression of rising industrial capitalism, wrestling for power. Its theoretical and practical thrust is not directed against the proletariat, which is still weak, but against the representatives of the old society, the feudal landowners and old-fashioned usurers. The feudal forms of ground rent and 'antediluvian' interest-bearing capital have 'yet to be subordinated to industrial capital and to acquire the dependent position which [they] must assume'.[6]

Ricardo's theory of ground rent, like Hume's critique before it,[7] is directed against feudal landownership. Ricardo's theory of value does, at the same time, articulate the struggle between the capitalist class and the waged proletariat, in theory. But the industrial bourgeoisie and its theory are still 'naive', that is, can afford to engage in the pursuit of truth, without regard for possible dangers and implications, as yet unsuspected and in fact not yet present, which follow from its own principles. So the labour theory of value is developed without fear of emphasising in theory the contradictions between the working class and the propertied class, which can be derived from it,[8] or of highlighting the distinction between productive and unproductive labour. For it was the representatives of the feudal occupations who were particularly ranked into the category of unproductive labour.

Those authors are 'classical', according to Marx, to the extent that they express this front line position; for example John Locke in his polemic against 'unproductive' feudal landownership and ground rent, which according to him 'is in no way different from usury'.[9] This front line position is particularly apparent in their theory of 'productive' and 'unproductive' labour, in which

4 Marx 1989c, p. 275.
5 Marx 1976b, p. 96.
6 Marx 1989c, p. 463. [Editor's interpolation.]
7 Hume 1889, Chapter 4, pp. 320–30; Marx 1994, pp. 390–1.
8 E.g. Adam Smith 1910b, p. 63, where he states that ground rent and profit eat away the wage.
9 [Marx 1994, p. 89, summarising Locke 1924, p. 36.]

the relationship of the rising bourgeoisie to preceding classes and outlooks is entirely clear. This theory starkly contradicts both the perspective of the ancient world, 'when material[ly] productive labour bore the stigma of slavery and was regarded merely as a pedestal for the idle citizen',[10] and that of the social classes and occupations carried over from the feudal period, declared to be unproductive.

The language of classical political economy is, Marx thinks,

> the language of the still revolutionary bourgeoisie which has not yet subjected to itself the whole of society, the state etc. All these illustrious and time-honoured occupations – sovereign, judge, priest, officer etc. – with all the old ideological castes to which they give rise, their men of letters, their teachers and priests, are *from an economic standpoint* put on the same level as the swarm of their [i.e. the bourgeoisie's] own lackeys and jesters maintained by the bourgeoisie and by idle wealth – the landed nobility and idle capitalists ... They live on the produce of other people's industry, therefore they must be reduced to the smallest possible number.[11]

So long as the bourgeoisie has not yet confronted the 'real productive labourers' in conscious, openly hostile antagonism, labourers who 'moreover tell it that it [the bourgeoisie] lives on other people's industry', it can still confront the 'unproductive classes' of the feudal period as 'the representative of productive labour'.[12]

When the bourgeoisie has consolidated its position of social power, in the course of economic development, in part taken possession of the state and in part concluded a compromise with the feudal classes and 'ideological castes' and, in addition, once the proletariat and its theoretical representatives arrive on the scene and draw egalitarian and socialist conclusions from the classical economists' labour theory of value (the right of the working class to the full fruits of its labour), 'things take a new turn'. Political economy 'tries to justify "economically", from its own standpoint, what at an earlier stage it had criticised and fought against'.[13] At this point classical political economy disappears from the historical stage and the hour of vulgar economics ([Thomas] Chalmers, John Ramsay McCulloch, Jean-Baptiste Say and Germain Garnier)

10 Marx 1989b, p. 197. [Editor's interpolation].
11 Marx 1989b, p. 197. [Marx also emphasised '*industry*' and '*other*'.]
12 [Marx 1989b, pp. 32, 197.]
13 Marx 1989b, p. 198.

has struck (the second phase of political economy). The vulgar economics of the 1820s and 1830s, the 'metaphysical period' of political economy,[14] is the expression of the existence of the victorious and now conservative bourgeoisie, which therefore apologetically obfuscated the prevailing order, and whose theoretical representative in England was Malthus. He combatted any tendency in Ricardo's work which was 'revolutionary in relation to the old society'.[15] Like Ricardo, Malthus did indeed wish to have 'bourgeois production' but only so long as 'it is not revolutionary ... but merely creates a broader and more comfortable material basis for the "old society"', a society with which the bourgeoisie had just struck a compromise.[16]

Now the classical theory of the distinction between productive and unproductive labour was abandoned (as in Say and Malthus) – out of fear of the proletarian critique that had already registered its demands – and replaced by the conception that all labour is equally productive. Malthus likewise turned the real meaning of Ricardo's theory of ground rent, aimed against the landowners, into its direct opposite, by introducing capitalism's problem of sales. Malthus does emphasise the inevitability of generalised overproduction, affecting all branches of production. He only does so, however, in order to prove the necessity of unproductive consumers and classes, i.e. 'buyers who are not sellers', so that the sellers can find a market in which they can dispose of what they supply. Hence the necessity of waste (including war).[17] Finally, Ricardo's labour theory of value is now also abandoned. By regarding the wage as a proportion of the total social product (relative wage), Ricardo articulated the class relation which is inherent in the capitalist economy.[18] With the development of the real antagonisms of capitalist production, the embryonic theoretical class antagonism contained in Ricardo's labour theory of value began to polarise. The (theoretical) opposition 'to political economy has [already] come into being in more or less economic, utopian, critical and revolutionary forms.'[19]

Thompson (1824), Percy Ravenstone (1824) and Hodgskin (1825, 1827),[20] the theoretical representatives of the working class in England, draw egali-

14 Marx 1989c, p. 217. Cf. also the postface to the second edition of *Capital*, in which Marx states that 1830 'sounded the knell of scientific bourgeois economics', Marx 1976b, p. 97.

15 Marx 1989c, p. 245.

16 Marx 1989c, p. 244.

17 Marx 1989c, pp. 216–43 [the phrase is italicised by Marx].

18 Marx 1989c, pp. 226–7.

19 Marx 1989c, p. 500.

20 [See Thompson 1824; Ravenstone 1924; Hodgskin 1827 and Hodgskin 1825.]

tarian conclusions and demands from Ricardo's labour theory of value.[21] In the face of such demands, as an 1832 text by Malthus openly admits,[22] the classical labour theory of value was abandoned through successive small changes and transformed into a meaningless theory of costs of production: the specific value-creating role of labour was obliterated. A particular productivity – a creation of value! – was now attributed to land and capital, *per se*,[23] and labour was now only acknowledged as another factor of production, alongside capital and land. In this way Ricardo's conception of the wage as a relation of the working class's share in total production which it has itself created was likewise overturned, justifying capitalists' profits as the result of the 'productivity' of their capital (not of labour). In similar fashion, ground rent was justified as the fruit of the productivity of the land, which meant that antagonism towards landownership which characterised classical theory now lapsed and became meaningless.

The third phase of political economy, the period in the 1830s and 1840s following the July Revolution,[24] was a period of sharpening class antagonisms and cumulative proletarian critique of the prevailing social order in England (John Gray, 1831 and Bray, 1839) and in France (Pecqueur), and also of the first attempts to organise the workers' movement politically: the Saint-Simonians, [Philippe] Buchez, Louis Blanc (*Organisation du travail*, 1839), and Proudhon's struggle against interest-bearing capital.[25] The result is an intensified phase of vulgarisation and transformation of classical economics.[26] The last remnants of the original content of the theory were eradicated: those real contradictions of capital which were still admitted and highlighted by Malthus and Say (Say's disproportionality theory of crisis; Malthus's theory of generalised crisis) are now denied and disappear from economic theory. In Frédéric Bastiat's work (1848) capitalism is transformed into a harmonious system.[27]

---

21 See 'Opposition to the economists (based on the Ricardian theory)', Marx 1989c, pp. 373–449.

22 Marx 1989c, pp. 253–46.

23 ['*Per se*' means 'in themselves'.]

24 [The French revolution of July 1830 overturned the monarchy of the House of Bourbon, which represented the power of landowners and replaced it with the reign of Louis-Philippe of the House of Orléans, who served broader, bourgeois interests, though not those of industrial capital.]

25 [See Gray 1831; Bray 1839; Blanc 1848; Proudhon 1868. The Saint-Simonians followed the teachings of the pioneering French utopian socialist Henri Saint-Simon.]

26 See Marx 1989c, pp. 499–503.

27 [See Bastiat 1873. But perhaps of greater of relevance here is Bastiat 1880.]

The fourth phase of political economy, after 1848, falls into the period during which fully developed class antagonisms became unmistakably visible during the June days in Paris,[28] as the working class first struggled for its own goals. The result was the complete dissolution of the Ricardian school and a departure from all genuine theory. Economic theory was abandoned and replaced by the historical description of phenomena (the older historical school with Wilhelm Roscher at its head).[29] Or economic theory was degraded to a pseudo-theory, as it departed entirely from the terrain of economic reality and took flight to the higher regions of psychology (first attempts at a subjective theory of value by Nassau Senior and Hermann Heinrich Gossen, 1854). This likewise achieved the desired end: the turn away from real class antagonisms and granting equal rank to capital and labour in the creation of value. The theory of costs of production, the equation of labour, land and capital as factors in the creation of value, was unsatisfactory as it represented a trivial circular argument. In attempting to explain the process of the creation of value, the value of products was reduced to the value of the factors jointly acting to produce the product, i.e. value is explained by value. (There is no such circle in Marx's labour theory of value, as it is labour which creates value, but is not itself a value: it is the use value of the commodity labour power). Under the pressure of the left Ricardians' critique, the theory of costs of production had to be abandoned. But, since a return to the labour theory of value was undesirable, a way out was found by transforming economics into psychology. In principle, Senior had already accomplished this change.[30] Basing himself on one of the two interpretations of labour provided by Smith, according to which labour is not seen as an objective expenditure of energy (measured by time) but rather as the subjective effort employed in producing an article, Senior treats labour as a psychological sacrifice. In order for capital to be granted equal status with labour as a parallel factor in the creation of value, it must also be turned into a psychological variable. If the wage is the reward for the effort of labour then the interest on capital is the reward for the subjective sacrifice of saving, the renunciation of immediate consumption of capital.

The 'development' of the individual phases of political economy, as sketched above, imposes the formulation of the following question: can Marx, the theoretician of the proletariat at an advanced stage of capitalist development, take

28 [In June 1848 the French government, brought to power by the revolution in February, brutally suppressed a workers' uprising provoked by its attack on state support for the unemployed.]

29 Marx 1989c, p. 502.

30 Senior 1965.

over and 'complete' the theories and categories of classical economics, in particular those of Ricardo, as the dominant conception maintains, if Ricardo, like classical economics in general, expressed bourgeois interests at a much lower stage of capitalist development, a stage of undeveloped class antagonisms? And the thesis that Marx's original achievement in his 'socialist critique' of capitalism is that he drew socialist conclusions inherent in Ricardo's labour theory of value, in short, that he was a 'Ricardo turned socialist' is just as much to be rejected. As pre-Marxist socialists also offered a socialist critique of capitalism, such a critique cannot be regarded as the specific essence of Marx's theory. But Marx reproaches the egalitarian, left Ricardians for the 'superficiality' of their critique; namely that they base their critique on Ricardo's theory and only attack 'particular results of the capitalist mode of production', instead of its 'manifold presuppositions'. An effective socialist critique could only be based on a specific, new theory and with the assistance of new economic categories.

In his critique, Marx proceeds from the mystifying character of the reified forms of value, that is the fact that relations that people enter into in the process of production appear as relations between objects, things, and that these reified forms conceal true relations between people. Marx therefore speaks of the deceptive appearance of all forms of value. In contrast to transparent, pre-capitalist forms, the relation between exploiter and exploited in the modern capitalist form of value is opaque because in the wage-relation, that is a form of value which regulates the 'exchange' between the wage labourer and the entrepreneur, it appears that the worker's wage fully compensates all his labour and no unpaid labour is performed.[31]

According to classical theory, all exchange transactions correspond strictly to the law of value, i.e. equal labour times always exchange for equal labour times. This principle also applies to the exchange relation between the worker and the entrepreneur. Now, according to Marx, it is quite evident that there is no exchange of equivalents between worker and entrepreneur. If workers were to receive as much in wages (measured in labour) from entrepreneurs as they give in labour then profit, surplus accruing to entrepreneurs, and hence also the capitalist economy, which is based on this profit, would be impossible.[32] Since both profit and capitalism do, however, exist, no exchange of equivalents can take place. Marx's entire effort is directed at showing that the transaction between capitalist and worker is as much an exchange of nonequivalents as

31 'On the surface of bourgeois society the worker's wage appears as the price of labour', Marx 1976b, p. 675.

32 Marx 1976b, p. 676.

of equivalents, depending on whether this transaction is regarded within the sphere of circulation (on the market) or during the process of production. The exchange of equivalents between worker and capitalist on the market is merely an appearance arising from the form of exchange. Despite the alleged exchange of equivalents,

> the laws based on the production of commodities ... become changed into their direct opposite ... The relation of exchange between capitalist and worker becomes a mere semblance belonging only to the process of circulation, it becomes a mere form, which is alien to the content of the transaction itself, and merely mystifies it. The constant sale and purchase of labour power is the form; the content is the constant appropriation by the capitalist, without equivalent, of a portion of the labour of others, which has already been objectified, and his repeated exchange of this labour for a greater quantity of the living labour of others.[33]

Marx regards it as one of Smith's great merits that he at least sensed that the exchange between capital and wage labour is a flaw in the law of value. Although Smith could not clarify it, he could see 'that in the actual result the law is suspended'.[34] According to Marx, it is precisely the form of exchange value which mystifies the real content. 'The wage form thus extinguishes every trace of the division of the working day into necessary labour and surplus labour, into paid labour and unpaid labour.'[35] Just as the wage form does, so too all the other forms of value that emerge in the process of exchange mystify.[36] The reified forms of value (exchange value, ground rent, profit, interest, wages and prices, etc.) conceal and invert the real relations between people, by making them appear as the 'fantastic form of a relation between things', 'a social hieroglyphic', 'something dark and mysterious'.[37]

Classical economics did seek to dissolve the mystifying categories of value into 'labour' and thought that in doing so it grasped the essence behind the deceptive appearance of phenomena. Marx wants to demonstrate that this attempted solution leads to contradictions which could not be overcome on the basis of classical political economy. Any glance back at earlier economic epochs shows that mystifying forms of value first arose in the period of com-

33 Marx 1976b, pp. 729–30.
34 Marx 1988a, p. 393.
35 Marx 1976b, p. 680.
36 Marx 1976b, pp. 169, 173–4; Marx 1987a, p. 289.
37 Marx 1976b, pp. 165, 167; Marx 1978b, pp. 430–1; Marx 1989c, p. 451.

modity production and exchange.[38] Resolving these forms of value into 'labour' turns their mystifying character into an eternal feature of all social processes, as 'labour' itself is definitely a 'nature-imposed necessity' of human existence.[39] Experience contradicts this view, however, and this contradiction is insoluble, from the standpoint of the classical economists.

For Marx, who wants to grasp the 'concrete' in thought, the mystifying categories of value cannot simply be eliminated or ignored, to be replaced by other 'true' categories. Even though the phenomena of exchange value are mystifying, they are still an important component of reality. The point is not to eliminate one mystifying factor and substitute another but rather to demonstrate the necessary connection between the two and to explain what is deceptive in the phenomena of value. Because capitalism has a dual reality, mystifying and non-mystifying sides, and binds them together in a concrete unity, any theory which reflects this reality must likewise be a unity of opposites.

It has become almost banal to assert that Marx taught that monetary processes should not be regarded as the primary elements in economic events, but only as their characteristic reflexive determinations, and that real processes should be sought behind the veil of money, on the side of commodities, within the process of production. The acknowledged polar opposition between commodity and money is repeated within the world of commodities itself as the opposition between the commodity's value and its use value. For it is not the metallic existence of money which is deceptive, but rather its character as value.[40] Marx sarcastically criticises the 'crude … vision' of political economy, which only perceives what is misleading in exchange value in its 'developed shape' *as money*, but not in its preexisting form of the *values of commodities*, to the extent that they appear as mutual equivalents for each other.[41] It is precisely this equivalent form which Marx sees as a puzzle: the 'internal opposition between use value and value' within the individual commodity becomes visible in the 'external opposition' of two commodities, in which one counts 'only as a use value' and the other commodity – money – 'only as exchange value'.[42]

The illusion is not due merely to the money form but to the value form in general. Consequently, real economic processes have to be sought not only behind the veil of money but behind the veil of value in general.

38 Marx 1976b, pp. 153–4.
39 Marx 1976b, p. 175.
40 Marx 1975a, pp. 213–14.
41 Marx 1976b, pp. 147–9.
42 Marx 1976b, p. 153.

2

In the section of first volume of *Capital* dealing with 'The fetishism of the commodity and its secret',[43] Marx attempts to penetrate the mystification involved in the exchange value form. Two different, [though] in their basic notion analogous, methods serve this end. The first is the method of historical comparison between the period of commodity production and earlier periods when there was no production or exchange of commodities and consequently no exchange value. In these periods there was, therefore, no mystification: personal relations of dependence appeared in unconcealed form and were not veiled by the process of exchange.[44] In order to illustrate this, Marx presents three different types of economy that do not produce commodities: Robinson Crusoe, medieval feudal lords with their serfs who perform compulsory labour and finally the patriarchal peasant family. In all these cases producers create useful objects for the satisfaction of their own needs. As there are no exchange values, 'All the relations between Robinson and these objects that form his self-created wealth are … simple and transparent'.[45] What is mysterious and mystifying about the production of commodities evidently does not derive from the use value side of commodities but is instead connected only with the process of exchange and exchange value.[46]

Marx arrives at the same result by the method of comparing various sides of commodity production itself, value side with use value side, the process of valorisation with the labour process. In short, the means of seeing through the mystifying character of the categories of exchange value is, in fact, use values! The use values of earlier historical periods are just as much the result of human labour as the products of the epoch of commodity production. But only in this contemporary period do products assume a mystifying character. The same source – labour – cannot yield such totally different results. It is not sufficient to say that commodities are the products of 'labour', as such, just as those of earlier economic epochs were. Instead, it is necessary to distinguish two different moments[47] of labour, its 'dual character'. First, labour which

43 Marx 1976b, pp. 163–77.

44 Marx 1976b, p. 169.

45 Marx 1976b, p. 170.

46 'The whole mystery of commodities, all the magic and necromancy that surrounds the products of labour on the basis of commodity production, vanishes therefore as soon as we come to other forms of production', Marx 1976b, p. 169.

47 ['Moment' is a Hegelian term, here with the sense of 'aspect'.]

is 'concrete', 'useful', creating not value but rather objects of use; the labour of the joiner, tailor, weaver, which functions in the technical labour process and as 'productive activity appropriate to its purpose' of the appropriation of the natural world, is a nature-imposed necessity for all social formations.[48] Secondly, general human labour 'that creates exchange value',[49] functioning in the process of valorisation, the moment of labour which only appears in one particular social formation (of commercial interaction). Only with the arrival of exchange value does the object of use become a commodity.[50] It is evident that only this second side of labour, the characteristic that it 'creates exchange value', is the origin of all that is mystifying and fetishistic. The reduction of the forms of value to 'labour' pure and simple, as carried out in classical economics, is false because labour as such is an unreal abstraction, a 'mere spectre'.[51]

In this way Marx arrived at the differentiation of the 'double character' of the labour represented in commodities, which in his own eyes constituted what was 'fundamentally new' in his theory.[52] With a pride which he seldom expressed, Marx emphasises the importance of his discovery: the examination of the twofold character of labour was the 'point ... crucial to an understanding of political economy'.[53] He saw in this element a decisive break between his conception and that of all his predecessors. And in fact, from the new standpoint of a two-dimensional conception of economic processes, he repeatedly criticises the classical political economists in principle, reproaching them for their one-dimensional theory, exclusively concerned with value. Time and again he raises the objection that classical political economists and their successors did not distinguish the dual character of labour. '[C]lassical political economy in fact nowhere distinguishes explicitly and with a clear awareness between labour as it appears in the value of a product, and the same labour as it appears in the product's use value.'[54] And then Marx makes this general objection more precise in specific criticisms of William Petty, Adam Smith, Ricardo

48 Marx 1976b, pp. 133, 174–5, 176, 179.

49 [Marx uses the phrase 'labour that creates exchange value' in Marx 1987a, p. 271.]

50 Marx 1976b, p. 153.

51 Marx 1981b, p. 954.

52 Marx 1987b, p. 514.

53 Marx 1976b, p. 132. Marx himself, in other places in his work and letters, also repeatedly identified precisely this theory as his original contribution to the understanding of economic events, the 'fundamentally new' element of his achievement. For example, in 1859, in Marx 1987a and, in 1867, in Marx 1976b.

54 Marx 1976b, p. 173. Similarly, Marx 1976b, p. 313 and frequently elsewhere.

and Hodgskin.[55] This alone is sufficient to show that we find ourselves here at the real centre of Marx's innovation in comparison with the classical political economists. The great significance of the new conception is that Marx found in it a means of eliminating what was deceptive in the pure categories of exchange value and thus created a foundation for his further research into capitalist production, which gave him the possibility of grasping the true interconnections of this production, behind the veil of value.

3

The results of our analysis are particularly confirmed by those statements by Marx in which he deals with his relationship with the classical political economists and indicates the place he claims for himself in the development of political economy.

Such statements in *Capital* as well as *A Contribution to the Critique of Political Economy* reveal that Marx regarded classical political economy as fundamentally concluded, completed by Ricardo because, in Ricardo, 'political economy ruthlessly draws its final conclusion and therewith ends'.[56] Marx judged John Stuart Mill's attempts to develop classical political economy beyond this limit and to accommodate the principles of classical theory to the demands of the working class as a 'shallow syncretism' and 'a declaration of bankruptcy by "bourgeois" economics'.[57] So, did Marx himself yet again complete what already had been completed and 'further develop' what had already been concluded? According to Marx's own conception, he stands in starkest opposition to clas-

55 Against Petty: 'Labour as the source of exchange value is confused with labour as the source of use value', Marx 1994, p. 248.

Against Adam Smith: 'He does not distinguish the twofold character of labour itself: labour that creates value, by the expenditure of labour power, and labour that creates objects of use (use values), as concrete useful labour', Marx 1978b, p. 453, similarly p. 460.

Against Ricardo: 'What Ricardo does not investigate is the specific form in which labour manifests itself as the common element of commodities ... Ricardo does not sufficiently differentiate between labour in so far as it is represented in use values or in exchange value', Marx 1989c, p. 325 [Marx emphasised '*specific*']. Similarly Marx 1976b, pp. 174 and 313.

Against Hodgskin: 'In his investigations into the productivity of capital, Hodgskin is remiss in that he does not distinguish between how far it is a question of producing use values or exchange values', Marx 1989c, p. 401. Also see Koepp 1911, pp. 32, 34, 39.

56 Marx 1987a, p. 301. He expresses himself similarly in the postface to the second edition of *Capital*, Marx 1976b, p. 96.

57 Marx 1976b, p. 98.

sical theory and not only as regards its specific theories (such as its theories of wages, ground rent, crises, etc.) but also to the very theoretical foundation of economics. He does not aim, therefore, 'to develop classical theory further' but rather to undertake a 'scientific attempt to revolutionise a science'.[58]

He expressed himself quite clearly about the nature of this 'revolutionising': after first developing the dual character of the commodity in the first chapter of the *Contribution*, in the section 'Historical notes on the analysis of commodities', he provides a characterisation of his theoretical position and its relation to those of his predecessors.

> The decisive outcome of the research carried on for over a century and a half by classical political economy, beginning with William Petty in Britain and Boisguillebert in France, and ending with Ricardo in Britain and Sismondi in France, is an analysis of the aspects of the commodity into two forms of labour – use value is reduced to concrete labour or purposive productive activity, exchange value to labour time or homogeneous social labour.[59]

The issue is therefore one of a contrast between two conceptions, one of which (the English) took exchange value as its main object, the other (the French) use value. That is, each only grasped one side of reality. Marx's actual theoretical position only emerges in sharp profile when it is seen from the perspective of this historical background. Only then is it understandable why Marx identified the discovery of the dual form of labour as the 'decisive discovery of the research carried on for over a century and a half by classical political economy'. Marx's theory of the dual character of labour is the critical synthesis and only as such a further development of both conceptions.

The following analysis is intended to show that Marx fundamentally transformed the most important categories inherited from classical economics based on the new viewpoint which he had elaborated. In Marx's work they all obtain a value and a material side.

The *commodity* is a dual entity, a unity of exchange value and use value. This is because its source, *labour*, has a twofold character, which of necessity reveals itself not only in the commodity, but in all the products of labour. The commodity is the unity of exchange value and use value.[60] The *capitalist production process* is the unity of the technical labour process and the valorisation

58 Marx 1985a, p. 436 [Marx emphasised '*scientific*'].

59 Marx 1987a, p. 292.

60 Marx 1976b, pp. 125–7.

process.[61] While the means of production, raw and auxiliary materials are transformed by human activity into material products, use values, during the labour process, the valorisation process is the site of the creation of new values, whose excess over the values used in production results in surplus value and its derivatives (industrial profit, ground rent, gains made through trade, interest, etc.). This dual character is also apparent in the *management of the capitalist production process*, the necessity of which results from the division of labour, the increasing scope of the means of production employed and the necessity of controlling their proper use.[62] On the one hand, the management function is necessary in any economic system, insofar as it arises from a social labour process with a division of labour, like the function of an orchestra conductor. On the other hand, under the capitalist mode of production the capitalist exercises the management function by virtue of ownership of capital; it is 'made necessary by the capitalist and therefore antagonistic nature of that process'.[63] The process of reproduction of total social capital is also 'not only a replacement of values, but a replacement of materials, and is therefore conditioned not just by the mutual relations of the value components of the social product but equally by their use values, their material shape'.[64] The *category of wages* has the same dual character. On the labour market, the worker does not sell 'labour', that is the activity, since labour does not take place on the market, but rather the commodity 'labour power', the capacity to labour. For this the worker receives as counter-value, as the wage, an exchange value (as in the sale of any other commodity). Only later in the labour process, thus outside the market, does this labour power become an activity, that is when it is used by the entrepreneur.[65] Surplus value is obtained precisely from this use value of labour. By splitting the classical category of (wage-) labour in this way into its use and exchange value sides, the contradictions in which the classical economists entangled themselves could be avoided.

The category of *capital* also has a dual character. The classical political economists already made the distinction between fixed and circulating capital. Marx took this distinction over, but gave it an entirely different meaning, in which, yet again, the difference between the value and use value sides of fixed capital became decisive. The difference between fixed and circulating [capital] in the sphere of circulation employed by the classical economists is meaning-

61 Marx 1976b, pp. 283, 304, 425.
62 Marx 1976b, p. 449.
63 Marx 1976b, p. 450.
64 Marx 1978b, p. 470.
65 Marx 1976b, p. 292.

less. It is only valid for productive capital, i.e. in the sphere of production, in the labour process.[66] As money or as a commodity, capital is neither fixed nor circulating.[67] The material bases of fixed and circulating components give rise to the distinct characteristics of the useful forms, in which they function as factors in the labour process.[68] Circulating capital is used up in a single working period, while fixed capital functions in a series of 'repeated labour processes', due to the durability of its natural form. The result of this difference in the duration of the lives of different capitals, i.e. the time aspect, is the completely different manner in which fixed capital is replaced, on one hand as value and on the other as use value, *in natura*.[69] Marx derived the necessity of periodic crises already under simple reproduction, from this difference in the mode of replacement.[70]

The category of the *organic composition of capital* changes in a similar way. Ricardo already made the distinction between capital-intensive and labour-intensive spheres of production, which was important for his theory of profit. But he conceived of it purely in terms of value. Marx split Ricardo's category into its use value and exchange value sides, in order to reunite them in a synthesis.[71] The category of organic composition, transformed in this way, takes on a completely different function, not only for the explanation of profit, as in Ricardo's work, but also as the 'most important factor' in the accumulation of capital.[72]

Finally, the same dual aspect is apparent in the category which occupies the central place in Marx's system: the *falling average rate of profit*, the 'driving force in capitalist production'.[73] Repeatedly in *Capital*, 'the internal opposition

66 Marx 1978b, pp. 246–7, 269–70, 282, 288–9.

67 Marx 1978b, pp. 270, 278.

68 Marx 1978b, pp. 237, 241, 246.

69 Marx 1978b, pp. 237, 298, 246, 302. ['*In natura*' means 'in its natural form'.]

70 Cf. 'Replacement of the fixed capital' (a) in the money form, (b) in kind, Marx 1978b, pp. 528–45.

71 'The composition of capital is to be understood in a twofold sense. As value ... [and a]s material, as it functions in the process of production ... I call the former the *value* composition, the latter the *technical* composition of capital'. The mutual relation between the two is called the *organic* composition, which is apparent in the *value* composition, 'in so far as it is determined by its technical composition and mirrors the changes in the latter', Marx 1976b, p. 762. Similarly Marx 1981b, pp. 244–5, 254, 264; and Marx 1989b, p. 493.

72 Marx 1976b, p. 762. The importance of the distinction between the technical and value composition of capital is already apparent in Marx's creation of entirely different terminological designations for them: the technical composition in its material form is expressed symbolically as MP:L (the relation of the means of production to labour) and the value-composition as c:v (the relation of constant to variable capital).

73 Marx 1981b, p. 368.

between use value and value, hidden within the commodity' is emphasised, and the development and growth of this contradiction as capitalist production develops is explained.[74] The nature of the opposition between use value and value in the commodity and why it constantly assumes ever greater dimensions was never previously treated as a problem. Now, when seen in connection with the presentation of the development of the productive power of labour in the first volume,[75] the presentation of the tendency of the rate of profit to fall in the third volume of *Capital*[76] shows that Marx also derives this category from the dual character of labour, namely the inverse movement of the mass of use values and values as a consequence of the increase in labour's productive power. The richer a society, the greater the development of labour's productive power, the larger the volume of useful things which can be made in a given labour time. At the same time, however, the value of these things becomes smaller. As with the development of labour's productive power, an ever growing mass of means of production (MP) is set in motion by a relatively ever falling mass of labour (L), the unpaid part of the labour (surplus value or profit) must also progressively fall [relatively]. In capitalist terms, growing social wealth is expressed in the tendency for the [the rate of] profit of a given capital to decline. The decline in [the rate of] profit, the factor that regulates and drives the capitalist mechanism, also calls the continued existence of this mechanism into question.[77]

74 Marx 1976b, pp. 153, 181, 198, 209; Marx 1989c, pp. 247–8.

75 Marx 1976b, pp. 136–7.

76 Marx 1981b, pp. 318–19.

77 For a more precise justification for this deduction it is noted that, with the development of the productive power of labour by which 'we always mean the productivity of concrete useful labour', the same labour produces a growing mass of useful goods, of material wealth. The rising mass of useful things can, however, correspond with a fall in the value of each thing and even of their total value. 'This contradictory movement arises out of the twofold character of labour', Marx 1976b, p. 137. Now, it is an empirical law of the capitalist mode of production that its development is accompanied by a relative decline in variable in relation to constant capital. 'This simply means that the same number of workers ... sets in motion, works up, and productively consumes, within the same period, an ever-growing mass of means of labour, machinery and fixed capital of all kinds, and raw and ancillary materials', Marx 1981b, p. 318. 'It is just another expression for the progressive development of the social productivity of labour', Marx 1981b, p. 318. Looked at in terms of use value, constantly growing masses of useful things arise, which, however, represent ever smaller amounts of value. 'Since the mass of living labour applied continuously declines in relation to the mass of objectified labour ... the part of this living labour that is unpaid ... must also stand in an ever-decreasing ratio to the value of the total capital applied', Marx 1981b, p. 319. In short, 'The progressive tendency for the general rate of profit to fall is thus simply the expression, peculiar to the capitalist mode of

The greater the mass of use values, the more pronounced the tendency for the rate of profit to fall (in value terms).

In its interpretation of Marxist economics the dominant theory has, however, expunged the entire theory of the dual character of labour indicated above, i.e. precisely what is specific to Marxism and what distinguishes it from classical political economy, in order, subsequently, to incorporate it into classical theory's lines of thought. That this 'incorporation' was no mere accident is apparent when Benedetto Croce virtually credits it as one of the merits of the dominant theory.[78] In showing the untenability of classical theory, the intention is to demonstrate *eo ipso* the invalidity of Marx's theory.[79]

4

From its origins, theoretical political economy was a theory of abstract exchange value: where it did concern itself with production it dealt solely with the value side, passing over the labour process.[80] Since the rise of marginal utility theory and the mathematical school, the analysis of the concrete production process was increasingly excluded as a component of theory, only considered in establishing its preconditions and overall framework. Analysis was concentrated almost exclusively on relations between given market variables. It therefore had a static character and was unable to explain dynamic structural changes in the economy. Marx's economic theory deviates in principle from both of these tendencies.

---

production, of the progressive development of the social productivity of labour', Marx 1981b, p. 319 [Marx emphasised '*the expression, peculiar to the capitalist mode of production*'.]

78 'It has even been possible to unite with the body of admitted economic doctrines those of Marx, which seemed revolutionary, for these are only definitions of a particular casuistry …', Croce 1913, p. 379.

79 In a book commemorating the 150th anniversary of the publication of *The Wealth of Nations*, Paul H. Douglas endeavours to show that 'the contribution of Adam Smith to the theory of value … [was] not great', which necessarily led to the failure not only of classical but also of Marx's theory. But 'the failure was not the failure of one man, but of a philosophy of value, and the roots of the ultimate contradiction made manifest to the world in the third volume of *Das Kapital* lie embedded in the first volume of the Wealth of Nations', Douglas 1927, p. 69. ['*Eo ipso*' means 'thereby'.]

80 'The pivots of any theory of the economic process are their teachings about value and interest … and four fifths of theoretical economic literature consists of research into or controversies about these subjects', Schumpeter 1925, p. 67.

The capitalist mode of production is governed by the relation: exchange value—increase in exchange value, (M–M′).[81] As a faithful expression of the bourgeois economic system, classical theory was always only a theory of abstract exchange value.[82] Adam Smith does begin his work *The Wealth of Nations* by emphasising the division of labour as the source of wealth. A people's wealth consists of an abundant supply of the results of labour, useful things. In the subsequent course of his work, however, he forgets use values; they are not used any further in the economic analysis.[83] Certainly, there are also presentations of material and structural relations. They have, however, an exclusively descriptive character. His theory is one of abstract exchange value. The social equilibrium between supply and demand, which yields the 'natural price', is an exclusively value equilibrium.[84] The same applies to Ricardo. Chapter 20 of his *Principles*,[85] where he elaborates the distinction between use value and value, and the importance of 'wealth', of use values, remains an alien body in the book. Ricardo's entire ingenuity is concentrated on value terms (profit) and the use value side of commodities plays no role in his analysis. The life of the working class depends on the mass of use values which can be bought with a capital. The entrepreneur, meanwhile, is only interested in exchange value, the expansion of exchange value, i.e. profit. Ricardo expressed this in the now famous dictum that for the employer who annually makes £2,000 profit on a capital of £20,000 – 10 percent – 'it would be a matter quite indifferent whether his capital would employ a hundred or a thousand men ... provided, in all cases, his profits were not diminished below £2,000'.[86] Whether a given capital employs 100 or 1,000 workers depends on the specific economic structure. Ricardo is indifferent to this. Marx emphasises that Ricardo is only concerned with net revenue (pure profit), with the excess, in value terms, of price over costs, not with gross revenue, i.e. the mass of use values necessary for the maintenance of the working nation. For Ricardo these are considered only as costs, to be pushed down as low as possible. Marx says: 'By denying the importance of gross

81 [Where M is the value represented by money capital laid out at the start of the circuit of capital; M′ is the expanded value of represented by money generated at the end of the circuit.]

82 Marx consequently speaks of the 'accentuation of quantity and exchange value' by the classical economists, in the 'most striking contrast' to 'the writers of classical antiquity' (Plato, Xenophon), 'who are exclusively concerned with quality and use value', Marx 1976b, p. 486.

83 Cf. Elster 1933, p. 213. Further, Bousquet 1927, p. 199; and Myrdal 1953, p. 61.

84 Elster 1933.

85 [Ricardo 1912, pp. 182–91.]

86 Ricardo 1912, pp. 234–5.

revenue, i.e. the volume of production and consumption apart from the value-surplus – and hence denying the importance of life itself – political economy's abstraction reaches the peak of infamy'.[87]

Ricardo's central interest is the theory of distribution: 'To determine the laws which regulate ... distribution is the principal problem in Political Economy.'[88] In a letter to Malthus he calls political economy a theory of laws which govern the proportional division of a given wealth among the various social classes. He regarded the determination of the mathematical relation between the parts of this given totality as 'the only true object of the sciences'.[89] This point of departure renders Ricardo's method aprioristic and deductive: his theories can be derived from a very small number of premises. Classical theory is more a system of logical deductions than research into and presentation of the objective economic relations of the capitalist mode of production.

In post-classical economics this tendency to avoid the real labour process becomes even more pronounced. In itself the principle of labour [as the source of] value contains a revolutionary element. It indicates, as the classical political economists themselves stated, that workers do not receive the full product of their labour under the prevailing social order, and that rent and profits on capital represent deductions [from it]. The egalitarian Ricardians in England merely drew the conclusion implicit in the classical labour theory of value when they explained that a social situation in which workers received the full product of their labour is, fundamentally, the only proper and 'natural' one.[90]

The reaction of right-wing students of Ricardo to this theoretical turn of the left Ricardians was to become ever more conservative. They scented a threat to class peace in Ricardo's theory of value.[91] Any analysis of the production

87 Marx 1981a, p. 421 [Marx emphasised 'infamy']

88 Ricardo 1912, p. 1.

89 'Political economy you think is an inquiry into the nature and causes of wealth; I think it should rather be called an inquiry into the laws which determine the division of the produce of industry amongst the classes who concur in its formation. No law can be laid down respecting quantity, but a tolerably correct one can be laid down respecting proportions', Ricardo 1887, p. 175.

90 See, in particular, the sharp formulation of workers' rights to the full product of labour in Hodgskin 1825.

91 See, for example, Charles Knight's book, which scathingly attacks all opponents of the prevailing rights of property, including Hodgskin, and characterises them as 'ignorant of mankind', 'destroyers' and 'ministers of desolation', Knight 1832, pp. 210, 212. Somewhat later, Carey formulated this view most clearly: 'Ricardo's system is one of discords ... its whole tends to the production of hostility among classes ... His book is the true manual of the demagogue, who seeks power by means of agrarianism, war and plunder', Carey 1848, pp. 74–5.

and labour processes was avoided, in order to avoid the awkward question of the labour theory of value and its dangerous implications for distribution and the prevailing social order. Analysis was restricted to market phenomena, exchange: 'Exchange', says Bastiat, 'is political economy'.[92] According to Léon Walras, the founder of the Lausanne school, political economy is '*la théorie de la valeur d'échange et de l'échange; au contraire il* [Walras] *nous interdit d'étudier objectivement la production et la répartition*'.[93]

For fear of ending up in opposition to prevailing propertied interests, every effort was made to give economic theory the most abstract and formal shape possible, abandoning any qualitative-concrete content.[94] In short, efforts were made to erect a theory of distribution based on a theory of markets, in order to furnish proof, by means of a theory of allocation, that all factors of production are rewarded in proportion to their contribution to the product and that, consequently, workers receive in wages full compensation for their labour.[95]

A second line of development also begins to become apparent just as early. Out of the same need to flee from reality, it pushes economic theory onto another terrain, that of psychology. This begins with Jean-Baptiste Say, who starts with the use values of commodities, understanding them not as physical phenomena but rather as psychological variables, the subjective utilities

---

92 [Bastiat 1880, p. 97.] Cf. Bousquet 1927, p. 226.

93 ['The theory of exchange of value and of exchange; on the contrary, he [Walras] forbade us to study production and distribution objectively'], Bousquet 1927, p. 208. Walras's analysis is in fact confined to exchange relations. He disposes of the entire 'production process' with one word. The production process is replaced by a symbol, the concept of 'coefficients of production', which means those quantities of productive goods used in the manufacture of one unit of output. In this purely formal manner, each unit of production is then allotted a corresponding 'production coefficient' and the 'production process' is thus disposed of.

94 August Walras makes this quite clear in a letter to his son Léon, on 6 February 1859: '*Une chose qui me plaît parfaitement dans le plan de ton travail, c'est le projet que tu as et que j'approuve de tous points, de te maintenir dans les limites les plus inoffensives á l'égard de MM. les propriétaires. Cela est très sage et très facile á observer. Il faut faire de l'économie politique comme on ferait de l'accoustique ou de la mécanique*' ['One thing which I find especially pleasing in the plan for your work is the project you have, of which I totally approve, to stay within the least offensive limits as regards property owners. This is very wise and very easy to observe. It is necessary to do political economy as one would do acoustics or mechanics'], see Leroy 1923, p. 289.

95 John Bates Clark constantly tried to prove the proposition that the formation of prices under free competition allocates to individual each exactly in accordance with his productive efforts. '[N]atural law, so far as it has its way, excludes all spoliation.' In a polemic against von Thünen he affirms that 'the natural law of wages gives a result ... [that is] morally justifiable.' Clark 1927, p. 324.

of the objects, and who constructed a subjective theory of value on [the basis of] this 'service'. From Say, through Senior (1836) in England, [Jules] Dupuit (1844) in France and Hermann Heinrich Gossen (1854) in Germany,[96] the subjective theory of value led on to the theory of marginal utility as a theory of general hedonism. In the process, political economy's object of inquiry shifted from the realm of things and social relations onto the terrain of subjective feelings. 'Böhm-Bawerk's analysis of subjective value is the purest and most rationalistic hedonism', as Böhm-Bawerk's tenth supplementary discussion 'On the "measurability" of sensations' particularly shows.[97] The process of production is passed over.[98] Analysis is confined to market phenomena, the explanation of which is sought in human nature.

An even higher level of abstraction is represented by those attempts to make economics into a mathematically 'exact' science that consequently disregard any qualitative content in economic phenomena. Market phenomena are one-sidedly regarded as mere 'economic quantities' and, where possible, are expressed in mathematical equations. This tendency in modern theory is, perhaps, formulated most clearly by Joseph Schumpeter.[99] The process of production, like all objective economic relations, lies outside the analysis. According to Schumpeter, the essence of economic relations rests on a relation 'between economic quantities', which is indeed reduced to the relation of exchange; all other relations among economic quantities are neglected as inessential.

96 [See Senior, 1965; Depuit 1969; Gossen 1983.]

97 Cf. Myrdal 1953, p. 98. Cf. Böhm-Bawerk 1959c.

98 One could easily respond that, on the contrary, there are the well-known sections on 'The capitalist production process' and 'Roundabout methods of production' in Böhm-Bawerk 1959b, pp. 79–88, 89–94. It would be self-deception, however, to anticipate that Böhm-Bawerk really does describe the capitalist production process. All that is learnt are general concepts which do not seek to grasp the specific features of the period of capitalist production but which are instead intended to apply, in their abstract universality, to all periods. Thus, for example, the statement that objects of use can be made in two ways: directly, such as picking wild fruit from a high tree; or indirectly, by first cutting a stick from another tree and then knocking the fruit down, Böhm-Bawerk 1959b, p. 82. The creation of such an 'intermediary product', a tool, is the creation of 'capital' and hence the conduct of 'capitalist production', which for Böhm-Bawerk is identical with any form of indirect production. This confusion rests on a trivial confusion of the technical labour process with the valorisation process, so that, for Böhm-Bawerk, every tool is already 'capital'. Hence the wild Indian or Zulu who uses a boat to catch fish is a capitalist and carries on 'capitalist production', Böhm-Bawerk 1959c, p. 81. According to Böhm-Bawerk's terminology, capitalist production was already present at the most primitive level of culture.

99 Schumpeter 1908, pp. 50 et seq.

Summarising, it can be said that although theoretical schools and tendencies have changed a great deal over the entire century since classical economics, they possess the common trait that the real labour process and the social relations entered into during its course are excluded from their theoretical analyses.[100]

Marx's critique is directed against political economy's abstract value approach, as was the contrasting critique made by the older historical school. The latter sought, however, to overcome the abstract 'absolute' character of classical theoretical deduction by means of superficially and indiscriminately drawing on concrete historical or statistical material about production, consumption, trade, tax, the conditions of workers or peasants etc. It remained purely descriptive, denying, in effect, the possibility of knowing theoretical laws. But Marx set himself the task of 'revealing the economic law of motion of modern society'.[101] This cannot be done, however, by abstracting from the 'real world' and merely clinging to its aspect as 'economic quantities'. Such a procedure is not political economy but the 'metaphysics of political economy', which the more it detaches itself from real objects by way of abstraction, 'the more [it] imagine[s] [itself] to be getting all the nearer to the point of penetrating to their core'.[102] As reality does not merely consist of values but is rather the unity of values and use values, Marx's critique begins from the twofold character of economic phenomena, according to which the essential character of the bourgeois economic system is given by the specific connection of the valorisation process to the technical labour process. Of course, subjectively, the entrepreneur is only interested in the value side, in the valorisation process of his capital, in profit. But he can only realise his desire for profit through the technical labour process, by making products, use values. And the capitalist period impresses its specific stamp on precisely the specific character of this labour process: from being a means of satisfying needs it becomes an instrument of the valorisation process.[103] Marx accuses previous economic theory of only looking at individual, isolated sectors, instead of grasping the concrete totality of economic relations.

100 With the possible exception of the [younger] historical school in Germany dominated by Schmoller, which, however, because of its descriptive and eclectic character and rejection of theory can be passed over here.

101 Marx 1976b, p. 92.

102 Marx 1976a, pp. 163, 165. [Editor's interpolation].

103 'In the capitalist mode of production the labour process appears only as a means towards the process of valorisation', Marx 1976b, p. 711, cf. Marx 1978b, p. 461.

The monetary system of the mercantilists merely analysed the circuit of capital in its money form within the sphere of circulation. The Physiocrats (Quesnay) grasped the problem at a deeper level, yet regarded the economic process as an eternal circuit of commodities, because the production of commodities was not actually the work of human beings but of nature. Finally, the classical economists (Adam Smith, Ricardo) did take the production process as the object of their analysis but only to the extent that it is a valorisation process. In this way, by detouring through production, they eventually arrive at the same formula that constituted the basis of mercantilism.[104] In contrast to his predecessors, Marx emphasises the decisive importance of the production process, regarded not merely as a process of valorisation but, at the same time, as a labour process. This does not mean, however, that the two other forms of the circuit of capital, as money and commodities, may be ignored. Capitalist reality is a unity of circuits: the process of circulation (of both money and commodities) and the process of production (as the unity of the valorisation and labour processes). Only to the extent that it is the unity of the labour and valorisation processes does the production process, according to Marx, constitute 'The basis, the starting-point for the physiology of the bourgeois system – for the understanding of its internal organic coherence and life process.'[105] When the production process is regarded as a mere valorisation process – as in classical theory – it has all the characteristics of 'hoarding', becomes lost in abstraction and is no longer capable of grasping the real economic process.[106]

---

104 According to Marx, the deep similarity between capitalist production and the mercantilist system becomes particularly evident in crises. When all values and prices are subject to enormous disturbances, there is suddenly a hunt for stable metallic currency, hoarding of gold, as the one secure thing in the midst of general insecurity, as the '*summum bonum*' [highest good] 'just as it is regarded by the hoarder'. This hoarding of gold expresses how 'the actual devaluation and worthlessness of all physical wealth' is the natural consequence of a mode of production based on abstract exchange value, because alongside abstract exchange value, 'all other commodities – just because they are use values – appear to be useless, mere baubles and toys', Marx 1987a, p. 378. Although political economy imagines itself to be superior to the mercantile system, and assails it as 'utterly wrong', as illusion, it shares the same 'basic presuppositions' as the mercantile system. As a consequence, the monetary system at present 'remains not only historically valid but retain[s its] full validity within certain spheres of the modern economy', Marx 1987a, p. 390 [editor's interpolation], cf. Marx 1981b, pp. 670, 706–7, 727.

105 Marx 1989b, p. 391.

106 Accordingly, for Marx, only concrete labour functioning in the technical labour process, creating use values is 'real', 'genuine' labour, Marx 1987a, pp. 293, 296–7. [This translation has been modified because it rendered '*real*' and '*wirklich*' as 'concrete' which did not capture the full nuance of Marx's expression, especially as earlier in the German text he also used the phrase '*konkrete Arbeit*', Marx 1980, pp. 115, 130–1.] Abstract labour creat-

Because Ricardo's categories of value are the expression, if only one-sided, of concrete reality, namely the valorisation process, they are taken over by Marx in principle and developed further. At the same time, however, he modifies them, by rounding their exclusively abstract value character out with the material side, and elaborates their dual character. The meaning of his critique of Ricardo's categories of value and the changes he made to them moves in the same direction as Marx's critique and transformation of Hegel's dialectic.[107] Both exhibit the same basic feature, being directed against the abstract and final character which Ricardo's categories of value and Hegel's dialectic share, because both abstract from 'real determinateness'. In his critique of Hegel's dialectic, Marx compares, in characteristic fashion, the logic with which Hegel begins the *Encyclopaedia*[108] with money and value: it is 'mind's coin of the realm' and the 'mental value of man and nature', because it is 'totally indifferent to all real determinateness' and has become 'thinking which abstracts from nature and from real man: abstract thinking'.[109] Similarly money represents the 'most irrational' form of capitalism and, in interest-bearing money capital, capital has achieved the 'pure fetish form' 'in which all its determining features are obliterated and its real elements [are] invisible; in this form it represents merely independent exchange value'.[110]

Marx also puts this decisive philosophical position into practice in economics: the abstract study of value obscures 'real determinateness', the qualitative content of the concrete labour process, which impresses its specific, differentiating features on the capitalist economy. These can only be grasped by demonstrating the specific connection of the valorisation process to the technical labour process in each particular epoch.[111] The 'value-form, whose fully

ing exchange values is merely the 'bourgeois form' of labour, Marx 1987a, p. 298; '… labour which creates exchange value is a specifically bourgeois feature', Marx 1987a, p. 298, and it is precisely this labour that sets exchange value which is responsible for all market catastrophes, devaluations, overproduction, stagnation, Marx, 1976a, pp. 135–8.

107 Marx 1976b, p. 103.

108 [Hegel 1991.]

109 Marx 1975b, p. 330 [Marx italicises '*mental value*' and '*abstract*'.]

110 Marx 1989c, p. 462 [editor's interpolation].

111 Hegel already criticised this tendency to mathematicisation, which only grasps one side, the relations between quantities, in the concrete totality of reality and neglects all the remaining qualitative moments. 'Its purpose or principle is quantity. This is precisely the relationship that is non-essential, alien to the character of the notion. The process of knowledge goes on, therefore, on the surface, does not affect the concrete fact itself, does not touch its inner nature or notion, and is hence not a conceptual way of comprehending', Hegel 1910, p. 41. He consequently emphasised that the task of economics consists not merely in representing quantitative but also, at the same time, qualitative relations and

developed shape is the money form, is very simple and slight in content'.[112] The category of exchange value leads an 'antediluvian existence'.[113] Exchange value can be found in ancient Rome, in the Middle Ages and under capitalism. Different contents are hidden behind each of these forms of exchange value. Marx emphasises that 'exchange value', detached from the concrete relations under which it has arisen, is an unreal abstraction, as exchange value 'cannot exist except as an abstract, one-sided relation of an already existing concrete living whole'. Whoever says 'exchange value' presupposes a 'population which produces under definite conditions'.[114] Of course, '[p]olitical economy ... is not technology'.[115] The point is not, however, to study the valorisation process in separation from the particular labour process, on whose basis it arose and with which it constitutes a unitary whole. 'The concrete is concrete because it is a synthesis of many determinations, thus a unity of the diverse.' The task of science consists of the 'reproduction of the concrete' 'by way of thinking'.[116]

Just as the paleontologist reconstructs the entire skeleton and even the presumed muscles and movements of an animal from a few excavated bones, Marx reads the necessary tendencies of capital which are peculiar to an epoch from the structure of the labour process in the particular epoch and the type of tools used in it. For '[t]echnology reveals the active relation of man to nature, the direct process of the production of his life, and thereby ... the social relations of his life'.[117] 'The hand-mill gives you society with the feudal lord; the steam-mill, society with the industrial capitalist.'[118] Since social relations are closely bound up with the forces of production, changes in the tendencies of capital can be read from changes in these forces.

The best illustration of Marx's theoretical thought is provided by chapters 14 and 15 of the first volume of *Capital*, the chapters on 'Manufacture' and

movements of their elements in their 'complexity', Hegel 2008, p. 187. [Grossman's original text has '*Verwirklichung*', i.e. 'realisation', but, given the passage he refers to and the structure of his own sentence, what seems to be meant is '*Verwickelung*', i.e. 'complexity'.]

112 Marx 1976b, p. 90.
113 Marx 1986b, p. 38.
114 Marx 1986b, p. 38.
115 Marx 1986b, p. 24.
116 Marx 1986b, p. 38.
117 Marx 1976b, p. 493.
118 Marx 1976a, p. 166. In a letter to Kautsky, Engels criticises him for having paid insufficient attention to the role of the labour process. 'You should not separate ... technology from political economy as you do ... The tools of the savage condition his society just as much as do more modern ones capitalist society', Engels 1995, p. 156, [Engels emphasised '*technology*' and '*his*'].

'Machinery and large-scale industry'.[119] They are by no means historical-descriptive depictions, in which Marx seeks to present genetically how large-scale industry arose out of manufacture. Both chapters have an eminently theoretical character, which is proven by the fact that they are merely subsections of the part of *Capital* dealing with 'The production of relative surplus value'. What characterises manufacture and large-scale industry by means of machines as two distinct phases of capitalist production? Both have a capitalist character, both are based on wage labour and are governed by the pursuit for profit. The technical labour process in each is, however, completely different. Manufacture represents a 'productive mechanism whose organs are human beings'.[120] In contrast, modern large-scale industry is based on machines. So precisely it [the technical labour process] marks the distinctness of capitalism's different phases. The example of the derivation of these objective tendencies of capital from the analysis of the concrete labour process and its instruments, machinery, illustrates the difference in principle between Marx and other theoretical tendencies in the study of economic events. Further consequences arising from this for the problem of crises and dynamics will be dealt with later.

While transformations in the mode of production during manufacture begin with labour, in large-scale industry they proceed from the instruments of labour, machinery.[121] The process is as follows: machinery makes muscle-power dispensable and thus facilitates the incorporation of women and children into the production process on a massive scale. It lowers the price of labour power and increases surplus value, because the wages of the entire 'parcelised family',[122] doing labour that is many times greater, are now no higher than that previously received by the individual head of the family alone. The degree of exploitation of labour increases in an avalanche.[123] Further, the tendencies to employ minors and immature people and simultaneously to strengthen the despotism of capital through the extensive employment of women and chil-

119 Marx 1976b, pp. 455–91 and 492–639. It is no accident that so large a part of the presentation in all the volumes of *Capital* is devoted to the technical labour process. The chapter on the shaping of the labour process by machinery, in the first volume alone, encompasses nearly 150 pages. But much space is also devoted to the presentation of the technical labour process in its connection with the valorisation process.

120 Marx 1976b, pp. 457, 468.

121 Marx 1976b, p. 517.

122 [This phrase is used by Marx in German but does not appear in Marx 1976b, p. 518. See Marx 1991a, p. 355.]

123 Marx 1976b, p. 517.

dren break down the resistance put up by the male workers.[124] The material consumption of the machinery, which represents a large capital-value and which must have interest paid on it and be depreciated, occurs not only when it is in use but also when it is not in use, as a result of the destructive effects of the elements. Hence the capitalists' tendency to make labour continue day and night. It is further strengthened by the circumstance that every new invention threatens to devalue machinery. Hence the capitalists' efforts to minimise the danger of the 'moral' depreciation of the machinery by reducing the period in which its total value is reproduced.[125] 'Hence too the economic paradox that the most powerful instrument for reducing labour time suffers a dialectical inversion and becomes the most unfailing means for turning the whole lifetime of the worker and his family into labour time at capital's disposal for its own valorisation.'[126]

A further impulse to the prolongation of labour time therefore comes from savings on outlays for additional machinery and buildings, otherwise normally required for the expansion of the scale of production. The expansion in the scale of production without these additional outlays signifies an increase in the mass of surplus value, with a simultaneous reduction in capital expenditure per unit of the commodity produced, which further increases the mass of profit.[127]

Machinery leads to the tendency for labour to become more intense and particularly in all areas where workers' resistance has made the extensive prolongation of the working day impossible because of legal prohibitions. In the factory, 'the dependence of the worker on the continuous and uniform motion of the machinery had already created the strictest discipline'.[128] The increased speed of machinery forces the worker to become more attentive and active.[129]

Here the tendency for the rate of valorisation to fall and to create an industrial reserve army also comes into play. At higher levels of capitalist development and with its general application, machinery, whose purpose is to enlarge relative surplus value and hence the mass of surplus value, brings about a countertendency, i.e. towards a fall in the rate of valorisation. For the mass of surplus value which can be obtained depends on two factors: the rate of surplus

124 Marx 1976b, p. 526. See pp. 489–90 on the insubordination of workers characteristic of the period of manufacture.
125 Marx 1976b, p. 528.
126 Marx 1976b, p. 532.
127 Marx 1976b, p. 529.
128 Marx 1976b, p. 535.
129 Marx 1976b, pp. 536–7.

value, and 'the number of workers simultaneously employed'.[130] In the hunt for increased relative surplus value, the capitalist is driven to constantly develop labour's productivity, by expanding the application of machinery in relation to living labour and he 'attains this result only by diminishing the number of workers employed by a given amount of capital'.[131] A part of the capital, which was previously variable and yielded surplus value, progressively becomes constant capital, which produces no surplus value. The result is apparent in the tendency to create an excess working population; on the other hand, in the tendency for the mass of surplus value attainable, in relation to the size of the capital employed, to fall. 'Hence there is an immanent contradiction in the application of machinery to the production of surplus value, since, of the two factors of the surplus value created by a given amount of capital, one, the rate of surplus value, cannot be increased except by diminishing the other, the number of workers.'[132] Finally, Marx underlines the dynamic impulses which emanate from machinery. While manufacture traditionally 'strives to hold fast to that [appropriate] form [of the division of labour] when once it has been found'[133] and was consequently unable to seize hold of society in its full extent and transform it in depth,[134] large-scale industry based on machinery is forced by the fall in the rate of profit to continually revolutionise the technology of the labour process and therefore the structure of society.

5

The second characteristic feature of the dominant theories since classical economics (the first was their one-sided view of the valorisation process) is their static character. No one disputes the static character of the theory of the Physiocrats, who discovered the 'economic circuit' (the '*tableau économique*').[135] The theories of Smith and Ricardo are both similarly static. All of their categories are based on the concept of an equilibrium, in which 'natural price' (value) asserts itself as an ideal point in economic activity, around which market prices oscillate. As a result, there is no room for crises in Ricardo's mechanism. For him, they are merely accidents, introduced from the outside (wars,

130 Marx 1976b, p. 530.
131 Marx 1976b, p. 531.
132 Marx 1976b, p. 531.
133 Marx 1976b, p. 485 [editor's interpolation.]
134 Marx 1976b, p. 489.
135 [Quesnay 1972.]

bad harvests, state intervention, etc.).[136] Left to itself, the economic circuit always moves in equilibrium and always follows the same path. The deceleration and cessation of capital accumulation in the distant future which Ricardo forecast must be described as mere pseudo-dynamics, because the 'dynamic' factor is not inherent in the economic process itself but is rather a natural force which influences the economic process from the outside (falling rate of profit as a consequence of a growing population and hence increased ground rents).

This is how it remained with Ricardo's students too. In France, Say's theory of markets, that is, the theory that every supply is simultaneously a demand, that consequently any production, through [its] supply *eo ipso* creates its own demand, leads to the conclusion that an equilibrium between supply and demand is possible at any time and on any scale of production. But this implies the possibility of the unlimited accumulation of capital and expansion of production, because there are no obstacles to the full employment[137] of all factors of production.

John Stuart Mill does make the first attempt to consider the dynamic character of the economy, by distinguishing between statics and dynamics. But this division of the scientific object into two, taken over from the mechanics of physics, proved disastrous for the further development of political economy. Mill's analysis has an entirely static character. After having first analysed the economic mechanism in a static state (with constant population, production, capital and, likewise, unchanged technology) and investigated its laws, he subsequently sought to add 'a theory of motion to our theory of equilibrium – the dynamics of political economy to the statics'.[138]

A certain number of corrections are introduced into the static picture: population growth, growth of capital, etc., as if such subsequent retouching removes the statically conceived character of the economic system's essence; as if there were two capitalisms, a static one and a dynamic one. But, if capitalism is dynamic, what is the point of investigating the laws of an imaginary static economy without, at the same time, demonstrating how the transition from statics to dynamics is to take place?[139]

As equilibrium theories, the dominant theories cannot, in principle, derive generalised crisis from the system because, for them, prices are an automatic mechanism for the restoration of equilibrium, for overcoming disturbances. Any attempt to incorporate into their system one of the empirically confirmed

136 Cf. Weiller 1934, p. 11; and Clark 1937, p. 51.

137 ['Full employment' is in English in the original text.]

138 Mill 1900, p. 461.

139 'The main problem now is to proceed from static to dynamic economics', Clark 1937, p. 46.

moments of disturbance, i.e. the tendency to break through equilibrium that is actually observed, necessarily suffers from a fundamental contradiction. Consistent application of the lines of thought employed in equilibrium theory can only demonstrate that such disruptions of equilibrium are only generated precisely 'from outside', i.e. by changes in economic data. From the standpoint of equilibrium theories, the economy can always only react in one direction, following changes in these data, by adjusting, i.e. by tending to create a new equilibrium. It is not apparent how a crisis can arise in such a system.[140]

Alfred Marshall (1890), who tries to combine classical theory with marginal utility theory, has a decidedly static construct. He does investigate shifts in a developing society. These merely constitute, however, an external framework for his analysis. It is only a matter of the adjustment of the economy to changing, external data, such as population, capital, etc., but not of economic developments which arise from the economy itself. Marshall's economy does not develop. At the centre of his system lies the concept of a general equilibrium enforcing itself in all parts of the economic mechanism.[141] Once it is achieved, no further changes take place. This basic idea is then applied to individual problems. Equilibrium is not an heuristic device in theory but a tendency asserting itself in reality.[142]

The whole system is governed by the idea of a general state of equilibrium (maximum satisfaction), towards which the economy, under free competition, tends. Marshall only arrived at this static picture thanks to his inadequate method because, despite his 'general theory of equilibrium', he does not provide any theory of the system as a whole which deals with all the sub-markets and the production process at the same time, that is one which grasps the overall interdependence of the system. What he offers, in reality, is a theory of partial equilibria in sub-markets, which is always concerned with relations between already existing economic variables, with the determination of the price level, (if supply and demand curves are given), or with the determination of the demand curve, if quantities and prices are known. So Henry Ludwell Moore, quite correctly, characterises Marshall's approach as 'static and limited to functions of one variable'.[143]

---

140 Cf. Grossmann 1929a, p. 284.

141 '[T]he general theory of equilibrium of demand and supply is a fundamental idea running through the frames of all the various parts of the central problem of distribution and exchange', Marshall 1890, p. ix.

142 'When demand and supply are in stable equilibrium, if any accident should move the scale of production from its equilibrium position, there will be instantly brought into play forces tending to bring it back to that position', Marshall 1890, pp. 404–5.

143 Marshall was conscious of the weaknesses of his construct, of its unrealistic character.

John Bates Clark, in Schumpeter's view the most influential American theorist of the previous generation, did 'take a significant step beyond Mill's standpoint, already mentioned, and carefully defined the static state ... he also energetically advanced the proposal for a specific theory of "dynamics"'.[144] But this remained a 'proposal'. In resignation, Clark says of dynamics: 'But the task of developing this branch of science is so large that the execution of it will occupy generations of workers.'[145] What he really gives is a picture of a fictional, static economy: year after year the mass of workers employed and the number of capitals remain unchanged, along with the tools and technologies in production. In this society, there are no transfers of capital or labour from one branch of production to another and consumer demand also remains constant. Under these assumptions he investigates the principle of distribution, and demonstrates the way that prices, wages and interest on capital are formed in a static situation. Commodities are sold at their 'natural', that is, cost prices, so that entrepreneurs gain no profit.[146] Clark admits that: 'This picture is completely imaginary. A static society is an impossible one.'[147] 'Actual society is always dynamic ... industrial society is constantly assuming new forms and discharging new functions.'[148] But no conclusions are drawn from this observation. Clark thinks that static forces, isolated in this way, do nevertheless possess real meaning: they also always operate as a fundamental component force in the dynamic world, they indicate real tendencies.[149] But there is more. Despite all the emphasis on the 'hypothetical' character of the 'static state' and despite all his references to the dynamic essence of reality, Clark almost totally abandoned dynamics

---

'He recognised the impossibility of solving real problems by his method unless his hypothetical, static constructions could be replaced by concrete, dynamic functions', which he hoped would follow the improvement of mathematical 'scientific machinery', Moore 1929, p. 93. Hicks also emphasises the static character of Marshall's construct, stating 'how reluctant he is to abandon static conceptions even in his dynamic analysis ... his dynamics are not made easier by running in terms of a very static equilibrium and by the fact that their central passage leads up to the introduction of the "famous fiction", the stationary state'. In addition, Marshall's distinction between 'short' and 'long periods', with the further assumption that 'a "full adaptation" of supply to demand' will occur in the latter, 'is not a concept that fits very well into a general dynamic theory', Hicks 1939, pp. 120–1.

144 Schumpeter 1912, p. 100. [The English translation of this work, Schumpeter 1983, is a revised version of the German edition and does not include the text quoted by Grossman.]

145 Clark 1927, p. 442.

146 Clark 1927, pp. 400 and vi–vii.

147 Clark 1927, pp. 400 and 29.

148 Clark 1927, pp. vi and 30.

149 'The static state which has here been pictured is the one towards which society is at every instant tending', Clark 1927, p. 402.

in his later, principal work, *Essentials of Economic Theory*. His picture of the economy and society is static. The static model asserts itself in a competitive economy – although not in an ideally pure form. As long as there is free competition, 'the most active societies conform most closely to their static model'.[150] The situation is not much different in contemporary society (with imperfect competition).[151] Precisely the mobility of the prevailing economy's elements enables a static state to be attained more quickly than if these elements were less mobile. The 'normal' (static) form asserts itself better in the highly industrialised society of [the United States of] America than in immobile Asian societies.[152] 'The static shape itself, though it is never completely copied in the actual shape of society, is for scientific purposes a reality.'[153] In short, 'static influences that draw society forever toward its natural form are always fundamental and progress has no tendency to suppress them'.[154] What the economy's 'dynamic' character consists of, and how disturbances can arise, Clark has not said. He presents 'dynamic' development, with its rapid changes in the economic organism, as a succession in time of different static states.[155]

This static character becomes even more pronounced in the pure theory of marginal utility. Dynamic changes in the structure can hardly be reconciled with such a construct, because it assumes that production is governed by consumers (demand), and that the economy can be reduced to subjective choices between various subjective uses. They are merely external data, which this theory assumes. But it does not investigate or explain their emergence. Schumpeter (1912) could therefore state that 'the static character of its theoretical edifice was unaffected by the great reform of theory, through the subjective theory of value ... In fact, the static character of the theory gained substantially in rigour and clarity as a result of the new analysis.'[156]

As [Maurice] Roche-Agussol states, the main object of marginal utility theory's analyses is an 'essentially static problem', namely the valuation and distribution of goods 'at a *given* level of needs and the means for satisfying needs

150 Clark 1915, p. 195.
151 'The actual form of a highly dynamic society hovers relatively near to its static model though it never conforms to it', op. cit.
152 Clark 1915, p. 195. [Editor's interpolation.]
153 Clark 1915, p. 197.
154 Clark 1915, p. 198.
155 Clark 1915, p. 196. A more recent critic of Clark says, quite correctly, that as a result of all his abstract assumptions, the picture he sketched is totally alien to reality. 'Such an isolation of static forces, it is admitted, gives to the study an unlifelike appearance and makes it "heroically theoretical"', Homan 1928, p. 38.
156 Schumpeter 1912, p. 100.

and of needs'.[157] With the introduction of movement through time, this theory has to fail, even from its own standpoint, because no statements about future needs and means for satisfying them can be made. Conscious of this fact, Menger declares that 'the conception of theoretical economics ... as a science of the ... "laws of development in economy", and other such things, is a one-sided monstrosity ... It is a living proof of the aberrations', etc.[158] The theory of William Stanley Jevons, the other founder of the marginal utility school, is also decidedly static. He operates with concepts borrowed from the science of mechanics (such as 'infinitely small quantities'), on which he erects his theory of exchange. '[T]he laws of exchange resemble the laws governing the equilibrium of a lever, as they are both determined by the principle of virtual velocities.'[159] Jevons does know that all economic phenomena are in motion and must, therefore, be dealt with in units of time. But, in chapter 3 of his book, he manages to exclude the time factor from his analysis by recourse to a methodological trick. From the outset, he dispenses with the idea 'of a complete solution to the problem in its entire natural complexity' (that would be 'a problem of motion – a problem of dynamics') and confines his analysis to 'the purely static problem' of establishing the conditions under which exchange ceases and equilibrium is achieved.[160]

The marginal utility school has consistently retained this character to the present; for reasons of space, we have to restrict ourselves to a few typical examples from various currents. Frank Hyneman Knight does emphasise that history does not stop and that 'evolution to other forms of organisation as the dominant type' is inherent in capitalism[161] but thinks that 'such a social development falls outside the scope of the economic theorist' because the notion of equilibrium is entirely inapplicable to such changes.[162] He refers the study of these changes to the science of history and comes to the conclusion that 'economic dynamics, in the sense which this expression should have in order to be applicable [in economic theory], does not exist. What is specified as being dynamic in it should be named evolutionary or historical economic theory.'[163] Ewald Schams's position is no different. According to him, economics is a the-

157 Roche-Agussol 1932, p. 36. [Grossman's emphasis.]

158 Menger 1985, p. 121. [This quotation is misleading. Menger's comments were not directed *against* subjective preference/marginal utility theory but rather *from* that position against the German historical school.]

159 Jevons 1879, pp. vii, 3.

160 Jevons 1879, pp. iv, 93–4.

161 Knight 1931, p. 25.

162 Knight 1931, p. 26.

163 Knight 1931, p. 7.

ory of 'economic variables' and understanding the relations among variables and dependent variables necessarily requires the construction of functional concepts and the specification of equations.[164] Since, however, the theory of functional relations, as is generally conceded today,[165] is necessarily static because it merely investigates relations between given value variables, Schams arrives at the conclusion (despite his acknowledgment of the dynamic character of the capitalist economy) that we must work with static conceptual tools. This is because we do not possess a specifically dynamic conceptual form which could grasp dynamic changes. The theory of economic variables [mathematical economics], as a theory of relations, has no more possibility of development than geometry. Quite independently of whether 'there is a stationary reality or simply an economy in full motion', 'logically defined statics will always be an assumption'.[166] Schams therefore directs his criticism against the twofold division of theory into statics and dynamics. 'Every theory of economic variables is entirely static.' Economic movement can only be understood as the succession and comparison of various static states of equilibrium, as 'comparative statics', as 'the comparison of the two states of dependent variables over a certain interval of time'.[167] There can be no specifically dynamic problems within the theory of economic variables but, at most, theoretical problems which are no longer questions of the theory of variables, and are thus theories of the development of economic data. But these lie outside the scope of economic theory.[168]

---

164 Schams 1931, pp. 46–8.

165 Cf. Mayer 1932.

166 Schams 1931, p. 49.

167 Schams 1931, pp. 49–50.

168 Yet another of the grounds advanced by Schams for the passionate struggle being waged against attempts to 'dynamise theory' and introduce the time factor directly into the analysis, despite acknowledgement of the dynamic nature of reality, is interesting. If economics is regarded as 'a theory of economic variables' then the mathematical method will prove indispensable in the 'exact' treatment of complex relations among variables, which cannot be mastered by means of 'conventional logic'. The most important methodological principle in the construction of systems of variables is the 'equivalence of relations, that is, the construction of equations in which the relationships among the variables can be expressed', Schams 1931, p. 48. This method, however, is located right in the centre of statics, as the functional method can only grasp relations between given values, quantities etc. but not their formation. If movement, i.e. change through time, is now introduced, it is apparent that 'the regularity of disproportional movement will destroy the equivalence of the relations', as Schams freely admits. 'The simultaneity of more than two independent movements cannot be dealt with mathematically', Schams 1931, p. 49. 'The use of differential and integral equations is scarcely possible with non-equivalent relations.' Not beginning with given prices and quantities, however, and introducing change

The realisation that several interdependent movements and non-equivalent relations cannot be grasped mathematically has apparently led one part of the dominant theory into an intensified struggle against attempts to 'dynamise' the theory and to a renaissance of static theories of equilibrium.[169] According to Conrad, an exchange economy without centralised management is a 'self-regulating mechanism, which tends toward a steady state, that is, seeks to assume uniform movement'. The essence of 'self-regulation' is that the 'mechanism is steered towards a stationary state' – 'a tendency that never actually reaches its goal but which is alone to be thanked if an exchange economy, lacking centralised management, does not fall into chaos'.[170] Conrad does know that there are crises and disturbances which cannot be regarded as movement towards a stationary state. The presupposition of the tendency towards equilibrium is therefore 'that the regulative apparatus functions correctly' (sic!). If this were not the case 'then it is possible that the approach toward the stationary state will be constantly impeded'.[171]

According to Conrad, movement should be understood as a succession of stationary states without making the intervening non-stationary states intelligible.[172] Alexander Bilimovic concedes that previously theory merely succeeded in determining equilibrium equations for a stationary economy but not for a dynamic economy. This explains why 'the schemas which have predominated until now do not express economic equilibrium in the real world'. These schemas are, nevertheless, held to be capable of improvement and Bilimovic hopes that it may also be possible to construct a mathematical 'model' of a

---

through time, means confronting the task of dealing with future changes and, instead of establishing exact relations between given variables, 'being content with the calculation of correlations and mathematical price expectations'. Doing this, however, means turning away from 'exact theory' and 'entering the company of the dice-throwing probability theorists', Schams 1931, p. 55. The 'mathematically exact' method, originally designated as indispensable on the grounds that it was supposed to be the best means for the exact investigation of reality, is here raised to the level of an end in itself. Reality is dynamic. As it is impossible to grasp dynamic movement by mathematical means, however, one is restricted to statics, in order to avoid having to dispense with the 'exact' method of mathematics.

169 On this cf. Conrad 1936, p. 243.

170 Conrad 1936, p. 236 [citing Conrad 1931, p. 286].

171 Conrad 1936, p. 239.

172 Lachmann (London) similarly understands 'a dynamic theory of equilibrium' as one 'which is concerned with changes in equilibrium through time and describes the complete process of transition from one equilibrium to the next'. The difficulties with which the theory of dynamics wrestles are difficulties in neither its principles nor content and are rather to be attributed to 'the deficiencies of our analytical tools', Lachmann 1937, pp. 33–4.

non-stationary economy, for previous attempts' lack of success in dynamising the schemas of a stationary economy cannot be attributed to any fundamental defect in these schemas.[173]

Doesn't this twofold division of theory recall John Stuart Mill's similar proposition? And won't it remain as futile as Mill's, in view of the basic fact that no bridge can lead from 'statics' to 'dynamics', even if this 'dynamics' is thought of as a succession of static states? For these are various static states, that follow one another. The static line of thought is unable to explain how successive new states arise precisely for the reason 'that the equilibrium of static analysis does not allow for growth, that this analysis can only describe an expanding system in terms of successive states of equilibrium, with the intervening stages of transition left, and left with danger to the validity of the argument, unanalysed'.[174]

These difficulties only really begin to accrue when statics are no longer regarded as a real tendency but as an heuristic device, because there is then even less of a bridge leading from this hypothetical state to reality, which moves in disequilibrium. 'If the economic cycle's entire course is movement in disequilibrium – neither cumulative downwards nor upwards – what is the point of regarding particular states of equilibrium as the point of departure or a transition point in this movement? If equilibrium is nowhere departed from, tended towards or passed through, why behave "as if" this was the case?'[175] Proceeding from the assumption of static equilibrium, the entire problem of dynamics is reduced to the question of which factors 'disturb' this supposed state. Thus, for [Gottfried] Haberler, there is an inherent tendency towards equilibrium in the economic system. Consequently, for him, only the downturn in the course of the economic cycle, the 'long swing' 'in the negative direction' but not the upswing, requires explanation, 'since the upward movement, the approach to full employment, might be explained as a natural consequence of the inherent tendency of the economic system towards equilibrium'.[176]

More recently still, criticisms of the concept of 'the stationary state'[177] as a superfluous, because economically unreal presupposition, have multiplied in another area of the dominant theory. As [John] Hicks says, this group is forced

173 Bilimovic 1937a, pp. 220–4.
174 Cf. Harrod 1937, p. 496.
175 Bode 1937, p. 599.
176 Haberler 1946, p. 265. [Quotations in English in the original text.]
177 [In English in the original text.]

to concede 'that the actual state of any real economy is never in fact stationary; nevertheless, stationary-state theorists naturally regarded reality as "tending" towards stationariness; though the existence of such a tendency is more than questionable'. 'The stationary theory itself gives no indication that reality does tend to move in any such direction.'[178] Still more, Hicks holds the concept of a stationary economy directly responsible for retarding the development of science, because it neglected problems of dynamics.[179]

We can deal with the mathematical tendency's lines of thought briefly, because our concern is not to offer an exhaustive critique of this school but rather to bring out its static character.[180] 'No presentation is more static than that of Léon Walras.'[181] As can be read on a memorial tablet in the Lausanne Academy, Walras was exalted as the theorist '*qui le premier a établi des conditions générales de l'équilibre économique*'.[182] According to Walras, the economy can be compared with a lake, whose waves may well be temporarily whipped up by a storm but which subsequently subsides to form a new, mirror-flat equilibrium. Similarly, economic disturbances to general equilibrium spread out through the entire economic system. But Walras simply regards them as oscillations, whose amplitude falls over time until equilibrium is restored.[183] The question of whether, perhaps, such a static state cannot be realised at all is not posed. On the contrary, Walras is convinced of the possibility of the realisation of an enduring equilibrium. 'The more we know of the ideal conditions of equilibrium, the better we shall be able to control or prevent these crises.'[184]

The same can be said of Pareto's work. Hicks calls Pareto's *Manual* 'the most complete static theory of value which economic science has hitherto been able to produce'.[185] Pareto distinguishes three areas of research: the theory of statics, the area of economic theory that is the most complete; the theory of successive equilibria, 'we have only a very few notions about the theory of successive equilibria'; finally the theory of dynamics, which deals

178 Hicks 1939, p. 119.
179 Hicks 1939, p. 119.
180 Hicks also includes Knut Wicksell in the Lausanne school, alongside Walras and Pareto, because he thinks just as statically as the other two. Wicksell's 'capital theory is limited to considering the artificial abstraction of a stationary state', Hicks 1939, p. 3.
181 Schumpeter 1912, p. 100.
182 ['Who first established the general conditions of economic equilibrium'.]
183 Walras 1954, pp. 380–1.
184 Walras 1954, p. 381.
185 Hicks 1934, p. 52.

with the investigation of the movement of economic phenomena, 'except for a special theory, that of economic crises, nothing is known about dynamic theory'.[186] Pareto himself contributed nothing to the investigation of dynamics and, rather, impeded it by assuming that the above threefold division of research actually corresponded to reality.[187] His attention is only directed towards statics; his central, indeed only, problem is that of equilibrium,[188] to which he devotes chapters 3 to 6 of his book. He never indicates the bridge which leads from statics to dynamics.[189] Pareto underscores the significance of Walras's equations for economic equilibrium and attributes to them an analogous role to Lagrangian equations in mechanics, in that he conceptualised reality as a system of 'continual oscillations around a central point of equilibrium' and thought that this centre of equilibrium moved.[190] The question of whether the concept of economic movement is compatible with that of equilibrium is never raised and is almost completely excluded by the untenable assumption that all economic phenomena share a simultaneous, uniform rhythm.[191]

This static trait of Pareto's theory is understandable if it is considered that he deals exclusively with relations between already existing values on the market or, in Pareto's later formulation, with choices between indifference combinations that already exist. According to his conception, equilibrium is achieved if two people possessing a certain number of goods exchange them with each other on the market up to the point at which both parties agree that no further exchange is possible. The state of equilibrium attained can therefore be defined as 'a state which would maintain itself indefinitely' if there is no change in its conditions or if this change is so slight that the system 'tends to re-establish itself, to return to its original position'.[192]

186 Pareto 1972, p. 105.

187 'This division corresponds to reality', Pareto 1972, p. 104. As if we had experienced two different objects, a static alongside a dynamic economy!

188 'The principal subject of our study is economic equilibrium.' Pareto 1972, p. 106.

189 Pareto 1972, pp. 103–290.

190 Consequently, Rosenstein-Rodan correctly says: 'No doubt mathematical, like any static theory only seeks to explain tendencies to equilibrium and understand the real course of the economy as deviations from the state of equilibrium.' 'In this it is supposed that, after numerous oscillations, a state of equilibrium, which continues to exist unchanged, will emerge', Rosenstein-Rodan 1929, p. 136.

191 The assumption that economic phenomena share a simultaneous rhythm was explicitly emphasised in Pareto 1972, p. 105. The same is true of a successor of Pareto, Pietri-Tonelli. [See, for example, Pietri-Tonelli 1927].

192 Pareto 1972, pp. 108, 109.

Pareto employs the concepts of 'statics' and 'tendency to equilibrium', borrowed from mechanics, without investigating whether they make sense in economics. The essence of his method of the general interdependence of all economic variables, long regarded as a modern miracle, like the essence of any functional approach which abstains from genetic explanation, is their static character. It only shows the relations between already given economic variables (be they utilities or indifference combinations), but not the capacity of the system for movement, the evolution of these variables, and hence the direction in which the system is moving. To do this, it is necessary to look at the process of production as the source of all changes in 'economic variables'. But this is excluded from the analysis at the outset.[193] Although Hicks thinks that Pareto's exchange equations could be extended to production processes, given certain corrections, he makes the reservation that they would only be valid for a stationary economy in which no capital accumulation (Hicks says no net saving) and no other changes in given economic data take place. But this makes Pareto's equations, as Hicks concedes, 'far from being a description of reality'. 'They are not a description of reality'.[194]

As early as 1846, Marx wrote against Proudhon that: 'The relations of production of every society form a whole.'[195] The same authors who emphasise the 'general interdependence' of all economic variables and reject methods which seek to single out and explain only individual groups of phenomena from the process of economic life themselves break this totality down into sectors. They separate market phenomena from the sphere of the labour process, and make this artificially separated sphere of exchange the main object of their analysis. Pareto could arrive at 'equilibrium equations' by dealing with

---

193 As Amoroso emphasises, '*a base della statica economica paretiana sono due concetti fondamentali: di richezza, di ofelimià. Non esistono differenze sostanziali fra produzione.*' ['two concepts underlie Pareto's economic statics: wealth and ophelimity. No substantial distinctions exist in production'. 'Ophelimity' is 'economic satisfaction'.] Amoroso asks: what about the former division of economics into production, exchange, consumption and distribution? And he answers the question, saying that according to Pareto, '*non esiste nella realità una distinzione di cose corrispondente a questa distinzione di parole … ma tutti i problemi economici sono compressi nelle condizioni generali dell'equilibrio, limitamente alla sola condizione che restano invariate le forze e gli vincoli quali esistono nella posizione iniziale.*' ['there is no distinction in reality which corresponds to this linguistic distinction … rather all the problems of economics are contained in the general conditions for equilibrium, amounting to the sole condition that forces and constraints do not change from their initial state.'], Amoroso 1924, pp. 46–7.

194 Hicks 1980, pp. 525, 526.

195 [Marx 1976a, p. 166.]

the functional connection between given market variables[196] and excluding the dynamic factor of the production process or, that is, by 'completely dedynamising the system'.[197]

At the same time, the above example shows how the accuracy of the mathematical process is invoked in the construction of the system of equilibrium equations. This accuracy is not related to the content of economic knowledge but rather to the technique of mathematical calculation. Despite the accuracy of these operations, mathematical treatment can be a source of the greatest errors, precisely because of the postulates which underlie the equations and which determine the value of the knowledge they yield.[198]

In its youthful enthusiasm, the mathematical school (Walras, Marshall, [Ysidro] Edgeworth, Pareto in his *Course* but also Böhm-Bawerk)[199] believed it could measure everything and constructed an edifice of equilibrium equations, whose basis was the assumption that utility is, in principle, a measurable variable, or would be a measurable variable if we had knowledge of enough facts at our disposal. After one generation, a more sober assessment was made. The objection initially raised by a few was generally acknowledged: utility, as an intensely psychological variable, cannot be measured and subjected to mathematical operations.[200] But if marginal utility is not measurable then nor is aggregate social utility, and hence all the 'equilibrium equations' constructed on this unreal basis, are invalid.

The critique of the marginal utility theory, which was initially made only by opponents of the mathematical school, is now pursued by its supporters

196 '[T]he circulation of commodities has of course only to do with already existing, given values', Marx 1978b, p. 297.

197 Mayer 1932, p. 239. Of course, Mayer is not consistent enough. As a marginalist he regards consumer demand as the 'driving force of the entire system', Mayer 1932, p. 239. Demand, however, as the most recent works of the Keynesian school admit, is not a driving factor but is instead only a result, a variable which depends on the extent of investment. Investments themselves are conditioned by the profitability which can be achieved in the process of production.

198 Mayer 1932, p. 205.

199 [Pareto 1896–7.]

200 'Utility is [and will remain] only a comparable but not a measurable magnitude.' 'Attempts to treat utility like an ordinary extensive magnitude, in our opinion are bound to fail.' 'One cannot subject utility to the ordinary arithmetic and algebraic operations', cf. Fischer 1892, p. 88. [The quotations, in modified form, in English, actually appears, with the interpolation, in Bernadelli 1938, p. 192. Bernadelli emphasised '*comparable*' and '*measurable*'. As the source of the quotations, Bernadelli cites Bilimovic 1929. It is not there but is in Bilimovic 1933, p. 178. The page in Fisher's work that Grossman referred to does not seem directly relevant, although the entire monograph is devoted to the subjection of utility to algebraic operations.]

and has led to the dissolution of marginal utility theory.[201] The breakdown of marginal utility theory did not, however, lead to the abandonment of equilibrium equations but rather to efforts to construct them on another basis. In his *Manual*, Pareto took refuge in the concept of 'ordinal' indifference curves, in order to use this as the basis, supposedly taken from experience,[202] on which to construct his theory of preference and its 'equilibrium equations'. Criticism proved the untenability of this theory by highlighting the arbitrary nature of the assumptions behind the equations. The mathematicians' procedure presupposes the infinite divisibility of goods and the unlimited substitutability of various goods (e.g. of nuts for apples), in the satisfaction of wants. Hence a gulf arose between the assumptions on which the indifference curves were based and reality.[203] Elevated to the status of a general rule, the assumption of the unlimited substitutability of goods 'leads to the most absurd conclusions'. For example, in the everyday consumption of a combination of bread and wine, a very little or even a minimum amount of bread can be 'replaced' by a lot of wine or increasingly small amounts of meat by more and more salt![204] These absurd results and the indifference curves, demand curves, price relations and equilibrium positions derived from them are not an approximate reflection, but 'in truth a distorted picture of reality'.[205]

Considering that even in the circumstances of a solitary individual with few commodities at his disposal there are an infinite number of possible indifference combinations, it is apparent that with 40 million people and several thousand different types of commodities, 'the time and energy of a whole generation would not suffice' to collect the incalculable amount of information needed to construct the hundreds of millions of indifference combinations.

---

201 'It is a curious process of a self-decomposition of a theory – a supreme example of Hegelian dialectics ... – which not so long ago had been hailed as the essential step in putting economics on a scientific basis', Bernadelli 1938, p. 192.

202 For example, someone who possesses 100 apples and 100 nuts can be asked how many nuts would compensate for giving up 10 or 20 apples. A combination of 80 apples and 140 nuts, for example, could result.

203 Mayer 1932, p. 214.

204 Mayer 1932, pp. 211–12.

205 Mayer 1932, p. 212, cf. p. 216. Cf. also Ricci 1924, p. 43. Cf., in addition, Schultz 1931 p. 77; and Mayer who stresses that the indifference combination only takes the form of a curve with two goods. With a combination of three goods, the diagram becomes three-dimensional; under real conditions, i.e. with thousands of goods, indifference diagrams would be 'inconceivable', thought of in a space of thousands of dimensions (!) – 'variétés dans l'hyperspace' ['diversities in hyperspace'] – which would be purely imaginary and have nothing more to do with reality, Mayer 1932, pp. 207–8.

And the time and energy of a further generation would not suffice to solve the equations which were constructed on this basis.[206]

The static character of the monetary theories of crisis, which spread during the postwar period – Wicksellian and neo-Wicksellian efforts to overcome economic cycles and stabilise the economy, the value of money and world prices in a purely monetary way, by means of the appropriate regulation of interest rates by central banks – is also apparent.[207] According to Wicksell, 'in principle' the real causes of crisis do lie on the commodity side. But this plays no role in his thinking because, according to him, the connection between the economy and credit has shifted the economic system's centre of gravity towards the monetary side. With an appropriate regulation of interest rates, 'the real element of the crisis' would fall away and be reduced to 'an even fluctuation'.[208] This holds not merely for individual countries but primarily for the world economy. 'It would then be the simple duty of each [central] credit institution to regulate its rate of interest, both relatively to, and in unison with, other countries, so as both to maintain in equilibrium the international balance of payments and to stabilise the general level of world prices.'[209] And it is precisely this static conception of the economy which is identified by [Friedrich] Hayek as 'the most important basis for all future monetary theory of the trade cycle'.[210] In fact, this conception underlies all monetary theories of crisis (Irving Fisher[211] and Ralph George Hawtrey). For the latter, eco-

206 In addition, the Lausanne School's method – the method of the general interdependence of all economic variables – so admired in its time, is today held responsible for the School never going beyond worthless generalities. It led to the School's 'theoretically idle state', Lange 1933, p. 56. Hicks underlines the 'apparent sterility of the Walrasian system', because of its great distance from reality, Hicks 1939, p. 60. As Husserl correctly says, the danger of such failures is inherent in the essence of mathematics itself. It is a technique which can be and often is applied to the most various and also irrelevant areas. 'The same thinkers who sustain marvellous mathematical methods with such incomparable mastery, and who add new methods to them, often show themselves incapable of accounting satisfactorily … for the limits of their right use', Husserl 2001, p. 16. Hence, in the field of economic theory, the dazzling application of mathematical methods and their miserable results.

207 Wicksell 1978, pp. 216, 223.

208 Wicksell 1978, p. 212.

209 [Wicksell 1936, p. 194.]

210 Hayek 1933, p. 116. Wicksell's neo-Malthusianism is also rooted in an undynamic conception of the productive forces, according to which a country can only support a particular optimum population, exceeding which must lead to the country's impoverishment. This conception represents an unambiguous relapse to the level of the outlook of the first half of the eighteenth century. Cf. Süßmilch 1761, p. 142.

211 Cf. Fisher 1925.

nomic fluctuations are not of necessity bound up with the essence of the capitalist mechanism but instead 'arise out of a world-wide contraction of credit'.[212]

The crisis cycle is consequently 'a purely monetary phenomenon' and changes in economic activity, 'the alternation of prosperity and depression', have as their sole cause 'changes in "the flow of money"'. 'If the flow of money could be stabilised, the fluctuations in economic activity would disappear',[213] and prosperity could continue indefinitely without limit.

Doubts within the dominant theory about the correctness of the static conception first arose under the pressure of the great crisis of 1900–1 and then the economic disturbances of the postwar period. More attention was paid to the problem of crises and to collecting empirical material on the course of past crises. Using this material, economic research institutes, founded to investigate these problems, attempted to establish the laws of the economic cycle's course and its phases. Only now was attention paid to the material elements of the production process, in addition to the value side, and the distinction between the production of means of production and the production of means of consumption was introduced into the analysis, emphasising their different roles in the course of the economic cycle. The specific role of so-called durable ('fixed') capital[214] was emphasised as a cause of crisis, for example by [Arthur] Spiethoff and [Gustav] Cassel.[215] The role of progressive technological improvements, the disproportion between the structure of the various branches of production[216]

212 Hawtrey 1923, p. 141.

213 Cf. Haberler 1946, pp. 15, 17; and Hawtrey 1928, p. 98.

214 Haberler 1946, p. 73.

215 [See Spiethoff 1955; and Cassel 1932.]

216 Haberler 1946, pp. 39 and 73. Haberler correctly says of non-monetary theories of overinvestment, whose representatives he names as Arthur Spiethoff and Gustav Cassel, 'In the writings of these two authors … we find the culmination of a very important line of thought which can be traced back to Marx', Haberler 1946, p. 72. On the now usual distinction between the production of means of production and the production of means of consumption, cf. first, in Marx, 'The two departments of social production', Marx 1978b, pp. 471–4; on the specific role of durable (fixed) capital, 'Replacement of the fixed capital', Marx 1978b, pp. 524–45; on the influence of the length of the construction period on the course of the cycle, see Marx 1978b, pp. 387, 445, 552–3. [These pages, as opposed to pp. 306–68, do not seem relevant. Marx does not refer to 'construction period' but distinguishes between 'working period' and 'production period'.] This distinction among material elements was first introduced into the recent literature by Tugan-Baranovsky's book on crises in England (Tugan-Baranowsky 1901) and subsequently by Spiethoff and others. They were influenced by Marx, as can immediately be seen from Tugan-Baranovsky's reproduction schemas which were copied from Marx. Tugan-Baranovsky, however, was

and the influence of the length of the period of construction on the course of the cycle (Aftalion)[217] were emphasised.

These attempts turned out to be unsatisfactory as each of the authors simply made one, individual, isolated material moment of the entire process the basis of his crisis theory, which gave these theories an accidental, eclectic character, resting on partial observations. The same can be said of the most recent attempts, by John Maurice Clark,[218] Simon Kuznets,[219] and Leonard Ayres,[220] to use the durability of the means of production as a possible basis for explaining periodicity itself and the more intense fluctuations in the industries producing 'capital goods' (the so-called accelerator principle). An attempt is made to explain the special problem of crises by means of individual observable correlations. This means abandoning any connection with the theoretical foundations of political economy, because of the feeling that the old static theories are of little use in explaining a dynamic process. As, on the other hand, no conclusive dynamic theory in which these material elements have been treated theoretically has been constructed, these more recent investigations of crisis have remained special theories of a subfield in economics, lacking a broader theoretical foundation.[221]

Only a very small circle within the dominant theory itself has perceived the lack of a general theory of dynamics. As Hans Mayer stated, 'the unsatisfactoriness and deficiency of previous theories' was felt 'more and more intensely', as was their fundamental error, that the apparatus of their system 'could not assimilate and deal with certain problems thrown up by the actual course of economic events'. 'The evidently dynamic problem of the economic cycle and crises' cannot be grasped by the 'previous, essentially static systems of price theory', as a consequence of its 'purely static approach' to relations of exchange between given economic variables, which merely describes 'existing price rela-

---

celebrated by Sombart as the 'father of modern crisis theory', Sombart 1904, p. 130, and his book was praised by Spiethoff as the 'first scientific monograph on crises', Spiethoff 1903, p. 700.

217 [See Aftalion 1913 and 1932.]

218 Clark 1917.

219 Kuznets 1935. [Grossman mistakenly attributes this essay to Roy Forbes Harrod, in both the main text and a footnote.]

220 Ayres 1939d. [Grossman reviewed this book, Grossman 1939.]

221 Thus Paul Thomas Homan writes in an essay entitled 'The present impasse': 'It is probably no exaggeration to say that recent investigations into the causes of cycles have done as much to destroy adherence to older types of theory as any other single cause. And it has led to the casting of their problems by many economists into terms of a changing process, rather than into terms of a static situation', Homan 1928, p. 453.

tions in a state of equilibrium, that has already been reached'. For the 'analysis of the processes of movement in economic reality' requires 'insight into the process of price formation'.[222] As shown above, all these systems abstained from grasping the economic system's overall trend in a definite direction, i.e. its developmental tendencies, and were also incapable of doing this, because they confined themselves solely to grasping exchange relations between given variables. But from the exchange equations it is apparent that all the quantities of goods or prices, which an economic subject disposes of, are received as increments by others. Hence all these (positive or negative) increments in the number of goods or prices result in a total sum of zero. There is no incalculable [sic] remainder which could be regarded as an index of a definite trend in the course of the system as a whole.[223] The relations of exchange of the 'economic variables' on markets are, likewise, not real processes of movement, a sequence over time. They are transfers, a timeless 'movement', a circular motion. If, however, the economic system's overall trend in a definite direction is to be grasped, not only the relations of exchange of given variables must be investigated but also their evolution, growth or passing away or (as Mayer says) the process of 'price formation'. It is insufficient to investigate exchange relations; the production process as well as the process of circulation, that is the process as a whole, must also be investigated. It is then apparent that positive and negative changes no longer balance out in the full account to yield zero but that they assume definite values (e.g. a falling rate of profit). That is, they reveal the direction of movement of the system as a whole, its developmental tendency. So the main task of theory for Marx in *Capital*, the investigation of 'economic laws of motion', which was banished from the realm of economic theory by the marginal utility school, finally steps into the foreground of the dominant theory too. Now, for the first time, a small group of theoreticians within the dominant theory – [Rudolf] Streller, [Luigi] Amoroso, [Paul] Rosenstein-Rodan, [Umberto] Ricci, [Oskar] Morgenstern, [Karl] Bode and others – turns, in principle, against the central line of thought of equilibrium theories, with their fictitious assumption of the simultaneous rhythm of economic events. The group's criticism is meant to prepare the ground for a dynamic theory. It maintains that 'with the realistic assumption of diverse rhythms ... of [economic] movements it would ... be a matter of coincidence if equilibrium came about'.[224] For the tendency toward equilibrium is *one* possibility; the alternat-

222 Mayer 1932, p. 148.

223 Cf. Schams 1931, p. 30.

224 Rosenstein-Rodan 1929, pp. 131, 134. [Grossman did not signal the ellipsis or interpolation and indicated that the quotation started with 'it'. Rosenstein-Rodan emphasised 'diverse'.]

ive is that due to non-simultaneous rhythms of movements, one change 'always brings about other changes; a *perpetuum mobile* of changes, the time coefficients do not equalise and no state of equilibrium emerges at all'.[225] Theories of equilibrium would have to prove that this second constellation of time coefficients cannot occur. They have not provided such a proof and, because of the assumption of the simultaneous rhythm of all economic processes, they have blocked the path to understanding the problem of dynamics.

The 'equilibrium system' of the mathematical school only exists thanks to the circumstance that it is 'economics without time'. 'The equilibrium system of the mathematical school, which includes neither time indices nor coefficients, can therefore in no way grasp the real state of equilibrium.'[226] And the critique of the mathematical school does not single out one particular aspect of the theory or a particular theorem but rather the theory itself, 'because it offers the most precise formulation of a line of thought common to all economic schools, so that its proven defect affects all other formulations even more acutely'.[227]

The fundamental error of equilibrium theories is not, therefore, only that 'they have regarded moving, changing variables, as fixed, as invariant'. For if these movements were of the same duration, if they were equitemporal, the real course of the economic process could indeed be grasped as a series of 'successive equilibria', each of which could be defined by the equilibrium system.[228] The moment the theory proceeds to grasp non-equitemporal movements, i.e. to explicitly express the time factor 't', however, as Shams states, 'the static system is struck at its weakest point: the assumption of the pseudo-constancy of economic periods'.[229] For the incorporation of the time element, i.e. divergent periods of movement, shatters the equivalence of the relations which constitute the basis of the mathematical system of the equations, and therefore cannot be managed mathematically.[230] So talk about the failure of

225 [Rosenstein-Rodan 1929, p. 131. '*Perpetuum mobile*' means 'perpetual motion'.]

226 Rosenstein-Rodan 1929, p. 129.

227 Rosenstein-Rodan 1929, p. 135.

228 Consequently the concept of 'moving equilibrium' is a contradiction, as the real movements of the elements of the economy are in constant disequilibrium. Nevertheless, Moore did try, in 'Moving equilibria', chapter 5 of his book, to prove that exchange, production, distribution and accumulation move in lock-step, 'as a moving general equilibrium', using empirical material from American potato production over a long period, Moore 1929, pp. 93–145. He did not, however, succeed. As Umberto Ricci showed in his critique, Moore did not describe a moving equilibrium, but rather a moving disequilibrium, Ricci 1930, p. 654.

229 Schams 1931, p. 42.

230 Schams 1931, p. 55, or, as Streller formulated this idea: the equilibrium equations would only have been possible at a level of higher abstraction from reality. It is apparent, however,

economic theory is understandable, because it progressively lost all relation to reality. A theory which regards capitalism as a mechanism tending, through 'self-regulation', towards equilibrium, is incapable of comprehending the economic developments of the last few decades, namely the attempts to establish such an equilibrium through conscious interventions of monopolistic regulation, which characterised this period.

So the dominant theory faces a dilemma. Mathematical economics could celebrate its 'triumph' as long as it was dominated by ideas of equilibrium. These, however, failed to explain the economy's dynamic movements. They regarded these movements as mere 'oscillations' around a state of equilibrium or as temporary 'disturbances' prior to the achievement of a new equilibrium,[231] while reality demonstrates long term disequilibrating movements, exhibiting increasing disequilibrium instead of a tendency towards equilibrium. The reason why all tendencies within the dominant theory emphasised the static character of the economy, its capacity to adjust to the changing needs of society, for over a century – from Ricardo to the present – has clearly been the need to justify the existing economic order as a 'reasonable', 'self-regulating' mechanism. The concept of 'self-regulation' serves to divert attention away from the actually prevailing chaos of the destruction of capital, the bankruptcy of entrepreneurs and factories, mass unemployment, insufficient capital investment, currency disturbances, and arbitrary redistributions of property.[232] Only in this way is the introduction into economic theory of concepts of 'statics' and 'dynamics', which originated in theoretical physics, without any justification of such a twofold division of theory, understandable.[233]

---

that 'an introduction of the time factor "t" into the equation immediately and clearly makes them insoluble', Streller 1928, p. 12.

231 Thus Carver also recently wrote: 'In fact every dynamic movement is either a disturbance of a static condition, or a series of movements by which the static condition is reasserting itself, or rather by which a new static condition is being established after the disturbance', Carver 1937, p. 29.

232 Ricardo stresses that, despite changing economic conditions, the mechanism of self-regulation will distribute capital among individual branches of industry exactly according to their respective needs, 'without often producing either the effects of a glut from a too abundant supply, or an enormously high price from the supply being unequal to the demand', Ricardo 1912, p. 49. Conrad similarly assures us that only the tendency to equilibrium is 'to be thanked if' an economy, 'lacking centralised management, does not fall into chaos', Conrad 1936, p. 236. Hayek's language is characteristic: he sees merely the economy's 'adjustments' but regards the intervals of disturbances and catastrophes between two 'adjustments' as 'unproblematic', Hayek 1931, p. 23.

233 So the concept of 'dynamics' is only vaguely indicated. Within the static line of thought, only statics had to be defined. Dynamics was then the other, the 'counterpart' which does

The untenability of such a division becomes clear when the fact that there are no 'immobile' economic processes is considered; that the so-called 'stationary' economy 'moves', is, namely, a circular process. Hence the characteristic distinction between statics and dynamics cannot be that one investigates immobile, the other mobile, changing phenomena. Instead, we characterise as 'static' a kinetic economic process which has reached complete equilibrium in its movements and, because all subjective and objective conditions persist, repeats itself forever in unchanging form, from one period to the next (a cyclical process).[234] Consequently, a dynamic economy is not to be understood just as an economy 'in motion' (a static economy also 'moves') but rather as an economic process which has not reached equilibrium in its movement and thus moves in disequilibrium over the course of time. This can only mean, however, that the conditions of this economic process change from period to period, hence the result of the economic process – the economic structure – also experiences continual changes.

Since John Stuart Mill, theory has been forced into this twofold division; but only statics, the tendency towards equilibrium, has been worked on. Dynamics and the necessity of 'dynamising' theory have only been talked about, without anyone being able to construct a complete theory of dynamics. Success in breaking away from the dictatorship of these traditional concepts has only come late and very slowly. Finally, as Bode states, it has been recognised that there is no point in clinging to the concept of an equilibrium state if, in reality 'equilibrium is nowhere departed from, tended towards or passed through'.[235]

Understanding that the equilibrium line of thought is untenable has not, however, made the position of the dominant theory any easier. On one hand, it states that a dynamic theory is needed to explain reality; on the other hand, however, it is forced to admit that the construction of such a theory generates fundamental difficulties.[236]

not have to be defined and which is somehow supposed to 'complement' statics, Streller 1928, p. 5.

234 Bilimovic 1937b, p. 298.

235 [Bode 1937, p. 599.]

236 'Only static theory can be regarded as being established, dynamic theory is almost totally uninvestigated and unformulated. To this point, apparently, only the necessity for such a theory could be demonstrated', Streller 1928, p. 26. John Maurice Clark assures us that: 'We possess a substantially complete static economics, while dynamics is in its infancy … and very possibly is destined always to remain in that stage', Clark 1937, pp. 46, 48. Similarly Hicks mentions: 'a dynamic theory – the theory which many writers had demanded, but which none, at that time, had produced', Hicks 1939, p. 4. Cf. Harrod 1937, p. 498; and many others.

6

The discovery, only made by the most advanced, minority wing of the currently dominant theory – and then only after the violent disturbances of the [First] World War – namely that a dynamic reality cannot be explained by arguments based on ideas of equilibrium, had already been enunciated by Marx in 1867 in the theory of the 'dual character of labour'. This theory was completed in the second volume of *Capital*, in the theory of the various circuits of capital and also of the turnover time of capital. Marx was obliged to set foot here, too, on terrain that had never been entered before. First, he had to create all the categories and concepts which were connected with the time element (circuit, turnover, turnover time, turnover cycles). He correctly raises the objection that classical theory has neglected the investigation of the time element, the form of the circuits and of turnover.[237] Such a disregard was understandable given their merely value-oriented approach. In contrast, Marx's conception of the dual character of all economic phenomena compelled him to look at the economy in its specific movement, not statically. For capital advanced in the form of money can only maintain and multiply itself by changing its natural form in the circuit, transforming itself from the money form into the shape of the elements of production and from these again into the shape of finished products, commodities. Capital must spend a given minimum period of time, objectively determined by the technologies of the processes of production and circulation, in each of these three stages before passing on to the next phase. Capital 'is a movement, a circulatory process through different stages ... Hence it can only be grasped as a movement, and not as a static thing.'[238] The 'production time' presented in the first volume of *Capital* is now supplemented in the second volume by an analysis of 'circulation time'.[239] This not only has consequences for the specific problem of the size of profit but also gives Marx the opportunity to deal with the naked form of motion as such,[240] the question of the duration of the circuits, whether they coincide or are sequential, i.e. the conditions for the undisturbed transition from one stage to the next. The circuit of capital proceeds normally only so long as its various phases pass into each other without delay.[241] Marx demonstrates the theoretically postu-

237 Cf. Marx 1978b, p. 234.
238 Marx 1978b, p. 185.
239 Marx 1978b, p. 200.
240 Marx 1978b, p. 185.
241 Marx 1978b, p. 133, cf. p. 183.

lated conditions for such a normal circuit, which in reality are only present by way of exception: the undisturbed course requires the co-existence of capital in all of its three natural forms. The normal 'succession' of each part is conditioned by the 'co-existence' of capital, i.e. by its constant availability in all three forms – as money-capital, productive-capital and commodity-capital – and by its proportional division into each of these forms.[242] This simple formulation conceals the problem of dynamics. The 'coexistence' of the three forms of capital is identical with their synchronisation and thus presupposes given values that are unchanged, because they all fall into the same unit of time. It is precisely only in this case that the 'unity of the three circuits' can really be spoken of.[243] In contrast, 'succession' is a process in time and consequently includes the possibility of revolutions in the value of the individual parts of capital, which must impede the smooth transition of capital from one phase to another.[244] Thus, according to Marx, equilibrium would only be possible under the unrealistic assumption that values and technology are constant.[245] Since in reality this condition cannot be realised, the circuit of capital must move 'abnormally', i.e. in disequilibrium.

The entire presentation is crowned by the analysis of the 'turnover of capital', where the circuit of capital through all three stages is understood 'not as an isolated act but as a periodic process'. The duration of this turnover, given by the sum of production time and circulation time, is called 'turnover time' and measures 'the periodicity in the capital's life-process, or, if you like, the time required for the renewal and repetition of the valorisation and production process of the same capital value'.[246] Finally, following the presentation of the turnover of individual capitals, Marx arrives at the presentation of 'The

242 Marx 1978b, p. 183.

243 Marx 1978b, p. 184.

244 'Further: since the circulation process of capital is not completed in one day but extends over a fairly long period until the capital returns to its original form, since ... great upheavals and changes take place in the market in the course of this period, since great changes take place in the productivity of labour and therefore also in the real value of commodities, it is quite clear that between the starting point, the prerequisite capital, and the time of its return at the end of one of these periods, great catastrophes must occur and elements of crisis must have gathered and developed', Marx 1989c, p. 126, [Marx emphasised '*market*' and '*value*'].

245 'In order for the circuit to run its normal course ... C-M-C [must] not just include the replacement of one commodity by another, but its replacement in the same value relations'. '[T]hus it is ... assumed that the commodities ... do not suffer any change of value during the circuit; if this is not the case, then the process cannot run its normal course', Marx 1978b, p. 153 [editor's interpolation].

246 Marx 1978b, pp. 235–6.

overall turnover of capital advanced. Turnover cycles',[247] in order, within this train of thought, to emphasise those elements which operate in the direction of disequilibrium.

In his reproduction schemas, Marx proceeds on the assumption of an identical turnover time of one year for all capitals in all branches of production. While for the dominant theory the synchronisation of all movements is a definitive approach, for Marx it is merely a preliminary, simplifying assumption, a first step in the method of successive approximation of reality. He later considers the circumstance that, in reality, 'the turnover times of the capitals vary according to their various spheres of investment'. This variation in turnover time depends on the natural and technical conditions of production of each kind of commodity (food crops, leather, etc.).[248] In addition to these circumstances, resulting from the process of production and 'which distinguish the turnover of different capitals invested in different branches of industry', there are others given by conditions in the sphere of circulation (e.g. improved means of transport and communication, which reduce the period during which commodities are moved about).[249] It is self-evident that all these differences in total turnover times must necessarily result in disequilibrium of the system, considering that the original equilibrium in the equations for the reproduction schemas only resulted on the assumption of an equal turnover time for all capitals.

In addition to these sources of disequilibrium, due to variations in the total turnover time of the capitals in the various branches of production, there are further differentiating factors within each branch of production, because the turnover times of the fixed and circulating parts of capital are different. With regard to circulating capital, Marx investigates the temporal relation between working period and turnover period, since the size of the circulating capital which functions during both of these periods is conditioned by their durations. Of the three possible cases – that the working period is the same as, longer than or shorter than the period of circulation[250] – only the first, 'in which the working period and the circulation time form two equal halves of the turnover period', allows the undisturbed transition of the capital functioning in the working period into the circulation phase.[251] The same applies in the

247 [This a chapter heading.] Marx 1978b, p. 262.

248 Marx 1978b, p. 236. Cf. the analysis of various turnover times for agriculture, Marx 1978b, p. 317; forestry, Marx 1978b, p. 321; and cattle-raising, Marx 1978b, p. 322.

249 Marx 1978b, p. 327.

250 Marx 1978b, pp. 343–55.

251 Marx 1978b, p. 339.

case in which both periods are indeed unequal but the turnover period 'is ... an exact multiple' of the working period, e.g. if the working period is three weeks and the circulation period six, nine or 12 weeks, etc.[252] The turnover process only proceeds 'normally', undisturbed, under this 'exceptional' 'assumption',[253] which in reality only occurs by chance.

In all the other cases, i.e. for the majority of social circulating capital, the necessary modification of the 'normal course' occurs during the annual or multi-year turnover cycle. As a result, the circulating capital advanced is 'set free' or 'tied up'.[254] This generates the objective basis for and subjective impulses to credit expansion or contraction and also the impulses to expand or contract the given scale of production itself, instead of the originally assumed 'normal' transition, on an unchanged scale, from the working period to the circulation period. These impulses do not come from outside but arise endogenously, 'simply by the mechanism of the turnover movement', i.e. from the temporal difference between the working period and the circulation period.[255] Far from being a primary cause of changes in the scale of production (as monetary theorists of crisis assume) credit expansion and contraction is a dependent variable, conditioned by the turnover mechanism.[256]

And, similarly, the time factor (the durability of the means of production) constitutes the basis for the distinction between fixed and circulating capital. The means of labour employed in the production process 'only form fixed capital to the extent that the time during which they are in use extends longer than the turnover period of the fluid capital',[257] i.e. to the extent that the 'turnover of the fixed component of capital, and thus also the turnover time needed by it, encompasses several turnovers of the fluid components of capital'.[258]

This difference in the length of the life of both types of capital results in the variation in the replacement of both kinds of the means of labour, to the extent that we do not consider the value side (as replacement of money) alone

---

252 Marx 1978b, pp. 353, 356–7.

253 [Marx 1978b, p. 339.]

254 Marx 1978b, p. 189.

255 Marx 1978b, p. 357.

256 Curiously, a misjudgement of the importance of Marx's analysis for the understanding of the dynamic course of the capitalist economy can even be found in Engels, who held the view that Marx had ascribed 'an undeserved significance to ... a matter of little importance', namely what Marx called the 'setting-free' of money capital and that this is the 'uncertain [result] of [his] tiresome calculation business'. See Engels's note, Marx 1978b, p. 359 [editor's interpolations].

257 Marx 1978b, p. 254.

258 Marx 1978b, p. 247.

but, at the same time, replacement in kind. While labour power and those means of production which represent fluid capital (raw materials) are used up in a shorter period of time and must therefore be continuously renewed, the replacement of fixed capital in kind does not occur continuously, but rather periodically.[259] Marx uses this divergence in the time periods necessary for the replacement of both types of capital, in the form of money and in kind, as one of the elements ('the material basis') of his explanation for the periodicity of crises.[260]

So long as the process of reproduction and the problem of equilibrium are regarded exclusively from the value side, the problem under consideration here won't be encountered at all, because the distinction between the lifetimes of fixed and fluid capital applies to their natural form, not their value. If Marx's schema for simple reproduction is regarded merely in terms of value and assumes an annual renewal of all the components of capital, the resultant synchronisation of all the movements in the schema would obliterate the specific difference between fixed and circulating capital[261] and hence the whole problem connected with their various replacement times. For both fixed and also circulating capital are renewed annually as values in the schema. The problem first arises when the schema is considered in terms of use value: only now does the difference in the life of each type of capital become apparent and hence also the problem of the different dates of their replacement. (The originally assumed synchronisation of replacement dates was only a preliminary approximation, which does not correspond with reality.) While raw materials have to be renewed annually, fixed capital (e.g. the 2,000 units in department II of the schema, the consumer goods industry) 'is not renewed for the whole of the period during which it functions' because it lasts for several years.[262] Consequently, there can be no sales from department I, which manufactures this fixed capital, to department II, for several years. Since, however, the annual productive capacity of department I remains 2,000 units, overproduction must necessarily take place in department I. 'There would be a crisis – a crisis of production – despite reproduction on a constant scale.'[263] 'Normal' production could then only occur in department I if (despite the assumption of simple reproduction in department I) department II was to be expanded over several

259 Marx 1978b, pp. 533 et seq.

260 Marx 1978b, p. 264.

261 In the schema of simple reproduction, 'total value is 9,000, the fixed capital that continues to function in its natural form being excluded by our assumption', Marx 1978b, p. 473.

262 Marx 1978b, p. 570.

263 Marx 1978b, p. 533.

years,[264] creating a new, additional market for department I each year (the accelerator principle).[265] This is, however, impossible. For the faster expansion of department II, on the basis of the given technology, presupposes an impossible increase in the working population. The second department in the schema would have to double in the second year and triple in the third; the working population employed there would have to grow by 100 percent in the second year of reproduction, 50 percent in the third, and 33 percent in the fourth!

In addition to the reasons for the absence of an equilibrium, previously mentioned, there is a much more fundamental and general one, resulting from the structure of the capitalist mode of production, from the tensions which are grounded in the dual character of this mode of production.

Theories both before and after Marx confine the conditions for 'equilibrium' to sub-markets[266] and merely in terms of value. The relation between quantities and values is only analysed from the perspective of the effect of variations in quantity on marginal values. 'Equilibrium' can always be achieved under such assumptions.[267] In contrast, Marx shows that the issue is not equilibrium in sub-markets (money market, labour market, commodity market for the means of production or consumption), just as little, equilibrium in the 'production process' or the 'circulation process'. Instead, because Marx regarded the capitalist process of production as a 'circuit' in which capital passes through its various stages, he highlighted the idea that equilibrium has to be grasped as an equilibrium within the overall interaction of all these stages. From this perspective, he was the first to carefully define the state of equilibrium in the 'process as a whole', and investigate the conditions under which it arises. At the same time, however, he showed that these conditions cannot be realised within the capitalist mode of production. For Marx, this signifies, however, that the 'normal course', the 'state of equilibrium', does not mean an 'average', 'typical' or 'most frequently occurring' process but instead only an imaginary, undisturbed course of reproduction (under fictitious conditions), which never comes about in reality and merely serves as a methodological tool of analysis. As a total social

---

264 'If things are to proceed normally, accumulation in department II must take place quicker than in department I', Marx 1978b, p. 588.

265 As we see, Marx's accelerator principle is the direct opposite of that propounded in the literature of the dominant theory, Marx 1978b, p. 588.

266 'By its essence, statics only studies one single market', Streller 1928, p. 39.

267 'Equilibrium must be considered as an equilibrium of prices.' 'There is always a solution of such a system admitting full employment of every factor of production', given only that the condition 'that prices must be high enough to equalise supply and demand' is maintained, Cassel 1937, pp. 438, 444.

process, the problem of reproduction has to be dealt with in its dual character, that is, 'the process of reproduction has to be considered from the standpoint of the replacement of the individual components of C′ both in value and in material'.[268] Consequently, equilibrium could only be realised if both sets of conditions, those on the value side and those on the use side, are simultaneously fulfilled.

Marx's specific crisis problematic and its solution arise from this comparison of the two series – 'the *value* components of the social product ... with its *material* components'. In the circuit C ... C′ 'the preconditions for social reproduction can be immediately recognised from the fact that it is necessary to demonstrate what becomes of each portion of the value of this overall product C′'.[269] This means not only that, in terms of value, all the commodities produced must be sold on the market, without a remainder. It is also necessary to investigate what then happens to the material mass of things, the use values, which have been purchased to see whether they can in fact be completely employed in the production process (equilibrium in production),[270] including individual consumption. It is therefore a matter of the 'transformation of one portion of the product's value back into capital, the entry of another part into ... individual consumption ... and this movement is not only a replacement of values, but a replacement of materials, and is therefore conditioned not just by the mutual relations of the value components of the social product but equally by their use values, their material shape'.[271]

From the above, it is already apparent that the assertion often made in the literature that, according to Marx, use values lie 'outside the consideration of political economy' is based on a misunderstanding. According to Marx, only 'use value as such', that is use value in the sense of subjective utility, lies outside political economy.[272] He counterposes to this use value as 'material shape', which is not a subjective utility but an objective thing with a definite, economically important form,[273] a natural form which is exchanged on the market or functions as a means of production in the labour process. Consequently Marx

---

268 Marx 1978b, p. 469. [C′ is the expanded value of commodities, after production, in the circuit of capital.]

269 Marx 1978b, pp. 469, 506. [C is the value of the commodities which go into the production process in the circuit of capital.]

270 Marx consequently speaks of the 'social balance of production', Marx 1981b, p. 1020. As the immediate employment of all factors of production is assumed, stocks lying unused in warehouses are disregarded.

271 Marx 1978b, p. 470.

272 Marx 1987a, p. 270.

273 Marx 1989c, p. 120.

speaks of 'use value or object of utility', of use value or 'material shape', of 'use value or its physical shape as a commodity', of the 'sensuous objectivity of commodities as physical objects' and of the 'mass of the means of production', as distinct from their values.[274] Use values, defined in this way, take on crucial importance in Marx's system.[275]

Under the influence of dominant theories, Marxist literature has regarded the problem of equilibrium – insofar as its conditions are specified in Marx's '*tableau économique*' – exclusively from the value side (Kautsky, Rudolf Hilferding, Otto Bauer, Rosa Luxemburg and Bukharin).[276] There have to be certain quantitative, value proportions in both of the departments in Marx's reproduction schemas if all the quantities of value supplied and demanded are to be exchanged without a remainder. The analysis of the material side of the labour process was reduced to the single proposition that in the process of reproduction, department I must produce means of production and department II means of consumption.

Marx's conception of equilibrium, however, is fundamentally different from the above. He shows that, in addition to value proportions, quite definite technical proportions must exist between the mass of labour and the mass of the means of production (machines, raw materials, buildings), in all the departments and sub-departments of the reproduction schemas. These depend on the particular character of the sphere of production under consideration. For the technical labour process, the amount of value which these use values represent is quite immaterial.[277] In factories, such a technical proportionality among factors of production is arranged directly by the technical management. In view of the reciprocal relations of the various branches of production within society, however, it is also the basic condition for the undisturbed course of the production process, because the social division of labour makes the various preceding and subsequent stages of the labour process dependent on one

274 Marx 1976b, pp. 152, 168, 158, 138, 754; also Marx 1978b p. 471; Marx 1981b, p. 137.

275 *Use value* can only be abstracted from to the extent that the matter at hand is the *process of valorisation*, the formation of surplus value: 'In considering surplus value as such, the original form of the product ... is of no consequence. It becomes important when considering the actual process of reproduction ... Here is another example of how use value as such acquires economic significance', Marx 1989c, p. 386. [Marx emphasised '*use value*']. Similarly Marx 1989c, p. 120.

276 [See Kautsky 1911b; Hilferding 1949, p. 130; Otto Bauer 1986; Luxemburg 1951; Bukharin 1972b, p. 63.]

277 'All these things serve in the real labour process because of the relationship which exists between them as use values – not as exchange values, and still less as capital', Marx 1989c, p. 398. [Marx emphasised '*use values*'.]

another, as 'element[s] of the total labour of society'. Despite all their apparent personal independence, producers soon discover that 'the independence of the individuals from each other has as its counterpart and supplement a system of all-round material dependence'.[278] Only insofar as there is such technical articulation and reciprocal, quantitative accord among individual branches of production is 'full employment'[279] of all productive factors in the technical labour process possible, without either unused capacity or shortages of raw materials, machines or labour power.

In short, the condition for equilibrium in the system of capitalist production as a whole is a dual proportionality of its basic elements. While sale on the market, without a remainder, requires value proportionality within the scope of individual branches of production, for the technical labour process quantitative proportionality of all productive factors, among all branches of production and within each branch, as conditioned by the state of technology, is necessary. This technical proportionality is no more present from the outset under the capitalist mode of production than value proportionality, as '[t]he quantitative articulation of society's productive organism ... is ... haphazard and spontaneous'.[280] Is there any possibility that this dual proportionality is realised at all? This question takes us to the heart of Marx's conception of the problem of equilibrium in the 'process as a whole', which is the unity of the technical labour process and the process of value circulation. The difference from the dominant conception is most clearly intelligible in the example of simple reproduction.

'The supposition is that a social capital ... supplies the same mass of commodity values and satisfies the same quantity of needs in both the current year and the previous year' (that is, supplies the same mass of use values). Does an equilibrium in reproduction now exist in the case, for example, of a bad harvest reducing the amount of cotton by a half, although it represents the same value as twice as much cotton did previously? In short, does 'value ... remain

278 Marx 1976b, pp. 168, 202–3. Marx therefore speaks of the 'interdependent branches of the collective production of a whole society' and of the 'bond' which holds it together. Not only are the branches of cattle-breeding, which produces hides, tanning, which produces leather, and shoemaking, which works leather up, quantitatively dependent on one another, but those branches which supply them with means of production are too, Marx 1976b, pp. 472, 274–5. What results from this and what is important for understanding the dynamics of capitalism is that revolutions in the mode of production in one individual sphere, e.g. machine spinning, will necessitate similar revolutions in other spheres, such as weaving and dyeing, otherwise incongruities arise in the technical proportionality between these branches of industry, Marx 1976b, p. 505.

279 [English in the original.]

280 Marx 1976b, p. 202.

the same, even though the volume of use values declines'?[281] Seen in terms of value, there would still be 'a market equilibrium' in the schema of simple reproduction. In contrast, the schema would necessarily exhibit large disturbances when looked at from the standpoint of the technical labour process: half the spindles and looms would have to be shut down due to the shortage of cotton, i.e. the technical scale would be halved. 'Reproduction cannot be *repeated* on the same scale.'[282] This example shows the inadequacy of the dominant theory's purely value perspective. It assumes that the conditions for equilibrium which are expressed in value equations can always be realised. It does know that capitals which are immobilised in one branch of industry can only be shifted to another branch with difficulty. It treats such instances, however, as 'frictions' which only impede the realisation of value equilibrium for short periods. In contrast, it regards 'adjustment' over longer periods as eminently possible, because the issue here is not so much the transfer of already immobilised old capitals, as of the investment of new capitals, thus of 'processes of adjustment' within production. These allow the subsequent re-establishment of the correct value proportions on both sides of the exchange equation. In contrast, Marx shows that the value equilibrium, asserted by all static theories, to which the economy is supposed to tend, can be established only exceptionally and by chance. This is because the technical labour process gives rise to objective and enduring resistances and blockages which, in principle, exclude the establishment of such an equilibrium. Even if, when seen from a purely physical point of view, complete freedom and mobility of capital existed and the transfers in the sense required by the value equations for the establishment of equilibrium took place, equilibrium in the system as a whole would not be achievable, due to the incongruence, in principle, between value proportions and technical, quantitative proportions. It may well be possible for a partial equilibrium to occur temporarily, e.g. a value equilibrium on the market. But then it becomes apparent that there is no equilibrium in production and various elements of production cannot find employment or, conversely, that although there is quantitative equilibrium in production, there is no value equilibrium on the market. It follows that with a definite quantitative, technical proportion, which is necessarily given by the scale of production and depends on the size of fixed capital,[283] a value proportion resulting from this technical proportion is also already given. It cannot be changed according to the free will of the entrepreneur so that the theoretically postulated conditions

281 Marx 1978b, p. 471. Cf. Marx 1989c, p. 145.
282 Marx 1989c, p. 146.
283 Marx 1978b, p. 245 [this reference is not relevant, unlike pp. 280–7].

for value-equilibrium are satisfied. In short, value proportionality is not very elastic because it is bound up with technical proportionality. Under these circumstances, the incongruence of the two series of proportions and hence the tendency towards the disequilibrium of the system as a whole is unavoidable. On the basis of capitalist production, equilibrium – the 'normal course' – is merely our abstraction, a conceptual fiction derived from the 'real movement', which is the opposite of this abstraction, namely constant disequilibrium. 'In political economy law is determined by its opposite, absence of law. The true law of political economy is chance.'[284]

Not only does Marx deny the regulatory function of the price mechanism, its supposed tendency to balance supply and demand but he also shows that once this mechanism has fallen into a state of disequilibrium,[285] it continually generates impulses which increase this disequilibrium. Because too much has been produced, there is an impulse to produce still more! From Adam Smith to the present, the dominant schools could only propound the theory of the tendency for the volume of production to adjust to demand with the aid of competition, because they presupposed competition as given, as a kind of '*ars qualitas occulta*',[286] without ever investigating its origins. 'Competition ... is burdened with explaining all the economists' irrationalities, whereas it is supposed to be the economists who explain competition.'[287]

In contrast to the dominant conception, Marx shows that there is no balancing mechanism, in the sense of the adjustment of production to demand. According to Marx, an orientation to consumption, i.e. adjustment of production to demand, was a characteristic of capitalism's youth, the period before the advent of modern large-scale industry, when there was as yet no large fixed capital.[288] There can be no talk of such an 'adjustment' of production to demand at present, when fixed capital constitutes a predominant and continuously growing share of total capital. The entrepreneur ignores the 'market's command' to curtail production, supposedly expressed in falling prices. An orientation towards production instead of consumption is precisely characteristic of the highly developed capitalist economy, i.e. production precedes demand. Hence,

284 Marx 1975a, p. 211. [Marx emphasised '*chance*'.]

285 'In actual fact, demand and supply never coincide, or, if they do so, it is only by chance and not to be taken into account for scientific purposes; it should be considered as not having happened', Marx 1981b, p. 291.

286 ['*Ars qualitas occulta*' means 'occult quality'.]

287 Marx 1981b, p. 1005.

288 Cf. Marx 1976a, p. 137. Cf. on the absence of expansionary economic cycles, cyclical booms with subsequent breakdowns under early capitalism, 'into the eighteenth century', see Sombart 1919, pp. 214 et seq. [The quotation is on p. 215].

for the reasons previously provided, there is an inherent tendency to periodically overproduce durable 'fixed' capital, for which no profitable employment can be found.[289] But because there is a persistent tendency to overproduce in the sphere producing fixed capital, a compulsion to compete necessarily arises, which does not operate to balance supply and demand. Where, as a consequence of overproduction there is insufficient living-space (market outlets) for all entrepreneurs, individuals are compelled to save themselves from collapse at the expense of the others. Far from curtailing output when prices and profits are falling, every entrepreneur with access to the necessary means seeks to produce more cheaply and, indeed, profitably than competitors, by introducing better and cheaper technologies and by expanding the scale of production. So the continual overproduction of fixed capital constitutes a permanent impulse to continually revolutionise technology and hence to continuous revolutions in value, which are characteristic of the capitalist mode of production.[290] Continuous improvements in technology and expansion of the scale of production make general overproduction even worse. The individual entrepreneur has, however, secured the profitability of and markets for his own progressive plant.[291]

So, under the pressure of initial overproduction, the transformation of the entire structure of the capitalist mechanism propagates over the whole breadth of society. At one pole, new, higher technology, together with the enlarged scale of the individual plant, is victorious. The extra profits achieved attract new entrepreneurs, the movement becomes more generalised and an 'upswing' occurs. At the other pole of society, simultaneously and as a direct consequence of the spread of improved technologies and associated revolutions in value (reduction in 'socially necessary' labour time), this does not prevent all plants with more backward technologies from being even more threatened by falling prices and overproduction, and pressured to withdraw from competition altogether. As, however, the scale of those few new large plants exceeds the productive capacity of the many small, failing plants, the end result of the

289 Marx 1976a, p. 137. 'What Ricardo cannot answer, and neither Mr Say for that matter, is where competition, and the resultant bankruptcies, trade crises etc. come from, if every capital finds its proper employ?' *'If capitals … were not so numerous in relation to the uses of capital – competition* would be completely inexplicable', Marx 1981a, p. 416, [Marx emphasised only '*competition*'.] The only one of the recent writers to have seen this problem is Willard L. Thorp: 'Under competition', he writes, 'it is certain that some degree of overcapacity will exist', Thorp 1935, p. 491.

290 Marx 1978b, p. 185.

291 Cf. Marx 1981b, pp. 231–2 [these pages do not seem relevant], 279 et seq.

movement is growth in the overall scale of social production. And this movement is repeated again and again, as the large new plants with the most modern technologies soon lose their privileged position because of the generalised application of technological innovations and the game must begin anew.

Under the pressure of periodically occurring overproduction, the impulse to constantly revolutionise technology and hence also to 'periodic revolutions in value' is strengthened. The entrepreneurs who yesterday were able to gain extra surplus value by introducing new processes are today threatened by newcomers with still better technologies and have to be content with the average profit. Tomorrow they may not even cover their costs or may indeed register a loss, and will have to pull out of the market.[292] There is an eternal hunt after extra profits for their own individual plants, a continual attempt to secure an at least temporary, privileged island of extra profit, by revolutionising technology. The 'real movement', presented above, shows that there can be no talk of an 'adjustment' of production to demand; rather, production constantly outpaces demand and the 'regulatory' function of the price mechanism does not exist at all. Far from leading to the curtailment of production, periods of falling prices were in the past and still are today periods of the greatest technological progress and expansion of production. In the face of this now self-evident failure in the construction of the existing economic mechanism, the dominant theory also begins to discover that instead of the alleged tendency towards equilibrium, there is a '*perpetuum mobile*' of change, a tendency towards disequilibrium;[293] that instead of the regulatory function of the price mechanism, balancing supply and demand, situations can arise in which 'once destroyed, equilibrium is lost forever'.[294]

A theory of dynamic movement must not only point out individual dynamic 'factors' but also make the disequilibrating movement of the system as a whole and its causes intelligible. Beyond that, it has to show the consequences of the dynamic movement for the whole system. In a self-contained theory, Marx sought to grasp not only the sequence of the economic cycle but also the structural changes in the whole system which were its result. Only thus could he show the direction of the overall course of the economic system, its 'developmental tendencies'. This is not contradicted by the fact that, at a particular level of development, the indicated direction of this course encounters a limit and approaches its end. The validity of the theory is not put in question if it is shown

292 Cf. Marx 1978b, p. 185.
293 Cf. Rosenstein-Rodan 1929, p. 131.
294 Ricci 1930, p. 655.

that this limit to the capitalist dynamic is conditioned by and derived from the basic conditions of the system, the 'dual character of labour'.[295]

We have seen how,[296] with the development of the capitalist mode of production, a tendency towards growth in the minimum size of plants prevails. Hence also growth in the capitals required to run a business under 'normal' conditions.[297] It follows that, at a given moment, the scale of production, the size of plant does not depend on the free will of the entrepreneur. 'The actual degree of development of the productive forces compels him to produce on such and such a scale.'[298] This is, therefore, something given by the technology. It is self-evident that this makes accord between the technical proportions and

---

295 Marx not only regarded a definite level of maturity in the development of the objective factor – the economy – as a precondition for the future higher form of society but also of the subjective factor, humanity itself. World history, for him, 'is nothing but the creation of man through human labour, nothing but the emergence of nature for man', Marx 1975b, p. 305, cf. pp. 292, 333. The 'conquest' of the world of objects is, at the same time, the first emergence of this world for humanity. For Marx, its domination, 'possessing' it [Marx 1975b, p. 299], does not happen because of a theoretical outlook but rather through labour, through human praxis. In this way, Marx distinguishes himself from Feuerbach, for example, cf. Marcuse 1972, p. 22. The labour, whose result is the subjection of nature and the evolution of humanity, is not, however, 'value-creating' labour but 'real', i.e. 'concrete' labour which creates useful things; in short, the development of human productive power. Since concrete labour is always bound together with value-creating labour in the present economic order, however, the degree of the progressive maturation of concrete labour can only be expressed in its value, in the fall of the rate of profit. It was shown above that the fall in the rate of profit is only the capitalist expression of the wealth of society, of the degree of development of labour's productive power, and hence is also a symptom of the approaching supersession of capital's rule itself. 'The decrease in the interest rate is therefore a symptom of the annulment of capital only inasmuch as it is a symptom of the growing domination of capital in the process of perfecting itself – of the estrangement which is growing and therefore hastening to its annulment.' Marx 1975b, p. 316.

296 Having shown elsewhere the consequences which arise for the problem of equilibrium by considering the process of accumulation in terms of value, Grossmann 1929a, I confine myself here to emphasising those moments which impede the attainment of a state of equilibrium from the material side of the technical labour process and increase the incongruence, already described, between material and value proportions even more.

297 Marx 1976b, pp. 777.

298 Marx 1976a, p. 118. The significance of this statement first becomes entirely apparent if we compare it with Böhm-Bawerk's view, according to which the scale of production can be determined arbitrarily, and is not technically given. According to Böhm-Bawerk, 'any given total of present goods, be it large or small, is sufficient to purchase and remunerate the total supply of labour existent in an economic community. All that is required is to bring about a corresponding contraction or extension of the production period', Böhm-Bawerk 1959b, p. 354. It is simply to be wondered why unemployment continues to exist, when it appears so easily abolished.

the required value proportions more difficult. In the course of capitalist development, the tendency towards growth in the organic composition of capital prevails. An ever larger part of a given capital is transformed into means of production (MP) and an ever smaller part into labour power (LP).[299] Looked at from the value side, the ratio c:v does grow, however, because of the slower pace of technological progress (cheapening, in value terms, of the means of production) than the quantitative growth in [the ratio of] MP to LP. The difference between capital's rates of growth in terms of the quantity [of commodities] and value makes the congruence of value and physical proportions even more difficult than previously.

Further, the analysis of the technical labour process yields the law of the uneven development of the individual branches of production.[300] It is precisely the example of this disproportionality in development that best illustrates the distinction between Marx's conception and that of the dominant theory. The latter represents uneven development as capital accumulation in different branches as being different in value terms, e.g. 20 percent in one, 35 percent in another, etc.; and disturbances as arising from such value disproportions. According to Marx, this can happen, but does not have to and does not get to the essence of the problem. Even if all spheres were to have accumulated evenly, in value terms, e.g. by 1 percent, disturbances must nevertheless arise if the expansion in material terms is not proportionally the same in all branches of production. For, with the same percentage growth in capital (e.g. 1 percent) in all branches, the material expansion in the various branches can vary in size and amount, for example, to 5 percent in one sphere and 20 percent in another. This is conditioned by the specific technological character of each sphere and, according to Marx, it is these characteristics which underlie leaps in technological development.[301]

---

299 Marx 1976b, pp. 773–5.

300 'The specific degree of development of the social productivity of labour differs from one particular sphere of production to another', Marx 1981b, p. 263.

301 'If all other capitals have accumulated at the same rate, it does not follow at all that their production has [also] increased at the same rate ... The same value is produced in both cases, but the quantity of commodities in which it is represented is very different. It is quite incomprehensible, therefore, why trade A, because the value of its output has increased by 1 percent while the mass of its products has grown by 20 percent, must find a market in trade B, where the value has likewise increased by 1 percent, but the quantity of its output only by 5 percent. Here, the author has failed to take into consideration the difference between use value and exchange value', Marx 1989c, pp. 306–7.

The contradiction, *in abstracto*,[302] between possible, continuous accumulation of value and the fact of discontinuous, jerky material expansion is related to, but not identical with, the above law. Vulgar Marxist literature is fond of looking at accumulation in purely value terms and assuming that any arbitrary amount of value can be accumulated (see, for example, Laurat);[303] that 50 percent of the surplus value is consumed by the capitalist, and the other 50 percent steadily accumulated each year. It does not ask whether this surplus value destined for accumulation is large enough to acquire the quantities of means of production required for the expansion of production. The assumption that any small increase in profit can correspond with an equally small growth in the technological apparatus of production, i.e. the presupposition of the infinite divisibility of goods, underpins this conception. In contrast, Marx emphasises that such a parallel relation between value accumulation and material accumulation does not exist, because not every dollar earned is accumulated, i.e. can be converted into the material elements of production. For the expansion of the scale of production, a certain minimum amount of capital is usually required, to buy a whole set of technically connected machines, making up a unit (e.g. in the textile industry).[304] Expansion can only take place, therefore, by this unit, or multiples of it.[305] Such material relations – and consequently also the value relations which they bear – consequently determine the minimum amount of money capital necessary for expansion and vary from industry to industry.[306] In short, according to Marx, 'the proportions in which the productive process can be expanded are not arbitrary, but are prescribed by technical factors'.[307] While, for example, the entire surplus value (or even part of it) suffices and is employed for the expansion of production in one branch, in others the surplus value is saved up for several years until it reaches the minimum size necessary for 'real accumulation'.[308] Consequently, while one branch of production may be expanded every year, expansion in others only occurs at intervals of several years.

The incongruence between the value side and the material side of the process of reproduction, which we have examined from the side of production, is increased still more by impulses, which come from the demand side. An

302 ['*In abstracto*' means 'in the abstract'.]
303 [Laurat 1932.]
304 Cf. Marx 1978b, pp. 162–3.
305 Marx 1976b, pp. 465–6.
306 Marx 1978b, pp. 162–3; and Marx 1976b, pp. 422, 424.
307 Marx 1978b, p. 158.
308 Marx 1978b, p. 565.

even, proportional expansion of all the spheres of production rests on the tacit assumption that demand (consumption) can be expanded just as evenly and proportionally. In contrast, Marx emphasises that the individual or productive use of certain commodities is constrained, inelastic, which must likewise result in an uneven material expansion of production in various spheres. No one who finds two tractors sufficient for the cultivation of their land will buy four simply because their price has fallen by a half. Demand for tractors is – *ceteris paribus* – not dependent on their price alone but is, rather, determined by the area to be cultivated, that is quantitatively. 'But the use value – consumption – depends not on value, but on the quantity. It is quite unintelligible why I should buy 6 knives because I can now get them for the same price that I previously paid for 1'.[309]

All these moments exclude symmetry in technical and value movements, consequently they impede the doubly proportional expansion of the productive apparatus, in both value and quantitative terms, that theory postulates as the condition for 'equilibrium'. The realisation of this equilibrium cannot be an enduring 'rule'. With the constant impulse to revolutionise technology and values, the coordination of the value and material sides of the productive apparatus must become more and more difficult and their incongruence constantly grow. The two sides of the productive apparatus move in opposite directions following technological change and the development of the productive forces: the values of individual commodities have a tendency to fall, while the mass of material goods increases. Under such circumstances equilibrium, the 'rule' presupposed by political economy, can only occur, as it were, by chance within the general irregularity, as a momentary point of transition in the midst of constant disequilibrium.[310]

---

309 Marx 1989c, p. 307. The fact of inelastic demand, along with the role of money, constitutes the main argument in Marx's critique of the James Mill-Say theory of the identity of demand and supply, by means of which the possibility of generalised crisis is denied, Marx 1989c, pp. 290–2.

310 '... a mode of production whose laws can only assert themselves as blindly operating averages between constant irregularities', Marx 1976b, p. 196.

CHAPTER 27

Review of Josef A. Schumpeter, *Business Cycles: A Theoretical, Historical and Statistical Analysis of the Capitalist Process**

Schumpeter, Josef A. 1939, *Business Cycles: A Theoretical, Historical and Statistical Analysis of the Capitalist Process*, two volumes, New York: McGraw-Hill (1050pp, $10.00).

Schumpeter's new book is an inexhaustible source of information on the economic facts and theories relevant to business cycles, and as such it is a meritorious work, certainly above the average. He is no newcomer to the realm of theory; his present work must therefore be judged in light of his previous theoretical studies.

Schumpeter is an adherent of the subjective theory of value, even though his first book, *The Nature and Content of Economic Theories* (1908), did not show in detail how a science of economics would be built on subjective valuations. Psychic data are intensive magnitudes and hardly appropriate to serve as primary cells of an exact scientific structure, and Schumpeter in that earliest work emphatically refused to explain economics through an analysis of the psyche and the motives of economic activity.[1] He preferred to build an 'exact discipline of human economy',[2] a mathematical, functional theory, on the basis of objectively existing market phenomena, the objective relations of exchange. He sought to formulate 'pure' economics 'in a way similar to that in which mechanics describes motions',[3] and to show that 'it is possible to conceive it exactly and indisputably and that scientific correctness in the physicist's sense is not unattainable in our domain too'.[4]

This exact basis of exchange relations could, according to him, be expressed in a 'girdle of equations'[5] that would describe the problem of equilibrium at

* [Originally published as Grossman 1941b.]
1 Schumpeter 1908, p. 77.
2 Schumpeter 1908, p. 117.
3 Schumpeter 1908, p. 128.
4 Schumpeter 1908, p. 131.
5 Schumpeter 1908, p. 132.

the centre of statics.[6] Schumpeter realised that 'statics' was nothing but a theoretical fiction. The reality was to be treated in the next book, *The Theory of Economic Development* (1912, second edition 1926).[7] The book, however, turned out to be but a temporary and preliminary sketch, the elaboration of which has come only with the present book. Here Schumpeter has moved still further from the Austrian School, and especially from the conception that the consumer – man and his Needs – is the initial factor in the study of economic phenomena and that the direction of the productive process and its changes are nothing but a reaction to the changes in the demand. Railroads have not emerged because any consumers took the initiative in displaying an effective demand for their service in preference to the services of mail coaches. Nor did the consumers display any such initiative, wish to have electric lamps or rayon stockings, or to travel by motor car or airplane, or to listen to radios or to chew gum. There is obviously no lack of realism in the proposition that the great majority of changes in commodities consumed has been forced by producers on consumers who, more often than not, have resisted the change and have had to be educated up by elaborate psychotechnics of advertising.[8]

If this is true, however, the whole subjective theory of value is done away with. For the value of the productive factors is not and cannot be deduced from the value of the final product given as the degree of satisfaction of the demand. The relation between the final product and the productive factor is reversed and the basis of the prevalent doctrine is thus abandoned. Since Schumpeter does not present a new theory of economic phenomena, what he offers here is not a general theory attempting a causal explanation, but at best a partial theory of a special domain. All it aims to be is a positivistic description of the phenomena, in an 'exact' mathematical disguise, nothing but a protocol statement: 'it is thus and so'.

But the book just published is remarkable for still another reason. The Schumpeter of 1908 planned to construct an 'exact' mathematico-functional theory of exchange relations and he owes his renown as a theoretician to precisely that intention; the Schumpeter of 1912 did not apply this principle to dynamics, but broke with his previous method. He did not succeed in passing from statics to dynamics while maintaining his 'exact' conception of exchange relations. The strict method of statics proved inapplicable to dynamic problems. For that reason Schumpeter took refuge, in his second work, in the method which he had previously deprecated as 'motivative' and 'psychological'.

6 Schumpeter 1908, p. 118.

7 Schumpeter 1983.

8 Schumpeter 1939, p. 73.

The promises of the first book were not fulfilled. The dynamic forces were not conceived 'exactly', in terms of exchange relations or 'a girdle of equations', but were deduced from the capitalist's psyche, from his constant urge for innovations: his 'joy of forms', his 'daring because of his very difficulties', his 'will to victory' in the 'the financial boxing match', in brief, from 'economic activity considered as a sport'.[9] Thus, Schumpeter's scientific fame as an exponent of 'exact' economic science was founded not on the accomplishments of his second book, but on the unfulfilled promises of his first.

The Schumpeter of 1939 revolutionises his methodological foundations for the third time: the motive force of all economic changes is no longer to be found in exact exchange relations nor in the capitalist's heroic personality, but in his banal, prosaic quest for profits, already stressed so much by Ricardo and later by Marx: the only thing that counts is the magnitude of profit and its changes. The capitalist no longer functions as the original dynamic force which spontaneously works changes. His activity is itself merely a result and he himself a mere stopping point in the automatic workings of the entire mechanism, aiming to restore a vanished rentability.[10] Methodologically it is interesting that through this inner tendency toward accumulation, and excluding all external influence, Schumpeter tries to explain both the expansion and the depression that follows. He rejects the opinion that the impulse towards the change and expansion of the economic mechanism, originally conceived as static, comes from the consumer and the change in his needs.

The author has many intelligent things to say here[11] about differences between saving, not spending, accumulation, investment, and real investment; his exposition is often more correct and clearer than, for example, similar passages in J.M. Keynes. He attempts a conceptual analysis of dynamic reality, choosing the methodological procedure, customary since J.S. Mill, which begins with a stationary, constantly reproduced system excluding all external disturbing influences. Then, the path to reality is sought by successive approximations. Schumpeter is interested above all in the real source of the dynamic changes, the 'prime mover in the process of internal economic change'.[12] The stationary system is so defined that there are no savings in it, and therefore no loans either; the rate of interest is thus equal to zero; lastly, there are no profits. Into this stationary phase the factor of savings is first introduced and the factor

9 Schumpeter 1983, p. 93. [The quotations are from the English translation of Schumpeter's book, rather than the versions in Grossman's review.]

10 [i.e. 'profitability'.]

11 Schumpeter 1939, pp. 76–7.

12 Schumpeter 1939, p. 72.

of accumulation, then inventions; the influence of each of these elements on the course of the process of reproduction is then examined.

As his first approximation, Schumpeter thus takes for his point of departure 'a society, stationary in every respect except in that it displays a positive rate of saving'. The productive functions follow the same course year after year; there are no external disturbances. The only form of investment opportunity that exists is that of loans to enterprises. Thus, credit exists only in the form of credit for productive ends. The only source of this credit and of the monetary capital offered for it is real savings. The creation of credit is thus excluded. It is true that credit expansion through the creation of credit is one of the chief sources of enterprising activity and therewith of the secondary wave of industrial and speculative activities, but Schumpeter is here endeavouring to reveal only the primary sources of cyclical motions, and the creation of credit must remain excluded. Within this pattern the means of payment is real gold passing from hand to hand in each transaction.[13] A state of competitive equilibrium exists at the beginning and Schumpeter's schematic model is intended exclusively, *ceteris paribus*, to show the effects of the factor of saving and of investment, and in particular to clarify the question whether savings as such can cause depression.

It is true that an influx of new savings offered to the enterprises would result in a constant expansion of the industrial apparatus through the constant addition of new plants or new machines. But as long as these machines and plants would be of the same type as the ones previously used, under the assumption of an unvarying technical and organisational set-up, this growth in the industrial apparatus would be accomplished in a relative equilibrium. True, this equilibrium would constantly be disturbed by the influx of new capital savings. But granted a given rate of savings the economic mechanism would continuously 'adapt' itself to this rate, i.e. would continuously absorb the disturbances. As a result of the savings, the rate of interest would necessarily drop, and therefore new investment opportunities would arise, opportunities which had not existed at the previous, higher rate of interest. On the other hand, the enlarged productive apparatus would 'certainly' find new buyers of merchandise, because every saving, just as it creates its own investment opportunities, also creates its own demand for the additional products manufactured in the new plants.

The proof of this wonderful harmonic development, however, is the author's bare assertion of it. The matter treated is eminently quantitative: the addi-

13 Schumpeter 1939, p. 79.

tional workers receive additional wages and additional purchasing power, and the new plants produce an added mass of commodities for the market. The problem consists in finding out whether the additional mass of values and the additional purchasing power can coincide. Here is a brilliant occasion for showing in an 'exact' mathematical manner, by means of a 'girdle of equations', how such an equilibrium could arise from the disequilibrium admitted by Schumpeter, how the consumer's social purchasing power each time just suffices to dispose of the increased mass of products thrown on the market by the producers. Instead of a proof, however, Schumpeter is content with a mere statement that the system has 'adapted' itself to the new savings rate; but he says nothing about how this 'adaptation' takes place, simply assuring us, 'the new producers' commodities are sure to find their buyers'.[14]

With a method such as this all the problems in the world could be solved on paper. Schumpeter has arrived at the old harmonistic theory of investments and '*débouchés*' of Ricardo and Jean-Baptiste Say[15] without supporting it by any new argument or weakening the 150-year-old critique of it.

So far, we have not taken into account the internal contradictions of Schumpeter's construction. It starts with the equilibrium and assumes an increase in production in a society which otherwise is 'in every respect stationary'; in particular it presupposes 'that production functions are invariant', that is, that the technical-organisational basis remains unchanged, or, in other words, that 'the same types of plants and machinery' are used as before.[16]

It is evident that these presuppositions are contradictory. We begin with a state of equilibrium in a stationary society wherein all the means of production and all the workers are occupied. If we assume an invariant technical-organisational basis, the additional plants and machines can be put into motion only by an additional number of workers. But in Schumpeter's stationary model the population, too, is stationary, for he counts the 'variations in population among external factors',[17] which are excluded from his stationary model.[18] Clearly no increase in production is possible in this model at all. In the second place Schumpeter assumes that in passing from the stationary phase to that involving increased production, the producers of consumers' goods suffer no

14 Schumpeter 1939, p. 79.

15 [Say's law or the law of markets, '*loi des débouchés*' in French, is that supply creates its own demand.]

16 Schumpeter 1939, p. 79.

17 Schumpeter 1939, p. 74.

18 Schumpeter 1939, p. 79.

losses. Every producer therefore will at all times be ready to absorb additional capital for an increase in production: 'this process can go on indefinitely',[19] so long as the rate of interest has not fallen to zero. This is again an unproved assertion, which is clearly false because every rearrangement of the stationary economy in the direction of increasing production necessarily restricts the production of consumers' goods and therefore also causes losses to the owners of the enterprises concerned.

But Schumpeter holds that even in the latter case no disturbance would ensue and the prices of consumers' goods would not fall. Accepting the famous Tugan-Baranovsky merry-go-round which 40 years ago was demonstrated as theoretically untenable, he believes that the equilibrium would be re-established because the increased production of production goods would take the place of the restricted production of consumer goods. 'The demand from the increased incomes in the machine industries steps into the place of the demand discontinued by savers', he says.[20] Thus, when there is a displacement of the demand for consumer goods, the total amount of consumption does not have to fall. And even if one is willing to grant – for the sake of the argument – that the asserted displacements actually take place, one finds that Schumpeter has not attempted to investigate the quantitative problem of the demand for substitutes and of the time factor, and that he has not tried to show that the missing consumption of one consumer group can be replaced in the same unit of time by the new demand of another group; also that the new demand, originating in the machine industry, is quantitatively equal to the previous demand in the consumer goods industry. Yet, it is known (only, Schumpeter does not take this into account) that machine industry occupies considerably fewer workers (the total amount of investments being the same) and therefore also creates less demand for consumers' goods than does the consumers' goods industry.

Since the savings process is not a single act, but continuous, the need for rearranging industry and increasing the production of means of production would not be a single act – this according to Schumpeter's own presuppositions – but would provoke a wave of successive rearrangements; in short, it would constitute a permanent disturbance.

Schumpeter solves all these theoretical difficulties with a word, 'adaptation'. He never describes the process of adaptation. The desired result of it – the equi-

19 Schumpeter 1939, p. 80.
20 Schumpeter 1939, p. 82.

librium – is introduced as a *deus ex machina*. If this 'adaptation' takes place, the system functions 'satisfactorily' and we are in 'equilibrium'.

The latter concept plays a fatal role in the whole exposition. At first, equilibrium is a sort of system of reference which enables us to measure how far removed the real system, afflicted with chronic disequilibrium, is from an ideal point of reference.[21] Schumpeter, however, does not stick to this ideal 'theoretical norm', but assumes a really existing tendency toward equilibrium,[22] to which he ascribes great diagnostic significance, though the equilibrium itself is never reached: 'the system approaches a state which would – if reached – fulfil equilibrium conditions'.[23] The mode of argumentation runs somewhat as follows: if we had to deal not with our reality, but with an imaginary world, then the conditions of equilibrium would easily be achieved! Schumpeter carries this unrealistic conception so far that he speaks of the constantly growing significance of the concept of equilibrium for economic theory! Here, too, Schumpeter is a victim of self-delusion. For more than 150 years – from the Physiocrats, Smith and Ricardo, to Walras, Marshall and Pareto – the concept of equilibrium lay at the basis of all economic theories. The result was that everyone spoke of the failure of economic theory, because it progressively lost all relation to reality and was no longer able to explain it. This sad state finally brought about a reaction; a theoretical opposition against the concept of equilibrium recently arose, an opposition which regarded the concept not only as superfluous but even as harmful and responsible for the retarded development of economic theory as such. Schumpeter has not considered this development in economic theory but continues to represent old, untenable views.

We do not want, however, to dwell any further on these important, though merely preliminary arguments. We shall now examine his main theory: the concept of business cycles. In contrast to the previously considered model of a stationary economy, this theory treats the problem of change as such: 'How the economic system generates evolution.' Here, too – for the sake of argument – the author starts from a stationary economy without savings and profits in order to determine how 'evolution' arises in such a model. We have seen above how he methodologically isolated the factor of savings and accumulation and tried to demonstrate that the influence of this factor alone would result in an 'increase', but an increase which would not disturb the equilibrium. This

---

21 Schumpeter 1939, p. 69.
22 Schumpeter 1939, p. 70.
23 Schumpeter 1939, p. 71.

time he wants to isolate another factor (though both are in reality connected and mutually influence one another), which is responsible for all the disturbances of the equilibrium and is at their root. This factor is 'innovation', by which Schumpeter means not only technological improvements, but all other organisational improvements (new methods in the production of the same goods, the introduction of new articles, the discovery of new markets or new sources of raw materials).[24] 'Innovation' is always merely the economic reaction of the system to a specific situation of the economy – non-profitability – and for that reason is, according to Schumpeter, the internal factor in the economic history of capitalist society.[25] To him production is nothing but a combination of various production factors. He builds his theory on the following assertion: 'the physical marginal productivity of every factor must (in the absence of innovation) monotonically decrease'. The monetary expression of this situation, if the prices of the production factors are constant, is increasing cost as compared to decreasing returns,[26] as a result of which the profitability of the enterprises falls or, in limit cases, vanishes entirely. Thus, falling profitability, which characterises the depression, is discussed without the help of external influences, it is true, but in a naturalistic-technical manner. In this central point of his theory – falling profitability – Schumpeter gives no proof, but dismisses the problem in the few words just quoted. At this point the innovation sets in. It is the capitalist's reaction to vanishing profitability. Its task is to restore profitability by a reorganisation of productive factors. The innovation interrupts the falling curve of returns, replacing it by another which begins on a higher level, only to fall again later. Wherever the cost of a commodity or a particular productive factor has decreased, we have a sign that the innovation has taken place. But, Schumpeter assures us, the costs will never fall constantly; there is no law of falling costs, such a law is but an optical illusion.[27] In reality costs fall only at intervals. For once the innovation has been introduced generally, it ceases to be an innovation;[28] its efficacy is exhausted, and cost begins to rise again. ('Law of increasing cost'). Thereby non-profitability breaks through anew.[29]

Thus Schumpeter believes he has arrived at one cause to explain, if not the periodicity, at least the process of alternating phases of prosperity and depres-

24 Schumpeter 1939, p. 84.
25 Schumpeter 1939, p. 86.
26 Schumpeter 1939, p. 88.
27 Schumpeter 1939, p. 91.
28 Schumpeter 1939, p. 89.
29 Schumpeter 1939, p. 90.

sion,[30] which he later differentiates into the four well-known phases of the cycle. He directs his criticism particularly against the so-called 'self-generating theories', according to which depression arises out of prosperity and prosperity out of depression. He denounces this theory as a theoretically inadmissible *perpetuum mobile*.[31] (This has been done before him, cf. Grossman, *The Law of Accumulation*).[32] This endogene[33] cyclical process develops only in the industrial sphere. As regards the stock exchange, the starting point of the depression, the falling of stock and bond prices is exogenous, provoked by the impulsion coming from the industrial sphere.[34]

Schumpeter seems convinced of the great originality of his innovation theory. The expert, however, will see at once that Schumpeter remembers on this point – and despite all other differences – more of Mill's and Marx's explanations of the cycle than he would care to admit, that capitalist production operates not for use, but for profit. When profitability disappears, the capitalist mechanism of production, and capitalist accumulation, come to a standstill and can be revivified only by a rearrangement of technical and organisational bases. The theory is not made any more original when the name of 'innovations' is assigned to what Mill and Marx called 'countertendencies'.[35] Nor is the theory made more original by projecting the innovations, which in Mill and Marx are objective reactions of the economic mechanism to a specific situation, into the realm of personality and by presenting them and glorifying them as the special merit of the capitalist, as his creative function. While Marx, on the basis of the law of value, deduces the periodic drop in profitability from the social process of accumulation, that is, from the increasing organic composition of capital, Schumpeter takes refuge in an untenable naturalistic-technical explanation, whose model he has found in the obsolete Ricardian doctrine of the decreasing yield of the soil and which he has merely transposed from agriculture to industry.

Schumpeter's theory of the falling profit is an *ad hoc* theory, unintegrated into any larger doctrine. Moreover this theory cannot be theoretically grounded on Schumpeter's own premises. It is therefore unnecessary to dwell on

30 Schumpeter 1939, p. 193.
31 Schumpeter 1939, p. 139.
32 Grossmann 1929, p. 229.
33 [i.e. 'endogenous'.]
34 Schumpeter 1939, p. 152.
35 Cf. the exposition of the 'countertendencies' in Mill and Marx in Grossmann 1992, pp. 73–4, 130–201.

Schumpeter's effort to illustrate the theory by statistical and historical data. In recent years, just as 120 years ago, the centre of the discussions has not been the problem of the business cycle. Ricardo and, later, John Stuart Mill and Simonde de Sismondi disputed not only about the causes and the inevitability of depressions, but about a wider question, that of the economic structure changing in the course of its contradictory development, that is, they discussed the tendencies in the evolution of capitalist economy. The question that interested them was thus whether this economic system is durable or whether it approaches its end as a result of its inner structural changes. This decisive problem, which has become even more important after the great depression of 1929, is not discussed by the author; not even the question of increasing 'structural' unemployment which may become the tragic fate of the existing economic order. On the contrary, Schumpeter tries to avoid a direct answer to such questions, in order to deal with them by the detour of his peculiar definition of 'evolution'. Economic 'evolution' is conceived in 'a quite narrow and particular sense, abstracting from all the concrete content of evolution'.[36] If this definition were to hold, of course there could be no definite direction of evolution in the sense indicated above. What would remain would be the abstract empty idea of a 'something' moving without any direction, and 'evolution' would here be identical with 'change'.

Nor does the new book go beyond that result. It is hence to be expected that Schumpeter would slur over such an important problem as that of overaccumulated capital which cannot be profitably invested, a problem particularly pressing in the USA. The fact that many billions of dollars remain idle for many years in the banks of the USA would not result from the objective situation of American capitalism, from a definite change in structure during a late phase of development, or from a saturation of the economy with capital for which no new and sufficiently profitable investments are at hand. Schumpeter hardly examines this problem – according to him, this is no problem at all. Instead, he describes how the bad government policies of the New Deal victimised the capitalists, declaring that the Roosevelt government has shaken the confidence of the capitalists as a result of its gigantic spending policy, its oppressive taxation and, above all, its open threats against the industrial middle class,[37] thus contributing to the paralysis of all creative enterprises without putting anything in their place. Here, instead of analysing the objective structure of American capitalism, Schumpeter offers us accusations against the government. He does

36 Schumpeter 1908, p. 95.

37 Schumpeter 1939, pp. 1044–9.

not make the simple reflection that similar phenomena of overaccumulation could also be observed in Europe (England, France, Switzerland, etc.) where the relations between government and industry were very different from those in the USA.

This central problem, which the author does not see, disappears in a mass of secondary details; he always deals with particular equilibria, for example, those between a producer and a buyer in an otherwise competitive society; the 'cases' are split into 'subcases', and each case must be treated separately, until the author finally gets lost in purely private considerations of the profitability of particular firms. For instance, when he takes up a bilateral monopoly he inquires under what conditions a monopolistic workers' union can obtain a maximum of wages and he believes he has proved that 'perfect equilibrium may … be compatible with the existence of unemployed resources'.[38]

It is evident that the concept of equilibrium is being abused here. A 'perfect equilibrium' involving unused production factors is an obvious contradiction, not to mention the significant omissions of the author, his failure to deal with the general equilibrium of the entire system, or even with a particular equilibrium of a particular market or industry branch, but only with the maximal profitability of two concerns!

Schumpeter's predilection for casuistry is demonstrated, for instance, in the treatment of the problem of monopolies. Capitalist reality reveals a general trend toward the concentration of enterprises and the formation of a few large monopolies dominating entire branches of industry. Thus the question spontaneously arises, how a society would function in which such monopolistic tendencies triumphed in all industrial branches so as to form a 'universal monopoly'. This problem has a great theoretical significance. But Schumpeter has his sympathies and antipathies: he does not like the New Deal, nor anything that means planning and organised economy. For that reason he dismisses this real and important problem with the bare assertion that such a universal monopoly 'would be inactive'.[39] He prefers to illustrate capitalist monopoly by the example of [Fridtjof] Nansen and [Fredrik Hjalmar] Johansen who, during their polar expedition, were left with only one remaining sled and could not agree about the direction of their voyage, but finally had to reach a compromise.[40]

We have seen that Schumpeter fights the theory of the shrinking of capital investment opportunities and sees the cause of the evil in the disastrous

38 Schumpeter 1939, p. 59.
39 Schumpeter 1939, p. 57.
40 Schumpeter 1939, p. 62.

government policy. It is true that he is not certain whether capital investment would flourish again if after the 1940 elections men more friendly to business were to assume power; and he says: 'The practical implications of our diagnosis do not differ much from those of the theory of vanishing investment opportunity in its usual acceptance'.[41] A similar lack of logic is revealed in Schumpeter's criticism of the government's currency and credit policies, in particular of its 'spending' program. According to him, these policies have not achieved their desired effect; they had nothing to do with restoring prosperity in the years 1935 to 1937, because this prosperity took place independently of government measures.[42] But a few pages later we read, to our surprise, that 'even government spending as a permanent policy could be rationally defended on our diagnosis'.[43]

If it is true that science consists in subsuming the complex mass of phenomena under general laws which express the true nature of things, then Schumpeter has not made use of a real theoretical idea. In spite of his great erudition and many stimulating details he loses himself in a bewilderment of detail.

Henryk Grossman (New York)

---

41 Schumpeter 1939, p. 1050.
42 Schumpeter 1939, p. 1031.
43 Schumpeter 1939, p. 1050.

CHAPTER 28

Review of Solomon Fabricant, *The Output of Manufacturing Industries 1899–1937**

Fabricant, Solomon, with the assistance of Julius Shirkin 1940, *The Output of Manufacturing Industries 1899–1937*, New York: National Bureau of Economic Research (xxi + 685pp, 66 tables, 24 charts; $4.50).

This report deals with the trend of production in American industry, with the exception of mining and public utilities. The period covered runs for 38 years since 1899. Since only from that year on have reasonably adequate data been collected in the US Census of Manufactures. The primary interest of this study is in physical output, the actual quantities of goods produced in American factories. It was only where other information was lacking that the census data on pecuniary value were used, and then merely to supplement the deficiencies in the information on physical output. So, freed of money-mysteries, this study offers extraordinarily important material – though such as should only be used critically – for an examination of changes that occurred in the material state of the population during the period from 1899 to 1937, changes measured not by gold but by quantity of goods actually on disposal. It is to be noted, thus, that the study has not treated cyclical changes but deals exclusively with the most persistent shifts in production.

Evaluation of the rich material offered by the book demands painstaking and detailed analysis. In this review, however, we shall limit ourselves to brief comment on the contents and chief results.

In chapter 3 the author deals with changes in the total manufacturing output. During the years 1899 to 1937 physical output grew 276 percent, representing an annual increase of 3.5 percent on the average, while increase in population during the same period ran to only 73 percent or 1.4 percent per annum. On the other hand, the Day-Thomas Index for the same years shows a rise of only 203 percent,[1] indicating that the greater rate of increase disclosed by the National Bureau index was based on a greater number of industries, many of

* [Originally published as Grossman 1941c.]

1 Fabricant 1940, p. 47.

them new, rapidly rising ones, such as rayon and rayon goods.[2] Were there the possibility of determining the improved quality of the product statistically, the rate of increase in output would be still greater. Calculated per capita of the population, the increase in manufacturing for the period designated comes to 120 percent. The author stresses that it does not follow from this rate of increase that there was an equivalent 'rise in the per capita consumption of finished processed goods'[3] since the total output includes not only consumers goods but capital goods as well. But – and this is a serious defect in the book – the author nowhere carries through a division of the physical output into the two familiar categories of producers goods and consumers goods on the basis of the statistical data, but merely states quite generally that 'it is probable that the rise of 120 percent in the per capita net output of manufacturing industries from 1899 to 1937 overstates the gain in per capita production of finished processed goods' and the probable increase is, quite arbitrarily, put at an estimate of about 100 percent per capita.

This result of the National Research Bureau's analysis must be sharply questioned. Did the material living standard of the broad mass of the population – expressed in goods – actually rise 100 percent during the latter 38 years? Since the mass of capital goods increased much more quickly in the course of productive development than the production of consumer goods, the average growth of the total manufacturing output of production must consequently be very strongly overstated. For example, the machinery group as a whole increased its value 'almost 50 percent more than did all manufacturing industries combined'.[4] This machinery group, considered by itself, shows a growth of close to 400 percent in the 38 year period under discussion.[5] The increase in total output of transportation equipment was even greater.[6]

It follows from this that the per capita increase in quantity of goods actually consumed must be considered significantly less than 100 percent. This seems to be confirmed by the data the author himself presents on the two most important consumer goods industries, food and textile[s]. In the food industry group, for example, the increase during the period reported comes to 156 percent[7] as against a population increase of 73 percent. This would signify a real increase of only 48 percent in consumer goods. Since, moreover, it is precisely in the

2 Fabricant 1940, p. 49.
3 Fabricant 1940, p. 52.
4 Fabricant 1940, p. 297.
5 Fabricant 1940, p. 298.
6 Fabricant 1940, p. 313.
7 Fabricant 1940, p. 142.

food industry that a stronger shift takes place from home made to factory made goods, the real increase in food production becomes even further reduced, and the author himself arrives at the result that the index of increase in per capita consumption of processed goods is overstated.[8] Incidentally, the author in a footnote further weakens the value of his calculation: 'If caloric content, rather than value added per unit, had been used as the coefficient, *it is possible that no increase in per capita consumption* would have been found'.[9] We must ask, therefore, what can be the value of the indices that show an increase of 100 percent in the output of consumer goods? The danger remains that they might become slogans which can be lightly used for political propaganda. According to Robert F. Martin[10] the realised national income per capita, adjusted by the general price level, increased from $456 in 1899 to $531 in 1938 (after it had passed through an artificial inflation in the postwar decade up to 1929). The per capita increase in real income thus came to barely 17 percent in these 38 years. The unusually great difference in Martin's and Fabricant's researches shows that the statistical methods of research are still in their beginning stages and require further improvement. Fabricant's work, however, is most welcome as a step along this path.

8 Fabricant 1940, p. 144.
9 Fabricant 1940, p. 144.
10 Martin 1939, pp. 6–7.

CHAPTER 29

Review of Lynn Thorndike, *A History of Magic and Experimental Sciences**

Thorndike, Lynn, 1941, *A History of Magic and Experimental Sciences. Volumes 5 and 6, The Sixteenth Century*, New York: Columbia University Press (695 + 766pp, $10.00).

With the appearance of these two volumes on the sixteenth century, a monumental series that began in 1923 comes to a conclusion. To give an idea of the prodigious research involved, the author's own compilation shows that in these last two volumes more than 3,000 names are cited – writers and men of learning, printers, princes, prelates and lay figures in the play of ideas. The index includes some 1,700 items. Treated or mentioned are Biblical and Jewish writers, church fathers, early medieval Latin writers, and so on through the long list.

The material with which the present two volumes deal is organised in 48 chapters. After an introductory characterisation of the century as a whole, the investigation opens with Leonardo da Vinci and proceeds according to individual subjects like astrology, anatomy, alchemy, medicine, chiromancy,[1] natural philosophy and natural magic, so that single chapters often bear in their titles the names of the leading personalities in the field under survey. One must marvel at the author's extensive reading and his knowledge of the vast material; he knows practically everything that was written during and concerning this time: books, manuscripts, pamphlets, and news articles. He lists not only all editions of the works he treats, but the translations and criticisms which they underwent or the discussions which they occasioned, their affinities with similar ideas of earlier writers or their open plagiarisms.

The examination that follows should offer an impression of the rich and interesting material that has gone into his work. We were informed of the extent of astrology, alchemy and occult arts before Thorndike published his work. For this reason it is of especial interest to learn from him what the

* [Originally published as Grossman 1941d.]

1 [Chiromancy is palm-reading.]

adversaries of these arts had to say. We know that a papal decree against alchemists existed. But how little material interest the church had in combatting alchemy is disclosed by what Thorndike reports concerning Johannes Pantheus, a Venetian priest. Despite the papal decree Pantheus published in 1518 a work on alchemy, *Art of Metallic Transmutation*,[2] and an edict of Pope Leo X gave him the exclusive right to print the work in the Papal States! Subsequently, when someone called the attention of the papal court to the existence of a decree against alchemists, Pantheus quietly wrote another alchemist work (1530), a sort of 'cabala of metals', only he was clever enough to say that this was not a work in alchemy but, as the title indicates, *Making Gold against Alchemy: An Art Different from Alchemy and Sophistry*.[3] Thereupon the apostolic legate again gave him permission to publish.[4]

Another 'adversary' of occult arts, the Frenchman Symphorien Champier, criticises magic, incantation, images, alchemy, and much of astrology, especially in medicine. His *Dialogue in Destruction of Magic Arts* (1500)[5] enters into the power of demons in magic and shows him to be convinced that men can free themselves of diabolic magic through prayer, confession, and fasting. Good angels can help, as can exorcism, or sorcery which employs demons of a superior order. If a melancholy person speaks languages previously unknown to him, that is a sure sign he is possessed by a demon. Aristotle offers a natural explanation even for this phenomenon, but he may not have encountered people possessed by demons. The *Bible* and other early Christian works convinced Symphorien that demoniacs exist. He repeats [Giovanni] Pico della Mirandola's arguments against astrology in general, but asserts that stars influence the weather, crops, disease, sedition and war, tempering this opinion with the observation that philosophers, farmers, and sailors can foresee these effects as well as astrologers can.[6]

Despite his rich collection of materials, Thorndike does not offer a definitive picture of the epoch. He excludes from his investigation fields of knowledge that were extremely characteristic of the time with which he is dealing: mathematics, physics, and especially mechanics, and justifies this procedure on the ground that it would 'avoid duplication of what has already been brought out by investigations of others, particularly Pierre Duhem'. If Thorndike nevertheless

2 [Pantheus 1518.]
3 [Pantheus 1530.]
4 Thorndike 1941a, p. 539.
5 [Champier 1500.]
6 Thorndike 1941a, pp. 111 et seq.

thinks that 'sufficient ground has been covered to indicate amply the relations between the magical and the scientific interests and methods in the sixteenth century',[7] he is labouring under an illusion. The most precise report out of a criminal court also gives only a picture of a section of life, not of life itself. As on the field of military conquest, so in the field of intellectual activity, not all provinces of knowledge are of equal weight. To hold sway, it is enough to take the key positions and it does not matter much that at many other points the enemy is still able to resist. During the sixteenth century such key positions were represented by mathematics, physics and above all mechanics. They constituted the basis for shaping the mechanistic conception which slowly emerged from the world of scholastic speculation to dominate the intellectual arena for four centuries. As a result of separating off this element that was so characteristic of the time, what remains – the province of astrology, alchemy, astrological medicine, and such – obtains an undue significance. For this reason, the very opening chapter on Leonardo da Vinci is not an accurate picture of the great scholar. Thorndike has a tendency to lay stress not on what was new in Leonardo but on what was old, what tied him in with the past, for example, 'the fact that Leonardo was to a large extent interested in the same topics as his predecessors'.[8] Thorndike even goes so far as to say that 'Leonardo's manuscripts are too disorderly and wanting in method to qualify as classified knowledge or science'.[9] The revolutionising of science, however, often comes not from the 'classified knowledge' of the university textbook but precisely from the 'disorderly' and unsystematic outsider. Thorndike does mention, though briefly, the pioneer activities of Leonardo in palaeontology and geology, attributing to Leonardo 'a determination to face all natural questions on a purely physical basis',[10] but he underscores the more strongly that he 'harboured many incorrect notions' and wishes to place these 'in balance against his instances ... of argument well sustained upon a strictly natural basis'.[11] An idle endeavour! We know, for instance, that Newton was largely interested and spent most time not in chemistry in the modern sense but in alchemy, that he was interested in the transmutation of metals, in the philosopher's stone and the elixir of life. And Newton's conception of matter, his atomic theory, made it possible that by rearrangement of these fundamental components

7 Thorndike 1941a, p. 12.
8 Thorndike 1941a, p. 23.
9 Thorndike 1941a, p. 18.
10 Thorndike 1941a, p. 36.
11 Thorndike 1941a, p. 29.

one element could he transmuted into another. 'The changing of bodies into light', he wrote, 'and light into bodies, is very comfortable to the cause of nature which seems delighted with transmutations.'[12]

This was perhaps the reason why Newton's distinguished contemporaries, [Christiaan] Huygens and Leibniz, who were aware of his alchemist leanings, suspected that he was seeking to revive occult faculties through his doctrine of attraction at a distance without the intermediary of matter. Huygens called the principle of attraction 'absurd' (1690) and Leibniz wrote against Newton his article *Against Barbaric Physics: Toward a Philosophy of What There Actually Is and Against the Revival of the Qualities of the Scholastics and Chimerical Intelligences*[13]. Newton's alchemy seems to have been connected less with his scientific than with his mystical meditations. Should we therefore stamp him an avowed representative of the Paracelsian period, or should we rather not maintain that Newton's chemical knowledge was rudimentary and that despite the fact that he was encumbered with obsolete ideas in the field of chemistry, his trail-blazing doctrine of gravitation was to become indisputable master in the intellectual world of the next 200 years?

What applies to Leonardo da Vinci is repeated in many other chapters, for example, in the one on Paracelsus. Thorndike seems to have a predilection for painting the irrational aspects of the human mind while the rational ones interest him little. Thus, he says of Paracelsus that he may be regarded as a specialist in hysteria, mountain diseases and syphilis. On the last he had more medical knowledge than anyone who lived before 1850. It would have been interesting to hear the ideas of the sixteenth century on hysteria or syphilis, but nothing is said on this subject, while the slogan attributed to Paracelsus, 'the sick should be doctors' books',[14] receives an entire page of polemical criticism. From the slogan Thorndike deduces that Paracelsus wished to renounce book learning together with profit through the experience of others. Is such an interpretation of the text correct, however? Just at this time, when so many physicians were prone to follow the humanist trend of relying on ancient Greek medical authorities, as Thorndike himself reports,[15] one must see nothing else in the slogan than the principle, so often extolled elsewhere, that nature should be the ultimate source of our experience. This in no case would involve renouncing the profit to be derived from the experience others have stored in their books.

12 Sullivan 1938, p. 52.
13 [Leibniz 1989.]
14 Thorndike 1941a, p. 441.
15 Thorndike 1941a, p. 435.

Thorndike mentions the book *Pirotechnia* (1540) written by Vanuccio Biringuccio,[16] and remarks, 'the text deals chiefly with metals and little with fireworks and artillery'. One gets the impression that we are dealing here with an alchemist work. Thorndike does say that 'the opening chapter is sceptical as to the possibility of transmutation', but he immediately adds, 'in general the book impressed me as a sixteenth century version in Italian of what one might find in Latin works of the three previous centuries'.[17] This would lead to an incorrect impression. Biringuccio is not the belated associate of the middle ages, but on the contrary the representative of modern times, of that new type of man who takes his starting point from practice and enriches his practical experience through theory. He was no alchemist but an engineer, founder of modern metallurgy and practical manager of mines and iron works, as the title of his book, chiefly a treatise on mining and metallurgy, would indicate. *De La Pirotechnia ... si tratta non solo di ogni sorte & diversita di miniere ma anchora quanta si ricera intorno a la prattica di quelle cose di quel che si appartienne a l'arte de la fusione ouer gito de metalli ...*[18] By virtue of his better understanding of frictional laws, Biringuccio introduced into a north Italian iron works a new arrangement of machinery, discovered by him, for the better utilisation of water power.

Thorndike sometimes presents facts without giving an explanation of the intellectual currents around them. For instance, he asserts that almost no alchemical treatises had been printed during the period of incunabula[19] and that they appeared slowly in the sixteenth century, that 'for the most part alchemy remained relatively quiescent in laboratory and manuscripts until the Paracelsan revival of the second half of the century'.[20] The rise of Paracelsanism went hand in hand with the development of occult philosophy and a benevolent attitude to natural magic. We read that this tendency continued briskly into the seventeenth century until 'by its excesses' it exhausted itself and was replaced by the sceptical rationalism and enlightenment of the eighteenth century,[21] though never uniformly in all provinces of knowledge. While Galileo, Descartes and Newton introduced clarity and precision into mathematics, physics and astronomy, the case was different in the fields of biology, chemistry, and medicine. Here, a good deal of the old feeling for occult

16 [Biringuccio 1959.]

17 Thorndike 1941a, p. 544.

18 [*On Pyrotechnics ... Wherein there Are Broadly Dealt with not only All Kinds and the Diversity of Minerals but also Much Research into the Practice of those Matters which Belong to the Art of Melting and Casting Metals ...*]

19 [Incunabula are early printed books, especially before the sixteenth century.]

20 Thorndike 1941a, p. 532.

21 Thorndike 1941a, p. 14.

nature persisted even in the age of reason.[22] Thorndike does not go beyond the assertion. We who are seeking an explanation already know from Duhem that for example as early as the twelfth century a wave of rationalism arose and continued into the thirteenth century, that for example Thierry of the school of Chartres gives, in the twelfth century, a rationalistic, purely physical theory of world genesis wherein the six days of the *Bible* are interpreted as six stages of becoming. *'L'oeuvre de six jours'*, Duhem says, *'s'est donc déroulée sans aucune intervention direct du Dieu, par le jeu naturel des puissances du feu … Dieu créât la matière pour que cette matière, livrée à elle-meme, produit le Monde tel qu'il est. Ni Descartes, ni Laplace ne dépasseront l'audacieux rationalisme de Thierry.'*[23]

Why did this rationalist upsurge of the twelfth and thirteenth centuries give way to anti-rationalist currents, only to reappear, in partial form, in the sixteenth and, in larger measure, in the seventeenth century? Why does this age of reason pursue its triumph only in a few strictly limited fields, in mathematics, physics, mechanics and astronomy, while the old forms of thinking continue to spread within the remaining provinces of knowledge? Thorndike leaves such questions open.

He establishes that, about a quarter century after the death of Paracelsus, a Paracelsian movement was growing. When Paracelsus's alchemist work, *Archidoxa*,[24] appeared in Cracow in 1569, it was followed in one single year, in 1570, by six other editions, in Basle, Munich, Cologne, and Strassburg. As to how this Paracelsus renaissance is to be explained, Thorndike answers that Paracelsus corresponds to the same spirit which produced [Bernardino] Telesio's *Natural Philosophy*[25] in Italy at the same time (1565). This answer shifts the problem: one must inquire why in Italy, Poland and Germany during the second half of the sixteenth century a demand should arise for books of this kind, and that notwithstanding the most extravagant statements to be found in Paracelsus, for example. Thus, Paracelsus avers that he had seen a man who lived without food for six months, and he adds that a man could live without food provided his feet are planted in the ground. And so on. There is no such thing for Paracelsus as a natural law or natural science. Even the most incurable disease can yield to

---

22 Thorndike 1941a, p. 14.

23 Duhem 1915, p. 185. ['The work of six days is conducted without god's direct intervention, by the play of the natural powers of fire … God may create the matter, so that matter, left to itself, produces the world as it is. Neither Descartes nor Laplace surpassed the audacious rationalism of Thierry.'

24 [Paracelsus 1656.]

25 [Telesio 1565.]

magic rites. Mystery is everywhere; everywhere there is animism and invisible power, and all this at a time when [Nicolaus] Copernicus was endeavouring to restore the movements of heavenly bodies to circular regularity and uniformity. Thorndike ends his discussion with the declaration, 'Such are the contrasts which are possible in the thought of the same period'. But instead of going on to clarify the trend and the contrast for us, he contents himself with the melancholy remark, 'It was indeed a discouraging contrast in intellectual history, ... the same half century which refused to digest and accept the solid demonstrations of *De Revolutionibus* of Copernicus[26] ... swallowed eagerly the innumerable ... tomes of Paracelsus and his followers.'[27]

Thorndike's magnificent work is nevertheless a mighty contribution to an extension of our knowledge. He has assembled the most wonderful materials for building a cathedral – marble, porphyry, granite. We owe him thanks for this and admiration. But even the most beautiful materials are not yet the cathedral.

These latest two volumes will be indispensable as handbooks for every scholar of the medieval and modern history of science, just as the earlier volumes have been. But are they a history of science and magic in the sixteenth century?

Henryk Grossman (New York)

---

26 [Copernicus 1992.]

27 Thorndike 1941a, p. 629.

CHAPTER 30

The Evolutionist Revolt against Classical Economics*

1 In France – Condorcet, Saint-Simon, Simonde de Sismondi

Any theoretical analysis of a contemporary economic system must lead to the formulation of a standard with which to evaluate the existing level of development. To have any validity such a standard must be worked out of the developmental process itself and not merely from the level attained at the moment of analysis. It will therefore be useful to the present-day theorist to look back and see how dynamic or evolutionary thinking actually entered the field of economic theory. The problem has not been adequately or at all accurately presented in our economic literature. Thus, Richard T. Ely writes: 'It is probably due to Herbert Spencer more than to any other person that we have come to recognise the applicability of evolution to the various departments of the social life of man'.[1] But the essay of Spencer to which he refers did not appear until 1857,[2] decades after others were already using evolutionary notions in the social sciences. John Bagnell Bury, to cite a more recent example, wrote a whole book on the idea of progress[3] without even mentioning Sismondi or Richard Jones – the two men who first worked out the idea of the historical succession of ever more advanced economic stages. In German economic literature either the problem is not discussed at all, as in [Karl] Bücher's widely known study of the rise of national economy,[4] which does not once mention feudalism or capitalism; or else the sole responsibility for what they call the 'sociologising' of economics is falsely attributed to Hegel and his school.[5] [Edmund] Whittaker,

---

* [Originally published in two parts as 'The Evolutionist Revolt Against Classical Economics: I. In France – Condorcet, Saint-Simon, Simonde de Sismondi' and 'The Evolutionist Revolt Against Classical Economics: II. In England – James Steuart, Richard Jones, Karl Marx', by Henryk Grossman in *Journal of Political Economy* 51, no. 5 and 6, University of Chicago Press (Grossman 1943a and Grossman 1943b).

1 Ely 1903, pp. 6–7.

2 Spencer 1878, pp. 1–60.

3 Bury 1920.

4 Bücher 1906.

5 Thus Kötschke 1923, pp. 12–15 has a section on the history of the idea of stages in economic

too, in a recent book, makes the mistake of overestimating the German representatives of historicism – the German historical school and Hegel. At the same time, speaking of the French and English, he mentions the economic views of Saint-Simon, Sismondi, James Steuart, and Richard Jones, but not their ideas on evolution. Condorcet is not mentioned at all.[6]

The purpose of the present study is to show the decisive role of French and English economists in laying the basis for modern evolutionary theories of economics, and particularly for the work of Karl Marx. It is fully consistent with the general neglect of our problem that Marx's contribution to the 'sociologising' of economics is also widely misconstrued. According to Sombart, for example, the importance of Marx lies not so much in the field of economic theory as in the field of sociology. 'Marx', he writes, 'applied evolutionary thinking to the social process'.[7] He gives us 'an insight into the historical character of the economy, into *its constant changeability in the course of history*. He first created the *concept of the economic system* and made it the subject of economic science.'[8] Sombart thus arbitrarily gives Marx credit for accomplishments he never claimed and thereby conceals and distorts the picture of Marx's real work.[9] Unfortunately, Sombart's view has been widely echoed, even in Socialist circles. Eduard Heimann, for example, repeats that Marx's decisive contribution to the growth of economics, his truly 'Copernican significance', does not lie in specific theories, such as the theory of surplus value, the theory of concentration, or the theory of crisis, but in his having for the first time 'historicised' or 'sociologised' economics. It was Marx, he writes, who 'first conceived [capitalism] to be historical, and therefore time bound, transformable and transitory'. Marx was able to discover this insight because he was the 'heir

---

development in which the names of Saint-Simon, Sismondi, James Steuart, and Richard Jones never appear. Kötschke, furthermore, follows Bücher's precedent in discussing the sequence not of complete economic structures, such as feudalism or capitalism, but only of partial units: village economy, town economy, territorial economy. Similarly, = Sombart speaks of individual economy, transition economy, social economy; and, according to Richard T. Ely, the various stages are not characterised by the different types of social organisation, rather various occupational activities, such as hunting or fishing, agriculture or cattle-raising, are just different historical 'stages' (hunting stage, fishing stage, etc.) Ely 1903, pp. 26, 39.

6 See Whittaker 1940.

7 Sombart 1909b, p. 16.

8 Sombart 1909b, pp. 53–54. Italics are mine.

9 It has frequently been pointed out that Sombart's historical statements simply do not stand up under close scrutiny. See, for example, Adolf Schaube's (1908) criticism of Sombart's account of certain early English developments.

and executor of Hegel's thinking' and because he possessed the 'political will' to attack static capitalism.[10]

We can easily dispose of the allegedly Hegelian basis for the 'historicising' of economics. All the great theorists of the French Enlightenment, with the exception of Rousseau, held the philosophic view that history was an endless progress marking man's path to reason.[11] Endless progress necessarily implies that the existing reality, the given state of affairs, will be negated and will not continue to exist indefinitely. Hegel, on the other hand, thought that history had reached its goal in his own day, that the idea and reality had found their common ground.[12] On this point, Marx was closer to the French tradition than to Hegel.

In the *Philosophy of Right*, Hegel patterns the notion of freedom after the free ownership of property.[13] The historical process thus becomes a glorification of the history of the middle class; and Hegel's *Philosophy of History* ends with the consolidation of middle-class society.[14] Here was a social system no longer to be transcended. We shall see that the French tradition from Condorcet through Saint-Simon and his disciples to Sismondi and Pecqueur was very different. For them the idea of historical progress ruled by reason tended to turn away from the possessing classes in favour of 'the great mass of those who live by their work' (Condorcet). They stood opposed to the existing oppressive social system. Progress does not end with middle-class society. Quite the contrary, it will continue to unfold in the future in new social structures. Whereas one trend in eighteenth-century thought, influenced by the religious tradition of the Garden of Eden, placed the golden age in the past, at the beginning of man's history, Saint-Simon turned the sequence around. 'The golden age', he wrote, following an idea of Condorcet's, 'which a blind tradition had always placed in the past, lies ahead of us'. Here, too, Marx is linked to French thought, not to Hegel.

We must remember that Hegel's *Philosophy of History* was a relatively late work, published posthumously in 1837, four years after Richard Jones had

10 Heimann 1931, pp. 165, 168.

11 Turgot, for example, in his second Sorbonne discourse, 'A Philosophical Review of the Successive Advances of the Human Mind', spoke of 'the whole human race, through alternate periods … of weal and woe, goes on advancing, although at a slow pace, toward greater perfection', Turgot 2011, p. 322.

12 Marcuse 1941, p. 226.

13 [Hegel 2008, pp. 50–1, 57 et seq.]

14 [Hegel 1914, pp. 472–7.]

already appeared with his historical study of economics.[15] Hegel, furthermore, as we shall see later, expressly rejected the concept that must lie at the base of any genetic theory of development, namely, that a higher, more developed phase proceeds from the preceding, lower phase.

On the other hand, a genuinely powerful influence on evolutionary thinking must be assigned to the revolution in astrophysics brought about by the publication of [Pierre-Simon] Laplace's *The System of the World* in 1796.[16] Laplace denied the unchanging character of 'eternal' nature and offered his famous theory of the evolution of the planetary system, through purely mechanical phenomena of the attraction and repulsion of atoms, from a rotating ball of gas which, by cooling and contraction, threw off segments of its surface. These segments in turn united to become the planets. Both the earth and the entire solar system were formerly nonexistent, and the time will come when the sun will be extinguished and the universe will break apart.[17] At one time the earth was an uninhabited and unformed mass of gas. It required millions of years for the cooling of the earth's crust to create the conditions which brought into existence the lower organic forms and eventually man himself.

This evolutionary theory of astrophysics had already appeared in 1755 in an anonymous publication by Immanuel Kant. It had failed to make headway against the biblical tradition of 'Genesis', however, and had passed unnoticed. Kant himself knew that he had 'travelled on a dangerous journey' and went to great pains in his preface to ward off the charge of atheism.[18] It required the intellectual atmosphere of the French Revolution to obtain recognition for such a work as Laplace's *System*.

Finally, it must be noted that the 'sociologising' of economics is not and cannot be regarded as a purely intellectual development flowing from Hegel's dialectics or any other book. While the thinkers of the Enlightenment strove to deduce the eternal laws of a rational 'natural order' from nature and from the properties of the human individual, the advocates of the evolutionary idea whom we are dealing with here based their universal laws and predictions on

15 [Hegel 1914.] Fifty years before Hegel, Gotthold Ephraim Lessing, the most prominent figure of the German Enlightenment, advanced certain evolutionist ideas in his essay *The Education of the Human Species* (1780) [Lessing 1883]; these ideas were strongly influenced by Adam Ferguson's, *Essay on the History of Civil Society*, (1767) [Ferguson 1809]. Later on, Lessing's essay, translated into French (1829), belonged to the Saint-Simonian propagandist literature.

16 [Laplace 1830.]

17 The influence of these views on Saint-Simon is clearly seen in his *Memorandum on the Science of Man* (1813), Saint-Simon 1964b, p. 294.

18 Kant 2009, p. 7.

history, on actually observed *evolutionary tendencies*. Their ideas are the theoretical reflection of such great historical phenomena as the French and American revolutions[19] and the industrial revolution in England. Above all, it was the outbreak of the French Revolution which, like the eruption of a volcano, exposed the weaknesses of eighteenth-century rationalism. What caused such an eruption? To answer that question, man turned to history.[20]

The classical economists had also made some investigations of the past. Adam Smith, for example, revealed considerable historical knowledge, as in chapter 4 of book 1, 'Of the origin and use of money', or chapter 11, 'Digression concerning the variation in the value of silver during the course of the four last centuries', and, above all, in book 3 on the 'Progress of opulence in different nations'.[21]

The classical economists never reached the point, however, of permitting the idea of development to bring order out of the chaos of economic facts. Adam Smith distinguished between advancing, stationary, or declining conditions of society,[22] and Ricardo talked about the 'progress' or 'natural advance of society', of 'an improving society' advancing from poverty to a flourishing condition.[23] But neither one knew of phases of development, only of datable conditions of one and the same capitalist society – conditions that varied in size of population, extent of capital accumulation, or knowledge of agricultural tech-

19 Contemporaries were astounded at the rapid post-revolutionary progress of the United States, both in size of population and in development of agriculture, as contrasted with its 'stagnation' under British rule. As one analyst phrased the problem, the United States was a country 'where from a few adventurers, a power is now rising.' And he continued: 'The history of the world has furnished few instances of so great a tract of country undergoing a change, from an uncultivated and barbarous, to a civilised state; and it will well merit the attention of mankind to observe the different steps and the progress upon so large a scale.' Playfair 1801, pp. 29–30. [See Grossman 1948, below pp. 600–623.]

20 The so-called German historical school of law, which received its programmatic statement in Savigny's *From the Vocation of our Age to Law Making and Legal Studies* 1814, was itself only a by-product of the French Revolution. It was the answer of the conservative elements in Germany to the revolutionary method of lawgiving. Against the latter they insisted upon the slow method of historical, organic evolution. They thus condemned progress in the name of continuity. Marx's 'The Philosophical Manifesto of the Historical School of Law' (1975c) against [Gustav] Hugo is a most penetrating criticism of the methodological presuppositions of the historical school of law (see Hook 1936, pp. 141–4).

21 [Adam Smith 1910a, pp. 19–25, 161–92, 336–74.]

22 Book I, chapter vii, Adam Smith 1910a, pp. 48–56.

23 Chapter 5, Ricardo 1912, pp. 52–63.

niques[24] and not in their fundamental structure.[25] In his chapter entitled 'On the accumulation of capital', Adam Smith's account of the historical development of England from the invasion of Julius Caesar is characteristic. He writes:

> When we compare the state of a nation at two different periods and find that the annual produce of its land and labour is evidently greater at the latter than at the former, that its lands are better cultivated, its manufactures more numerous and more flourishing, we may be assured that its capital must have increased during the interval between the two periods.[26]

'In different stages of society', wrote Ricardo in a similar vein, 'the accumulation of capital ... is more or less rapid', so that in new settlements with little capital, for example, it is very slow.[27] The 'different stages' are thus nothing but levels of the same capitalist system of economy. Marx commented sarcastically that 'the bourgeois form of labour is regarded by Ricardo as the eternal natural form of social labour. Ricardo's primitive fisherman and primitive hunter are from the outset owners of commodities who exchange their fish and game in proportion to the labour time which is objectified in these exchange values.'[28]

The classical economists lacked an understanding of the real developmental sequence and changes of economic systems. Just as Rousseau in the *Social Contract*[29] explained the origin of social institutions rationalistically, the classicists took a rationalistic rather than a genetic approach to the past. All previous societies were measured with the rational yardstick of free trade. That is why they knew of only two ideal states: the 'original state of things', occurring before the

24 Chapter 1, Ricardo 1912, pp. 5–32.

25 Richard Schueller did not succeed in clearing the classics of the charge of unhistoricism. All he shows is that Smith and Ricardo emphasise the temporal, local, or cultural differentiations, Schueller 1895, p. 16, which result in modifications of the general laws of prices, average profits, rents, and wages. But such differentiations can occur within a given economic system regarded as permanent and have nothing in common with the fundamental idea of the theory of evolution, that is to say, with the theory of successive and different economic structures – an idea which is entirely absent from the classics and which Schueller does not discuss at all.

26 Adam Smith 1910a, p. 307.

27 [Grossman's paraphrase is inaccurate. Ricardo wrote: 'In new settlements, where the arts and knowledge of countries far advanced in refinement are introduced, it is probable that capital has a tendency to increase faster than mankind', 1912, pp. 55–6.]

28 Marx 1987a, p. 300.

29 [Rousseau 1920.]

fall from grace, as it were, and the bourgeois state in their own days, of more or less free trade and competition. All intervening epochs, with their severe limitations upon trade and industry, were condemned as unfit and erroneous. They were never discussed in terms of the limitations and conditions of their own time.[30]

We have become so accustomed to the idea of historical development that it is difficult for us to imagine such a lack of historicism. How did the change in our thinking come about? It must be stressed that we are not concerned with individual, isolated representatives of the evolutionary idea; such representatives appeared as early as the Middle Ages[31] and the Renaissance (Vico).[32] The subject of our analysis is a current of thinking which emerged in the social sciences during the last third of the eighteenth century and became triumphant during the first half of the nineteenth century: the concept of the evolution of human society through a succession of economic stages, each superior to the preceding one. Six men are the main representatives of this current: Condorcet, Saint-Simon, and Sismondi in France; Sir James Steuart and Richard Jones in England; and, finally, Karl Marx, who synthesised and completed the whole development. Thereafter the theory of evolution through the succession of definite economic structures was not further developed and fell into discredit with the dominant school.[33]

The great revolution in thought brought about by the French Revolution was most notable in the handling of social problems. Ever since Descartes, the notion of the unity of all knowledge had been generally prevalent. All phenomena, it was believed, no matter how complicated, can ultimately be understood by the same method – the mathematical method of the natural sciences. With the French Revolution, however, the idea arose that social phenomena constitute a special class, requiring special treatment and a special methodology. Eternally unchanging laws may be valid for the natural sciences, because nature

30 It was this attitude which Marx had in mind when he wrote: 'Hence the pre-bourgeois forms of the social organisation of production are treated by political economy in much the same way as the Fathers of the Church treated pre-Christian religions'. From such a point of view, feudal institutions are 'artificial', bourgeois institutions 'natural', Marx 1976b, p. 175.

31 Ibn Khaldun (1332–1406) in his work *Muqaddimah* (*Prolegomena*), 1967.

32 [Vico 1948.]

33 Whittaker approvingly quotes the opinion of the English historian, Frederic William Maitland, directed against 'architects of stage-systems', who are 'prescribing a normal program for the human race in decreeing that every portion of mankind must move through one fated series of stages', Whittaker 1940, p. 3.

is eternal and unchanging, but human society undergoes constant change (progress) from epoch to epoch. The particular task of the social sciences is therefore not to seek for eternal laws but to find the law of change itself.

It is true that the application of eternal natural laws to human society was still given formal recognition; but, in actual practice, men like Condorcet, Saint-Simon, and Richard Jones began to make sharp differentiations. Eventually, with the further spread of new sciences, such as chemistry and biology, in which mathematical analysis played no role, an open revolt set in against the applications of the methods of natural science to the study of society. Auguste Comte waged a bitter struggle against the 'metaphysical prejudice that no real certainty can exist outside mathematics' and the 'empty scientific overlordship temporarily granted the mathematical spirit'. In the last 'lesson' of his *Course*, Comte wrote: 'Instead of seeking blindly for a sterile scientific unity, as oppressive as it is chimerical, in the reduction of all phenomena to a single order of laws, the human mind will eventually consider the different classes of events as having their special laws'. He went on to say that 'the laws of organic phenomena or social phenomena are established by the predominance of specific methods: the comparative method in biology, the historical method in sociology'.[34]

The pioneer of the new approach is Condorcet (1743–94). According to him, the great revolution of his own time can be understood only through 'the picture of revolutions which preceded and prepared the way for it'.[35] Historical development 'is subject to … general laws … The result which every instant presents, depends upon that offered by the preceding instants, and has an influence on the instants which follow … This picture, therefore, is historical; since subjected as it will be to perpetual variations, it is formed by the successive observation of human societies at the different eras through which they have passed.' The student's task is to discover 'the laws of … change' of the steady progress of spiritual and social development 'towards knowledge and happiness'. Progress, Condorcet continues, 'may doubtless be more or less rapid, but it can never be retrograde'.[36] The certainty of progress can be derived from the fact of the American and French revolutions. By freeing themselves from their tyrannical rulers, the two countries give us the symbol of progress and free us from anti-

34 Comte 1908b, pp. 413, 521 [the first quotation and the first part of the final quotation cannot be located, although they do express Comte's position; the words after the colon are at p. 397].

35 Condorcet 1796, p. 22.

36 Condorcet 1796, pp. 9–11.

quated preconceptions. We must construct 'an art ... of foreseeing the future improvement of the human race, and of directing and hastening that improvement', and 'history ... must form the principal basis of this art'.[37] 'From these observations on what man has heretofore been, and what he is at present, we shall be led to the means of securing and of accelerating the still further progress, of which, from his nature, we may indulge the hope.'[38]

We have already seen that the idea of development, of history as a continuous movement of causally linked processes, was worked out before the French Revolution. There was no place in such a conception for a theory of historical stages, however. The spokesmen of the eighteenth-century Enlightenment were convinced that, as soon as reason had discovered the truth, the existing irrational state of affairs would immediately be replaced by a state of perfection. The prevailing irrational conditions were nothing more than the unnecessary products of 'error' or 'prejudice'. The rationalists therefore believed that, with the progress of reason, there would be an unbroken, straight-line rise to perfection. Then came the French Revolution, with its tremendous political and social upheavals, its frightful party and class conflicts; yet it failed to bring about a state of perfection. Rationalism received a mortal blow. The revolution and its aftermath demonstrated that moral and legal relationships did not depend on reason alone, that economic interests were a more important factor in determining the political position of each group in the population.

Condorcet, himself a member of the Girondist party, promptly incorporated this disillusioning experience into his conception of history.[39] The ultimate aim of a state of perfection was not abandoned, but the idea of progress became more differentiated into a succession of stages and periods. He now saw that historical development was an uneven process, in which desirable progressive aims are constantly, though temporarily, being turned into their opposite, into backward steps, until they are finally realised in a new and higher stage. The French Revolution failed to accomplish what its spokesmen had hoped because both the ideas and the social relationships were incomplete *and not yet ripe* for a state of perfection.[40] The conclusion was therefore inevitable that it is not possible to move directly from any given condition to perfection through the demands of reason. Certain specific preconditions must first be fulfilled. And that means that past history should be looked upon not as merely an error that

37 Condorcet 1796, p. 21.
38 Condorcet 1796, p. 11.
39 See Mannheim 1936, p. 200.
40 See Cunow 1920, p. 158.

could have been avoided by proper insight but as historically determined and therefore as necessary and unavoidable. In other words, historical development encompasses not only the elements of rational progress but also those of irrational progress. '[T]he history of general errors ...': 'the manner in which general errors are introduced, propagated ... among nations, forms a part of the picture of the progress of the human mind.'[41] Thus Condorcet arrived at his stage theory. The 'errors' of the past, and especially of the revolution, were a necessary part of a transitional stage in the road to perfection.

After formulating this general theory, Condorcet proceeded to sketch the social evolution of human progress in nine epochs, each representing a higher stage than its predecessor, concluding with a preview (the tenth epoch) of the 'future progress of the human spirit'. He found two fundamental tendencies in history.

1. There is a certain regularity in the development of mankind, so that the backward nations will eventually go through the same process of growth which the most advanced nations have already traversed.[42] Condorcet was therefore convinced that the immense distance which separates these people (the most enlightened) from 'the slavery of countries subjected to kings, the barbarity of African tribes, and the ignorance of savages' will 'gradually vanish', until historical development has accomplished 'the destruction of inequality between different nations ... every nation[will] one day arrive at the state of civilization attained by those people who are most enlightened ... as the French, for instance, and the Anglo-Americans'.[43] This goal is realisable because 'The march of these people will be less slow and more sure than ours has been, because they will derive from us that light which we have been obliged to discover, and because for them to acquire the simple truths ... we have obtained after long wandering in the mazes of error, it will be sufficient to seize upon ... proofs in our ... publications'.[44]
2. The development of social progress is uneven as compared with the progress of knowledge. 'We perceive', he wrote, 'that the exertions of these last ages have done much for the progress of the human mind, but little for the perfection of the human species ... We behold vast countries groan-

41 Condorcet 1796, pp. 19–20.
42 Bury's statement that 'Condorcet cannot be said to have deduced any law of social development' is completely false, Bury 1920 p. 212.
43 Condorcet 1796, p. 251. [Editor's interpolation.]
44 Condorcet 1796, pp. 257–8.

> ing under slavery ... In a few directions, our eyes are struck with a dazzling light', while the great mass of mankind is 'consigned over to ignorance and prejudice'.[45]

What is responsible for this lag? Up until now history was the history of individuals instead of being the history of the masses. 'The mind of the philosopher reposes with satisfaction upon a small number of objects' and forgets 'the spectacle of the stupidity, the slavery, the extravagance, and the barbarity' that characterises the great majority of people.[46] 'Hitherto, ... history ... has been merely the history of a few men. That which forms in truth the human species, the mass of families, which subsist almost entirely upon their labour, has been forgotten ... the chiefs only have fixed the attention of historians'. This is all wrong. Whether we are concerned with a discovery or an important theory, a legal system or a political revolution, we must always examine its effects on the largest section of each society, 'the true object of philosophy'. Until now, that is precisely the part of 'the history of the human species' which is 'the most obscure, the most neglected'.[47] Condorcet proceeded to explain this neglect in a purely intellectual way, as the failure of science and knowledge to pay sufficient attention to the social condition of the great mass of working people, who, during the two revolutions, had taken their first active role on the stage of history and thereby demonstrated their importance. Behind the intellectual explanation, however, there was an important insight into historical development, which necessarily brought the economic factor into the foreground. With Condorcet the idea of natural laws of historical development and the collectivist view of history as a history of the masses were born.[48]

Leaning heavily on Condorcet,[49] Saint-Simon (1760–1825) sought to give history the strictly scientific character and certainty that marked astronomy and chemistry.[50] As his starting-point Saint-Simon takes the fact of the French Revolution, which he seeks to fit into the whole sequence of historical changes. By this method he hopes to discover the basic forces of history. His ultimate purpose

---

45 [Condorcet 1796, p. 245.]

46 Condorcet 1796, p. 245.

47 Condorcet 1796, pp. 246, 248.

48 See Hayek 1941b.

49 In *L'Organisateur* (1819) Saint-Simon praises Condorcet's *Outlines* [1796]: 'It is the first attempt to constitute history ... by treating it as a real science', he says, 'but this attempt, sufficient to indicate the goal of history, will not suffice to achieve it', Saint-Simon 1964a, pp. 72–3.

50 Saint-Simon 1964b. For the following discussion, see Bazard 1958; Muckle 1920; Weill 1896; Spühler 1925; Volgin, 1926; and Hayek 1941b [also Hayek 1941a].

is to found a *politique scientifique* based on systematised historical observations and destined to replace the hitherto current *politique métaphysique* based on abstract hypotheses, which in reality is only a kind of theology.[51] History, Saint-Simon thinks, can be made into a science only if the student learns from historical experience and 'laws' how to predict the future on the basis of the past. 'The wise [or knowing] man ... is the man who foresees.'[52]

Saint-Simon's philosophy of history has a history of its own. Originally he too accepted a purely intellectual theory and considered the growth of knowledge to be the determining factor in the historical transformations of society. After 1814, however, he turned to an economic conception. Retaining the formal framework of his earlier view, that is, the idea of the progressive development of historical phenomena causally determined by some basic force, Saint-Simon substituted the economic factor for intellectual enlightenment as the driving force. Material production and the law of property, he now stated, were the base of society. In all social changes the strongest determining factor is not the spiritual element but the organisation of property: 'The National character is powerless against objective developments ... there is no change in the social order without a change in property'.[53] In his *Views on Property and Legislation* (1818),[54] Saint-Simon develops his idea of the dependence of the legal superstructure upon the economic base: he emphasises that, while parliamentary government is merely a *form*, it is the structure of property relations which is the fundamental thing and therefore 'this structure is the *real foundation* of the social edifice', implying that with the revision of property relations the whole

51 Saint-Simon 1964c, p. 20 ['*politique scientifique*' means 'scientific politics'; '*politique métaphysique*' means 'metaphysical politics'].

52 Saint-Simon 1964e, p. 36. In the *Memorandum on the Science of Man* Saint-Simon criticised previous historical writing: 'It is a collection of facts ... These facts are not bound together by any theory ... they do not provide the means for determining what will happen from what has happened.' 'The future is made up of the last terms of a series of which the past constitutes the first term', Saint-Simon 1964b, pp. 246 and 172.

Enfantin insisted later that the theory of history was the most complete and elaborate part of Saint-Simonism and that it 'justified our claim that it was *science* ... We demonstrated ... a LAW, ... a REGULAR ORDER where only *chaos* and *confusion* had been seen ... we showed the steady march of humanity toward UNIVERSAL ASSOCIATION', Enfantin 1964a, pp. 55, 60 [emphases in Enfantin's original text, but not Grossman's translation]. The Saint-Simonians were also the first (in 1832) to raise the important problem of the uneven development of the West and the Orient. How was it possible, they asked, to reconcile the stationary or retrogressive conditions in Asia and Turkey with the law of continuous progress? Enfantin 1964b, pp. 135–40 and Enfantin 1964c, pp. 167–8 [the pages Grossman refers to in Enfantin 1964c are not relevant;].

53 Saint-Simon 1964f, pp. 241–2.

54 [Saint-Simon 1841b.]

social order can be changed.[55] 'Thus putting it briefly, politics is the *science of production*, whose object is to discover the order of things most favourable to all sorts of production.'[56]

The exposition of Saint-Simon's ideas on the historical sequence of various economic structures must be preceded by a short summary of his philosophy of history. 'The universe', says Saint-Simon, 'is ruled by a single immutable law',[57] and the science of man is part of physical science. The study of history enables us to demonstrate the sequence of organic and critical epochs in the life of nations.[58] In the organic epochs mankind moved with regularity under the sway of common beliefs', as well as common institutions, whereas during the critical epochs 'all forces were engaged in destroying the principles and institutions which had guided the preceding society',[59] because new facts have emerged and society has new needs that cannot be satisfied within the narrow frame of old institutions and beliefs.[60] In such epochs, dominant religious and political institutions and ideas binding together the culture of a given epoch lose their harmonious unity and organic character; they are undermined by new critical elements, and the society enters a revolutionary crisis: the old creeds and institutions become the targets of attack. At first weak, the new elements, by repeated assault, shake the old order to its foundations and in the end overthrow it. Thus a fundamental change in the basic factor of a given period destroys the superstructure, and society is driven into anarchy. The crisis is overcome only after a reconstruction of the foundations has created the conditions for the development of new cultural elements, common institutions, and beliefs; then a new organic period begins. Thus the historical process does not

55 Saint-Simon 1964g, pp. 43, 82–3.

56 Thierry 1964, p. 188 [Grossman implies that this was a work by Saint-Simon. It was written, under Saint-Simon's influence, by his student and adopted son Augustin Thierry]. This new conclusion was forced upon Saint-Simon by the course of the French Revolution, which preserved the economic-legal structure of the bourgeoisie, and thus of the society, throughout the rapid series of changes in the political constitution, when between 1789 and 1814 France changed its political constitutions ten times (see Saint-Simon 1964f, p. 228).

57 Saint-Simon 1964b, pp. 173, 309; also Saint-Simon 1964e, p. 55.

58 Only the technical terms 'organic' and 'critical' epochs were introduced by the school (Buchez, Bazard); the distinction between these epochs was introduced by Saint-Simon himself. More generally it must be stated against the views of Hayek, who gives too much credit to the Saint-Simonian school, that almost all the important doctrines of the school can be found in Saint-Simon himself; the school only developed and systematised them [Hayek 1941a, p. 135 et seq.].

59 Bazard 1958, pp. 206–7.

60 Bazard 1958, pp. 207–8.

follow a straight and continuous line but is interrupted by periodic setbacks. Nevertheless, Saint-Simon regards this succession of progressive and regressive periods as useful and necessary. For each setback is only the expression of new forces facilitating the transition from the existing to a more advanced social system.[61]

Particularly interesting are the concrete illustrations of this theory given by Saint-Simon and further developed by [Saint-Amand] Bazard. Pre-Socratic Greece, dominated by polytheism, constituted an 'organic' period. This was followed by a long 'critical' period, from Socrates to the barbarian invasions, during which ancient religion suffered a slow process of disintegration. The Middle Ages, says Saint-Simon, are generally regarded as a period of barbarism and ignorance; what is overlooked is that with the Middle Ages mankind entered a new organic period, after Charlemagne had created the social organisation and Pope Gregory VII the spiritual organisation that gave European society a homogeneous character for centuries to come.[62] These institutions proved advantageous as a whole; this was the 'period of splendour of the feudal system',[63] during which Europe waged few wars, and these unimportant. The modern critical period began with Copernicus, who destroyed the scientific armour of the Christian religion, and with Luther, who undermined the political power of the papacy, thus breaking the bond that united all the European countries. Carried further by [Francis] Bacon, Descartes, Galileo, Newton, and Locke, this spiritual revolution led finally to the French Revolution – the peak of critical dissolution, the collapse of the power of Catholicism.[64] Simultaneously with that dissolution of European unity there began the struggle of the European powers for the domination of the world, from Karl V through Philip II and Louis XIV until Napoleon.[65]

It is against the background of this succession of organic and critical epochs that Saint-Simon shows us the sequence of the various socio-economic systems – his most brilliant contribution. In contrast to the theoretical individualism of the classical economists and the eighteenth-century Enlightenment, Saint-Simon regards history as an objective process, as the slow, century-

61 Saint-Simon 1964f, p. 166.

62 Saint-Simon gives a particularly interesting analysis of the organic period of the Middle Ages in *On the Industrial System* (1821), Saint-Simon 1964d, p. 90 [the page Grossman refers to does not seem relevant]; Saint-Simon 1964b, pp. 170, 243; Saint-Simon 1964f, p. 173; Saint-Simon 1964a, p. 89; Saint-Simon 1964h, p. 174.

63 Saint-Simon 1964a, p. 88.

64 Saint-Simon 1964b, pp. 191–4; Saint-Simon 1964a, p. 99 et seq.

65 Saint-Simon 1964f, p. 174.

long maturation of successive, ever more advanced social systems. The whole population contributes to this process, but not as separate individuals; Saint-Simon stresses *the primacy of the class* over the individual and the nation; he regards historical development, 'the march of civilisation', as the result of class relations. The so-called 'creators', or great men of history, such as Luther, [John] Wycliffe, [Jan] Hus, merely express the new that had slowly come into being. 'Nobody creates a system of social organisation; the concatenation of interests and ideas which had been formed is noticed and pointed out, that is all.'[66] The 'real constitution' cannot be *invented* but only *described*. The 'veritable constituent power' belongs neither to the king nor to the constituent assembly but to the 'march of civilisation' observed and formulated into a 'general law' by the philosopher.[67] The seemingly unlimited power of kings is in reality limited by the existing social structure; when general conditions are not ripe, even absolute kings cannot accomplish much, as is shown by the failure of Emperor Joseph II's (1780–90) attempt to restrict the privileges of the nobility and the church in Austria.[68] Every social organisation of the past, however deficient it may seem to us, was justified at the time of its birth because it corresponded to the degree of scientific enlightenment and to the productivity of social labour conditioned by it.[69] That for Saint-Simon the economic factor is predominant can also be seen from the fact that, according to him, the leading class in *production* must also be the *politically* ruling class. In the Middle Ages, because the nobility played a leading part in agriculture, it also wielded political power beginning with the eleventh century (in alliance with the clergy as representatives of spiritual power), and these classes subjugated the rest of the population 'to exploit it for their own profit'.[70] But after Louis XI (died 1483) the kings, alarmed by the power of their big feudal vassals and desirous of strengthening their own power, allied themselves with the new class of *industriels* that had arisen in the womb of feudal society, against the nobility.[71] In their class strategy directed against the nobility, the kings encouraged the nobles to live in luxury, to settle at the royal court, etc.; this led to the farming-out of the noblemen's estates and deprived them of any active function in the productive process. Thus it alienated them

66 Saint-Simon 1964a, pp. 178–80.
67 Saint-Simon 1964d, p. 188.
68 Saint-Simon 1964h, p. 54.
69 Saint-Simon 1964c, p. 72; and Saint-Simon 1964a, p. 38; also Saint-Simon 1964h, p. 170 [the page Grossman refers to does not seem relevant].
70 Saint-Simon 1964a, p. 41.
71 Saint-Simon 1964h, p. 21.

from the nation. 'From that time on they ceased to have any *political* importance in the country, because they were no longer the leaders of the people in their everyday *labours*.'[72]

After the kings had thus succeeded in destroying the power of the nobility, they turned against the growing power of the industrial class. Under Louis XIV, with the establishment of banking in France, the power of the industrial class grew tremendously and surpassed that of all other classes. Louis XIV, changing the previous class strategy of the French kings, went over to the side of the nobility and pursued a policy directed *against* the *industriels*. As a result, the monarchy came into contradiction with historical development;[73] it allied itself with a class doomed to perish in its struggle with the new class, which to an ever increasing extent concentrated in itself all the economic and spiritual forces of the nation. When the French Revolution broke the power of feudalism and the nobility, the end of the monarchy allied with the nobility was inevitable.

The revolution was a gigantic destructive force; room was now made for the unfettered development of industry. But the revolution, says Saint-Simon, is not yet completed, for the task of every social movement is the creation of a superior social and political organisation,[74] and up until now no unified social and cultural organisation of society has been created. Production through competition has prevailed and created a wavering chaos, which lacks any principle of integration; self-interest is triumphant everywhere. However, 'no system can be replaced by the *critique* that overthrows it; only a *new system* can replace an old one'. Saint-Simon tried to develop this positive system of the future in *L'Organisateur*, whose very name was a program.[75]

He does not, however, condemn capitalism, with its base in individual freedom and its dispersal of forces. He regards capitalism as a necessary stage of evolution, which won its right to existence through its victory over the restrictive feudal economy. But capitalism cannot last long. The restoration period will not bring stabilisation, and the danger of new disorder will be present as long as the leading class in production – the industrial class – is not also the leading political class. The term 'industrial class' is taken here not in its modern meaning but as denoting all those who do productive work, including the entrepreneurs, not in their character as capitalists but as the technical and commercial directors and organisers of industry, in opposition to the *oisifs*, or

72 Saint-Simon 1964h, p. 24. Italics are mine.
73 Saint-Simon 1964h, pp. 25, 30, 32; and Saint-Simon 1964a, pp. 103–4.
74 Saint-Simon 1964c, pp. 28, 39–40.
75 Saint-Simon 1964a, p. 6.

the idle (the unproductive wing of the bourgeoisie: *rentiers*, the *military*, *bureaucrats*). The majority of the industrial class, however, consists of the 'least educated and poorest men'. This class is 'the only useful one'.[76] Economic evolution shows that 'this class is increasing steadily at the expense of the others; it must end by becoming the only class'.[77]

According to Saint-Simon the restoration period is a *period of transition*. A parasitical group, consisting of the unproductive portions of the bourgeoisie mentioned above (*rentiers*, etc.), the *classe intermediaire*, has wedged itself between the old defeated nobility and the industrial class; this intermediate class seized power during the revolution and concluded a compromise with the old nobility during the restoration; at present it forms the royal bureaucracy and exploits the industrial class.[78] Such a situation is untenable for any length of time, because it is based on '*two antagonistic principles*': economic and social power is held by one class, while political power is held by another. 'The nation is essentially industrial and its government is essentially feudal.'[79] The time is now nearer for a new organic period which will overcome the present disorganisation. The economy of the future, he explains, will be a system of association completely different from all previous systems. Its main task will be to improve the lot of the class whose sole means of subsistence is the work of its hands, which constitutes the majority of the population. For the time being, no one is concerned about this class kept in silent subjection by the ruling classes.[80] But the increasing significance of the new organisation 'will make them pass from the governed to the governing'.[81] The people will no longer be subjects; men will cease to command one another and will be partners, and there will no longer be any need for 'government' but only for 'administration'. The repressive functions of the state are needed only when the majority of the population is exploited by the ruling class. With the abolition of exploitation the repressive functions of the state will disappear.[82] The social organisation

76 Saint-Simon 1964g, p. 74.

77 Saint-Simon 1964g, p. 74. Elsewhere Saint-Simon says that the industrial class comprises 29.5 million of the 30 million Frenchmen, Saint-Simon 1964d, p. 187.

78 Saint-Simon 1964h, pp. 8, 34–9, 41, 67.

79 Saint-Simon 1964h, pp. 33–4 [emphasised in Saint-Simon's text]. This passage contains the germ of the important (Lenin's) theory that transitional periods are characterised by dual rule.

80 Saint-Simon 1964c, p. 81.

81 Saint-Simon 1841a, p. 14.

82 Saint-Simon 1964h, pp. 44, 106. This passage foreshadows the Marxist theory of the 'withering away' of the state in the classless society. [The phrase, now widely used in English, has been rendered as 'dies out' in more recent translations of Engels 1987, p. 268 and its

will have only one purpose: the fullest possible satisfaction of human needs and the increase in social wealth.

The rise of this system is not a utopian dream of an individual but the necessary outcome of the development of civilisation during the last 700 years. Mankind has always moved in the direction of the industrial system, and, once constituted, 'this system will be the *final system*'.[83]

Saint-Simon's philosophy of history unquestionably exerted a great influence on the further development of evolutionary thinking in France, England, and Germany. There is a widespread belief that evolutionary ideas in France and in England were developed under German influence; it is important to stress that the exact opposite is true and that particularly after the July Revolution (1831) Paris became the Mecca of the Liberals of all Europe and that many young Hegelians and members of the Young Germany movement were strongly influenced by the Saint-Simonians.[84]

With regard to the further development of the historical approach to political economy, it is particularly interesting to note that Friedrich List's 'natural law of historical development', according to which social evolution must necessarily pass through definite stages – an idea readily accepted by the historical school of German economists – is of Saint-Simonian origin.[85] That Bruno Hildebrand, another German economist of the historical school, who propounded the theory of definite stages of economic development, derived his ideas from the Saint-Simonians has been pointed out by Johann Plenge.[86]

A real pioneer was Simonde de Sismondi (1773–1842), who was not only a historian but also a remarkable theorist.[87] He made important contributions in various fields of economic theory and especially in his critique of the static, harmonistic conceptions of Ricardo, Jean-Baptiste Say, and Malthus. Against their abstract, deductive method, he insists upon experience, history, and observation.[88] Rejecting the prevailing glorification of free competition, Sismondi

condensation into Engels 1989a p. 321, which was for a long time the main introductory Marxist text in the German-speaking world. Grossman exaggerates: Saint-Simon argued that, instead of being dominant in government, in the future society the military and legal officials would be subordinate to the most capable administrators.]

83 Saint-Simon 1964c, p. 166; also Saint-Simon 1964h, p. 42.

84 See especially Hayek 1941b, pp. 283 et seq.; also Suhge 1935, pp. 47, 87; and Shine 1940, chapter 4.

85 Hayek 1941b, p. 291.

86 Plenge 1919, p. xv.

87 See Grossman 1924a, above pp. 55–119.

88 See the standard biography, Salis 1932, p. 407. While Saint-Simon had developed the his-

points to the crises of 1814 and 1818, the transformations in England during the first two decades of the nineteenth century, the poverty of the working class that grew out of free competition, the concentration of masses of workers in the new industrial centres, the flight from the soil, the growth of the slums, and the creation of the modern proletariat. This dark picture is very different from the rosy pictures painted by his contemporaries. More than that, Sismondi draws an equally dark view of the future, in his first theory of crises. Crises, he argues, are not something accidental, the product of noneconomic factors, such as drought or war, as Ricardo taught, but are storms necessarily resulting from the very nature of capitalism. They will become increasingly severe with the future development of capitalism. Since the purchasing-power of the working class is never large enough to take all of one year's production and since the productive power of industry grows more rapidly than the limited purchasing-power of the workers, this gap must grow wider as capitalism develops.[89]

This is the point at which Sismondi's theory merges with his 'sociologising' of economics. Just as he gave a preview of future developments, so he also examined the past systematically; and in 1819 he offered the first general explanation of the development of the existing economic system of the most advanced countries (England and France) out of the conditions of the past – conditions which had by no means disappeared from the world. Modern capitalism is thus conceived as a sort of island in a sea of other, older forms of economy.

Sismondi traced the history of agriculture, for example, from patriarchal exploitation at the dawn of cultural history through slave exploitation in antiquity, serfdom in the Middle Ages, *métayer* system (share farming) and *corvée* labour in the early modern period to modern capitalism in which large-scale

---

torical, evolutionary theory, showing the transitory character of the existing social order, his economic critique of existing society remained unelaborated and lacking in precision. (See Henri 1925, p. 6). It was only Sismondi who completed the historical criticism by adding the elements of an economic critique of society, namely, the theories of concentration of capital, periodical crises, unemployment, economic exploitation, pauperism, and insecurity of the working masses – all necessarily resulting from the existing social organisation (see Grossman 1924a, above p. 93–94).

89 There are, of course, other important distinctions between Sismondi and his contemporaries. Thus, against Ricardo's differential land-rent theory, according to which rent arises from better soil but not from the less fruitful, Sismondi shows that even the worst land gives rise to rent. 'All land', he said, 'yields rent', Sismondi 1991d, p. 229 [Sismondi expressed this idea but did not use the words Grossman attributes to him on the page he cites]. It is no wonder that Ricardo's disciple, McCulloch, bitterly attacked this work in the *Edinburgh Review*. [In fact, the anonymous review of books by Robert Owen, which included a critique of Sismondi, was written by Robert Torrens 1819.]

exploitation (*bail à ferme*) reveals its tremendous superiority over small-scale exploitation because the former can 'substitute capital for human forces'.[90] This superiority means that small-scale production will ultimately disappear. Sismondi then traces industrial production from the guild organisation in the towns of the Middle Ages to the development of capitalism. He shows how the capitalist system follows from the separation of the independent handworker from the means of production. In its pure form this system would involve the coexistence of but two classes – the wage-earners and the owners of the means of production. In actual fact, however, there still remains a third group held over from the earlier stage – the peasants and craftsmen.[91]

Underlying Sismondi's account of the historical development of agricultural and industrial production is his notion of the difference between dominant and subordinate economic forms. When specific institutions are carried over into a new system, their relation to the whole is altered, and a decisive change occurs in their function. Thus the once dominant role of the peasant and craftsman has disappeared. What remains is merely a fragment of the past, occupying a subordinate role in the new capitalist economy.

Sismondi was also a pioneer historian. Before his work appeared, the history of medieval Italy was virtually unknown. To the eighteenth-century rationalists the Middle Ages appeared as an era of barbarism and darkness, of interest to none but antiquarians. Sismondi was one of the first to understand that the liberation of the medieval Italian towns prepared the foundation of bourgeois society in Italy earlier than anywhere else.[92] Sweeping aside the classical evaluation of these earlier economies as 'irrational', he showed the historical justification for their existence. Each of these earlier systems grew spontaneously out of contemporary conditions, spread without compulsion, and eventually became a dominant form because, from the standpoint of the development of liberty, it represented an economic and social advance over its immediate predecessor. Only when the dominant system passed the peak of its development and creativity did it degenerate and become a hindrance to further progress. It then sought to maintain itself by force against the rise of new economic forms, only to be compelled to give way in the end to a new and more progressive

90 Sismondi 1991d, pp. 143–96. [The closest expression, in both the original French and the published English translation, to the text Grossman quotes is 'Cultivation on the great scale … invents machines, in which the wind, fall of water, the expansion of steam, are substituted for the power of limbs', Sismondi 1991d, p. 185. '*Corvée*' was feudal vassals' unpaid labour for their lords; '*bail à ferme*' was an agricultural lease.]

91 See Grossman 1924a, see above p. 64–65.

92 See Grossman 1934, p. 69.

system.[93] The economic development of man is thus not a mere succession of different economic systems but a development toward even greater progress and freedom.[94]

Characteristic of Sismondi's insight is that he projected this historical development into the future. In view of the long process of the rise and decline of economic systems, he argues, we cannot assume that the existing bourgeois wage-labour system represents the final form of society.[95] On the contrary, we must assume that 'our actual organisation ... the dependency of the worker',[96] will also be transcended and replaced by a better system in the future.

Sismondi is thus a forerunner of the Marxist doctrine of the historical development of different economic systems in the direction of a progressive unfolding of the forces of production. 'It is one of the civilizing aspects of capital', Marx wrote, 'that it extorts this surplus labour in a manner and in conditions that are more advantageous to social relations and to the creation of elements for a new and higher formation than was the case under the earlier forms of slavery; serfdom, etc'.[97] What escaped Sismondi, however, was a realisation of precisely which factors constitute the driving force of historical development. His investigations into the history of the free Italian towns from the twelfth to the sixteenth century convinced him that the characters of nations, their energy or weakness, their culture or backwardness, are not the products of climate or racial peculiarities but the results of social organisation and political institutions. The real motive power of politics and the interdependence between politics and economics he did not see, however.

Sismondi's doubts about the permanence of the capitalist system could not be forgiven by the representatives of the official doctrine. Among his contemporaries he was recognised chiefly as a historian and historian of literature. Later on, after 1850, the protagonists of social reform, exaggerating Sismondi's really limited faith in reform measures, hailed him as a precursor. But as a theorist he fell into oblivion for more than a century.

---

93 See Grossman 1924a, see above p. 107–108.

94 In a recent article, Anthony Babel 1938, pp. 298 et seq., criticises Sismondi for failing to give a precise definition of progress. As a matter of fact, Babel failed to discover not only the definition but also the very conception itself, as outlined above. He does not see Sismondi's discussion of the historical sequence of progressively freer economic systems as a whole and loses himself in a mass of details about technical, religious, or political progress.

95 See Grossman 1924a, see above p. 107–108.

96 [Sismondi 1991d, p. 558.]

97 Marx 1981b, p. 958.

2 In England – James Steuart, Richard Jones, Karl Marx

Alongside the trend of thought linked with the French Revolution, another important movement grew out of the industrial revolution in England. Every year new technical processes were increasing the productivity of industry. The equilibrium of society was overthrown, to the detriment of the country districts and to the advantage of the towns, which were rapidly increasing both in number and in size. The workmen affected by the rapid introduction of machinery were in revolt against the novel conditions.[98] England was steadily moving away from the Continental type of agricultural nations, and this rapid process of differentiation demanded an explanation of its historical roots. 'Why have not all civilized societies', wrote [James Maitland] Lord Lauderdale, 'derived equal benefit from them [that is, from the new technical inventions] – and what are the circumstances that retard the progress of industry in some countries, and that guide its direction in all?'[99]

The tremendous leap in production, on the other hand, particularly during and after the Napoleonic Wars, resulted in a marked increase in trade and extension of the world market. One of the consequences was the establishment of close economic and cultural contact between Western European capitalism and the more backward economies of southern and Eastern Europe, South America, and, above all, Asia. A clear understanding by means of historical comparison was thus afforded of the different economic systems still existing in different parts of the world and of the changeability of specific economic institutions, such as property. These new insights, together with the influence of the French Revolution previously discussed,[100] inevitably led to a better understanding of the historical development of all social institutions and to the formulation of the inductive method in the field of history and economics, which in the field of history is associated with the name of Auguste Comte.[101]

---

98 Halévy 1937, pp. 79–80.

99 Lauderdale 1804, p. 304.

100 Cf. pp. 560 and 564 above.

101 We need not spend any more time on Comte, because he made no contribution to the particular problem under discussion. In his remarks on the method of historical comparison he assumes the validity of the same law of evolution for all peoples, since he holds that they all go through the same successive stages. His 'three-stage' theory, however, has nothing to do with the succession of constantly higher, objective economic systems but deals only with intellectual advances. Man's interpretation of facts advanced from the attribution of all phenomena to supernatural agencies to the use of metaphysical abstractions and finally to scientific laws of succession and similitude. The 'law' of the three stages is thus no historical law at all. It offers no causal, genetic explanation of development

The chief representative of evolutionary ideas in the field of economics in England is the Reverend Richard Jones; but the way was prepared for Jones by the work of Sir James Steuart (1712–80), whose *Inquiry into the Principles of Political Economy*[102] reveals an evolutionary approach to economic problems. He argues that the 'speculative person' or theorist must use not only deduction but also the inductive method grounded on observation. On the one hand, he must consider the universal factors – he must 'become a citizen of the world'.[103] In analysing individual branches of the economy – population, agriculture, trade, industry, interest, or money – he cannot remain satisfied with mere description, 'the nature of the work being a deduction of principles, not a collection of institutions'.[104]

On the other hand, Steuart warns against too easy generalisations that are not properly based on experience, against the 'habit of running into what the French call *systèmes*. These are no more than a chain of contingent consequences, drawn from a few fundamental maxims, adopted, perhaps, rashly'.[105] 'If one considers the variety … in different countries, in the distribution of property … of classes, [etc.] … one may conclude, that … principles, however universally true, may become quite ineffectual in practice …'.[106]

Political economy must be adjusted to these differences. That is why, in approaching political economy, Steuart conducts 'himself through the great avenues of this extensive labyrinth' of facts 'by this kind of historical clue';[107] and he promises to treat the subject 'in that order which the revolutions of the last centuries have pointed out as the most natural'.[108]

In the second chapter of Book I, entitled 'Of the spirit of a people', Steuart offers a sketch of the historical development of Europe 'from the experience of what has happened'.[109] The 'great alteration in the affairs of Europe within these … centuries, by the discovery of America and the Indies', namely, the rise of industry and learning and the introduction of trade, led to the 'dissolution of the feudal form of government' and the introduction of 'civil and

---

but merely a schematic description of historical sequences, see Lesson 48, Comte 1908a, pp. 151–247; Maudit 1929, p. 89; Krynska 1908, p. 78.

102 Steuart 1767.
103 Steuart 1767, p. 3.
104 Steuart 1767, p. viii.
105 Steuart 1767, p. ix.
106 Steuart 1767, p. 3.
107 Steuart 1767, p. 16.
108 Steuart 1767, p. 150.
109 Steuart 1767, p. 16.

domestic liberty'.[110] These, in turn, 'produced wealth and credit; these again debts and taxes; and all together established a perfectly new system of political economy'.[111] All these factors 'have entirely altered the plan of government everywhere ... From feudal and military, it is become free and commercial'.[112]

The social transformation has led, in turn, to corresponding changes in 'the manners of Europe';[113] and the two together are changing the spirit of the people, slowly to be sure, but nonetheless unmistakably, when we compare any two succeeding generations.[114]

The 'sociologising' of economic categories and institutions was carried through still more penetratingly and systematically by the Reverend Richard Jones (1790–1855), a man who has not been properly appreciated except by Marx.[115] Jones was the first Englishman to criticise the classical economists from the standpoint of the historical school. He sharply attacked their attempts to deduce economic laws valid for all times and all countries. He wrote:

> We must get comprehensive views of facts, that we may arrive at principles which are truly comprehensive ... [If] we determine to know as much as we can of the world as it has been, and of the world as it is, before we lay down general laws as to the economical habits and fortunes of mankind or of classes of men: there are open to us two sources of knowledge – history and statistics, the story of the past, and a detail of the present condition of the nations of the earth. [On the other hand, i]f we take a different method, if we snatch at general principles, and content

110 Steuart 1767, p. 150.
111 Steuart 1767, p. 150.
112 Steuart 1767, p. 10.
113 Steuart 1767, p. 11.
114 Steuart 1767, p. 11.
115 Marx's evaluation is restated by Rudolf Hilferding, 1912a; and by Eric Roll 1938, pp. 309–16. We have already noted that Marx never claimed credit for having first introduced the historical factor into political economy. He pointed, besides Sismondi, to two men: James Steuart (1767) and, even more important, Richard Jones (1831), who, though ignorant of the Hegelian dialectic, was thoroughly familiar with the historical conditions of earlier epochs and with the economic conditions of the backward spheres of Eastern Europe and Asia. Richard Jones, a friend of Malthus and his successor as a professor of economics at East India College, Haileybury, was an expert on Asiatic conditions, particularly in India, Persia, and Turkey. In his *Essay on the Distribution of Wealth* (1831), book 1, 'Rent', Jones lists as [the] source of his historical analysis in an appendix a copious literature about Asiatic and South American countries. Particularly amazing is the knowledge of Asiatic economic conditions that Jones revealed in a work published 20 years later, Jones 1859.

> ourselves with confined observations, two things will happen to us. First: what we call general principles will often be found to have no generality ... at every step of our further progress, we shall be obliged to confess [that they] are frequently false; and, secondly ...[116]

Jones was especially sharp in his criticism of the supposed universality of Ricardo's laws. He held that they have but limited historical validity, specifically only where Ricardo's presuppositions agree with the actual conditions. They are valid neither for the past nor for the future, because in different epochs the conditions change and no longer coincide with Ricardo's premises.[117]

This approach is genuinely epoch-making when contrasted with the 'eternal' laws of the classicists. Just before the publication of Jones's major work,[118] his friend William Whewell hailed him as the founder of the inductive system of political economy, in contrast to Ricardo, the master of the deductive method, and expected that Jones's book would *faire époque*.[119] Actually, the work received scant notice. Among the classical economists, only [John Ramsay] McCulloch gave it some attention, and he dismissed it as 'superficial' and unimportant. John Stuart Mill describes Jones's 'essay on distribution'[120] as a 'copious repertory of valuable facts on the landed tenures of different countries'; Jones's evolutionary ideas are not mentioned.[121] Much more recently Böhm-Bawerk, in his history of economic theory, the third German edition of which appeared in 1914, that is, after the publication of Marx's study of Jones in his *Theories of Surplus Value*, could not say more than that Jones 'contribute[s] nothing of great consequence to our subject'.[122] Marian Bowley disposes of him briefly by saying that he 'looked upon sociology as a branch of economics, thus revising Comte's treatment of economics as a branch of sociology', and that he 'criticised the classics for ignoring the relativity of economic laws'.[123]

---

116 Jones 1833a, pp. 31–2. The extracts given above have been rearranged somewhat.

117 A theory of rent, for instance, based on the English type of land system, which assumes individual ownership and free competition, cannot be applied to oriental societies, in which joint ownership and absence of competition are the rule.

118 Jones 1831.

119 [*Faire époque* means 'make history'.]

120 [i.e. Jones 1831.]

121 Mill 1900a, p. 176.

122 Böhm-Bawerk 1959a, p. 69; see also the recent monograph of Hans Weber 1939; and Marx 1991b.

123 Bowley 1937, p. 40. We have already called attention to Eric Roll's discussion of Jones, which does benefit from Marx's analysis but does not discuss Jones's position with respect to

Though Jones's influence on his immediate contemporaries was thus slight, he exercised a powerful indirect influence through Marx. He is one of the few economists of whom Marx speaks with deep acknowledgement, despite the fact that Jones, a friend of Malthus, was very conservative in his political thinking and rejected Ricardo's doctrine of the opposition of class interests in favour of a faith in class harmony.[124] Marx recognised the limited bourgeois character of Jones's horizon but called him the last representative of the 'true science of political economy'[125] and made a special analysis of each of his major works; we find in this analysis frequent references to Jones's superiority over the classical economist.[126]

Jones was not a theorist in the classical sense of developing categorical concepts by sharp, logical deduction from a given set of presuppositions. He was a historian. But, unlike the discredited school of Roscher, who substituted for theoretical laws an unthinking, chronological accumulation of unanalysed descriptive material, Jones considered it his function to test and correct the prevalent theories against actual historical developments and to formulate concrete experience into new theoretical viewpoints and categories. With Thomas Hodgskin, for example, he was one of the earliest opponents of McCulloch's wage-fund theory, which held that there is a special fund of fixed magnitude for the employment of workers. Unlike Hodgskin, however, whose critique (1825) of this theory was a beautiful exercise in logic, Jones went to history to show that such a wage fund never really existed in fact. Quite the contrary, given a fixed amount of capital, there is continual fluctuation between its constant (for machines and raw material) and its variable (for wages) elements.[127] To this important theoretical conclusion Marx

our particular problem. Mr Nai-Tuan Chao's thorough-going thesis deals only with Jones's system of political economy: his theory of production and distribution, rent, wages, and profit, Chau 1930, pp. 45 et seq. Jones's evolutionary theories, particularly his theory of the succession of economic stages, are not mentioned.

124 Jones 1831, p. 328.

125 Marx 1991b, p. 345.

126 E.g. 'Jones marks a substantial advance on Ricardo', Marx 1991b, p. 322; 'It is here that Jones' superiority is most striking', Marx 1991b, p. 322; 'One can see what a great leap forward there was from Ramsay to Jones.' Marx 1991b, p. 344. Altogether, Marx devoted 70 pages to the discussion of Jones [in the third volume of the edition of *Theorien über den Mehrwert*, Marx 1910a–d, edited by Karl Kautsky which is now superseded by the *Collected Works* edition of Marx's economic manuscripts of 1861–3; for the extensive discussion of Jones, see Marx 1991b, pp. 320–71].

127 'The amount of capital devoted to the maintenance of labour may vary, independently of any changes in the whole amount of capital', Jones 1833a, p. 52.

appended the gloss: 'This is an important point';[128] and he developed it still further in critical opposition to the classical school in a chapter on 'The so-called labour fund'.[129]

Jones went still further. Whereas the wage-fund theory held that there is a rigid law of wages, that is, that wages can rise only if the number of workers decreases or if the amount of capital increases,[130] Jones showed by historical evidence that it is possible – and at given historical moments it actually occurs – that 'great fluctuations in the amount of employment, and great consequent suffering, may sometimes be observed to become more frequent as capital becomes more plentiful'.[131] This happens in the 'periods of transitions of the labourers from dependence on one fund to dependence on another',[132] that is to say, in the period of the transition from an economy of independent peasants and handicraftsmen to a system in which those groups become a propertyless proletariat. Such a 'transfer' – the loss of economic independence through the loss of ownership of the means of production – obviously cannot be accomplished without serious disturbances.[133] Marx commented that Jones had here hit upon the germ of the idea of 'primitive accumulation', that is, the antecedent of capital formation, and had thus begun the necessary process of replacing the 'absurd' and rationalistic notion of capital formation through 'savings' by a more realistic and historically correct view.[134]

Even more important insights into the historical roots of the capitalist system are to be found in Jones's discussion of various systems of production. He

128 Marx 1910d, 476. [Although it was not apparent to Grossman, this phrase is Kautsky's rather than Marx's. Marx prefaces the quotation from Jones with 'Richard Jones sums up correctly in the following passage', Marx 1991b, p. 371].

129 'It has been shown in the course of this inquiry that the capital is not a fixed magnitude', Marx 1976b, p. 758.

130 McCulloch 1825, pp. 61–2.

131 Jones 1833a, p. 52.

132 'Transfer of the labouring cultivators to the pay of capitalists ... Transfer of non-agricultural classes to the employ of capitalists', Jones 1833a, pp. 52–3 [Jones emphasised '*labouring cultivators*'].

133 Jones 1833a, pp. 52–3. The uprising of propertyless peasants in Norfolk, in the middle of the sixteenth century, when enclosures were made on a tremendous scale, is well known. This uprising was crushed, and 'multitudes of dispossessed and impoverished villagers flocked to the towns', Gibbins 1897, pp. 88–9. It is not hard to see why just in this period there occurs for the first time in history the application of the word 'proletarii' in the modem sense, to denote propertyless day labourers, wage-workers, and 'poore husbandmen' as a 'fourth sort or classe' of society, see book 1, chapter 24, Thomas Smith 1906, pp. 12–13.

134 'What Jones calls "transfer" here, is what I call "primitive accumulation"', Marx 1991b, p. 336.

was well aware of the fact that different systems have succeeded one another in the past; and sought to work out their essential characteristics. The decisive factor in differentiating these various systems is *the way in which human labour is organised.* As this factor changes, the whole economic system changes. That is why Jones does not follow a chronological arrangement in describing the succession of economies but begins with the capitalist system as a yardstick with which to measure and differentiate earlier systems.

Like Sismondi, he considered the 'transfer', i.e. the separation of the once independent producers (peasants and craftsmen) from their means of production, to be the necessary historical precondition for capitalism. Through the 'transfer' process they became wage-workers dependent on the capitalist. 'The first capitalist employers', he wrote, 'those who first advance the wages of labour from accumulated stock, and seek ... profits ... have been ordinarily a class distinct from the labourers themselves.'[135] This development had so far been limited pretty much to England,[136] and even there it was historically a late phenomenon.[137] In previous centuries the handworkers were supported not by advances from capital but by land revenue, 'the surplus produce' of the land.[138] This surplus produce 'may be handed over to individual landowners' or it 'may be paid to the state'.[139] In the latter case 'the wages of such workmen were obviously derived directly from the revenue of their great customer, and not from an intermediate class of capitalists', and it 'is in Asia that we observe this particular fund ... in full and continued ... predominance'.[140] In Europe the number of workers paid out of land revenues is still large, but no longer predominant, and 'in England itself, ... the body is comparatively small'.[141]

Jones shows the superiority of the capitalist system over preceding forms. In China and throughout the East, for example, tailors and other artisans wander all over the city, day in and day out, seeking work in their customers' homes, and thus waste a great deal of time, while under capitalism the workers became sedentary and 'can now labour continuously'. Finally, on this basis, where one capitalist employs many workers, an organised division of labour becomes possible.[142]

135 Jones 1859, pp. 444–5.
136 Jones 1833a, p. 52.
137 Jones 1859, p. 454.
138 Jones 1859, p. 440.
139 Jones 1859, p. 440.
140 Jones 1859, pp. 442, 444.
141 Jones 1859, p. 443.
142 Jones 1859, pp. 395, 396, 397, 455 [Jones emphasised '*can*'.]

It is on the basis of such concrete historical material that Jones developed his idea of the *sequence of economies through which every nation must pass, though at different tempos* according to their varying conditions. After a given economy becomes dominant, it begins to lose that position while still remaining very widespread, and it slowly becomes more and more subordinate to a new form. When Jones says that 'England is much in advance of other nations', he does not mean that English conditions are better but merely that, 'in arriving at our present position, we have passed through and gone beyond those, at which we see other nations … *The future of all other people will, however, at some time, be like our present.*' This succession theory has exceedingly broad implications, as he himself recognised: 'the prophecy is bold'.[143] Following Condorcet, he sees an easier road ahead for the younger nations. They have 'better hopes for the future' because, 'if they assume our economic organisation and power, [they] may escape many of the evils that have afflicted our progress, or from which we suffer now'.[144]

Jones goes still further. Not only does he predict that every nation must ultimately attain the highest economic form so far developed – capitalism – but he sees the possibility of still further development in the future to a socialised form of production in which the separation of the wage-worker from the means of production will be ended. Capitalism is thus a historical and transitory, though necessary, stage on the road to a more advanced economy of the future.

> … a state of things may hereafter exist, and parts of the world may be approaching to it, under which the labourers and the owners of accumulated stock, may be identical; but in the progress of nations, which we are now observing, this has never yet been the case … [The present system in which] a body of employers pay the workers by advances of capital … may not be as desirable a state of things as that in which labourers and capitalists are identified; but we must still accept it as constituting a stage in the march of industry, which has hitherto marked the progress of advancing nations.[145]

Having shown the way in which historical economies succeed one another, Jones then tried to differentiate those elements in the economy which are particularly active and decisive in the process of transformation from the more

143 Jones 1833a, pp. 19, 21. Italics are mine.
144 Jones 1859, p. 412.
145 Jones 1859, p. 445.

passive and secondary ones. He was not interested in the traditional categories of political economy – profit, rent, wages, etc. – but in the changes in production in so far as they influence the growth of productive power and the character of the economy itself. His study of history led him to the conclusion that 'changes in the economical structure of nations' teach us to understand the secrets of ancient and of modern history;[146] on the other hand, that changes in the structure of the economy are closely linked with changes in the institution of property and that the differing property relations correspond to different stages in the development of productive power.[147] For Jones, therefore, the

> economical structure of nations [is made up of] relations between the different classes which are established in the first instance by the institution of property in the soil, and by the distribution of its surplus produce; afterwards modified and changed (to a greater or lesser extent) by the introduction of capitalists, as agents in ... feeding and employing the labouring population ... An accurate knowledge of that structure can alone give us the key to the past fortunes of the different people of the earth, by displaying their economical anatomy, and showing thus, the most deeply-seated sources of their strength, the elements of their institutions, and causes of their habits and character. It is thus we must learn the circumstances which divide them into classes.[148]

In other words, the economic structure, as thus defined, is the key to social relationships:

> There is a close connection between the economical and social organisation of nations ... Great political, social, moral, and intellectual changes, accompany changes in the economical organisation of communities ... These changes necessarily exercise a commanding influence over the different political and social elements to be found in the populations where

146 Jones 1833a, p. 34.

147 Marx 1991b, p. 321.

148 Jones 1833a, pp. 21–2. With the expression 'economical anatomy' Jones foreshadows the famous phrase of Marx in the preface to *A Contribution to a Critique of Political Economy* that legal relations and forms of state cannot be understood by themselves and that they are rooted in material conditions of life, that 'the anatomy of this civil society ... has to be sought in political economy', Marx 1987a, p. 262. It was Sir William Petty who first (1672) introduced the expression 'political anatomy' to denote the knowledge of the economic structure of a country, its 'Symmetry, Fabrick and Proportion', as the basis for understanding the 'Body Politick', see Petty 1899, p. 129.

> they take place: that influence extends to the intellectual character, to the habits, manners, morals, and happiness of nations.[149]
>
> As communities change their powers of production, they necessarily change their habits too. During their progress in advance, all the different classes of the community find that they are connected with other classes by new relations, are assuming new positions, and are surrounded by new moral and social dangers, and new conditions of social and political excellence.[150]

This superstructure, in turn, 'react[s] on the productive capacities of the body'.[151]

Only after he has shown the historical relationship of capitalism to earlier systems does Jones turn to the problem of modern land rent. Here, too, he resorts to historical study and shows how modern ground rent developed out of earlier forms. Rent takes on a completely different character within each economy. In one case it is the dominant institution; in another it becomes subordinate to capital, and the landowning class no longer participates directly in production. Jones differentiates five historical types of rent: (1) labour rent, i.e. slave and serf rent; (2) an intermediate form of rent, which is the transition from type 1 to type 3; (3) rent in kind; (4) money rent of the precapitalist period; and, finally, (5) in the capitalist period, farmer's rent (in the Ricardian sense). The latter differs from all others and can exist only in a society based on the capitalist mode of production, because rent, as a surplus above the average profit, requires as its precondition the development of the industrial average profit rate. In sum, every specific form of property has its corresponding form of labour and of rent.[152]

Jones rejected Ricardo's theory of a 'continuous diminution in the returns to agriculture, of its assumed effects on the progress of accumulation'.[153] By historical illustrations he showed that rents were actually highest in countries where agriculture was very productive, and he thus destroyed the *historical* basis of Ricardo's theory of rent. As the classical theory of profits and wages was closely

149 Jones 1859, pp. 405–6. Rearranged.

150 Jones 1859, pp. 410–11.

151 Jones 1859, p. 406 [editor's interpolation.]

152 Jones 1859, pp. 185, 188. Marx 1991b, p. 321 points out that in Jones's work *On Rent* (Jones 1831) he starts with the different forms of real property, whereas two years later in his *Syllabus* (Jones 1833b) he analyses the different forms of labour that correspond to those types of property.

153 Jones 1859, p. xiii.

connected with the theory of rent, the collapse of the latter endangered the classical theory as a whole.

It is not hard to see why Jones earned the enmity of the classical school and, on the other hand, the strong approbation of Marx. Jones, the latter wrote, is characterised

> by what has been lacking in all English economists since Sir James Steuart, namely, a sense of the historical differences in modes of production.[154]
>
> What distinguishes Jones from the other economists (except perhaps Sismondi) is that he emphasises that the essential feature of capital is its socially determined form [*Formbestimmtheit*].[155]

Probably the highest praise Marx could give Jones was to contrast his presentation of genetic developments with Ricardo, who 'developed nothing'.[156]

It is worth noting here the emphasis placed by John Stuart Mill on the intellectual backwardness of England – the country which in his judgement was 'usually the last to enter the general movement of the European mind'.[157] Mill underscored the charge that, whereas 'the doctrine that … the course of history is subject to general laws … has been familiar for generations to the scientific thinkers of the Continent' (France), it was opposed in England well into the second half of the nineteenth century because it conflicted with 'the doctrine of Free Will'.[158] The fate of the new science of geology is particularly revealing in this context. The foundation for a rational evolutionary system of geology was laid in Italy by [Cirillo] Generelli (a Carmelite friar) in 1749; in France by [Nicolas] Desmarest (1777) and [Jean-Baptiste] Lamarck (1802); in England by [James] Hutton (1785). Hutton, however, was accused of heresy; evolutionary ideas were condemned as incompatible with the biblical account of Genesis.

It was in such an antievolutionary atmosphere that Jones, like Sismondi before him, had the courage to attack the whole structure of the classical economists, not merely specific doctrines, and to cast doubts upon the permanence of the capitalist system. Their critique of the existing economic order,

---

154 Marx 1991b, p. 320 [Marx emphasised '*historical*'].

155 Marx 1991b, p. 341. [In the original published version, the word '*Formgestimmtheit*' was used, a typographical error not apparent in a late draft of the translation of the article.]

156 Marx 1910d, pp. 451 and *passim* [the phrase quoted is not present at the point indicated by Grossman in either Kautsky's edition of *Theorien über den Mehrwert*, Marx 1910d, or Marx 1991b, although Marx writes there that 'Jones' analysis … distinguishes him from, and shows his superiority over, all his predecessors', Marx 1991b, p. 321.]

157 Mill 1900b, p. 643.

158 Mill 1900b, p. 644.

their emphasis upon its historical, transitory character was considered a heresy, which could not be forgiven. *As theorists*, both men were ignored by the representatives of the dominant school and left in oblivion for nearly a century.

It is apparent that by the time Karl Marx (1818–83) began his work, in the forties of the last [nineteenth] century, the application of evolutionary concepts to economic institutions and the formulation of the doctrine that economic systems are historical in character had been basically accomplished. Marx himself pointed that out repeatedly, though it was left to him to complete and sharpen the analysis. He took over the heritage of Saint-Simon and Sismondi in France, of James Steuart and Richard Jones in England, and of certain elements in Hegel's philosophy of history and, introducing certain new ideas of his own, created an integrated, original theory.

We need not underline the point and we assume it as well known that, for Marx, the Hegelian 'development' meant something quite different from what the eighteenth-century Enlightenment, the Saint-Simonians, or even Sismondi, Jones, and positivists like August Comte understood by this term. To men oriented to the natural sciences of their day, development meant nothing more than the generalisation of an empirically and inductively constructed series of particular observations,[159] whereas Marx, like Hegel, understood the relationship between the particular and the universal quite differently, viewing the historical 'object' as made up not of individual observations but of the '*cultural whole*' of social-collective unities.[160] Using the genetic method of the dialectic, with its constant creation and synthesis of opposites, Marx sought to grasp the evolution of these collective unities in their historical necessity. Every present moment contains both the past, which has led to it logically and historically, and the elements of further development in the future.

At the same time there is a fundamental point at which Marx is joined with Sismondi and Jones against Hegel – one which must not be overlooked in ascribing the 'historicising' of economics to Hegelian influence. For the former, historical development, occurring in the external world in time, is a succession of objective economic stages of different economic structures, whereby the higher stage develops out of the lower. In other words, history has not a

159 See Troeltsch 1919, pp. 6–7. From the antipositivists' viewpoint, the relationship between the particular and the universal is presented in the excellent book by Cohen 1931, p. 161.

160 'Just as generally in the case of any historical, social science, so also in examining the development of economic categories it is always necessary to remember that the subject [is] … modern bourgeois society …', Marx 1986b, p. 43 [Marx did not use the phrases 'cultural whole' or 'cultural totality' in this publication].

relativistic character, it does not depend on the accident of the observer's point of view, ideals, or standards. What Marx did was to remove the study of history from that subjective level to a higher one, where objective, measurable stages of development are perceived. He fulfilled Saint-Simon's hope of making history a science.

Hegel was flatly opposed to such a doctrine. The German word *Entwicklung* has two different meanings, translated into English (and French) by two distinct words – 'development' and 'evolution'. Hegel always used the term in the first sense, meaning the unfolding and dissection of the various component elements (*Gedankenbestimmungen*) contained in the *Begriff* ('notion of the essentials of a thing'). Development is possible only under the rule of the *Begriff* and *hence takes place in the sphere of logic*. 'Metamorphosis', Hegel wrote, 'pertains only to the Notion as such [i.e., to the notion of the essential in contrast to the notion of phenomena], since only its alteration is development'.[161] Hegel therefore attacked the concept of the natural philosophers (and thus also of the sociologists) that evolution as an objective process in history is the 'external real production' of a higher stage from a lower one. He insisted, on the contrary, that it is 'the dialectical Notion which leads forward the stages, is the *inner side* of them'.[162] That is why in *The Philosophy of History* he saw the various stages in world history, not as an objective process in the *sphere of real history*, but as a process within the *sphere of logic*.[163] World history is to Hegel the progress within man's *consciousness* of the idea of freedom, and it is this development of consciousness which determines the four principal levels achieved by the various peoples: the oriental world, the Greek, the Roman, and the Germanic world.[164]

Marx, on the contrary, uses the term *Entwicklung* mostly in the second sense, meaning not development within the sphere of *logic* but, like Sismondi and Richard Jones, evolution as an objective process in the sphere of *real History*.[165]

With such a point of view, writes [Georg] Lasson, 'Hegel *must* reject the theory of [biological] evolution. Long before Darwin he had discarded all of Dar-

161 Hegel 2004, paragraph 249, p. 20 [Hegel emphasised '*Metamorphosis*' and '*its*'].

162 Hegel 2004, paragraph 249, p. 20. Italics are mine [Hegel emphasised '*stages*'].

163 Hegel 1914, pp. 58–9.

164 Hegel 1914, pp. 109–16; and Fischer 1901, p. 748.

165 For that very reason Marx directs his criticism against Proudhon's notion of 'evolution': Proudhon, he says, has accepted the 'Hegelian trash' and is '[u]nable to follow the real course of history … The *evolutions* of which Mr Proudhon speaks are presumed to be evolutions such as take place in the mystical bosom of the absolute idea', Marx 1982a, p. 97; Marx 1976a, pp. 168 and 169.

winism as an unclear confusion of the *notion* and external *existence*.'[166] Hegel himself said of the idea of evolution as an objective process in the external world: 'A thinking consideration must reject such nebulous ... ideas as in particular the so-called ... origination of the more highly developed animal organisms from the lower and so on'.[167]

Marx, on the contrary, accepts the idea of the rise of more developed structures from the lower, and for this reason he was one of the first to acknowledge the importance of Darwin's work. In a similar way, as Darwin uses nature's technology, i.e. the formation of the organs of plants and animals, as instruments to explain the origin and development of species, Marx wishes to use the history of human technology as an instrument 'that *distinguishes different economic epochs*',[168] as the 'productive organs of man in society ... are the material basis of every particular organisation of society'[169] and the 'instruments of labour ... supply a *standard of the degree of development* which human labour has attained'.[170]

In sum, Marx refuses to follow Hegel on the basic question of the concept of development but works rather from the conception of Sismondi and Richard Jones. For Marx, evolution is an objective process of history, whereby each historical period or social structure is *marked by specific objective tendencies*,[171] which can be discovered from the nature of the technological instruments and from the social organisation of labour in the use of those instruments.[172]

---

166 Lasson 1920, p. xvii.

167 Hegel 2004, paragraph 249, p. 20 [Hegel emphasised '*origination*']; see also Renouvier 1912, p. 271.

168 Marx 1976b, p. 286 [Grossman's emphasis]. Long before the publication of Darwin's work, in one of his earliest works – the critique of Proudhon (1847) – Marx had already emphasised the fundamental significance of human technology for the characteristics of a given society [Marx 1976a].

169 Marx 1976b, p. 493.

170 Marx 1976b, p. 286 [Grossman's emphasis]. Alongside this technological factor, the social factor is equally significant for the distinction of economic epochs from one another, namely, 'The particular form and mode in which this connection [between labourers and means of production] is effected', Marx 1978b, p. 120.

171 As early as 1847, Marx wrote, against Proudhon: 'The hand-mill gives you society with the feudal lord; the steam-mill, society with the industrial capitalist.' Marx 1976a, p. 166.

172 Elsewhere, in the section 'The capitalistic character of manufacture', Marx 1976b, pp. 480–91, Marx differentiates the specific tendencies of the manufacturing period from the trends under industrial capitalism and lays the basis for the differences in the fact that 'In manufacture the transformation of the mode of production takes *labour power* as its starting point. In large-scale industry, on the other hand, the *instruments* of labour are the starting point', Marx 1976b, p. 492. [Grossman's emphasis. This quotation and Marx's

From the basic point of view, Marx saw that the history of economic organisation is a series of economies, each more advanced than its predecessor because of changes in the method of production: 'In broad outline, the Asiatic, ancient, feudal and modern bourgeois modes of production may be designated as epochs marking progress in the economic development of society'.[173]

Throughout Marx's writings there are scattered, but nonetheless profound, characterisations of each of these epochs.[174] His main efforts, however, were not directed to the precapitalist forms but to a systematic analysis of the genesis and development of the specific historical phases of capitalism[175] and to the transition from capitalism to socialism.[176] Marx views 'the development of the economic formation of society ... as a process of natural history',[177] and his aim 'lies in the illumination of the special laws that regulate the origin, existence, development and death of a given social organism and its replacement by another, higher one',[178] whereby society 'can neither leap over the natural phases of its development nor remove them by decree. But it can shorten and lessen the birth-pangs'.[179]

Marx showed, for instance, that industrial capitalism did not develop out of handicraft or out of accumulated rent from landed property (as Max Weber and Sombart later taught) but from the merchant. The latter, by progressively subordinating the production of the craftsman and transforming him into a proletarian, brought about the transition from mercantile to industrial capitalism. Starting with the decentralised workshop under command of the merchant-capitalist (domestic system), production moved into the various phases of

account of the difference between manufacture and large-scale industry actually come from the following section, the first in the next chapter of *Capital*.]

173 Marx 1987a.

174 Thus he contrasted the unceasing technical revolutionising of our economy with the *static economic structure of Asiatic societies*, notably India, and saw the explanation in the fact that production was there organised in self-sufficing communities 'based on possession of land in common, on the blending of agriculture and handicrafts and on an unalterable division of labour', Marx 1976b, pp. 477–8. In this connection the form of taxes, namely, taxes in kind, played an important role, Marx 1976b, p. 239. In countries where central governments, by the use of artificial irrigation, made it possible to transform deserts into fertile fields, 'a single war of devastation has been able to depopulate a country for centuries, and to strip it of all its civilization', Marx 1979b, p. 127.

175 For a good historical application of Marx's theory of the earlier stages of capitalism, see Pirenne 1914.

176 Marx 1989a.

177 Marx 1976b, p. 92.

178 Marx 1976b, p. 102.

179 Marx 1976b, p. 92.

the period of manufacture (cooperative, heterogeneous, and organic manufactures), and finally into modern large-scale industry based on the machine. Marx did not stop with the delineation of the broad lines of historical development, however. He continued the application of the genetic method to the individual organs, institutions, and functions of the capitalist mechanism.

We cannot go into the details of Marx's historical analysis. The important point to emphasise is that Marx never remained within the narrow framework of historical description but always made use of historical insights to deepen his theoretical understanding of the laws of development. *This close link between history and theory* is one of the factors that differentiate Marx from all his predecessors. An example will serve to illustrate this point. A study of the demography of antiquity, the Middle Ages, and the modern world led Marx to the insight that there is no universally valid law of population, as Malthus had taught, but that the modern trend toward the creation of a relatively surplus population 'is a law of population peculiar to the capitalist mode of production; and in fact every particular historical mode of production has its own special laws of population, which are historically valid within that particular sphere'.[180]

This type of historical analysis also led to important conclusions in economic theory. When Sombart raises the accusation that Marx 'hardly ever *defines* ... his concepts ... such as capital, factory, plant, accumulation',[181] he shows that he misses the true sense of Marx's historicism and even of Marxist terminology: he uses the word *Begriff* in the sense of 'definition'; the word 'concept' or 'notion' (*Begriff*), however, is used by Marx in the specifically Hegelian sense, as notion of essence of a thing, as contrasted with the definition as merely the notion of the phenomenon.

Marx rejects the view that knowledge consists in classifying and defining, and that the task of science is simply to discover a rational criterion for classification. This is the static approach of the classicists, looking upon social phenomena as unchangeable structures. Marx, on the other hand, is a spokesman of the new, dynamic approach. That is why social phenomena, in his judgement, are actually indefinable. They have no 'fixed' or 'eternal' elements or character but are subject to constant change. A definition fixes the superficial attributes of a thing at any given moment or period, and thus transforms these attributes into something permanent and unchanging.[182] To understand

180 Marx 1976b, pp. 783–4.

181 Sombart 1909b, p. 52.

182 Marx made his point of view quite clear in his polemic against Cherbuliez: 'Previously profit ought to have been explained. But nothing emerged except a *definition* of it which merely states the form in which it appears ... a statement that profit and rate of profit exist,

things it is necessary to grasp them genetically, in their successive transformations, and thus to discover their essence, their 'notion' (*Begriff*). It is only a pseudo-science that is satisfied with definitions and the phenomenal aspects of things.[183] Without devoting more space to a characterisation of Marx's analysis, we turn to an examination of the fruits of his analysis. By attributing to Marx the first application of evolutionary thinking to economics, critics have obliterated the original contribution that Marx really did make to our understanding of history and the specific differences between Marx and his predecessors. They have reduced his historical conceptions to a level that does not go beyond the horizon of bourgeois liberalism, that is, beyond the idea of evolution in the direction of constant progress 'from the incomplete to the complete' – to quote Hegel.

The fundamental characteristic of Marx's historicism and the mark that distinguishes it from his predecessors is not the doctrine of the historical succession of economic systems but a special theory which, in addition to evolutionary changes *within* a given system, explains the objective and subjective conditions necessary for the *transition from one system to another*. Briefly stated, it is that within the existing economy a new economic form arises and grows, that the two enter into ever sharper conflict with each other, and that through the violent resolution of the conflict, the new economy finally takes over.

Within this general theory there are three special theories: (1) a doctrine of a 'universal social dynamic' of structural changes in society, valid for all 'antagonistic' societies; (2) the theory of the *objective developmental tendencies of capitalism*; and (3) the theory of the subjective bearer of change, that is, the class struggle theory. Obviously the second, unlike the two others, deals only with the special historical phenomenon of the transformation from capitalism to socialism. Like Condorcet and Saint-Simon, Marx teaches that the idea of

---

without, however, anything being said about their nature', Marx 1991b, pp. 296–7. Elsewhere, in speaking of the economists, Marx says that their 'definitions ... are expanded into trivial tautologies'; whereas the task of science is not the construction of abstract definitions but 'by way of thinking ... the *reproduction of the concrete*', Marx 1986b, pp. 24 and 38 [Grossman's emphasis]. There are, therefore, no 'eternal' economic categories; every category is only 'the theoretical expression of historical relations of production, corresponding to a particular stage of development in material production', Marx 1985b, p. 29 [Marx emphasised the entire text].

183 '[T]he vulgar economists confine themselves to systematising [the phenomena] in a pedantic way, and proclaiming [them] for everlasting truths', Marx 1976b, p. 175 [the second interpolation is Grossman's, the others are made necessary by the difference between this and the translation of *Capital* Grossman used].

evolution must be applied to the future as well as to the past, for one must seek in the perceptible structural changes of the present the lines of future development.[184]

We have already seen that Saint-Simon and his school knew that the industrial system grew up within, and as a bitter enemy of, the feudal system of the later Middle Ages. For the Saint-Simonians, however, this insight was no more than a singular historical observation. Marx developed this observation into what we might call a universal birth story of a social system. Every new economic system, he taught, is born directly within the old and goes through a long process of maturation before it can displace its predecessor and become dominant. '[N]ew superior relations of production never replace older ones before the material conditions for their existence have matured within the framework of the old society.'[185] The displacement of the old system by the new is not an arbitrary process, to be accomplished at any chance moment. It requires the existence and slow maturation of certain necessary subjective and objective factors.[186]

For the first time in the history of ideas we encounter a theory which combines the evolutionary and revolutionary elements in an original manner to form a meaningful unit. Gradual changes in the productive forces lead at some point in the process to sudden changes in the social relations of production, that is to say, to political revolution. By underlining the evolutionary aspects, Marxism sharply distinguishes itself from the voluntarism of the utopian socialists as well as from the pseudo-revolutionarism of putschists or partisans of the *coup d'état*. At the same time, Marxism does not give up the idea of revolution, but regards it as the necessary conclusion of the evolutionary process and as the instrument for achieving the transition to a new economic

---

184 As early as 1843, Marx wrote to Arnold Ruge that we must not be concerned with 'constructing the future' or 'dogmatically anticipat[ing] the world, but only want to find the new world through criticism of the old one', Marx 1975b, p. 142 [editor's interpolation]. Twenty years later Marx wrote to Schweitzer that Proudhon and the utopians were hunting for a 'science' by which the social question was to be solved *a priori* 'instead of deriving their science from *a critical knowledge of the historical movement*, a movement which itself produces the material conditions of emancipation', Marx 1985b, p. 29 [Grossman's emphasis; Marx emphasised '*material conditions of emancipation*'].

185 Marx 1987a, p. 263. Elsewhere Marx emphasised (May, 1871) that the working class can expect no 'ready-made utopias ... They have no ideals to realise, but to set free elements of the new society with which the old collapsing bourgeois society itself is pregnant', Marx 1986a, p. 335.

186 'They [the working class] know that in order to work out their own emancipation ... they will have to pass through long struggles, through a series of historic processes, transforming completely circumstances and men', Marx 1986a, p. 335.

structure. This theory rests primarily on the fact that productive forces, legal property relations, and political power are subject to the law of uneven development.

Changes in the productive forces release a relatively rapid and dynamic element, out of which grows the assault against the structure of the old society as a whole. Legal property relations, on the other hand, and political power, which rests upon them, constitute the passive, conservative, static element, guarding the existing society against change. The latter element changes slowly, long after the changes in the productive forces and as the result of those changes. The new economic forces thus clash with the antiquated political and property relations, which no longer correspond to the new needs and fetter further progress. 'Then begins an era of social revolution',[187] in which the antiquated legal and political relations are broken and replaced by new ones that are appropriate to the new economic forces. Since the antiquated laws express only the vested interests of their creators and since these will never voluntarily renounce their privileges, the disappearance of the old laws entails the disappearance of their creators, the former ruling classes.

In his second special theory, dealing with *the objective developmental trends within capitalism*, 'the natural laws of its movement',[188] Marx tries to show that there is a limit to the development of capitalism, that it must reach a peak after which a *declining phase* will set in and that at a certain point the further functioning of the system will become impossible and its collapse inevitable. The system must be transformed not only because the working people reject it but also because the ruling classes cannot find any way out. During this critical period, despite progress in restricted sectors (technology, chemistry), the system as a whole loses its progressive character, and the symptoms of its disintegration grow more and more numerous; the system becomes a fetter on further development and can preserve itself only by violence and increasingly severe repression of the newly emerging social forces. In the end, however, it must be defeated in the conflict with these forces and yield to them. Thus progress is achieved only at the price of the misery and humiliation of individuals and entire peoples.

---

187 Marx 1987a, p. 263.

188 Marx 1976b, p. 92. It must be stressed that Marx does not use the word 'trend' or 'tendencies' in the usual sense of the term; by 'trend' he means 'tendencies winning their way through and working themselves out *with iron necessity*', Marx 1976b, p. 91 [Grossman's emphasis]. The other factors and counter-trends can weaken or slow up the dominant trend but not prevent it from asserting itself. Elsewhere Marx speaks about 'that higher form to which present society is *irresistibly tending* by its own economical agencies', Marx 1986a, p. 335 [Grossman's emphasis].

No predecessor of Marx had a similar theory. It is true that the Saint-Simonians wanted to make history an exact science and conceived the future to be a necessary product of the past; but they never got beyond the mere postulate and never attempted to work out a theory of the future tendencies of capitalism. Nor did Sismondi or Richard Jones. Their prediction that capitalism would be replaced by a higher form of economy did not rest upon theoretical arguments but merely on historical analogy: since all previous economic systems were transitory, they argued, we must assume the same to be true of capitalism.

Marx undertook to demonstrate the historical necessity of the decline and final disintegration of capitalism. When the process of accumulation reaches a certain point, he shows, there will be a transformation of quantity into quality. A condition of oversaturation with capital will arise, and no adequate new possibility for capital investment will be available. All further accumulation of capital will become impossible, and society will enter a permanent period of growing accumulation of idle capital, on the one hand, and of large-scale permanent unemployment, on the other. Thus the process of disintegration will begin. The property-owners' fear of losing their privileges gives the spiritual and political life of this period a reactionary character. In short, the whole structure of capitalism will be shaken to its roots, and the basis will have been laid for great political and economic transformations.[189] It is true, of course, that Bazard and later Pecqueur, following Sismondi, foresaw the crises, the misery, and the uncertainty of the working class. These insights remained mere particular observations with them, however, and not, as with Marx, elements of a steadily worsening disease of the system from epoch to epoch that would lead to ultimate paralysis.

The third element in Marx's general theory is that no economic system, no matter how weakened, collapses by itself in automatic fashion. It must be 'overthrown'. The theoretical analysis of the objective trends leading to a paralysis of the system serves to discover the 'weak links' and to fix them in time as a sort of barometer indicating when the system becomes ripe for change. Even when that point is reached, change will come about only through active operation of the subjective factors. This part of the theory Marx developed in his study of the class struggle. Marx has frequently been charged with a 'fatalistic' theory of the 'historical necessity' of social development in some given direction. Such a charge rests on a serious misunderstanding of the theory of the class struggle. In all his writings Marx characteristically emphasises the

189 For a detailed study of this theoretical analysis, see Grossmann 1929a.

unity of theory and practice. This so-called 'historical necessity' does not operate automatically but requires the active participation of the working class in the historical process. This participation, however, is itself not something arbitrary but follows from the pressure of the objective factors. The student of history and the forward-looking practical politician must therefore consider this subjective factor as in fact another objective condition of the historical process.[190]

While, for instance, Saint-Simon and his school do not give the working class any political role in the transformation of society, the main result of Marx's doctrine is the clarification of the historical role of the proletariat as the carrier of the transformative principle and the creator of the socialist society. To Marx, activity is an integral part of thinking, and truth cannot be discovered by a merely contemplative attitude, but only by action. This is the meaning of Marx's eleventh thesis on Feuerbach: 'The philosophers have only interpreted the world in various ways; the point is to change it.'[191] If philosophers from Montesquieu to [Ludwig] Feuerbach taught that man is a product of his natural and social environment, Marx observes that to an even greater extent man is influenced by his action on his environment. In changing the historical *object*, the *subject* changes himself.[192] Thus the education of the working class to its historical mission must be achieved not through theories brought in from outside but through the everyday practice of the class struggle. This is not a doctrine but a practical process of existing conflicts of interests, in which doctrines are tested and accepted or discarded. Only through these struggles does the working class change and re-educate itself and become conscious of itself. Marx's attack on the '*fatalist* economists'[193] is only an illustration of the fact that his dialectical concept of history has a twofold significance. In this he follows Hegel, for whom history has both an objective and a subjective meaning, the history of human activity (*historia rerum gestarum*) and human activity itself (*res gestas*).[194] The dialectical concept of history is not merely an instrument with which to explain history but also an instrument with which to make history. 'Men make their own history, but they do not make it ... under circum-

190 Of course, 'class struggle' is not to be understood in the primitive sense that the workers must blindly attack the entrepreneur class wherever the two come into contact. Both the content and the form of the class conflicts are themselves determined by the attained level of historical development and by the concrete historical situation.

191 [Marx 1976c, p. 5, Marx emphasised '*interpreted*' and '*change*'.]

192 Marx 1976b, p. 283.

193 Marx 1976a, p. 176.

194 Hegel 1914, p. 63; Fischer 1901, p. 739.

stances chosen by themselves, but under circumstances directly encountered, given and transmitted from the past.'[195]

It is in this double sense that the Marxist theory of the class struggle is to be understood. On the one hand, it is an expression of the existing conflict of interests between classes. At the same time, it transcends the mere statement of an existing factual condition, not as a fatalistic expectation of evolution, but as a guide to the active participation of the working class in the historical process. By this activity the objective tendencies can be realised and the forces of a reactionary but powerful minority that stand in the way of further development and progress overcome. In this latter sense the class struggle has always been a decisive subjective factor in history.[196]

It is worth repeating that no one before Marx understood history in this way. It is true that in the first third of the nineteenth century the ideologists of the victorious revolutionary French bourgeoisie – the historians Augustin Thierry, [François] Mignet, and, above all, François Guizot – clearly recognised that the past centuries were dominated by class interests and class struggles. But they never went beyond the description of actual conditions, i.e. the struggles of the rising bourgeoisie against the landowning feudal class. They recognised class struggles only in the past and failed to see their continuation in their own time, in the existing relations between the working class and the bourgeoisie. In Marx the class struggle is not merely a description of actual facts but a part of an elaborated historical theory: he explains genetically the necessary emergence of class conflicts in various historical epochs and explains their origin, form, and intensity by the development of the productive forces in each period and by the position individuals and classes occupy in the productive process. This endows the doctrine of the class struggle with a concrete and profound meaning.[197]

On the other hand, Saint-Simon and his school, as we have seen above, had also recognised past class struggles only in a factual sense and did not admit them for their own time. The Saint-Simonians feared to arouse the hopes of the proletariat; and, convinced that progress must come through the elite of the upper classes, they wanted above all to win these upper classes over to their

195 Marx 1979a, p. 103.

196 Sismondi, for instance, says that 'the freedom of the Occident results from the rebellion of the non-owners' (against a small minority of landowners) … 'Between the tenth and the twelfth centuries, people without land reconquered freedom for the future generations', Sismondi 1840, pp. 499, 107.

197 See Plekhanov 1976c, pp. 466–7. *Neue Zeit*, 31 (1903), pp. 298, 304; and Tiumenev 1935.

views.[198] Though the writings of Bazard, [Barthélemy Prosper] Enfantin, and later Pecqueur contain references to the struggle of the working class against the dehumanising effects of capitalism,[199] these remain isolated statements of fact. In principle, the Saint-Simonians accepted the idea that progress was a continuous transition from antagonism to peaceful association. Thus Pecqueur regards class struggle as an evil, like every other form of struggle, and compares it to war. He expects that in the future all forms of struggle will be less violent and that peaceful methods of production and distribution will develop. There is a wide gap between this view and the over-powering generalisation of the *Communist Manifesto*: 'The history of all hitherto existing society is the history of class struggles'. Here, class struggle is not regarded as an evil but as a dynamic force, the lever of history. By fighting for its rights against the ruling class, the exploited and oppressed class creates a new historical situation. New rights are wrested from the ruling class, and the whole of society is thereby raised to a new and higher level. In this conception, class struggle does not end with the abolition of feudalism by the bourgeoisie; it is also typical of the relations between the bourgeoisie and the working class. According to Marx, the process of history on the road of progress, far from becoming increasingly peaceful, increases in violence with the development of capitalism, and class conflicts become the decisive instrument in the transition from capitalism to collectivism.

198 Weill 1896, pp. 56, 293.

199 'One fact is certain, general ... it is the silent but very decisive struggle of the workers against their masters ... with a view to forcing the captains of industry to raise their wages ...', Pecqueur 1839b, p. 126; 'How can one not see that to leave [the wage-earners] dependent on the insufficiency of a fluctuating wage is to wish to find oneself surrounded in times of crisis and general unemployment by a famished multitude, to create riot and civil war, and perhaps to arm new Spartacuses ...', Pecqueur 1839b, p. 108 [Grossman's translation mistakenly has 'Spartans' instead of 'Spartacuses'].

CHAPTER 31

William Playfair, the Earliest Theorist of Capitalist Development*

Simonde de Sismondi is regarded as the earliest representative of the doctrine of the objective tendencies of capitalist development. But Sismondi reflects not so much the French as the English industrial experience, and we know that in 1817 he went to England, the home country of the Industrial Revolution, to collect material for his *New Principles*. This is not surprising: British capitalism was the most developed at that time. It would be surprising, however, if the basic trends of capitalism, which manifested themselves in early nineteenth-century England more clearly than anywhere else, had not left any trace in English economic literature. In Playfair we rediscover a missing link; it shows that the English industrial experience found its expression not only indirectly, via Sismondi in France, but also directly in England.

'Trend spotting', or discovery of the objective developmental trends of capitalism, is the primary aim of modern economic science. It is also one of the essential elements of Marxian economics. Nevertheless, there prevails great confusion about the genesis of this important doctrine. Some writers attribute the first formulation of the fundamental tendencies of capitalism to Karl Marx; others maintain that Marx borrowed them from his forerunners, particularly Sismondi.

Can one agree with Professor Charles Rist who declares that of all the ideas that Marx took over from Sismondi '[t]he most fertile idea borrowed by Marx was that which deals with the concentration of wealth in the hands of a few powerful capitalists, which results in the increasing dependence of the working classes. This conception … forms a part of the very foundation of Marxian collectivism'?[1]

Nothing is more contrary to truth than this assertion. The concentration of wealth, the trend toward large-scale production, and the growing proletarianisation of the working classes in the first half of the nineteenth century were not theoretical conceptions, but statements of empirically observable facts. Marx did not have to 'borrow' from Sismondi facts that could be easily

* [Originally published as Grossman 1948.]

1 Rist 1915, p. 198.

ascertained from contemporary English industrial statistics and that served as the common starting-point for all critiques of capitalism by the leaders of the working-class movement in France in the middle of the nineteenth century.

Who was the first to discover and to establish these objective tendencies? In the preface to the first volume of *Capital* (1867) Marx declares that 'it is the ultimate aim of this work to reveal the economic law of motion of modern society', namely, to show 'its tendencies', which Marx regards as 'the natural laws of capitalist production'.[2] He is referring to objectively ascertainable tendencies, which Marx and Engels describe elsewhere as the concentration of capital and land in a few hands; the ruin of the petty bourgeoisie and peasants; the misery of the proletariat; the crying inequalities in the distribution of wealth; and the industrial war of extermination among the nations.[3]

However, Marx and Engels were not the first to establish the existence of such tendencies. As early as 1843, Victor Considerant, the Fourierist leader in France,[4] clearly formulated all these tendencies in his pamphlet, *Principles of Socialism, Manifesto of Democracy in the 19th Century*.[5] Particularly important are paragraphs VII, VIII and XI.

Paragraph VII (the tendency to the destruction of the small and medium industries): the result of free competition 'is the direct reduction of the proletarian masses to collective serfdom ... the progressive crushing ... of small and medium industry ... under the weight of big property, under the colossal wheels of big industry and big trade'.[6]

Paragraph VIII (concerning the tendency to the concentration of capital and the impoverishment of the working masses): 'Society tends more and more distinctly to be divided into two great classes: a small number possessing everything or almost everything ... and the great number possessing nothing, living in absolute collective dependence upon the owners of capital and the

---

2 Marx 1976b, pp. 92, 91.

3 Marx and Engels 1976, pp. 489–91.

4 [Considerant led the followers of the utopian socialist Charles Fourier.]

5 First published as a programmatic statement in the issue 1 of *Democratie Pacifique*, the daily organ of L'École Sociétaire (1 August 1843). The quotations refer to the second edition, Considerant 1847. A few months after the appearance of Considerant's *Manifesto* of 1843, Parke Godwin, an American Fourierist, published a pamphlet, *Democracy Constructive and Pacific*, which follows closely Considerant and in which the developmental trends of capitalism are defined, Godwin 1844. I am indebted to Mr Maurice Buchs who is preparing a new study in French, entitled 'Fourierism in the United States', for having drawn my attention to Godwin, Buchs 1948.

6 Considerant 1847, p. 9.

instruments of production, compelled to hire for precarious and ever decreasing wages their hands, talents, and energies to the feudal lords of modern society.'[7]

Finally, Considerant emphasises the fact in paragraph XI, that as an inevitable result of free competition there arises the tendency to the formation of big monopolies in every branch of business.[8]

Nor was Considerant the first to discover these tendencies. Several years before him, all the tendencies described above had been formulated, with masterful conciseness and precision, by Constantin Pecqueur. In his *Social Economics* this writer predicts that as a result of the introduction of machines, 'the various small industries, agricultural, manufacturing and commercial, will disappear quite generally ... As small industry will disappear, the small industrialists ... will degenerate into wage labourers, a mass of serfs working day by day in the manufactures, into proletarians without a future; and all the big industries will be monopolised exclusively by an industrial feudalism.'[9]

A few other authors propounding similar ideas could be quoted. Their primary source in France was Sismondi's book, *New Principles*, in which the fundamental developmental tendencies of capitalism were clearly stated as early as 1819. As regards the tendency to concentration, Sismondi shows that as capitalism progressively accumulates, it concentrates in large-scale manufactures.[10] He formulates the tendency to the destruction of small and medium enterprises in industry and trade.[11] As for the tendency to the impoverishment of the labouring masses, he observes that, as a result of the technological advances that extend to a growing number of branches of industry, new masses of workers constantly become unemployed; to find employment they are ready to work for starvation wages and as a result become physically and morally degraded, sinking below the level of beasts. Every technological revolution is followed by a new deterioration of the status of labourers.

7 Considerant 1847, p. 11.

8 Considerant 1847, p. 13.

9 Pecqueur 1839b, p. 101. See also Pecqueur 1839a, p. 269. [Here 'manufactures' means 'factories'.]

10 'It is worthy of mention that ... the effect increasing capital is generally to concentrate labour in very large manufactories', Sismondi 1991d, p. 275. 'Discoveries in mechanical arts have always the remote result of concentrating industry within the hands of a smaller number of merchants', Sismondi 1991d, p. 561. [Here 'manufactures' means 'factories'.]

11 'They discover the economy which exists in management on a greater scale ... the employment common to a greater number of men at once, of light, fuel, and all the powers of nature. Thus small merchants, small manufacturers disappear', Sismondi 1991d, p. 562.

However, Sismondi too had a predecessor. This article attempts to show that the true originator of the doctrine of the objective developmental trends of capitalism was William Playfair (1759–1823), a British economist, who until now has remained completely unnoticed.

Such revaluation of a forgotten economist has more than a merely personal significance. If it can be established that the conception of the objective fundamental tendencies of capitalism, the ideas of the growing accumulation of capital in a few hands, of the disappearance of the middle classes, of the necessity of capital export, etc. can be found for the first time not in Sismondi, 1819, but in Playfair, as early as 1805, this means that all these tendencies had become sufficiently perceptible in England and objectively ascertainable 14 years before the publication of Sismondi's book, and for that very reason could be formulated at that early date.[12]

Furthermore, it is noteworthy that while the previously known French theorists of the objective trends of capitalism were utopian or petty bourgeois socialists, or semi-socialists, who sharply criticised capitalism and proposed to replace it by another more or less socialist form of society, Playfair was a spokesman for the petty bourgeoisie. He too criticises the failings of capitalism, but his critique is purely sentimental. He does not conceive of any way out of the situation; despite all the failings of capitalism that he points out, he wants to preserve it, and does not propose to replace it by another system.

Playfair is not a theoretician comparable to the classical economists, that is to say, he is not an analyst. He does not precede his exposition by any general principles, such as a theory of value, from which he might draw inferences by way of logical deduction. He applies the reverse procedure – the method of the historical school. He describes the real processes and the observed devel-

---

12 William Playfair, known as an anti-Jacobin pamphleteer and statistician has remained entirely unnoticed in the history of economic ideas, although his book, *Inquiry into Permanent Causes of the Decline and Fall of Powerful and Wealthy Nations*, 1805, had some success in his time and was published in a second edition in 1807 – Playfair is not even mentioned in any early or recent history of economic theories. Furthermore, Playfair's name is not mentioned in the *Encyclopaedia Britannica*, 1941, nor in the American *Encyclopaedia of the Social Sciences*, Seligman 1930–35, nor in James Bonar's monograph *Malthus and His Work*, 1924, although it deals with a period in which both Malthus and Playfair were active. Only two English dictionaries contain short biographical and bibliographical notices on Playfair – Robert Palgrave's *Dictionary of Political Economy*, 1913, p. 116, and *The Dictionary of National Biography*, Stephen and Lee, 1921–2, p. 1300. But even these notices are confined to enumerating the titles of Playfair's writings; his economic theories are not mentioned. *Economic Journal* (*Economic History Supplement*), [Funkhouser and Walker] 1935, contains an article.

opmental tendencies, and theorises rarely. In this 'inquiry ... there has been an invariable rule, never to oppose theory and reasoning to facts but to take experience as the surest guide'.[13] The result is a surface treatment, and a lack of depth and analysis. But he is an excellent observer. Playfair is interested above all in the fate of the British Empire and its future economic development as a basis for its political power. In order to foresee that future fate, Playfair first strives to discover a general law of historical development, a law valid for all nations and all times, from antiquity to the modern era, so that Britain would represent only a special case in the application of the general law, only its modification under the particular circumstances of modern capitalism, which can be understood only as such. For that reason Playfair's exposition of Britain's developmental trends would be difficult to understand without a discussion of his general historical law of the rise and decline of nations.

1 The Dominant Tendencies of Capitalism

While contemporary French evolutionists such as Turgot (1750), Condorcet (1795) and Count Saint-Simon (first publication in 1802) assumed the existence of a law of continuous cultural and economic progress, Playfair rejects such an idea.[14] His law of the rise and decline of nations is based on the idea that mankind marks time without moving forward; that states, just like individuals, go necessarily through periods of infancy, manhood and decrepitude and then die; that all of them begin with 'their original state of poverty',[15] that they subsequently gradually develop into centres of wealth and power and that in the end, after reaching the climax of their wealth, through the operation of the same general law, they inevitably relapse into barbarism and poverty; their place is then taken by other, culturally and economically backward nations, so 'that the greatness of nations is but of short duration'.[16]

To prove the existence of such an historical law, Playfair briefly outlines the rise and fall of all the civilisations he knows for a period of more than 3,000 years, covering Antiquity, the Middle Ages and Modern Times. Under 'the pres-

13 Playfair 1805, p. 276.
14 [Turgot 1808; Condorcet 1796; Saint-Simon 1964e. See Grossman 1943a and Grossman 1943b, above pp. 556–599.]
15 Playfair 1805, p. iv.
16 Playfair 1805, p. iv.

sure of necessity'[17] the poor countries with 'superior energy' attack the wealthy nations either by peaceful methods or by war, producing always the same effect: 'the triumph of poverty over wealth'.[18] 'The effeminacy and luxury of the rich'[19] operating persistently 'from generation to generation'[20] undermines the energy and activity of the wealthy.

This General Law of historical development works in 'modern' (i.e. capitalist) industrial countries only with some modifications, because of the presence of 'some particular causes that operate in some modern nations'.[21] One of these 'particular causes' is the tremendous development of modern military technique and mechanical warfare. In the past, the triumph of poverty over wealth was possible because the backward nations under the pressure of necessity were energetic, martial and brave. In modern times, however, wars no longer favour poor nations [as] 'bodily strength has but little effect, while the engines of war can only be procured by those resources which wealth affords.' To constitute and equip an army with modern engines 'a very considerable degree of wealth is necessary'.[22] Courage and bravery, the fighting qualities of the poor nations, no longer prevail against modern weapons. While in the past, wealth and luxury led to the decline of the wealthy nations, in modern times the situation is reversed: victory is decided not by martial virtues but by wealth; therefore, the main task of the government is now to preserve wealth and prosperity.

Having formulated the general law in Book 1, Playfair confines his analyses in Books 2 and 3 to the 'modern', i.e. capitalist nations, inquiring into the specific causes that determine the rise and fall of such nations. He eliminates 'a variety' of local or accidental causes (e.g. wars) and attempts to deal only with fundamental causes 'operating in all of them', namely, 'the interior causes of the decline of wealthy nations, arising from the wealth itself',[23] i.e. from the degree of accumulation of capital achieved in a given period. Playfair distinguishes three phases of such accumulation: in the first, less capital is available than can be invested; in the second, there is sufficient capital; in the third – on which he concentrates almost exclusively – there is more available capital than can be profitably invested. Therefore, capital reaches insuperable limits – 'its bounds'[24] – to further accumulation. All nations begin their development as

17 Playfair 1805, p. 167.
18 Playfair 1805, p. 19.
19 Playfair 1805, p. 177.
20 Playfair 1805, p. 81.
21 Playfair 1805, p. 164.
22 Playfair 1805, p. 18.
23 Playfair 1805, p. 90.
24 Playfair 1805, p. 200.

agrarian countries, then become manufacturing countries and finally change into creditor nations which must export the available surplus capital.[25]

According to Playfair, Britain has entered, or is about to enter, this third phase, and he analyses it in the light both of arguments drawn from observation of contemporary conditions in Britain and of arguments drawn from the experience of previous centuries, particularly from the history of Holland, Genoa and Venice. In the course of this analysis he attempts – and he is the first economist to do so – to formulate the developmental trends of capitalist accumulation.

During the whole period embracing the first two phases of capital accumulation, which is identical with the period of progressive industrialisation, Playfair observes three fundamental tendencies of development:

1. The tendency of capital to concentrate in a few hands.
2. The tendency of the productive classes to become poorer.
3. The tendency of the middle classes to disappear. When the third phase, that of superabundance of capital, is reached, a fourth fundamental tendency begins to operate – the tendency of every industrial nation to become a creditor or investor nation.

But this means the end of progressive industrialisation and expansion, that is, a tendency to a stationary state and the beginning of disintegration and decline. Thus the general law of rise and decline remains valid also for 'modern' (capitalist) states, although its outward form is modified.

The Natural Tendency of Wealth to Accumulate in the Hands of a Few

The tendency of wealth to accumulate in the hands of a few was often asserted as a fact. Thus [Paul Henri Thiry] d'Holbach wrote in 1773: 'Wealth … gradually accumulates in a small number of hands; to favour a few shrewd citizens, all others are reduced to indigence'.[26] Playfair – and this is his contribution – does not confine himself to a vague general statement that seems to apply to all epochs, and he does not explain the concentration of capital by the personal shrewdness of a few, but regards it as the natural and inevitable result of the accumulation process in modern industrial states. In contrast to the belief of eighteenth-century economists that fundamental economic structures are the result of legislation, he shows that parallel to this accumulation, the differentiation and inequality of possessions increase as a natural result of the economic process, quite independently of existing legislation or the political

---

25 Playfair 1805, pp. 161, 200, 270.
26 Holbach 1773b, p. 74.

form of the state (that is, both in despotic and free states). Moreover, he shows the effects of concentration of capital on all social classes – the enrichment of a few big entrepreneurs, the ruin of numerous small entrepreneurs who lose their economic independence, the decline of wealth based on rentier income, the automatic enrichment of the landowning class, the specific role of credit in the centralisation of big fortunes, and, as a consequence of the concentration process as a whole, the widening of the gap between the impoverished and degraded classes and the wealthy upper classes.

'In the career of wealth, in its early state, when individual industry is almost without any aid from capital, men are as nearly on an equality as the nature of things can admit. But in proportion as capital comes into the aid of industry, that equality dies away, and men, who have nothing but industry, lose their means of exerting it with advantage; some become then incapable of maintaining their rank in society altogether.'[27] 'In every country, the wealth ... has a natural tendency to accumulate in the hands of certain individuals, whether the laws of the society do or do not favour this accumulation', as a result of which the 'unequal division of property' is accentuated.[28]

This tendency of productive industrially employed capital to concentrate is intensified by the specific function of credit. Profits are primarily created by productive activity. But this mode of enrichment is relatively slow. Big fortunes can be accumulated with the help of long-term credits:

> In countries where the common practice is to sell, chiefly, for ready money, great fortunes are seldom gained ... But in a country that gives long credits, or in a branch of trade on which long credits are given, we always see some individuals gaining immense fortunes.[29]

On the basis of the observation that as capital accumulates the rate of interest sinks (Turgot, Adam Smith),[30] Playfair concludes that in the course of the accumulation process the relative position of an owner of a definite amount of money capital deteriorates. If the rate of interest drops from 4 to 2%, a capital of £1,000 brings in the same income as previously a capital of £500. Capital accumulation is thus accompanied by depreciation of money capital and as a

27 Playfair 1805, p. 156.
28 'Of the internal causes of decline, arising from the unequal division of property, and its accumulation in the hands of particular persons', Playfair 1805, p. 125.
29 Playfair 1805, pp. 181–2. Cf. Marx '[T]he credit system ... is ... an enormous social mechanism for the centralisation of capitals', Marx 1976b, pp. 777–8.
30 Adam Smith 1910a, pp. 313–20.

result of this tendency to depreciation, large money fortunes are not permanent; they shrink after two or three generations. To counteract this tendency, and maintain the former relative position of money capital, much energy, work, shrewdness, and willingness to take risks are required.[31]

In contrast to this constantly threatened position of the moneylender, the relative position of the landowning class grows progressively stronger. As capital accumulation in industry increases and the rate of interest falls, the value of land automatically rises, without the intervention or work of the landowner. Therefore, this form of property and its concentration in a few hands is the most dangerous.[32]

The Tendency of the Number of Poor to Increase in Countries Advancing in Wealth

In the seventeenth century, England was faced with a chronic problem of pauperism – pauperism in an agricultural country. The new pauperism was very different; it was a consequence of industrialisation. What distinguishes Playfair from his predecessors in calling attention to this fact is that, in contrast to the countless remedies proposed by older economists for curing idleness by corrective or punitive legislation, he regards the increase in the number of the poor as a natural consequence of concentration of capital and wealth: 'The alarming and lamentable increases of the poor in proportion, as a nation becomes rich'.[33]

Playfair calculates that the number of the poor has grown faster than the total population.[34] These victims of poverty, he says sarcastically, are 'filling

31 'A fortune lent at interest, diminishes as the value of money sinks'. 'The depreciation of money that takes place in every country that grows rich, falls nearly all on the lender at interest', Playfair 1805, pp. 129, 162–3. 'A fortune engaged in trade is liable to risks, and requires industry to preserve it: but industry … never is to be found for any great length of time in any single line of men', Playfair 1805, p. 129. '[W]e find that wealth seldom goes amongst people of business past the second, and almost never past the third generation', Playfair 1805, p. 89.

32 The 1,000 pounds laid at interest, after 30 years is always worth 1,000 pounds. But land bought for 1,000 pounds would be worth 2,000 pounds, Playfair 1805, p. 163. 'An estate in land augments in value, without augmenting in extent, when a country becomes richer'. 'Of all the ways in which property accumulates, in particular hands, the most dangerous is landed property', Playfair 1805, p. 129.

33 Playfair 1805, pp. 87–8.

34 Playfair 1805, p. 88. Playfair's contemporary, James Mill, states 'that the paupers are equal to nearly one third of the whole male population, including old men, young men, or children', Mill 1808, p. 101.

prisons, poor houses and hospitals', 'illustrating the effect of wealth', and he devotes a whole chapter to the problem 'Of the increase of the poor, as general affluence becomes greater'.[35]

Playfair distinguishes between two types of poverty. The first, which exists 'in every nation', comprises people who are poor for general, demographic, natural reasons, such as 'the lame, the sick, the infirm, the aged, or children unprovided for'. The number of those 'in proportion to the total number of inhabitants, will be pretty nearly the same at all times; for it is nature that produces this species of helpless poverty'. 'There is another species of poverty, not of nature's creation ... That new species of poverty is occasioned by the general wealth, since it increases in proportion to it'. 'As this tendency is uniformly felt ... over the whole country when it advances in wealth ... it must operate, in length of time, in producing the decline of the whole nation'.[36]

For even though the enrichment of some and the impoverishment of others takes place in such a way that they 'change places gradually and without noise' the final result is nevertheless that 'such changes are attended with ... violent commotion'. '[T]he lower classes become degraded and discouraged, as is universally found to be the case in nations that have passed their meridian'. While some men remain idle because of their wealth, 'others, who are depressed below the natural situation of men, are bringing them [their children] up to feel the extreme pressure of want ... Neither the powers of their body, nor of their mind, arrive at maturity'. 'Whilst the foundation of idleness ... is laid in, for one part of a nation, from the affluence of their parents, another portion seems as if it were chained down to misery from the indigence in which they were born and brought up'.[37]

This social sickness is not the result of accidental external causes, but of 'the interior cause' – the accumulation of capital. That is why this sickness is inherent in the nature of the economic organism, and it becomes accentuated with the growth of this organism – a process that Playfair illustrates by quoting from [Alexander] Pope:

> The great disease that must destroy at length,
> Grows with our growth, and strengthens with our strength.[38]

35 Playfair 1805, pp. 87, 88, 156–60.

36 Playfair 1805, pp. 88–9.

37 Playfair 1805, pp. 89, 132, 156.

38 Playfair 1805, p. 90. [Playfair paraphrased Pope's couplet, 'The young disease, which must subdue at length,/Grows with his growth, and strenthens with his strength', Pope 1869, p. 204.]

> In all new and rising states the higher orders … [a]s they increase in wealth and have lost sight of its origin, which is industry, they change their mode of thinking; and by degrees, the lower classes are considered as only made for the convenience of the rich. The degradation into which the lower orders themselves fall, by vice and indolence, widens the difference and increases the contempt in which they are held. This is one of the invariable marks of the decline of nations.[39]

But the rich consider only their own advantage; the richer they become, the more selfish they are; they hold the poor responsible for their poverty and treat them worse than beasts:

> It has been noticed that in every society, as wealth increases, hospitality [which existed in a less advanced state of society] dies away … The social feelings become less active, and men turn selfish and interested, thinking for themselves and careless for the community; while, on the one hand, the causes for poverty increase, on the other, the means of relief are misapplied, neglected.[40]

The Tendency of the 'Middling Classes' to Disappear

Concentration of wealth on the one hand, and the growing number of impoverished masses on the other, take place at the expense of the middle classes, i.e. 'those immediately above' 'the inferior classes'.[41] These middle classes gradually disappear. 'The consequence of great fortunes, and the unequal division of property, are that the lower ranks … become degraded, disorderly and uncomfortable, while the middling classes disappear by degrees.' Such an exasperation of economic antagonisms as a result of the unequal division of property is dangerous and leads the nation to inevitable ruin.[42]

Playfair is not a radical. He praises the middle class and believes in their great task of assuring economic and political progress, the material and spiritual elements of which are concentrated in that class. The rich have always managed to shift burdens to the others; as for the large masses of the productive workers, they have neither the leisure nor the resources to steer the ship of state. Nor has Playfair a high opinion of the landowners, rentiers and all those who receive a fixed unearned income. He contrasts 'the most use-

39 Playfair 1805, p. 263.

40 Playfair 1805, p. 159. [In the original the 'one' was 'other', Grossman corrected this.]

41 Playfair 1805, p. 133.

42 Playfair 1805, pp. 126, 128.

ful class', i.e. 'those whose income is regulated by their efforts ... that is to say, the productive labourers of the country', with 'those whose incomes are fixed, that is principally the unproductive labourers ... the drones of society'.[43] 'Where there is no regular gradation of rank and division of property, emulation, which is the spur to action ... is ... destroyed'.[44] 'The higher classes can never be made to contribute their share towards the prosperity of a state ... The higher class ... can never be very numerous; and being above the feeling of want ... there is nothing to be expected of them towards the general good'. 'From the working and laborious classes, again, little is to be expected ... they have neither leisure, nor other means of contributing to general prosperity as public men; they, indeed, pay more than their share of taxes in almost every country; but they cannot directly, even by election, participate in the government of the country'. 'It is in the middling classes that the freedom, the intelligence, and the industry of a country reside ... where there are no middling classes to connect the higher and lower orders ... a state must gradually decline'.[45]

The rapid disappearance of the middle class is particularly dangerous, because this increases the distance between the mass of the poor and the class of the wealthy, and the contrasts between want and riches are brought into sharp focus:

> the strongest bond of society is thereby broken; the bond that consists in the attachment of the inferior classes to those immediately above them. Where the distance is great there is but little connection ... The whole society becomes, as it were, disjointed.[46]

Despite Playfair's sympathy for the middle classes, he has no illusions about the actual development of capitalism. He knows that the wheel of history cannot be stopped. The middle classes are disappearing and social inequality operates permanently, even in the opening stages of capital accumulation, when the nation is still poor in capital; but it operates with particular intensity at the higher stages of accumulation and capital saturation: '[the] tendency to [inequality] increases very rapidly of late years'. 'But if this progress goes on, while a nation is acquiring wealth, how much faster does it not proceed when

43 Playfair 1805, pp. 167–8.
44 Playfair 1805, p. 132.
45 Playfair 1805, pp. 131–2.
46 Playfair 1805, pp. 132–3.

it approaches its decline? It is then, indeed, that the extremes of poverty and riches are to be seen in the most striking degree'.[47]

The Tendency of Agricultural Nations to Change into Industrial Nations and Later into Creditor (Investor) Nations. Superabundance of Capital and Lack of Investment Opportunities in Old Industrial Countries as Factors of Disintegration and Decay

We have shown that, according to Playfair, capitalism, from its very beginning, has been accompanied by the three developmental trends described above. We shall pass now to the most important section of Playfair's theory of accumulation – his view that at a specific stage – capital accumulation reaches a maximum limit. This results in a profound structural change of the whole economy. It is at this late stage of accumulation that a fourth trend appears – the tendency of industrial nations to change into creditor (investor) nations, which ultimately leads to the disintegration of the whole economic system. For, if capital accumulation reaches the third phase (characterised by superabundance of capital), the profits earned in the existing enterprises cannot be profitably absorbed at home; they become 'surplus' capital, and must therefore be exported: 'When capital becomes over abundant ...'[48] '[i]f there is not sufficient means of employing capital within a nation or country ... there are plenty of opportunities furnished by poorer nations'.[49]

In other words, the 'surplus' capital which cannot be invested at home must be exported to other, economically undeveloped countries. If the 'surplus' capital is nevertheless invested in the home country and the manufactures are expanded, an unsaleable surplus of commodities is inevitably produced, which again can be marketed only in undeveloped countries. Such countries 'afford us much reason for hope, and do away one of the causes for fearing a decline that has been stated, namely ... by not having a market for our increasing manufactures'.[50] '[T]he United States promise to support the industry of England now ... far more than both the Indies ... a market for British manufactures [will be] insured for ages to come'.[51]

Here we have in germ a formulation of a specific underconsumption theory deriving from 'surplus' capital, a theory that was later developed by Sismondi

47 Playfair 1805, pp. 129, 131.
48 Playfair 1805, p. 161.
49 Playfair 1805, p. 135.
50 Playfair 1805, p. 269.
51 Playfair 1805, p. 268.

(1819) and Hegel (1820) and that was popularised in the twentieth century by J.A. Hobson (1911) and Rosa Luxemburg (1913).[52]

Ricardo, in 1817, criticised such a 'surplus' theory. According to him, there can be no 'surplus' capital in a country, because any amount of capital can always find profitable investment.[53] Unlike Ricardo, Adam Smith explicitly defended the theory of overabundance of capital inherited from his predecessors, John Locke and David Hume.[54]

This theory of Adam Smith of a possible saturation of capital, i.e. of a 'mature economy', which has acquired 'its full complement of riches', was quite current in Playfair's lifetime. Locke (1692) and Hume (1752) had advanced it before Smith in England; in France, it was held by Turgot (1766) and Condorcet (1794).[55] But Playfair goes beyond his predecessors in one very important respect. Smith, for instance, confines himself to stating that in Holland many moneylenders or rentiers lived on the interest of capital lent to foreign nations. Playfair, however, not only refers to investors or rentiers, but also is the first to define all the characteristic features of a parasitic creditor (investor) nation living not on productive work but 'without labour',[56] on the interests of capital lent abroad. At the same time Playfair conceives of the investor state as the necessary and ultimate phase of industrial development of any country, a phase which inaugurates decline and decay.

According to Playfair, there is a fundamental difference between an individual creditor and a creditor nation. Individuals can withdraw from productive activity at any time. They can sell their real estate and lend their capital abroad against interest. On the contrary, a nation cannot completely cease productive activities and must always put to use its real estate, factories, mines, cultivated land, etc.; only movable goods and money capital can be exported abroad. Therefore only part of a nation can function as a creditor: '[T]he whole nation could not become idle. Such a case never can exist, as that of all individuals in a country becoming sufficiently rich to live without labour'. 'A nation can never retire; it must always be industrious'.[57]

---

52 [Hobson 1911, pp. 85–6. Hobson had, however, been propounding underconsumptionist arguments since 1894 at the latest: Hobson 1894, pp. 167–219. Luxemburg 1951.] Simonde de Sismondi 1991d, pp. 264, 276, 561; Hegel 2008, paragraphs 245, 246 and additions to paragraphs 244, 248, on pp. 221–2, 223–4.

53 [Ricardo 1912, p. 193.]

54 Adam Smith cites the example of the Dutch, who lent large amounts of capital to the English, French and other nations, Adam Smith 1910a, p. 82.

55 [Adam Smith 1910a, p. 86; Locke 1924; Hume 1906; Turgot 1898; Condorcet 1796.]

56 Playfair 1805, p. 82.

57 Playfair 1805, pp. 82, 89.

However, although not all individuals in a creditor nation can live comfortably, 'without labour', the number of such idle individuals who live on interest coming from abroad is steadily increasing.

Once the state of overabundance of capital is attained, there begins a slow disintegrating process, a retrogression of the industrial state, which in the end must lead to its decline. Two types of change take place: a structural change in the economic basis, and parallel to it, a far-reaching change in the spiritual superstructure.[58]

Playfair is a realist; his analysis of the economic disintegration and ultimate decay of a creditor state are not wishful speculations or conclusions reached by deduction from abstract presuppositions; they have a realistic character, for he takes as a basis of his analyses the historical example of the decline of Holland, a creditor state, and he thinks that if in the future other, for the time being backward, nations ever reach the stage of capital superabundance, they will produce analogous symptoms of material and moral disintegration.

According to Playfair, the economic disintegration and decline of Holland was not accidental. Accidents play a great part in the lives of individuals or small human groups, but not in the life of a whole nation. Playfair obviously has in view the statistical law of big numbers, which he was the first to apply to history. The accidental forces inclining in different directions cancel one another, and only the fundamental forces common to the total mass of the nation assert themselves and can be considered the dominant trends. A whole nation can perish only if 'interior causes' have prepared it for decay:[59]

> [A]n inquiry into the causes of the revolutions of nations is more perfect ... than when directed to those of individuals ... Nations are exempt from those accidental vicissitudes which derange the wisest of human plans upon a smaller scale. Number and magnitude reduce chances to certainty. The single and unforeseen cause that overwhelms a man in the midst of prosperity, never ruins a nation: unless it be ripe for ruin, a nation never falls ... [A]ccident has only the appearance of doing what, in reality, was already nearly accomplished.[60]

58 In another context Playfair illustrates the parallelism of economic and spiritual development by the following remark which is reminiscent of Max Weber [1968]: 'The reformation in religion, and the establishment of manufactures in England date from nearly the same period ... There are, therefore many reasons, from experience, for believing that the Protestant religion is particularly favourable to industry ...', Playfair 1805, p. 265. [Grossman was very familiar with this issue, see Grossman 2006.]

59 Playfair 1805, p. 185.

60 Playfair 1805, pp. xi–xii.

Playfair analyses the rise and decline of Holland from that standpoint:

As for the Dutch, they continued to increase in wealth til the end of the seventeenth century ... In addition to their great industry, the fisheries and art of curing fish, the Dutch excelled in making machines of various sorts, and became the nation that supplied others with materials in a state ready prepared for manufacturing: this was a new branch of business and very lucrative, for, as the machines were kept a secret, the abbreviation of labour was great.[61]

But when Dutch industry became saturated with capital, there were no further profitable investments at home. The additional capital could function only as commercial agent between foreign nations; the Dutch became a nation of intermediaries: 'But, when they became affluent ... [t]he manufacturers became merchants, and the merchants became agents and carriers ... Dutch capital was employed to purchase goods in one country and sell them in another; the Dutch became carriers of others, instead of manufacturing ... for themselves'. Thus 'the solid sources of riches [i.e. production] disappeared ... The merchants preferred safe agencies for foreigners to trading on their own'. '[S]uperiority in manufactures over other countries was continually diminishing; consequently, industry was not so well rewarded, and less active'.[62]

According to Playfair, the structural transformation of the country did not stop there. The manufacturer who regressed to the status of a merchant later became a rentier; the industries were neglected, and the nation changed from an industrial into a creditor nation.

> Manufacturers aspire to become merchants, and merchants to become lenders of money or agents ...
>
> The Dutch were the greatest example of this ... They had long ceased to give that great encouragement to manufactures which had, at first, raised them to wealth and power ... They had, in the latter times, become agents for others rather than merchants on their own account; so that the capital, which, at one time, brought in, probably, twenty or twenty-five percent annually, and which had, even at a late period, produced ten or fifteen, was employed in a way that scarcely produced three.[63]

This economic transformation was accompanied by a parallel change of mentality, which reacted on the economic basis and further accentuated its weak-

61 Playfair 1805, p. 66.

62 Playfair 1805, pp. 66–7. This picture of the decline of Dutch industry is essentially confirmed by a modern historian C.H. Wilson 1939.

63 Playfair 1805, p. 134.

ness. In an investor nation 'it is not merely a neglect of industry ... that is hurtful; the general way of thinking and acting becomes different'.[64]

The mentality of an idle class of rentiers who despise productive work leaves its impress on the whole life of an investor nation. This 'degradation of moral character' of an investor nation is again illustrated by Holland. In an industrial country, her manufacturers are a class of robust, active entrepreneurs; in an investor country, wealthy, well-established firms avoid risks, withdraw from productive activity and live on interest.[65]

> Whatever, therefore, tends to accumulate the capital of a nation in a few hands ... not only increases luxury, and corrupts morals, but diminishes the activity of the capital and industry of the country.
>
> In all the great places that are now in a state of decay, we find families living on the interest of money, that formerly were engaged in manufactures or commerce. Antwerp, Genoa and Venice, were full of such; but those persons would not have ventured a single shilling in a new enterprise.[66]

In this way, both for objective and subjective, psychological reasons, capital expansion is brought to a standstill, productivity deteriorates, and industry disintegrates. Holland's position deteriorated as a result of an internal development, not of unfavourable external circumstances: 'There was no violent revolution no invasion by an enemy; it was the silent operation of that cause of decline which had been already mentioned'.[67]

The foregoing outline of the economic evolution of Holland from an industrial to a parasitic creditor nation is, according to Playfair, not a casual excursion into the history of a specific country. It is on the contrary conceived of as an illustration of a general law of the rise and decline of all modern industrial nations. The economic transformation and the attending processes of material and moral degradation are seen as an inevitable historical stage in the development of every industrial state, which begins the moment its capital accumulation has entered the phase of superabundance and capital export.

Thus Playfair was the first – and for a whole century he remained the only one – to describe this characteristic tendency in the evolution of modern industrial states, the tendency to capital export and to transformation into creditor

64 Playfair 1805, p. 90.
65 Playfair 1805, pp. 91, 162.
66 Playfair 1805, p. 135.
67 Playfair 1805, p. 67.

states. Economic theory neglected this problem during the entire nineteenth century. Only at the beginning of the twentieth century was the problem raised again by John Atkinson Hobson, whose work gave rise to a whole literature; but it is interesting to note that Hobson's economic interpretation of investment, his theory of surplus capital formulated in 1911[68] does not go an inch beyond Playfair's views expressed as early as 1805.

2 Counteracting Tendencies

What consequences does Playfair draw from his theory of the fundamental developmental trends of capitalism?

The prospect of decay presented Playfair, who assumed it to be a proven truth as regards the whole historical past of more than 3,000 years, with considerable theoretical difficulties, insofar as he dealt with the future evolution of Britain, then the leading industrial country in the world. The French evolutionists, Condorcet, Sismondi and particularly Saint-Simon, or utopian socialists like Pecqueur and Considerant, were able to point out the contradictions and inadequacies of capitalism because they not only criticised such inadequacies, but also rejected the existing social organisation and wanted it replaced by a higher form.[69] But Playfair, who criticises the contradictions of capitalism with equal keenness, is a partisan of capitalism, and wants to preserve it despite its evils. The idea of a transition to another, socialist organisation, is outside his horizon because in his eyes the existing capitalist form is the highest, and he violently criticises the French Revolution for its 'levelling' tendencies. But if the capitalist basis is retained, then, according to Playfair's own general historical law valid for all epochs, society is threatened with decay, because these tendencies originate in wealth, i.e. in the very essence of capital accumulation. The danger is all the more to be feared because history shows that wealth and power 'never have been renewed when once destroyed'.[70]

Thus the theoretical problem has a practical implication, and Playfair raises the question whether England cannot avert such a tragic end: 'It is then worth while to inquire into the causes of so terrible a reverse', [whether] that 'degradation which naturally follows, and which has always followed hitherto, may be averted'.[71]

68 Hobson 1911.

69 See Grossman 1943a and 1943b, above pp. 556–599.

70 Playfair 1805, p. 79.

71 Playfair 1805, pp. iv–v.

He solves this problem by distinguishing between 'necessity' and 'tendency', and by a new methodological construction in which the dominant tendency is weakened by one or more counteracting tendencies. These do not eliminate the main tendency but check its effectiveness and postpone its ultimate triumph.

If decay were a historical necessity impossible to avert the 'inquiry would be of no utility. It is of no importance to seek for means of preventing what must of necessity come to pass: but if the word necessity is changed for tendency or propensity, then it becomes an inquiry deserving attention'. 'It merits investigation, whether it is or is not possible to counteract the tendency to decline ... after having attained the summit of wealth, we may remain there instead of immediately descending'.[72]

We know that later Ricardo (1817), John Stuart Mill (1848) and Karl Marx (1867) resorted to the same methodological instrument of a dominant tendency and counteracting tendencies.[73]

Economic theory recorded this as a fact but has never raised the problem of the origin of this idea, and has never inquired into the circumstances that led to making such a distinction between the tendencies. The foregoing passage from Playfair's book shows that he is the originator of the idea and casts light on the circumstances that led him to this important methodological construction. Playfair, the petty-bourgeois theorist, elaborates the counteracting tendencies because he regards them as the theoretical justification of an effort to preserve the existing capitalist society from disintegration and decay, or at least to postpone them for several generations.

This does not mean that Playfair places his subjective wish for the preservation of capitalism above the objective developmental trends; he still thinks that history is governed by necessity. Just as he tries to show the objective inevitability of decline on the basis of the internal structure of the economic organism, 'the interior causes', so remaining true to his methodological principles, he inquires whether objective countertendencies are not active within the economic organism. Only if such objective counter-tendencies can be discovered, is there room for the intervention of the subjective factor – the deliberate effort to strengthen them.

According to Playfair, the task of strengthening and directing these objective countertendencies is incumbent not upon individuals, but upon the government: 'Government can never be better employed than in counteracting this

72 Playfair 1805, pp. ix, 169.

73 [Ricardo 1912, e.g. p. 52; Mill 1900a, pp. 481–91; Grossman refers to the first volume of *Capital*, Marx 1976b. Marx's extensive discussion of the tendency for the rate of profit to fall and its countertendencies is, however, in the third volume, Marx 1981b, pp. 317–48.]

tendency to decay'.[74] This does not eliminate the inevitability of decline, but – and this is all that Playfair expects from his *Inquiry* – it might be possible 'to find the means by which prosperity may be lengthened out,[75] and the period of humiliation procrastinated to a distant day'.[76]

With the help of such a distinction between 'necessity' and 'tendency', and between 'tendency' and 'counteracting tendency', Playfair's general law of rise from barbarism to civilisation and subsequent decline can be upheld theoretically with regard not only to the past but also to Britain's future, and at the same time the decline of England, even though the existing capitalist basis is maintained, can be averted or at least postponed for long generations.

What are these counteracting tendencies? Playfair enumerates several,[77] of which we shall discuss the most important – export of capital.

Superabundance of capital in an industrial nation entails consequences that Playfair describes in a special chapter entitled 'Of the tendency of capital and industry to leave a wealthy country'.[78] 'If there is not sufficient means of employing capital within a nation or country ... there are plenty of opportunities furnished by poorer nations'. This withdrawal of capital 'that operate[s] ... in some modern nations, is counteracting this effect, so far as it is occasioned by a superabundance of capital'. '[A]s it raises the poor nation nearer the level of the rich one, its effect gradually becomes less powerful'.[79]

Nations with superabundant capital indulge in comforts, keep numerous servants, and work less than the poorer nations, just as the sons of a well-to-do father work less than the father worked in his youth.

But the export of capital, though it counteracts the effects occasioned by superabundance of capital, does not eliminate the dominant tendency to decline. These counteracting tendencies relieve the situation of capital-saturated countries only temporarily. In the long run 'the intercourse between nations is ... in favour of the poorer one'. 'The capital of a rich nation is employed in fostering a rivalship in a poorer nation'.[80]

---

74 Playfair 1805, p. 172.

75 Playfair emphasises this idea in the subtitle of his book: *An Inquiry ... Designed to Show How the Prosperity of the British Empire May Be Prolonged.*

76 Playfair 1805, p. iv.

77 The counteracting tendencies listed here – export of commodities and of capital, decentralisation of capital, further various forms of unproductive expenditure and waste – are the same as those mentioned forty years later by John Stuart Mill, 1900a, pp. 487–8. This fact suggests that Mill carefully read Playfair.

78 Playfair 1805, pp. 161–5.

79 Playfair 1805, pp. [135], 164, 183. [Editor's interpolation.]

80 Playfair 1805, pp. 179, 180.

Young nations which appear as rivals of older and wealthier nations enjoy a number of advantages that enable them to rise faster and even to overtake their models. Elaborating on an idea that Condorcet formulated ten years earlier, Playfair observes that the leading nations can develop technology and invent new methods of work only by the hard way of trial and error. The rival young nations need to imitate only the successful inventions, thus saving a great deal of time and expenditure. 'The nation that is highest, treads in discovery, invention, etc. a new path … Those who follow have, in general, but to copy, and in doing that, it is generally pretty easy to improve'. 'So far as method of working and machinery are concerned, the imitating nation has the advantage; it copies the best sort of machine and the best manners of working at once'.[81] This, according to Playfair, explains the fact that whereas the old industrial nations, which improved their technique step by step, are burdened with many obsolete machines, 'the nations that have improved in manufactures the latest have always carried them to the greatest perfection'.[82]

In this manner the relief experienced by capital-saturated nations through export of capital to backward nations is of short duration. Their economic and technical advantage is only temporary, it disappears by degrees, and England 'cannot be expected long to maintain its superiority over others'.[83]

It is of little avail to possess a legal or factual monopoly in order to secure superiority: 'Holland, Flanders, and France were all originally superior, in the arts of manufacturing most goods, to England'.[84]

Nevertheless, these countries lost their superiority to England, because while the rising nation's industrialisation is stimulated by high profits, the low profits earned by the advanced nation 'which is about being rivalled' produces 'a sort of discouragement and dismay'.[85] Such nations with superabundant capital cease accumulating, they tend to a stationary state in which no capital investments take place: 'At all events, a day must arrive when the nation that is highest, ceasing to proceed, the others must overtake it'.[86] 'From this it is very evident, that the nation the farthest advanced in inventions has only to remain stationary a few years, and it will soon be overtaken, and perhaps surpassed'.[87]

81 Playfair 1805, pp. 208, 212.
82 Playfair 1805, p. 211.
83 Playfair 1805, p. 204.
84 Playfair 1805, p. 203.
85 Playfair 1805, p. 212.
86 Playfair 1805, p. 208.
87 Playfair 1805, p. 203.

Thus the export of capital which brought temporary relief and advantage to the industrial country exporting capital in time undermines its long-range interests, because the exported capital helps in the industrialisation of the rival country: 'In this manner it is, that the capital of a rich country supplies the want of it in poorer ones, and that, by degrees, a nation saps the foundation of its own wealth and greatness, and gives encouragement to them in others'.[88]

Playfair illustrates this development by the example of Holland:

> the Dutch, for the last century, employed their capital in this manner, and, at one time, were the chief carriers ... giving credit largely ... [t]hey ruined many of their own manufactures in this manner ... There are many manufactures in England that originally rose by means of Dutch capital.[89]

Thus Playfair shows that there is an insoluble antagonism of interest between the industrial and merchant capital of a country. At first the Dutch merchants 'ruined many of their own manufactures' by giving large credits to foreigners, earning large profits as merchants and carriers of raw materials and finished commodities; but later 'they sunk both as a commercial and manufacturing people'.[90]

However, Playfair does not reproach the Dutch merchants with lack of patriotism; he considers their conduct inevitable in a nation that has reached the creditor stage. Every merchant is under pressure of competition and must take the constantly changing circumstances into account. He cannot stop to consider whether he serves or harms his nation; he is guided and driven by the profit incentive, the principle on which the system of private enterprise rests. Should he allow himself to be guided by other motives, he would soon be ruined. The transfer of capital and industry abroad is not the result of the merchant's personal decision, but of an objective tendency of industry in a nation that has reached the creditor stage.

The counteracting tendencies, therefore, bring only temporary relief; in the long run, the backward agricultural and colonial countries are industrialised with the help of exported capital and attain the level of the wealthy countries; they too enter a stage at which they have accumulated sufficient capital of their own or even have begun to suffer from superabundance of capital. At such a future stage of development, all international credit operations will inevit-

88 Playfair 1805, p. 181.
89 Playfair 1805, p. 181.
90 Playfair 1805, p. 181.

ably stop: 'If the time should ever come that capital should be abundant in all nations ... obtaining credit will not be an object ...'.[91]

For despite the operation of all counteracting trends, the dominant trend, if the changes and rebounds caused by wars are disregarded, asserts itself in the end; all nations will ultimately reach the state of capital saturation, or the stationary state.

The fact that as early as the first half of the nineteenth century, before Karl Marx, a number of authors such as Playfair (1805), Sismondi (1819), Pecqueur (1837), and Victor Considerant (1843) described the objective developmental trends of capitalism raises the question of Marx's relation to his forerunners.[92] If he is not the originator of the idea, what is Marx's contribution to that doctrine?

Marx approached the problem of the developmental tendencies of capitalism not as a historian but as a theoretician. His purpose was not once again to describe these tendencies that had repeatedly been described in contemporary French literature, but to explain them. Marx's *Capital* does not contain a single chapter or section in which the above-mentioned developmental trends are described – as is the case with Sismondi, Pecqueur or Considerant – as empirical facts. In chapter 32, 'The historical tendency of capitalist accumulation', and in chapter 25, 'General law of capitalist accumulation', Marx strives to show *why* the trend to concentration (and the associated trends to centralisation and to the destruction of the small and medium industries) is the *inevitable* result of capitalist accumulation on the basis of the law of value; his purpose is to show that all these trends are dominated and explainable by the law of accumulation.[93]

At the same time Marx developed an idea that was completely alien to all his forerunners and that is the focal point of Marx's theory of the developmental trends of capitalism – the idea that the trends to concentration and centralisation, as well as the disappearance of small industry, follow *one* direction, and that they are only the outward expression of the slow, gradual, long process of socialisation of labour – even under capitalism – a process that paves the way for the socialised economy, of the future. This process begins with the 'scattered

91 Playfair 1805, p. 181.

92 [Sismondi 199d; Pecqueur 1839a and 1839b; Considerant 1847.]

93 [Marx 1976b pp. 762–870, 927–30.] It must be stressed that Marx does not use the word 'trend' or 'tendencies' in the usual sense of the term; by 'trend' he means 'tendencies winning their way through and working themselves out with iron necessity', Marx 1976b, p. 91. The other factors and counter-trends can weaken or slow up the dominant trend but not prevent it from asserting itself.

private property resting on the personal labour of individuals'; it continues with the 'centralisation of the means of production and socialisation of labour'; and it ends with the transformation 'of capitalist private property, which in fact already rests on the carrying on of production by society, into social property' – a result that looms only at the end of a long historical transformation of social labour.[94] What Playfair, Sismondi, Pecqueur and Considerant could not see were the far-reaching implications of this historic process. It is true that many writers before Marx referred to the regularity of crises and the precarious condition of the working class. However, these insights remained mere observations until Marx showed them to be the inevitable result of another long-term fundamental tendency, which he discovered – the tendency of capital, as technology advances, to increase its so-called 'organic composition', i.e. the amount of invested fixed capital per worker.

New York City

94 [Marx 1976b, pp. 929–30.]

CHAPTER 32

Letters to Bill Blake and Christina Stead*

3 March 1947

521 W. 111 St
New York City

Dear Christina and Bill

Our thought crossed: you wrote your letter February 14, and the same day I sent you my letter. It was really no letter, but rather a short report, I wanted be sure that the letter will reach you at your new address in Brussels.

I am very glad to hear that all is all right with you; from the letter I see that you, Christina, are writing your new novel. Only Bill does not say if he is working on his 'normal' job, and if he is 'settled'. Of course I am thrilled deeply to see how you, dear Bill, have the time, now, to promote my affairs in spite that you have probably more than enough personal troubles.

Here, we have had in the past week two journalistic sensations. Edgar Snow published in Saturday Evening Post 3 articles on Russia where he demonstrated how a eminently peacful election speach of Stalin (February 1946) was falsified in a speach threatening with war. Besides this there are many facts, which – after Snow – shall prove, that Stalin gave up many revolutionary slogans and is believing in the possibility of a long peaceful co-operation with capitalistic states. One of such a slogan is – after Snow – is the theory of the 'withering away of the state'; and another such an obsolete slogan is theory of the 'breakdown of capitalism' neither in western countries, and not in retrograded eastern states.[1] In the preface to the new edition (1946) of his works, Stalin calls such beliefs 'youthful indiscretions'. And the other was a series of articles by [Walter] Lippmann in Herald Tribune, where he shows, that in such cases allway comes the war as a instrument or 'regulation' of the problem of spoils.[2] (3 days after Lippmanns article, Dorothy Thompson in the '[New York] Post' and [William Philip] Simms in '[New York] World-Telegr[am]'[3] robbed every idea

* [Selection from original letters in Grossman 1947c. Grossman's idiosyncratic expression, spelling and punctuation have not been corrected.]

1 [Snow 1947, pp. 120–1; Stalin 1950.]

2 [Lippmann 1947.]

3 [Editor's interpolations.]

and argument of Lippmann without quoting him. This shameless plagiarism, even here, is astonishing!)

Another interesting remarque of Snow: 'Everyone knows that since [President Franklin Delano] Roosevelt's death our foreign policy has more and more been determined by generals and admirals on the basis ... in a hypothetical war with Russia'.[4] I wrote in the last time an longer article 'An early middle class theorist of development trends of capitalism' (in German). There the origin of such ideas, (conception of capital, disappearing of middle-classes etc. back to the year 1805 – fourteen years before Sismondi!

Dear Bill, you mention your friendship. You shall be sure that I have the same feeling. Sometime seems to me superfluous to express how much I love you and Christina. You must have the feelings; the words are unable to express the real things.

With affection
Henryk

Between 3 March and 20 April 1947

Dear Christina and Bill

I am really afraid, because of your prolonged silence. At the time of your departure, the weather was rough and I am afraid to think, that you have caught cold. On the other hand I do well understand, that a settlement in a new city and country is connected with difficulties.

Here everything develops – 'according to plan'. Anti-labor legislation in preparation. A complete deroute of the 'liberals' who are split in 2 subdivision and attack themselves mutually.

But you are there neighbours of big events in collapsing 'gradually socialization'. Your friend, Bill, Mr [Manny] Shinwell is not doing just the best. Mr Lippmann in Herald Trib[une] is afraid. The collapse of this English socialism, he thinks will isolate US from Europe and Asia and will annihilate the moderates and strengthen the right- and left-wing extremists all over Europe.

Here, I was one evening invited to Mrs Lina Lewin; it was a charming evening; a musical soirée. Mr [Max] Kotlarsky was at his best. Another excellent pianist, and a opera singer, a lady. There I met many our common friend and all expressed their love for you both, but specially Christina (I hope Bill will not be jalous).

4 [Editor's interpolation.]

Bill, do you know an English economist Playfair? He is here and there quoted as statistician but never as economist. Is not mentioned in Encyclop. Britanica. I have written an Article on his theory.

And secondly – do you know Brooks Adams? He wrote 'The law of civilisation and decay, London 1895, New York 1896, Paris 1898. Charles Beards published 1943 a new ed.[5] With introduction where he gloryfies Adams book as the most important contribution to American historical thought. What do you think about Adams? I think it is a incredible exageration. Is Adams so much known in America?

I am reading with passion (but in small daily doses) Letty Fox; in small doses, to avoid to crush my 'moral' prejudices, as Christina warned me *not* to read the book.

All my best wishes to you both and for your new home.

Henryk

20 April 1947

New York

Dear Christina and Bill

Christina's last letter was for me a mystery-story! I was surprised because I know Christina as a novelist and not as a mystery writer! And it is difficult to understand, that your travel is in some connection with my person. I have only one interpretation, that you have a there in Brussels troubles because of me.

If in general, you both, are excellent psychologists, so in this special case, I regard it as a little unpsychological effort of Bill to propose me for a professorship there. Bill, have you forgotten, what I wrote about the last Congress of the Second International in Vienna 1931, and specially about the Chairman of this Internat – Mr [Louis] De Brouckère? Every word, I wrote, is true. These gentlemen never protested, because they know, that every word, I wrote, is exact. But no, you, Dear Bill, you gave them a cheap opportunity for revenge and humiliation for you and me. (Please, Bill read again in Wörterbuch der Volkswirtschaft vol. II. p. 16–17, Art. 'Internationale'.)[6]

In all this changes of your travels, I have forgotten, Bill, to thank you for your (and Christinas) magnificent gift – the wunderful collection of records

5 [Adams 1943.]
6 [Grossman 1932c.]

of Beethoven's quartets, quintets and sextets. It is a real pleasure to have them at hand. My traditional Sunday morning visitor prof [Rafał] Taubenschlag just helped me to admire Beethoven's music today.

Your short remarks about Belgium are very interesting. I regret that you went to England, I would prefer to see you on the Continent.

Thanks for your information on Playfair and Brooks Adams. I know all on them and asking you I wanted only to be sure, that I did not neglect something essential. You will be surprised: I wrote on Playfair an Essay: He is the earliest theorist of capitalist developmental trends. I enclose for you the content of matter. I will try to publish here – perhaps in Journal of polit. Economy. Unfortunately my paper is relatively long, perhaps one third, are quotations from Playfair, I show that 14 years *before* Sismondi and 12 years before Ricardo, he sees correctly the fundamental tendencies of capitalism. I concentration of capital, II growing misery of proletariat, III disappearing of the middle-classes. Finally the IV tendency, the transformation of an industrial nation in Investor-Nation. As regards this point – he, Playfair, was the *unique* theorist for a century, until beginning of twentieth when Hobson arised the problem of a 'Rentierstaat'.

Here in U.S. does not exist a magazine for history of doctrines, which would be able to print a larger essay, perhaps 60 pages in print. Besides, in the 'conclusions' I deal the problem of the *originality* of Marx as regards the 'Entwicklungstendenzen' of capitalism, when before Marx, Playfair, Sismondi, Pecqueur and Victor Considerant, they all have correctly these trends stated. So, it is possible, they will reject my paper.

I am expecting your promised 'really interesting' letter with impatience, and I am terribly sorry if I contributed in some way to your discomfort.

Cordially
Henryk

W. Playfair, the earliest theorist of capitalist development
Introduction: Three Problems

1. Foreign and Colonial markets as instruments of the old mercantilist policy and their new function in the frame of an underconsumption theory. Who is the originator of this change in the theoretical attitude?
2. Developmental trends of capitalism as seen by precursors of K. Marx: Victor Considerant, Constantin Pecqueur and Sismondi. Who is the earliest theorist of such trends?
3. The origin of the methodological conception of a dominant tendency of capitalism and of counteracting tendencies. The application of this conception by Ricardo, John St. Mill and K. Marx. Who is the first originator of this methodological conception?

Part I. The dominant tendencies of capitalism

A. Playfair's General Historical Law of Rise and Decay of Nations.

B. Modification of the General Law for the period of capitalism

   I. The natural Tendency of Wealth to accumulate in the hands of few. *Credit* as an accelerating factor of accumulation of capital.

   II. The Tendency to increase the number of indigent in a country when it advances in wealth.

   III. The Tendency to disappearing of the 'middling' classes, what widens the distance between rich and poor and contributes to the disintegration of society.

   IV. The Tendency to Transformation of agricultural nations into industrial ones, and later of the industrial nations into creditor (investor) nations. The superabundancy of capital and lack of investment possibilities in old industrial countries as factors of disintegration and of decay.

Playfair's methodological excurse on the decay of nations: No accidents in the History of Nations. Historical necessity and the rule of the Law of big numbers.

Part II. The counter-acting Tendencies

1. Export of Commodities at the cheapest prices. The new function of foreign markets: they supply to the exporting country additional consumers and thus make additional investments of capital in the exporting country possible. The idea of a *General Congress of Nations* as an Body for peaceful regulation of Colonial problems.
2. Export of capital
3. Various forms of unproductive expenditures, of waste and decentralisation of capital.

Part III. Only temporary character of counteracting Tendencies

Gradual industrialisation of retrograded countries arises again the problem of superabundancy of capital and of decay of nations, this time on a world scale: What will be the future of foreign investment? The views of W Playfair and John A. Hobson.

Conclusions

4 and 5 May 1947

521 W. 111 St. (N.Y.C.)

Dear Christina

Thanks for your long letter; I see that the winter in Bruxelles was for you not too pleasant. And your explorations of the 'afferie' In spite that they are technically (letter to the Maison Communale) chair, seem to me more mysterious than ever. An old friend of more than 20 years, who is intent to make you trouble? For such acts must be always a special motive. For that reason I thought on de Brouckère. I have had in Frankfurt a pupil, a man about 30, married, Belgian, former pupil of de Brouckère, who became leftist; I helped him much in his study and gave him various services. Later, he went back to Belgium. After Collapse of belgian Currency, (crisis, in mal speculation all Belgian banks in longs, the banks were practically bankrupt so they in purpose to save themselves, preferred collapse of belgian currency) I wrote him, he may send me the printed *report* of the Chambre des Deputés. The answer was: 'I will not send you, because you will make only bad use upon'. And in Frankfurt he was my 'admirer'. Eternally thankful etc. This was the influence of de Brouckère clique!

May 5th

I was interrupted to finish the letter and today received Bill letter. I am glad to see your vitality, dear Bill, your quick adjustment to new environment. You are right in jugement about the Horkheimer etc. now terribly 'antisowjet'. They are 'directors' of Institute, living all the time *in Hollywood*! Here is now only *bureau* (accountant etc.). No publications, nothing doing at all. [Herbert Marcuse] Markuse, [Otto] Kirchheimer, [Franz] Neumann all help the Government in Germany. Neumann came back because he became ... professor at Columbia! Never was a man with less theoretical ability than he. A second class attorney. But he knows business.

My 'Playfair' is with [Norbert] Guterman for translation. I think that the paper itself is better than the 'content'. The point is: Sismondi went to England, to collect materials for his book on the basis of higher development of Engl. capitalism. So the English Capitalism influenced through Sismondi *French* economic literature. This must astonish, why this higher developed engl. capitalism *did not influenced english* economic literature? Now, I found the missing link, the *direct* trace in english literature. If Laski could help publish in an english quarterly, would be better, than here in Journal of Polit. Economy. If you wish, I will send you a copy of MSS.

I hope that after this storm in an glass water you will have, both, a pleasant spring in London – the only good season there in Regent Park, Hampstead etc. I am not decided what to do now: finish Descartes? or the book on Marx simple reproduction (which I regard as my chief contribution to Marxist theory).

My most cordial regards for you both,

Henryk

On your 'Imperialism' in next letter.

1 June 1947

521 W. 111 St, N.Y.C.

Dearest Christina and Bill

It is so long as I have had news from you, that I am worry that you have perhaps another trouble, because they come always uninvited. Dr Kurz had the plan to return in May to Vienna. Now he is ill, in Hospital, he has liver-trouble (jauness), the recovery is very slow, nearly invisible and he mus have much patience.

But I return to you both. I am advising you Christina, that you have finished your novel at time under such adverse conditions as in past Winter, so more as I know that the smallest trouble bring me out of equilibrium and I cannot work. I hope, Christina, that you will not start immediately a new book, and will rather have a nice time in the spring in London.

From our common friends I have not seen anybody. Once I have called Harry Bl[oom]. His daughter told me that he is on a business trip. May 20, prof Taubenschlag left N.Y. for Gdynia with the Polish motorboat 'Batory'. Again an friend less. Here, our friend [Friedrich Georg] Alexan (you remember him Bill?) arranged an exhibition of 40 modern Japanese painting brought directly from Tokio. They signify a revolution, have abandoned their old style and imitate completely Europeans. I was lastly at an cocktail party with my polish friends. On friend, who returned from Warsaw, told me that 80 percent of popul. against government. Why? because government is friendly to Russia. They recognise that the government is the best possible, that material improvement is all over visible (rather they are dissatisfied that the government has so much plans!) Only the *workers* – socialists & communists support the government with enthusiasm and inspite they made the biggest material sacrifices. Philharmonic society gives no concert, because their building was bombed, and no movie theatre has a good accustic in Warsaw.

The author of the wonderful story of Nana-performance in Mongolia, published just a pamphlet about fascism, imperialism etc. In spite that it has many excellent ideas, it will have little success, because it is badly written, chaotic; without separating the criticism of the present situation from positive program etc.

About your intention to write a book on Imperialism I am not clear what will be your leading idea. Of course it is not so difficult to show that at all time was imperialism and that they all have something in common. 1) imperialism of Alexander the Great, 2) imperialism of Feudal France in the time of the crusades; as the church swallowed much of land remained too little for younger sons. So they went for conquest in Asia, where they erected a feudal Empire on the model of French motherland etc.

But the conclusion is, that every imperialism has the specific form impressed (or rooted in) the specific economic condition of the period. In our time, this is the struggle for investment possibilities. This was described in many books e.g. Herbert Feis Europe, the World Banker 1870–1914 (New Haven, 1930) or Eugene Staley War and the private investor (New York 1935) who collected seven years his materials and is proud *not* to have any theory.[7] Many pages of Staley's book I can regard as illustrations of my book, because if any capital can be invested at home, then is not understandable why the struggle for investment opportunities abroad?

So, as this kind of books was written, I do not know what is your intention. Only one thing is clear: A book on Imperialism in 1947 *must be differently written than a book in 1935*. It must deal with *New problems* of today. And this demands much research work.

But enough of this professional jargon for today. Please, write me how you feel in new surrounding. I miss you both now even more than after you left.

But I do not wish to be sentimental. I great you

Most cordially

Henryk

10 July 1947

521 W. 111 St. New York City

Dear Bill

This time I am late in answering your interesting letter from June 7. I was in vacation, i.e. I decided that I am on vacation. I did not look at economic

7 [Feis 1930; Staley 1935.]

books etc. went every day on River Drive, Hudson promenade and read to end Christinas Letty Fox.[8] It is an excellent novel full of deep psychological truth and richness of various human characters. Letty is for me too much passive, waiting for the first serious proposition, and marry the man who make the proposition. I prefer little Jacky who loves Godynch inspite of that everything in him is repugnant. She reacts emotionally not with brain like Letty. Anyhow I have had a big pleasure reading the book, a real vacation.

Regarding your book on Imperialism: I am very obliged to you, for your intention to dedicate your book to me; it would be a big honour to me, indeed. From your few words about your plan I see how tremendous research-work must be done. In reality it would be necessary a group-work, because the task is to big for a single person. I would be curious to know how would you characterise in two or three sentences the leading idea of your book: what do you wish to prove or disprove. Have you already such idea – or will she be only the result of your research?

It is not so important for me to write a letter against the distortions of Mr Sweezy. If I will not be able to publish an English book on Marx, such a letter will not help. If I will publish a book, than I will crush him all bones and the reader will be able to judge himself which book give really superior interpretation of Marx theory. It happens that the day ago I lunched together with Mr [Philip] Vaudrin, manager of Oxford press here. It was *his initiative*: he told me he was interested to speak me, he has heard so much about me, and that he would be interested in publication of my book. We were 2 hours or longer together. I told him my views about the present world situation and probable development in the future. He encouraged me to write such a book, asked me to write an outline. I was very reserved, I am not too enthusiastic after my former American experiences. But I will write such an outline. The best is to wait and see.

In your book you should *avoid every direct criticism* of Lenin. You can make your different view clear, without attacking him – otherwise your book will be doomed as heretic. You can say 'older Marxian theorist told this and that. Today situation is changed', etc.

That this charming girl Ruth [Blech] did not forget me, being in Paris is very flattering to me and please Bill, express to her on my behalf *mes sentiments les plus deservés*.[9]

For Christina and you my love
Henryk

8 [Stead 2001.]
9 [*'Mes sentiments les plus deservés'* means 'my feelings which are most deserved'.]

CHAPTER 33

Letters to Walter Braeuer*

Translated from German by Ben Fowkes

25 June 1948

New York

Dear friend Braeuer

I hasten to reply to your letter of 27 May to prevent any misunderstanding from arising. Should I perhaps draw the conclusion from the critique of my book that you enclosed that, as Dean of the Faculty, he [Fritz Behrens] opposed my appointment?[1] Are my scientific and political qualifications not sufficient for me to receive a professorial position and am I obliged to agree with Professor Behrens in all theoretical questions? I would like to remind you that after my book appeared I was named, by Resolution of 1 November 1930 (number 360/44), an honorary member of the International Agrarian Institute in Moscow, which indicates that my book was considered to be a valuable achievement.

The reproach has been levelled against me that I present breakdown 'mechanistically', whereas I have always emphasised the contrary. Also, in the English article you have in your possession, I wrote that Marx's theory comprises two fundamental elements: 'the theory of the *objective developmental tendencies* of capitalism' and, in addition to this, the second element, 'the *subjective* factor, i.e. the class struggle'.[2] My book ends with the section on the class struggle. In the dictionary entry 'Fifty years of struggle over Marxism', I say that the objective tendency towards collapse has the function of showing when capitalism has ripened sufficiently for the decisive struggle for power to have a prospect of success.[3] Marx too – and Engels – evidently have 'mechanistic' views. Thus Engels says in the *Anti-Dühring*, in the section 'Socialism, 2, Theoretical',[4] that the cap-

* [A selection of original letters in Grossman 1947–9.]
1 [Possibly a reference to Behrens 1948, p. 43.]
2 [Grossman 1943b, see above p. 598.]
3 [Grossmann 1932f/1933a, see above p. 385.]
4 [Engels 1987, pp. 254–71.]

italist mode of production 'is never able to get out of that vicious circle' which progressively gets smaller so 'that the movement becomes more and more a *spiral*, and *must come to an end*'.[5]

I am very moved and grateful for your repeated invitations to come to Rostock. But I cannot come to Germany under circumstances in which I am not acceptable in Leipzig and so to speak smuggle myself into Rostock. Quite apart from that, I [would] feel bad in a small town. I have no family. My wife and son were murdered by Hitlerites. I cannot work at home the whole time and be solitary. I must have the possibility of attending symphony concerts and visiting theatres.

If there is opposition to me on grounds of theory, there is nothing left for me but to abandon the idea of returning to Germany. I am the more astonished by this situation because the original proposal to me came from Leipzig (via a roundabout route), namely from Professor Albert Schreiner (Leipzig N24, Hänisch Strasse 45), who has lived in New York and knows me.

You can keep the two English articles. A German translation is *not* needed. Who would publish it? I still have not received (paper shortage) any offprints of my English article on the objective tendencies of capitalism, which was published in Cambridge (England) in the *Economic History Review*.[6] That essay would be for translation, if a *publisher* could be found for it.

With my best regards
H. Grossman

24 December 1948

New York City

Dear friend Braeuer

I have received your letters of 1 and 13 November, which arrived simultaneously. I am glad that the parcel for October has arrived. Two further parcels are on their way for November and December, and, apart from this, you will receive a letter from the Swiss Oversea Co. at Christmas or shortly afterwards

5 [Engels 1987, p. 361.]
6 [Grossman 1948.]

and, after you have proved your identity, the contents enumerated in the letter will immediately be handed out to you.

I informed you some time ago that I wanted to travel to Poland (Gdynia) on the 10 December. I have received a fellowship from the Institute to carry out a scientific investigation into the 'Future outlook of industrialisation of agricultural countries of Europe'.[7] This would have offered me the opportunity of travelling and I would have been delighted with the opportunity to see you and your wife. But it was unfortunately humanly impossible to equip myself in such a short time for a Baltic journey in winter. I informed you and other friends in a letter of 26 November from Washington that I had been compelled to postpone the voyage on the 'Batory' until 3 February. The ship will arrive in Gdynia on 15 February.

As regards the article you are planning to write about me, I cannot prevent you from writing it but I am very doubtful about its usefulness. *The time is too short* to write an article of this nature. You do not have all my works to hand, such as, for example, my long article against Borkenau: 'The Social Foundations of the Scientific Conception of the World [of Descartes] and Manufacture', in which I demonstrate that a whole philosophical system, 'the mechanical conception of Descartes and Galileo' is 'a reflection of the actual application of machinery' from the thirteenth century to the seventeenth century.[8]

And my accumulation book![9] The whole of the debate has centred on breakdown, whereas this only constitutes *one* of the results. In contrast, there has been *absolutely no discussion* of the *most important problem*, which I examine in the preface and later, in 'The Change in the Original Plan', 'The Value-Price Transformation' and the introductory section of 'Gold Production'.[10] These *methodological* problems signify a turning-point in Marxist research. What does the first volume of *Capital* deal with? Reality? Have you seen 'surplus value' (in its totality) in empirical reality? You see *only parts* of surplus value: profit, rent, the profits of trade, interest, etc. Surplus value in its totality is a product of Marx's act of abstraction. The parts of surplus value just mentioned lie on the surface; they are *phenomena* visible to everyone. Surplus value as a totality is the *hidden essence*, first discovered through analysis.

---

7 [English in the original.]

8 [Grossman did not cite the title accurately, and summarised rather than quoted his own work Grossman 2009. Editor's interpolation.]

9 [Grossman 1929a.]

10 [Grossman 1929b, see above pp. 183–209; Grossman 1932a, see above pp. 276–283; 1932b, see above pp. 304–331.]

That is my objection to your review of the new edition of the first volume of *Capital*. You treat it *as if* surplus value existed at the same level as interest, rent, etc., whereas in reality a *long path* of successive transformations precedes it: the *method of progressive concretisation*. I do not want to go into details. Anyone who does not understand this question of method will misunderstand a number of Marxism's essential points of. But it is difficult to formulate all these matters correctly in the short time you have to complete the article.

I said earlier that 'breakdown' was only *one* of the results I was dealing with (NB I am not waiting with my hands in my pockets for this. I explicitly *stressed* this in the last article in [Elster's] *Dictionary*,[11] where I give a short presentation of my theory.)

What about the other results? For example, *speculation?* Hilferding treats speculation as nothing more than 'the speculation by promoters' [who float companies on the stock exchange] which spread, for example, in Germany after 1871, that is to say, the historical moment when private firms were converted into joint stock companies. That gave the hyenas of the stock exchange the opportunity to plunder wealth earned over decades of hard work, since the original entrepreneurs were unfamiliar with the tricks of the stock exchange and were plundered by the hyenas. That happens *only once* on a large scale in every nation.

I, however, deal with speculation – for the first time in the Marxist literature – as an *essential element of the cycle*. If industry is *expanding*, the paper of the stock exchange has the *opposite* tendency. (I treat this problem in a 'pure' form, hence in an *isolated* country. In reality the 'pure' form is distorted by influences from abroad.)

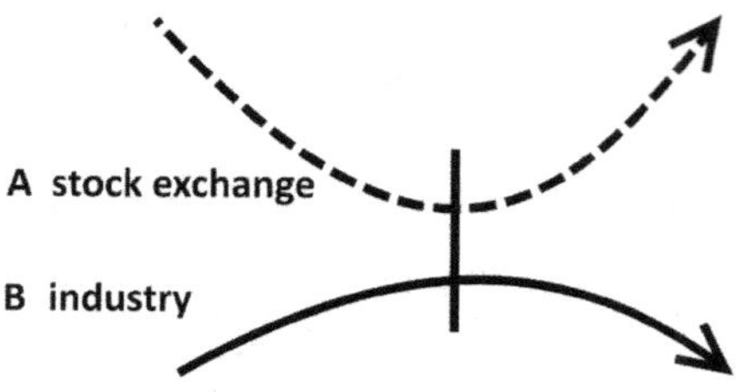

If industry is making good profits, the industrialist does not speculate: he is not inclined to risk his property. The growth in the magnitude of production (*more* workers, raw materials, machines) requires *more* capital, speculation contracts

11 [Grossman 1932f/1933a, see above pp. 332–388.]

and becomes restricted to professional speculators. The stock exchange displays a declining tendency.

Inversely, when an industrial depression sets in, workers and along with them wages, raw materials, *capital is released*, and cannot be profitably employed. Only then does this released capital flow towards the stock exchange; speculation revives.

No one before me has even mentioned this problem of speculation as an element in the cycle. And the situation is similar with many other problems. (See my presentation of ground rent.)

In this connection, you do not know my most important work on the *relation of Marx to classical economics*. Was Marx *merely the highest point* reached by classical economics, as Hilferding asserts (in the preface to *Finance Capital*),[12] or does he have a *fundamentally new conception* of political economy?

(I have examined this point in a typewritten study which was reproduced in 80 copies.)

In short: what is the difference between Marx and the classical political economists? New conclusions derived from the classical presuppositions? Or did Marx reject the presuppositions of the classical political economists and replace them with others?

These are tremendous questions – and, in view of the small amount of time at your disposal, they cannot be grasped very well and there is a danger that this may indirectly do harm to me. (My opponents are only waiting for such an opportunity.) But you have the final decision. I am restricting myself here to pointing out the difficulties.

Sincerest regards to you
your
Henryk Grossman

12 [Hilferding 1981, p. 21.]

References

Adams, Brooks 1943 [1895], *The Law of Civilization and Decay: An Essay on History*, introduced by Charles A. Beard, New York: Knopf.

Adler, Max 1904, *Kausalität und Teleologie im Streite um die Wissenschaft*, Wien: Verlag der Wiener Volksbuchhandlung Brand.

Adler, Max 1908, *Marx als Denker: zum 25. Todesjahre von Karl Marx*, Berlin: Verlag Buchhandlung Vorwärts.

Adler, Max 1913, *Marxistische Probleme: Beiträge zur Theorie der materialistischen Geschichtsauffsung und Dialektik*, Stuttgart: Dietz.

Adler, Max 1925, *Kant und der Marxismus*, Berlin: Laub'sche Verlagsbuchhandlung.

Adorno, Theodor W. 2002 [1936], 'On Jazz', in Theodor W. Adorno, *Essays on Music*, Berkeley, CA: University of California Press, pp. 470–95.

Adorno, Theodor W. and Max Horkheimer 2011 [written 1956], *Towards a New Manifesto*, London: Verso.

Aeschylus 1906, *The Lyrical Dramas of Aeschylus*, translated by John Stuart Blackie, London: Dent.

Aftalion, Albert 1899, 'L'oeuvre économique de Simonde de Sismondi', doctoral thesis, Paris: Faculté de Droit de Paris.

Aftalion, Albert 1913, *Les crises périodiques de surproduction*, Paris: Rivière.

Aftalion, Albert 1932, 'Les crises économiques et financières', *Recueil des cours, Académie de droit international de La Haye*, 39: 273–350.

Amoroso, Luigi 1924, 'La meccanica economica', *Giornali degli Economisti*, 64: 45–54.

Andler, Charles 1901, *Introduction historique et commentaire au* Manifeste communiste, Paris: Rieder.

Anonymous 1821, *Observations on Certain Verbal Disputes in Political Economy*, London: R. Hunter.

Anonymous 1907, 'Dos 40 yohriger yubileum fun *Kapital*', *Sotsial-demokrat*, 19 July: 1.

Arbeitgeber, Der 1927, 17.

Aristophenes 1907, *The Plutus of Aristophenes*, London: Bell.

Aristophenes 1913, *The Peace of Aristophenes*, London: Bell.

Aristotle 1905, *Aristotle's Politics*, translated by Benjamin Jowett, Oxford: Clarendon.

Aucuy, Marc 1908, *Les systèmes socialistes d'échange*, Paris: Alcan.

Avenel, Georges d' 1910, *Découvertes d'Histoire sociale*, Paris: Flammarion.

Ayres, Leonard P. 1939, *Turning Points in Business Cycles*, New York: Macmillan.

Babel, Anthony 1938, 'La Notion de progrès chez Sismondi', *Revue international de sociologie*, 46: 296–328.

Bachofen, Johann Jacob 2003 [1861], *An English Translation of Bachofen's Mutterrecht*

(*Mother right*) (*1861*): *A Study of the Religious and Juridical Aspects of Gynecocracy in the Ancient World*, translated by David Partenheimer, Lewiston: Edwin Mellen Press.

Ballod, Carl 1927, *Der Zukunftsstaat: Wirtschaftstechnisches Ideal und volkswirtschaftliche Wirklichkeit*, fourth edition, Berlin: Laubsche Verlagsbuchhandlung.

Basu, Deepankar and Panayiotis T. Manolakos 2012, 'Is there a tendency for the rate of profit to fall? Econometric evidence for the U.S. economy, 1948–2007', *Review of Radical Political Economics*, 45, 1: 76–95.

Bastiat, Frédéric 1873 [1845, 1848], *Economic Sophisms*, Edinburgh: Oliver and Boyd.

Bastiat, Frédéric 1880 [1850], *Harmonies of Political Economy*, translated by Patrick James Stirling, Edinburgh: Oliver and Boyd.

Bauer, Helene 1929, 'Ein neuer Zusammenbruchstheoretiker', *Der Kampf*, 22, 6, June: 270–80.

Bauer, Otto 1906, 'Marxismus und Ethik', *Neue Zeit*, 24, 2 (41): 485–99.

Bauer, Otto 1907, 'Mathematische Formeln gegen Tugan-Baranowsky', *Neue Zeit*, 25, 1 (24), 18 March: 822–3.

Bauer, Otto 1956 [written 1927–8], *Einführung in die Volkswirtschaftslehre*, Wien: Verlag der Wiener Volksbuchhandlung.

Bauer, Otto 2012 [1913], 'The Accumulation of Capital', in *Discovering Imperialism Social Democracy to World War I*, translated, edited and introduced by Richard B. Day and Daniel Gaido, Leiden: Brill, pp. 719–43.

Bazard, Saint-Amand 1958 [1828–9], *The Doctrine of Saint-Simon: An Exposition. First Year, 1828–1829*, Boston: Beacon Press.

Behrens, Fritz 1948, *Alte und die neue Probleme der politischen Ökonomie: Eine theoretische und statistische Studie über die produktive Arbeit im Kapitalismus*, Berlin: Dietz.

Benjamin, Walter 2008 [1936], 'The Work of Art in the Age of its Technological Reproducibility' (second version), in *The Work of Art in the Age of Its Technological Reproducibility, and Other Writings on Media*, second version, Cambridge, MA: Harvard University Press, pp. 19–55.

Bernadelli, Harro 1938, 'The End of the Marginal Utility Theory?', *Economica*, new series, 5, 18, May: 192–212.

Bernstein, Eduard 1894–5, 'Der dritte Band des *Kapital*', *Neue Zeit*, 13, 1 (11, 12, 13, 14, 17, 18, 20): 333–8, 364–71, 388–98, 427–32, 485–92, 516–24, 624–32.

Bernstein, Eduard 1896, 'Sozialistische Oekonomie in England', *Neue Zeit*, 15, 1 (2): 46–54.

Bernstein, Eduard 1898, 'Der Kampf der Sozialdemokratie und die Revolution der Gesellschaft', *Neue Zeit*, 16, 1 (16, 18): 484–97, 548–57.

Bernstein, Eduard 1899, 'Antwort', *Vorwärts*, 26 March: 9–10.

Bernstein, Eduard 1901a, *Zur Geschichte und Theorie des Socialismus: gesammelte Abhandlungen*, Berlin: Edelheim.

Bernstein, Eduard 1901b, *Wie ist wissenschaftlicher Socialismus möglich? Ein Vortrag*, Berlin: Verlag der Socialistischen Monatshefte.

Bernstein, Eduard 1909, *Der Revisionismus in der Sozialdemocratie: ein Vortrag gehalten in Amsterdam vor Akademikern und Arbeitern: Mit einem Anhang: Leitsätze für ein sozialdemocratisches Programm*, Amsterdam: Cohen.

Bernstein, Eduard 1993 [1899], *The Preconditions of Socialism*, translated by Henry Tudor, Cambridge: Cambridge University Press.

Bilimovic, Alexander 1929, 'Irving Fishers statistische Methode für die Bemessung des Grenznutzens', *Zeitschrift für Nationalökonomie*, 1, 1, May: 114–28.

Bilimovic, Alexander 1933, 'Ein neuer Versuch der Bemessung des Grenznutzens', *Zeitschrift für Nationalökonomie*, 4, 2, January: 161–87.

Bilimovic, Alexander 1937a, 'Zur Verteidigung der Gleichgewichtsidee', *Zeitschrift fur Nationalokonomie*, 8, 2: 220–8.

Bilimovic, Alexander 1937b, 'Zins and Unternehmerginn im Gleichungssystem der stationären Wirtschaft', *Zeitschrift fur Nationalökonomie*, 8, 3: 297–32.

Biringuccio, Vanuccio 1959 [1540], *Pirotechnia*, translated by Cyril Stanley Smith and Martha Teach Gnudi, New York: Basic Book.

Blanc, Louis 1848 [1839], *The Organization of Labour*, London: Clarke.

Blanqui, Adolphe 1885 [1860], *History of Political Economy*, New York: G. Putnam's Sons.

Bode, Karl 1937, 'Prosperität und Depression' *Zeitschrift für Nationalökonomie*, 8, 5: 597–614.

Bogdanov, Aleksandr 1925 [1896], *A Short Course of Economic Science*, second edition, translated by J. Fineberg, London: Communist Party of Great Britain.

Böhm-Bawerk, Eugen 1959a [1884], *Capital and Interest. Volume 1: History and Critique of Interest Theories*, translated by George D. Huncke and Hans F. Sennholz, South Holland, IL: Libertarian Press.

Böhm-Bawerk, Eugen 1959b [1888, 1921], *Capital and Interest. Volume 2: The Positive Theory of Capital*, translated by George D. Huncke, South Holland, IL: Libertarian Press.

Böhm-Bawerk, Eugen 1959c [1888, 1921] 'On the "Measurability" of Sensations', in *Capital and Interest. Volume 3: Further Essays on Capital and Interest*, translated by Hans F. Sennholz, South Holland, IL: Libertarian Press, pp. 124–36.

Böhm-Bawerk, Eugen 1975 [1896], *Karl Marx and the Close of his System*, London: Merlin.

Boissier, Gaston 1885 [1875], *L'opposition sous les Césars*, second edition, Paris: Hachette.

Bonar, James 1924, *Malthus and His Work*, second edition, London: Allen & Unwin.

Bordaz, Robert 1933, *La loi de Marx sur les capitaux à la lumière des événements contemporains*, Paris: Rodstein.

Borkenau, Franz 1938, *The Spanish Cockpit: An Eye-witness Account of the Political and Social Conflicts of the Spanish Civil War*, London: Faber & Faber.

Borkenau, Franz 1971 [1934], *Der Übergang vom feudalen zum bürgerlichen Weltbild:*

Studien zur Geschichte der Philosophie der Manufakturperiode, Darmstadt: Wissenschaftliche Buchgesellschaft.

Bortkiewicz, Ladislaus 1907, 'Zur Berichtigung der grundlegenden theoretischen Konstruktionen von Marx im III. Band des *Kapital*', *Jahrbücher für Nationalökonomie und Statistik*, 34: 319–35.

Bortkiewicz, Ladislaus 1949 [1907], 'On the Correction of Marx's Fundamental Theoretical Construction in the Third Volume of *Capital*', translated by Paul Sweezy, in Eugen von Böhm-Bawerk and Rudolf Hilferding, *Karl Marx and the Close of his System* and *Böhm-Bawerk's Criticism of Marx*, New York: Kelley, pp. 199–221.

Bortkiewicz, Ladislaus 1952, 'Value and Price in the Marxian System', translated by J. Kahane, *International Economic Papers*, 2, London: Macmillian.

Boudin, Louis B. 1907a, *The Theoretical System of Karl Marx in the Light of Recent Criticism*, Chicago: Kerr.

Boudin, Louis B. 1907b, 'Mathematische Formeln gegen Karl Marx', *Neue Zeit*, 25, 1 (16, 17, 18): 524–35, 557–67, 603–10.

Boudin, Louis B. 1909 [1907], *Das theoretische System von Karl Marx*, Stuttgart: Dietz.

Bourguin, Maurice 1893, 'Des rapports entre Proudhon et Karl Marx', *Revue d'économie politique*, 7, 3, March: 177–207.

Bourguin, Maurice 1901, 'La valeur dans le système collectiviste', *Revue politique et parlementaire*, 28, 82, 83, 84, April, May, June: 18–60, 335–52, 479–523.

Bourguin, Maurice 1925, *Les Systèmes socialistes et l'évolution économique*, third edition, Paris: Armand Colin.

Bousquet, Georges-Henri 1927, *Essai sur l'évolution de la pensée économique*, Paris: Giard.

Bowley, Marian 1937, *Nassau Senior and Classical Economics*, London: Allen & Unwin.

Branting, Hjalmar 1909, 'Der Massenstreik in Schweden', *Neue Zeit*, 27, 2, 47: 708–13.

Brauer, Theodor 1929, *Der moderne deutsche Sozialismus*, Freiburg im Breisgau: Herder.

Braunthal, Alfred 1929, 'Der Zusammenbruch der Zusammenbruchstheorie', *Die Gesellschaft*, 6, 2, 10: 289–304.

Braunthal, Alfred 1930, *Wirtschaft der Gegenwart und ihre Gesetze: Ein sozialistisches Lehrbuch der Nationalökonomie*, Berlin: Laubsche Verlagsbuchhandlung.

Brousse, Paul 1882, *Le Marxisme dans l'Internationale*, Paris: Le Proletaire.

Bray, John Francis 1839, *Labour's Wrongs and Labour's Remedy*, Leeds: David Green.

Bucharin, Nikolai 1929 [1917], *Imperialismus und Weltwirtschaft*, Wien: Verlag für Literatur und Politik.

Bücher, Karl 1906, *Die Entstehung der Volkswirtschaft*, fith edition, Tübingen: Laupp.

Buchs, Maurice 1948, 'Le fourriérisme aux Etats Unis', doctoral thesis, Paris: Université de Paris.

Buckmiller, Michael 1981, 'Bibliographie der Schriften von Paul Maitick 1924–1981', *Internationale Wissenschaftliche Korrespondenz zur Geschichte der deutschen Arbeiterbewegung*, 17, 2: 197–224.

Budge, Siegfried 1920, *Der Kapitalprofit*, Jena: Fischer.
Bukharin, Nikolai 1929 [1917], *Imperialism and World Economy*, London: Lawrence.
Bukharin, Nikolai 1972a [1919, written 1914], *The Economic Theory of the Leisure Class*, New York: Monthly Review.
Bukharin, Nikolai 1972b [1925–6], *Imperialism and the Accumulation of Capital*, with Rosa Luxemburg, *The Accumulation of Capital: An Anti-Critique*, edited by Kenneth Tarbuck, translated by Rudolf Wichmann, New York: Monthly Review Press.
Bukharin, Nikolai 1979 [1920], *The Politics and Economics of the Transition Period*, London: Routledge & Kegan Paul.
Bukharin, Nikolai 2012 [1922], 'The Programme of the International and the Communist Parties', in *Toward the United Front: Proceedings of the Fourth Congress of the Communist International, 1922*, translated and edited by John Riddell, Leiden: Brill, pp. 479–501.
Burkett, Paul 2004, 'Marx's Reproduction Schemes and the Environment', *Ecological Economics*, 49, 42: 457–67.
Bury, John Bagnell 1920, *The Idea of Progress*, London: MacMillan.
Cairnes, John Elliott 1875 [1857], *The Character and Logical Method of Political Economy*, New York: Harper.
Canard, Nicolas-François 1801, *Principes d'économie politique*, Paris: F. Buisson.
Carchedi, Guglielmo 1991, *Frontiers of Political Economy*, London: Verso.
Carchedi, Guglielmo 2009, 'The Fallacies of "New Dialectics" and Value-form Theory', *Historical Materialism*, 17, 1: 145–69.
Carchedi, Guglielmo and Michael Roberts 2013, 'The Long Roots of the Present Crisis: Keynesians, Austerians, and Marx's Law', *World Review of Political Economy*, 4, 1, Spring: 86–115.
Carey, Henry Charles 1848, *The Past, the Present and the Future*, Philadelphia: Carey & Hart.
Carver, Thomas Nixon 1937, 'The Static State and the Technology of Economic Reform', in *Economic Essays Contributed in Honour of John Bates Clark*, edited by Jacob Hollander, New York: Macmillan, pp. 29–45.
Cassel, Gustav 1932 [1918], *The Theory of Social Economy*, London: Unwin.
Cassel, Gustav 1937, 'Keynes' "General Theory"', *International Labour Review*, 36, 4, October: 437–45.
Chaloupek, Günther 1986, 'Marxistische Kritik an der Österreichischen Schule', in *Die Wiener Schule der Nationalökonomie*, edited by Norbert Leser, Wien-Köln-Graz: Böhlau-Verlag, pp. 195–221.
Chamisso, Adalbert von 1842 [1832], 'Roland ein Roß kamm', in *Adalbert von Chamisso's Werke. Band 3*, second edition, Leipzig: Weidmann, pp. 194–5.
Champier, Symphorien 1498, *Dialogus in magicarum artium destructionem*, Lyon: Guillaume Balsarin.

Chao, Nai-Tuan 1930, 'Richard Jones: An Early English Institutionalist', PhD dissertation, New York: Columbia University.

Chaptal, Jean-Antoine 1819, *De l'industrie française. Tome second*, Paris: Antoine-Augustin Renouard.

Charasoff, Georg 1910, *Das System des Marxismus: Darstellung und Kritik*, Berlin: Bondy.

Chayanov, Alexander Vasilyevich 1930 [1921], *Die optimalen Betriebsgrössen in der Landwirtschaft*, Berlin: Parey.

Chayanov, Alexander Vasilyevich 1991 [1919], *The Theory of Peasant Co-operatives*, Columbus: Ohio State University Press.

Chayanov, Alexander Vasilyevich 1966 [1923], *The Theory of the Peasant Economy*, Homewood: Irwin.

Clark, George Norman 1937, *Science and Social Welfare in the Age of Newton*, London: Oxford University Press.

Clark, John Bates 1915, *Essentials of Economic Theory*, New York: Macmillan.

Clark, John Bates 1927 [1899], *The Distribution of Wealth*, New York: Macmillan.

Clark, John Maurice 1917, 'Business Acceleration and the Law of Demand', *Journal of Political Economy*, 25, 3, March: 217–23.

Clark, John Maurice 1937, 'The Relation between Statics and Dynamics', in *Economic Essays Contributed in Honour of John Bates Clark*, edited by Jacob Hollander, New York: Macmillan, pp. 48–70.

Cliff, Tony 1974 [1955], *State Capitalism in Russia*, London: Pluto.

Cliff, Tony 1957, 'The Economic Roots of Reformism', *Socialist Review*, 6, 9, www.marxists.org/archive/cliff/works/1957/06/rootsref.htm, accessed 25 June 2017.

Cohen, Hermann 1896, 'Einleitung mit kritischem Nachtrag', in Friedrich Albert Lange, *Geschichte des Materialismus seit Kant*, fifth edition, Leipzig: Baedeker.

Cohen, Morris Raphael 1931, *Reason and Nature: An Essay on the Meaning of Scientific Method*, New York: Harcourt, Brace.

Cole, George Douglas Howard 1920b, *Guild Socialism*, London: Fabian Society.

Cole, George Douglas Howard 1921, *Selbstverwaltung in der Industrie*, Berlin: Engelmann.

Cole, George Douglas Howard 1920a [1917], *Self-government in Industry*, London: Bell and Sons.

Cole, George Douglas Howard and William Mellor 1918, *The Meaning of Industrial Freedom*, London: Allen and Unwin.

Cole, George Douglas Howard and William Mellor 1921, *Gildensozialismus*, Köln: Rheinland.

Colquhoun, Patrick 1814, *A Treatise on the Wealth, Power, and Resources, of the British Empire*, London: Joseph Mawman.

Comte, August 1908a [1838], *Cours de philosophie positive. Tome quatrième*, Paris: Schleicher Frères.

Comte, August 1908b [1842], *Cours de philosophie positive. Tome sixième*, Paris: Schleicher Frères.
Condorcet, Jean-Antoine-Nicolas de 1796 [1795], *Outlines of an Historical View of the Progress of the Human Mind*, New York: Carey, Price.
Conrad, Otto 1931, *Der Mechanismus der Verkehrswirtschaft*, Jena: Fischer.
Conrad, Otto 1936, 'Die Grundannahme der Gleichgewichtstheorie', *Zeitschrift fur Nationalökonomie*, 7, 2: 234–43.
Considerant, Victor 1847 [1843], *Principes du socialisme, manifeste de la democratie au XIXe Siecle*, Paris: Librairie Phalanstérienne.
Copernicus, Nicholas 1992 [1543], *On the Revolutions*, translated by Edward Rosen, Baltimore: Johns Hopkins University Press.
Cossa, Luigi 1809, *Histoire des doctrine économiques*, Paris: V. Briard & E. Brière.
Croce, Benedetto 1913 [1909], *Philosophy of the Practical: Economic and Ethic*, London: Macmillan.
Croce, Benedetto 1914 [1899], *Historical Materialism and the Economics of Karl Marx*, London: George Allen and Unwin.
Cunow, Heinrich 1898, 'Zur Zusammenbruchstheorie', *Neue Zeit*, 17, 1 (12, 13, 14): 356–64, 396–403, 424–30.
Cunow, Heinrich 1920, *Die Marxsche Geschichts-, Gesellschafts- und Staatstheorie: Grundzüge der Marxschen Soziologie*, Berlin: Buchhandlung Vorwärts.
David, Eduard 1903, *Socialismus und Landwirtschaft*. Berlin: Verlag der Socialistischen Monatshefte.
Day, Richard B. 1976, 'The Theory of the Long Cycle: Kondratiev, Trotsky, Mandel', *New Left Review*, I, 99, September–October: 67–82.
Day, Richard B. 1981, *The 'Crisis' and the 'Crash': Soviet Studies of the West (1917–1939)*, London: NLB.
Delbrück, Hans 1903, *Preußische Jahrbücher*, 113: 333–50.
Denis, Hector 1907, *Histoire des systèmes économiques et socialistes. Volume 2*, Paris: Giard & Brière.
Deutsche Arbeit 1927 [further information about this publication could not be found].
Deutsche Bergwerkszeitung 1929, 'Inventory Problems', Düsseldorf, 10 November.
Diehl, Karl 1898, *Über das Verhältnis von Wert und Preis im ökonomischen System von Karl Marx*, Jena: Fischer.
Diehl, Karl 1921, *Sozialwissenschaftliche Erläuterungen zu David Ricardos Grundgesetzen der Volkswirtschaft. Band 1*, third edition, Leipzig: Meiner.
Dietzgen, Josef 1934 [written 1867], 'Letter to Karl Marx, 7 November 1867', in Karl Marx, *Karl Marx, Letters to Dr Kugelmann*, London: Martin Lawrence, pp. 56–7.
Dobb, Maurice 1937, *Political Economy and Capitalism: Some Essays in Economic Tradition*, London: George Routledge and Sons.
Dollard, John 1936, Review of *Studien über Autorität und Familie: Forschungsberichte*

aus dem Institut für Sozialforschung, edited by Max Horkheimer, Paris: Alcan, 1936, *American Sociological Review*, 1 (2), April: 302–5.

Douglas, Paul H. 1927, 'Smith's Theory of Value and Distribution', *University Journal of Business*, 5, 1, January: 53–87.

Duhem, Pierre 1915, *Le système du monde: histoire des doctrines cosmologiques de Platon à Copernic Tome 3*, Paris: Hermann.

Duprat, Guillaume-Léonce 1932, 'Introduction a l'étude de la *prévision* sociologique', *Revue internationale de soclologie*, 3–4.

Dupuit, Jules 1969 [1844], 'On the Measurement of the Utility of Public Works', in *Readings in Welfare Economics*, edited by Kenneth J. Arrow and Tibor Scitovsky, Homewood, IL: Richard D. Irwin, pp. 255–83.

Duret, Jean 1933, *Le Marxisme et les crises*, Paris: Gallimard.

Eckstein, Gustav 1902, 'Die vierfache Wurzel des Satzes vom unzureichenden Grunde der Grenznutztheorie: Eine Robinsonade', *Neue Zeit*, 20, 2 (26), 24 September, pp. 810–16.

Eckstein, Gustav 1904, 'Zur Methode der politischen Ökonomie', *Neue Zeit*, 28, 1 (10, 11, 14): 324–32, 367–75, 489–97.

Eisenhart, Hugo 1910 [1881], *Geschichte der nationalökonomik*, third edition, Jena: Fischer; Périn, Charles 1880, *Les doctrines économiques depuis un siècle*, Paris: Lecoffre.

Elster, Ludwig 1887, 'J.Ch.L. Simonde de Sismondi: Ein Beitrag zur Geschichte der Volkswirtschaftslehre', *Jahrbücher für Nationalökonomie und Statistik*, 48, new series 14, 4/5: 321–82.

Elster, Ludwig (ed.) 1931–3, *Wörterbuch der Volkswirtschaft*, three volumes, fourth edition, Jena: Fischer.

Elster, Ludwig 1933, 'Smiths Lehre and die Lehren der sogenannten "Klassiker der Volkswirtschaftslehre"', in *Wörterbuch der Volkswirtschaft. Band 3*, edited by Ludwig Elster, fourth edition, Jena: Fischer, pp. 211–33.

Ely, Richard T. 1903, 'The Idea of Evolution in Society,' in *Studies in the Evolution of Industrial Society*, New York: Macmillan.

Encyclopaedia Britannica 1941, London: Encyclopaedia Britannica.

Enfantin, Barthélemy Prosper 1964a [1831], *Deuxième enseignement: l'histoire*, in Henri Saint-Simon and Barthélemy Prosper Enfantin, *Œuvres de Saint-Simon et d'Enfantin. Tome 14*, Aalen: Otto Zeller, pp. 45–74.

Enfantin, Barthélemy Prosper 1964b [1832], *Dix-huitième enseignement: l'histoire*, in Henri Saint-Simon and Barthélemy Prosper Enfantin, *Œuvres de Saint-Simon et d'Enfantin. Tome 17*, Aalen: Otto Zeller, pp. 103–40.

Enfantin, Barthélemy Prosper 1964c [1838], *Les mémoires d'un inustriel de l'an 2240*, in Henri Saint-Simon and Barthélemy Prosper Enfantin, *Œuvres de Saint-Simon et d'Enfantin. Tome 17*, Aalen: Otto Zeller, pp. 103–40.

Engels, Friedrich 1976 [1885], 'Postface to the Second Edition', in Karl Marx, *Capital: A Critique of Political Economy. Volume 3*, translated by David Fernbach, Harmondsworth: Penguin, pp. 94–103.

Engels, Friedrich 1978a [1885], 'Preface', in Karl Marx, *Capital: A Critique of Political Economy. Volume 2*, translated by David Fernbach, Harmondsworth: Penguin, pp. 83–102.

Engels, Friedrich 1978b [1850], 'The Peasant War in Germany', in Karl Marx and Frederick Engels, *Marx and Engels Collected Works. Volume 10*, New York: International Publishers, pp. 396–482.

Engels, Friedrich 1979 [1851–2], *Revolution and Counter-Revolution in Germany*, in Karl Marx and Frederick Engels, *Marx and Engels Collected Works. Volume 11*, New York: International Publishers, pp. 3–96.

Engels, Friedrich 1987 [1878], *Anti-Dühring: Herr Eugen Dühring's Revolution in Science*, in Karl Marx and Frederick Engels, *Marx and Engels Collected Works. Volume 25*, New York: International Publishers, pp. 1–309.

Engels, Friedrich 1989a, *Socialism: Utopian and Scientific*, in Karl Marx and Frederick Engels, *Marx and Engels Collected Works. Volume 24*, New York: International Publishers, pp. 281–325.

Engels, Friedrich 1990a [1891], 'A Critique of the Draft Social-Democratic Programme of 1891', in Karl Marx and Frederick Engels, *Marx and Engels Collected Works. Volume 27*, New York: International Publishers, pp. 217–33.

Engels, Friedrich 1990b [1895], 'Introduction', to Karl Marx, *The Class Struggles in France*, in Karl Marx and Frederick Engels, *Marx and Engels Collected Works. Volume 27*, New York: International Publishers, pp. 506–24.

Engels, Friedrich 1990c [1884], *The Origin of the Family, Private Property and The State in the Light of the Researches by Lewis H. Morgan*, in Karl Marx and Frederick Engels, *Marx and Engels Collected Works. Volume 26*, New York: International Publishers, pp. 129–276.

Engels, Friedrich 1995 [1884], 'Letter to Karl Kautsky, 26 June 1884', in *Marx and Engels Collected Works. Volume 47*, New York: International Publishers, pp. 155–7.

Engels, Friedrich 2001a [1888], 'Letter to Nikolai Danielson, 5 January 1888', in *Marx and Engels Collected Works. Volume 48*, New York: International Publishers, pp. 135–7.

Engels, Friedrich 2001b [1890], 'Letter to Joseph Bloch, 21 September', in Karl Marx and Frederick Engels, *Marx and Engels Collected Works. Volume 49*, New York: International Publishers, pp. 33–6.

Engels, Friedrich 2001c, 'Letter to Nikolai Danielson, October 15, 1888', in Karl Marx and Frederick Engels, *Marx and Engels Collected Works. Volume 48*, New York: International Publishers, pp. 228–30.

Engels, Friedrich 2001d, 'Letter to Victor Adler, 16 March 1895', in Karl Marx and Frederick Engels, *Marx and Engels Collected Works. Volume 50*, New York: International Publishers, pp. 468–70.

Engländer, Oskar 1928, 'Böhm-Bawerk und Marx', *Archiv fur Sozialwissenschaft and Sozialpolitik*, 60: 368–81.

Epstein, Ralph C. 1934, *Industrial Profits in the United States*, New York: National Bureau of Economic Research in cooperation with the Committee on Recent Economic Changes.

Espinas, Alfred Victor 1891, *Histoire des doctrines économiques*, Paris: Colin.

Fabricant, Salomon 1940, *The Output of Manufacturing Industries 1899–1937*, New York: National Bureau of Economic Research.

Federal Trade Commission 1926, *National Wealth and Income*, Senate Document 126, Washington.

Feiler, Arthur, 1974 [1926], *America Seen Through German Eyes*, New York: Arno Press.

Feis, Herbert 1930, *Europe, the World Banker 1870–1914*, New Haven, CT: Yale University Press.

Ferguson, Adam 1809 [1767], *Essay on the History of Civil Society*, seventh edition, Boston: Hastings, Etheridge and Bliss.

Fichte, Johann Gottlieb 2012 [1800], *The Closed Commercial State*, Albany, NY: State University of New York Press.

Fischer, Kuno 1901, *Hegels Leben, Werke und Lehre. Theil 2*, Heidelberg: Carl Winter's Universitätsbuchhandlung.

Fisher, Irving 1892, *Mathematical Investigations in the Theory of Value and Prices*, in *Transactions of the Connecticut Academy of Arts and Sciences*, 9: 1–124.

Fisher, Irving 1925 [1920], *Stabilising the Dollar*, New York: Macmillan.

Fontaine, Jean de La 1896 [1674], 'The Eel Pie', in Jean de La Fontaine, *Tales and Novels in Verse. Volume 1*, London: Society of English Bibliophiles, pp. 153–7.

Fontaine, Jean de La 2009 [1674], 'Clymene', in Jean de La Fontaine, *La Fontaine's Complete Tales in Verse: An Illustrated and Annotated Translation*, translated by Randolph Runyon, Jefferson, NC: McFarland.

Ford, Henry 1922, *My Life and Work*, New York: Doubleday.

Foreign Bondholders Protective Council 1938, *Annual Report 1937*, New York.

Foster, John Bellamy and Robert W. McChesney 2010, 'Listen Keynesians, it's the system! Response to Palley', *Monthly Review*, 61, 11, April: 44–56.

Fourier, Charles 1996 [1808], *Theory of the Four Movements*, Cambridge: Cambridge University Press.

Foxwell, Herbert 1899, 'Introduction', in Anton Menger, *The Right to the Whole Produce of Labour*, London: Macmillan.

Freudenthal, Gideon and Peter McLaughlin (editors) 2009, *The Social and Economic Roots of the Scientific Revolution: Texts by Boris Hessen and Henryk Grossmann*, Dordrecht: Springer.

Funkhouser, H.G. and Helen M. Walker 1935, 'Playfair and his Charts', in *Economic History*, supplement to *Economic Journal*, pp. 103–9.

Ganilh, Charles 1815, *La théorie de l'économie politique. Tome Premier*, Paris: Deterville.
Gibbins, Henry de Beltgens 1897 [1890], *The Industrial History of England*, London: Methuen.
Gide, Charles and Charles Rist 1915 [1909], *A History of Economic Doctrines*, Boston: Heath.
Godwin, Parke 1844, *Democracy Constructive and Pacific*, New York: Winchester.
Gonnard, René 1922, *Histoire des doctrines économiques. Volume 3*, Paris: Nouvelle Librairie Nationale.
Gorter, Herman 1915, *Der Imperialismus, der Weltkrieg und die Sozial-demokratie*, Amsterdam: Sozial-demokratische Partei Hollands.
Gossen, Hermann Heinrich 1983 [1854], *The Laws of Human Relations and the Rules of Human Action Derived Therefrom*, Cambridge, MA: MIT Press.
Gottl, Friedrich 1901, *Die Herrschaft des Wortes*, Jena: Gustav Fischer.
Grandeau, Frédéric 1937, *Économie sociale: théorie des crises*, Paris: Éditions A. Pedone.
Gray, John 1831, *The Social System. A Treatise on the Principle of Exchange*, Edinburgh: Tait.
Graziadei, Antonio 1923, *Prezzo e sovrapprezzo nell'economia capitalistica. Critica alla teoria del valore di Carlo Marx*, Milano: Societa editrice Avanti!
Grimm, Robert 1927, 'Bauer und Arbeiter', *Rote Revue*, 6, 6/7, February/March: 192–203.
Grossman, Henryk n.d.a, manuscript starting 'Die Entwertung sollen die Zusammenbruchstendenz aufheben ...', manuscript, original Folder 45, 'Stellungnahme zur Kritik am Hauptwerk', 'Henryk Grossman III-155' collection, Archiwum Polskiej Akademii Nauk, Warszawa.
Grossman, Henryk n.d.b, 'Marx Classical National Economy and Problem of Dynamics', manuscript, Folder 74, 'Henryk Grossman III-155' collection, Archiwum Polskiej Akademii Nauk, Warszawa.
Grossman, Henryk 1905, *Proletariat wobec kwestii żydowskiej z powodu niedyskutowanej dyskusyi w 'Krytyce'* Kraków: Drukani Wladyslawa Teodorczuka,
Grossman, Henryk 1912, 'Polityka przemysłowa i handlowa rządu Terezynansko-Józefińskiego w Galicyi 1772–1790: Referat na V. Zjazd prawnikow i ekonomistow polskich' *Przeglad prawa i administracyi*: 1–43.
Grossman, Henryk 1914, *Österreichs Handelspolitik mit Bezug auf Galizien in der Reformperiode 1772–1790*, Wien: Konegen.
Grossman, Henryk 1922, 'Teorja kryzysów gospodarczych (The Theory of Economic Crisis). Meeting of June 16, 1919' *Bulletin International de l'Académie Polonaise des Sciences et des Lettres. Classe de Philologie. Classe d'Histoire et de Philosophie. 1 Partie. Les Années 1919, 1920*, Kraków, pp. 285–90.
Grossman, Henryk 1923a, 'Przycznek do historji socjalizmu w Polsce przed laty czterdziestu' in Karol Marks, *Karol Marks: Pisma niewydane, 1 Listy Marksa do Kugelmana, 2 Przyczynek do Krytyki socjaldemokratycznego programu partyjnego. Przełożył, wstę-*

pem i uwagami zaopatrzył, translated by Henryk Grossman, Warsaw: Książka, pp. iii–xxvii.

Grossman, Henryk 1923b, 'Ekonomiczny system Karola Marksa' *Kultura Robotnicza* 2, 10 (32), 17 March: 295–9.

Grossman, Henryk 1924a, *Simonde de Sismondi et ses théories économiques. Une nouvelle interprétation de sa pensée*, Warszawa: Bibliotheca Universitatis Liberae Polniae.

Grossman, Henryk 1924b, 'Zur Dynamik Des kapitalistischen Wirtschaftsmechanismus', manuscript, Folder 37, 'Henryk Grossman III–155' collection, Archiwum Polskiej Akademii Nauk, Warszawa.

Grossman, Henryk 1924c, Manuscript 'Inhalt', December 6, originally in the collection's Folder 39, Archiwum, Polskiej Akademii Nauk, Warszawa.

Grossman, Henryk written circa 1929–32, Manuscripts in folder labelled 'Stellungnahme zur Kritik am Hauptwerk', Materiały Henryka Grossmanna, III-155, originally in the collection's Folder 45, Archiwum, Polskiej Akademii Nauk, Warszawa.

Grossman, Henryk written circa 1930, 'Zum Abschluss des Streites um die Wert- und Preisrechnung im Marxschen System', manuscript, Folder 61, 'Henryk Grossman III-155' collection, Archiwum Polskiej Akademii Nauk, Warszawa.

Grossman, Henryk 1931–7, Letters to Paul Mattick, in Paul Mattick Collection, International Institute of Social History, Amsterdam.

Grossman, Henryk 1932, *Shihon no chikuseki narabi ni hokai no riron*, Tokyo: Kaizosha.

Grossman, Henryk 1933a, Letter to Paul Mattick, in Paul Mattick Collection, International Institute of Social History, Amsterdam, 16 September.

Grossman, Henryk 1933b, Letter to Paul Mattick, in Paul Mattick Collection, International Institute of Social History, Amsterdam, 17 June.

Grossman, Henryk 1933–9, Na 4 Nachlass Leo Löwenthal, A325, Universitätsbiliothek, Goethe Universität Frankfurt am Main, Frankfurt am Main.

Grossman, Henryk 1934–43, Na 1 Nachless Max Horkheimer, IV 10.1–94, VI 9, VI 10, IX 58, IX 59.3, Universitätsbiliothek, Goethe Universität Frankfurt am Main, Frankfurt am Main.

Grossman, Henryk 1934, 'Sismondi, Jean Charles Leonard Simonde de (1773–1842)', in *Encyclopedia of the Social Sciences. Volume 14*, edited by Edwin R.A. Seligman, New York: Macmillan, pp. 69–71.

Grossman, Henryk 1935a, Letter to Paul Mattick, in Paul Mattick Collection, International Institute of Social History, Amsterdam, 19 February.

Grossman, Henryk 1935b, Letter to Ernst Schachtel, Na 4 Nachlass Leo Löwenthal, A325, Universitätsbiliothek, Goethe Universität Frankfurt am Main, Frankfurt am Main, 11 July.

Grossman, Henryk 1936 Letter to Max Horkheimer, Na 1 Nachless Max Horkheimer, VI 9.346, Universitätsbiliothek, Goethe Universität Frankfurt am Main, Frankfurt am Main, 1 October.

Grossman, Henryk 1937a, 'Marx u d klassische Oekonomie oder die Lehre von Wertfetisch', manuscript, Folder 68, Archiwum Polskiej Akademii Nauk.

Grossman, Henryk 1937b, Letter to Paul Mattick, in Paul Mattick Collection, International Institute of Social History, Amsterdam, 18 July.

Grossman, Henryk 1937c, Letter to Max Horkheimer, Na 1 Nachlass Max Horkheimer, VI 9.320, Universitätsbiliothek, Goethe Universität Frankfurt am Main, Frankfurt am Main, 30 June.

Grossman, Henryk 1937d, Letter to Max Horkheimer, Na 1 Nachlass Max Horkheimer, VI 9.314, Universitätsbiliothek, Goethe Universität Frankfurt am Main, Frankfurt am Main, 1 August.

Grossman, Henryk 1938a, Review of G.N. Clark, *Science and Social Welfare in the Age of Newton*, New York and London: Oxford University Press, 1937; and George Sarton, *The History of Science and the New Humanism*, Cambridge, MA: Harvard University Press and London: Oxford University Press, 1937, *Zeitschrift für Sozialforschung* 7, 1/2: 233–7.

Grossman, Henryk 1938b, Review of Karl Marx and Friedrich Engels, *The Civil War in the United States*, edited by Richard Enmale, New York: International Publishers, 1937, *Zeitschrift für Sozialforschung*, 7, 1/2: 259–63.

Grossman, Henryk 1938c, *Plan i metod 'Kapitala'*, translated by Mara Fran Zemun: Graficki zavod 'Rotacija'.

Grossman, Henryk 1939a, Review of F. Grandeau, *Théorie des crises*, Paris: Pedone, 1937, *Zeitschrift für Sozialforschung* 8, 1/2: 300–1.

Grossman, Henryk 1939b, Review of Cleona Lewis, assisted by K.T. Schotterbeck, *America's Stake in International Investments*, Washington D.C.: Brookings Institution, London: Faber and Faber, 1938, *Zeitschrift für Sozialforschung*, 8, 1/2: 304–6.

Grossman, Henryk 1939c, Review of Jürgen Kuczynski, *Hunger and Work*, New York: International Publishers and London: Lawrence & Wishart, 1938, *Zeitschrift für Sozialforschung* 8, 1/2: 318–20.

Grossman, Henryk 1939d, Review of L.P. Ayres, *Turning Points in Business Cycles*, New York: Macmillan, 1939, *Zeitschrift für Sozialforschung*, 8, 3: 490–2.

Grossman, Henryk 1941a, *Marx, die Klassische Nationaloekonomie und das Problem der Dynamik*, mimeograph, New York: Institut für Sozialforschung.

Grossman, Henryk 1941b, Review of Josef A. Schumpeter, *Business Cycles. A Theoretical, Historical and Statistical Analysis of the Capitalist Process*, two volumes, New York: McGraw-Hill, 1939, *Studies in Philosophy and Social Science*, 9, 1: 181–9.

Grossman, Henryk 1941c, Review of Salomon Fabricant, *The Output of Manufacturing Industries 1899–1937*, New York: National Bureau of Economic Research, 1940, *Studies in Philosophy and Social Science*, 9, 2: 352–4.

Grossman, Henryk 1941d, Review of Lynn Thorndike, *A History of Magic and Experi-*

mental Sciences. Volumes 5 and 6, The Sixteenth Century, New York: Columbia University Press, 1941, *Studies in Philosophy and Social Science*, 9, 3: 514–19.

Grossman, Henryk 1943a, 'The Evolutionist Revolt against Classical Economics. I. In France – Condorcet, Saint-Simon, Simonde de Sismondi', *The Journal of Political Economy*, 51, 5, October: 381–96.

Grossman, Henryk 1943b, 'The Evolutionist Revolt against Classical Economics. II. In England – James Steuart, Richard Jones, Karl Marx', *Journal of Political Economy*, 51, 6, December: 506–22.

Grossman, Henryk 1947a, Letter to Christina Stead and Bill Blake, Box 17, Folder 125, Stead Collection, National Library of Australia, 4 and 5 May.

Grossman, Henryk 1947b Letter to Bill Blake, 1947, Box 17, Folder 125, Stead Collection, between 3 March and 20 April.

Grossman, Henryk 1947–9, Letters from Henryk Grossman to Walter Braeuer, Braeuer Nachlaß, von Thünen Museum, Teltow, Meklenberg-Vorpommern.

Grossman, Henryk 1948, 'W. Playfair, the Earliest Theorist of Capitalist Development', *Economic History Review*, 18, 1/2: 65–83.

Grossman, Henryk 1977 [1941], 'Marx, Classical Political Economy and the Problem of Dynamics', translated by Pete Burgess, *Capital and Class*, 2, Summer: 32–55, and 3, Autumn: 67–99.

Grossman, Henryk 1990, 'The Evolutionist Revolt against Classical Economics', in *Karl Marx's Social and Political Thought: Critical Assessments. Volume 1*, edited by Bob Jessop, London and New York: Routledge, pp. 253–74.

Grossman, Henryk 1991, 'The Evolutionist Revolt against Classical Economics', in *Thomas Tooke (1774–1858), Mountifort Longfield (1802–1884), Richard Jones (1790–1855)*, edited by Mark Blaug, Aldershot: Elgar, pp. 1–16.

Grossman, Henryk 2000 [1922], 'The Theory of Economic Crises', in *Value, Capitalist Dynamics, and Money*, edited by Paul Zarembka and Susanne Soederberg, *Research in Political Economy 18*, New York: Elsevir Science, pp. 171–80.

Grossman, Henryk 2006 [written 1934], 'The Beginnings of Capitalism and the New Mass Morality', *Journal of Classical Sociology*, 6, 2: 201–13.

Grossman, Henryk 2013 [1929], 'The Change in the Original Plan for Marx's *Capital* and its Causes', translated by Geoffrey McCormack, *Historical Materialism*, 21, 3: 138–64.

Grossman, Henryk 2014 [1932], *Fifty Years of Struggle over Marxism*, translated by Rick Kuhn and Einde O'Callaghan, Melbourne: Socialist Alternative.

Grossman, Henryk 2015 [1941], *Marx, Classical Political Economy and the Problem of Dynamics*, translated by Rick Kuhn, Melbourne: Socialist Alternative.

Grossmann, Henryk 1914, *Österreichs Handelspolitik mit Bezug auf Galizien in der Reformperiode 1772–1790*, in series *Studien zur Soziale-, Wirtschafts- und Verwaltungsgeschichte, herausgegeben von Carl Grünberg, 10. Heft*, Wien: Konegen.

Grossmann, Henryk 1916, 'Die Anfänge und geschichtliche Entwicklung der amtlichen Statistik in Österreich', *Statistische Monatsschrift*, new series 21: 331–423.

Grossmann, Henryk 1928a, 'Eine neue Theorie über Imperialismus und die soziale Revolution', *Archiv für die Geschichte des Sozialismus und der Arbeiterbewegung* 13: 141–92.

Grossmann, Henryk 1928b, Review of Othmar Spann, *Die Haupttheorien der Volkswirtschaftslehre*. twelth to fifteenth editions, Leipzig: Quelle & Meyer, 1923, *Archiv für die Geschichte des Sozialismus und der Arbeiterbewegung* 13: 341–4.

Grossmann, Henryk 1928c, Review of Maurice Bourgin, *Les systemes socialistes et l'évolution économique*, third edition, fourth printing, Paris: Armand Colin, 1925, *Archiv für die Geschichte des Sozialismus und der Arbeiterbewegung* 13: 344–5.

Grossmann, Henryk 1929a, *Das Akkumulations- und Zusammenbruchsgesetz des kapitalistischen Systems (zugleich eine Krisentheorie)*, Leipzig: Hirschfeld.

Grossmann, Henryk 1929b, 'Die Änderung des ursprunglichen Aufbauplans des Marxschen *Kapital* und ihre Ursachen', *Archiv für die Geschichte des Sozialismus und der Arbeiterbewegung*, 14: 305–38.

Grossmann, Henryk 1931a, 'Anarchismus', in *Wörterbuch der Volkswirtschaft. Band 1*, edited by Ludwig Elster, fourth edition, Jena: Fischer, pp. 97–109.

Grossmann, Henryk 1931b, 'Bolschevismus', in *Wörterbuch der Volkswirtschaft. Band 1*, edited by Ludwig Elster, fourth edition, Jena: Fischer, pp. 421–44.

Grossmann, Henryk 1932a, 'Die Goldproduktion im Reproduktionsschema von Marx und Rosa Luxemburg', in Max Adler et al., *Festschrift für Carl Grünberg zum 70. Geburtstag*, Leipzig: Hirschfeld, pp. 152–84.

Grossmann, Henryk 1932b, 'Die Wert-Preis-Transformation bei Marx und das Krisenproblem', *Zeitschrift für Sozialforschung*, 1: 55–84.

Grossmann, Henryk 1932c, 'Internationale: Die Zweite Internationale', in *Wörterbuch der Volkswirtschaft. Band 2*, edited by Ludwig Elster, fourth edition, Jena: Fischer, pp. 432–9.

Grossmann, Henryk 1932d, 'Internationale: Die dritte Internationale', in *Wörterbuch der Volkswirtschaft. Band 2*, edited by Ludwig Elster, fourth edition, Jena: Fischer, pp. 439–49.

Grossmann, Henryk 1932e, 'Jaurès Jean' in *Wörterbuch der Volkswirtschaft. Band 2*, edited by Ludwig Elster, fourth edition, Jena: Fischer, pp. 382–3.

Grossmann, Henryk 1932f, *Fünfzig Jahre Kampf um den Marxismus 1883–1932*, Jena: Fischer.

Grossmann, Henryk 1932g, 'Das Problem der Durchschnittsprofitrate in der modernen wirtschaftlichen Theorie', a student's typed-up notes from Grossman's course, Folder 60, 'Henryk Grossman III–155' collection, Archiwum Polskiej Akademii Nauk, Warszawa.

Grossmann, Henryk 1932h, 'Lenin (Pseud. für Uljanow), Wladimir Iljitsch', in *Wörter-*

buch der Volkswirtschaft. Zweiter Band, edited by Ludwig Elster, fourth edition, Jena: Fischer, pp. 828–31.

Grossmann, Henryk 1932i, 'Plechanow, Georg', in *Wörterbuch der Volkswirtschaft. Zweiter Band*, edited by Ludwig Elster, fourth edition, Jena: Fischer, pp. 1140–1.

Grossmann, Henryk 1933a, '7 Die Fortentwicklung des Marxismus bis zur Gegenwart', in *Wörterbuch der Volkswirtschaft. Band 3*, edited by Ludwig Elster, fourth edition, Jena: Fischer, pp. 313–41.

Grossmann, Henryk 1933b, 'Sozialdemokratische und kommunistische Parteien', in *Wörterbuch der Volkswirtschaft. Band 3*, edited by Ludwig Elster, fourth edition, Jena: Fischer, pp. 238–57.

Grossmann, Henryk 1933c, 'Sorel, Georges', in *Wörterbuch der Volkswirtschaft. Band 3*, edited by Ludwig Elster, fourth edition, Jena: Fischer, pp. 236–7.

Grossmann, Henryk 1934a, Review of Elie Halévy, *Sismondi*, Paris: Alcan, 1933, *Zeitschrift für Sozialforschung*, 3, 2: 291.

Grossmann, Henryk 1934b, Review of Robert Bordaz, *La loi de Marx sur les capitaux à la lumière des événements contemporains*, Paris: L. Rodstein, 1933, *Zeitschrift für Sozialforschung*, 3, 2: 314–5.

Grossmann, Henryk 1969 [1941] *Marx, die klassische Nationalökonomie und das Problem der Dynamik*, with appendix 'Briefe Henryk Grossmanns an Paul Mattick über Akkumulation', Frankfurt am Main: Europäische Verlagsanstalt.

Grossmann, Henryk circa 1970 [1941] *Marx, die klassische Nationalökonomie und das Problem der Dynamik*, unauthorised edition.

Grossmann, Henryk 1971 [1941], *Marx, l'economia politica classica e il problema della dinamica*, translated by Gigio Backhaus, Bari: Laterza.

Grossmann, Henryk 1971b [1928–1943], *Aufsätze zur Krisentheorie*: Frankfurt: Archiv sozialistische Literatur.

Grossmann, Henryk 1972 [1941], 'Marx en de klassieke politieke economie', *Te Elfder Ure*, 19, 7/8: 308–33.

Grossmann, Henryk 1975a [1941], *Marx, l'économie politique classique et le probleme de la dynamique*, Paris: Champ Libre.

Grossmann, Henryk 1975b [1941], *Marx, den klassiske nationaløkonomi og dynamikken*, København: Rhodos.

Grossmann, Henryk 1985a [written 1937], theses, in 'Diskussionen aus einem Seminar über Monopolkapitalismus', in Max Horkheimer, *Gesammelte Schriften. Band 12: Nachgelassene Schriften 1931–1949*, Frankfurt am Main: Fischer, pp. 418–20.

Grossmann, Henryk 1985b [written 1937], minutes of a seminar on 20 November 1937, 'Diskussionen aus einem Seminar über Monopolkapitalismus', in Max Horkheimer, *Gesammelte Schriften. Band 12: Nachgelassene Schriften 1931–1949*, Frankfurt am Main: Fischer, p. 429.

Grossmann, Henryk 1992 [1929], *The Law of Accumulation and Breakdown of the Cap-*

italist System: Being also a Theory of Crises, abridged English translation by Jairus Banaji, London: Pluto Press.

Grossmann, Henryk 2007 [1941], 'Marx, Classical Economics, and the Problem of Dynamics', translated by Paul Mattick Jr., *International Journal of Political Economy*, 36, 2, Summer: 6–83.

Grossmann, Henryk 2009a [1935], 'The Social Foundations of Mechanistic Philosophy and Manufacture', translated by Gabriella Shalit, in *The Social and Economic Roots of the Scientific Revolution: Texts by Boris Hessen and Henryk Grossmann*, edited by Gideon Freudenthal and Peter McLaughlin, Dordrecht: Springer, pp. 103–56.

Grossmann, Henryk 2009b [written 1930s and 1940s], 'Descartes and the Social Origins of the Mechanistic Concept of the World', in *The Social and Economic Roots of the Scientific Revolution: Texts by Boris Hessen and Henryk Grossmann*, edited by Freudenthal and Peter McLaughlin, Dordrecht: Springer, pp. 157–229.

Grossmann, Henryk 2017a, *Schiften aus dem Nachlass. Mit weiteren Materialien und Dokumenten*, edited by Jürgen Scheele, 47–94, Baden-Baden: Tectum.

Grossmann, Henryk 2017b [1930?], 'Zum Abschluss des Streites um die Wert- und Preisrechnung im Marxschen System', in Henryk Grossmann, *Schiften aus dem Nachlass. Mit weiteren Materialien und Dokumenten*, edited by Jürgen Scheele, 269–90, Baden-Baden: Tectum.

Grossmann, Henryk 2017c [written 1932], 'Das Problem der Durchschnittsprofitrate in der modernen wirtschaftlichen Theorie', in Henryk Grossmann, *Schiften aus dem Nachlass. Mit weiteren Materialien und Dokumenten*, edited by Jürgen Scheele, 95–139, Baden-Baden: Tectum.

Grossmann, Henryk 2017d [written 1937], 'Marx u d klassische Oekonomie oder die Lehre von Wertfetisch (Auszug)', in Henryk Grossmann, *Schiften aus dem Nachlass. Mit weiteren Materialien und Dokumenten*, edited by Jürgen Scheele, 155–86, Baden-Baden: Tectum.

Grünberg, Carl 1911a, 'Sozialdemokratie', in *Wörterbuch der Volkswirtschaft. Band 2*, edited by Ludwig Elster, third edition, Jena: Fischer, pp. 799–827.

Grünberg, Carl 1911b, 'Sozialistische Ideen und Lehren', in *Wörterbuch der Volkswirtschaft. Band 2*, edited by Ludwig Elster, third edition, Jena: Fischer, pp. 876–9.

Grünberg, Carl 1932, 'Internationale: Die Erste Internationale (Internationale Arbeiterassociation – IAA)', in *Wörterbuch der Volkswirtschaft. Zweiter Band*, edited by Ludwig Elster, fourth edition, Jena: Fischer, pp. 430–2.

Grünberg, Carl and Henryk Grossmann 1931, 'Christlicher und religiöser Sozialismus', in *Wörterbuch der Volkswirtschaft. Erster Band*, edited by Ludwig Elster, fourth edition, Jena: Fischer, pp. 538–59.

Grünberg, Carl and Henryk Grossmann 1933, 'Sozialdemokratische und kommunistische Parteien', in *Wörterbuch der Volkswirtschaft. Band 3*, edited by Ludwig Elster, fourth edition, Jena: Fischer, pp. 238–57.

Gumperz, Julian 1931, *Die Agrarkrise in den Vereinigten Staaten*, Leipzig: Buske.
Gurland, Arkadij 1930, 'Absatz und Verwertung im Kapitalismus: Zur neueren Diskussion des Zusammenbruchsproblems', *Klassenkampf*, 4, 3: 75–83.
Guyot, Yves 1894 [1893], *The Tyranny of Socialism*, London: Swan Sonnenschein.
Haberler, Gottfried 1946 [1937], *Prosperity and Depression*, third edition, Lake Success, NY: United Nations.
Halévy, Élie 1933, *Sismondi*, Paris: Alcan.
Halévy, Élie 1937, *A History of the English People. Volume 2: Economic Life*, Harmondsworth: Penguin.
Harrod, Roy Forbes 1937, 'Studies in the Theory of Economic Expansion', *Zeitschrift fur Nationalökonomie*, 8, 4: 494–8.
Hasbach, Wilhelm 1891, *Untersuchungen über Adam Smith*, Leipzig: Duncker.
Hauser, Henri 1927, *Les débuts du capitalisme*, Paris: Alcan.
Hauser, Henri and Augustin Renaudet 1929, *Les débuts de l'âge moderne: la renaissance et la réforme*, Paris: Alcan.
Hawtrey, Ralph George 1923, *Currency and Credit*, second edition, London: Longmans, Green.
Hawtrey, Ralph George 1928, *Trade and Credit*, London: Longmans, Green.
Hayek, Friedrich August 1931, *Preise und Produktion*, Wien: Springer.
Hayek, Friedrich August 1933 [1929], *Monetary Theory and the Trade Cycle*, New York: Harcourt, Brace.
Hayek, Friedrich August 1941a, 'The Counter-revolution of Science', *Economica*, 8: 30, May: 119–50.
Hayek, Friedrich August 1941b, 'The Counter-revolution of Science', *Economica*, 8: 31, August: 281–320.
Haynes, Mike 2002, *Russia: Class and Power 1917–2000*, London: Bookmarks.
Hegel, Georg Wilhelm Friedrich 1910, *Phenomenology of Mind. Volume 1*, translated by J.B. Baillie, London: Swan Sonnenschein.
Hegel, Georg Wilhelm Friedrich 1914 [1837], *Lectures on the Philosophy of History*, translated by J. Sibree, London: Bell.
Hegel, Georg Wilhelm Friedrich 1991 [1817], *The Encyclopaedia Logic: Part 1 of the Encyclopaedia of Philosophical Sciences*, translated by T.F. Geraets, W.A. Suchting and H.S. Harris, Indianapolis: Hackett.
Hegel, Georg Wilhelm Friedrich 2004 [1830], *Hegel's Philosophy of Nature: Being Part Two of the Encyclopaedia of the Philosophical Sciences*, translated by Arnold V. Miller, Oxford: Oxford University Press.
Hegel, Georg Wilhelm Friedrich 2008 [1821], *Outlines of the Philosophy of Right*, translated by T.M. Knox, Oxford: Oxford University Press.
Heimann, Eduard, 1922, *Mehrwert und Gemeinwirtschaft*, Berlin: Engelmann.
Heimann, Eduard, 1931, 'Karl Marx' Bedeutung für die Entwicklung der Nationalökonomie', *Kapitalismus und Sozialismus*, Potsdam: Protte.

Heimann, Eduard, 1932, *Sozialistische Wirtschafts- und arbeitsordnung*, Potsdam: Protte.

Herkner, Heinrich 1894, *Die Arbeiterfrage: Eine Einfuhrung*, Berlin: Guttentag.

Herkner, Heinrich 1921 [1894], *Die Arbeiterfrage: Eine Einführung. Band 2*, seventh edition, Berlin: de Gruyter.

Hessen, Boris 2009 [1931], 'The Social and Economic Roots of Newton's *Principia*', translated by Phillipa Shimrat, in *The Social and Economic Roots of the Scientific Revolution: Texts by Boris Hessen and Henryk Grossmann*, edited by Gideon Freudenthal and Peter Mclaughlin, Dordrecht: Springer, pp. 41–101.

Hicks, John Richard 1980 [1933], 'Equilibrium and the Trade Cycle', *Economic Inquiry*, 18, 4, October: 523–34.

Hicks, John Richard 1934, 'A Reconsideration of Value. Part 1', *Economica*, new series 1, 1: 52–76.

Hicks, John Richard 1939, *Value and Capital: An Inquiry into Some Fundamental Principles of Economic Theory*, Oxford: Clarendon.

Hilferding, Rudolf 1912a, 'Aus der Vorgeschichte der Marxschen Ökonomie: 3 Richard Jones', *Neue Zeit*, 30, 1 (10): 343–54.

Hilferding, Rudolf 1912b, Review of Ludwig Mises, *Theorie des Geldes und des Umlaufsmittel*, *Neue Zeit*, 30, 2 (52), 27 September: 1024–7.

Hilferding, Rudolf 1927, *Die Aufgaben der Sozialdemokratie in der Republik*, Berlin: Vorstand der Sozialdemokratischen Partei Deutschlands, http://library.fes.de/prodok/fa-59843.pdf, accessed 4 February 2012.

Hilferding, Rudolf 1949 [1904], 'Böhm-Bawerk's Criticism of Marx', translated by Eden Paul and Cedar Paul, in Eugen von Böhm-Bawerk and Rudolf Hilferding, *Karl Marx and the Close of his System* and *Böhm-Bawerk's Criticism of Marx*, edited by Paul Sweezy, New York: Kelley, pp. 121–96.

Hilferding, Rudolf 1981 [1910], *Finance Capital: A Study of the Latest Phase of Capitalist Development*, translated by Morris Watnick and Sam Gordon, London: Routledge & Kegan Paul.

Hillquit, Morris 1909, *Socialism in Theory and Practice*, New York: Macmillan.

Hobson, John Atkinson 1894, *The Evolution of Modern Capitalism*, London: Walter Scott.

Hobson, John Atkinson 1911, *An Economic Interpretation of Investment*, London: The Financial Review of Reviews.

Hobson, Oscar Rudolph and W. Manning Dacey 1937, 'The Function of Foreign Lending', 9th Congress of the International Chamber of Commerce, Berlin, Document number 3, Paris: Lahure.

Hodgskin, Thomas 1825, *Labour Defended against the Claims of Capital*, London: Knight and Lacey.

Hodgskin, Thomas 1827, *Popular Political Economy*, London: Tait.

Holbach, Paul-Henri Thiry d' 1773a, *Système Social. Tome Premier*, London [actually Amsterdam].

Holbach, Paul-Henri Thiry d' 1773b, *Système Social. Tome troisième*, London [actually Amsterdam].

Homan, Paul T. 1928, *Contemporary Economic Thought*, New York: Harper.

Honegger, Hans 1936, 'Väterliche Gewalt und Familie', *Neue Zürcher Zeitung* 116, 28 June: 4.

Hook, Sidney 1936, *From Hegel to Marx: Studies in the Intellectual Development of Karl Marx*, London: Gollancz.

Horkheimer, Max 1933, 'Zum Problem der Voraussage in den Sozialwissenschaften', *Zeitschrift für Sozialforschung*, 2, 3: 407–12.

Horkheimer, Max 1936a, Letter to Henryk Grossman, 9 September, VI 9, Max-Horkheimer-Archiv, Frankfurt am Main, p. 349.

Horkheimer, Max (ed.) 1936b, *Studien über Autorität und Familie: Forschungsberichte aus dem Institut für Sozialforschung*, Paris: Alcan.

Horkheimer, Max 1943, Letter to Leo Löwenthal, 21 January, VI 16, Max-Horkheimer-Archiv, Frankfurt am Main, p. 105.

Horkheimer, Max 1993a [1935], 'On the Problem of Truth', in Max Horkheimer, *Between Philosophy and Social Science: Selected Early Writings*, Cambridge, MA: MIT Press, pp. 177–218.

Horkheimer, Max 1993b [1933], 'Materialism and Morality', in Max Horkheimer, *Between Philosophy and Social Science: Selected Early Writings*, Cambridge, MA: MIT Press, pp. 15–48.

Horkheimer, Max 1993c [1936], 'Egoism and the Freedom Movements: On the Anthropology of the Bourgeois Era', in Max Horkheimer, *Between Philosophy and Social Science: Selected Early Writings*, Cambridge, MA: MIT Press, pp. 49–110.

Horkheimer, Max 1995a, *Gesammelte Schiften Band 15: Briefwechsel 1913–1936*, Frankfurt am Main: Fischer.

Horkheimer, Max 1995b, *Gesammelte Schiften Band 16: Briefwechsel 1937–1940*, Frankfurt am Main: Fischer.

Horkheimer, Max 1995c [1936], Letter to Henryk Grossman, 12 October 1936, in Max Horkheimer *Gesammelte Schiften. Band 15, Briefwechsel 1913–1936*, Frankfurt am Main: Fischer, p. 660.

Horkheimer, Max 1996a, *Gesammelte Schiften Band 17: Briefwechsel 1941–1948*, Frankfurt am Main: Fischer.

Horkheimer, Max 1996b [1943], Letter to Friedrich Pollock, 9 June 1943, in Max Horkheimer, *Gesammelte Schiften. Band 17, Briefwechsel 1941–1948*, Frankfurt am Main: Fischer, pp. 453–4.

Horkheimer, Max 2002 [1937], 'The Latest Attack on Metaphysics', in Max Horkheimer, *Critical Theory: Selected Essays*, New York: Continuum, pp. 132–87.

Horkheimer, Max 2005 [1934], 'On Bergson's Metaphysics of Time', *Radical Philosophy*, 131, May/June: 9–19.

Horkheimer, Max and Theodor Adorno 1985 [written 1939], 'Diskussion über die Differenz zwischen Positivismus and materialistischer Dialektik', in Max Horkheimer, *Gesammelte Schiften. Band 12, Nachgelassene Schriften 1931–1949*, Frankfurt am Main: Fischer, p. 438.

Horkheimer, Max and Samuel H. Flowerman (eds) 1950, *Studies in Prejudice*, series of five books, American Jewish Committee, http://www.ajcarchives.org/main.php?GroupingId=1380, accessed 10 September 2018.

Husserl, Edmund 2001 [1900/01], *Logical Investigations. Band 1*, translated by J.N. Findlay, London: Routledge.

Hume, David 1889 [1742], *Essays, Moral, Political, and Literary. Volume 1*, London: Longmans, Green.

Hume, David 1906 [1752], *Hume's Political Discourses*, London: Walter Scott.

Hyndman, Henry 1921 [1896, written 1894], *The Economics of Socialism*, Boston: Small, Maynard & Company.

Ibn Khaldun 1967 [written 1377], *The Muqaddimah: An Introduction to History*, three volumes, translated by Franz Rosenthal, second edition, New Haven, NJ: Princeton University Press.

Ingram, John Kells 1915 [1888], *A History of Political Economy*, London: Black.

International Institute of Social Research, American Branch [probably 1934], *International Institute of Social Research: A Short Description of its History and Aims*, Columbia University Archives, New York.

Jaurès, Jean 1891, *De primis socialismi germanici lineamentis apud Lutherum, Kant, Fichte et Hegel*, Toulouse: Chauvin.

Jaurès, Jean 1924, *Histoire socialiste de la révolution française. Tome 7*, revised by A. Mathiez, Paris: Librairie de l'Humanité.

Jessen, Jens 1933, 'Sozialistische Ideen und Lehren (II National Sozialismus)', in *Wörterbuch der Volkswirtschaft. Band 3*, edited by Ludwig Elster, fourth edition, Jena: Fischer, pp. 341–59.

Jevons, William Stanley 1879 [1871], *The Theory of Political Economy*, fifth edition, London: Kelley.

Jones, Richard 1831, *Essay on the Distribution of Wealth*, London: John Murray.

Jones, Richard 1833a, 'An Introductory Lecture on Political Economy', in Richard Jones, *An Introductory Lecture on Political Economy to Which Is Added a Syllabus of a Course of Lectures on the Wages of Labor*, London: John Murray, pp. 1–42.

Jones, Richard 1833b, 'A Syllabus of a Course of Lectures on the Wages of Labor', in Richard Jones, *An Introductory Lecture on Political Economy to Which Is Added a Syllabus of a Course of Lectures on the Wages of Labor*, London: John Murray, pp. 43–59.

Jones, Richard 1859 [1852], *Textbook of Lectures on the Political Economy of Nations*, in Richard Jones, *Literary Remains Consisting of Lectures and Tracts on Political Economy, of the Late Rev. Richard Jones*, London: John Murray, pp. 339–537.

Kant, Immanuel 2009 [1755], *Universal Natural History and Theory of the Heavens or an Essay on the Constitution and the Mechanical Origin of the Entire Structure of the Universe Based on Newtonian Principles*, translated by Ian C. Johnston, Arlington, VA: Richer Resources Publications.

Kautsky, Karl 1886, '*Das Elend der Philosophie* und *Das Kapital*', *Neue Zeit*, 4 (1, 2, 3, 4): 7–19, 49–58, 117–29, 157–65.

Kautsky, Karl 1897, 'Vorwort', in Karl Marx, *Zur Kritik der Politischen Oekonomie*, Stuttgart: J.H.W. Dietz.

Kautsky, Karl 1899a, 'Bernstein über die Wertheorie und die Klassen', *Neue Zeit*, 17, 2 (29), 5 April: 68–81.

Kautsky, Karl 1899b, *Bernstein und das sozialdemokratische Programm: Eine Antikritik*, Dietz: Stuttgart.

Kautsky, Karl 1899c, Letter, *Petite Republique*, 28 September.

Kautsky, Karl 1901, 'Der sozialistischen Kongresse und der sozialistische Minister', *Neue Zeit*, 19, 1 (2): 36–44.

Kautsky, Karl 1902, 'Krisentheorien', *Neue Zeit*, 20, 2 (2, 3, 4, 5): 37–47, 76–81, 110–18, 133–43.

Kautsky, Karl 1903 [1902], *The Social Revolution*, translated by A.B. Askew, Clerkenwell Green: Twentieth Century Press.

Kautsky, Karl 1906, *Ethics and the Materialist Conception of History*, translated by John B. Askew, Chicago: Kerr.

Kautsky, Karl 1908a [1889], *Die Klassengegensätze im Zeitalter der französischen Revolution*, Stuttgart: Dietz.

Kautsky, Karl 1908b, 'Verelendung und Zusammenbruch: Die neuste Phase des Revisionismus', *Neue Zeit*, 26, 2 (42, 43): 540–51 and 607–12.

Kautsky, Karl 1909, *The Road to Power*, translated by A.M. Simons, Chicago: Bloch.

Kautsky, Karl 1911a [1901], *Handelspolitik und Sozialdemokratie*, Berlin: Buchhandlung Vorwärts.

Kautsky, Karl 1911b, 'Finance-Capital and Crises', *Marxists Internet Archive*, www.marxists.org/archive/kautsky/1911/xx/finance.htm, accessed 4 February 2012.

Kautsky, Karl 1914, *Der politische Massenstreik*, Berlin: Buchhandlung Vorwärts Paul Singer.

Kautsky, Karl (ed.) 1919 [1908], *Die Historische Leistung von Karl Marx: Zum 25. Todestag des Meisters*, Berlin: Buchhandlung Vorwärts.

Kautsky, Karl 1921 [1887], *Karl Marx' Ökonomische Lehren*, Stuttgart: Dietz.

Kautsky, Karl 1925a [1887], *The Economic Doctrines of Karl Marx*, translated by H.J. Stenning, London: Black.

Kautsky, Karl 1925b [1889], *Foundations of Christianity: A Study in Christian Origins*, translated by Henry F. Mins, New York: International Publishers.

Kautsky, Karl 1926, 'Vorwort', in Karl Marx, *Das Kapital: Kritik der politischen Ökonomie. 2. Der Zirkulationsprozeß des Kapitals*, Berlin: Dietz.

Kautsky, Karl 1927 [1888], *Thomas More and his Utopia*, London: Black.

Kautsky, Karl 1988a [1899], *The Agrarian Question*, two volumes, translated by Pete Burgess, London: Zwan.

Kautsky, Karl 1988b [1927], *The Materialist Conception of History*, translated by Raymond Meyer and John H. Kautsky, abridged, annotated and introduced by John H. Kautsky, New Haven, CT: Yale University Press.

Kautz, Julius 1860, *Theorie und geschichte der national-oekonomik. Zweite Teil: Literatur-Geschichte der National Oekonomik*, Wien: Gerold.

Kleinwächter, Friedrich 1885, *Grundlagen der wissenschaftlichen Sozialismus*, Innsbruck: Wagner.

Kliman, Andrew 2007, *Reclaiming Marx's 'Capital': A Refutation of the Myth of Inconsistency*, Lanham, MD: Lexington Books.

Kliman, Andrew 2012, *The Failure of Capitalist Production: Underlying Causes of the Great Recession*, London: Pluto.

Knapp, Georg Friedrich 1924 [1895], *The State Theory of Money*, London: Macmillan.

Knies, Karl 1885, *Das Geld*, second edition, Berlin: Weidmannsche Buchhandlung.

Knight, Charles 1832 [1831], *The Rights of Industry: 1 Capital and Labour*, Philadelphia: Carey & Hart.

Knight, Frank Hyneman 1931, 'Statik and Dynamik', *Zeitschrift für Nationalökonomie*, 2, 1: 1–26.

Knight, Frank Hyneman 1940, Review of *A History of Economic Thought* by Erich Roll, *American Journal of Sociology*, 46, 1, July: 104–5.

Koepp, Carl 1911, *Das Verhältnis der Mehrwerttheorien von Karl Marx and Thomas Hodgskin*, Wien: Konegen.

Komitet organizacyjny żydowskiej Partyi socyalno-demokraticycznej w Galicyi 1905, *Czego chcemy?* Kraków.

Kötschke, Rudolf 1923, *Grundzüge der deutschen Wirtschaftsgeschichte bis zum 17. Jahrhundert*, Leipzig: Teubner.

Korsch, Karl 1922, *Kernpunkte der materialistischen Geschichtsauffassung: Eine quellenmäßige Darstellung*, Berlin: VIVA Vereinigung internationaler Verlags-Anstalten.

Korsch, Karl 1929, *Die materialistische Geschichtsauffassung: Eine Auseinandersetzung mit Karl Kautsky*, Leipzig: Hirschfeld.

Korsch, Karl 1970 [1923], 'Marxism and Philosophy', in *Marxism and Philosophy*, translated by Fred Halliday, New York: Monthly Review Press, pp. 29–85.

Korsch, Karl 1971 [1933], 'Some Fundamental Presuppositions for a Materialist Discussion of Crisis Theory', translated by Karl-Heinz Otto and Andrew Giles-Peters, in Karl Korsch, *Karl Korsch: Revolutionary Theory*, Austin: University of Texas Press, pp. 181–6.

Kowalik, Tadeusz 2014 [1971], *Rosa Luxemburg: Theory of Accumulation and Imperialism*, translated and edited by Jan Toporowski and Hanna Szymborska, Houndsmills: Palgrave Macmillan.

Krynska, Salomea 1908, *Entwicklung und Fortschritt nach Condorcet und A. Comte*, Berne: Scheitlin, Spring.

Kuczynski, Jürgen 1938, *Hunger and Work*, London: Lawrence & Wishart.

Kuhn, Rick 2006, 'Introduction to Henryk Grossman's Critique of Franz Borkenau and Max Weber', *Journal of Classical Sociology*, 6, 2: 195–200.

Kuhn, Rick 2007, *Henryk Grossman and the Recovery of Marxism*, Chicago: University of Illinois Press.

Kuhn, Rick 2013, 'Introduction to "The Change in the Original Plan for Marx's *Capital* and Its Causes"', *Historical Materialism*, 21, 3: 117–37.

Kuhn, Rick 2014, 'Introduction', in Henryk Grossman, *Fifty Years of Struggle over Marxism: 1883–1932*, Carlton South: Socialist Alternative, pp. 1–15.

Kuhn, Rick 2015, 'Introduction', in Henryk Grossman, *Marx, Classical Political Economy and the Problem of Dynamics*, Carlton South: Socialist Alternative, pp. 1–22.

Kuhn, Rick 2016a, 'Sismondi, Marx and Grossman: Method, Contradictions of the Commodity and Crisis', *Marxism 21*, 13, 1, Spring: 262–82.

Kuhn, Rick 2016b, 'Henryk Grossman and Critical Theory', *History of the Human Sciences*, 29, 2: 42–59.

Kuhn, Rick 2016c, 'Introduction to Henryk Grossman, "The Value-Price Transformation in Marx and the Problem of Crisis"', *Historical Materialism*, 24, 1: 91–103.

Kunze, Walter 1926, *Der Aufbau des Phönix-Konzerns*, Nassau: Dillenburg.

Kuznets, Simon 1935, 'Relations between Capital Goods and Finished Products in the Business Cycle', in Asher Achinstein et al., *Economic Essays in Honour of Wesley Clair Mitchell*, New York: Columbia University Press, pp. 209–67.

l.d. 1936, 'Kapitalismus und mechanistische Naturwissenschaft', *Der Kampf: Internationale Revue* (Prag), series 2, 3: 255–8.

Labriola, Antonio 1910 [1908], *Karl Marx l'économiste, le socialiste*, Paris: Rivière.

Labriola, Arturo 1907, *La speculazione economica*, Napoli: Società Editrice Partenopea.

Labriola, Arturo 1924, *La dittatura della borghesia e la decadenza della società capitalistica*, Napoli: Morano.

Labriola, Arturo 1926 [1908], *Studio su Marx*, second edition, Napoli: Morano.

Lachmann, Ludwig M. 1937, 'Preiserwartungen and intertemporales Gleichgewicht', *Zeitschrift fur Nationalokonomie*, 8, 1: 33–46.

Lafargue, Paul 1909, *Le déterminisme économique de Karl Marx: recherches sur l'origine et l'évolution des idées de Justice, du Bien, de l'Ame et de Dieu*, Paris: Giard et Brière.

Lange, Oskar 1933, 'Die allgemeine Interdependenz der Wirtschaftgrössen und die Isoliermethode', *Zeitschrift fur Nationalökonomie*, 4, 1: 52–78.

Laplace, Pierre Simon 1830 [1796], *The System of the World*, two volumes, translated by Henry H. Harte, Dublin: Longman, Rees, Orme, Brown and Green.

Lasson, Georg 1920 [1905], 'Vorwort', in Georg Wilhelm Friedrich Hegel, *Enzyklopädie der philosophischen Wissenschaften im Grundrisse*, second edition, Leipzig: Meiner.

Lauderdale, James 1804, *An Inquiry into the Nature and Origin of Public Wealth*, Edinburgh: Constable.

Laurat, Lucien 1932, *Un système qui sombre*, Paris: l'Églantine.

Lederer, Emil 1922, *Grundzügen der ökonomischen Theorie*, Tübingen: Mohr (Siebeck).

Lederer, Emil 1925, 'Konjunktur und Krisen', *Grundriß der Sozialökonomie*, IV, i, Tübingen: Mohr (Siebeck), pp. 355–413.

Lefebvre des Noëttes, Richard 1931 [1924], *L'attelage, le cheval de selle à travers les âges, contribution à l'histoire de l'esclavage*, two volumes, Paris: Picard.

Leibniz, Gottfried Wilhelm 1989, *Against Barbaric Physics: Toward a Philosophy of What There Actually Is and Against the Revival of the Qualities of the Scholastics and Chimerical Intelligences*, in Gottfried Wilhelm Leibnitz, *Philosophical Essays*, edited and translated by Roger Ariew and Daniel Garber, Indianapolis: Hackett, pp. 312–20.

Lenin, N. and G. Sinowjew 1921 [1918], *Gegen den Strom. Aufsätze aus den Jahren 1914–16*, Hamburg: Verlag der Kommunistischen Internationale.

Lenin, Vladimir Ilyich 1960a [1897], *A Characterisation of Economic Romanticism (Sismondi and our Native Sismondists)*, in Vladimir Ilych Lenin, *Collected Works. Volume 2*, Moscow: Progress, pp. 129–265.

Lenin, Vladimir Ilyich 1960b [1899], *The Development of Capitalism in Russia*, in Vladimir Ilych Lenin, *Collected Works. Volume 3*, Moscow: Progress.

Lenin, Vladimir Ilyich 1962a [1905], *Two Tactics of Social-Democracy in the Democratic Revolution*, in Vladimir Ilych Lenin, *Collected Works. Volume 9*, Moscow: Progress, pp. 15–140.

Lenin, Vladimir Ilyich 1962b [1909], *Materialism and Empiriocriticism*, in Vladimir Ilych Lenin, *Collected Works. Volume 22*, Moscow: Progress, pp. 17–362.

Lenin, Vladimir Ilyich 1964a [1915], 'The Collapse of the Second International', in Vladimir Ilych Lenin, *Collected Works. Volume 21*, Moscow: Progress, pp. 205–59.

Lenin, Vladimir Ilyich 1964b [1916], 'The Junius Pamphlet', in Vladimir Ilych Lenin, *Collected Works. Volume 22*, Moscow: Progress, pp. 306–19.

Lenin, Vladimir Ilyich 1964c [1917], *Imperialism, the Highest Stage of Capitalism: A Popular Outline*, in Vladimir Ilych Lenin, *Collected Works. Volume 22*, Moscow: Progress, pp. 185–304.

Lenin, Vladimir Ilyich 1964d [1916], 'The Discussion on Self-determination Summed up', in Vladimir Ilych Lenin, *Collected Works. Volume 22*, Moscow: Progress, pp. 320–60.

Lenin, Vladimir Ilyich 1964e [1917], *Letters from Afar*, in Vladimir Ilyich Lenin, *Collected Works. Volume 23*, Moscow: Progress, pp. 297–342.

Lenin, Vladimir Ilyich 1964f [1917], 'The Chain is no Stronger than its Weakest Link', in Vladimir Ilyich Lenin, *Collected Works. Volume 24*, Moscow: Progress, pp. 519–21.

Lenin, Vladimir Ilyich 1964g [1918], *The State and Revolution*, in Vladimir Ilyich Lenin, *Collected Works. Volume 25*, Moscow: Progress, pp. 385–498.

Leroy, Louis-Modeste 1923, *Auguste Walras, sa vie, son œuvre*, Paris: Pichon et Durand-Auzias.

Lessing, Gotthold Ephraim 1883 [1780], *The Education of the Human Species*, translated by Frederic W. Robertson, London: Kegan Paul, Trench and Company.

Lewis, Cleona, assisted by K.T. Schotterbeck 1938, *America's Stake in International Investments*, Washington, D.C.: Brookings Institution.

Liebknecht, Karl 1919, 'Trotz alledem', *Rote Fahne*, 15 January: 1–2.

Liebknecht, Wilhelm 1963, 'Letter to Frederick Engels, 20 January 1868', in *Wilhelm Liebknecht: Briefwechsel mit Karl Marx und Friedrich Engels*, Hague: Mouton.

Liefmann, Robert 1923, *Beteiligung- und Finanzierungsgesellschaften: eine Studie über den modernen Effektenkapitalismus in Deutschland, den Vereinigten Staaten, der Schweiz, England, Frankreich und Belgien*, fourth edition, Jena: Fischer.

Lindemann, Hugo 1906a [1897], *Städteverwaltung und Munizipal-Sozialismus in England*, Stuttgart: Dietz.

Lindemann, Hugo 1906b [1901], *Deutsche Städteverwaltung: ihre Aufgaben auf den Gebieten der Volkshygiene*, des Städtebaus und des Wohnungswesens, Stuttgart: Dietz.

Lippmann, Walter 1947, *The Cold War: A Study in US Foreign Policy*, New York: Harper.

Locke, John 1924 [1691], *Some Considerations on the Lowering of Interest and Raising the Value of Money*, in *The Works of John Locke in Nine Volumes. Volume 4*, London: Rivington et al., pp. 1–116.

Löwenthal, Leo 1933 'Zugtier und Sklaverei: Zum Buch Lefebvre des Noettes, *L'attelage. Le cheval de selle à travers les âges*', *Zeitschrift für Sozialforschung*, 2, 2: 198–212.

Löwenthal, Leo 1939, Letter to Henryk Grossman, 30 July 1939, VI 9, Max-Horkheimer-Archive, p. 286.

Löwenthal, Leo 1996 [1941], Letter to Max Horkheimer, 26 November, in Max Horkheimer, *Gesammelte Schiften. Band 17, Briefwechsel 1941–1948*, Frankfurt am Main: Fischer, pp. 220–3.

Lucan 1962 [written 1961–5], *The Civil War. Books I–X*, with a translation by J.D. Duff, London: Heinemann.

Lukács, Georg 1970 [1924], *Lenin: A Study on the Unity of His Thought*, translated by Nicholas Jacobs, London: New Left Books.

Lukács, Georg 1971 [1923], *History and Class Consciousness: Studies in Marxist Dialectics*, translated by Rodney Livingstone, London: Merlin.

Luxemburg, Rosa 1913, *Die Akkumulation des Kapitals: Ein Beitrag zur ökonomischen Erklärung des Imperialismus*, Berlin: Buchhandlung Vorwärts Paul Singer.

Luxemburg, Rosa 1921 [written 1915], *Die Akkumulation des Kapitals oder Was die Epigonen aus der Marxschen Theorie gemacht haben: Eine Antikritik*, Leipzig: Franke.

Luxemburg, Rosa 1925a, *Gegen Reformismus*, introduced by Paul Frölich, Berlin: Vereinigung Internationaler Verlags-Anstalten.

Luxemburg, Rosa 1925b, *Einführung in die Nationalökonomie*, Berlin: Laub.

Luxemburg, Rosa 1951 [1913], *The Accumulation of Capital*, translated by Agnes Schwarzschild, London: Routledge and Kegan Paul.

Luxemburg, Rosa 1972 [1921, written 1915], *The Accumulation of Capital: An Anti-Critique*, in Rosa Luxemburg, *The Accumulation of Capital: An Anti-Critique* and Nikolai Bukharin, *Imperialism and the Accumulation of Capital*, translated by Rudolf Wichmann, edited by Kenneth Tarbuck, New York: Monthly Review Press, pp. 45–150.

Luxemburg, Rosa 2008a [1899, 1908], *Social Reform or Revolution*, translated by Integer, in Rosa Luxemburg, *The Essential Rosa Luxemburg: Reform or Revolution and The Mass Strike*, Chicago: Haymarket, pp. 41–104.

Luxemburg, Rosa 2008b [1907], 'The Mass Strike', in Rosa Luxemburg, *The Essential Rosa Luxemburg: Reform or Revolution and The Mass Strike*, Chicago: Haymarket, pp. 111–81.

MacDonald, James Ramsay 1905, *Socialism and Society*, London: Independent Labour Party.

MacDonald, James Ramsay 1912, *Sozialismus und Regierung*, with a foreword by Eduard Bernstein, Jena: Diederichs.

Maito, Esteban Ezequiel 2015, 'The Historical Transience of Capital: The Downward Trend in the Rate of Profit Since the XIX Century', https://www.academia.edu/6849268/Maito_Esteban_Ezequiel_-_The_historical_transience_of_capital_The_downward_trend_in_the_rate_of_profit_since_XIX_century_final_draft_, accessed 13 January 2016.

Majewski, Erazm 1914, *Kapitał: rozbiór podstawowych zjawisk i pojęć gospodarczych. Nauka o cywilizacyi. Tom 3*, Warszawa: Wende.

Makarov, Nikolai Pavlovich 1920, *Krestianskoe khozyaistvo i ego evolyutsiya*, Moscow: Zheludkovoi.

Malthus, Robert 1836 [1820], *Principles of Political Economy, Considered with a View to Their Practical Application*, London: Pickering.

Mannheim, Karl 1936 [1929], *Ideology and Utopia: An Introduction to the Sociology of Knowledge*, translated by Louis Wirth and Edward Shils, London: Routledge & Kegan Paul.

Marcuse, Herbert 2009 [1937], 'The Affirmative Character of Culture', in Herbert Marcuse, *Negations: Essays in Critical Theory*, London: Mayfly, pp. 65–98, 212–16.

Marcuse, Herbert 1941, *Reason and Revolution: Hegel and the Rise of Social Theory*, New York: Oxford University Press.

Marcuse, Herbert 1972 [1932], *Studies in Critical Philosophy*, translated by Joris de Bres, London: NLB.

Marshall, Alfred 1890, *Principles of Economics*, London: Macmillan.

Martin, Robert F. 1939, *National Income in the United States 1799–1938*, New York: National Industrial Conference Board Studies, 241.

Marx, Karl 1910a [written 1861–3], *Theorien über den Mehrwert: Aus dem nachgelassenen Manuskript 'Zur Kritik der politischen Ökonomie' von Karl Marx. Band 1*, edited by Karl Kautsky, Stuttgart: Dietz.

Marx, Karl 1910b [written 1861–3], *Theorien über den Mehrwert: Aus dem nachgelassenen Manuskript 'Zur Kritik der politischen Ökonomie' von Karl Marx. Band 2, Teil 1*, edited by Karl Kautsky, Stuttgart: Dietz.

Marx, Karl 1910c [written 1861–3], *Theorien über den Mehrwert: Aus dem nachgelassenen Manuskript 'Zur Kritik der politischen Ökonomie' von Karl Marx. Band 2, Teil 2*, edited by Karl Kautsky, Stuttgart: Dietz.

Marx, Karl 1910d [written 1861–3], *Theorien über den Mehrwert: Aus dem nachgelassenen Manuskript 'Zur Kritik der politischen Ökonomie' von Karl Marx. Band 3*, edited by Karl Kautsky, Stuttgart: Dietz.

Marx, Karl 1975a [written 1844], 'Comments on James Mill, *Éléments d'économie politique*', in Karl Marx and Frederick Engels, *Collected Works. Volume 3*, New York: International Publishers, pp. 211–34.

Marx, Karl 1975b, 'Economic and Philosophic Manuscripts of 1844', in Karl Marx and Frederick Engels, *Collected Works. Volume 6*, New York: International Publishers, pp. 229–346.

Marx, Karl 1975c [1842, 1927], 'The Philosophical Manifesto of the Historical School of Law', in Karl Marx and Frederick Engels, *Collected Works. Volume 1*, New York: International Publishers, pp. 203–10.

Marx, Karl 1975d [1844, written 1843], Letter to Arnold Ruge, March, May and September 1843, in Karl Marx and Frederick Engels, *Collected Works. Volume 3*, New York: International Publishers, pp. 141–5.

Marx, Karl 1976a [1847], *The Poverty of Philosophy: Answer to the Philosophy of Poverty by M. Proudhon*, in Karl Marx and Frederick Engels, *Collected Works. Volume 6*, New York: International Publishers, pp. 105–212.

Marx, Karl 1976b [1867], *Capital: A Critique of Political Economy. Volume 1*, translated by Ben Fowkes, Harmondsworth: Penguin.

Marx, Karl 1976c [written 1847], 'Theses on Feuerbach', in Karl Marx and Frederick Engels, *Collected Works. Volume 5*, New York: International Publishers, pp. 3–8.

Marx, Karl 1977 [1849, 1891], 'Wage Labour and Capital', in Karl Marx and Frederick Engels, *Collected Works. Volume 9*, New York: International Publishers, pp. 197–228.

Marx, Karl 1978a [1850], *The Class Struggles in France, 1848 to 1850*, in Karl Marx and Frederick Engels, *Collected Works. Volume 10*, New York: International Publishers, pp. 45–147.

Marx, Karl 1978b [1885], *Capital: A Critique of Political Economy. Volume 2*, translated by David Fernbach, Harmondsworth: Penguin.

Marx, Karl 1979a [1852], *The Eighteenth Brumaire of Louis Bonaparte*, in Karl Marx and

Frederick Engels, *Collected Works. Volume 11*, New York: International Publishers, pp. 99–197.

Marx, Karl 1979b [1853], 'The British Rule in India', in Karl Marx and Frederick Engels, *Collected Works. Volume 12*, New York: International Publishers, pp. 125–33.

Marx, Karl 1980 [1859], *Zur Kritik der politischen Ökonomie*, in Karl Marx and Friedrich Engels, *Marx-Engels-Gesamtausgabe, Ökonomische Manuskripte und Schriften. Abteilung 2, Band 2*, Berlin: Dietz, pp. 95–245.

Marx, Karl 1981a [1932, written 1845], 'Aus David Ricardo: *Des principes de l'économie politique et l'impôt*', in Karl Marx and Friedrich Engels, *Marx-Engels-Gesamtausgabe, Exzerpte und Notizen, 1843 bis Januar 1845. Vierte Abteilung, Band 2*, Berlin: Dietz: pp. 392–427.

Marx, Karl 1981b, *Capital: A Critique of Political Economy. Volume 3*, translated by David Fernbach, Harmondsworth: Penguin.

Marx, Karl 1982a, Letter to Pavel Vasilyevich Annenkov, 28 December 1846, in Karl Marx and Frederick Engels, *Collected Works. Volume 38*, New York: International Publishers, pp. 95–106.

Marx, Karl 1982b, Letter to Friedrich Engels, 7 January 1851, in Karl Marx and Frederick Engels, *Collected Works. Volume 38*, New York: International Publishers, pp. 258–62.

Marx, Karl 1984a [14 June 1862] 'English Humanity and America', in Karl Marx and Frederick Engels, *Collected Works. Volume 41*, New York: International Publishers, pp. 209–12.

Marx, Karl 1984b [11 January 1862], 'English Public Opinion', in Karl Marx and Frederick Engels, *Collected Works. Volume 41*, New York: International Publishers, pp. 137–42.

Marx, Karl 1984c [18 September 1861], 'The American Question in England', in Karl Marx and Frederick Engels, *Collected Works. Volume 41*, New York: International Publishers, pp. 7–16.

Marx, Karl 1984d [20 October 1861], 'The North American Civil War', in Karl Marx and Frederick Engels, *Collected Works. Volume 41*, New York: International Publishers, pp. 32–42.

Marx, Karl 1984e, 'American Affairs', in Karl Marx and Frederick Engels, *Collected Works. Volume 41*, New York: International Publishers, pp. 178–81.

Marx, Karl 1984f, 'A Criticism of American Affairs', in Karl Marx and Frederick Engels, *Collected Works. Volume 41*, New York: International Publishers, pp. 226–9.

Marx, Karl 1985a, Letter to Ludwig Kugelmann, 28 December 1862, in Karl Marx and Frederick Engels, *Collected Works. Volume 41*, New York: International Publishers, pp. 435–7.

Marx, Karl 1985b [1865], 'On Proudhon' (Letter to J.B. Schweitzer 24 January 1865), in Karl Marx and Frederick Engels, *Collected Works. Volume 20*, New York: International Publishers, pp. 26–33.

Marx, Karl 1985c [1865], 'Value, Price and Profit', in Karl Marx and Frederick Engels, *Collected Works. Volume 20*, New York: International Publishers, pp. 101–49.
Marx, Karl 1985d, Letter to Frederick Engels, 6 July 1863, in Karl Marx and Frederick Engels, *Collected Works. Volume 41*, New York: International Publishers, pp. 483–7.
Marx, Karl 1985e, Letter to Frederick Engels, 15 August 1863, in Karl Marx and Frederick Engels, *Collected Works. Volume 41*, New York: International Publishers, pp. 488–91.
Marx, Karl 1986a [1871], *The Civil War in France*, in Karl Marx and Frederick Engels, *Collected Works. Volume 22*, New York: International Publishers, pp. 307–60.
Marx, Karl 1986b [1903, written 1857], 'Introduction', in Karl Marx and Frederick Engels, *Collected Works. Volume 28*, New York: International Publishers, pp. 17–48.
Marx, Karl 1986c [1939, written 1857–8], 'Outlines of the Critique of Political Economy (Rough Draft of 1857–1858) [First Instalment]', also known as *Grundrisse*, in Karl Marx and Frederick Engels, *Collected Works. Volume 28*, New York: International Publishers, pp. 49–537.
Marx, Karl 1987a [1859], *A Contribution to the Critique of Political Economy. Part One*, in Karl Marx and Frederick Engels, *Collected Works. Volume 29*, New York: International Publishers, pp. 257–417.
Marx, Karl 1987b [written 1868], Letter to Frederick Engels, 8 January 1868, in Karl Marx and Frederick Engels, *Collected Works. Volume 42*, New York: International Publishers, pp. 514–16.
Marx, Karl 1987c, Letter to Ludwig Kugelmann, 29 November 1864, in Karl Marx and Frederick Engels, *Collected Works. Volume 42*, New York: International Publishers, pp. 45–6.
Marx, Karl 1987d, Letter to Ludwig Kugelmann, 13 October 1866, in Karl Marx and Frederick Engels, *Collected Works. Volume 42*, New York: International Publishers, pp. 327–9.
Marx, Karl 1987d, Letter to Frederick Engels, 24 August 1867, in Karl Marx and Frederick Engels, *Collected Works. Volume 42*, New York: International Publishers, pp. 407–8.
Marx, Karl 1987e, Letter to Frederick Engels, 30 April 1868, in Karl Marx and Frederick Engels, *Collected Works. Volume 43*, New York: International Publishers, pp. 19–20.
Marx, Karl 1988a [1905–10], 'Economic Manuscript of 1861–63' [Notebooks I to VII], in Karl Marx and Frederick Engels, *Collected Works. Volume 30*, New York: International Publishers.
Marx, Karl 1988b, Letter to Ludwig Kugelmann, 11 July 1868, in Karl Marx and Frederick Engels, *Collected Works. Volume 43*, New York: International Publishers, pp. 67–70.
Marx, Karl 1989a [1875], *Critique of the Gotha Programme*, in Karl Marx and Frederick Engels, *Collected Works. Volume 24*, New York: International Publishers, pp. 75–100.
Marx, Karl 1989b [1905–10], 'Economic Manuscript of 1861–63' [Notebooks VII to XII], in Karl Marx and Frederick Engels, *Collected Works. Volume 31*, New York: International Publishers.

Marx, Karl 1989c [1905–10], 'Economic Manuscript of 1861–63' [Notebooks XII to XV], in Karl Marx and Frederick Engels, *Collected Works. Volume 32*, New York: International Publishers.

Marx, Karl 1991a [1890], *Das Kapital: Kritik der Politischen Ökonomie. Band 1*, Fourth Edition, in *Marx-Engels-Gesamtausgabe. Abteilung 2, Band 10*, Berlin: Akademie.

Marx, Karl 1991b [1905–10], 'Economic Manuscript of 1861–63' [Notebooks XV to XX], in Karl Marx and Frederick Engels, *Collected Works. Volume 33*, New York: International Publishers.

Marx, Karl 1994 [1905–10], 'Economic Manuscript of 1861–63' [Notebooks XX to XXIII], in Karl Marx and Frederick Engels, *Collected Works. Volume 34*, New York: International Publishers.

Marx, Karl and Friedrich Engels 1927–41, *Historisch-kritische Gesamtausgabe*, Frankfurt am Main and Berlin: Marx-Engels-Archiv, Verlagsgenossenschaft ausländischer Arbeiter in der UdSSR and Marx-Engels-Verlag.

Marx, Karl and Friedrich Engels 1937, *The Civil War in the United States*, edited by Richard Enmale, New York: International Publishers.

Marx, Karl and Friedrich Engels 1976 [1848], *Manifesto of the Communist Party*, in Karl Marx and Frederick Engels, *Collected Works. Volume 6*, New York: International Publishers, pp. 477–519.

Marx, Karl and Friedrich Engels 1978, *Address of the Central Authority to the League, March 1850*, in Karl Marx and Frederick Engels, *Collected Works. Volume 10*, New York: International Publishers, pp. 277–87.

Masaryk, Tomáš Garrigue 1972 [1899], *Masaryk on Marx*, translated by Erazim V. Kohak, Lewisburg: Bucknell University Press.

Mattick, Paul 1931, 'Die Krise und ihre Ursachen. Einleitung zu einer Diskussion', *Chicagoer Arbeiterzeitung*, 1, 5, May: 4.

Mattick, Paul 1932, 'Die Bienen', in *Dreissig neue Erzähler des neuen Deutschland. Junge deutsche Prosa*, edited by Wieland Herzfelde, Berlin: Malik, pp. 205–14.

Mattick, Paul 1934a, Review of Sidney Hook, *Towards the Understanding of Karl Marx: A Revolutionary Interpretation*, New York: John Day, 1933, *Zeitschrift für Sozialforschung*, 2, 1: 101–2.

Mattick, Paul 1934b, 'Die Streikwelle', *Neue Deutsche Blätter*, 2, 1 and 2, 2, October–November and December: 35–45, 87–99.

Mattick, Paul 1934c, 'One Step Forward, Two Steps Backward. Critical Remarks on the Statement of Programmatic Orientation by the American Workers' Party', *Modern Monthly*, 8, 10, December: 623–8, 631 and 640.

Mattick, Paul 1934d, 'Die Kommunistische Wirtschaft', *Kampfsignal*, New York, 15 November.

Mattick, Paul 1935a, *The Inevitability of Communism: A Critique of Sidney Hook's Interpretation of Marx*, New York: Polemic Publishers.

Mattick, Paul 1935b, Review of H. Parker Willis and John M. Chapman, *The Economics of Inflation*, New York: Columbia University Press, 1935, *Freidenker*, September.
Mattick, Paul 1935c, Review of Lewis Corey, *The Decline of American Capitalism*, and John Strachey, *The Nature of Capitalist Crisis*, London: Gollancz, 1935, *Zeitschrift für Sozialforschung* 4, 3: 475–7.
Mattick, Paul 1937, 'Nature and Significance of "Overproduction"', *International Council Correspondence*, 5–6, June: 23–8.
Mattick, Paul 1969 [written 1936], *Arbeitslosigkeit und Arbeitslosenbewegung in den USA 1929–1935*, Frankfurt: Neue Kritik.
Mattick, Paul 1973 [1934], 'Zur Marx'schen Akkumulations- und Zusammenbruchstheorie', in Karl Korsch, Paul Mattick and Anton Pannekoek, *Zusammenbruchstheorie des Kapitalismus oder Revolutionäres Subject*, Berlin: Karin Kramer, pp. 47–70.
Maudit, Roger 1929, *Auguste Comte et la science économique*, Paris: Alcan.
Mayer, Hans 1932, 'Der Erkenntniswert der funktionellen Preis-theorien', in *Wert, Preis, Produktion, Geld und Kredit: Die Wirtschaftstheorie der Gegenwart. Band 2*, edited by Hans Mayer, Wien: Springer, pp. 147–239.
McCulloch, John Ramsay 1825, *Discourse on Political Economy*, Edinburgh: Constable.
Mehring, Franz 1898a, 'Sozialistische Selbstkritik', *Leipziger Volkszeitung*, 9 February.
Mehring, Franz 1898b, 'Das sozialistische Endziel', *Leipziger Volkszeitung*, 10 February.
Mehring, Franz 1898c, 'In Sachen Bernstein', *Leipziger Volkszeitung*, 10 March.
Mehring, Franz 1938 [1893], *The Lessing Legend*, translated by A.S. Grogan, New York: Critics Group Press.
Mehring, Franz 1913a [1897], *Geschichte der deutschen Sozialdemokratie. Band 1*, fifth edition, Stuttgart: Dietz.
Mehring, Franz 1913b [1897], *Geschichte der deutschen Sozialdemokratie. Band 2*, fifth edition, Stuttgart: Dietz.
Mehring, Franz 1920 [1902], *Aus dem literarischen Nachlass von Karl Marx and Friedrich Engels. Band 1*, third edition, Stuttgart: Dietz.
Menger, Carl 1985 [1883], *Investigations into the Method of the Social Sciences with Special Reference to Economics*, translated by Francis J. Nock, New York: New York University Press.
Mill, James 1808, *Commerce Defended*, London: Baldwin.
Mill, John Stuart 1900a [1848], *Principles of Political Economy*, London: Routledge.
Mill, John Stuart 1900b [1843], A *System of Logic Ratiocinative and Inductive*, eighth edition, New York: Harper.
Mirowski, Philip 1989, *More Heat than Light: Economics as Social Physics, Physics as Nature's Economics*, Cambridge: Cambridge University Press.
Mitchell, Margaret 1936, *Gone with the Wind*, New York: Macmillan.
Mitchell, Wesley Clair 1927, *Business Cycles: The Problem and its Setting*, New York: National Bureau of Economic Research.

Montesquieu, Charles de Secondat, Baron de 1873 [1748], *The Spirit of Laws. Volume 2*, London: Nourse and Vaillant.

Monthly Review 1936, (Midland Bank), May–June.

Moore, Henry Ludwell 1929, *Synthetic Economics*, New York: Macmillan.

Morgan, Lewis Henry 1877, *Ancient Society or, Researches in the Lines of Human Progress from Savagery, through Barbarism to Civilization*, Chicago: Kerr.

Moseley, Fred 2005, *Marx's Theory of Money: Modern Appraisals*, Houndmills: Palgrave Macmillan.

Moseley, Fred 2016, *Money and Totality: A Macro-Monetary Interpretation of Marx's Logic in Capital and the End of the 'Transformation Problem'*, Leiden: Brill.

Muckle, Friedrich 1920, *Die grossen Sozialisten. Band 1, Owen, Fourier, Proudhon*, Leipzig: Teubner.

Muhs, Karl 1931, 'Das Gesetz der fallenden Profitrate und die Zusammenbruchstendenz des Kapitalismus', *Jahrbuch für Nationalökonomie und Statistik*, 135, 1, July: 1–29.

Myrdal, Gunnar 1953 [1932], *The Political Element in the Development of Economic Theory*, London: Routledge & Kegan Paul.

Neisser, Hans 1931, 'Das Gesetz der fallenden Profitrate als Krisen- und Zusammenbruchsgesetz', *Die Gesellschaft*, 8, 1: 72–85.

Neurath, Wilhelm 1892, *Die wahren Ursachen der Überproduktion*, Wien: Klinkhardt.

Nomad, Max 1932, *Rebels and Renegades*, New York: Macmillan.

Normand, Charles 1908, *La bourgeoisie française au XVIIe siècle*, Paris: Alcan.

Okishio, Nobuo 1961, 'Technical Change and the Rate of Profit', *Kobe University Economic Review*, 7: 85–99.

Olschki, Leonard 1927, *Galilei und seine Zeit*, Halle: Niemeyer.

Oncken, August 1902, *Geschichte der Nationalökonomie*, Leipzig: Hirschfeld.

Oppenheimer, Franz 1903, *Das Grundgesetz der Marxschen Gesellschaftslehre*, Berlin: Reimer.

Oppenheimer, Franz 1919, *Kapitalismus, Kommunismus, Wissenschaftlicher Sozialismus*, Berlin: de Gruyter.

Oppenheimer, Franz 1926, *Grundriß der theoretischen Ökonomik*, Jena: Fischer.

Oppenheimer, Franz 1927, 'Fritz Sternberg's *Imperialismus*', *Archiv für Sozialwissenschaft und Sozialpolitik*, 57: 496–526.

Oppenheimer, Franz 1932, *Weder Kapitalismus noch Kommunismus*, Jena: Fischer.

Owen, Robert 1813, *A New View of Society or Essay on the Principle of the Formation of the Human Character*, London: Cadell and Davies.

Palgrave, Robert Harry Inglis 1913, *Dictionary of Political Economy. Volume 3*, London: Macmillan.

Pannekoek, Anton 1910, 'Herrn Tugan-Baranowskys Marx-Kritik', *Neue Zeit*, 28, 1 (22) 25 February: 772–83.

Pannekoek, Anton 1977 [1934], 'The Theory of the Collapse of Capitalism', *Capital and Class*, 1: 59–81.

Pantheus, Joannes Antonius 1518, *Ars transmutationis metallicae*, Venice: Tacuinus.

Pantheus, Joannes Antonius 1530, *Voarchadumia contra alchimiam: ars distincta ab alchimia et sophia*, Venice: Giovanni Tacuinus.

Paracelsus 1656 [1569], *Archidoxes of Magic*, translated by Robert Turner, London: Brook and Harison.

Pareto, Vilfredo 1896–7, *Cours d'économie politique*, Lausanne: Rouge.

Pareto, Vilfredo 1902, *Les systèmes socialistes. Tome 2*, Paris: Giard & Brièr.

Pareto, Vilfredo 1972 [1906], *Manual of Political Economy*, London: Macmillan.

Parvus 1898, 'Bernsteins Umwälzung des Sozialismus', *Sächsiger Arbeiter-Zeitung*, 27, 28 January; 8, 9, 12, 18, 22, 24, 26 February; 9, 11, 24, 26 March.

Parvus 1901, *Die Handelskrisis und die Gewerkschaften*, München: Ernst.

Parvus 1907, *Die Kolonialpolitik und der Zusammenbruch*, Leipzig: Leipziger Buchdruckerei Aktiengesellschaft.

Parvus 1908, *Der gewerkschaftliche Kampf*, Berlin: Buchhandlung Vorwärts.

Parvus 1910, *Der Sozialismus und die soziale Revolution*, Berlin: Buchhandlung Vorwärts.

Pawlicki, Stefan 1874, *Lassalle i przyszłość socjalizmu*, Kraków: Księgarni S.A. Krzyżanowskiego.

Pecqueur, Constantin 1839a [1837], *Économie sociale des interets du commerce de l'industrie et de l'agriculture. Tome 1*, second edition, Paris: Dessesart.

Pecqueur, Constantin 1839b [1937], *Économie sociale des interets du commerce de l'industrie et de l'agriculture. Tome 2*, second edition, Paris: Dessesart

Petty, William 1899 [1672], 'The Political Anatomy of Ireland', in *The Economic Writings of Sir William Petty. Volume 1*, edited by Charles H. Hull, Cambridge: Cambridge University Press, pp. 121–231.

Pevsner, Nikolaus 1937, *Pioneers of the Modern Movement: From William Morris to Walter Gropius*, London: Faber & Faber.

Pietri-Tonelli, Alfonso de 1927, *Traité d'économie rationnelle*, Paris: Giard.

Pirenne, Henri 1914, 'The Stages in the Social History of Capitalism', *American Historical Review*, 19: 494–515.

Playfair, William 1801 [1786], *The Commercial and Political Atlas: Representing, by Means of Stained Copper-plate Charts, the Progress of the Commerce, Revenues, Expenditure, and Debts of England, during the Whole of the Eighteenth Century*, third edition, London: Wallis.

Playfair, William 1805, *Inquiry into Permanent Causes of the Decline and Fall of Powerful and Wealthy Nations*, London: Greenland and Morris.

Plechanow, G. 1908 [1906], *Henrik Ibsen*, Stuttgart: Neue Zeit.

Plekhanov, Georgi 1976a [1896], *Essays on the History of Materialism, Selected Philosophical Works. Volume 2*, Moscow: Progress Publishers, pp. 31–182.

Plekhanov, Georgi 1976b [1908], *Fundamental Problems of Marxism*, in Georgi Plekhanov, *Selected Philosophical Works. Volume 3*, Moscow: Progress Publishers, pp. 117–83.

Plekhanov, Georgi 1976c [1900], 'The Initial Phases of the Theory of the Class Struggle', in Georgi Valentinovich Plekhanov, *Selected Philosophical Works. Volume 2*, Moscow: Progress Publishers, pp. 427–73.

Plenge, Johann 1919, *Stammformen der vergleichenden Wirtschaftstheorie*, Essen: Baedeker.

Pöhlmann, Robert von 1912, *Geschichte der sozialen Frage und des Sozialismus in der antiken Welt*, two volumes, second edition, München: Beck.

Poincaré, Henri 1905 [1902], *Science and Hypothesis*, London: Walter Scott.

Pollock, Friedrich 1932, 'Sozialismus und Landwirtschaft', in Max Adler et al., *Festschrift für Carl Grünberg*, Leipzig: Hirschfeld, pp. 397–431.

Pollock, Friedrich 1933, 'Bemerkungen zur Wirtschaftskrise', *Zeitschrift für Sozialforschung*, 2, 3: 321–54.

Pollock, Friedrich 1971 [1929], *Die planwirtschaftlichen Versuche in der Sowjetunion 1917–1927*, Frankfurt am Main: Neue Kritik.

Pope, Alexander 1889 [1733], 'Essay on Man', in Alexander Pope, *The Poetical Works of Alexander Pope*, Macmillan: London, pp. 191–226.

Post, Charles 2010, 'Exploring Working-Class Consciousness: A Critique of the Theory of the "Labour Aristocracy"', *Historical Materialism*, 18: 3–38.

Proudhon, Pierre-Joseph 1868, *Œuvres complètes de P.-J. Proudhon, Tome VI*, Paris: Lacroix, Verboechoven.

Quesnay, François 1972 [1758], *Quesnay's Tableau Économique*, London: Macmillan.

Rambaud, Joseph 1902 [1899], *Histoire des doctrines économiques*, second edition, Paris: Librairie de la Société du Recueil Général des Lois et des Arrêts et du Journal du Palais.

Rageot, Gaston 1936, 'Le "Dolorisme"', *Le Temps*, 9 August: 3.

Ramsay, George 1836, *An Essay on the Distribution of Wealth*, Edinburgh: Adam and Charles Black.

Ravenstone, Piercy 1824, *Thoughts on the Funding System and its Effects*, London: Andrews.

Renner, Karl 1918 [1917], *Marxismus, Krieg und Internationale*, Stuttgart: Dietz.

Renouvier, Charles 1912, 'L'Evolutionisme de Hegel', in Charles Renouvier, *Les principes de la nature*, Paris: Colin.

Ricardo, David 1887, 'Letter to Thomas Malthus, 10 October 1820', in David Ricardo, *Letters of David Ricardo to Thomas Robert Malthus 1810–1823*, edited by James Bonar, Oxford: Clarendon, pp. 173–7.

Ricardo, David 1912 [1817], *The Principles of Political Economy and Taxation*, London: Dent.

Ricardo, David 1952, 'Letter to Jean-Baptiste Say, 11 January 1820', in *The Works and Correspondence of David Ricardo. Volume 8*, Cambridge: Cambridge University Press.

Ricci, Umberto 1924, 'Pareto e l'economia pura', *Giornali degli Economisti*, 64: 27–44.

Ricci, Umberto 1930, 'Die "synthetische Ökonomie" von Henry Ludwell Moore', *Zeitschrift fur Nationalökonomie*, 1, 5: 649–68.

Rist, Charles 1915 [1909], 'Sismondi and the Origins of the Critical School', in Charles Gide and Charles Rist, *A History of Economic Doctrines*, translated by R. Richards, Boston: Heath, pp. 170–98.

Robb, David and Eckhard John 2011, '"A Man's a Man for a' that" and "Trotz Alledem": Robert Burns, Ferdinand Freiligrath, and Their Reception in the German Folksong Movement', *Modern Language Review*, 106, 1, January: 17–46.

Roberts, Michael 2016, *The Long Depression: Marxism and the Global Crisis of Capitalism*, Chicago: Haymarket.

Roche-Agussol, Maurice 1932, 'Die Werttheorie', in *Wert, Preis, Produktion, Geld und Kredit: Die Wirtschaftstheorie der Gegenwart. Band 2*, edited by Hans Mayer, Wien: Springer, pp. 27–38.

Rodbertus, Karl 1898 [1850], *Overproduction and Crises*, London: Swan Sonnenschein.

Roland-Holst, Henriette 1906 [1905] *Generalstreik und Sozialdemokratie, mit einem Vorwort von Karl Kautsky*, Dresden: Kaden.

Roll, Eric 1938, *A History of Economic Thought*, London: Faber and Faber.

Rosdolsky, Roman 1977 [1968], *The Making of Marx's Capital*, London: Pluto.

Rosenstein-Rodan, Paul 1929, 'Das Zeitmoment in der mathematischen Theorie des wirtschaftlichen Gleichgewichtes', *Zeitschrift fur Nationalökonomie*, 1, 1: 129–42.

Roth, Gary 2014, *Marxism in a Lost Century: A Biography of Paul Mattick*, Leiden: Brill.

Rothwell, Charles Easton 1938, 'Rosa Luxemburg and the German Social Democratic Party', PhD thesis, Stanford University, August.

Rousseau, Jean-Jacques 1920, *Rousseau's Social Contract and Discourses*, translated by G.D.H. Cole, London: Dent.

Royal Institute of International Affairs 1937, *The Problem of International Investment*, London: Oxford University Press.

Rubin, Isaac Ilych 1973, *Essays on Marx's Theory of Value*, translated by Miloš Samardźija and Fredy Perlman, third edition, Detroit: Black and Red.

Saco, José Antonio 1932, *Historia de la esclavitud de los indios en el nuevo mundo: seguida de la Historia de los repartimientos y encomiendas*, two volumes, Habana: Cultural.

Saco, José Antonio 1938, *Historia de la esclavitud de la raza africana en el nuevo mundo y en especial en los países americo-hispanos*, in four volumes, Habana: Cultural.

Saint-Simon, Henri 1841a [1823], *Catéchisme politique des industriels*, in Henri Saint-Simon, *Œuvres de Saint-Simon*, edited by Olinde Rodrigues, Paris: Capelle, pp. 1–173.

Saint-Simon, Henri 1841b [1818], *Vues sur la propriété et la législation*, in Henri Saint-

Simon, *Œuvres de Saint-Simon*, edited by Olinde Rodrigues, Paris: Capelle, pp. 241–364.

Saint-Simon, Henri 1964a [1819, 1820], *L'Organisateur*, in Henri Saint-Simon and Barthélemy Prosper Enfantin, *Œuvres de Saint-Simon et d'Enfantin. Tome 20*, Aalen: Otto Zeller.

Saint-Simon, Henri 1964b [1813], *Mémoires sur la science de l'homme*, in Henri Saint-Simon and Barthélemy Prosper Enfantin, *Œuvres de Saint-Simon et d'Enfantin. Tome 40*, Aalen: Otto Zeller.

Saint-Simon, Henri 1964c [1821], *Du système industriel*, first part, in Henri Saint-Simon and Barthélemy Prosper Enfantin, *Œuvres de Saint-Simon et d'Enfantin. Tome 21*, Aalen: Otto Zeller.

Saint-Simon, Henri 1964d [1821], *Du système industriel*, second part, in Henri Saint-Simon and Barthélemy Prosper Enfantin, *Œuvres de Saint-Simon et d'Enfantin. Tome 22*, Aalen: Otto Zeller.

Saint-Simon, Henri 1964e [1802], *Lettres d'un habitant de Genève*, in Henri Saint-Simon and Enfantin, *Œuvres de Saint-Simon et d'Enfantin. Tome 15*, Aalen: Otto Zeller, pp. 7–60.

Saint-Simon, Henri 1964f [1814], *De la réorganisation de la sociéte européenne*, in Henri Saint-Simon and Barthélemy Prosper Enfantin, *Œuvres de Saint-Simon et d'Enfantin. Tome 15*, Aalen: Otto Zeller, pp. 155–248.

Saint-Simon, Henri 1964g [1817], *L'industrie ou discussion politiques, morales et philosophiques. Tome 2*, in Henri Saint-Simon and Barthélemy Prosper Enfantin, *Œuvres de Saint-Simon et d'Enfantin. Tome 19*, Aalen: Otto Zeller, pp. 11–174.

Saint-Simon, Henri 1964h [1823–4], *Catéchisme des industriels*, in Henri Saint-Simon and Barthélemy Prosper Enfantin, *Œuvres de Saint-Simon et d'Enfantin. Tome 37*, Aalen: Otto Zeller.

Salis, Jean Rodolphe de 1932, *Sismondi, 1773–1842: la vie et l'œuvre d'un cosmopolite philosophe*, two volumes, Paris: Champion.

Salz, Arthur 1913, *Geschichte der böhmischen Industrie in der Neuzeit*, München: Duncker & Humblot.

Sandemose, Jørgen 2008, 'Golden Howlers: Grossmann's Attack on Luxemburg', *Science & Society*, 72, 1, January: 103–14.

Sarton, George 1937, *The History of Science and the New Humanism*, London: Oxford University Press.

Sartorius, Georg 1806, *Abhandlungen die Elemente des Nationalreichtums betreffend*, Göttingen: Röwer.

Savigny, Friedrich Carl 1814, *Vom Beruf unserer Zeit zur Gesetzgebung und Rechtswissenschaft*, Heidelberg: Mohr und Zimmer.

Say, Jean-Baptiste 1867 [1803], *A Treatise on Political Economy*, sixth edition, translated by C.R. Prinsep, Philadelphia: Lippincott.

Schams, Ewald 1931, 'Komparative Statik', *Zeitschrift für Nationalökonomie*, 2, 1: 27–61.

Schapiro, Meyer 1938, Review of Nikolaus Pevsner, *Pioneers of the Modern Movement: From William Morris to Walter Gropius*, London: Faber & Faber, 1937, *Zeitschrift für Sozialforschung*, 7, 1/2: 291–3.

Schaube, Adolf 1908, 'Die Wollausfuhr Englands vom Jahre 1273', *Vierteljahrschrift fur Sozial- und Wirtschaftsgeschichte*, 6, 1: 39–72.

Scheele, Jürgen 2017, 'Bibliographie', in Henryk Grossmann, *Schiften aus dem Nachlass. Mit weiteren Materialien und Dokumenten*, edited by Jürgen Scheele, Baden-Baden: Tectum, pp. 269–90.

Schmidt, Conrad 1889, *Die Durchschnittsprofitrate auf Grundlage des Marx'schen Werthgesetzes*, Stuttgart: Dietz.

Schmidt, Conrad 1892, 'Die psychologische Richtung in der neueren National-Oekonomie', *Neue Zeit* 10, 2 (40, 41), 22 and 29 June 1892: 421–9, 459–64.

Schmidt, Conrad 1899, 'Nachträgliche Bemerkungen zur Bernstein-Diskussion', *Sozialistische Monatshefte*, 3, 10, October: 493–9.

Schmidt, Conrad 1901, 'Zur Theorie der Handelskrisen und der Ueberproduction', *Socialistische Monatshefte*, 5, 9, September: 669–82.

Schmidt, Conrad 1910, 'Positive Kritik des Marxschen Wertgesetzes', *Sozialistische Monatshefte*, 16, 10, 19 May: 604–18.

Schmidt, Conrad 1915, 'Zur Methode der theoretischen Nationalökonomie', *Sozialistische Monatshefte*, 21, 10, 27 May: 492–502.

Schueller, Richard 1895, *Die Klassische Nationalökonomie und ihre Gegner*, Berlin: Heymann.

Schultz, Henry 1931, 'The Italian School of Mathematical Economics', *Journal of Political Economy*, 39, 1: 76–85.

Schulze-Gävernitz, Gerhart 1906, *Britischer Imperialismus und englischer Freihandel zu Beginn des zwanzigsten Jahrhunderts*, Leipzig: Duncker & Humblot.

Schumpeter, Joseph Alois 1908, *Das Wesen und der Hauptinhalt der theoretischen Nationalökonomie*, Leipzig: Duncker & Humblot.

Schumpeter, Joseph Alois 1912 [1911], *Theorie der wirtschaftlichen Entwicklung*, Leipzig: Duncker & Humblot.

Schumpeter, Joseph Alois 1925, 'Eugen von Böhm-Bawerk', in *Neue oesterreichische Biographie. Band 2*, edited by Anton Bettelheim, Wien: Amalthea.

Schumpeter, Joseph Alois 1939, *Business Cycles: A Theoretical, Historical and Statistical Analysis of the Capitalist Process*, two volumes, New York: McGraw-Hill.

Schumpeter, Joseph Alois 1954 [1934], *Economic Doctrine and Method*, New York: Oxford University Press.

Schumpeter, Joseph Alois 1983 [1912], *The Theory of Economic Development: An Inquiry into Profits, Capital, Credit, Interest, and the Business Cycle*, translated by Redvers Opie, New Brunswick: Transaction.

Sée, Henri 1925, *La notion de classes chez les Saint-Simoniens*, Paris: Rivière.

Sée, Henri 1933, *La France économique et sociale au XVIIIe siècle*, Paris: Armand Colin.

Segal, Lev Khonanovich 1934 [1932], *Lehrbuch der politischen Ökonomie*, Zurich: Ring.

Seligman, Edwin R.A. 1930–5, *Encyclopedia of the Social Sciences*, 15 volumes, New York: Macmillan

Senior, Nassau 1965 [1836], *An Outline of the Science of Political Economy*, New York: Kelley.

Shaw, George Bernard 1896, *Report on Fabian Policy and Resolutions Presented by the Fabian Society to the International Socialist Workers and Trade Union Congress, London, 1896*, Fabian Tract 70, London: Fabian Society.

Shibata, Kei 1933a, 'Marx's Analysis of Capitalism and the General Equilibrium Theory of the Lausanne School', *Kyoto University Economic Review*, 8, 1: 107–36.

Shibata, Kei 1933b, 'The Meaning of the Theory of Value in Theoretical Economics', *Kyoto University Economic Review*, 8, 2: 49–68.

Shine, Hill 1940, *Carlyle and the Saint-Simonians*, Baltimore: Johns Hopkins Press.

Sinowjew, Grigorii 1924 [1916], *Der Krieg und die Krise des Sozialismus*, Wien: Verlag für Literatur und Politik.

Sismondi, Jean Charles Léonard Simonde de 1801, *Tableau de l'agriculture toscane*, Genève: Paschoud.

Sismondi, Jean Charles Léonard Simonde de 1803, *De la richesse commerciale*, two volumes, Genève: Paschoud.

Sismondi, Jean Charles Léonard Simonde de 1807–18, *Histoire des républiques italiennes au moyen âge*, 16 volumes, Zurich: Gessner, Paris: Treuttel et Würtz.

Sismondi, Jean Charles Léonard Simonde de 1813, *De la littérature du midi de l'Europe*, four volumes, Paris: Treuttel et Würtz.

Sismondi, Jean Charles Léonard Simonde de 1821–44, *Histoire des Français*, 31 volumes, Paris: Treuttel et Würtz.

Sismondi, Jean Charles Léonard Simonde de 1827, *Nouveau principes d'économie politique. Tome second*, second edition, Paris: Delaunay.

Sismondi, Jean Charles Léonard Simonde de 1836, *Études sur les constitutions des peuples libres*, Paris: Treuttel et Würtz.

Sismondi, Jean Charles Léonard Simonde de 1837, *Études sur l'économie politique. Tome premier*, Paris: Treuttel et Würtz.

Sismondi, Jean Charles Léonard Simonde de 1838, *Études sur l'économie politique. Tome second*, Paris: Treuttel et Würtz.

Sismondi, Jean Charles Léonard Simonde de 1840 [1809], *Histoire des républiques italiennes du moyen âge. Tome 3*, Paris: Furne.

Sismondi, Jean Charles Léonard Simonde de 1852 [1823], *Historical View of the Literature of the South of Europe*, two volumes, translated by Thomas Roscoe, London: Bohn.

Sismondi, Jean Charles Léonard Simonde de 1991a [1820], 'Analysis of a Refutation of *New Principles of Political Economy* published in the *Edinburgh Review* by a follower of Mr. Ricardo', in Jean Charles Léonard Simonde de Sismondi, *New Principles of Political Economy*, translated by Richard Hyse, New Brunswick: Transaction, pp. 599–616.

Sismondi, Jean Charles Léonard Simonde de 1991b [1824], 'On the Balance of Consumption with Production', in Jean Charles Léonard Simonde de Sismondi, *New Principles of Political Economy*, translated by Richard Hyse, New Brunswick: Transaction, pp. 617–39.

Sismondi, Jean Charles Léonard Simonde de 1991c [1824], 'Notes on an Article by M. Say, entitled "On the Balance of Consumption with Production"', in Jean Charles Léonard Simonde de Sismondi, *New Principles of Political Economy*, translated by Richard Hyse, New Brunswick: Transaction, pp. 645–8.

Sismondi, Jean Charles Léonard Simonde de 1991d [1827], *New Principles of Political Economy*, translated by Richard Hyse, New Brunswick: Transaction.

Sismondi, Jean Charles Léonard Simonde de 1991e [1827], 'Clarification Relative to the Equilibrium of Consumption with Production', in Jean Charles Léonard Simonde de Sismondi, *New Principles of Political Economy*, translated by Richard Hyse, New Brunswick: Transaction, pp. 595–7.

Skarbek, Fryderyk 1829, *Théorie des richesses sociales. Tome premier*, Paris: A. Sautelet.

Smith, Adam 1910a [1776], *The Wealth of Nations. Volume 1*, London: Dent.

Smith, Adam 1910b [1776], *The Wealth of Nations. Volume 2*, London: Dent.

Smith, Thomas 1906 [1583, written about 1565], *De republica Anglorum, a Discourse of the Commonwealth of England*, Cambridge: Cambridge University Press.

Snow, Edgar 1947, *Stalin Must Have Peace*, New York: Random House.

Sombart, Werner 1903, *Die deutsche Volkswirtschaft im neunzehnten Jahrhundert*, Berlin: Bondi.

Sombart, Werner 1904, 'Die Störungen im deutschen Wirtschaftsleben während der Jahre 1900 ff.', *Verhandlungen der General-versammlung in Hamburg, 14., 15. und 16. September 1903 ... Referate von Werner Sombart, F. Hecht, J. Jastrow*, Schriften des Vereins fur Sozialpolitik, 113, Leipzig: Duncker & Humblot, pp. 121–36.

Sombart, Werner 1913, *Krieg und Kapitalismus*, München: Duncker & Humblot.

Sombart, Werner 1909a [1896], *Socialism and the Social Movement*, London: J.M. Dent.

Sombart, Werner 1909b, *Das Lebenswerk von Karl Marx*, Jena: Fischer.

Sombart, Werner 1919, *Der Moderne Kapitalismus*. Zweiter Band, Erster Halbband, Leipzig: Duncker & Humblot.

Soden, Julius 1815 [1805], *Die National-Oekonomie, Ein philosophischer Versuch*, second edition, Wien: B.Ph. Bauer.

Sorel, Georges 1925 [1908], *Reflections on Violence*, London: George Allen and Unwin.

Spann, Othmar 1918, *Die Haupttheorien der Volkswirtschaftslehre*, third edition, Leipzig: Quelle & Meyer.

Spann, Othmar 1923, *Die Haupttheorien der Volkswirtschaftslehre*, twelth–fifteenth edition, Leipzig: Quelle & Meyer.

Spann, Othmar 1930 [1929], *Types of Economic Theory*, translated from the nineteenth edition of 1929 by Eden and Cedar Paul, London: Routledge.

Spiethoff, Athur 1903, 'Die Krisentheorien von M. Tugan-Baranowsky und L. Pohle', *Schmollers Jahrbuch*, new series, 27: 679–708.

Spiethoff, Athur 1955 [1925], 'Business Cycles', *International Economic Papers*, 3: 75–171.

Spencer, Herbert 1878 [1864], 'Progress: Its Law and Causes', in Herbert Spencer, *Illustrations of Universal Progress*, New York: Appleton.

Spühler, Willy 1925, *Der Saint-Simonismus: Lehre und Leben von Saint-Amand Bazard*, Zurich: Girsberger.

Staley, Eugene 1935, *War and the Private Investor*, New York: Doubleday, Doran.

Stalin, Joseph Vissarionovich 1950 [1946], 'Speech Delivered by J.V. Stalin at a Meeting of Voters of the Stalin Electoral District, Moscow: February 9, 1946', in Joseph Stalin, *Speeches Delivered at Meetings of Voters of the Stalin Electoral District, Moscow*, Moscow: Foreign Languages Publishing House, pp. 19–44.

Stalin, Joseph Vissarionovich 1954 [1929], 'A Necessary Correction', in Iosif Vissarionovich Stalin, *Works. Volume 12, April 1929–June 1930*, Moscow: Foreign Languages Publishing House, pp. 143–5.

Stammler, Rudolf 1896, *Wirtschaft und Recht nach der materialistischen Geschichtsauffassung: eine sozialphilosophische Untersuchung*, Leipzig: Veit.

Staudinger, Franz 1899, *Ethik und Politik*, Berlin: Dümmler.

Staudinger, Franz 1907, *Wirtschaftliche Grundlagen der Moral*, Darmstadt: Roether.

Stead, Christina 2001 [1946], *Letty Fox: Her Luck*, New York: New York Review of Books.

Stephen, Leslie and Sir Leslie Lee (eds) 1922, *The Dictionary of National Biography. Volume 15*, London: Oxford Uniersity Press.

Sternberg, Fritz 1929, *'Der Imperialismus' und seine Kritiker*, Berlin: Soziologische Verlagsanstalt.

Sternberg, Fritz 1930, *Eine Unwältzung der Wissenschaft? Kritik des Buches von Henryk Grossmann 'Das Akkumulations- und Zusammenbruchsgesetz des kapitalistischen System'. Zugleich eine positive Analyse des Imperialismus*, Berlin: Prager.

Sternberg, Fritz 1971 [1926], *Der Imperialismus*, Frankfurt: Neue Kritik.

Steuart, James 1767, *Inquiry into the Principles of Political Oeconomy*, London: Millar and Cadell.

Strachey, John 1935, *The Nature of Capitalist Crisis*, London: Gollancz.

Stone, Nahum Isaac 1904, 'Preface', in Karl Marx 1904, *A Contribution to the Critique of Political Economy*, translated by N.I. Stone, Chicago: Kerr.

Streller, Rudolf 1928, *Die Dynamik der theoretischen Nationalökonomie*, Tübingen: Mohr.

Suhge, Werner 1935, *Saint-Simonismus und Junges Deutschland, Germanische Studien*, 164, Berlin: Ebering.

Sullivan, John William Navin 1938, *Isaac Newton 1642–1727*, London: Macmillan.

Süßmilch, Johann Peter 1761, *Die Göttliche Ordnung in den Veränderungen des menschlichen Geschlechts. Band 1*, Berlin: Verlag des Buchladens der Realschule.

Sweezy, Paul 1962 [1942], *The Theory of Capitalist Development*, London, Dobson.

Tarnow, Fritz 1928, *Warum arm sein?*, Berlin: Allgemeiner Deutscher Gewerkschaftsbund.

Taylor, George Robert Stirling 1921, *Guild Politics: A Practical Programme for the Labour Party and the Co-operators*, London: Palmer.

Tazerout, Mohand 1932, 'Théorie économique et sociologie économique', *Revue internationale de sociologie*, 40, 5–6, May–June: 303–20.

Telesio 1565, *De natura iuxta propria principia liber primus et secundus*, Rome: Antonium Bladum.

Teppe, Julien 1936, *Dictature de la douleur ou précisions sur le dolorisme*, Paris: La Caravelle.

Tertullian 1956 [ca. 206], *Tertullian's Treatise on the Incarnation*, with a translation by Ernest Evans, Cambridge: Cambridge University Press.

Thierry, Augustin 1964 [1817], *L'industrie ou discussion politiques, morales et philosophiques. Tome 1*, in Henri Saint-Simon and Barthélemy Prosper Enfantin, *Œuvres de Saint-Simon et d'Enfantin. Volume 18*, Aalen: Otto Zeller.

Thompson, William 1824, *An Inquiry into the Principles of the Distribution of Wealth Most Conducive to Human Happiness*, London: Longman.

Thorndike, Lynn 1941a, *A History of Magic and Experimental Sciences. Volume 5, The Sixteenth Century*, New York: Columbia University Press.

Thorndike, Lynn 1941b, *A History of Magic and Experimental Sciences. Volume 6, The Sixteenth Century*, New York: Columbia University Press.

Thorp, Willard L. 1935, 'The Problem of Overcapacity', in Asher Achinstein et al., *Economic Essays in Honour of Wesley Clair Mitchell*, New York: Columbia University Press, pp. 477–95.

Thünen, Johann Heinrich von 1921 [1842], *Der isolirte Staat in Beziehung auf Landwirthschaft und National-Ökonomie*, Jena: Fischer.

Tillich, Paul 1981 [1923], *The System of the Sciences According to Objects and Methods*, East Brunswick, NJ: Associated University Presses.

Troeltsch, Ernst 1919, *Die Dynamik der Geschichte nach der Geschichtsphilosophie des Positivismus*, Berlin: Reuther und Reichard.

Trotsky, Leon 1941 [1923], 'The Curve of Capitalist Development', *Fourth International*, 2, 4, May: 111–14.

Trotsky, Leon 1969 [1906], *Results and Prospects*, in Leon Trotsky, *The Permanent Revolution and Results and Prospects*, translated by John G. Wright and Brian Pearce, New York: Pathfinder, pp. 125–281.

Trotsky, Leon 1971 [1914], *The War and the International*, Colombo: Young Socialist.

Trotsky, Leon 1975 [1933], 'The German Catastrophe: The Responsibility of the Leadership', in Leon Trotsky, *The Struggle Against Fascism in Germany*, Harmondsworth: Penguin, pp. 397–404.

Tudor, Henry and Josephine M. Tudor (eds) 1988, *Marxism and Social Democracy: The Revisionist Debate 1896–98*, Cambridge: Cambridge University Press.

Tugan-Baranowsky, Michael 1901 [1894], *Studien zur Theorie und Geschichte der Handelskrisen in England*, translation of second Russian edition, Jena: Fischer.

Tugan-Baranowsky, Michael 1904, 'Der Zusammenbruch der kapitalistischen Wirtschaftsordnung im Lichte der nationalökonomischen Theorie', *Archiv für Sozialwissenschaft und Sozialpolitik*, 19: 273–306.

Tugan-Baranowsky, Michael 1905, *Theoretische Grundlagen des Marxismus*, Leipzig: Duncker & Humblot.

Tugan-Baranowsky, Michael 1908, 'Gesunder Menschenverstand und wissenschaftliche Wahrheit: Eine Erwiderung', *Neue Zeit*, 26, 1 (19), 7 February: 640–58.

Tugan-Baranowsky, Michael 1910 [1908], *Modern Socialism in Its Historical Development*, London: Sonnenschein.

Tugan-Baranowsky, Michael 2000 [1901], 'Chapter I. The Fundamental Causes of Crises in the Capitalist Economy' and 'Chapter VII. Marx's Theory of Crises' of *Studien zur Theorie und Geschichte der Handelskrisen in England*, translated by Alejandro Ramos-Martínez, in *Value, Capitalist Dynamics and Money, Research in Political Economy 18*, edited by Paul Zarembka, New York: Elsevier, pp. 53–80, 81–110.

Turgot, Anne Robert Jacques 1898 [1769–70, written 1766], *Reflections on the Formation and Distribution of Wealth*, London: Macmillan.

Turgot, Anne Robert Jacques 2011 [1750], 'A Philosophical Review of the Successive Advances of the Human Mind', in Anne Robert Jacques Turgot, *The Turgot Collection*, Auburn (Alabama): Ludwig von Mises Institute, pp. 320–43.

Universität Frankfurt am Main 1928, *Verzeichnis der Vorlesungen Sommer-Halbjahr 1928 und Personalverzeichnis.*

Universität Frankfurt am Main 1930 *Verzeichnis der Vorlesungen Sommer-Halbjahr 1930 und Personalverzeichnis.*

Vandervelde, Émile 1901 [1900], *Collectivism and Industrial Evolution*, translated by Charles H. Kerr, Chicago: Kerr.

Vandervelde, Émile 1902, *Essais sur la question agraire en Belgique*, Paris: Éditions du Mouvement Socialiste.

Vandervelde, Émile 1906, *La Belgique ouvrière*, Paris: Cornély.

Vandervelde, Émile 1908, *Le socialisme agraire ou le collectivisme et l'évolution agricole*, Paris: Giard & Brière.

Vandervelde, Émile 1925, *Le Parti Ouvrier Belge, 1885–1925*, Bruxelles: Maison Nationale d'Édition l'Églantine.

Varga, Eugen 1930, 'Akkumulation und Zusammenbruch des Kapitalismus', *Unter dem Banner des Marxismus*, 4, 1: 60–95.

Varoufakis, Yanis 1998, *Foundations of Economics: A Beginner's Companion*, London: Routledge.

Vico, Giambattista 1948, *The New Science of Giambattista Vico*, translated by Thomas Goddard Bergin and Max Harold Fisch, Ithaca, NY: Cornell University Press.

Vives, Juan Luis 1979 [1520], 'Against the Pseudodialecticians' in Juan Luis Vives, *Juan Luis Vives Against the Pseudodialecticians*, translated by Rita Guerlac, Dordrecht: Reidel, pp. 47–109.

Volgin, Vjačeslav Petrovič 1926, 'Über die historische Stellung Saint-Simons', *Marx-Engels Archiv. Band 1*: 82–118.

Vollmar, Georg von 1891, *Ueber die nächsten Aufgaben der Deutschen Sozialdemokratie: zwei Reden, gehalten am 1. Juni und 6 Juli 1891 im 'Eldorado' zu München*, München: M. Ernst.

Vollmar, Georg von 1892, *Ueber Staatssozialismus*, Nürnberg: Wörlein.

Vorländer, Karl 1900, *Kant und der Sozialismus unter besonderer Berücksichtigung der neuesten theoretischen Bewegung innerhalb des Marxismus*, Berlin: Reuther & Reichard.

Vorländer, Karl 1920, 'Zu den philosophischen Grundlagen unseres Parteiprogramms', in Sozialdemokratische Partei Deutschlands, *Das Programm der Sozialdemokratie, Vorschläge für seine Erneuerung*, Berlin: Buchhandlung Vorwärts, pp. 10–17.

Vorländer, Karl 1926a [1911], *Kant und Marx: Ein Beitrag zur Philosophie des Sozialismus*, second edition, Tübingen: Mohr.

Vorländer, Karl 1926b, *Von Machiavelli bis Lenin: Neuzeitliche Staats- und Gesellschafts-theorien*, Leipzig: Quelle & Meyer.

Walras, Léon 1954 [1874], *Elements of Pure Economics*, translated by William Jaffé, London: Allen and Unwin.

Walter, Emil 1930, 'Liquidation der Arbeitswertlehre?', *Der Kampf*, 23, 10, October: 429–30.

Webb, Sidney and Beatrice Webb 1894, *History of Trade Unionism*, London: Longmans, Green and Company.

Webb, Sidney and Beatrice Webb 1895 [1894], *Die Geschichte des Britischen Trade-Unionismus*, translated by Richard Bernstein, afterword by Eduard Bernstein, Stuttgart: Dietz.

Webb, Sidney and Beatrice Webb 1897, *Industrial Democracy*, two volumes, London: Longmans, Green.

Webb, Sidney and Beatrice Webb 1911, *The Prevention of Destitution*, London: Longmans, Green.

Webb, Sidney and Beatrice Webb 1920, *A Constitution for the Socialist Commonwealth of Great Britain*, London: Longmans, Green.

Webb, Sidney and Beatrice Webb 1923, *The Decay of Capitalist Civilisation*, London: Fabian Society.

Weber, Hans 1939, *Richard Jones: Ein früher englischer Abtrünniger der klassischen Schule der Nationaloekonomie*. Zurich: Girsberger.

Weber, Max 1968 [1904–5], *The Protestant Ethic and the Spirit of Capitalism*, translated by Talcott Parsons, London: Unwin.

Weill, Georges 1896, *L'École saint-simonienne*, Paris: Alcan.

Weiller, Jean 1934, *La Conception classique d'un équilibre économique*, Paris: Rivière.

Westermarck, Edvard 1921 [1891], *The History of Human Marriage*, Macmillan, London.

Whittaker, Edmund 1940, *A History of Economic Ideas*, New York: Longmans, Green and Company.

Wicksell, Knut 1936 [1898], *Interest and Prices: A Study of the Causes Regulating the Value of Money*, translated by R.F. Kahn, London: Royal Economic Society.

Wicksell, Knut 1978 [1913], *Lectures on Political Economy. Volume 2*, translated by E. Classen, Fairfield: Kelley.

Wilbrandt, Robert 1919 [1918], *Karl Marx: Versuch einer Würdigung*, third edition, Leipzig: Teubner.

Willis, H. Parker and John M. Chapman 1935, *The Economics of Inflation*, New York: Columbia University Press.

Wilson, C.H. 1939, 'The Economic Decline of the Netherlands', *Economic History Review*, 9, 2, May: 111–27.

Wirtschaft und Statistik 1927, 1.

Wittfogel, Karl August 1931, *Wirtschaft und Gesellschaft Chinas: Versuch einer wissenshaftlichen Analyse einer großen asiatischen Agrargesellschaft. Band 1, Produktivkräfte, Produktions- und Zirkulationsprozeß*, Leipzig: Hirschfeld.

Wittfogel, Karl August 1936 'Wirtschaftsgeschichtliche Grundlagen der Entwicklung der Familienautorität', in *Studien über Autorität und Familie: Forschungsberichte aus dem Institut für Sozialforschung*, edited by Max Horkheimer, Paris: Alcan, pp. 473–522.

Woltmann, Ludwig 1900, *Der historische Materialismus: Darstellung und Kritik der marxistischen Weltanschauung*, Düsseldorf: Michels.

Woytinsky, Wladimir 1927, *Magazin der Wirtschaft*, 3.

Zeisl, Hans 1930, 'Ein Einwand gegen die Marx'sche Wertlehre', *Der Kampf*, 23, 9, September: 391–4.

Zinoviev, Grigory 1952–3, 'Two Eras of War', *New International*, 18 (5, 6) and 19, 1, September–October 1952, November–December 1952, January–February 1953: 233–44, 323–7, 42–51, http://www.marxists.org/archive/zinoviev/works/1916/war/2eras-index.htm, accessed 17 June 2013.

Index and Abbreviations

CPSIA information can be obtained
at www.ICGtesting.com
Printed in the USA
JSHW020954140120
3568JS00003B/4

9 781642 590449